LIVERPOOL AS IT WAS:
1775 to 1800

by
Richard Brooke

The City of Liverpool

2003

First published 1853

This edition specially produced by
Cedric Chivers Limited, Bristol
for the publisher
Liverpool Libraries and Information Services
William Brown Street, Liverpool L3 8EW
2003

ISBN 0 902990 22 5

Printed in Great Britain by Antony Rowe Ltd.,
Chippenham, Wilts.

FOREWORD

I am delighted that Liverpool Libraries and Information Services has reproduced this book. It is the third in a series of reprints building up to the 800th anniversary of Liverpool in 2007.

The book was first published in 1853 as "Liverpool as it was during the last quarter of the eighteenth century, 1775 to 1800" by Richard Brooke. It presents a fascinating picture of Liverpool on the eve of the Industrial Revolution. The information in the book came from many sources including recollections of the author's father, also called Richard Brooke, who lived until the age of ninety two. He witnessed great changes in the town as the population grew at an incredible rate.

I am very grateful to Jane Longmore, who has written an introduction to this reprint. Jane has been familiar with the Liverpool skyline and dock frontage for many years, having been born and educated in Wallasey. She has been Head of the School of Humanities at the University of Greenwich since 1999. Her undergraduate degree was a BA (Hons.) in Modern History from the University of Oxford. She then completed a PGCE at the University of Durham followed by a doctorate at the University of Reading. Her thesis was a study of the development of eighteenth and early nineteenth century Liverpool.

Illustrations have been added to the original edition from the extensive collections of Liverpool Record Office and Local Studies.

I would like to thank the Liverpool Association of the British Federation of Women Graduates for their generous grant towards the cost of providing copies of the book for all Liverpool Libraries.

I would also like to thank David Stoker, Kay Parrott and all of the staff of Liverpool Record Office for their work in seeing this reprint through. Thanks are also due to Eileen Organ, a former member of staff, for her picture research.

I am sure that you will enjoy this book and find the information useful.

Councillor Warren Bradley
Executive Member for Leisure and Tourism

August 2003

THE BRITISH FEDERATION OF WOMEN GRADUATES

4 Mandeville Courtyard
142 Battersea Park Road
LONDON SW11 4NB
www.bfwg.org.uk

AIMS

To maintain an organization representing women graduates and
enabling them to take concerted action
To encourage and help women graduates to serve the community
especially in all spheres of public life
To work for conditions in which women can combine careers and
domestic responsibilities
To promote friendship and understanding amongst women graduates
throughout the world
To help women in all countries towards fuller opportunities for
education, training and research
To take part in the work of international organizations in advancing
world peace and progress

Membership of BFWG includes membership of IFUW (International
Federation of University Women) which is open to all women
graduates and women with equivalent professional qualification, as
agreed by BFWG and IFUW

ELEANOR RATHBONE
IN 1908
FOUNDED THE LIVERPOOL ASSOCIATION OF GRADUATE
WOMEN
(The local group of BFWG)

INTRODUCTION
TO THE 2003 EDITION

The growth of towns transformed Britain between 1660 and 1860, contributing to industrial change, acting as a catalyst for the development of mass politics and generating a radical alteration of the social structure. Since the pioneering work of H.J. Dyos in the 1960s and early 1970s[i], much historical research has been devoted to the study of individual towns and to aspects of urbanisation. Extensive work has been undertaken on the physical growth of towns, concentrating on both population growth and the urban economy. This has demonstrated the exceptional rate of urban growth in eighteenth-century England, which accounted for 70% of European urban growth between 1750 and 1800.[ii] Higher agricultural productivity in England sustained the growth of the towns by producing sufficient surplus to feed this expanding urban population. London, the largest city in western Europe, almost doubled in size during the eighteenth century, reaching nearly one million inhabitants by 1801; elsewhere, the proportion of the English population living in towns of more than 10,000 inhabitants quadrupled between 1600 and 1800, while the comparable figures for the rest of Europe showed only a minimal increase.

This extraordinary growth in the urban population was not a monolithic process. There were wide variations in regional patterns of development.[iii] Southern Britain and East Anglia deindustrialized during the eighteenth century, as the old iron industry of the Weald and the textile centres of East Anglia and the West Country gave way to the emerging Atlantic ports of Bristol and Liverpool and the industrial centres of the West Midlands, Lancashire, West Yorkshire, the north-east of England, south Wales and Clydeside. Even within the centres of urban growth there were different phases of economic development; the eighteenth-century port, for example, was often more economically diverse than its nineteenth-century successor. Recent research has identified a range of industrial concerns in eighteenth-century Liverpool, such as sugar-processing, watch-making, pottery production and shipbuilding. These early industries slowly disappeared in the nineteenth century as the city concentrated on the core business of its port.

In the 1980s, Penelope Corfield's groundbreaking study shifted the historical focus from purely economic and demographic concerns to the study of the political and cultural dimensions of the eighteenth-century town.[iv] The study of urban politics, parliamentary elections (until 1801, 405 out of 558 MPs were returned by borough constituencies) and civic government has extended our understanding of the relationship between the central state and the locality in Georgian England.[v] Peter Borsay has devoted attention to urban culture and civic identity, arguing that England experienced an urban cultural 'renaissance' between 1660 and 1820. Civic identity was strengthened by the establishment of a plethora of cultural and charitable institutions, often financed by the subscriptions of the more affluent residents in place of a single, aristocratic patron.

Few British towns in the eighteenth century experienced as dramatic a rate of growth and change as Liverpool. Figures drawn from the monumental *Cambridge Urban History of Britain* reveal that Liverpool had the highest average percentage rate of growth per annum (138.69%) through the seventeenth and eighteenth centuries, albeit starting from a low point of approximately 1200 inhabitants in the 1660s.[vi] Newcomers were drawn by the rising prosperity of the Atlantic port with its innovative dock system and its improved transport links with the emerging industrial regions of Lancashire and the West Midlands. The population growth was outstanding in the last quarter of the eighteenth century, with numbers more than doubling from about 35,000 in 1775 to 82,295 in the 1801 census. This period was therefore of pivotal significance in the transformation of Liverpool from a relatively obscure borough (one of only three incorporated boroughs in medieval Lancashire) to 'the first town in the kingdom in point of size and commercial importance, the Metropolis excepted'.[vii]

The preliminary stages of the transformation from village to city have tended to be overshadowed by the historical phenomenon of nineteenth-century Liverpool, at once the 'second city of Empire' and 'the black spot on the Mersey'. Brooke's *Liverpool as it was during the last quarter of the eighteenth century, 1775 to 1800* helps to refocus attention on these formative years prior to the Victorian heyday. It is a curious book; part scholarly history, part recollection and part antiquarian study. Rather unflatteringly, sixty years later, Ramsay Muir, Professor of Modern History at the University of Liverpool, referred to Brooke's account as a 'hodge-podge'.[viii] However justified this criticism in purely academic terms, it missed both the purpose and the fascination of the book. As the author stressed in his preface 'the chief object of the work is to preserve, unimpaired, the knowledge of various particulars and events relating to Liverpool, most of which would, perhaps, otherwise soon have been forgotten' (page ii). He also had an extremely personal motive for compiling the account: his father had arrived in Liverpool in January 1776 at the age of 14 and, having lived to over ninety, was able to provide clear recollections of Liverpool people and places during the last quarter of the previous century. The book was therefore Brooke's tribute to his father, who died just prior to its publication in 1853.

Brooke was a fellow of the Society of Antiquaries and his work was entirely in keeping with the mid-Victorian passion for collecting information about the past. Other antiquarian books on Liverpool were published during the 1850s and 1860s: J.Aspinall, *Liverpool a few years since* (1852), W.G.Herdman, *Pictorial Relics of Ancient Liverpool* (Liverpool, 1856), J.A.Picton, *The Architectural History of Liverpool* (Liverpool, 1858) and J.Stonehouse, *Recollections of Old Liverpool by a Nonagenarian* (Liverpool, 1863). Yet he was more than an antiquarian with a strong sense of filial duty. He made use of existing histories of Liverpool to supplement the material gathered from the discussions with his father. Throughout the text there are numerous reference to J.Aikin, *A Description of the Country within forty miles of Manchester* (1795),W.Enfield, *An Essay towards the History of Liverpool* (Warrington, 1773), H.Smithers, *Liverpool: its Commerce, Statistics and Institutions* (Liverpool, 1825) and the anonymous *History of Liverpool* published in 1810 by the bookseller Thomas Troughton. Brooke also had access to various archival sources, including the records of the Corporation of Liverpool, the Underhill Papers (a manuscript collection assembled between 1828 and 1834 for an abortive history of Liverpool), and local newspapers such as *Gore's General Advertiser*. There is, however, no reference to the one work on Liverpool actually published in the last quarter of the eighteenth century, *The Liverpool Guide, 1796* written by William Moss, surgeon to the Liverpool Lying-In Charity. Brooke possibly dismissed this delightful survey on the grounds that it was intended for tourists and therefore lacked any scholarly pretensions.

On occasion, his own work veers too much in the other direction, particularly when discussing the early charters or the armorial bearings of the Liverpool Corporation. Here his immense enthusiasm for historical detail produces pages of tedium and tends to overwhelm the text with footnotes. The structure is occasionally idiosyncratic as, for example, in the introduction, which covers the period from the Norman Conquest to the late fourteenth century at length and then makes passing reference to four centuries in a single page. However, there is much of interest in the remaining chapters for both the academic and lay reader. Brooke offers a useful description of the state of Liverpool at the beginning of this critical quarter of a century, with the onset of dramatic population growth and the extension of its medieval core as new streets radiated from the seven, central lanes across the wasteland or 'Common' owned by the Corporation. Although he refers to 'little or nothing calculated to excite admiration or interest' in the physical appearance of Liverpool in 1775 (p.118), he provides memorable glimpses of the vitality of the mercantile community: for example, the image conveyed by the copy of the bill for the annual mayoral dinner held at St James' Coffee-House in October

1775 which included a 37 lb turtle and £5 for wine and punch (page 165).

Although Brooke does not, of course, focus explicitly on the issues of current interest to historians identified above, it is possible to extract much useful material from his work. Take, for example, the question of identity. His account provides support for the argument recently advanced by Rosemary Sweet that urban identity and culture were emerging in the eighteenth century rather than, as previously thought, first appearing as civic pride in the Victorian period.[ix] The energy of the group of merchants who dominated the self-elected Corporation of Liverpool in the early eighteenth century had led to the establishment of the strong commercial identity of the port. This energy was channelled into the construction of the first commercial wet dock in 1709-15 and four further docks by 1800, as well as support for improvements in the major road and river links with Liverpool's hinterland and the construction of the Liverpool to Leeds canal. By the last quarter of the eighteenth century Liverpool had outstripped its local rival, Chester and its competitor in the slave trade, Bristol. It was an extraordinary commercial success story.

Unlike the leading citizens of Leeds or Manchester, Liverpool's mercantile elite remained socially and politically distinct from the gentry of its hinterland, devoting attention to building the port and town through membership of the Corporation rather than relying on the political influence exerted by the surrounding gentry. Throughout the eighteenth century merchants comprised a majority of the 41 member of the Corporation of Liverpool and managed corporate finances that were the largest outside London. Towns such as Hull, York and Bath had annual incomes of only a few thousand pounds in 1800: Liverpool Corporation enjoyed an income of over £20,000 from dock duties alone at the same date. Seven years earlier its total property had been valued at over £820,000. The bulk of this property was the 1000-acre estate, formerly the Liverpool Common, which provided land for house building and dock construction, as well as offering ample security to investors.

Although Brooke is slightly dismissive of the role of the Corporation prior to the Municipal Reform Act of 1835, commenting 'It is not necessary to discuss here whether the members of the old Council were, as a body, remarkable for talent or otherwise' (p.201), he goes on to recount a number of aspects of the work of the Corporation which contributed directly to the prosperity of the town. He notes the work of the Corporation as Dock Trustees, encouraging commercial growth by raising the capital to double the acreage of dock space in this period. In contrast, the private London Dock Company expected to achieve a profit of between 10-20% per annum for the benefit of its owners. The Corporation also needed to maintain commercial confidence during the periodic slumps that accompanied the repeated outbreaks of war in the eighteenth century. Their strong sense of civic responsibility was particularly evident during the financial crisis of 1793 precipitated by the French Revolutionary Wars, when they issued bonds on security of their property as a means of stabilising the local economy. The commercial community and civic government were deeply intertwined in eighteenth-century Liverpool, ensuring the rapid creation of a strong identity for a town that was unable to draw on centuries of tradition or a distinguished history for its sense of place.

Contemporary critics observed that commerce dominated the activities of the population of Liverpool to the exclusion of more cultural pursuits: in a letter dated May 1804, for example, the Liverpool physician, James Currie, referred to 'busy, noisy, smoky, money-getting Liverpool'.[x] There is little surviving evidence of the time-consuming pursuit of mercantile wealth in eighteenth century Liverpool but the papers of the Tarleton family provide a rare and evocative insight. The Tarletons built up a fortune as merchants during the eighteenth century, with considerable property in the West Indies. John Tarleton's annual profit and loss accounts are held in the Liverpool Record Office.[xi] This series of manuscripts commences in 1748 and records the details of 'the money I have employed in trade'. At this point his fortune totalled £5,874. Within ten years it had almost quadrupled to just under £23,000. Five years later, in 1763, he estimated his fortune at £53,900, including the value of his sugarhouse, his profits from voyages to the West Indies and various items of stock, such as sugar and rum. Yet he does not record any subscriptions to charities, any shares in the construction of public buildings, such as the Infirmary (1745-8), or any membership of cultural organisations such as the Liverpool Library (1758), appearing to confirm the view that interests in culture and commerce could not be reconciled.

Brooke's account of the cultural and charitable institutions of late eighteenth-century Liverpool suggests a different interpretation. He demonstrates that cultural activities of particular relevance to a mercantile community were supported and provides extensive details of a dining society called 'The Unanimous Club'. The membership included many prominent merchants, some of whom were also members of the Corporation, and weekly meetings were held from September to April. It is revealing that this club survived for at least 25 years from 1753, whilst the demands of the Literary and Philosophical Societies that were fashionable elsewhere could not be sustained in Liverpool. Less time-consuming and more relaxing theatrical and musical entertainments were well supported. The Liverpool Theatre had been built in 1772 by subscriptions totalling a massive £6000 with merchants comprising two-thirds of the original subscribers. The Music Hall, which opened in Bold Street in 1786, was capable of holding 1300 persons: concerts were well attended by Liverpool's wealthier residents. Leading merchants were willing to play a role in such organisations: Brooke notes the example of Thomas Staniforth, a merchant dealing in the Greenland fishery trade, who was one of the early Presidents of the Music Hall.

Local histories and guidebooks often stressed the charitable activities of their citizens as a means of emphasizing their moral integrity.[xii] The eighteenth century saw the rise of charitable institutions built and financed by subscriptions from the increasingly affluent 'middling sorts'. Liverpool's slow start in this regard may have been linked to the need for the mercantile elite to secure their own wealth and the facilities of the port prior to seeking public approval for their benevolence. There was certainly no shortage of investment in the infrastructure of the port: a contemporary estimate suggests that, by 1811, £1 million had been spent on the erection of warehouses in the centre of the town[xiii] and merchants were the heaviest investors in the bonds issued by the Corporation to raise money for dock construction. Thus, before 1775 the town had few charitable institutions: only the Blue-Coat Hospital and the Liverpool Infirmary were supported by voluntary contributions and the Seaman's Hospital was financed by monthly deductions from the wages of Liverpool seamen. The pace of charitable activity quickened in the last quarter of the century, with the establishment of the Dispensary for supplying medical assistance to the poor, the Blind Asylum and philanthropic societies such as the Benevolent Society and the Ladies' Charity. Occasionally, merchants were involved in the administration of charitable organisations (Ralph Earle, a leading timber merchant, was treasurer of the Infirmary in 1770[xiv],) but, on the whole, the mercantile elite preferred to give money rather than time.

Much time was, of course, devoted to the business of trade. The growth of Liverpool in the first half of the eighteenth century owed much to the lucrative West Indian trade in sugar and tobacco but, by the mid-century, Liverpool merchants had also established a significant foothold in the notorious 'Africa Trade'. In the next quarter of a century Liverpool outstripped its main competitors, London and Bristol, completing a total of about 1909 slave voyages between 1750 and 1779.[xv] Brooke covers this 'odious and inhuman source of emolument' in his survey of the commercial and industrial life of late eighteenth-century Liverpool, including his personal recollection of the sale in the town of irons for branding slaves (p.233). Although he confirms that spectacular profits were made from slave voyages, he adds little to the recent debates about the relative value of the trade to the town, apart from an interesting aside about the rapid dissolution of fortunes derived from slavery. This was, perhaps, a deliberate attempt to distance contemporary Liverpool from any remaining connection with this discredited source of wealth. He also makes no reference to the black community, whether free or enslaved, in eighteenth-century Liverpool, apart from an incidental reference in a footnote to the discovery of 'a little negro boy...concealed in a clockcase, whither he had fled for safety' during the riots of 1775 (p.341). As the child was found in the home of one of the leading merchants involved in the slave trade, Mr William James, it is likely that he was an imported slave. There is little evidence to suggest that slaves were regularly brought into Liverpool, although an advertisement in the *Liverpool Courier* in 1768 offered 'A Fine Negro Boy, of about 4 feet 5 inches high. Of a sober, tractable, humane Disposition, Eleven or Twelve Years of Age, talks English very well, and can Dress Hair in a tolerable way'[xvi]

Other facets of Georgian Liverpool were more enlightened, especially given the absence of the guilds, monopolies and restrictive practices of more established urban communities. Brooke's father was one of the many immigrants from the surrounding counties who were drawn to Liverpool by this freer and more entrepreneurial environment. There is also some indication that this less restrictive and more dynamic atmosphere was of advantage to another of the 'hidden' communities of the eighteenth-century: women. Buried in the mass of detail of people and places provided by Brooke, there are occasional references to the activities of prominent women. The list of 103 subscribers to the newly established Dispensary, published in 1779, included four women. One of these, Frances Waterworth, sister of the sugar refiner Stephen Waterworth, died in 1803 and, according to Brooke, left an endowment of £4000 to provide free education for poor children at a school built by her brother.

It was, of course, inevitable that women, often as the widows or bereaved daughters of successful merchants, would hold a proportion of the wealth generated in the growing port. The Clayton family built a mercantile fortune at the beginning of the century: the wills of Margaret Clayton, spinster, dated March 1735, and Elizabeth Clayton, her sister-in-law and widow of William Clayton, dated May 1740, give some indication of the wealth at the disposal of such women.[xvii] Both left a large number of legacies to female relatives, godchildren and maids, often circumscribed with specific conditions to prevent husbands from acquiring these funds. Elizabeth Clayton's daughter, Sarah, was named as the sole executrix of the will of her mother. The spirited approach of the Clayton women may have been exceptional but there is evidence that a number of other women in eighteenth-century Liverpool were controlling their funds, depositing significant sums of money on bond with the Corporation for dock construction and gaining a solid return of 4% interest or above.[xviii] Yet, by the end of the period, Liverpool appeared to be rather more restrictive for women than half a century earlier: whereas the Liverpool Library, founded in 1758, was open to both men and women who could afford the entry fee of one guinea, by 1797 the proposal to establish the Athenaeum library was circulated only to the town's leading male citizens and women were not admitted.[xix]

Brooke also reveals little of the life of Liverpool's less affluent citizens, although they are mentioned briefly in his account of elections and in his description of their 'rude and coarse' amusements (p.266). The one significant exception is his reconstruction of the details of the sailors' riots of late August and early September 1775, drawn mainly from the London press. Riots were common in eighteenth-century England due to the lack of effective channels of communication for the views of the less privileged members of the community. Although two-thirds of all popular disturbances in this period were connected with food shortages or high food prices, especially during the turbulence of the American War or the French Revolutionary Wars, wage disputes could also trigger riots. Brooke's account reveals the extent to which the town could be terrorized by a mob of angry sailors, who attacked the Exchange and the homes of the merchants who had attempted to lower their wages. Troops had to be called from Manchester to suppress the disturbances. Brooke suggests that the local mismanagement of the whole affair led to its suppression in the local press until the subsequent trial of fourteen sailors at Lancaster in April 1776. The whole incident demonstrates the frailty of local government in the eighteenth century, especially during the recurring periods of war, which caused severe fluctuations in trade and employment.

Although Brooke's book is entirely a product of its time in terms of its antiquarian approach, it is also of wider significance. He does capture the excitement of a town growing by 130% in twenty-five years during which, undeterred by wars and riots and unashamed of their uneventful history, the citizens of Liverpool laid the foundations of her Victorian prosperity. It is therefore fitting that the lives of the late eighteenth-century men and women who contributed so much to this phenomenal success story should begin to emerge from the shadows.

Jane Longmore
University of Greenwich

[i] See especially H.J.Dyos (ed.), *The Study of Urban History* (London, 1968).

[ii] E.A.Wrigley, *People, Cities and Wealth* (Oxford, 1987), 177, 179.

[iii] M.J.Daunton, *Progress and Poverty: An Economic and Social History of Britain 1700-1850* (Oxford, 1995), 136-145.

[iv] P.Corfield, *The Impact of English Towns, 1700-1800* (Oxford, 1982).

[v] D.Eastwood, *Government and Community in the English Provinces, 1700-1870* (Basingstoke, 1997).

[vi] P.Clark (ed.), *The Cambridge Urban History of Britain, Volume II, 1540-1840* (Cambridge, 2000), 474 .

[vii] W.Moss, *The Liverpool Guide* (Liverpool, 1796), 1.

[viii] R.Muir, *Bygone Liverpool* (Liverpool, 1913). It is worth noting that in his earlier *A History of Liverpool* (Liverpool, 1907), 348, he had referred to Brooke's work as 'a useful collection of fragments and documents'.

[ix] R.Sweet, *The Writing of Urban Histories in Eighteenth-Century England* (Oxford, 1997), 253

[x] W.W.Currie (ed.), *Memoir of the Life, Writings and Correspondence of James Currie M.D. of Liverpool* (London, 1831), 360.

[xi] Liverpool Record Office (LRO), Tarleton Papers, 920 TAR / 2.

[xii] P.Borsay, *The English Urban Renaissance: Culture and Society in the Provincial Town, 1660-1770* (Oxford, 1989), 265.

[xiii] LRO, 942 HOL/34 Holt Papers.

[xiv] LRO, Underhill Papers, 920 UND/3

[xv] J.Black, *Eighteenth Century Britain* (Basingstoke, 2001), 73.

[xvi] Quoted in G.Gerzina, *Black England. Life Before Emancipation* (London, 1995), 7.

[xvii] LRO, Tarleton Papers, 920 TAR 1/5 and 920 TAR 1/7.

[xviii] LRO, 352 MIN/DOC 1/1 Dock Committee Minute Book, January 1793-June 1811.

[xix] A.Wilson, 'The Cultural Identity of Liverpool 1790-1850: The Early Learned Societies', *Transactions of Historic Society of Lancashire and Cheshire, Volume 147,* (Liverpool, 1998).

Illustrations added to the 2003 edition

Cover

A view of the town and harbour of Leverpool, taken from the Bowling Green, near the Public Walk, 1770.
Coloured lithograph by Edward Rooker, after Michael Angelo Rooker.
Local Illustrations Collection 294.

Colour illustrations

1.   St. George's Church, Derby Square.
        Lithograph by W. G. Herdman.
        In: Pictorial relics of Ancient Liverpool by W. G. Herdman, 1843, plate 18.
        Hf 942.7214 HER

2.   The Royal Liverpool Umpire, Horn and Co.'s light post coach,1817.
        Engraving by R. Havell, from a drawing by James Pollard.
        Binns Collection D 313.

3.   View of Everton, 1817.
        Engraving by Daniel Havell, from a drawing by W. Cowen.
        Binns Collection D 305A.

4.   James Street c.1822/23.
        Lithograph by W. G. Herdman.
        In: Pictorial relics of Ancient Liverpool by W. G. Herdman, 1843, plate 19.
        Hf 942.7214 HER.

5.   Old Infirmary and Almshouses, showing the Folly Fair, held on the site of
        what is now St. George's Hall.
        Lithograph by W. G. Herdman.
        In: Pictorial relics of Ancient Liverpool by W. G. Herdman, 1843, plate 38.
        Hf 942.7214 HER.

Black and white illustrations

1. Plan of Liverpool, c.1795.
   Engraved by Palmer.
   Photographs and Small Prints Collection.

2. Chapel Street in 1797.
   Lithograph by W. G. Herdman.
   In: Pictorial relics of Ancient Liverpool by W. G. Herdman, 2nd series,
   1857, plate 6.
   Hf 942.7214 HER.

3. Old Dock and Custom House, 1773.
   Lithograph by W. G. Herdman.
   Local Illustrations Collection 264.

4. Lord Street in 1798, from Doran's Lane to Whitechapel.
   Lithograph by W. G. Herdman.
   In: Pictorial relics of Ancient Liverpool by W. G. Herdman, 2nd series,
   1857, plate 13.
   Hf 942.7214 HER.

5. Liverpool in 1770, showing the Town Hall, St. Nicholas Church,
   St. George's Church and the old Goree Warehouses.
   Lithograph by W. G. Herdman.
   In: Pictorial relics of Ancient Liverpool by W. G. Herdman, 1843, plate 49.
   Hf 942.7214 HER

6. Sir Banastre Tarleton, (1754-1833), M.P. for Liverpool 1790-1812.
   Engraved and published by J. R. Smith, after the painting by Sir Joshua
   Reynolds, 1782.
   Binns Collection C25.

7. High Street, from the corner of Tithebarn Street, looking towards Dale
   Street, 1797.
   Watercolour by W. Herdman.
   Herdman Collection 1266.

8.   Old Fish Market, James Street, 1822.
      Lithograph by W. G. Herdman.
      In: Pictorial relics of Ancient Liverpool by W. G. Herdman, 1843, plate 20.
      Hf 942.7214 HER.

9.   Blue Coat School and School Lane.
      Lithograph by W. G. Herdman.
      In: Pictorial relics of Ancient Liverpool by W. G. Herdman, 2nd series 1857,
      plate 26.
      Hf 942.7214 HER.

10.   Frontispiece to the 'Lecture on heads' delivered at Mr. Wrigley's New
      Room by George Alexander Stevens on 12th December 1766.
      Hq 655

11.   Custom House (4th) and Old Dock.
      Lithograph by W. G. Herdman.
      In: Pictorial relics of Ancient Liverpool by W. G. Herdman, 2nd series 1857,
      plate 18.
      Hf 942.7214 HER.

12.   William Roscoe.
      Drawn and engraved by J. Thompson.
      From the European Magazine, 1822.
      Photographs and Small Prints Collection.

13.   Playbill for the Theatre Royal, 2nd August 1798.
      Performance of 'The Stranger', with a note of the death of Mr. Palmer
      during the performance. The next night's performance was cancelled.
      In: Liverpool playbills: Theatre Royal 1797-1798.
      Hf 792.1 THE.

14.   Castle Street from the Exchange, looking south, 1786.
      Watercolour.
      Herdman Collection 1268.

15.   Balloon ascent: V. Lunardi, Mrs. Sage and C. Biggin Esq., 1785.
      Engraved by F Bartolozzi, after the painting by Rigaud.
      Binns Collection D 61.

LIVERPOOL

as it was

DURING THE LAST QUARTER

of

THE EIGHTEENTH CENTURY,

1775 TO 1800.

BY

RICHARD BROOKE, Esq. F.S.A.

LIVERPOOL:

J. MAWDSLEY AND SON, CASTLE-STREET.

LONDON: JOHN RUSSELL SMITH, 36, SOHO-SQUARE.

1853.

Printed by J. Mawdsley and Son, Castle-street, Liverpool.

PREFACE.

To trace the progressive increase of the commerce, population, and size, of any flourishing city or town, and to record information, communicated by persons now in their graves, which would otherwise have perished, constitute pursuits, certainly of a harmless, and possibly of a useful, nature.

The rapid and surprising changes which have occurred in Liverpool, even within the memory of man, and the commercial magnitude and prosperity which it has attained, induced the author, years ago, to devote some time and exertions, in collecting information respecting it; and he has succeeded in obtaining some original and interesting particulars, not only from sources of a documentary nature, but also from several old persons who were well acquainted with the town during the concluding quarter of the last century.

Amongst the persons who have furnished him with much valuable information, he may be allowed to particularize an aged individual, who was well known to many of the old inhabitants of Liverpool, and who, during the early part of a very long life, was well acquainted with the town, and possessed a remarkable fund of knowledge relative to its commerce and statistics, and the pursuits of its inhabitants. He was a person of the strictest veracity, and gifted with a very retentive memory, which it pleased Providence to permit him to enjoy until the period of his death. That individual was the author's father.*

In laying this Treatise before the public, the author may be permitted to observe, that, in undertaking it, he did not seek private gain, but he considered that its publication might probably be attended with the advantage, of preventing the information so acquired, from being lost to the public.

It is only proper to mention, that this work has not any pretensions to be a history of Liverpool; but it contains a descriptive acccount of the town, with an outline of its commerce and statistics, of the principal occurences, and of the habits, pursuits, and manners of its inhabitants, during the 25 years which elapsed between the commencement of the year 1775 and the termination of the 18th century; and the chief object of the work is to preserve, unimpaired, the knowledge of various particulars and events relating to Liverpool, most of which would, perhaps, otherwise soon have been forgotten.

RICHARD BROOKE.

LIVERPOOL, 7th November, 1853.

---

* He was born on the 14th of June, 1761, and died on the 15th of June, 1852, after having just entered his 92nd year. He had resided in Liverpool from the 13th of January, 1776; and it is believed that he was the last, or one of the last, surviving persons who had been resident there during most of the American Revolutionary War. Some rather remarkable particulars respecting him and his knowledge of Liverpool, appeared in an account published in one of the Liverpool newspapers soon after his death, a copy of which will be found in the Appendix, No. XIV.

LIVERPOOL

AS IT WAS,

During the last Quarter

OF

THE EIGHTEENTH CENTURY,

1775 TO 1800.

INTRODUCTION.

DURING the present, and a considerable part of the last century, Liverpool has advanced in commercial greatness and prosperity, with a rapidity which is almost unprecedented; and from being a place comparatively unimportant, it has become one of the most populous and prosperous commercial towns in Europe. Its origin, however, is enveloped in obscurity, and so little is known of the early history of this modern Carthage, that it is very doubtful whether it existed during the period of the Anglo-Saxon sway; if it did then exist, it was probably nothing more than a collection of mean hovels, inhabited by poor fishermen and herdsmen. The same uncertainty presents itself at the period of the Norman Invasion. Liverpool is not even named in Domesday Book, which is one of the most authentic and curious relics of antiquity connected with this country; nor is there any account of Lancashire, as a distinct county, in it, which may possibly be accounted for, from the circumstance, that at the time when William the Conqueror caused it to be compiled,

B

the devastation which had been committed by the Normans, in that, and parts of the other northern counties, had made vast tracts of country depopulated and waste; and the part of Lancashire which lies between the Ribble and the Mersey is included in the survey of Cheshire, in that book. The contractions and peculiar marks which abound, render it not an easy task to read it; but the following are extracts *in extenso*, from the portions, which relate to that part of Lancashire where Liverpool now stands[1]:—

" In Cestre Scire tenet Episcopus ejusdem civitatis de Rege quod ad suum pertinet episcopatum.   Cum suis hominibus totam reliquam terram comitatus tenet Hugo Comes de Rege.   Terram inter Ripam et Mersham tenuit Rogerius Pictavensis—modo tenet Rex."[2]

[TRANSLATION.]

" In Cheshire, the Bishop of the same city holds of the King what appertains to his bishoprick.   All the remaining land of the county, Hugh, the Earl,[3] holds of the King, with his men.   The land between the Ribble and the Mersey, Roger of Poictou held—now the King holds it."

Further on, we find in the same ancient book of record, the following statement :—

" Inter Ripam et Mersham."

" Terram infra scriptam tenuit Rogerius Pictavensis, inter Ripam et Mersham.   In Derbei hundredo."

[TRANSLATION.]

" Between the Ribble and the Mersey."

" Roger of Poictou held the underwritten land, between the Ribble and the Mersey.   In the hundred of Derby."

---

(1) The contractions and peculiar marks introduced in Domesday Book render it besides very difficult to procure a type adapted to a *fac simile* copy.   The survey of the lands, &c. comprised in the book, was completed in 1086.—Sir Henry Ellis's Introduction to Domesday Book, vol. 1, page 4.   Many of the Latin words used at that period, and for centuries afterwards, are very strange, and often seem invented to express some local custom, tenure, or duty ; indeed, the mediæval Latin is entirely a dialect *per se*, the terms used being always unclassical and often barbarous.

(2) Domesday Book, vol. 1, edition of 1783, published by the direction of the Commissioners of Public Records.

(3) Hugh Lupus, Earl of Chester.

It then proceeds to mention Roby, Knowsley, Kirkby, Crosby, Maghull, Aughton, Huyton, Torbock, Toxteth, Sefton, Kirkdale, Litherland, Ince Blundell, Thornton, Meols, Woolton, Allerton, Speke, Childwall, Wavertree, Bootle, and other places in the neighbourhood, amongst which we find Walton mentioned :—

" Winestan tenebat Waletone. Ibi duæ carucatæ terræ et tres bovatæ : valebant octo solidos."[1]

[TRANSLATION.]

" Winestan held Waletone [Walton]. There are two carucates of land, and three bovates : they were worth eight shillings."

From the circumstance of Liverpool not being named, whilst so many places in its vicinity are mentioned, it has been surmised, that from its then insignificance, it was included with Walton,[2] of which parish it remained a part for centuries, and was only separated from it by an Act of Parliament[3] in 1699.

If historical records fail us, so that we cannot trace out any authentic account of Liverpool immediately after the Norman Invasion, we may well be ignorant of all matters relating to it, or to the part of Lancashire near it, at a far more remote period; yet, in various places in the county, there have occasionally been discovered, the graves, mortal remains, weapons, implements, and even the rude canoes[4] of wild and

---

(1) As some slight difference as to the construction to be put upon the contractions, which exist in the passage in Domesday Book, may be observed in the works of some writers, the author has judged it best to give the above extract *in extenso*, as it is given by Dr. Whitaker, F.S.A. in his History of Whalley, 3rd edition, book 1, chap. 3, page 38, he being a high authority upon such points. The figures and word in contractions, " VIII sol " are inserted above the end of the line, in the printed copy published in 1783.

(2) Although commonly called Walton, the correct name is Walton-on-the-Hill.

(3) Act of 10 and 11 William III, c. 36.

(4) Upon draining Martin Mere, in Lancashire, there were discovered no less than eight canoes, in figure and dimensions not much unlike those used in America,

uncivilized tribes, of great antiquity, whose very names have
been forgotten in the lapse of ages.

Not long before the Norman Conquest, that part of Lancashire which lay to the eastward of the Mersey, was principally either forest land, or swampy and unproductive. To the
northward and north-eastward, with the exception of some
rather elevated ground near Ormskirk, the country between
the Mersey and the Ribble was almost entirely flat and
marshy; and, from the numerous trunks of trees, which are
even now frequently dug up in that district, many parts of it
must, in remote times, have been covered with woods of
considerable size. Some other parts of Lancashire consisted
of wild tracts, in most of which were extensive forests, moors,
and swamps, and a small portion only was cultivated. "Could
a curious observer" says the eloquent historian of Whalley,
"of the present day carry himself nine or ten centuries back,
and ranging the summit of Pendle, survey the forked vale
of Calder on one side, and the bolder margins of Ribble and
Hodder on the other, instead of populous towns and villages,
the castle, the old tower-built house, the elegant modern
mansion, the artificial plantation, the park and pleasure
ground, or instead of uninterrupted inclosures, which have
driven sterility almost to the summit of the fells, how great
must then have been the contrast, when ranging either at a

---

one of which had some plates of iron upon it; and in a morass at Sawick, about nine
miles distant from the mere, a stone instrument resembling a whetstone, and with it
one of the ancient weapons, or implements, (antiquaries differ as to their use,) called
celts, of mixed metal.—Dr. Leigh's Natural History of Lancashire, page 18, and
also page 181, where engraved representations of one of the canoes, the stone instrument, and the celt, are given. Dr. Leigh also states that a human body had been found
in a moss, near Meols, in Lancashire.—Ibid. page 65 and 119. It is supposed to have
been that of one of the early inhabitants of the country. Since Dr. Leigh wrote that
work, in 1700, other human remains, apparently of very remote antiquity, as well as
other celts, and implements of the ancient inhabitants, have occasionally been discovered
in Lancashire.

distance, or immediately beneath, his eye must have caught
vast tracts of forest ground, stagnating with bog, or dark-
ened by native woods, where the wild ox, the roe, the stag,
and the wolf, had scarcely learned the supremacy of man;
when directing his view to the intermediate spaces, to the
windings of the valleys, or the expanse of plain beneath, he
could only have distinguished a few insulated patches of culture, each encircling a village of wretched cabins, among which
would still be remarked one rude mansion of wood, scarcely
equal in comfort to a modern cottage, yet then rising proudly
eminent above the rest, where the Saxon lord, surrounded
by his faithful Cotarii, enjoyed a rude and solitary independence, owning no superior but his sovereign."[1]

To the southward and eastward of the part where
Liverpool now stands, there were extensive forests, and with
but a limited space cultivated, and that in a rude and imperfect manner; and there is every reason to believe that it
remained in the same state until after the commencement of
the 14th century.[2]

Long after the Norman Invasion, Lancashire abounded
with forests, the haunts of wild animals of the chace; and it
will perhaps surprise a modern sportsman, who never pursued any nobler game than foxes or hares, to be informed,
that more than a century after that event, the hunter

---

(1) Whitaker's History of Whalley, book 3, chap. 1, page 171; 3rd edition. About
a fourteenth part of the Parish of Whalley was cultivated at the date of Domesday
Book—Hallam's View of the State of Europe during the Middle Ages, vol. 2, page 421,
(in notis); 8th edition, 8vo.

(2) In the 2nd year of Edward the 3rd, (1328,) the forests of Toxteth, Croxteth,
and Simmonswood, are mentioned in the proceedings in Parliament of that year.—
Rotuli Parliamentorum, anno 1328, vol. 2, page 29. Even as late as the year 1485,
(and probably much later,) we find that a person filled the office of Master Forester, in
respect of those forests, and that Thomas Scaresbreke, servant to Sir Edward Stanley,
Knight, then held that office by letters patent.—Rotuli Parliamentorum, 1st Henry
the 7th, vol. 6, page 363.

might have roused the wild boar from his lair, and the stag and the roe-buck from their coverts, in Lancashire. The fact, however, cannot well be disputed, for we have the evidence of the Parliamentary Rolls,[1] that in the reign of Edward the Second, a petition, in Norman French, was presented from the inhabitants of Lancashire, stating that the Earl of Morton, afterwards King John, by his Charter, granted to them the privilege of cutting wood, and of pursuing and taking every kind of wild animal, except the stag, the hind, the roe-buck, and the wild hog, "*forpris cerf, e bisse,*[2] *chevereil, e pork salvage,*" in his forest, in that county.[3]

Leland, the antiquary, who wrote in the reign of Henry the Eighth, mentions Blakeley, which is near Manchester, in his "Itinerary," and states that wild boars, bulls (by which he is usually considered to mean wild cattle), and falcons bred there, "in times paste."[4] He also mentions, that at

---

(1) Rot. Parl. 18th Edward the 2nd, A.D. 1324 and 1325, vol. 1, page 421.

(2) *Biche*, in modern French, is the word for the hind, the female of the stag.

(3) "A n're seigneur le Roi monstre ses liges de Counte de Lancastre, qe com le Roi Johan tant com il estoit Conte de Moreton, par sa chartre les graunta, qe eus e lour heires, sans chalenge de luy e de ses heires, lour propres boys poient assarter, vendre e doner, a lour voluntez, e que eus fuissent quitts de reward de forest; e ensement q'il puissent chaser e prendre, levre, e gupyl, e chescune manere de beste de salvagine, forpris cerf, e bisse, chevereil, e pork salvage, tutes partes dedeinz sa forest en le dit Counte, dehors ses demeynes hayes. Est puys apres, mesmes cele chartre en le primer an de son regne conferma. E ensement le Roy Henry, l'an de son regne trezisme, les dites chartres recita e confirma. Dount il prient a n're Seigneur le Roi, q'il luy pleise celes chartres confermer, e commander p: Bref a ces Ministres en celes parties, qe eus ne soient sur les ditz pointz grevez ne chalengez."
Responsio.—"Veignent en Chauncellerie, & monstrent lur chartres, & les confermements, et le Roy se avisera. Coram Rege."—Rotuli Parliamentorum, 18th Edward the 2nd, A.D. 1324 and 1325, vol. 1, page 421.

(4) Leland's Itinerary, vol. 7, folio 57. Dr. Whitaker, in his History of Whalley, 3rd edition, page 205, states that tradition records, that the wild cattle, mentioned by Leland, were transported from Blakeley into the Dean's or Abbot's Park of Whalley, and that they were removed, after the dissolution of Whalley Abbey, to Gisburne Park, in Yorkshire, where their descendants still remain. Dr. Whitaker also adduces

the time when he wrote, there were in Lancashire three forests of red deer, Wyersdale, Bowland, and Bleasdale, which were partly woody and partly heathy;[1] and we learn from Dr. Whitaker, that the last stags of Bowland Forest

---

many reasons for the belief, that not only wild cattle, but wolves, stags, fallow deer, and roe deer, were to be found wild in various parts of England, long after the period of the Norman Conquest. Those persons who are curious upon such a topic will find it dwelt upon by Dr. Whitaker, in his History of Whalley, 3rd edition, page 197 to 205.

The Author does not consider it digressing too far from the subject, to mention here, though not particularly relating to Lancashire, that however King Edgar might have flattered himself with the idea, that the annual tribute of wolves' heads, which, it has been said, he imposed upon the Welsh princes, if indeed the account be not an exaggerated or idle tale, had effected the destruction of the race of those animals, it is certain, that in the reign of Edward the 1st, they existed, and had so increased, in many parts of England, that a commission was issued by him, to Peter Corbet, for the destruction, by means of men, dogs, and engines, of wolves, in all forests, parks, and other places, in Gloucestershire, Worcestershire, Herefordshire, Shropshire, and Staffordshire, and a royal mandate or precept was issued in 1281, the 9th of Edward the 1st, to all bailiffs, &c. commanding them to be aiding and assisting Peter Corbet in the destruction of wolves, in those counties. The commission is alluded to by Bingley, the naturalist, but he has omitted to give the date, or any reference where an account of it was to be found. Dr. Whitaker has not noticed it in his work above mentioned. As the mandate is a curiosity, it is considered advisable to publish it, precisely as it appears in the Fœdera :—

A.D. 1281. " Rex omnibus Ballivis etc : Sciatis quod injunximus dilecto &
An : 9 Edwd. I. fideli nostro Petro Corbet, quod in omnibus forestis, & parcis, &
Pat : 9 Edwd. I. aliis locis, infra comitatus nostros Gloucestr' Wygorn' Hereford'
m 20. Salop' & Stafford' in quibus lupi poterunt inveniri, lupos, cum
in Turr : Lond : hominibus, canibus & ingeniis suis, capiat, & destruat, modis omnibus quibus viderit expedire.

" Et ideo vobis mandamus quod eidem Petro in omnibus, quæ ad captionen luporum in comitatibus prædictis, pertinet, intendentes sitis & auxiliantes, quotiens opus fuerit, & prædictus Petrus vobis scire faciet ex parte nostra.

" In cujus &c. duratur' quamdiu nobis placuerit. Teste Rege apud Westm' decimo quarto die Maii."

Fœdera (modern edition) Tome 1, pt. 2, p. 591 ;
Ibid. folio edition of 1705, Tome 2, p. 168.

(1) Leland's Itinerary vol 5, folio 84. He also mentions a large inclosed Park at Myerscough, on the Moor side, stocked with red deer.—Ibid.

were destroyed within the memory of the then keeper, a fine old forester of more than four-scoro.[1]

In consequence of the barbarous state of England, immediately before the Norman Conquest, it would be in vain to expect to find many traces of commercial pursuits, at that period, in Lancashire.

The higher classes of the Anglo-Saxons, consisting of the great landowners, were a powerful body; there was no middle class; for the small landowners or inferior thanes, were too insignificant to merit such an appellation; and the common people were the vassals of the great landowners, by whom they were considered of no account, except so far as they could be made useful to them, and contributed to their power, or to the cultivation of their lands. The mutual relation of lord and vassal, strongly partaking of the nature of the feudal system, appears to have existed;[2] the natural effect of which, was to give almost despotic power to the owners of large possessions, and to depress and reduce the common people to a very low state of degradation. Under whatever form, and wherever the feudal system prevailed, it followed as a necessary consequence, that true liberty, the rational freedom of all classes, could not exist; and the only class who possessed even a semblance of it, was that of the great landowners who enjoyed, in the plenitude of their power, a wild and turbulent licence, which induced them to consider themselves rather as the equals, than the subjects of the sovereign. Liberty was unknown to the common

---

(1) Dr. Whitaker's History of Whalley, 3rd edition, published in 1818, page 235, (note *). He also states, ibid. page 237, that in the year 1805, a fine herd of wild deer, the last vestage of feudal superiority in the domains of the Lacies, were destroyed at Bowland.

(2) Hallam's View of the State of Europe during the Middle Ages, vol. 2, page 85 and 89; 8th edition, 8vo.

people, who ranked no higher in the scale, than "hewers of wood, and drawers of water," and it may well be more than doubted, whether they were sufficiently well informed, to appreciate such a blessing.

Immediately before the Norman Invasion, so generally profound was the ignorance, and so universal was the mental darkness, which prevailed, that there is every reason to believe, that in the whole of England, Scotland, and Ireland, there then were very few individuals amongst the higher, and not one of the lower classes, who could read or write.[1]

After the Norman Conquest, the common people of England were much more oppressed than before. The feudal system, and forest laws were carried out in a most severe and cruel manner.[2] Human beings were transferred as appertinent to the land which they tilled, much in the same manner in which cattle change hands; nearly all the lower classes were serfs or vassals; and instances have occurred, where freemen were so oppressed and degraded, and their condition rendered so intolerable, that many of them in despair surrendered their liberty, and voluntarily consented to become the vassals of some powerful noble, in order to ensure protection against more dangerous individuals, and

(1) See Hallam's View of the State of Europe during the Middle Ages, vol. 2, 8th edition, 8vo. pages 66, 68 and 79, for various proofs of the barbarous and degraded state, in which the Anglo-Saxons were with respect to their laws. See also, on the same subject, Robertson's Charles the 5th, vol. 1, page 16 and page 451, (in notis:) and also Carte's History of England, edition of 1747, vol. 1, page 366, and the authorities there cited.

(2) The penalty for killing a stag or boar, was the loss of eyes.—Hallam's View of the State of Europe during the Middle Ages, vol. 2, page 94, 8th edition. The destruction of a deer, within the limits of the forest, was as penal as the death of a man. —2 Blackstone's Com. chap. 27, page 416, 14th edition. In the Charter of the Forest of the 9th Henry the 3rd, chap. 10, A.D. 1224-5, it was declared, that thenceforth *no man should lose life or limb for killing the King's deer*, but that a grievous fine should be imposed on him, if he had any means of payment; and if not, that he should lie a year and a day in prison.

c

to obtain the means of subsisting themselves, and their families. As has been before observed, one great feudal potentate, Roger of Poictou, at one time owned all the land between the Ribble and the Mersey.[1]

Under circumstances so depressing to commerce, it was impossible that it could flourish, therefore it can scarcely be expected, that antiquaries, or historians, should find Liverpool mentioned, as a trading town, or even be able to discover any certain trace of its existence, before or soon after the Norman Conquest. Even for some time after that event, commerce was on a most insignificant scale. England had few superfluities to dispose of, and few necessities of which the supply was imperative; navigation was unsafe, in consequence of the unskilfulness of the seamen, the want of the mariner's compass, and the seas being exposed to the incursions of pirates; nor was it certain that foreigners bringing commodities to England, could rely on protection, in a barbarous age, or be secure of a friendly reception, in the ports of an uncivilized country. Even between different parts of England, the communication was difficult and unfrequent, in consequence of the bad and dangerous state of the roads, bridges, ferries, and fords, and the disorganized state of society.

Although it is true, that for sometime after the Norman Conquest, the commerce of England was on a most limited scale, still some little commerce did exist, which England carried on principally with France, the Low Countries, and Spain. Some articles were in demand, which either could not be produced or manufactured, in this country, or which were produced or manufactured, on a very small scale; such as wine for the drunken carousals of the Norman nobles,

---

(1) Domesday Book, vol. 1, edition of 1783. In some works he is called Roger of Poictiers.

vessels and utensils of silver for ornament or entertainments, manufactured silks, and rich furs for dresses, armour, military weapons, bowstaves, fruits, of which scarcely any were then grown in England, spices and drugs, which came from the East, by way of Venice and Genoa. Sugar was even about that period brought into Europe, from the East, where it was then and had long previously been produced. It probably was brought into Western Europe in very small quantities, as an article of curiosity or medicine.[1]

England, in return for articles of commerce which she received from abroad, had not much to send. The English manufactured some coarse woollen clothing, and a little linen; but probably not much more than was needed for their own consumption. They had not many articles to export, except wool, hides, skins, some metals, and perhaps salt and cattle. The balance of trade with the nations of the continent, would, therefore, be against the English, who would, consequently, have to pay the difference in silver, the only metal then used for the purposes of commerce. Some commercial intercourse, however limited, was even then kept up between England and Ireland, we are, however, much in the dark as to its nature or extent.[2] From the middle of the twelfth century to that of the thirteenth, the trade of England became more extensive and prosperous.

---

(1) The sugar cane was cultivated in Sicily, about 100 years after the Norman Conquest, though perhaps only to a limited extent. It may here be remarked, that the sugar cane is believed to be mentioned in the Holy Scriptures by the name of sweet cane.—43rd chap. Isaiah, ver. 24; and 6th chap. Jeremiah, ver. 20.

(2) In England, it was very common even after the Conquest, to export slaves to Ireland, until, in the reign of Henry the 2nd, the Irish came to a non-importation agreement, which put a stop to the practice.—Hallam's View of the State of Europe during the Middle Ages, vol. 2, page 379; 8th edition, 8vo.

William of Malmsbury accuses the Anglo-Saxon nobility of selling their female servants, even when pregnant by them, as slaves, to foreigners.—Ibid. (in notis,) page 379.

The towns on the southern coast exported tin and other metals, in exchange for the wines of France ; those of the eastern coast sent corn to Norway ; the Cinque-ports bartered wool against the stuffs of Flanders.[1]

The fisheries also of England, were, after the Norman Invasion, a source of occupation and gain, at a time when, from the peculiar tenets of the prevailing creed, fish either fresh or cured, formed no inconsiderable portion of the diet of a great part of the population, and gave employment to many of the industrious classes. Commerce and fishing cannot be carried on, even on a small scale, without ports or havens ; and the inlet or creek called, in comparatively modern times, the " Pool," on the eastward side of the estuary of the Mersey, upon the site of which a part of Liverpool now stands, formed a commodious natural harbour for the purpose.

However indifferent the ignorant Anglo-Saxon, or illiterate Norman might be to the fields of coal, the mineral treasures of Lancashire and Cheshire, the value of which he could not appreciate, still he was alive to the utility of the springs of salt in Cheshire, which were then worked and had been worked for ages previously ; and it is fair to suppose, that the portion of the salt made in Cheshire, which had to be sent by sea to Scotland, Ireland, Wales, the western coast of England, and the Isle of Man, would be brought for some distance at least down the Mersey, and not any place could be found there, so eligible as a place of shipment, or as a depôt, preparatory to its final exportation, as the spot where Liverpool now stands. From those and various other causes, though imperceptibly and by slow degrees, Liverpool, from a petty hamlet of hovels, at length

---

(1) Hallam's View of the State of Europe during the Middle Ages, vol. 2, page 157 ; 8th edition, 8vo.

became a small town and obscure seaport, at a period most probably not long after the Norman Conquest.

The name Liverpool has been spelt in a great variety of modes;[1] but it seems most probable, that it is a corruption of the words " Lower Pool ;" the pool, which will be afterwards described, having remained until about the commencement of the 18th century; and the name " Pool," occurs in various places,[2] on the banks of the Mersey, and nearly all of them are higher up the estuary than Liverpool.

In the rude age which succeeded the Norman Conquest, feudal castles and monastic establishments, near a sea port town, had a tendency, in some degree, to promote its increase, by the constant demand of their inmates and visiters upon the productions of its mechanics, and the industry and skill of its mariners and other inhabitants. The castle of Liverpool, erected soon after the Conquest, as it is said by Roger of Poictou,[3] that of Halton, in Cheshire, built about the same period by one of the barons of Halton, the Priory of Birkenhead, and the Abbey of Stanlow, in Cheshire, also erected about the same time, would probably have some slight effect in promoting the increase of Liverpool.

When England began to enjoy a more settled form of government, under succeeding kings, and its population and commerce increased, and a more frequent intercourse took place with Ireland, and the Isle of Man, Liverpool

---

(1) In the various muniments and documents given in evidence, on the important Trial of the Corporation of Liverpool against Bolton and others, in the Queen's Bench, 14th February, 1833, twenty-five varieties in the spelling of its name occur.—See the printed Report of the Proceedings of the Associated Merchants, and of the Bill of Exceptions, in that cause.

(2) Over Poole, Nether Poole, Bromborough Pool, Otterspool, Tranmere Pool, and Wallasey Pool; the two latter have been recently drained, and docks occupy the site of Wallasey Pool.

(3) Camden's Britannia, vol. 3, page 128 ; edition of 1789.

could hardly fail to benefit by those events, and to increase in some degree in size and importance.

Although many of the circumstances may have been fortuitous, which caused the rise and increase of Liverpool, it could not well have been an accident, which induced its first settlers to select the spot on which it stands. The pool, which has been appropriately called the cradle of Liverpool, was situated on the eastern shore of the estuary of the Mersey, and was formed by nature, as a convenient and comparatively secure harbour for vessels, such as they were. It was larger and more commodious, than any other inlet or pool, on either shore of the Mersey, or in that part of South Lancashire; it extended in a curved direction, round the south and east sides of the elevated ground on which the town was originally built, forming not only a harbour, but a natural defence on those two sides, whilst the Mersey formed one on the westward; and though Liverpool never was (as far as is now known) fortified, until the troubles of the 17th century, and then only for a short period, still by barricading the narrow streets on the north side, it might be rendered tolerably secure from the nocturnal attacks of any rude rabble, or gangs of outlaws; a class of men who, it is a matter of history, were not unfrequently driven, by the oppression of the Norman barons, to a desperate and criminal mode of life.

The pool at high water extended round a considerable part of the town, and a stream of fresh water, called, in comparatively modern times, the Brook, flowed into the pool and contributed to keep it open. Their position and extent, will be best understood, by mentioning the tract of ground over which they flowed, by the modern names which have been given to the streets and places afterwards made there. The pool extended in a curved direction from the Mersey, over the places where the Old Dock, now the site

of Canning-place, the old Custom-house, and the yard
behind it (on the eastward) stood, and along the low
ground, part of which is now occupied by Coopers-row,
(a portion of) King-street, Paradise-street, and Whitechapel,
and the lower parts of the contiguous streets. The stream
of fresh water called the Brook, flowed into it, a few yards
to the westward of the point of junction of Byrom-street,
with the old Haymarket or Shaw-place. The water supplying it came principally from the swampy ground, called
in the last century, and even in the present one until not
many years back, the Moss Lake fields, now the site of
Falkner-square, Falkner-street, Abercromby-square, Grove-
street, Chatham-street, Oxford-street, &c., crossed the tract
of land now occupied by Brownlow-hill, the upper end of
Pembroke-place, Daulby-street, London-road, the north
end of Norton-street, the south end of St. Anne-street, the
middle part of Clare-street and Christian-street, and from
thence flowed down the declivity of the hill, to a low spot
or valley, formerly called the Dingle, where Downe-street
now is, to the foot of Richmond-row, where it received a
tributary stream, collected from near Everton and from the
northward, and then flowed a little to the westward of what
is now Byrom-street, into the low tract of ground at present
called Shaw-place or the old Haymarket, where it joined
the Pool.

Although Liverpool, from a petty hamlet, at length
became a small town and sea-port, still she wanted much,
before she attained any rank, amongst the other cities and
towns of England. An institution had however taken root
in Europe, which, whether new, or an ancient one revived,
it is not requisite to discuss here, had a great effect in
encouraging commerce, and did more in England towards
the formation of a middle class of society, and the weaken-
ing of the despotic power of the monarchs and feudal nobles,

than any other civil institution, and which also had a large share in the formation of our present constitutional limited monarchy.

That institution was the forming of cities and towns into communities, by granting them charters of incorporation with perpetual succession. Various kings, feeling to their cost, that there was not any middle class, and that the nobles were too powerful, both for the welfare of the crown and of the common people, soon perceived that the inhabitants of cities and towns if enjoying peculiar privileges, and possessing within themselves a municipal force, trained even in a slight degree to arms, formed some kind of counterpoise to their common adversaries. In England, the oppressive part of the feudal system, appears only partially to have reached the inhabitants of the cities and towns, who, consisting almost entirely of artificers or mechanics, were, in some degree, protected by their insignificance; besides which, in their several vocations, they were useful to the nobles, and it was not their policy, to destroy those who conduced to their comforts or convenience. Charters of incorporation, were originally granted to bodies of men comparatively humble; but great changes in England resulted from the system, which, after towns had obtained charters, soon realised, and more than realised, in beneficial results, the anticipations of the sovereigns who granted them, and who found it their interest to make common cause with such bodies, against their mutual enemies the feudal nobles of England.

At length the period arrived, when Liverpool became a place sufficiently important, to receive charters of different kinds, from various sovereigns. The first charter[1] of any

---

(1) See the examination, in November, 1833, of the then Town Clerk of Liverpool, taken before the Commissioners of Inquiry into the state of Municipal Corporations, in the printed report of the proceedings; on which occasion all the Charters of the

description which Liverpool obtained, is one which was granted by King John; that, however, is not considered to be a charter of incorporation, but a mere grant of a privilege. It was not at all unusual, in former ages, for privileges to be granted to the inhabitants of various towns and places, without incorporating them ; the common cases of grants of the right to hold fairs and markets are instances, and many others might be adduced. The charter is in a good state of preservation, and is dated the 28th of August, in the 9th year of his reign (1207). It is on parchment, and, notwithstanding the lapse of centuries, is fairly legible ; but, as was the custom of the age, it abounds with rather difficult contractions ; and it is very small and of an irregular shape.

The size, shape and general appearance of the charter

---

town were produced on oath, by the Town Clerk. A petition was presented in 1751, by the Mayor, Bailiffs and Burgesses of Liverpool, to King George the 2nd, praying for a new Charter, and in it they distinctly stated that King John granted to the town its first Charter: the petition was read in evidence on the trial of the cause, the Mayor, Bailiffs and Burgesses of Liverpool against Golightly, before Mr. Baron Thompson, at Lancaster, in 1791.[*] In Mr. T. Troughton's History of Liverpool, a copy of a pretended Charter of Henry the 2nd is set out. It was a fabrication of a Mr. James Williamson, a retired solicitor, who possessed a certain degree of shrewdness and talent, and in his way was a character, (the word, according to its common acceptation, being defined as peculiar and original,) and he probably thinking that Mr. T. Troughton was going to write a dull book, thought it an excusable act to play off a hoax. In doing so, however, he, perhaps without intending it, mislead others : even the late Mr. William Statham, formerly the Town Clerk, a gentleman of talents, who possessed much information on such subjects, once in a conversation with the Author of this Work, expressed himself as if staggered, after seeing the pretended copy in print in Troughton's History. The late Mr. Egerton Smith, the talented Editor of the *Liverpool Mercury*, appears to have been the first person who publicly disputed the genuineness of such a Charter. Mr. Baines, the author of the History of Lancashire, was not aware of the fabrication until after a considerable portion of the History had been printed, in which he mentioned it as if it had been genuine. The Author of this Work was in correspondence with Mr. Baines respecting some antiquarian matters, connected with the county, whilst his History of Lancashire was in the press, and

(*) See the printed Report of that Trial, where it is given at length.

D

of John, are as shown by the accompanying wood-cut : it would have been a laborious task to have given a *fac simile* of it.

It is a trifle more than seven inches long, and is three inches wide at the widest end, but only two inches wide at the narrowest end ; and a thin strip of the parchment has been partly detached from the bottom, in order to form a label, to which a seal has evidently

drew his attention to the imposture, and in the course of their correspondence, the

once been attached.   The strip, though much shrivelled, still
hangs to it, but the seal is gone.[1]

Author received a letter from Mr. Baines, dated Leeds, September 27, 1835, of which
the following is an extract relative to the spurious Charter :—

" Whilst I am investigating the matter relating to the Charter of Henry the 2nd,
here, and in London, will you do me the favour to make such enquiries in Liverpool,
as you think calculated to shed any light that may be cast upon it in Liverpool,
and to communicate to me the result as soon as convenient ?   In particular may I beg
that you will enquire of the Record Keeper of the Corporation, and ascertain his views
on the subject.   Before I quit the History of Liverpool, which will be in the 57th
part, I must set at rest the claims of the Charter to authenticity."

In consequence of that letter the Author made some inquiries, the result of
which threw further discredit upon the authenticity of the pretended Charter ; he also
waited upon the then Town Clerk, who was the Record Keeper, for information on the
subject, and was assured by him, that not any thing was known of any Liverpool Charter
previous to that of King John ; and the Author communicated the result of his inquiries
to Mr. Baines : and from inquiries which the latter also pursued, he ascertained that
a draft, in Mr. James Williamson's hand-writing, from which he had made the copy
of the pretended Charter for Mr. Troughton, had been found after Mr. Williamson's
death amongst his papers ; and also, that there was no such Bishop of London at the
alleged date of it, as " Robertus," mentioned in it.   The fabrication was, consequently,
exposed, in a note in the fourth volume of the History of Lancashire.—See Baines's
Lancashire, vol. 4, page 185, (note *).

The statement in a letter of 25th September, 1789, from Mr. Henry Brown,
formerly Deputy Town Clerk, to Mr. Francis Hargrave, the then Recorder of Liverpool, which will be more particularly noticed afterwards, contains this important
passage : " The first Charter we know of is one granted in the 9th of John."   On
the occasion of the investigation by the Commissioners of Inquiry into the Municipal
Corporations, in 1833, a copy of a case, drawn up in 1824, by Mr. William Statham,
the then Town Clerk, and laid before Mr. Tindal, afterwards Lord Chief Justice Tindal,
was also produced before the Commissioners, which contains the following passage :
" The earliest Charter in existence, granted to the Borough of Liverpool is one
of King John, in the year 1208," [quære, meant for 1207] " and the next is one of King
Henry the 3rd, in the year 1229."(†)   But that is not all ; for Mr. Troughton's Work
was only published in our own time, in 1810, many years after the date of the statement
of Mr. Henry Brown ; yet no person pretends that he ever saw such a Charter, or
possessed a copy of a Charter of Henry the 2nd, before Mr. Troughton's Work was
published ; nor did the latter give his authority for it, or state from whom he obtained
it ; from which it may not uncharitably be inferred, that he either knew or had some
suspicion, that it was not genuine.

(†) Printed Report of the Proceedings of the Commissioners of Inquiry into the
Municipal Corporations, page 251.

(1) The Author has been kindly permitted to inspect several of the Charters of the
Borough, and many other documents, in the Town-hall.   Amongst others, he examined,

The following is a copy of the charter, but as the contractions would make it unintelligible to many, it is given here almost wholly *in extenso*[1]:—

"Johannes Dei gratia, Rex Angliæ, Dominus Hiberniæ, Dux Normandiæ, Aquitaniæ, et Comes Andegaviæ, omnibus fidelibus suis qui burgagia apud villam de Lyr'pul habere voluerint, Salutem; Sciatis quod concessimus omnibus fidelibus nostris qui burgagia, apud Lyr'pul ceperint, quod habeant omnes libertates et liberas consuetudines, in villa de Lyr'pul, quas aliquis liber burgus super mare habet in terra nostra.   Et ideo vobis mandamus quod secure et in pace nostra, illuc veniatis ad burgagia nostra, recipienda et hospitanda.   Et in cujus rei testimonium has literas nostras patentes vobis transmittimus.—Teste Simone de Pateshill apud Winton, 28º. die Augusti anno regni nostri nono." [2]

[TRANSLATION.]

"John, by the Grace of God, King of England, Lord of Ireland, Duke of Normandy and Aquitaine, Earl of Anjou, To all his faithful people who would wish to have burgages at the town of Lyverpul, Greeting;   Know ye

in November, 1852, during the Mayoralty of Mr. Samuel Holme, the Charter granted by King John, and gladly avails himself of this opportunity of tendering his sincere thanks, to Mr. Holme, and his predecessor in office, Mr. Littledale, and also to Mr. Shuttleworth, the Town Clerk, for the facilities and courtesy afforded to the Author, whilst he pursued some researches at the Town-hall, during the present and the last mayoralties.

(1) A copy of an instrument, erroneously called a copy of the Charter, appears in the Appendix, page 1, No. 1, to the printed Report of the Proceedings of the Commissioners of Inquiry into the Municipal Corporations of 1833, but it is only a copy of the inrolment of the Charter in Chancery, of which the original is in the Tower of London. A copy of that inrolment is in the possession of the Corporation of Liverpool.

(2) A copy of the Charter, *in extenso*, (except the name of the town in contractions, and the day of the month in figures,) is preserved in the Town-hall, in a book belonging to the Corporation, vol. 16, page 59, from which the above is given; and the Author, having also had access to and examined the original Charter, considers that after allowing for the difficulties, arising from a great number of contractions, and the peculiar writing of so ancient a document, the copy *in extenso* is correct.

that we have granted to all our faithful people who shall have taken burgages at Lyverpul, that they shall have all the liberties and free customs in the town of Lyverpul which any free borough on the sea hath in our land; and we therefore command you that ye shall securely and in our peace come there to receive and inhabit our burgages; and in testimony hereof we send you our letters patent.—Witness, S. de Pateshill, at Winchester, the 28th day of August, in the ninth year of our reign."[1]

Simon de Pateshill was Justiciar of England, from 1206 to 1213, and was re-appointed in 1232. He was also a Baron of the Exchequer in the 4th and 5th years of the reign of John.

It is an important point to observe, that, although by the charter, King John gave to Liverpool the privileges and liberties of a free port, yet it is merely addressed to his faithful people, and does not mention the burgesses, nor does it recognize or provide for a mayor, bailiffs, or any other description of officers, the usual constituent parts of a corporation, nor does it contain any expression calculated to declare the town to be a corporate borough; in fact, it is totally silent on those points. It is important to bear in mind, that an aggregate body of men, not being a corporation,[2] cannot legally use a common seal; and there is not the

---

(1) This translation corresponds with a translated copy of the Charter preserved in the Town-hall, made for the use of the plaintiffs' counsel in the important cause, The Mayor, Bailiffs and Burgesses of Liverpool against Bolton and others, tried in 1833, relative to the right of the Corporation to the Town's Dues: and Mr. William Statham, the then Town Clerk, who prepared the papers and got up the cause for trial, though he did not live to try it, was no common authority, as to the interpretation of charters and other corporate muniments.

(2) Of course it will be understood that the Author is writing of an aggregate temporal corporation, but that rule is also equally applicable to a spiritual corporation aggregate; for example, abbeys, when they legally existed in England, had common seals, because the abbots and monks of the same house were an aggregate spiritual corporation.

slightest reason to suppose, that the town possessed such a
seal until long after the charter of John, nor is it intelligible
how a common seal could be used for Liverpool, before the
town was by charter constituted a corporate town.   There is
a very high legal opinion, which has never been disputed by
any lawyer, which is in the possession of the Corporation of
Liverpool, to the effect, that the charter of King John is not
a charter of incorporation, but a mere grant of a privilege.
That opinion was given by the late Mr. Henry Brown, the
deputy Town Clerk of Liverpool, and solicitor to the Corporation, a gentleman of great legal talents, of whom the late
Lord Chief Justice Ellenborough when Mr. Law, K.C. has
been known to say, that there was not a better corporation
lawyer in existence.   Mr. Brown's opinion is contained in
a statement in a letter from him, of 25th September, 1789,
to Mr. Francis Hargrave, the then Recorder of the town,[1]
from which the following are extracts:—" The first charter
we know of, is one granted in the 9th of John, and even

---

(1)   [OPINION OF MR. HENRY BROWN.]

" With respect to the Corporation being by prescription, I have great doubt;
for I cannot meet, either by search at the Tower or elsewhere, with any Charter of
Incorporation of Liverpool before time of legal memory ; but, on the contrary, the
charters which we have, or know of, very strongly imply the reverse ; for the first
charter we know of is one granted in the 9th of John, (copy of which, as also of all
the other charters thought material, is now laid before you,) and even this charter seems
to be no more than a *mere grant of a privilege*, and *not a Charter of Incorporation.*
The second charter, you will see, is in the 13th Henry the 3rd, and from the words,
" habeant gildam mercatoriam, &c." I presume it is a Charter of Incorporation ; and
from this circumstance, and also, because in our charter of 6th Edward the 3rd, and
other subsequent charters, the earliest inspeximus begins with the Charter of John,
and then proceeds to that of Henry the 3rd, I am strongly led to think that the
Charter of *Henry the 3rd* is the *first Charter incorporating us.*"—Extracted from a
copy of the opinion of Mr. Brown, kept in the Town-hall.   The opinion has also
been published in the printed Report of Proceedings before the Commissioners of
Enquiry into Municipal Corporations, in 1833, page 249.

this charter seems to be no more than *a mere grant of a privilege,* and *not a charter of incorporation;"* and also, "I am strongly led to think, that the charter of *Henry the Third is the first charter incorporating us."* The very limited nature of the charter of John, and the opinion of Mr. Brown, seem very unfortunate for some theories, which have formerly been brought forward, to the effect, that the seal is as old as the time of John, and that his name in contractions is engraved upon it.

However unimportant as a town Liverpool may have ranked, still it appears to have been a port of shipment as early as the reign of John, because in the Sheriff's account, of 13th John, 1212, (in the accounts of the Sheriffs of Lancashire,) the Sheriff took credit for the carriage of men, cattle, hogs, and a great variety of articles, bought and forwarded to the army in Wales, and sent from Lancaster to Liverpool, and so to Chester.[1]

In the 13th year of the reign of King Henry the Third, March 24th, 1229, another charter was granted to Liverpool, by which it became an incorporated borough. This charter abounds in contractions, and contains not a few uncouth words and obsolete expressions. It distinctly recognizes the burgesses of Liverpool. The following is a copy *in extenso*[2]:—

Henricus Dei gratia, Rex Angliæ, Dominus Hiberniæ, Dux Normandiæ et Aquitaniæ, Comes Andegaviæ, archiepiscopis, episcopis, abbatibus, prioribus, comitibus, baronibus,

---

(1) A copy in English accompanied the brief for the plaintiffs' counsel, in the cause, The Corporation of Liverpool against Bolton and others, in 1833.—See Appendix, No. I.

(2) After allowing for the difficulties arising from the contractions, the above copy is as nearly accurate as it could readily be made: it is impossible to say that it is correct in all minute particulars.

justiciariis, vicecomitibus, præpositis, ministris, et omnibus ballivis, et fidelibus suis, Salutem ;

Sciatis nos concessisse, et hac cartâ nostrâ confirmasse, quod villâ nostrâ de Leverepul liber burgus sit in perpetuum, et quod burgenses ejusdem burgi habeant gildam mercatoriam, cum hansâ, et aliis libertatibus, et liberis consuetudinibus, ad gildam illam pertinentibus; et quod nullus qui non sit de gildâ illâ, mercandisam aliquam in prædicto burgo faciat, nisi de voluntate eorundem burgensium. Concessimus etiam eisdem burgensibus et eorum hæredibus, quod habeant soc et sac, et thol et theam, et infangenethef, et quod quieti sint per totam terram nostram, et per omnes portus maris de theloneo, lastagio, passagio, pontagio, et stallagio, et quod nullam sectam comitatuum et wapentaciorum faciant de tenuris suis, quas tenent intra burgum prædictum. Concessimus etiam eisdem burgensibus et eorum hæredibus, quod quicumque mercatores petierint burgum prædictum cum mercandisis suis de quocumque loco fuerint sive extranei, sive alii, qui de pace nostrâ fuerint, vel de licentiâ nostrâ, in terram nostram venerint, salvo et secure ad prædictum burgum, cum mercandisis suis veniant et salvo ibidem morentur, et salvo inde recedant, faciendo inde rectas et debitas consuetudines. Prohibemus etiam, ne quis prædictis burgensibus injuriam, damnum, vel molestiam faciat, super forisforcuram nostram decem librarum. Quare volumus et firmiter præcipimus, quod prædicta villa de Leverepul liber burgus sit, et quod prædicti burgenses habeant prædictam gildam mercatoriam, cum hansâ et aliis libertatibus, et liberis consuetudinibus ad gildam illam pertinentibus, et quod habeant omnes alias libertates et liberas consuetudines, et quietantias, sicut prædictum est.—His testibus H. de Burgo, Comite Kanciæ Justiciario Angliæ, Philippo de Albiniaco, Radulfo filio Nicholai, Nicholao de Molis, Johanne filio Philippi, Galfrido Dispensareo, et aliis.—

Datum per manum venerabilis patris R Cicestriæ Episcopi
Cancellarii nostri, apud Merlebergiam, vicesimo quarto die
Martii, anno Regni nostri tertio decimo.

[TRANSLATION.]

Henry, by the grace of God, King of England, Lord of
Ireland, Duke of Normandy and Aquitain, and Earl of
Anjou; to the archbishops, bishops, abbots, priors, earls,
barons, justices, sheriffs, reeves, ministers, and all his
bailiffs and faithful people, Greeting; Know ye that we
have granted, and by this our charter have confirmed,
that our town of Leverepul shall be for ever a free
borough; and that the burgesses of the same borough
shall have a merchants' guild, with a hanse, and other
liberties, and free customs, to the same guild appertaining, and that no one who is not of the same guild shall
transact any merchandize in the aforesaid borough, unless
by consent of the same burgesses. We have also granted
to the same burgesses and their heirs, that they may have
soc and sac, and tol and theam, and infangenethef, and
that they shall be quit throughout our whole land, and
through all sea-ports, of toll, lastage, passage, pontage, and
stallage; and that they shall do no suit of counties and
wapentakes, for their tenures, which they hold within the
borough aforesaid. We have granted also to the same
burgesses and their heirs, that whatsoever merchants shall
seek the borough aforesaid, with their merchandize, of whatsoever place they may be, whether strangers or others, who
may be of our peace, or with our licence, may have come
into our land, may safely and securely come to the aforesaid
borough with their merchandize, and safely remain there,
and safely thence depart, doing, therefore, the right and due
customs. We prohibit also, any one from injuring, damaging,
or molesting the aforesaid burgesses, upon forfeiture to us of
ten pounds. Wherefore we will and firmly command, that

E

the aforesaid town of Leverepul shall be a free borough, and that the aforesaid burgesses shall have the aforesaid merchants' guild, with a hanse and other liberties, and free customs to that guild appertaining, and that they shall have all other liberties and free customs and acquittances as is aforesaid.—These being witnesses, H. de Burgh, Earl of Kent Justice of England, Philip d'Aubeney, Ralph, son of Nicholas, Nicholas de Moles, John, son of Philip, Geoffrey Despenser, and others.—Given by the hand of the venerable Father R., Bishop of Chichester, our Chancellor, at Marl-borough, the twenty-fourth day of March, in the thirteenth year of our reign.

In the next year, the 13th of Henry the Third, (25th March, 1229,) he granted, the town of Liverpool, for four years, to the *honest men* of Liverpool, at a rent of £10 a year.[1]

It will be remarked, on referring to the charter of Henry the Third, that although it is considered to be a charter of incorporation, and declares Liverpool to be a free borough for ever, contains a grant to the burgesses of a merchants' guild, and of soc and sac, and toll and theam, and infan-genethef,[2] and freedom of lastage, passage, pontage and stallage, and confers other privileges upon the town; yet, this charter does not provide for or notice either a mayor, bailiffs, or any other corporate officer. Officers, known by the title of the bailiffs of Liverpool, were, however, in existence, as will be presently shown, as early as in 1326, the 20th year of Edward the Second.

---

(1) See Appendix, No. II.

(2) It may be advisable to mention, for the information of those, who are not conversant with the above obsolete words, that according to the interpretation put upon them by old writers, "*Soc*" means power or liberty to minister justice and execute laws; also a circuit or territory wherein such power is exercised. Whence

It is certain, from the frequent mention made of Liverpool soon afterwards, that it must, at a very early period, have become well known as a town and port; and we have evidence that in the 17th year of the reign of Edward the Second, (1323,) that monarch visited Liverpool; a royal mandate or precept having been issued by him, concluding thus, " Teste Rege apud Liverpol xxiiii die Octobris."[1]

In tracing the origin and gradual rise of Liverpool, it is interesting to find at what an early period Liverpool was recognized as a port and a borough. Some few instances will therefore be given.

On the 24th September, in the 20th year of King Edward the Second, (1326,) mandates were sent to several ports of the kingdom, including Liverpool, for the searching for letters, either coming into or going out of the kingdom, and

---

the word *soca* is used for a seigniory or lordship infranchised by the King, with the liberty of holding a court of sockmen.

" *Sac*," *saca*: an ancient privilege which a Lord of a Manor claims to have in his court, of holding plea in causes of trespass, arising amongst his tenants, and of imposing fines and amercements touching the same. It is sometimes used to signify the amercement itself.

" *Toll*," *toluctum*: signifies, generally, a payment in markets and fairs, for goods sold therein.

" *Them*," *team*, *or theame*, was a royalty or privilege granted by the King's Charter to the Lord of a Manor, for the having, restraining, and judging of bondmen and villeins, with their children, goods, and chattels.

"*Infangthief*:" or *infangenethef*, from the Saxon *fang*, to take, signifies a privilege or liberty granted to the Lords of certain Manors, to try any thief taken within their fee.

(1) It appears impossible to read those words without admitting, that neither King William the 3rd (as has been said), or our beloved monarch, Queen Victoria, was the first sovereign who visited Liverpool. Edward the 2nd appears to have been at Skipton, in Yorkshire, on the 2nd October, 1323, and at Liverpool, on the 24th of that month, probably on his way southward from the north of England. In consequence of some pretended miracles wrought in Bristol, at the place where two rebels, Henry de Monteforte and Henry de Wylyngton, had been executed and gibbeted; a royal mandate or precept was issued by the King, at Skipton, and another at Liverpool, condemnatory of such fictitious miracles, and for punishing the parties implicated in the fraud.—See Fœdera, (modern edition,) 17th Edward the 2nd, 1323, tome 2, part 1, page 537 ; see also, the copy set out in the Appendix, No. III.

for arresting all suspected persons who should be found in the same ports ; and these orders, as far as respected Liverpool, were directed to the Bailiffs and Commonalty of the town of Liverpool.[1]

Many circular precepts, mandates and proclamations were issued during the reign of Edward the Third, addressed to the local authorities of Liverpool, and to those of a considerable number of other cities and places ;[2] and the following references will give the reader some idea of the nature and objects of those documents :—

1st Edw: 3rd, 1327, April 3.	To the Bailiffs of Liverpool.	Not to permit any abbot, friar, or other religious person to depart out of the kingdom, without licence.[3]
7th Edw: 3rd, 1333, June 26.	To the Bailiffs of Liverpool.	For the detention of ships of the burthen of 50 tons, and for the owners of ships which were absent from port, to cause them to return, and to be prepared for the defence of the realm.[4]
9th Edw: 3rd, 1335:	To the Bailiffs of Liverpool.	For arresting ships carrying 40 tons and upwards.[5]
9th Edw: 3rd, 1335:	To William de Werdill.	For providing two ships in the port of the town of Liverpool.[5]
10th Edw: 3rd, 1336:	To the Bailiffs of the Town of Liverpool.	Commanding all ships of the fleet, of the West of England, to assemble at Portsmouth.[6]

---

(1) Appendix, No. IV. and Fœdera, (modern edition,) tome 2, part 1, page 642.

(2) Amongst others were the neighbouring city and towns of Chester, Wigan, Preston, and Lancaster.

(3) Fœdera, (modern edition,) tome 2, part 2, page 701.

(4) See Appendix, No. V.

(5) Copies, in English of the above, of 9th Edward the 3rd, (1335,) respectively, are in the Town-hall.

(6) Fœdera, (modern edition,) tome 2, part 2, page 950.

21st Edw: 3rd, 1347:	To the Collectors of the Impost, &c. in the ports of the city of Chester, and town of Liverpool.	Concerning an impost for providing ships.[1]
29th Edw: 3rd, 1356, May 19.	To the Mayor & Commonalty of the Town of Liverpool.	Licence to acquire, give and assign lands, &c. to certain chaplains, and for the chaplains to receive from the before named Mayor and Commonalty, the said lands, in order to perform divine service for the souls of the faithful deceased in the chapel of the blessed Mary and St. Nicholas, for ever.[2] [This is the earliest known document in which the Mayor of Liverpool is named.]
30th Edw: 3rd, 1356:	To all Admirals, Sheriffs, Mayors, Bailiffs, &c.	For arresting ships in the ports of Conway, Beaumaris, Chester, and Liverpool, for the passage of Thomas de Rokeby, Justiciar, to Ireland.[3]
35th Edw: 3rd, 1361, May 10.	To the Justice, Chancellor, Treasurer, &c. in Ireland.	Concerning Lionel, Earl of Ulster's being sent to Ireland, and that the navy, completely armed, should be sent to the ports of Liverpool, Chester, &c.[4]
36th Edw: 3rd, 1362:	To the Bailiffs of Liverpool.	Against carrying corn, cloths, &c. out of the kingdom.[5]
37th Edw: 3rd, 1363:	To the Bailiffs of Liverpool.	Against carrying horses, falcons, thread, wool or linen out of the kingdom.[6]

---

(1) Fœdera, (modern edition,) tome 3, part 1, page 124.

(2) See Appendix, No. VI.

(3) Fœdera, (modern edition,) tome 3, part 1, page 332.

(4) See Appendix, No. VII. and Fœdera, tome 3, part 2, page 617.

(5) Fœdera, (modern edition,) tome 3, part 2, page 683.   (6) Ibid. page 694.

37th Edw: 3rd, 1363:	To the Bailiffs of Liverpool and the Collectors there.	Concerning corn, cloths, &c.[1]
38th Edw: 3rd, 1364:	To the Bailiffs of the Town of Liverpool.	Against carrying gold, silver, or jewels, out of the king-dom.[2]
38th Edw: 3rd, 1364, July 5.	To all Admirals, Sheriffs, Mayors, Bailiffs, &c.	For arresting ships and sending them to the port of Liverpool, for the pass-age of Lionel, Duke of Clarence, to Ireland.[3]
38th Edw: 3rd, 1364, August 8.	Same.	Same.[4]
41st Edw: 3rd, 1367, Feb. 8.	To the Bailiffs of Liverpool.	Prohibiting persons from leaving the kingdom.[5]
41st Edw: 3rd, 1367, Dec. 8.	To the Mayor and Bailiffs of the Town of Liverpool.	Concerning the money of the kingdom.[6]
42nd Edw: 3rd, 1368, Nov. 1.	To the Justices, Chancellor, and Treasurer of Ireland.	Letters patent for arresting ships, in the ports of Dub-lin, Drogheda, and Water-ford, and sending them to the port of Liverpool, in the county of Lancaster, for the passage of William de Wyndesore and men at arms to Ireland.[7]
44th Edw: 3rd, 1370. May 10.	To all Admirals, Sheriffs, Mayors Bailiffs, &c.	For arresting ships in the port of Liverpool, and other places, and sending them to Southampton and Plymouth. [8]

---

(1) Fœdera, (modern edition,) tome 3, part 2, page 710.

(2) Ibid. page 728.   (3) Ibid. page 740.

(4) Ibid. page 746.   (5) Ibid. page 818.

(6) Ibid. page 838.   In the above mandates of 41st Edward the 3rd, (1367,) Feb. 8, and 41st Edward the 3rd, (1367,) Dec. 8, the years are inserted as they appear in the margin of the Fœdera, but, ought not the year 1366 to be given instead of 1367?

(7) See Appendix, No. VIII, and Fœdera, (modern edition,) tome 3, part 2, page 850.

(8) Fœdera, (modern edition,) tome 3, part 2, page 891.

47th Edw: 3rd. 1373, Oct. 8.	To all Admirals, Sheriffs, Mayors, Bailiffs, &c.	For arresting ships of the burthen of 20 tons and upwards to 200 tons, in the port of Bristol, and in all ports and places from thence to the port of the town of Liverpool, and causing the same to be brought to the said port of Liverpool, for the passage of William de Wyndesore, Governor of Ireland, and men at arms and others in his retinue, to Ireland.[1]

The Author's object in noticing those ancient documents, has been to show the early period at which Liverpool was known and recognized as a borough and port. There are several others relating to it, of dates in, and previous to, the reign of Edward the Third; those which have already been referred to, however, furnish abundant evidence of its recognition, at a very early period, as a borough and port, and it has not been considered necessary to adduce any instances after his reign, or during the remainder of the 14th century. It is not intended to trace the gradual rise of the town from that period, which, indeed, would scarcely be within the scope of a work professing to give a descriptive account of Liverpool, from 1775 to the close of the 18th century.[2]

There were other charters granted to the town by subsequent monarchs, a list of which, with their dates, will be given in another place.

The earliest return of members for the borough, is said to have been in the 24th of Edward the First, 1296,

---

(1) See Appendix, No. IX, and Fœdera, (modern edition,) tome 3, part 2, page 991.

(2) The 18th century terminated with the last hour of the 31st December, 1799. There have been plausible arguments occasionally brought forward, with a view to show that it did not terminate until the 31st of December, 1800; they, however, appear to the Author not to have any good foundation. In one of the Liverpool

on the occasion of the return of Adam Fitz Richard and
Robert Pinklowe being elected to serve in parliament for
Liverpool; and though there have been intervals, during
which, either writs did not issue for elections at Liverpool,
or the returns have been suspended, the names of the
members who have represented Liverpool, from that period
to the present time, have been preserved.

It is a matter of history, that the sheriffs of Lancashire,
after several returns that they had no boroughs within their
county, though, in truth, Wigan, Liverpool, and Preston
were such, alleged at length, that none ought to be called
upon, on account of their poverty. This return was con-

---

newspapers, which has been conducted with a degree of talent not surpassed by any
other provincial paper, the following paragraph appeared on the 13th of November,
1846:—

"Century signifies a full hundred years; and that, after 1800, or eighteen
centuries, the nineteenth must begin with January 1st, 1801, just as the first century
began with January 1st, in the year one."

In reckoning centuries, as from the birth of our Saviour,* persons who support the
above line of argument, are liable to fall into an error from their not adverting to the
fact, that at the time when our Saviour was born, or when the first century commenced,
there was not any "year one." He merely, on his birth, (which we will suppose to
have occurred on the 1st of January,) entered upon or commenced his first year; but
though he then commenced the first year, it was not until 365 days and the odd number of hours and minutes had elapsed after the day of his birth, that there was any
complete "year one," or one year from his birth. After the first year had completely
elapsed, then, and not before, there was a "year one," and the second year
commenced.

The rule is just the same with a century as with a year from our Saviour's birth;
and any person who happened to have been born at the same time with him, and who
was living on the morning of the 1st of January, 99, then commenced his 100th year,
and if he had lived until *midnight* of the 31st December, at *the end* of the year 99, he
would have lived 100 complete years, or one full century; in other words, 99 years
and 365 days after our Saviour's birth.

The familiar case of the 1st, 2nd, or any other year of a king's reign, may also be
referred to, as calculated from the day of his accession on the same principle.

* The Author does not offer any opinion, whether our centuries are reckoned from
the true date of, or about the time of, our Saviour's birth, or on what day that event
occurred; it is quite enough for the present occasion, that, by common consent in
this country, a year or a century is always treated as commencing on the 1st January.

stantly made, from 36th of Edward the Third, to the reign of Henry the Sixth.[1]

During the 14th, 15th and 16th centuries,[2] and part of the 17th century, the progressive increase of the commerce and population of Liverpool was extremely slow, but after the expulsion of the despotic and infatuated Stuarts, and the accession of William the Third, a decided impulse was given, and the town began more rapidly to advance in size, population, and commerce. After the commencement of and during the 18th century, whilst the manufacturing districts were becoming eminent for ingenious inventions, occupied in sending forth the productions of their workshops and looms to foreign countries in exchange for the raw materials; and, increasing in wealth and importance, they were dependent, in a great degree, upon Liverpool, in consequence of its commodious and unrivalled situation, as a

---

(1) Hallam's View of the State of Europe, during the Middle Ages ; vol. 2, page 246 ; 8th edition, octavo. Mr. Hallam might also have mentioned Lancaster, which was then a borough.

(2) To persons who may feel an interest in learning what was said about Liverpool, in the reign of Henry the 8th, by a writer of authenticity, the following passage from the *Itinerary* of Leland, the antiquary, may be interesting :—

" At Lyrpole is smaule custume payid that causith marchantes to resorte.

A v. mile on the other side in Lancastreshire is . . . . wlliam Runco . . . . . . e Water.

Good marchandis at Lyrpole, and moch Yrisch Yarn that Manchester men do by ther."

" Lyrpole, alias Lyverpoole, a pavid Towne hath but a Chapel. Walton a iiii miles of nat far from the Se is Paroche Chirch. The King hath a Castelet there, and the Erle of Darbe hath a stone Howse there. Irisch Marchauntes cum much thither, as to a good Haven. After that Mersey Water cumming towards Rumcorne in Chesshire lisith amonge the commune People the name, and to Lyrpole."— Leland's *Itinerary*, vol. 7, folio 56.

And the following passage from Camden's *Britannia*, relates to Liverpool, as it was in the reign of Elizabeth :—

" Where is the most convenient and most frequented passage to Ireland ; a town more famous for its beauty and populousness than its antiquity. Its name occurs in no ancient writer, except that Roger of Poitou, who was Lord, as then styled, of the honour of Lancaster, built a Castle here."*

* Camden's *Britannia*, edition of 1789, vol. 3, page 128. The first edition was published in 1586, in the reign of Elizabeth, and the last edition was in 1607, in the reign of James the 1st, which is the edition from which the several English translations are said to have been made."

F

port and outlet for all that portion of their trade, which was directed from the northern and central counties, towards the westward. The additional advantage of communication between one part of the kingdom and another by means of canal navigation, an improvement by which Liverpool largely benefitted; the facilities of receiving the products of the salt districts and coal fields; the opening of new branches of commerce; the purchases of some important rights and privileges from the ancient family of Molyneux; and the formation of commodious docks; combined with various other causes, as years rolled on, have all added to the prosperity of Liverpool; and have formed, under Providence, the principal sources of the commercial greatness and eminence which it now enjoys in the 19th century.

CHAPTER I.

EXTENT OF LIVERPOOL, CHURCHES, CHAPELS, CHARITIES, PUBLIC
BUILDINGS, THEATRE, POST-OFFICE, LIBRARIES, NEWSPAPERS,
DIRECTORY, PORT, DOCKS, CANALS, FAIRS, AND MARKETS,
IN 1775.

AT the commencement of the last quarter of the 18th
century, Liverpool was a seaport town of very moderate
pretensions, and a stranger, whose attention is drawn to its
present commercial greatness, and vast extent, may well
feel surprised at being told that, at that period, it was
neither pre-eminent for commerce, population, or size.

In 1775, Liverpool possessed only three floating docks;
Castle-street was so narrow that it was with difficulty that
two carriages could pass ; on the south side of Church-street
there was a large orchard, and one end of the street opened
into the country; Bold-street did not exist; Clayton-square,
though laid out, had only a few houses erected in it ; part
of the east side of Whitechapel was bounded by a hawthorn
hedge; the town could merely support two weekly newspapers ; there was only one chapel belonging to the
Methodists, two places of worship of the Baptists, one
very small meeting-house of the Society of Friends, two
chapels of the English Presbyterians, one of a congregation
of Protestant dissenters, called Octagonians, one Roman
Catholic chapel, which was of exceedingly limited size ;
and a very small synagogue of the Jews ; but not one place
of worship of the Scotch Presbyterians ; there was a theatre,
but neither amphitheatre, circus, or music-hall. The population of the town and parish was little more than 35,000 ;
between the house now called the Three Sixes, in Toxteth-
park, and the village of Garston, a large district, at present
covered with splendid mansions and beautiful villas, only

three dwelling-houses stood; and there were two houses only on Edge-hill, where there is now a large and populous suburb. The mail bags of letters were conveyed to and from the town on horse-back; there were only two charitable institutions supported by voluntary contributions; there was not one Sunday or day school for the gratuitous instruction of the children of the poor; and there were only six places of worship of the Church of England, in Liverpool, or within three miles of the Exchange, on the Lancashire side; there are now fifty-one.[1]

The town terminated on the north side at Oldhall-street; on the south at the lower end of Park-lane and Pitt-street; and on the east at Whitechapel and Church-street. The neighbourhood beyond those streets was then quite a rural district, with fields, country lanes, orchards, and gardens on every side, except on the westward, where it was bounded by the Mersey. There were, however, a number of detached houses erected in various spots beyond those limits, but not in the form of regular streets[2] or rows of houses; they had evidently been built with the double object of being near the seat of business, and of being in salubrious or rural situations; the large houses then and still standing on the south side of Mount-pleasant may be mentioned as examples.

Several of the streets which are now populous, and are in the heart of the town, were then rural lanes, amongst which

---

(1) Exclusive of the Mariner's Church.

(2) Ranelagh-street and Shaws-brow were both built, or nearly so, but being principal outlets from the town into the country, they can scarcely be considered as exceptions, because the town did not then extend to the right and left of them, and the main outlets of nearly every town are usually built before the masses of houses and buildings reach so far; there were, however, some streets partially laid out, beyond the above mentioned limits; but, being merely contemplated streets, and in some instances having only one or two houses erected, and sometimes not any, it is not considered necessary to describe them here.

may be particularised, the upper end of Mount-pleasant, (formerly called Martindale's-hill,) a large portion of which was then unpaved;[1] Byrom-street, which though containing some houses was then little more than a country road leading towards Walton; Folly-lane, where Upper Islington now stands, which was the way towards West Derby; the road to Prescot, now London-road; and the two roads to Toxteth-park, one of which afterwards formed the site of Great George-street, in which a few houses only had been erected, on the east side, at the end opening into Duke-street, and the other was where St. James'-street is now built. Another rural lane, then called the Everton-road, on the site of which Richmond-row now stands, extended from the town to Everton: on the south side was a tavern, called, the Loggerheads, with a garden attached to it, which was the property of, and was afterwards occupied as a private residence by several gentlemen named Nicholson, successively, and is now again a tavern, called by the old name, the Loggerheads, and stands on the south side of Richmond-row, nearly opposite the end of Fox-street.

Liverpool, when viewed from the estuary of the Mersey, did not exhibit either a commanding or handsome appearance. It presented to the view a seaport town of moderate size, possessing three floating docks, and a dock which was empty at low water, all of which will be more particulary described afterwards; a tolerably sized basin, and three graving docks. The spires of the churches of St. Nicholas, St. George, and St. Thomas; the towers of those of St. Peter, St. Ann, and St. James,[2] and the cupola of that of St.

---

(1) It joined Brownlow-hill road as at present, behind the spot where the Fever Hospital now stands, and after that junction they formed a country lane, which passed over Edge-hill towards Wavertree.

(2) The walls of St. James' Church were built, but it was not completed or used for Divine service until in the Summer of 1775.

Paul; the ancient embattled Tower at the bottom of Water-street; the Town-hall; the parish Workhouse on Brownlow-hill; the old Custom-house on the east side of the Old Dock, and the more ancient Custom-house,[1] then used as the tide-surveyor's office, at the south-west corner and lowest end of Water-street; a large number of windmills in different parts of the town and neighbourhood; and several cupola-like chimneys of earthenware works, and of glass works, were the most conspicuous objects seen from the Mersey. There were neither Goree warehouses nor any other commercial buildings then standing on the east side of the quay of George's Dock; but there was an unbuilt piece of ground extending a considerable distance on the south side of the tide-surveyor's office, before mentioned. A timber-yard of Mr. Moss, and a cooperage of Mr. Chaffers, occupied the space of ground where many of the Goree warehouses, to the southward of Water-street, now stand.[2] Liverpool could not then boast of extensive piers, or handsome marine parades fronting the river, but George's parade, on the east side of the Mersey, existed; it was, however, a narrow walk when compared with the one which now bears that name. The parade formed a very pleasant walk 320 yards in length, and was fenced and bounded on the east by wooden palisades. It was destroyed on enlarging George's Dock; and the present George's parade was formed in lieu of the

---

(1) The Author has seen an old abstract of a deed, a marriage settlement, dated the 7th of April, 1758, upon the intended marriage of Thomas Walmsley and Elizabeth Turner, which described some property in Water-street, where the old Custom-house stood, late rented " by Alderman Moorcroft at £4:5s, and 12 lbs. of prunes per annum."

(2) It is remarkable, that in a view of the west side of Liverpool, taken in 1770, by Mr. George Perry, of which some copies were engraved, the Goree warehouses were introduced by anticipation; and the Author has been informed by a member of the family of Mr. Perry, that he obtained for that purpose the elevations of the ware-houses from London, from the architect employed respecting them. In his curious and accurate plan of Liverpool, of 1769, he calls them " new intended warehouses."

old one, but further from the dock, and on ground inclosed from the shore of the river.   In a book of poems, written about the end of the last century, by Mr. William Colquitt, who was the brother of the Town-clerk of that name, one on Liverpool contains the following extraordinary lines: if the style should amuse the reader, he, in common candour, ought not to imagine that the literary productions of all the Liverpool poets, who lived at the close of the last century were precisely of the same class :—

> "Behold the esplanade near George's Dock,
> Where you may see ships sailing round the Rock,
> And Cheshire's distant sylvan shades and fields,
> That for this plenteous market so much yields." [1]

On the north end of the parade was a small slip and pier; and afterwards, in the French revolutionary war, a battery of guns was mounted on the latter.

The fort and barracks which subsequently stood on the North Shore, at the north end of Bath-street, had not been then erected; but a battery was made in the American revolutionary war on the pier on the north side [2] of the entrance or gut leading into George's basin, consisting of thirty-two pounders and eighteen pounders, which were said to have been removed from St. Nicholas' Church yard, where they had previously been mounted.   It had not originally any breast-work, but one was afterwards hastily formed of balks of timber in consequence of an alarm of an enemy being in the Irish sea.

In proceeding to describe the public buildings and

---

[1] Poems by William Colquitt, A.B. late of Christ College, Cambridge, page 27, lent to the Author, by an estimable, kind-hearted and much-lamented gentleman, the late Sir Thomas Brancker, whose death occurred after a part of this Work had been sent to the press.   The Author embraces this opportunity of expressing his respect for the memory of that gentleman, and also his obligations for much valuable information received from him whilst this Work was in progress.

[2] It was not until the French revolutionary war that a battery was erected on the pier, on the south side of the entrance or gut.

institutions which existed in Liverpool, in 1775, the places of worship will be first mentioned.

The Church of " Our Lady and St. Nicholas," usually called " St. Nicholas' Church," and occasionally " The Old Church," standing on the east side of George's Dock basin, and south side of Chapel-street, was a conspicuous object from the Mersey. It was formerly a chapel under the parish church of Walton-on-the-Hill, usually called Walton, but it is impossible to ascertain the time when it was built; it must, however, have been of very great antiquity. It has been already shown that it stood there in the 29th year of the reign of Edward the Third, (1356,)[1] and it was probably there at a much earlier period. Liverpool remained a part of the parish of Walton-on-the-Hill until 1699, when it was elevated to the rank of an independent parish by virtue of the Act of Parliament of the 10th and 11th of King William the Third, chap. 36.

The church was, in 1775, a plain Gothic building without any pretensions to beauty, with a square tower, on which stood a small spire.

There was a neat-looking white tavern (Hinde's) then standing in the church yard, close to the tower, and between it and the spot, where the Gothic arch and the steps communicating with the lowest end of Chapel-street now stand. This tavern was of considerable antiquity, commanded an interesting marine prospect, and was at that period much frequented by respectable persons. It remained standing a considerable time after the commencement of the present century.

In 1749 the church yard was enlarged on the west side, a space of ground being added, which is distinguishable by being on a lower level than the other parts.

---

(1) Introduction, page 31; and see Appendix, No. VI.

S! NICHOLAS' CHURCH.

and the old Tavern in the Church Yard.

G. Jarman sc.

The ancient tower of the church had the small spire erected upon it in 1750, which is said to have been an ill-judged measure, and one of the causes of a dreadful accident, which will shortly be noticed. There was a peal of six bells in the belfrey, which were ordered in 1724, in lieu of the old bells, and appear to have been first used in 1725.[1] In 1759 or 1760, a battery of fourteen guns (which remained for several years) was formed, for the protection of the town, in the enlarged part of the church yard, opposite the place where George's Dock basin now is, in consequence of apprehensions of an attack from an enterprising French commander, Monsieur Thurot, who was afterwards defeated and killed in action off the Isle of Man, in 1760.

In 1774 the church underwent considerable repair,[2] all the exterior parts of the body were completely re-built, and some of the interior parts were much altered.

On Sunday morning, the 11th of February, 1810, just as the bells ceased ringing before the commencement of Divine service, the spire gave way at the point where it joined the tower-part of the steeple; brought down with it a portion of the latter, and part of the roof, fell into the church, and destroyed twenty-three persons on the spot, and another died soon afterwards in the Infirmary : three of the sufferers were adults, and the others were female children of the Moorfields Charity School. Several persons had most providential escapes; amongst whom may be mentioned Mrs. Gibson, the wife of Mr. William Gibson, of St. Anne-street, who was in the church at the time; the Rev. H. Roughsedge, the rector, and the Rev. L. Pughe, the officiating

---

(1) History of Liverpool, Anon: printed by J. M'Creery, Houghton-street, Liverpool, in 1795, page 114, the authorship of which has been attributed to an individual of the name of Moss : copies of it were also printed by R. Phillips, Castle-street, Liverpool, of which one copy is in the Library of the Liverpool Athenæum.

(2) Smither's Liverpool, page 24.

minister of the day, both of whom were on the point of entering the church.

By the fall of the tower a curious font, with the following inscription, on the upper fillet of the octagon, was destroyed:—

Nemo potest cœlum, sed Christo munere fontis nostri scandere.[1]

On the face of the pedestal:—

P : E T E R , L
V R T I N G.
Major T.I.T.A.B.

I. B. ⎫
R. H. ⎬ C. W.

1644.

It seems extraordinary that Peter Lurting, whose name appears inscribed on it as mayor, was not elected until 1663; therefore, if he acted as mayor, in 1644, it could only have been as deputy mayor.[2]

In 1815 the present handsome Gothic tower and lanthorn were erected. In early times the image of St. Patrick stood in the church yard,[3] and mariners going to sea used to offer up vows and prayers before it; but, with the decline of an ignorant and superstitious age, the image disappeared.

---

(1) Troughton's Liverpool, page 63 and 75.

(2) History of Liverpool, Anon: printed by J. M'Creery, in 1795, page 119.

(3) There are some remarkable inscriptions in the church yard, as for example: one on a gravestone to the memory of Richard Blore, or Shore, (the inscription is a little obliterated,) of the date of 1789, lies to the south-westward of the church, and very near the sun-dial :—

"This Town's a Corporation full of crooked Streets,
Death is the Market-place where all men meets;
If Life was merchandise that men could buy,
The rich wou'd always live, the poor must die."

Another inscription, conveying the same sentiment, but differently expressed, to the memory of James Scallion, who died on the 18th July, 1786, may be found on the south side of the church yard, close to the principal gate :—

"This world is a bubble and all full of streets;
The Grave is the Market where all men meets;
If Life were merchandise to sell and buy,
The rich would live, and the poor would die."

Colonel Robert Broadneux, or Broadnax, an extraordinary personage, aged 109 years, was interred here. He was a lieutenant in the reign of King Charles the First; colonel of horse, and gentleman of the bedchamber to Oliver Cromwell; a major and lieutenant-colonel under King William the Third; he retained his memory to the last, but lost his sight a little before his death;[1] which event occurred on the 27th of January, 1727-8. He was born in 1617. His grave is opposite the south door of the church, and not far from the sun-dial. An inscription, much worn but still tolerably legible, on his gravestone, concisely mentions that "Colonel Robert Broadneux died Jan^y." [the day, if it ever were cut, is now obliterated,] "1727, aged 109 years."[2]

Another, to the memory of "Rebecca, wife of William Brown, died on the 27th of July, 1786, aged 80 years":—

> "Farewell, vain world, I've known enough of thee,
> And careless am of what thou say'st of me;
> Thy smiles I court not, nor thy frowns I fear,
> My cares are past, my head lies quiet here."

One to the memory of Mr. Henry Newsham, who was a member of a club called the Holly and Ivy Club, is remarkable for the conceit of commemorating his club:—

"In remembrance of Henry Newsham, wine merchant, who departed this life 14th May, 1800, aged 65 years.

> "To Hollie and Ivy,
> And Friendship, adieu."

Another, to the memory of a medical practitioner, of 1700, which may be seen near the gate of the middle of the south side of the church yard:—

"Here lyeth the body of Alexander Norres, of Leverpoole, professor of physick and chirurgery, who departed this life the 5th day of July, was buried the 8th, 1700."

There are few inscriptions of considerable antiquity in the church yard, but the following, on the south side of the church, are of the 17th century:—

"Here lieth interred the body of Richard Maule, who departed this life 3rd day of May, Anno Christi 1695."

"Here lieth intered the body of John Woodward, who departed this life the 2d of March, 1696."

"Here lietht Richard Formby, the Son of Gilbert Formby, decesed the 11th of October, 1698."

(1) Salmon's Chronological Historian, vol. 2, page 193.

(2) In the History of Liverpool, Anon: printed by J. M'Creery in 1795, page

From the church register it appears, that at the time of his death he was residing in George-street, Oldhall-street.[1]

Before the dissolution there were four chantries connected with this church, for prayers or masses for the souls of various persons.

The earliest entry in the parish register which has been preserved, is dated in 1661.

On the south side, a little to the eastward of an imaginary line, drawn from the south door to the north end of Stringers-alley, (now called Prison-weint,) and about half way between them, is the grave of Timothy Horsfield, who was the first parish-clerk after Liverpool was separated from

---

130, there is an erroneous statement respecting the inscription on the gravestone; the statement is as follows; " In the church-yard are two inscriptions on flat stones, that may not be thought undeserving notice; the one is near the erect dial, recording the death of Colonel Robert Broadneux, at the age of one hundred and nine, and relates the following singular anecdote: when he was about eighty-three years of age, having been attacked by a slight indisposition, he appeared to have anticipated his decease, and ordered his own coffin, in which, from that period, he generally slept, and had it rubbed and polished in common with the household furniture."

It is not necessary to discuss here, whether so improbable an occurrence as that which is alleged to have been so related, ever took place. It is sufficient here to mention, that nothing of the kind is recorded on the gravestone; nor is there space for it, because there are other inscriptions on the same stone, mentioning the interments or deaths of other persons, and not more than a couple of inches intervene between the inscription mentioning the death of the Colonel, and the latter inscriptions. Besides which, the date of one of those interments or deaths is recorded on the stone as having occurred in 1757; consequently, the strange inscription above mentioned could not have been on the stone after that date; and it seems scarcely credible, that if it ever were there, it could have been obliterated, in so short a period as intervened between the death of Colonel Broadnax or Broadneux in 1727 and the year 1757. Under any circumstances, instead of its having been on the stone in 1795, no such alleged inscription can possibly have been there for nearly 100 years past. It seems to have been written in error by the anonymous Author of the History of Liverpool of 1795; an error which has been followed in Baines' Lancashire, vol. 4, page 98.

(1) The following is an extract from the Church Register of St. Nicholas:—

" Burials, Anno Dom. 1727.
" January 29 : Robert Broadnax, Geo : Str : Gentleman."

Walton-on-the-Hill; his grave-stone contains the following inscription :—

"Here Lyeth the Body of Timothy Horsfield, First Parish Clerk of Liverpoole, departed this life, yᵉ 13th October, 1709."

It is easily distinguished by being close to another grave covered with a remarkably white gravestone.

St. Peter's Church, on the south side of Church-street, was built of soft stone, once yellowish, which, from the smoke, dust, and lapse of years, has become of a dingy brown hue. It was consecrated in 1704, and may be correctly called of the nondescript style. It has an octangular tower; upon each angle of which is a pinnacle representing a candlestick, with a gilt vane resembling the flame. The church is the reverse of handsome, and is remarkable for each of its four door-ways (two on each side of the church) being of a different description, which is said to have occured from the architect having introduced them in the plan and sections to be selected from ; and the contractor or builder, having the plan and sections before him, copied them exactly as they appeared there. The church contains a font of white marble, on which is cut the following inscription :—"The Gift of Robert Heysham, Esq. 1702."

Liverpool was by the Act of 10th & 11th William the Third, chap. 36, separated from the parish of Walton-on-the-Hill, and made a distinct parish, and the Rectory was declared to consist of two medieties. The Corporation then became patrons of the Rectory, and, by virtue of the act, the Common Council presented to it on every vacancy. The Rectors became entitled under the act, to have houses and gardens provided for them by the parish; an advantage which they relinquished in 1786, in consideration of an increase of their salaries by the parish.

The preamble to the Act of the 10th & 11th William

the Third, is singularly worded, and commences as follows:—

" Whereas, the parish of Walton, in the county of Lancaster, is a parish of large extent, and hath *several villages* therein, amongst which the Town of Liverpool *is one,* which by reason of its conveniency of situation, being near the sea, is become a place of great trade and commerce, and very populous ; and although *they* have had a parochial Chapel, yet, by reason of increase of people, the same is not sufficient for *them,*" &c.

The act directed a new church to be erected, and a church yard or cemetery to be provided and inclosed ; and enacted that they " shall be the parish church and church yard of the said parish of Liverpool," and declared the Rev. Robert Stith and Rev. William[1] Atherton to be the first Rectors of the new parish church, and of the parochial chapel.

Under this act St. Peter's Church was erected ; and since that event, one of the Rectors has generally taken the duties at the parochial chapel usually called St. Nicholas' Church, and the other at St. Peter's Church. The vestry-room of the latter contains a small library, which will be more fully noticed in another place.

The following is a List of the Rectors of Liverpool, from the time it became a parish distinct from Walton, and during the 18th century :—

Rev. Robert Stith................and Rev. WilliamAtherton, June 24, 1699
Rev. Henry Richmond..........*vice* Rev. William Atherton 1700
Rev. Thomas Bell................*vice* Rev. Robert Stith 1719
Rev. Thomas Baldwin ....*vice* Rev. Henry Richmond ...July, 1721
Rev. John Stanley ....*vice* Rev. Thomas Bell ....Nov. 1725
Rev. Robert Brereton ....*vice* Rev. John Stanley, Sept. or Oct. 1750
Rev. Henry Wolstenholme ...*vice* Rev. Thomas Baldwin............ 1752
Rev. Thomas Maddock..........*vice* Rev. H. Wolstenholme, Dec. 20, 1771
Rev. Thomas Dannett ....*vice* Rev. Thos. Maddock, Mar. 12, 1783
Rev. George Hodson ....*vice* Rev. Robert Brereton...Nov. 7, 1784
Rev. Samuel Renshaw..........*vice* Rev. George Hodson ...May 7, 1794
Rev. R. H. Roughsedge ......*vice* Rev. Thomas Dannett...July 6, 1796

---

(1) His Christian name is called William in the Act, but in some Works he is called Henry, and his surname is called Atherstone.

St. George's Church, in Derby-square, at the south end of Castle-street, was finished and consecrated in 1734, under an Act Parliament passed in 1715 : it stands on the site of the old Castle of Liverpool. The circumstance is alluded to in the extraordinary poem on Liverpool, published by Mr. William Colquitt, before mentioned, and the following extract may perhaps be amusing to the reader :—

> " Here was an ancient Castle fortified,
> With guns in embrasures plac'd on each side,
> Where now Saint George's Church stands, here the Mayor
> And Magistrates their praises oft declare." [1]

The Castle having been dismantled, and having remained some time in that state, its walls and ruins were pulled down about the year 1721. Part of the moat of the castle was, not many years ago, exposed to view [2] on excavating the ground, prior to laying the foundation of the present spire, and re-building part of the church : it had been a dry ditch cut in the rock, and in width and depth resembled one of those often seen near the ruined feudal castles in England. Another part of the moat, and the foundations of a tower and walls, [2] were laid open to view in 1827, near where the buildings on the east side of Derby-square formerly stood, when the labourers were excavating the foundations of the shops and houses now forming the north wing of St. George's-crescent ; and a small portion of the moat was laid open not long since, on the north side of Derby-square, [2] in digging the foundations of the North and South Wales Bank.

The exterior of St. George's Church and the whole of its present spire have been re-built within little more than thirty years past. The body of the church, in 1775, was of stone,

---

(1) Poems, by William Colquitt, A.B. late of Christ College, Cambridge, page 34.

(2) Seen by the Author.

and of the Doric order, with an attic wall above, ornamented with vases. The foundation of the old spire being laid in the moat of the castle, it had become unsafe and was the cause of its being taken down, and the present spire being built. The tower part of the steeple was on a square plan, and consisted of three heights of different orders, the Doric, Ionic and Corinthian. By an unlucky proportion of the Corinthian pilasters, the steeple, when viewed at a distance upon the plane of any of the sides, appeared larger above than below. From these pilasters and their cornice, rose an octangular tower of the composite order, between the pilasters of which, in niches, were the remains of eight paintings of saints, which, as might have been expected, had been defaced.[1] In the inside, the church was neatly pewed and fitted up with great elegance. The galleries were supported by slender pedestals, and the roof by handsome Corinthian columns. The pulpit, the altar-piece, the organ loft, and the front of the galleries were of mahogany. The whole was enriched with carving and gilding in modern taste.[1] Beneath the church were the vaults of many of the Liverpool families, which are still used for interments. This church was the Corporation chapel, at which the Mayor, Aldermen, and Common Council usually attended Divine service; a custom which is yet kept up by the Mayor and some of the corporate officers; and, since the Assizes have been held in Liverpool, the Judges also attend Divine service there.

It must not be supposed that the appearance of St. George's Church at that period bore much resemblance to the present building; perhaps it is not too much to say that it surpassed the present one in beauty, and certainly it had not the unsightly projection at the chancel end, which the

---

(1) Enfield's Liverpool, page 44.

want of taste in the architect has caused to protrude beyond
the line of the street, and which is a great eye-sore when
viewed from Castle-street. The church has been much
altered and rebuilt, and it has been remarked with great
truth[1] that it was re-built piece-meal. Instead of throwing
it down entirely, and then commencing the work of reconstruction, first one wall was taken down and then another;
the renovation of the exterior thus going on gradually, and
the interior in the mean while being allowed to remain.[1]
These proceedings rather conveyed the impression that the
alterations were "jobs," a class of abuses sometimes laid to
the charge of both new and old municipal corporations.
In its present form, the church was re-opened for Divine
service on Sunday, September 11, 1825.

Most of the Rectors of Liverpool have been lecturers and
afterwards chaplains of this church, and have been successively
promoted from the living of St. George's to the incumbency
of the parish.[2] The present much-respected Rectors of
Liverpool both officiated at St. George's: the Rev. Jonathan
Brooks, M.A., Archdeacon of Liverpool, was formerly lecturer,
but succeeded the Rev. Frodsham Hodson, D.D. as chaplain,
about 1822, and was elected one of the Rectors of Liverpool
in 1829; and also the Rev. Augustus Campbell, M.A.
who held the appointment of lecturer of St. George's, was
elected by the Common Council one of the Rectors about
1829. The Rectors who preceded them were the Rev.
Samuel Renshaw, M.A. and the Rev. Robert Hankinson

---

(1) By the Rev. Dr. Thom, in his interesting Paper on the Liverpool Churches
and Chapels, read before the Historic Society of Lancashire and Cheshire, 10th
June, 1852.

(2) The names and other particulars of the different Clergymen who have officiated
at St. George's, have been clearly and ably given by the Rev. Dr. Thom, in the paper
which has been mentioned in a previous note, and, as that has appeared so recently
before the public, it is not considered requisite to give many of the names in this work.

H

Roughsedge, M.A. both well known to many of the readers. Having mentioned Dr. Hodson, it may be correct to add that he was a native of Liverpool, his father having been in succession lecturer and chaplain of St. George's, and afterwards one of the Rectors of Liverpool, from 1784 to 1794. Dr. Hodson also first held the appointment of lecturer of St. George's, to which he was elected in 1795,[1] and afterwards that of chaplain.[2] About 1809 he was appointed to the dignified and important office of Principal of Brazenose College, in the University of Oxford. Dr. Hodson died in 1821 or 1822, and in losing him the Church and the University lost a dignitary and member of great abilities and attainments. However men may differ as to various points in his character, it is admitted on all hands, that he was a man of first-rate talents and scholastic acquirements. The Author, however, never heard him represented as a particularly pious or zealous clergyman. Two faults have been alleged against him; one, that he was too much addicted to courting the notice of, or currying the favour of, "great men," and the other, that he was proud and haughty. The Author had some acquaintance, though not much intimacy with him, but has no means of judging whether the first of those allegations is well founded or otherwise; with respect, however, to the last of them, the Author is bound in common candour to state, that he never, in his intercourse with Dr. Hodson, perceived indications of pride or haughtiness in him, and his deportment appeared to the Author, rather to be agreeable and free from either of those objectionable defects. One great fault, however, in his conduct cannot be denied; he persevered in holding

---

(1) Rev. Dr. Thom's Paper, before mentioned, on the Liverpool Churches.

(2) The Author has heard that Dr. Hodson, in early life, had been Tutor to one of Lord Grenville's family.

the chaplaincy of St. George's, and receiving the emoluments, after his appointment as principal of Brazenose
College ; and, although he occasionally visited Liverpool, his
constant residence in the town, and his discharge of the
duties of St. George's Church, were impracticable. He was
by that conduct the more exposed to censure as a pluralist,
because, he must have been conscious, when he was elected
chaplain of the church, that the congregation, and many of
the Council who voted for him, had a right to expect him
to perform the duties of it in person, and his residence
at Oxford seems, therefore, scarcely consistent with the rule
of good faith, or with his duty as chaplain of St. George's.

A terrace, raised considerably higher than the street,
extended on each side of the church, forming, as it is at
present, a small raised church yard ; and, on the south-
east corner of it, was a small octangular edifice, which was
the watch-house and lock-up night prison, and which had the
fire-bell over it. Another octangular edifice, corresponding
to the one before described, was used for the clerk of the
market, and stood at the south-west corner of the church
yard; and under the south side of the terrace was an arcade,
consisting of a range of six arches which extended beneath
the terrace from one of the octangular edifices to the other.

St. Thomas' Church, at the lower end and on the east
side of Park-lane, was consecrated in 1750; the body of the
church was built of stone, and consisted, as it still does, of a
rustic base and two rows of windows, having Ionic pilasters
between them, and above them a cornice and balustrade terminated with a variety of vases. Its spire, when it existed,
was very tall, slender, and tapering, and a beautiful object
when seen from a little distance. The following account is
given of it by Mr. Enfield :—" Its steeple and spire are well
proportioned and lofty; it is 216 feet from the ground, of
which the spire is above one-half. The pedestal which sup-

ports it consists of windows and ornaments in the Grecian style, but upon four couplets of Corinthian columns the architect has placed four Gothic pinnacles, which seem to have no affinity with the rest of the structure." Upon the whole, however, notwithstanding that architectural error, the spire was very handsome. It underwent many vicissitudes; on the 15th March, 1757, in a hurricane, about 42 feet of the spire were blown down,[1] and, on being rebuilt, it was reduced in height 18 feet; it was many years afterwards struck by lightening, and also injured by storms, and at length became so unsafe and rocked so much during high winds, that its vibrations were perceptible, even from the distance of Castle-street,[2] and after having been much reduced in height, the whole, except the tower part of the steeple, was taken down in 1822, in order to prevent mischief.

St. Paul's Church, in St. Paul's-square, (of stone,) was consecrated in 1769; the main body is of the Ionic order, with a bold Ionic portico and a projecting pediment, on the west side. The south and north fronts have each a pediment supported in the like manner, but not projecting so much. In the centre, upon an octangular base, rises a large dome, on which is placed a lanthorn, terminated by a large ball and cross.

St. Ann's Church, on the north side of Great Richmond-street, was erected in 1772, several years before St. Anne-street was opened, and was consequently quite in the country.

---

(1) *Williamson's Liverpool Advertiser*, of Friday the 18th March, 1757, after mentioning great damage done at sea, and on land near Liverpool, by the storm, (from the west), states that, " about 42 feet of the lofty spire of St. Thomas' Church, (which was esteemed one of the most beautiful in Europe), fell upon the body of the church, broke through the roof, and tore down the west galleries."

(2) The Author, as well as many others, witnessed the vibrations in a storm from the great distance of Castle-street, when opposite the *Courier Office.*

It is a brick edifice without any pretensions to beauty, with a low tower, ornamented with pinnacles, and is remarkable for not being built according to the usual canonical rule; its altar being at the south end and its tower at the north; it stands north and south, instead of east and west, according to usage.

St. James' Church, on the south side of Parliament-street, in the extra-parochial place of Toxteth-park;[1] a plain brick building, with a tower; though built in 1774, was not used for Divine service until the summer of 1775, as will be further noticed in another place.

The patronage of those churches will be mentioned in a subsequent chapter.

Besides the churches of the Establishment, there were nine other places of worship.

The Methodist Chapel, on the west side of Pitt-street, erected by the Wesleyan Methodists, was a plain brick edifice. There, that truly good and pious Christian, the Rev. John Wesley, the founder of one class of Methodists, has occasionally preached[2]; and as he never spared his labours in the conscientious discharge of his religious duties, he has been known to preach there when divine service commenced as early as at six o'clock in the morning.[3]   The

---

(1) It is often called, though erroneously, in the parish of Walton-on-the-Hill, even in the Register Book of that Church. A large portion of Toxteth-park is now, by the Municipal Reform Act, within the Borough of Liverpool, including the part where the Church stands.

(2) *Gore's General Advertiser*, of 29th March and 5th April, 1776, mentions his preaching in Liverpool in April, in that year.

" Wesley's life was extended far beyond the usual term of human life, to the year 1791, and to the age of eighty-eight. He has left behind him a Journal, giving a full account of his unwearied travelling and preaching, during more than half a century, together with occasional remarks on the towns he visited, or the books he read."—Lord Mahon's History of England from the Peace of Utrecht to the Peace of Aix la Chapelle, v. 2, p. 385.

(3) The Author's father, actuated by a natural wish to hear so good and so extraordinary a man, more than once heard Mr. Wesley preach there, and has attended

chapel was built in 1766, but was taken down and rebuilt of brick on a much larger scale in 1800.[1] It was the first chapel which the Methodists erected in Liverpool, but they had a society in the town, and used to meet in temporary places of worship, prior to 1754.[1]

The Chapel in Benns-garden was a brick building of unpretending exterior, frequented by a congregation who then and for some years afterwards were of the Presbyterian persuasion. It had been in use since 1727. In 1811 the congregation having much increased, they removed to the new chapel on the east side of Renshaw-street, and profess the Unitarian creed. The chapel in Benns-garden is now used by a congregation of Welsh Methodists.

Another Chapel, of which the frequenters were also originally of the Presbyterian persuasion, was on the western side of Key-street, formerly called Kaye, or Kay-street. After it ceased to be frequented by a congregation of Protestant dissenters, it was for many years licensed, and was consequently used by the members of the Church of England, and called St. Matthew's Church.[2] This edifice is considered to have been one of the oldest, if not the oldest place of worship which had been used by Protestant Non-conformists, in the borough of Liverpool.[3]

Divine service when Mr. Wesley officiated there before breakfast. The service commenced early, probably in order to accommodate the working-classes and others who could not conveniently attend later in the day.

(1) From a communication to the Author by Mr. Thomas Crook.

(2) Amongst many other clergymen who officiated at St. Matthew's Church was the Rev. Dr. Pulford, afterwards of St. George's. He was a good classical scholar, and at one period kept a school of some celebrity. Few of the readers, who happen to have been his pupils, can have forgotten the strictness of his discipline ; at all events, the Author, who was under his tuition, has a very lively recollection of it. The Rev. Dr. Tattershall, a person of great talents and learning, was another of the clergymen there.

(3) It is said that immediately after the Revolution of 1688, a chapel for Protestant Non-conformists was built within the borough, in Castle-hey, now called Harrington-street.—History of Lancashire by J. Baines, vol. 4, page 104.

The old chapel in Toxteth-park was beyond the then limits of the Borough, and

The Key-street Chapel was erected about the year 1707,[1] and frequented by a congregation of the Presbyterian denomination; the first minister was the Rev. Christopher Basnett; the Rev. — Brekell and the Rev. Philip Taylor were also successively ministers there.

In 1777 the Rev. John Yates succeeded to the pulpit, in the room of the Rev. Philip Taylor, who removed to the Eustace-street Congregation in Dublin, and in 1791 the congregation emerged from the Key-street Chapel to the spacious and handsome chapel in Paradise-street, which will be mentioned in another chapter. St. Matthew's Church was pulled down in May, 1849, in consequence of the changes effected by making the station of the Lancashire and Yorkshire Railway.

The Baptists had a chapel, on the east side of the lane, now Byrom-street, leading towards Ormskirk. The original Baptist congregation in Liverpool was a branch of a society at Hill Cliff, near Warrington, and came to Liverpool about 1700.[2] In 1714, they built a chapel in Everton-lane, where their burial ground yet remains.[2] From thence the congregation, about 1722, removed to the before-mentioned chapel, then newly erected in the lane, now Byrom-street. Its pulpit was occupied in 1775, by the Rev. Samuel Medley, a person of talents, and much respected. He became the minister of the chapel in 1772, and in consequence of the increase of the congregation, it was enlarged in 1773; their numbers increased, and it became necessary for the congregation to have a larger place of worship; and, in 1789, they

is said to have formerly belonged to the Church of England, but to have been used by Dissenters during the time of the Commonwealth. It is also said that Thomas Crompton, the Non-conformist minister of the Toxteth-park Chapel, was not disturbed in consequence of the Act of Uniformity. It has ever since that period been used as a place of worship by Protestant Non-conformists.

(1) History of Lancashire, by J. Baines, vol. 4, page 104.

(2) History of Lancashire by J. Baines, vol. 4, page 105.

removed to a new and more commodious chapel at the north
end of Byrom-street and corner of Gerard-street. Mr.
Medley continued to officiate as the minister there until his
death, which occurred in 1799. After the congregation had
left their old chapel, the latter was sold, and it was then
licensed for the solemnization of the Church of England
service, and is now St. Stephen's Church.

A Chapel in Stanley-street, at the corner of Derby-street,
was also used in 1775 as a place of worship by the Baptists,
of which the Rev. John Johnson was the minister. It was
erected and first used in 1750. The congregation were an
off-shoot from that of the old Baptist's Chapel, (now St.
Stephen's Church, in Byrom-street,) of which Mr. Johnson
was appointed minister in 1741, and quitted it in 1748. The
chapel in Stanley-street was afterwards used as a place of
worship by dissenters of some other persuasion, and the
building is still standing, but is now made into shops.

Neither the Independents, nor the Scotch Presbyterians
had in 1775 any place of worship, peculiarly for their
respective creeds, in Liverpool.

The Chapel called the Octagon stood at the bottom of
Temple-court, nearly on the site of the present Fire Police
Station. It was frequented by a congregation of Protestant
Non-conformists, called Octagonians; and, contrary to the
general usages amongst dissenters, they made use of a prayer-
book, of which one or two of the prayers had a resemblance to
some of those of the Established Church. It was first opened
in 1763, in consequence of a secession of members, who
favoured the use of a printed book of prayers and psalms,
both from the chapel in Key-street and from that in Benns-
garden, and who, with a view to the improvement of religious
worship, had engaged several gentlemen of learning and
ability to draw up a liturgy for their use. It was a brick
building, (except the front portico and pediment, which were

of stone,) of an octagonal form.   The interior space, where
Divine service was performed, was also of the octagonal form,
and it had on each side large windows, which gave the building within a light and cheerful appearance.   This place of
worship exhibited the rare instance of the vestry-room being
on a level with, and also communicating with the gallery,
instead of being, as is usual, on the ground floor.   The
vestry-room was decidedly the most commodious, light, and
comfortable of any in the town.   On the front of the
building, facing Temple-court, was a small stone portico,
from which a flight of stairs passed on each side into the
gallery.   Above this portico were three large windows,
and over the entrance to it was the vestry-room, with
an ante-room, access to them being obtained through a
door under the organ, (the Octagonians used that instrument); and the vestry-room was so contrived that the
minister passed from it through the ante-room, and from
thence, by a very short space, to the pulpit, without having
the inconvenience of descending from the gallery into the
body of the chapel, or of passing through the midst of the
congregation.   He could not, however, get from the vestry-
room to the reading-desk without passing down the stair-
case into the portico outside, and from thence through the
general door, which was in the centre of it, leading into the
body of the chapel.   Between the windows and on the
angles were Ionic pilasters, supporting a neat stone pediment.   The building was surrounded by a burial ground,
and enclosed by a wall and a handsome pair of gates
fronting Temple-court.   The Rev. Nicholas Clayton[1] was

(1) He married a daughter of Mr. James Nicholson, merchant, of Dale-street,
Liverpool, and received a diploma as Doctor of Divinity from the University of Edinburgh, in 1782. He died in 1797, and was buried in a vault at the Octagon Chapel,
but his remains were removed by Mr. James Boardman, one of his relatives, in 1819,
in consequence of the improvements then contemplated, to another place of interment,
the Cemetery of the Unitarian Chapel, in Renshaw-street.

I

the minister. He preached the first sermon at the opening of the chapel on 5th June, 1763, and his farewell sermon on 25th February, 1776, on the closing of the chapel.[1] It was soon afterwards disposed of, and used as a place of worship of the Church of England from 1776 until 1820, as will be noticed in another place.

The Roman Catholics had a chapel of small size in Lumber-street, which, to the disgrace of the police and of a portion of the inhabitants of Liverpool, had been attacked and destroyed by a mob in 1759. There had been a disputed succession; one of the infatuated and tyrannical race of Stuart still lived, who professed the creed of the Church of Rome, and was a claimant to the throne; party spirit ran high, and a furious mob completely destroyed the interior of the chapel, but it had been restored, and though very small, was then the only place of worship in Liverpool for persons of the Roman Catholic creed, at the period we are describing; and was dedicated to St. Mary. It has lately been re-built, and much enlarged, and its front now faces Edmund-street.

The Quakers had a meeting-house, on a small scale, as early as 1709, on the east side of Hackins-hey, where they remained until they removed from it to their present place of worship, in Hunter-street, in 1791; the old meeting-house still remains, but is now used as a charity school.

Of that ancient and interesting race, the Jews, there were very few in Liverpool, in 1775. They had then a synagogue at the lower end of Cumberland-street, on the south side, which had been originally principally established by some Germans of that persuasion, but there are not any records to show at what date it was first opened. The Jews afterwards left it for one on the south side of the Old Dock,

---

(1) The Author has one of the Prayer-Books used in the Chapel. It once belonged to one of the leading members of the congregation.

where it is believed that they remained only a short period.[1] They afterwards removed to a synagogue on the north side of Upper Frederick-street, where they also had a very small cemetery; the latter still remains, though it is no longer used. The date of the last interment there was about 1794, after which they used a larger cemetery in Oakes-street. Several years ago an old Hebrew tomb-stone was discovered near the lowest end of Stanley-street, from which it has been conjectured that they had a small cemetery there, at the time when the neighbouring synagogue in Cumberland-street was used; but if so, all knowledge of it is lost by lapse of time. The building which was used as the synagogue in Upper Frederick-street, is No. 151, and is made use of as a kind of committee-room, where the business connected with the synagogue is now transacted. In 1808, they removed to the present synagogue in Seel-street; and some years ago they opened a second synagogue in Pilgrim-street. The cemetery in Oakes-street being filled, their present cemetery in Deane-street, Prescot-road, was formed, and the first interment took place there in 1837.

The charitable and benevolent institutions of Liverpool must now be noticed; and it cannot be concealed that there were very few in 1775: and of those which existed, two only, the Blue-Coat Hospital, and the Liverpool Infirmary, were supported by voluntary contributions.

A striking contrast presents itself, between the degree of support given by the inhabitants of Liverpool to public institutions for charitable purposes, in 1775, and the present time. Now, in 1853, there are thirty-two benevolent and charitable institutions in Liverpool, supported by voluntary contributions, exclusive of missionary, bible, and other reli-

---

(1) The Author has been unable to learn at what date the Synagogue was opened at the Old Dock; but his Father, from curiosity, was once present during Divine service there, which is believed to have been between seventy and eighty years ago.

gious societies, and of such as are for ecclesiastical and educational purposes, and also exclusive of Sunday and day schools for the children of the poor, of which societies and schools the number is considerable.

As a proof of the spirit with which arrangements for charitable objects are now made and supported in Liverpool, it may not be improper concisely to notice here the Fancy Fair for charitable purposes, held in August, 1849, during the mayoralty of Mr. J. Bramley-Moore. It was held in the Prince's-park, near Liverpool, which the proprietor, Mr. Richard Vaughan Yates, had kindly allowed to be the arena of the festival, and realised the large sum of £9593 6s 2d, nett; which was divided between three of the public charities—the Liverpool Infirmary, the Northern Hospital, and the Southern and Toxteth Hospital.[1]

The Alms-houses of Liverpool must now be noticed. A range of alms-houses existed at the lowest part of the south side of Shaws-brow, near the Old Haymarket, now Shaw-place. Another range of them stood at the upper end of St. John's-lane, where the New Haymarket now is, and opposite the station of the London and North-western Railway; and a third range stood near the bottom of

---

(1) It commenced on Wednesday, the 8th, was continued on the 9th and 10th, and terminated on Saturday, the 11th of August. The tables or stalls were presided over by twelve ladies, who, with the assistance of others, were kind enough to give their services in disposing of the various articles exhibited for sale, which were in a great measure of that nature which are generally on sale at a *fete* of this kind, principally produced by the skill and ingenuity of the ladies who preside at the stalls and their friends, ranging from articles of the simplest description to those of the most elaborate design and costly execution. It is believed that at no previous *fete* of this nature a larger quantity of richly-wrought articles, beautiful in design and elegantly executed, was ever exhibited. Chairs, cushions, ottomans, specimens of fancy knittings, children's drapery, dolls, curiously-wrought devices, pictures, prints, &c. were heaped in profusion on the various stalls, each of which might lay claim to some article of a unique kind or great value.

Besides the Fancy Fair, strictly so called, there were a Flower Show, tents for the sale of refreshments, balloon ascents, a boat race, camera obscuras, exhibitions of ledger-

Ranelagh-street, opposite the end of Hanover-street, and near the eastward end of Church-street, close to the spot where the north front and garden of the Lyceum News-room now stand. All were destroyed when the new range of alms-houses was erected in St. Mary's-lane, Mount-pleasant, in 1787, as will be mentioned in a subsequent chapter, in noticing the events of that year.

---

demain, puppets, fantoccini, ventriloquism, bands of music, sports and pleasures, such as a foot hurdle race, a sack race, a race blindfold, and swarming greased poles for prizes, and the Festival closed with fire-works in the evening.

The following is a list of the names of the fair Presidents, and of the sums received by each from the sale of various articles at the stalls :—

Stall	£.	s.	d.
No. 1, Mrs. Bramley-Moore, (the Lady of the Mayor)	684	12	5
2, Mrs. Yates, Mrs. Moss, Mrs. R. V. Yates, and Mrs. Thompson..................................	632	10	2
3, Mrs. Alison and the Misses Wraith	174	16	0
4, Mrs. G. H. Lawrence	80	1	11
5, The Misses Fry...............................	101	6	1
6, Mrs. Campbell	46	3	5½
7, Mrs. Sutton and the Misses Pritt	170	0	0
8, Mrs. Rotherham	124	8	4
9, Mrs. Morris, Mrs. Robert Lucas and Mrs. M. Lucas..	317	8	8
10, Mrs. Howell, Mrs. George Wright and Mrs. Samuel Hope......................................	135	17	2
11, Mrs. Troughton and Miss Petrie..................	155	0	0
12, Mrs. E. Moon	205	15	2
	£2,827	19	4½
The Raffle.........................	163	15	0
	£2,991	14	4½

SUMMARY OF THE PAYMENTS AND RECEIPTS OF THE FANCY FAIR.

PAYMENTS.	£.	s.	d.	RECEIPTS.	£.	s.	d.
Music Committee	162	17	0	Admission Tickets	5,407	17	0
Amusements	177	0	4	Ladies' Bazaar........	2,991	14	4½
Floral....................	56	17	1	Refreshments	1,117	3	11
Refreshments	316	8	8	Plants	18	4	10
Printing..................	126	15	9	Concert	71	2	6
Tent	619	19	11	Amusements	239	15	11½
Gardens..................	83	3	0	Omnibus Proprietors ..	75	8	10
Medals	151	18	3	Donations	1,500	3	6
Raffle...................	16	7	1				
Sundries	44	17	8				
	£1,828	4	9				

Infirmary £3197 15 5
Northern Hospital 3197 15 5
Southern and Tox-
    teth Hospital.. 3197 15 4
——————— 9,593 6 2

£11,421 10 11   £11,421 10 11

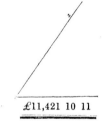

The origin of the old alms-houses is stated to have been as follows:—

In the year 1692, Dr. Silvester Richmond gave £100 to erect alms-houses, on Shaws-brow, for poor sailors' widows; and, in 1706, Mrs. Sarah Richmond gave £50 for repairing the same. In 1723, Mr. John Scarsbrick gave £70 towards completing them. In 1706, Mr. Richard Warbrick vested £120 in the Corporation of Liverpool for building alms-houses for poor sailors' widows, in Hanover-street, and the interest of £30 for repairing them, in addition to which, he also gave two houses in Castle-street and two houses in Moor-street, towards the support of such poor women as should thereafter inhabit them.[1]

The charity called Mrs. Ann Molyneux's Charity, had its origin from that lady, having by her will, dated 19th January, 1727, bequeathed £200 to the Mayor and Rectors of Liverpool, to be placed out at interest on landed security, for the benefit of the poor prisoners confined for debt in the gaol of Liverpool; and she also left £300, to be placed out at interest, the interest to be disposed of for the benefit of old sailors and sailors' widows inhabiting Liverpool, especially those who dwelt in the alms-houses, in such proportions as the Rectors should think fit. She appointed Ralph Williamson and Robert Whittle executors, and died in March, 1729. Probate of the will was granted by the Consistory Court of Chester, on the 8th May, 1729.[2] With that money five fields, known by the name of the Rectors' Fields, (then near the Moss-lake Fields, now built upon,) which adjoined Falkner-street, were purchased; and several other legacies for those purposes have been given.

The Blue-Coat Hospital, on the south side of School-lane, for the education of orphan and fatherless children, and

---

(1) History of Liverpool, Anon: printed by J. M'Creery, in 1795, page 163.
(2) Corporation Records.

of those who have indigent but honest parents, was first established under the name of the Charity School, in 1709.[1] The original part of the present building was commenced in 1716 and finished in 1717, and although it has been subsequently much enlarged, its front presents the same appearance now as it originally did. It is a brick building, of which the angles and windows are ornamented with stone. It has a large court-yard in front, inclosed with iron rails and gates; has wings projecting considerably towards School-lane, and has a large yard behind, in which the children play. The apartments are numerous and convenient. In the principal body of the building is a good hall, and stair-case leading to a large room, fitted up and used as a chapel. The charity clothes, feeds, lodges and educates the children, and at a proper age puts them out as apprentices to various trades or occupations.[2] The boys are taught reading, writing,

---

(1) Enfield's Liverpool, page 48.

(2) The following is a list of the Governors and Trustees of the Blue-Coat Hospital, in 1741, kindly furnished by Mr. Anthony Swainson, one of the present Trustees. It is curious as containing the names of some of the then principal merchants, and other inhabitants of Liverpool :—

1, The Worshipful the Mayor for the time being.
2, ⎫ The Rev. the Rectors of the new
3, ⎬ Church of St. Peter, and of
   ⎭ St. Nicholas.
4, The Rt. Hon. Edw. Earl of Derby.
5, James, Lord Strange.
6, Thos. Henry Ashurst.
7, Foster Cunliffe.
8, John Goodwin.
9, Bryan Blundell.
10, Thos. Brereton.
11, Richard Gildart.
12, Thos. Bootle.
13, Captain Robert Bootle.
14, John Blackburn.
15, John Radcliff.
16, Richard Clayton.
17, Francis Price.
18, Isaac Green.
19, Wm. Shaw.
20, John Plumb.
21, Thos. Case.
22, Daniel Willis.
23, Samuel Powell.
24, Roger Brook.
25, Richard Houghton, merchant.
26, Ralph Peters.
27, Dr. George Dickin.
28, Wm. Sudlow.
29, Wm. Williamson, the elder.
30, Charles Pole.
31, John Entwisle.
32, John Atherton.
33, Edward Markland.
34, John Williamson, clerk.
35, William Williamson, junior.
36, Ellis Cunliffe.
37, Thos. Tyrer.
38, Wm. Blundell.
39, Caryl Fleetwood.
40, Thos. Seel.
41, John Parr.
42, Edward Parr.
43, James Bromfield, surgeon.
44, Thomas Steers.
45, Owen Prichard.
46, Thomas Parks.
47, Robert Whittle.
48, John Okill.
49, William Marsh.
50, James Haydock.

and arithmetic, the elements of the English grammar, and the outlines of geometry and astronomy; those intended for the sea, navigation; the girls reading, writing, arithmetic, sewing, knitting and housewifery. The girls knit their own and the boys' stockings and make their own clothes. There are now 250 boys and 100 girls; total, 350 in the institution.

An ancient Free School, which then existed on the south side of School-lane, in Liverpool, but is now discontinued, towards the support of which a grant of £5 6s 8d[1] was formerly made out of the revenues of the Duchy of Lancaster, will be noticed in the chapter[2] upon the municipal affairs of the town, and the patronage of the Corporation.

The Liverpool Infirmary was a conspicuous object, on the south side and upper end of Shaws-brow. The design for erecting it was first formed in 1745, when subscriptions were entered into. The Corporation gave a field for 999 years, and the work commenced, but the progress was, from several circumstances, so much retarded, that it was not finished until the latter end of 1748, when the two upper wards were furnished with thirty beds. It was opened and patients admitted on the 15th of March, 1749. It was a brick building, with a large garden behind, used principally for convalescent patients, and had an extensive court in front, enclosed with iron rails and a gate. Its wings were formed by the Seamen's Hospital, built on each side of it.

The Seamen's Hospital, adjoining and extending on each side of the Infirmary, was built of brick. The design for it was first formed in 1747, but it was only carried into effect in 1752, in which year land was contracted for, and proper edifices erected. It was a hospital for decayed

---

(1) It is stated to have been £5 6s 8d in the printed Report of the proceedings before the Commissioners of Inquiry into the Municipal Corporations of 1833, page 104. In other accounts it has been stated to have been £5 13s 4d.

(2) Chapter 3.

seamen, their widows and children, and supported by the monthly allowance of sixpence, which every seaman from the port of Liverpool was obliged, by Act of Parliament, to pay out of his wages. The business of the hospital was conducted by a committee, who were chosen at the beginning of each year.[1]

The Lunatic Asylum, which was subsequently erected and was entered from St. John's-lane, behind the Infirmary, will be noticed in another place. The Infirmary and Seamen's Hospital were pulled down in 1826, and the Lunatic Asylum not very long afterwards; the present Infirmary, which was opened in 1824, in Brownlow-street, and the Lunatic Asylum, on Brownlow-hill, being then in use.

On Monday, the 27th of September, 1824, a ball took place in the Town-hall, on the occasion of the opening of the New Infirmary, in Brownlow-street. It has been remarked as an extraordinary circumstance connected with the ball, that Mrs. Linacre, aged 97, attended it. "The old lady was brought to the ball by Miss Backhouse, into whose carriage she was lifted from the door of her house, on the east side of Oldhall-street, where she was born, amidst the surprised assemblage of her neighbours. On entering the Town-hall, she refused to be carried up the multitude of steps of the grand staircase, but walked up, leaning on the arms of Dr. Brandreth and of Mr. W. H. Atherton, by whose grand-father, John Atherton, Esq. of Walton-hall, she had been taken in his carriage, the only one then kept in Liverpool, seventy-five years before, on the opening of the then new and now old Infirmary. She remained in the rooms upwards of two hours, during which period she was several times very kindly accosted by the Countess of Derby, and the other

---

(1) Enfield's Liverpool, page 55.

K

ladies of rank, and was surrounded from time to time, by the sons, grandsons, and perhaps great grandsons of the acquaintance of her youth."[1]

When the excavations were making for the foundations of the old Infirmary, the vestiges of an entrenchment, and various other *indicia* of the siege of Liverpool, in 1644, by Prince Rupert, were discovered; they are believed to have been his advanced works. His camp was at Everton, near the ancient beacon, from whence he brought a detachment every day to open the trenches and erect batteries.[2] From the trenches and batteries, which were relieved from the camp twice in every twenty-four hours, the Prince frequently attacked the besieged and their works, but he was always repulsed with great slaughter of his men for nearly the space of a month.[3] The siege commenced about the 2nd of June, and on the 26th of that month Prince Rupert attacked the town, on the north side, about three o'clock in the morning, and took it by assault.[3]

Prince Rupert's batteries were placed on an elevated ridge of ground, in the fields above the old Infirmary. They extended in the direction from the upper end of Shaws-brow,[4] and near the place where the old Infirmary was afterwards erected, and upon the high ground above the present Railway Station, in Lime-street, towards the place where the copperas works on Copperas-hill afterwards stood, and occasionally discoveries have been made throwing a light upon them. When the foundations of the old Liverpool Infirmary were sunk, the marks of trenches which the Prince had thrown up, and some gardevin bottles, cartouches, &c. which the besiegers had left behind, were discovered.[5]

---

(1) Liverpool Courier, of 29th September, 1824.

(2) Enfield's Liverpool, page 13.   (3) Ibid. page 13 and 14.

(4) Enfield's Liverpool, page 13.   (5) Ibid. page 14.

In 1805, on digging up the ground for the foundation of the houses which form Seymour-street, Silver-street and the upper part of Gloucester-street, evident marks were discovered of a line of entrenchments and of a battery. The following account of the discovery is given in the *Gentleman's Magazine*:—"The inquisitive antiquary now has an opportunity of gratifying himself with the examination of the traces of the intrenchment thrown up by Prince Rupert, when he laid siege to Liverpool in the year 1644, and described by Enfield in his history of that town. It is situated about twenty yards from the present London-road, and opposite the end of St. Ann's-street, on the east side of a road recently cut[1] leading to Rodney-street. Here the rock has been evidently excavated and filled up again with loose earth. Other traces are discernible in the field above, as well as on the other side of a lane nearer the town, at the top of a new street, (now planned), to be called Gloucester-street, and at the corner of another intended street, to be denominated Silver-street, all just below the copperas works, and on the site of the old mill blown down about the year 1795. There has likewise been traced, and may be now seen as the workmen are removing the earth, the situation of the fort or battery so accurately pointed out by Enfield; and, in the trench have been found many bones, broken glass, old bricks, remnants of a wall and leaden balls. The lower trenches mentioned by the same writer were discovered about sixty years ago, when the Infirmary was dug, and in them were found gardevin bottles, cartouches, and various other articles left behind by the besiegers."[2]

The Parish Workhouse or Poorhouse, on the south side of Brownlow-hill, was commenced in 1770, and finished in

---

(1) Evidently meant for the site of Seymour-street.

(2) Gentleman's Magazine for March, 1805, vol. 75, part 1, page 376.

1771. It was erected in lieu of an old one which stood on the north side of College-lane, and corner of Hanover-street,[1] of which the court-yard and principal part of the building still remain, and are approached from College-lane, by a large gate, which is very near the corner of Hanover-street, and opens into the court-yard, on the opposite side of which the old building stands. It is of brick, and has had large cottage windows, now built up, and is used as a ware-house. The more modern workhouse or poor-house on Brownlow-hill was a brick building, four stories high, the windows of which were ornamented with stone, and it had projecting wings and a very large court, which had iron rails, and large iron gates in front. It was afterwards consider-ably enlarged, and in 1796 one of its wings was destroyed by fire, but it was soon re-built. As the population of Liverpool increased, that building, like its predecessor, was not found sufficiently commodious, and it became necessary to have a workhouse on a larger scale. A commencement was made, in 1846, in gradually taking it down, and erecting, on its site, the extensive pile of buildings now the Parish Workhouse. As new portions were erected and made fit for use, from time to time, a part of the former building was pulled down, and the last portion of it was removed in 1852, except a very small part which is intended to be taken down in the present year, (1853.) The edifice contains at present 2040 pauper inmates, but it can accommodate as many as 2348; and, when completed, there will be accommodation for 3000. An extensive range of offices and buildings con-nected with the parish, was built in 1849 and 1850, upon Brownlow-hill, in front of the workhouse.

---

(1) This was first used as a Parish Workhouse about 1732.—See Underhill's M.S. in the possession of Joseph Mayer, F.S.A., who kindly allowed the Author to inspect it.

The other public edifices standing in 1775, of a secular nature, now require notice.

The present Town-hall, then called the Exchange, stood conspicuously at the north end of Castle-street; the first stone of its foundation was laid in 1748, and it was first used in 1754,[1] in the mayoralty of Mr. Joseph Clegg; it had then neither the present portico, balustrade, or cupola. The edifice had in front an elegant range of Corinthian columns, supporting a pediment, and supported by a well-proportioned rustic basement. Between the capitals were placed, in basso-relievo, heads and emblems of commerce.[2] Above the centre of the south, or principal front, and the pediment, a low, ill-proportioned and small dome originally stood, upon which was a turret with a seat inside, from whence an extensive and beautiful view of the sea, the town and its environs, might be obtained. The dome was generally condemned as in bad taste, and it has been correctly stated that it was a massive dome covered with lead, which incumbered the building and disgraced the Corinthian architecture which supported it.[2]   It was, however, got rid of on Sunday, the 18th January, 1795, when the interior, the roof and the dome were completely destroyed by fire. Upon the pediment of the south or Castle-street front were carved some strange absurdities, consisting of figures[3] intended to

---

(1) In 1755, the old Exchange, which stood in Castle-street, in front of and very near the new building, was taken down. It had been erected in 1674.

(2) Enfield's Liverpool, page 58 and 59.

(3) The following extraordinary description of the figures is given in *Troughton's Liverpool*, page 286 :—" On the left angle of the pediment appears the Genius of Commerce, the Liver, the Genius of Liberty, the Cap of Liberty, and the Fasces. On the right we discover Neptune, a trident, and an aqueous urn. The principal figure is contiguous to Neptune, and seems to represent the Genius of Liverpool, with the appropriate emblems, a cornucopia resting on a shield, the figure of a Liver beneath his right arm, the hand of which holds a flaming sword ; the left arm of the figure is extended to direct the attention of Neptune to the Genius of Commerce ; " and

be allegorical. It is said that the whole[1] was executed from the designs of the late Mr. Woods, architect of Bath. To the credit of his memory, it is to be hoped that so extraordinary an exhibition of absurdities, anachronisms, and bad taste, as the so-called allegorical figures in the pediment, was forced upon him by some committee of the Corporation, and was adopted contrary to his better judgment. The edifice was built of stone, and was upon the whole handsome. Access to the interior was obtained, as now, from Castle-street, through the principal entrance, which was by three arched door-ways, ornamented with handsome iron work; these led to a spacious covered piazza, surrounding a square

---

the following interpretation is attempted to be given of it in that work :—"The Genius of Commerce is the proper representative of the prosperity and importance of this town, and of which the erection of this magnificent pile is a memorable instance ; the Liver is the emblem of Liverpool, the Genius of Liberty holding the cap on a rod, indicates that to give full scope to the human powers, freedom is absolutely requisite, and that where freedom is denied, the arts will languish, ingenuity be paralized, and commerce decay. The Fasces were badges of Roman magisterial power, twelve being carried by lictors or town sergeants, before a supreme magistrate, and six before an inferior one. They were composed of rods bound round an axe, indicating the appropriate rewards of licentiousness and of crimes. Neptune the God of the Sea is made the protector of the River Mersey, of which the aqueous urn is the type. The Trident according to Cornutus, is an exact resemblance of the fuscinæ or spears, which the ancient fishermen used in the prosecution of their employments, and if it be considered that almost all the towns and cities which have been famed for commercial greatness, were once the hamlets of fishermen, or only treacherous stations for ships, it will clearly appear, that Neptune was originally the patron and protector of fishing, and that he is now, by a transition very natural and easy, become the patron and protector of commerce. As to the Genius of Liverpool, the cornucopia, the shield, and the flaming sword, plenty and protection are the natural imports. The whole is designed with spirit, the allusions are judicious, and the execution bold and masterly." In that florid description there is however an omission ; certain bales of merchandise, apparently intended to represent Manchester cotton or Yorkshire woollen goods, were prominently introduced amongst the figures ; they certainly were not in worse taste, or more ridiculous, than the shield, fasces, flaming sword, &c. and perhaps they ought not to have been omitted when the other absurdities were described.

(1) Troughton's Liverpool, page 286, the word "whole" probably is here meant to apply to the whole edifice, including the pediment and its figures.

area in the middle. This covered walk was supported by couplets of Doric columns, without pedestals. The under part of the entablature, and the body of the building, under the piazza, were crowded with a variety of ornaments, except the ceiling of the chief or south walk. The area was so small as to have somewhat the appearance of a well, and to give a gloomy cast to the walks that surrounded it.[1] The principal stair-case, which was spacious and easy of ascent, led to the Town-hall, which was a large and handsome room, well lighted, and elegantly fitted up with a semi-circular range of seats, &c. all of mahogany. Behind the Town-hall was the Council-room, and adjoining to that was the Assembly-room. That room was 65 feet in length and 25 in breadth; it was everywhere enriched with carving and other ornaments.[1] In the open space, or area, in the interior before-mentioned, the merchants were intended to have assembled; it was, in fact, to have been the public exchange, but it was never used for that purpose, and they were accustomed to meet on High Change, at the north end of Castle-street, opposite Mr. Gore's shop, (now Messrs. Mawdsley and Son's,) until the new Exchange-buildings were opened, when the latter were adopted as their place of meeting. Although the fire destroyed the interior, the dome, and the roof of the edifice, yet the outside walls did not suffer much injury, and the appearance of the east and west sides still remains as before the fire. The interior was re-built on a different plan, and the present cupola erected, but the balustrades, and the portico on the south front, were added afterwards; the latter in 1811. In building the portico, the absurd allegorical figures before mentioned were taken away. The wing on the north side, in which the large ball-room now is, was erected some time after the principal part of the edifice.

---

(1) Enfield's Liverpool, page 58 and 59.

The immediate neighbourhood of the Town-hall was, in 1775, a principal scene of one of the most extraordinary and dangerous riots that occurred in England during the last century, which lasted several days, and was remarkable from the circumstance of the rioters using cannon and other fire-arms during the continuance of their violence. A full account of the riots will be found in a subsequent chapter.

The Custom-house, on the east side of the Old Dock, now Canning-place, was built about 1700,[1] and was a brick building, with slightly-projecting wings; the angles and windows were ornamented with stone. It had the royal arms carved in stone, in front, and was entered by a wide flight of steps in the centre, through arches, into an arcade or piazza, out of which several doors opened, and a staircase led to the long-room, which was above the piazza, and to several other offices. The Custom-house yard and warehouse (the latter fronted Paradise-street) were at the back, and access to them for carts was obtained by a passage on the south side of the Custom-house. The whole were pulled down in 1839, when the new Custom-house in Canning-place was opened.

LIST OF THE COLLECTORS OF CUSTOMS OF THE PORT OF LIVERPOOL, FROM 1698 TO 1823.

Edward Scarborough	1698.	John Colquitt, jun.	1749.
Luke Singleton	1705.	Henry Hardwar	1773.
Sir Barnabas Scudamore, Bart.	1707.	John Kennion	1782.
Edmond Smith	1709.	Arthur Onslow	1785.
Nathaniel Smith	1710.	John Timothy Swainson	1807.
John Colquitt	1726.	Elias Arnaud	1823.

The ancient Tower at the lower end of Water-street, on the north side, between Tower-garden and Stringer's-alley, was the Gaol of Liverpool, and continued to be so used until

(1) It is said to have been built by Mr. Silvester Moorecroft, who was Bailiff in that year, and was afterwards Mayor in 1706.—Underhill's M.S.

3rd of July, 1811. It had formed a portion of the possessions of the Stanleys, in the feudal times, but the date of its
erection is not clearly known. It was a heavy stone building,
with towers, on which some remains of the old machicolations
might be perceived, with a large open space in its interior, in
which the prisoners took exercise. On its east side a large
gothic arch extended from it across Tower-garden to the
house opposite. This gaol was used for the confinement of
both debtors and criminals, who were, as lately as 1810,
allowed to meet promiscuously in the open space allotted for
exercise,[1] an instance of gross neglect on the part of the
authorities, which has been noticed with the reprobation
which it merited. In the war with France, which broke out
in 1756, it was also used as a place of confinement for the
prisoners of war.[2] On the 3rd of July, 1811, the criminals
and debtors were removed to the new goal, in Great Howard-
street, and in 1819, the felons were removed from the latter
to the County Prison at Kirkdale.

Amongst the purposes for which a room in the old Tower
had been used, it may be mentioned, that whilst it was a gaol,
but long anterior to 1775, the room was made use of, amongst
other purposes, as a chapel, and also as a general assembly-
room. It is said that the ladies went there from their houses
in blue cloaks and pattens,[3] coaches and cabs not being then
in use.

At the close of 1819, or commencement of 1820, the
old Tower was pulled down, and warehouses now stand on

---

(1) Troughton's Liverpool, page 319.

(2) Communicated by Miss Park, whose father, the eminent and well-known
surgeon of that name, attended, in his professional capacity, when a very young man,
the French prisoners there.

(3) From an old manuscript note in the Author's possession ; the date is not given
in it, but in the *Directory* the circumstance is in part noticed under the date 1755. The
manuscript note calls the room, so used as a chapel, the Debtors'-room.

L

its site.[1]   It had been the place of confinement of several of the unfortunate adherents of the Pretender, implicated in the rebellion of 1715, and many of them having been tried and convicted at Liverpool, under a special commission, four of those who were convicted, were executed near Gallows Mill, which was one of three white wind-mills which many persons now living recollect standing near London-road.   Two of these mills remained standing long after the commencement of the present century.[2]   They stood a little distance from the north side of London-road, behind the spot where Stafford-street now is, and near where Audley-street is now built.

The persons executed were Mr. Collingwood, Mr. Bennett, or Burnet, Mr. Drummond and Mr. Hunter.   Mr. Collingwood had a landed estate of £2000 a year.[3]

There were 70 of the Pretender's adherents, who had been taken prisoners at Preston, tried at Liverpool, under a special commission of Oyer and Terminer, of whom 66 were convicted of high treason, and 22 of them were executed in different towns, and others acknowledged their offence and solicited transportation, which was granted to some of them, but many died in prisons by the severity of the season and the want of necessaries.[4]   Besides the persons convicted at Liverpool, a number of prisoners implicated in that rebellion, and taken at Preston, seem to have been brought, after

---

(1) The materials, together with those of an adjoining house had previously been sold by auction in December, 1819, for £200.

(2) As there were three wind-mills standing near the same spot and very near together, it is perhaps impossible to say which of them in particular was called the Gallows Mill; or all of them might, perhaps, correctly be called the Gallows Mills. The public-house at the corner of Stafford-street takes its name from the above circumstance.

(3) Salmon's Chronological Historian, page 60, 61, and 68.

(4) Salmon's Chronological Historian, page 59.

conviction, from other places to Liverpool in 1716, as £1000 was agreed to be paid to Sir Thomas John, in that year, to transport 130 of them to the plantations. Thirty of the Preston prisoners were put on board a ship, in order to be transported from Liverpool to the West Indies; but they rose and over-matched the crew, and affidavits were made before the Mayor of Liverpool that they had mastered the ship's crew and carried the ship to France, where they sold both ship and cargo.[1] This does not appear to have been the same shipment of prisoners as that in which Sir Thomas John was engaged, as the dates do not tally; that of Sir Thomas John apparently being in May, and the other in November, 1716. In 1788, two men, Patrick Burns and Silvester Dowling, were executed in Water-street, opposite the old Tower, for robbing Mrs. Graham's house, in Rose-hill, near St. Ann's Church; one of them is said to have been a painter, who had been employed at the house. These were the only executions since those of the rebels of 1716, and the last which took place at or near Liverpool, until the assizes were held there in August, 1835, when a man was tried there and executed at Kirkdale for murder.

The old Tower was visited by John Howard, the philanthropist, in 1775; it was then the Borough Gaol. He describes it as out of repair, and states that the apartments were close and dirty; that there were seven close dungeons ten steps under ground, each six feet and a half by five feet nine inches, and six feet high. That three prisoners were locked up in each of them at night; that there was another dungeon larger but not secure, and that there was no infirmary. He also mentions that the dungeons were offensive, and

---

(1) Salmon's Chronological Historian, page 61 and 68. In January, 1717, one hundred of the Preston prisoners, who had been confined in the *Savoy*, were put on board a ship to be transported to the West Indies.—Ibid. page 69.

that the prison was surrounded with other buildings, and that it could not be made healthy and convenient, and that the gaol fever had recently been prevalent in it.[1]   He also states, apparently with some satisfaction, that he had heard that the Corporation intended to build a new gaol.[2]   He also visited the old Tower in 1779, and again in 1782, and stated that it was much cleaner than at his first visit; the court paved, the act for preserving the health of prisoners hung up, but that the unhealthy dungeons were still in use. The prisoners were then as follows :—1779, November 30 : prisoners 25, deserters 2, impressed men, 2 ; 1782, September 5 : debtors 19, felons, &c. 14, deserter 1.[3]   The Corporation on the occasion of one of the visits presented him with the freedom of the town.[3]

A letter written in October, 1803, by a philanthropic individual, Mr. James Neild, which has been published, gives a lamentable account of the condition of the gaol and of the want of attention to the prisoners :—

" This prison, at the bottom of Water-street, was formerly part of an old tower, and contains a court-yard twenty yards by ten, paved with brick, well supplied with water, and two necessaries appertaining to it. All descriptions of prisoners, young and old, debtors and felons, men and women, mix promiscuously together. For criminals there are seven close dungeons, in a passage eleven feet wide, ten steps under ground; each 6½ feet by 5 feet 9 inches, and 6 feet high, lighted and ventilated by apertures in the door, eleven inches by six. Four prisoners are locked up in each of five of these dungeons, & 3 in each of the other 2, every night. Adjoining, there is another dungeon, which is larger, with an iron-grated window to the street; 12 criminals are confined in it. The gaoler told me this dungeon was not secure, and therefore, it was principally made use of for deserters, and that he had sometimes 40 confined in it for 4 days. One small room for the

---

(1) Howard's State of Prisons in England and Wales, page 440.

(2) The new Gaol, then in contemplation, was the House of Correction on Mount-pleasant, built in 1776.

(3) Howard's Appendix to the State of the Prisons in England and Wales, p. 258.

sick. Poor debtors are lodged in one of the towers, on straw, on the floor. Those who can pay for beds 1s per week each, if 2 lie together, are furnished by the gaoler with rooms in the other tower. This prison is so surrounded by old buildings called the Tower Garden, that without pulling them down, it cannot be made healthy and convenient. The whole prison is filthy in the extreme; nor is it to be wondered at, when a large dunghill, with ducks, poultry, &c. are suffered in the court. From the licentious intercourse of the sexes, which I had observed on my several visits, I imagined little attention was paid to the chaplain, and therefore requested two of the magistrates to accompany me to the chapel, (taking care no previous notice of our intentions should reach the prison) when out of 109 prisoners, 6 only attended divine service !"[1]

Although neither of the prisons which will now be mentioned was used as such in 1775, yet the following short notice of each of them may perhaps be introduced without impropriety in this place. One of them, a building which was soon destined to become a prison, in Liverpool, was standing in 1775. It was an old brick edifice which stood on the north side of Brownlow-hill, and was used for the confinement of prisoners of war, during the American Revolutionary War; and it will be more particularly noticed in another place. It was pulled down many years ago. The other was the old Bridewell of Liverpool,[2] which was not built in 1775, and the date when it was erected or first used cannot be ascertained. It was, however, used during a considerable period before the termination of the last century, and it will be convenient to notice it here, although not in the strict order of dates. It stood on the north side of George's Dock basin. It is said that it was originally intended to be used as a magazine for the battery,[3] which formerly stood near it.

---

(1) Gentlemen's Magazine, for December, 1803, vol. 73, part 2, page 1104.

(2) See Mr. James Neild's Remarks on the Gaols of Liverpool, in the Gentleman's Magazine, for December, 1803, vol. 73, part 2, page 1104.

(3) See also ibid. page 1104, where Mr. James Neild alludes to the circumstance, but erroneously states that it was "built as a magazine for the Fort." Its distance, however, from the Fort, rendered that impossible. He must have meant the Battery.

This bridewell was a small brick embattled building, which has been thus described by Mr. James Neild: "two very damp offensive dungeons, eight steps under ground, the one 18 feet by 12, the other 12 feet by 7½; lighted, and each ventilated by an iron-bar grated window. No straw, bedstead, or bedding of any kind. Above stairs, two rooms, one 18 feet by 10, the other 10 feet by 9, and six feet high. Adjoining to these are two cells, totally dark, and without ventilation, 5 feet by 3, and 6 feet high. The Corporation allow fire. No employ —no court yard—no water accessible to the prisoners." [1]   It ceased to be used in 1804, when the present bridewell, in South Chapel-street, was first used, and the old one was soon afterwards taken down.

It has been before mentioned that a small octangular edifice, on the south-east corner of the raised terrace of St. George's Church, was the watch-house and lock-up night prison.

The Theatre-Royal, in Williamson-square, was opened in June, 1772, with a prologue written by Mr. George Coleman, and spoken by Mr. Younger, one of the managers; but the interior has been re-built, and a front of stone brought forward, into Williamson-square, and it was re-opened with "Speed the Plough," on the 6th of June, 1803. The drama will be more fully noticed afterwards, when the amusements of the town come under consideration.

The exact period when the first play-house was erected in Liverpool is unknown. During the reign of Charles the First, a small building for the exhibition of dramatic entertainments stood in a court at the bottom of James-street; but at the time of the Civil War it was shut up, and con-

---

(1) Mr. James Nield's Remarks on the Gaols of Liverpool, in the Gentleman's Magazine, for December, 1803, vol. 73, part 2, page 1104.

tinued unoccupied until the Restoration.[1] Plays were afterwards represented by a strolling company, in a building in Moor-street, which was, even as late as after the commencement of the present century, frequently used as a cock-pit.[2]

In 1775 an old theatre, though disused, stood on the east side of Drury-lane, near the place where it now joins Brunswick-street, and which was opened in June, 1759,[3] with the tragedy of " The Orphan."[4] It was used for dramatic performances until the opening of the theatre on the north side of Williamson-square, in 1772, and remained standing many years after 1775.

Whether the theatre in Drury-lane stood on the site of a still older theatre there, or whether an older theatre had recently stood in some other quarter of the town cannot now be ascertained; but it is certain that about the middle of the last century, and several years before 1759, a theatre, or a building used as a theatre, existed somewhere in Liverpool; because, in *Williamson's Liverpool Advertiser*,[5] published in the summer of 1756, there are many advertisements of the performance of dramatic entertainments, such as tragedies, comedies, and farces, "at the Theatre, in Liverpool." In the first number of that newspaper, published on Friday, May 28, 1756, the following advertisement appears,

---

(1) Troughton's Liverpool, page 98.

(2) " In a building in Moor-street, which is now" [1810] " frequently used for a cock-pit."—Troughton's Liverpool, page 98.

(3) See Troughton's Liverpool, page 141, where it is stated that the Theatre, in Drury-lane, opened in the beginning of June, 1759. See also the Annals published in Gore's Liverpool Directory.

(4) It is stated in the Annals published in Gore's Liverpool Directory, that the Theatre in Drury-lane opened in 1759, without mentioning the month, with the Tragedy of The Orphan.

(5) Williamson's Liverpool Advertiser, 1756, vol. 1.

announcing the opening of the theatre for the season :—

> " By Comedians from the Theatres-Royal, in London,
> at the Theatre in Liverpool.
> During the months of June, July, and August next, will be perform'd variety of the best Plays.   N.B. The days of acting will be Mondays, Wednesdays, and Fridays."[1]

Another number of that newspaper of June 4, 1756, contains an advertisement of the performance, "at the Theatre in Liverpool," on Friday, the 4th June, of the comedy of the "The Constant Couple," with the farce of "The Virgin Unmask'd;" and on Monday, the 7th of June, of the tragedy of "George Barnwell," with the farce of "The Cheats of Scapin."   Price of admission—to the pit, two shillings; gallery, one shilling.   The performance commenced at seven o'clock.[2]

In those of June 11 and of June 18, 1756, there are also advertisements of dramatic performances, and from the latter we find, that the company advertised Shakespeare's comedy of "Much ado about Nothing."   In that of 2nd July, 1756, we find advertisements of the performance of "As you Like it," "Romeo and Juliet," and "The Suspicious Husband"; and in that of 9th July, 1756, the tragedy of "Hamlet."

---

(1) Williamson's Liverpool Advertiser, 28th May, 1756.

(2)   By Comedians from the Theatres-Royal, in London,
At the Theatre in Liverpool,
This present Friday, June the 4th, will be acted
A Comedy call'd
THE CONSTANT COUPLE,
OR
A TRIP TO THE JUBILEE,
With a Farce call'd
THE VIRGIN UNMASK'D.

And on Monday, June the 7th, will be acted
A Tragedy call'd
THE LONDON MERCHANT,
OR THE
HISTORY OF GEORGE BARNWELL ;
With a Farce (never perform'd there before) call'd
THE CHEATS OF SCAPIN.
Pit, Two Shillings ; Gallery, One Shilling.
To begin exactly at Seven o'clock.
N.B. The Days of acting are Mondays, Wednesdays, and Fridays."

There were other performances of plays of Shake-speare, and other dramatic writers of eminence, advertised during that summer, from which we seem fairly justified in supposing, that the plays were performed by a regular company. The advertisements in the newspapers also show that some of the members of the company had then the usual benefits, and that the last day of their performing for the season was Monday, the 6th of September. The last advertisement on dramatic subjects, which appears for the season of 1756, is in the paper of 3rd of September, viz :—

> " The last night but one of acting.
> For the benefit of Mr. Holtom and Mrs. Copen,
> By Comedians from the Theatres-Royal, in London,
> At the Theatre in Liverpool,
> This present Friday, September 3rd, will be acted
> A Comedy call'd
> AS YOU LIKE IT,
> Written by Shakespear;
> With a Farce call'd
> THE ENGLISHMAN IN PARIS,
> AND SEVERAL ENTERTAINMENTS.
> N.B. Monday next will be positively the last day of playing this Season."

It is remarkable that not one of those advertisements notice the street or place where the theatre stood, and its locality cannot now be satisfactorily ascertained. Is it not possible that the building in Moor-street (before mentioned) may have been the only Liverpool theatre, such as it was, in 1756? As the only places mentioned for seeing the performances were the pit and gallery, it must be inferred that there were not any boxes in the theatre for the audience.

The following advertisement relating to performances at the Liverpool Drury-lane Theatre, appears in the Liverpool newspaper of Friday, June 13th, 1766 :—

> By Comedians,
> From the Theatres-Royal,
> in
> London,
> at the
> Theatre in Drury-lane,
> Liverpool,

M

This present Friday, being the 13th of June, will be acted
A Tragedy call'd
HAMLET,
PRINCE OF DENMARK,
Written by Shakespear.
At the end of the Play,
A Pantomime Dance, call'd
JEALOUSY,
By Mr. Fischar and Mrs. Thompson.
To which will be added
A Farce call'd
THE MOCK DOCTOR.
Boxes, 3s; Pit, 2s; Gallery, 1s.
To begin exactly at Seven o'clock.
No Person whatever can be admitted behind the Scenes.
VIVANT REX & REGINA.
⁎ The Company will act on Mondays, Wednesdays, and Fridays, during the
Summer.(1)

The following is a copy of an old play-bill of the Liverpool Theatre, in Drury-lane, issued in 1767 :—

" By Comedians from the Theatres-Royal, in London,
At the Theatre, in Drury-lane.
This present Monday, being the 13th of July, 1767, will be acted
a Tragedy call'd
ROMEO AND JULIET,
Written by Shakespeare.

Romeo	Mr. Bensley.	Escalus	Mr. Wignell.
Mercutio	Mr. King.	Sampson	Mr. Parsons.
Capulet.......	Mr. Gibson.	Apothecary	Mr. Holtom.
Friar Lawrence.. by	Mr. Morris.	Balthazar...... by	Mr. Wild.
Benvolio	Mr. Mattocks.	Page..........	Master Besford.
Paris	Mr. Packer.	Juliet	Mrs. Mattocks.
Tibalt	Mr. Cushing.	Lady Capulet ..	Mrs. Parsons.
Montague	Mr. Fox.	Nurse	Mrs. Bennet.

With a Masquerade Scene,
In which will be introduc'd a Minuet, by Mr. Fishar and Mrs. Mattocks,
And a Scene representing the Monument of the Capulets.
With the following Entertainments,
End of Act the 4th,
A MINUET,
By Mr. Fishar and Miss Besford, Scholar to Mr. Fishar.
End of the Play,
THE PROLOGUE TO THE APPRENTICE,
Will be spoken by Master Besford.
After which
THE TURK'S DANCE,
By Mr. Fishar and Mrs. King.

---

(1) From Gore's Liverpool General Advertiser, of Friday, June 13th, 1766.

To which will be added a Ballad Farce, called
THE CONTRIVANCES.

Rovewell				1st Mob		Mr. Holtom.
Argus			Mr. Mattocks.	2nd Mob		Mr. Wignell.
Hearty	by	Mr. Parsons.	3rd Mob	by	Mr. Fox.
Robin		Mr. Morris.	Arethusa		Mrs. Mattocks.
Boy		Mr. Cushing.	Betty		Mrs. Evans.
		Master Besford.			

Not any money under the Full Price to be taken during the whole
Performance, nor any Servants admitted into the Gallery without
paying.

Boxes, 3s; Pit, 2s; Gallery, 1s.

The Doors to be open'd at Five.   To begin exactly at Seven.

Tickets to be had at the Golden Lyon, in Dale-street; at E. Smith's, in Cable-street; of Mr. Besford, at Mrs. Glover's, in Peter's-alley, Castle-street; and at Mr. Cox's, in Fenwick-street, where places for the Boxes may be taken.

No Person whatever can be admitted behind the Scenes.

N.B.—Tickets deliver'd out by Master Besford, will be taken.

VIVANT REX & REGINA."[1]

The Theatre in Drury-lane remained standing, as has
been already mentioned, many years after the theatre on the
north side of Williamson-square was built; and on one
occasion, after 1776, a dramatic performance took place in
the former for the benefit of Mr. Leverton, of Pool-lane, an
optical instrument maker, but the performers were principally
amateurs, or at least not a regular company.[2]

A portion of this theatre was afterwards used as an
engine house for the fire engines before they were kept in
the arcade at St. George's Church, and another part was
for a short time used as a carrier's warehouse.

The old theatre in Drury-lane, Liverpool, was a plain
and neat brick building, about twenty-seven yards in front
and sixteen yards deep: it had, as is shown by the advertisement and play-bills, boxes, a pit, and a gallery. The land
was held for a term of 900 years. It was purchased, in
1788, with other property, from Mrs. Chapman, and pulled
down, and part of its site forms a portion of the site of
Brunswick-street.

---

(1) The original was kindly lent to the Author by Mr. Thomas B. Gibbons.

(2) The Author's Father recollected the performance.

The Theatre-Royal, in Williamson-square, was originally erected at an expense of £6000, in thirty joint shares, by a subscription of thirty gentlemen, each proprietor being entitled to receive from the managers £5 per cent. for his share, and a silver ticket of free admission.[1]

The structure was, in its original form, built from a design of Sir William Chambers. It was a brick edifice, with stone ornaments to the windows, and had a pediment in front on which the royal arms were sculptured. A stone portico, a little higher than the door-ways, was afterwards added. The theatre was almost entirely re-built, and its present form adopted in 1803.

The Ranelagh Gardens must be mentioned whilst noticing the places of public amusement in Liverpool.

In the open space, now called Ranelagh-place, at the upper end of Ranelagh-street, was a tavern usually called the White-house, and occasionally Ranelagh-house; the ground on which it stood now forms part of the site of the Adelphi Hotel; at the back were public gardens called the Ranelagh Gardens, with seats and an orchestra in the centre, where entertainments of music, vocal and instrumental, and fireworks, something in the Vauxhall style, occasionally took place, to which the public were admitted on payment of a small sum. The gardens were also a favourite place of resort in the strawberry season for parties who wished to partake of strawberries grown there.

This place of amusement bore no resemblance to the London Ranelagh, which was a large circular covered building, in which the company used to assemble and promenade during the performance of pieces of music.

The following is a copy of a handbill of one of the evening performances, at the Ranelagh Gardens, in Liverpool:—

---

(1) Enfield's Liverpool, page 62.

" For the Benefit of Mrs. Ellis.
At Ranelagh Gardens,
To-morrow Evening, August 29, will be a
GRAND CONCERT,
of Vocal and Instrumental
MUSIC :
The Vocal Part by
Mrs. Ellis.
The first Violin, with a Solo, by
Mr. Morgan,
And the other Instrumental Parts
By the Best Performers.

Act I.	Act II.
Overture	Overture
A New Hunting Song, accompanied with the Horn	The favourite Hunting Song, in Mr. Dryden's Secular Masque, with the Horn
Concerto, Hargreave	A Duett Violincello and Bassoon Concerto
The favourite Ballad of Thro' the Wood Laddie	Violin Solo
Bassoon Concerto	Song, Ellen Aroon
Full Piece	Full Piece

To begin exactly at Six o'clock.

After the Concert will be exhibited some curious
FIREWORKS,
Very different from any of the former.

Twelve Rockets	Two Vertical Water Wheels
Two Horizontal Wheels	Two Water Flower Pots
Two Vertical Wheels	Two Water illuminating Showers
Two fierce Flower Pots	Water Rockets

Admittance, One Shilling.

Tickets to be had of Mrs. Ellis, at the Ship, near the Gardens ; and at the Angel, in Dale-street.

[Sadler, Print.]"[1]

It has not been found practicable to ascertain the date when the Ranelagh Gardens were first laid out or used in Liverpool, but it appears to have been some years before 1775, because performances there were advertised in 1766,[2] and they are laid down in Mr. John Eyes's Map of Liverpool, of 1768, and also in that of Mr. Perry, of 1769, and in the latter they are called "Ranelagh Gardens"; and the White House is called Ranelagh House, in one of

---

(1) Copied from the original printed hand-bill, in the possession of Mr. Thomas B. Gibbons.

(2) See Gore's Liverpool General Advertiser of 16th May, 1766.

the Liverpool Turnpike Acts, 11th George the Third, chap. 91, passed in 1771, which mentions a road passing "through Lime Kiln Lane"[1] to Ranelagh House, in Liverpool. The gardens had ceased to be used as a public place of amusement before the close of the last century.

There was not any Amphitheatre or Circus in Liverpool, in 1775, nor for many years afterwards. A Circus, in Christian-street, for the exhibition of equestrian performances, was, however, in existence at least as early as the year 1795, because, both the circus and the street of that name leading to it, are laid down in the Map of Liverpool of that date, published in Aikin's Description of the Country from Thirty to Forty Miles round Manchester. It is now the Adelphi Theatre.

The Post-office was, in 1775, and for some years after that date, in (North) John-street, on the east side, between Dale-street and the opening leading into Princes-street. It was like the post-offices still seen in small country towns, a plain dwelling-house, with an aperture for receiving letters, and a moveable square or little door-like opening in the window for the delivery of letters. Mr. Thomas Statham, the postmaster, lived there, and the establishment was afterwards removed to Lord-street, where it remained until 1800, when it was established in Postoffice-place, and in 1839 it was removed to Canning-place. In 1775 there was only one letter carrier for all Liverpool, and a greater number than one, was not then allowed to any town out of London.[2]

The mail bags were carried in 1775, and for some years afterwards, in and out of Liverpool, on horseback. At present the average number of letters and newspapers combined, and average number and weight of bags, sent from and

---

(1) Lime-street was sometimes called Lime Kiln Lane even within the Author's recollection.

(2) Gore's General Advertiser of 17th July, 1775.

received at the Post-office of Liverpool, daily, are as follows:—

Letters and Newspapers, about 115,000

Bags 460

Average weight of Bags, about .... 6 tons.[1]

which forms a wonderful contrast with the insignificant number and weight at the period when the post-office letters and newspapers were conveyed on horseback to and from Liverpool, a mode of conveyance in use during many years of the lifetime of an individual[2] yet living.

A laudable commencement of the formation of a Library was made in 1715, by John Fells, a mariner, who gave a sum of £30, to found a small theological library, in St. Peter's Church. It received some additions by one of the Rectors, and a few years ago the books were newly bound, repaired, and placed in glass cases; for, originally, they were on open shelves, and fastened together with rods and chains.[3] They are in good preservation, and are placed in the vestry of that church, where they may be consulted any day in proper hours; a catalogue, made out in 1818, shows that they then consisted of 217 volumes; 107 folio, 56 quarto and 54 octavo; consisting principally of ancient divinity and early church history; a considerable number of works of various kinds have, however, been since added by donations.

There was also a public Library of books existing in 1775, the ground-work of the present Liverpool Library, which had its origin in the following manner. A number of gentlemen were accustomed to meet in a conversation club, chiefly for the discussion of literary subjects, at the house of Mr. Wm. Everard, a schoolmaster in St. Paul's-square; the exact year when these meetings commenced is not known,

---

(1) Politely communicated to the Author in 1852, by Mr. Charles B. Banning, Postmaster, and since confirmed by a note from him to the Author, of 8th March, 1853.

(2) The Author's Father. He died after the above was written, and whilst this Work was in preparation for the press.

(3) Smithers' Liverpool, page 319.

but it is supposed to have been about 1756 or 1757. Soon after the first publication of the *Monthly Review*, it was agreed to take it in to read at their meetings. Other books were from time to time added, and kept in a large chest in Mr. Everard's parlour, from whence they were circulated amongst the members. In 1758 they were removed to a room in Princes-street, and the institution now assumed the form of a general subscription library. The first catalogue, containing twenty pages, published 17th November, 1758, gives the titles of 177 works and 48 pamphlets, altogether 450 volumes. There were at that time 109 subscribers, including most of the chief persons in the town. The annual subscription was then five shillings. In the following year the establishment was removed to (North) John-street,[1] where Mr. Everard had built himself a good school-house, of which the principal portion of the first floor then became occupied as the library, to which access was obtained by ascending some steps or stairs from a passage or lobby in the centre of the building, leading from (North) John-street.[2] The building was a uniform neat-looking edifice, of reddish brick, three stories in height, and the library-room occupied the middle portion of the first floor up stairs, and the whole of the interior was entered by a common door-way, and by the passage or lobby leading out of (North) John-street.

A catalogue was printed in 1760, of 650 volumes; and by the year 1770, they had increased to 1547.

Mr. Everard was appointed secretary and librarian of the Liverpool Library at the general meeting, in May, 1769; a serious dispute occurred with him, and he was removed from

---

(1) The situation of the Library, on the west side of John-street, is shown in Perry's Map of Liverpool, 1769.

(2) Some parts of the building, especially the ground-floor, were let off to one or more other persons.

his office on the 8th May, 1770, and Mr. Broderick was appointed in his stead, at a salary of £15 per annum; and a lease of the room was taken from Mr. Everard, in 1770, for seven years, at a rent of £10 per annum. In 1776, it was voted that the president should treat with Mr. Everard for a new lease, to commence on the expiration of the subsisting one, and at the same rent.

The earliest minutes on record are of a committee meeting held on 9th May, 1769, the Rev. Nicholas Clayton, (who has been mentioned before,) president. The affairs were then managed by a president and committee annually chosen.

Mr. Broderick held the office until 1772, when Mr. George Barker was appointed in his room.[1]

The accommodations in John-street were afterwards found small and insufficient. A scheme for a new building, on the north side of Lord-street, a little below John-street, to be devoted to public purposes, was set on foot in 1786, by some gentlemen, most of whom were subscribers to the library, and an arrangement was made by the promoters of the new undertaking with the subscribers to the library, by which a spacious room on the first floor of the building, twice the size of the old one in John-street, was appropriated to the library at a rent of £18 per annum. The new undertaking was subscribed for by individuals in 75 shares, on the principle of a tontine, each subscriber nominating one life for each share,

---

(1) The undermentioned particulars are from the Books of the Committee :—

1772. Mr. George Barker appointed Librarian.—(His portrait, painted by Williamson, is in the Library.)

,,   The Subscription was raised to 6s.

1775. The Committee adjourned to 17th July, in consequence of the occurrence of Crosby Races.

1776. Mr. Roscoe was elected one of the Committee. In 1789, he became President.

It may be here mentioned that before Castle-street was widened, the annual meetings of the subscribers were occasionally held at the St. George's Coffee-house, which stood on the west side of Castle-street.

Mr. Barker was succeeded, in 1817, by Mr. Phœnix, and on his retirement, in 1844, Mr. John Perris succeeded him.

N

with the benefit of survivorship as each life dropped off; and from an original list[1] of the names published in 1789, it is remarkable out of so large a number as 75 lives, who were almost invariably chosen from amongst very young persons, how very few are now in existence.

The subscribers to the library paid 4s 6d each for the purpose of fitting up the library-room in Lord-street; and in 1787 the library was removed to Lord-street; and, in 1803, it was again removed to the Lyceum, in Bold-street, where it still remains.

Out of the numerous gentlemen who were active members of the committee in the last century, it perhaps may be allowable to particularise the following: Mr. Roscoe, Dr. Currie, Mr. William Rathbone, the Rev. Henry Dannett, Dr. Bostock, Dr. Brandreth, the Rev. John Yates, Dr. Worthington, Dr. Rutter, Dr. Lyon, Mr. Evans, (afterwards Sir William David Evans, Recorder of Bombay,) Mr. Daulby, and Mr. Brooke.[2]

The Library contained, in 1850, when the last catalogue was printed, 36,761 volumes.

The Newspapers of Liverpool which were published in 1775 must be noticed here; but before doing so it may not be uninteresting to mention, that, as early as the year 1712 a Liverpool newspaper was then published by S. Terry, called the *Liverpool Courant*, of which the author has seen one part, (No. 18). The title or heading was as follows:—

" No. 18.
THE LEVERPOOLE COURANT,
being an Abstract of London and other News.
From Tuesday, July the 15th, to Friday, July the 18th, 1712."

It contains an announcement of the ships arrived and

---

(1) The Author is indebted to the kindness of Mr. Anthony Swainson for access to the list.

(2) Mr. Brooke, who is now dead, was the Author's Father, and survived every one of his colleagues who were upon the committee in the last century.

outward-bound. There was only one announced as arrived, " The Dragon, of Newcastle, Robert Holmes, Master, from Carlingford, with kelp," and only one outward bound, " The Catherine, of Leverpoole, Robert Laurence, Master, for Dublin, laden with tobacco, sugar, coals, &c."

There are only two advertisements in it; one from a governess, or female teacher, from London, notifying that she taught children to read by a plain and easy method, " also learneth young gentlewomen to mark, work, point, make plain work, floroushing, embroidery, and dressing of heads, after the newest mode, and to the best advantage." The other is from John Jackson, " teacher in mathematicks, in Castle-street, Leverpoole," of an intended publication, by subscription, of a new work on practical arithmetic.

The rest of the paper consists principally of the London political news of the day; and it was printed on two pages only, each about the size of a page of the present *London Gazette*. It concludes with the name and address of the editor thus : " Leverpoole, printed by S. Terry, in Dale St. where all persons willing to subscribe, by sending their names and places of abode, may be constantly served herewith every Tuesday and Friday morning."[1]

In 1775, and for several years afterwards, there were only two Liverpool newspapers published. One was called *Williamson's Liverpool Advertiser, and Mercantile Register,* and the other *The General Advertiser,* edited by J. Gore; the former was first published on the 28th May, 1756,[2] and

---

(1) That number of the newspaper belonged to the late Mr. Samuel Staniforth, and in June, 1848, the Author inspected and took the above extracts and particulars from it ; and Mr. Staniforth has informed him that it was presented to him (Mr. Staniforth) by Mrs. Swainson, the widow of Mr. John Timothy Swainson, who was many years ago the Collector of Customs for Liverpool.

(2) An error occurs in Baines's History of Lancashire, vol. 4, page 92, (note,) in stating that Robert Williamson published the first newspaper ever issued in Liverpool. The *Liverpool Courant*, of 1712, before mentioned, one number of which the Author

in the subjoined note is a copy of its title and of the first article or introductory paragraph which appeared in it.[1]

This newspaper was published weekly, and its name was many years ago changed to that of *Billinge's Liverpool Advertiser*, being called after Mr. Billinge, the then editor. Some years ago its name was again changed to that of the *Liverpool Times*, which is still continued.

In December, 1765, a second weekly newspaper made its appearance, called *The Liverpool General Advertiser, or The Commercial Register.* Its title was afterwards changed to the *The General Advertiser.* It is still published under

---

has seen, is a proof to the contrary; it was a perfect number, not a mutilated fragment, but in good order, and was in the possession of the late Mr. Samuel Staniforth.

(1)

" [Vol. 1.]   " WILLIAMSON'S LIVERPOOL ADVERTISER
                  AND MERCANTILE REGISTER.   [Numb. 1.]

" This paper is circulated through London, Bristol, Edinburgh, Glasgow, Dublin, Cork, Hull, Scarborough, Whitehaven, Chester, Lancaster, Manchester, Warrington, Preston, Blackburn, Bolton, Kendal, Shrewsbury, Wrexham, Flint, Denbigh, Northwich, Namptwich, the adjacent neighbourhood, and many other capital Places, in Great Britain, Ireland, and the Isle of Man.

FRIDAY, MAY, 28, 1756.

To the Public.

It hath, a long Time, been matter of surprise to many, that a place so respectable in its Inhabitants, so Advantageous in its Situation, and so important in its commercial concerns as Liverpool, shou'd be without those weekly and public methods of conveying Intelligence, which are to be met with in Towns of less considerable note. Influenced, therefore, not more by a View to their own Interest, than by a benevolent Regard for Society in General, the Proprietors have undertaken the Collecting of Materials for a Weekly Paper; the Design of which is, to inform, at once, and to please their Readers. A Scheme so comprehensive and which must necessarily require much attention, cannot, they are sensible, be carried successfully into execution, so as to furnish out a regular and constant supply, of Instruction and Amusement, without the kind assistance, and encouragement of others.

To the Men of Letters,

Therefore, and those of vacant hours, they beg leave to address themselves, intreating them, to contribute their favours, in order to render this plan, more extensively beneficial.

From the hope, that this request will be complyed with, and from the promises of assistance, from some Gentlemen of eminence, in the learned world, (which have already been generously given to them,) the Proprietors doubt not, but that sprightliness of wit, and humour, purity of morals, and soundness of good sense, will occasionally enrich and embellish the *Liverpool Advertiser.*

They mean not by this their attempt, to depreciate the merit of other performances of a similar kind, still however they must ingenuously confess, they are actuated by a principle of emulation, such as they doubt not, all will approve."

the name of *Gore's General Advertiser,* and was for 67 years edited by two persons in succession of the name of Gore.

A newspaper called the *Liverpool Chronicle* was also published at one period in the last century, but though the author has seen one of the numbers of it,[1] he has been unable to ascertain when it was first established, or at what date it was discontinued. That number is dated October 5th, 1769, printed by T. Cowburne, of Falcon-alley, Castle-street, and from its being numbered 98, and being a weekly paper, it is fair to suppose that it was first published in 1767.

In 1766, a Liverpool Directory was, for the first time, published, called *Gore's Directory of Liverpool,* containing, in alphabetical order, the names of the merchants, trades-men, and principal inhabitants of Liverpool, the local authorities, and other matters of information, printed by William Nevett and Company, in Princes-street. The publication of this directory was repeated, with additions, at irregular intervals, during the remainder of the last century, and is still published under the same title.

In 1787, another Liverpool Directory was published by William Bailey, but it probably was not found to answer, and does not appear to have ever been published after that year; at least the author never met with any copy of a directory by Bailey[2] of a subsequent date.

The legal boundaries of the port of Liverpool extend far beyond the mere harbour of the Mersey, and were fixed by a Royal commission.

The records of the Court of Exchequer of the 13th of September, 1723, the 10th of George the First, declare them to extend, "from Red Stones, in Hoylake, on the Point of Worral, southerly, to the foot of the River called

---

(1) Belonging to Mr. H. Leatherbarrow, printer.

(2) The copy of 1787 was obligingly lent to the Author by Miss Leatham, of Liverpool.

Ribble Water, in a direct line northerly, and so upon the south side of the said River to Hesketh Bank easterly, and to the River Astland and Douglas there, and so all along the sea coast of Meoles and Formby into the River Mersey, and all over the Rivers Mersey, Irwell, and Weaver."

The Docks of Liverpool, in 1775, were the following: The Old Dock, made on the site of part of the old Pool, on the spot which is now Canning-place, and where the new Custom-house and Revenue-buildings stand.

A slight attempt at forming something like a dock, in the old Pool, appears to have been made, in 1561, as a shelter to the shipping from the weather, at the entrance of the old Pool, by defending it with massive stone piers, and turning the fresh water, from the stream before mentioned, into it. From the bottom of what is now South Castle-street, (formerly Pool-lane, and said to have been more anciently called Water-street,) to the opposite side, a weir at one time crossed it, for the accommodation of foot passengers to Toxteth-park. For more than a century this harbour was sufficient for the limited trade of Liverpool, at that early period.[1]

The want of a regular dock was, however, afterwards experienced, and an Act of Parliament was passed in the 8th of Anne, chap. 12, (1709,)[2] entitled, "An Act for making a convenient Dock or Bason, at Leverpoole, for the security of all ships trading to and from the said Port of Leverpoole;" by virtue of which, "the Mayor, Aldermen, Bailiffs, and Common Council" of Liverpool, and their successors, were appointed trustees for carrying the undertaking into effect; and, in consequence of it, the first Liverpool dock (the Old Dock) was commenced. It was at one time called the Custom-house Dock. The time allowed by

---

(1) Underhill's M.S. Account of Liverpool, page 83.

(2) See Statutes at Large, (J. Raithby's edition,) vol. 4, page 43.

that act, for completing the works and undertaking, was enlarged by an act passed in the 3rd year of the reign of King George the First, (1716,) which recites that the trustees for making the dock had begun to make it, and had so far carried on the undertaking that it was capable of receiving and harbouring ships, but that the same, and the works belonging to it, were not finished, nor were any land-marks, buoys, &c. placed as mentioned in the act of Queen Anne; and that £11,000 had already been expended upon the undertaking. When completed, the walls or sides were of brick with stone work above. This dock was laid out in the direction which the old Pool had formerly taken, running eastward and westward; the westward part being rather wider than the eastward portion of the dock, and if it had not being for that irregularity, the form would have been that of a long square. In 1811, an Act of 51st of George the Third, passed, empowering the Dock Trustees to fill it up for the purpose of having a custom-house, com-mercial-buildings, police-office, and (notwithstanding the strange and out-of-the-way situation) a general market on its site. It was not, however, until the 31st August, 1826, that it was cleared of shipping for the purpose of closing it for ever, and the schooner Dispatch was the last vessel which left it. Upon its site the present structure was erected, called Revenue-buildings, containing the Custom-house, Excise-office, Post-office, Stamp-office, and Dock-office. The dock had been the general receptacle of West Indian and African ships, and also of Irish traders, and vessels from Spain, Portugal and the Mediterranean. Its form was irregular, and it measured 195 yards in length, 80 yards at the east, and 95 yards at the west end. Appended to the dock was a small gut or passage, and a slip.[1]

---

(1) Underhill's M.S. Account of Liverpool, page 86.

In October, 1829, trunks of trees, fibres of plants, decomposed leaves, branches and roots, and a pair of stag's horns were discovered, in excavating for the western wing of the new Custom-house. Below these lay a quantity of black peat, in which nutshells, fibrous particles of timber and leaves lay closely compressed together, and about a foot in thickness, and lay on the rock 40 feet below the level of the quay, and 20 feet below the bed of the Pool.[1]

In March, 1830, the root of a large oak was found about 27 feet below the level of the quay, and about 6 feet below the level of the Old Dock: near this spot another pair of stag's horns, and fragments of bones were found, and a short distance from them, more to the northward, a large trunk of a tree, measuring about 20 inches in diameter and 40 feet in length, lay horizontally in the clay, even deeper than the root before mentioned.[1]

The Salthouse Dock or South Dock, as it was once called, was made pursuant to an Act of the 11th of George the Second, chap. 32, (1738,) which authorized the making of an additional dock and the building of a pier, on ground belonging to the Corporation, adjoining the entrance into the Old Dock, on the north and south sides of the entrance. It was opened in 1753, and the pier mentioned in that act formed the sea wall or westward boundary of the intermediate space, then called the Dry Dock, extending from the Old Dock gut to the river.

Near the end of Ansdell-street, (now destroyed,) on the west side of the dock, was a shipbuilder's yard. The last ship built there, was at the time when the Salthouse Dock was being made, and which was so far completed, as to make it necessary that the ship should be launched into the dock, consequently, the wheys were laid across the quay

---

(1) Underhill's M.S. Account of Liverpool, page 7.

the day before the launch.   On the launch taking place, about midway between the yard and the dock, the ways yielded under the weight, and the vessel struck on the quay ; but that night was occupied in screwing her upright, and the next day she made a fine launch into the dock in the sight of thousands of spectators, highly gratified with the novelty of the scene.[1]   The dock received its name from the large salt works on the east side of it, and which, after having been for many years a great annoyance to the town, were removed in 1793; the proprietor, John Blackburne, Esq. M.P. having obtained an Act of Parliament for their removal to a creek at Garston, with the privilege of being nearer to the town than any other salt works.   The form of this dock was irregular, being adapted to the surrounding streets.   It was the depôt for Irish vessels laden with provisions, and the smaller class of ships from France, Spain, and the Mediterranean.

The Dry Dock was constructed under the Act of 11th George the Second, chap. 32, between the Old Dock and the Mersey, with which it communicated by a gut or passage, which opened into the Mersey.   It had not flood gates, and was, of course, empty at low water, from which circumstance it was rather strangely called the Dry Dock.   It was originally small, but was afterwards enlarged and extended to the northward.   An Act of Parliament of 1811, (51st George the Third, chap. 143,) empowered the Dock Trustees to convert this dock into a wet dock, which was effected when the Old Dock was closed as before mentioned.

George's Dock, at one time called the North Dock, or the New Dock, was the next dock made in Liverpool.   The Parliamentary authority was obtained on the 19th May,

---

(1) Underhill's M. S. Account of Liverpool, page 87.

o

1761, by an Act of 2nd George the Third, chap. 86. This Act vested the property in all the docks, piers, buoys, landmarks, beacons, lighthouses, &c. &c. formed under it or under the former acts, in the Mayor, Bailiffs, and Common Council of Liverpool, as trustees, and empowered them to bring actions, or prefer bills of indictments, by the name or style of "the Trustees of the Docks and Harbour of Liverpoole." The work was soon commenced on the eastward side, but a violent hurricane on the 1st October, 1762, blew down about 30 yards of the wall on that side, which was the only part then completed, and otherwise damaged the works. This accident materially delayed the undertaking, but on the 1st April, 1767, it was resumed, the first stone being laid on that day, by Mr. Thomas Johnson, mayor. The cost was £21,000.[1]

An act was obtained in 1799, (39th George the Third, chap. 59,) which, amongst other matters relating to the docks, authorised the widening of the quays of this dock; but twenty-three years elapsed before that measure was fully carried out. On the 6th August, 1822, the foundation of the new work was laid, and the dock was re-opened upon its completion, on the 30th April, 1825, having been almost entirely re-built, and 21½ yards added to the width of it.[1]

This dock was the principal resort of West Indian and South American shipping, It had a very large tidal basin attached to it, which still remains, and which communicates also with the Prince's Dock.

From George's pier and slip near this place, the majority of the packets and ferry-boats took their departure, so that George's parade was, at most times, a scene of general bustle and excitement.

---

(1) Underhill's M.S. Account of Liverpool, vol. 2, page 87.

George's Dock and its basin have more than once been altered and enlarged.

There were also three Graving Docks, which have all been destroyed in the modern improvements.

The small narrow dock, called the Duke's Dock, extending from the Mersey to Wapping, between the Salthouse Dock and the King's Dock, was made by the Duke of Bridgewater for the reception of flats or barges, and it is so named in consequence of his making it; he also erected a spacious warehouse there for the security of goods.[1] As the dock was used in connexion with the Duke of Bridgewater's canal, after mentioned, it is reasonable to conclude that it must have been made about the time when the canal was completed. The Duke's Dock was afterwards enlarged by the formation of a short branch or cut from the south side of it, and carried underneath a large and handsome modern range of lofty warehouses, for the convenience of loading and unloading the flats or barges; and the large yard adjoining was made as a depôt for goods.

It may not be out of place, whilst describing the docks of Liverpool, to mention a meritorious individual who, for nearly forty years during the last century, was closely connected with them: Mr. William Hutchinson, was born at Newcastle-upon-Tyne, he was originally a seafaring man, and went to sea early in life in a small collier. In 1750 he obtained the command of the *Leostaffe*, a government vessel; and, in 1760, he was appointed dock master at Liverpool.

He wrote, and presented to the Liverpool Library, a manuscript series of valuable observations on the tides, barometer, weather, and winds, from the 1st January, 1768, to the 18th August, 1793. It is preserved in the library,

---

(1) Troughton's Liverpool, page 127.

and is in a complete state except the first eleven sheets, which, to use his own words, written on a blank leaf at the commencement, were " cut out to give Mr. Richard Holden, to make out the 3000 observations, mentioned in his preface of his tide-table, by which he found theory from natural causes to agree with them."

In 1794 he published a treatise on naval architecture. He died 11th February, 1801, and was buried in the church yard of St. Thomas. He was succeeded by Mr. James Finchett.

Mr. Hutchinson held for many years the appointment of dock master, afterwards that of harbour master, and his duties at one time comprised both those now exercised by the harbour master and those of a dock master, yet his stipend was never more than 100 guineas per annum.[1]   He was a man of considerable talents and ingenuity, a scientific person, and some of his inventions were useful; amongst others, reflecting mirrors for lighthouses were invented by him ; and in 1763 he erected, at Bidston, the first mirror of that kind which was ever used, consisting of small reflectors of tinned plates soldered together, and he also made larger ones as far as 12 feet diameter, formed of wood and lined with numerous plates of looking-glass.[2]

---

(1) He will be mentioned in another place as a liberal contributor to the establishment of the Liverpool Marine Society.

(2) Underhill's M.S. Account of Liverpool, vol. 3, page 134.   In Gore's Directory for 1777, it is mentioned that Mr. Hutchinson and Mr. John Ward were then Dockmasters of the Old Dock, Dry Dock, South Dock, and Graving Dock, and that Mr. John Phillips was Dockmaster for St. George's Dock.

It is said that Mr. Hutchinson was accustomed to observe a particular day in each year, as one of strict devotion, in commemoration of his providential and merciful deliverance at one period of his life, when, after the loss of the vessel in which he sailed, he, and others of the crew of the vessel wrecked, being without food, had drawn lots to ascertain which of them should be put to death, in order to furnish a horrible and revolting meal to the survivors; the lot fell upon Mr. Hutchinson, but he and his fellow-sufferers were providentially saved by another vessel which hove in sight.

The Canals and Navigable Rivers which, in 1775, were in connexion with Liverpool, and upon which part of the traffic of the town with the interior of the country was carried on, will now be noticed.

By means of the tide, which flows with rapidity up the channel of the Mersey, small vessels were enabled, without any artificial aid, to navigate the Mersey as far as the neighbourhood of Warrington, and also the tributary river, the Weaver, to about six miles above Frodsham-bridge.

In order to effect a communication, by means of the Rivers Mersey and Irwell, for the conveyance of goods by water between Liverpool and Manchester, an Act of Parliament, the 7th of George the First, chap. 15, was passed in 1720, by which power was given to make those rivers navigable to Manchester, from a place near the Mills, situate a short distance above Warrington, to which small vessels sailed up the Mersey at high water. This was effected by the usual contrivance of weirs, locks, &c. and the very winding course of the river has, in several places, been corrected, by cuts across the principal bends. The want of water in droughts, and its too great abundance in floods, are circumstances under which this, as well as most other river navigations have laboured. A great inconvenience was experienced, from the circumstance that vessels could not get from Liverpool to the before-mentioned place, during low tides, which, whilst they prevailed, caused a suspension of the navigation. In order to remedy that inconvenience, an Act of Parliament was passed the 34th George the Third, chap. 37, (1794,) which authorised the extension of the navigation by the cutting of a canal from the place in question to a spot a short distance above Runcorn, in Cheshire, where the canal now locks into the Mersey. The distance from Liverpool to Manchester by that conveyance is about

50 miles, viz : 21 to Runcorn, and 29 from thence to Manchester.[1]

In 1719, an Act of Parliament, 6th of George the First, chap. 28, was passed for making the river Douglas, otherwise called Astland, navigable, from the mouth of the river Ribble to Wigan. The neighbourhood of Wigan is particularly rich in coal, and the little river Douglas flows past that town to the estuary of the Ribble. By means of this undertaking, which was not effected until 1727, the northern parts of Lancashire, and also Westmoreland, which do not produce coal, were supplied coastwise with fuel ; and limestone and slate from thence, were brought back in return. In 1783, the powers of the act were altered and varied by an Act of 23rd George the Third, chap. 47, under the provisions of which the Douglas navigation was purchased, in that year, by the proprietors of the Leeds and Liverpool Canal, who have, in part, substituted an artificial cut for the natural channel of the river.

In the year 1720, a number of gentlemen, at the head of whom were the Honourable Langham Booth and Sir George Warburton, Baronet, entered into a subscription for the purpose of procuring an act to make the river Weaver navigable from Frodsham Bridge to Winsford Bridge, near Northwich, a distance of about 20 miles : in its natural state it was navigable only at high tides, and not more than six miles above Frodsham Bridge. An Act of Parliament, the 7th George the First, chap. 10, (1720,) was accordingly obtained, under the provisions of which the Weaver was made navigable. It was intended principally for the conveyance of salt, cheese, and grain, from Cheshire, and

---

(1) On the 21st December, 1804, the Rochdale Canal was opened, which unites the Mersey and Irwell Navigation, at Manchester, with the Calder Navigation at Sowerby Bridge, in Yorkshire.

especially from near Northwich.   The subscribers, in a most liberal and patriotic spirit, agreed, and the act provided, that, after payment of the amount of the subscription, and interest at 5 per cent. with 1 per cent. yearly profit for their risk, the whole, with the income arising from the tonnage, &c. should be applicable to the like purposes as the county rate of the county of Chester.   In consequence of the great extension of traffic, and especially of the increased tonnage on salt, conveyed by that navigation, the revenue has been augmented to a surprising extent, and the expense of many magnificent and useful public works, buildings, highways, bridges, and improvements, most valuable to the county, has been defrayed out of the revenues of the Weaver navigation. In 1734, an Act of 7th George the Second, chap. 28, was passed, for extending the navigation of the river Weaver from Winsford Bridge to Nantwich.   Besides which, the act has been subsequently altered and amended by the Acts of 33rd George the Second, chap. 49, and 47th George the Third, Sess. 2nd, chap. 82.

In the year 1755, an undertaking was entered into which, under the general powers of an act for making navigable a small river in Lancashire, virtually gave rise to the first canal navigation made in England.   In that year the Sankey Navigation Act of the 28th of George the Second, chap. 8, was passed, by which some private individuals were authorised to make a small river, the Sankey Brook, navigable from the Mersey, about two miles below Warrington, up its three branches, viz: to Boardman's Stone Bridge, near St. Helens, on the south branch ; to Gerrard's Bridge, on the middle branch; and to Penny Bridge, on the north branch.[1]   In consequence of the prejudice and ignorance

---

(1) Aikin's Description of the Country from Thirty to Forty Miles round Manchester, page 109 and 110.

which then prevailed respecting canal navigation, the pro-
jectors were afraid of applying for an act to make a navigable
canal, and therefore called it an act to make Sankey Brook
navigable; but the canal, in fact, runs close to, and entirely
separate from, Sankey Brook, except crossing and mixing
with it in one or two places, about two miles from Sankey
Bridges.[1]   Sankey Brook was so inconsiderable a stream
that the Sankey Canal was, virtually, the first canal navigation in the kingdom, cut through solid land.   A subsequent
act, in 1761, the 2nd of George the Third, chap. 56, states,
that the navigation was completed from the lowest lock on
Sankey Brook to Gerrard's Bridge and Penny's Bridge, but
that in neap tides the navigation was rendered impracticable
for want of water in the brook; the act therefore authorised
the making of a canal, to be begun within 250 yards from
the lowest lock and carried to join the Mersey at a place
called Fiddler's Ferry.   This new part was accordingly completed, and is about one mile and three quarters in length.
The chief article carried on the Sankey Canal navigation
is coal, besides which, slate is brought down; and corn,
deal timber, paving and lime stone are carried up.[1]

This canal extends about twelve miles, besides its several
branches; it has proved beneficial to the public, and very
lucrative to the proprietors.   Its traffic has been much increased by large copper works for smelting copper ore, from
Anglesea, which were erected on one of its branches, and by
the plate glass manufactory, and other works established
near it, in the neighbourhood of the village of St. Helens.

It is worthy of notice that a great many years before
Mr. Macadam, or a macadamised road, so called, was ever
heard of, a portion of the turnpike-road from Liverpool to

---

(1) Aikin's Description of the Country from Thirty to Forty Miles round Manchester, page 110 and 111.

Warrington, for a considerable distance, near Sankey, was made on that principle. The road was made from the slag or dross from the large copper works before mentioned, near St. Helens, broken with hammers into small pieces. It made an excellent and durable road.[1]

An act of Parliament was obtained in 1761, the 2nd George the Third, chap. 11, enabling Francis, Duke of Bridgewater, to cut a canal, so as to effect an inland water communication from his estate at Worsley, in Lancashire, and also from Manchester to the river Mersey, at Hempstones, in the township of Halton, near the village of Runcorn, in Cheshire. This canal, called the Duke of Bridgewater's Canal, however, was not the first of those plans which have immortalised him in the history of canal navigation. By an Act of 10th George the Second, chap. 9, (1737,) passed at the instance of his predecessor, Scroop, Duke of Bridgewater, the power was given to render Worsley Brook navigable from Worsley Mill to the river Irwell. Worsley Brook is a small river flowing from the vicinity of his coal mines, at Worsley, into the river Irwell; a work of comparative insignificance, as the length of that navigation would not have exceeded about six miles, and it was only intended by that plan to have water carriage from the Worsley coal field to Manchester.

The original plans of the celebrated Francis, Duke of Bridgewater, were on a comparatively humble scale; they commenced in the years 1759 and 1760, when the Acts of 32nd George the Second, chap. 2, and 33rd George the Second, chap. 2, were passed, enabling him, first, to make a canal from a meadow in Salford to Worsley Mill, and

---

(1) The Author remembers seeing the road so formed, when he was quite a youth, and during many years afterwards; and it is mentioned as constructed of those materials in Aikin's Description of the Country from Thirty to Forty Miles round Manchester, (published in 1795,) page 308.

also to Hollinsferry on the Irwell; and, secondly, to deviate from that course and construct his canal so as to continue it from Worsley across the river Irwell by an aqueduct at Barton, in the township of Stretford, to Manchester and to Longford Bridge, in Lancashire. Before his original designs were completed, a much grander and more important plan occupied the mind and talents of the Duke, which was the extension of his canal by a branch, which, running through Cheshire, parallel in some degree with the Mersey, should at length terminate in that river, below the limits of its artificial navigation; and thus afford a new and most eligible water carriage, from Manchester and its vicinity to Liverpool.[1] In projecting this grand design he had the prudence to consult Mr. James Brindley, as an engineer. Mr. Brindley was originally of a humble sphere in life, born in 1716, at Tunsted, in the Parochial Chapelry of Wormhill, in Derbyshire,[2] almost destitute of education, but he was a self-instructed genius, and possessed extraordinary talents; and to him the Duke committed the management of this arduous undertaking. The execution of this bold idea was authorised by the before-mentioned Act of 1761, which enabled the Duke of Bridgewater to make a canal from Longford Bridge in the township of Stretford, in Lancashire, to join the river Mersey at Runcorn, in Cheshire. During the preparations for and the progress of this grand undertaking, the Duke was considered by most persons as an eccentric nobleman, full of strange crotchets and absurd schemes respecting canals, and he was frequently distressed for want of sufficient funds: the result has, however, proved his talents and judgment, and he now deservedly ranks amongst the benefactors of this country.

---

(1) Aikin's Description of the Country from Thirty to Forty Miles round Manchester, pages 112, 115, 116, and 139.   (2) Ibid. 139.

The canal, after leaving Worsley, enters Cheshire near Ashton-on-the-Mersey, passes near Altrincham, Dunham Massey, Bollington, Lymm, Grappenhall, Higher Walton, Preston-on-the-Hill, Moor, through Sir Richard Brooke's grounds at Norton, to Runcorn, where it joins the Mersey, passing through a series of numerous locks. The rise at that place is 95 feet, being the only deviation from the level in the course of the canal, except at the vale of Bollin, between Lymm and Altrincham, where an embankment has been made for the purpose of preserving it.[1]

The canal was begun in 1761, a communication (probably an imperfect one) between Liverpool and Manchester, is said to have been opened in 1772,[1] and the whole of the works, as first projected, were finished in 1776 : and in March, in that year, several barges and other vessels, with numbers of gentlemen on board, went from Liverpool to Runcorn, passed through the locks there, and navigated completely through the whole course of the canal to Manchester.[2] This canal is more than 29 miles in length to its termination at Runcorn Gap, which place was preferred to the Hempstones on account of the superior advantage it offered of entering the mouth of the canal at neap tides.[3] When the Duke of Bridgewater undertook this great design, the price of carriage on the river navigation was 12s per ton from Manchester to Liverpool, whilst that of land carriage was 40s per ton. The Duke's charge on his canal was limited to 6s per ton ; and, together with this vast superiority in cheapness, it had the speed and regularity of land carriage.[4]

The Trent and Mersey, or Grand Trunk Canal, was

---

(1) Lyson's Mag. Brit. title Cheshire, page 423.

(2) Gore's General Advertiser, 29th March, 1776.

(3) Aikin's Description of the Country from Thirty to Forty Miles round Manchester, page 115.   (4) Ibid. 116.

made under the Act of 6th George the Third, chap. 96, passed in 1766,[1] in order to effect a junction of the river Mersey with the Trent, and to unite, by an inland water conveyance, Liverpool and Hull, and, by means of the Grand Junction Canal, London and Bristol also.

The Trent and Mersey Canal communicates with the Duke of Bridgewater's at Preston Brook, (at Preston-on-the-Hill,) in Cheshire, and passes by Dutton, Barnton, Little Leigh, Northwich, Shipbrook, Middlewich, and (not far from Sandbach) by Lawton, a little beyond which it enters Staffordshire, and passes through that county, and Derbyshire, to Wilden Ferry in the latter county, where it communicates with the river Trent. In the course of this canal there are five tunnels; one through the hill at Harecastle, 2880 yards long; one at Preston-on-the-Hill, 1241 yards in length; another at Barnton in the parish of Great Budworth, 560 yards long; another at Saltenford, in the same parish, of 350 yards, and another at Armitage, of 130 yards.[2]

The Ellesmere Canal was made, in order to have a navigable water communication from the river Severn to the river Mersey, under an Act of the 33rd of George the Third, chap. 91, passed in the year 1793.[3] It communicates with the river Mersey at Whitby, in Cheshire, five miles from Eastham, at a place now called Ellesmere Port. It passes across the east end of the hundred of Wirral, and the south-

---

(1) The Act has been amended by several subsequent Acts : 10th George the 3rd, chap. 102 ; 15th George the 3rd, chap. 20 ; 16th George the 3rd, chap. 32 ; 23rd George the 3rd, chap. 33 ; 25th George the 3rd, chap. 99 ; 37th George the 3rd, chaps. 36 and 81 ; 42nd George the 3rd, chap. 25 ; 49th George the 3rd, chap. 73.

(2) Aikin's Description of the Country from Thirty to Forty Miles round Manchester, page 119.

(3) See also the Acts 36th George the 3rd, chaps. 71 and 96; 41st George the 3rd, (U.K.) chap. 70 ; 42nd George the 3rd, chap. 20 ; 44th George the 3rd, chap. 54 ; 50th George the 3rd, chap. 24.

east part of Broxton, passing through Whitby, Great Stor-
mey, Stoke, Croughton, Chorlton, Coghull, Moston, and
Upton, to Chester, (where it joins the river Dee and the
Chester Canal,) and from Chester through Denbighshire,
and after crossing the Dee, by a noble aqueduct near
Llangollen, and a tributary river by a smaller aqueduct at
Chirk, it passes into Shropshire; and from the main line it
has a branch to Ellesmere and Whitchurch, and another
branch to Llanymynech, in Wales.

The Leeds and Liverpool Canal was designed in 1767,
by Mr. Longbotham. The success of the Duke of Bridgewater's canals, excited in Mr. Longbotham the design of
making a communication between Leeds and Liverpool, by
similar means. He made surveys of the line, and estimates
of the probable expenditure, which he submitted to a meeting
held at Liverpool, in December, 1768, and, on the favourable
report of Mr. Brindley, who was consulted, application was
made to parliament for an act for carrying the scheme into
execution, which being obtained in 1770, (the 10th George
the Third, chap. 114,)[1] the work was immediately commenced. The first turf was cut at Halsall, on the 5th of
November, in that year, by the Hon. Charles Lewis Mor-
daunt, of Halsall-hall.

The design was the greatest and most adventurous of the
kind that had then been undertaken. The great direct distance
between the two extremities, much augmented by the very
winding course which the nature of the country demanded,
together with the high elevation of the tract on the borders
of the two counties of York and Lancaster, rendered the
work most difficult and expensive.[2] A considerable part at

---

(1) See also 23rd George the 3rd, chap. 47.

(2) Aikin's Description of the Country from Thirty to Forty Miles round Manchester, page 124.

the Liverpool end, and also a portion at the Leeds extremity, being about thirty-four miles in all, were completed at an early period after obtaining the act; the rest remained unfinished for several years. The former portion was opened in 1774. Under the powers of the Act of 23rd George the Third, chap. 47, passed in 1783, the proprietors purchased the Douglas River Navigation, and so incorporated and consolidated the two navigations. The unfinished part of the work remained in that state, until by an Act of 30th of George the Third, chap. 65, passed in 1790, they were enabled to raise a further sum of money, and also to make a variation in the course of the line, from the north to the south side of the river Calder. A further and much more considerable variation in the course of the canal was authorised to be made under the powers of an Act of 34th George the Third, chap. 94, passed in 1794,[1] by which the line was changed so as to pass by Burnley, Accrington, Blackburn, Chorley, Adlington, Blackrod, West Houghton, Ince, and so to Wigan.[2] Again, on the 31st June, 1819, an additional Act (the 59th George the Third, chap. 105) was obtained for a cut from Wigan to Leigh, in Lancashire, there to unite with the Duke of Bridgewater's Canal.

The whole length of the course, from Leeds to Liverpool, is 107¾ miles: the fall from the central level, on the Lancashire side, is 525 feet; on the Yorkshire, 446 feet. The canal, after leaving Liverpool, and after making a large circuit round Ormskirk, crosses the river Douglas, and, proceeding north-easterly, runs for some miles parallel and near to the Ribble; then follows the course of the Lanca-

---

(1) The Haslingden Extension, which unites this with the Manchester, Bolton and Bury Canals, was constructed under the powers of an Act of Parliament passed in 1793.

(2) Aikin's Description of the Country from Thirty to Forty Miles round Manchester, page 126.

shire Calder, which it crosses and re-crosses until it arrives at its head, at the great basin of Fouridge, near Pendle Hill, and the town of Colne; soon after passing which, it enters Yorkshire; thence, declining on the Leeds side, it passes north-eastward to the banks of the Aire, near Gargrave; which river it crosses, and, afterwards, closely accompanies it in its whole course to Leeds, passing the towns of Skipton and Bingley. Of two side branches, that to Wigan is upwards of seven miles and a half, with a fall of 36 feet; that to Bradford, is little more than three miles, with a fall of 87 feet 6 inches.[1]

The Liverpool Fair will be mentioned in another place; it was held (as it is nominally yet held) near the Exchange or Town-hall, on the 25th of July and 11th of November, and on ten days previously and subsequently: but the purchase and sale of goods there, and the other usual transactions of a fair, have long been discontinued. A hand, carved in wood, was exhibited on the front of that edifice, during the days on which the fair was held; a custom which is still kept up. A large stone, which may yet be seen in Castle-street, nearly in front of Messrs. Mander and Allender's hat-shop, is the southward limit of the ground on which the fair was held.

A fair, called Folly Fair, was also held in the lanes and fields near London-road and Folly-lane, (now Islington,) at Easter, which was frequented by the lower classes: it has gradually gone into disuse.

The Market days of Liverpool were Wednesday and Saturday, and they still remain so; they will be noticed in another place, when the tolls from the markets are mentioned.

We can scarcely doubt that Liverpool had a market

---

(1) Aikin's Description of the Country from Thirty to Forty Miles round Manchester, page 125.

In the Autum of 1820, the Branch Canal was opened from the Leeds and Liverpool Canal, at Wigan, to the Duke of Bridgewater's Canal, at Leigh, in Lancashire.

from about the time of its becoming a borough; but it is not known where the market was held, until after the middle of the 16th century, when it was established at the High Cross, for butcher's meat, fish, and vegetables. This cross was at the junction of the four main streets of the town, and was removed, in 1673, on the occasion of the preparations for the building of the then Exchange or Town-hall. The general market was held for a considerable time in the vicinity of High-street, and of the Exchange; and another was established at the White Cross, little more than about a hundred yards distant, at the upper part of Chapel-street, near the place where the north entrance of the Exchange-buildings now is. The latter was, for a long time, the principal market for potatoes, supplied for the most part from Formby and its vicinity, which are considered by many, even to this day, the best in Great Britain. The place for holding the White Cross Market was changed to St. John's Market, in 1822.

Another market, which afterwards became the principal one for the sale of provisions, vegetables, butter, and other articles usually sold in a market, was established early in the last century, in Derby-square, and on the south side of St. George's Church, where Alderman Tarleton afterwards erected an obelisk of red stone, which was called "The Red Cross," or "Tarleton's Obelisk;" and, after its establishment, the more ancient market in the vicinity of High-street and the Exchange, became disused, except as to the butchers' shambles, which remained there many years after 1775.

At that date the only markets for general purposes were two; of which the principal was the general one already mentioned, held in Derby-square and near St. George's Church.

The other general market has also been mentioned

before, and was called the White Cross Market; it was on a very small and reduced scale.[1]

Cleveland-square was not then used as a market-place, but it was so used not many years afterwards.

The Pig Market was at the south end of Preesons-row.

A market for the sale of potatoes, was held in the street then called the Potato Market, but in the present century called Castle-ditch, now destroyed, on the site of which part of St. George's-crescent at present stands.

The market for corn was on a very limited scale, and sacks of corn used to be exhibited for sale at the north end of Castle-street, near the Exchange, (now the Town-hall,) in the open space where the old Exchange had formerly stood, and which space was usually called the Corn Market.[2] There was not any building of the nature of a Corn Exchange connected with it.

---

(1) The Author has been unable to obtain the correct prices of provisions and other necessaries of life, wages, &c. in 1775; but a statement is given below of payments in respect of some of them, in different years, about that period; they are extracted from the receipt and account book of Mr. Joseph Brooks, who is mentioned in several places in this Work, and the Author is indebted to the kindness of Mr. Richard Vaughan Yates (who was a relative of Mr. Brooks) for the particulars contained in the book :—

Potatoes ..1776.. 1s 2¼d per measure.	Salary— Clerk { 1776 to 1778 } £30 per annum.	
,, ..1777.. 1 4 ,,		
Beans ....1778.. 3 10		
Hay ......1767.. 0 3½ per stone.	Wages—	
,, ...1768.. 0 4 ,,	Footman { 1776 to 1778 } £5 5s per annum.	
,, ...1778.. 0 5 ,,		
,, ...1779.. 0 4½ ,,	,, 1779.. 6 6 ,,	
Clover Hay.1777.. 0 6 ,,		
Straw ....1776.. 0 2 ,,	Gardener { 1777 and 1778 } 4 4 ,,	
,, ...1779.. 0 1½ ,,		
Oats ......1768.. 1 5 per bushel.	Labourer..1768..1s 4d to 1s 6d pr day.	
,, ...1777.. 2 2 ,,	Seaman .. ,, ..25s to 37s 6d pr mo.	
,, ...1779.. 2 6 ,,	Suppl. mate .. £3 ,,	
Coals ....1768..10 0 per ton.	Molecatcher 1776.. { 2s 6d for catching 43 moles, in the garden.	
,, ...1776.. 7 6 ,,		
Lime......1768.. 7 6 per hhd.		
Cartage....1776.. 5 6 } per cart,		
,, ...1777.. 6 4 } per day.		

(2) Perry's Map of Liverpool, of 1769, shows that between Sweeting-street and Dale-street, and the Exchange, Castle-street was considerably wider than elsewhere. The widest part is called in the map, the Corn Market.

Q

The Fish Market was held at the fish-stones, at the upper ends of Pool-lane and of Redcross-street, it having been removed thither from the bottom of Chapel-street, in 1764, where it had previously been held. It was removed, in 1786, to the Goree, near the bottom of James-street; afterwards from thence, in 1792, to a covered building used as a fishmarket, at the upper end of James-street, on the north side, and contiguous to St. George's Market; again, in 1822, to St. John's Market; and, afterwards, in 1837, to the new fishmarket connected with the latter on the east side of Great Charlotte-street.

There were shambles for the sale of butcher's meat in various parts of the town; the principal were those already mentioned to the northward of the Exchange; as well as others at the south corner of the upper end of Redcross-street and Pool-lane, now South Castle-street; and there were also butchers' shambles at the upper end and east side of Pool-lane, and extending from thence, in the form of the letter L reversed, in an angle, into Cable-street; and also a small range of shambles on the west side of Castle-street, opposite the end of Cook-street; and some small shambles, in Dale-street, in front of the White Bear Tavern, at the corner of Hockenhall-alley, Cunliffe-street, nearly opposite Sir Thomas'-buildings.

The market for hay and straw was in the space now called Shaw-place, or the Old Haymarket, at the north end of Whitechapel, where it remained many years, and until it was removed to the open space between Lime-street and the upper end of St. John's-lane.

There could scarcely be said to be any regular Cattle Market in 1775; but about the year 1780, a Cattle Market was established on the west side of the part of the road which is now St. James'-place, opposite St. James' Church. It was held in a farm-yard, and the farm-house there was soon

converted into a tavern or inn, for the frequenters of the
market; it is still standing, and was lately separated from
the road by a small garden, to which there was a descent
from the road of several steps; but houses and shops were
built in the garden in 1847, which at present mask the
house, and prevent its being easily seen from St. James'-
place.   Cattle, sheep, and pigs were sold there, until cattle
pens were erected some years afterwards at Kirkdale, near
the Liver Tavern, and then the Cattle Market was removed
to Kirkdale, where it continued to be held until its final
removal in 1830, to its present situation near the Old Swan
village, about three miles from the Town-hall.[1]   The reason
of its removal from St. James'-place was, that there was
not then any considerable trade in cattle or pigs from Ireland,
and the cattle brought to Liverpool were, with the exception
of some from Wales, principally driven from Scotland and
the North of England; and Kirkdale, being on the north
road, it was, consequently, a more convenient situation.

---

(1) For a short period a Cattle Market was also held in a large yard, in Lime-
street, before the Station of the London and North-Western Railway, which now
occupies its site, was made.

CHAPTER II.

APPEARANCE OF LIVERPOOL, STREETS, SQUARES, TOXTETH PARK,
EDGE HILL, MOUNT VERNON, LOW HILL, EVERTON, KIRKDALE,
FERRIES, OLD NAMES OF STREETS, PROJECTED STREETS, POPULA-
TION, WALKS, HIGH ROADS, INNS, COFFEE HOUSES, PUBLIC
CONVEYANCES, AND PRIVATE CARRIAGES, IN 1775.

IN 1775, the interior of Liverpool presented to the eye
little or nothing calculated to excite admiration or interest;
nearly every house, and, with the exception of the Old
Tower in Water-street, and the Town-hall, then called the
Exchange, all the public buildings of a secular nature, were
built of dingy brick; and though the churches of St.
Nicholas, St. Peter, St. George, St. Thomas, and St. Paul,
were of stone, yet, all the other Liverpool edifices, for Divine
worship, were of brick.[1]   Every street near the Town-hall
was then narrow, irregular, and ill built; nor is it fair to
judge of the streets in that neighbourhood by their present
width and appearance, because all of them have since been
very much widened and improved.

Numerous dirty, confined, and mean courts and alleys
were to be met with, communicating with the principal
streets in the old parts of the town, near the Town-hall;
most of them, however, in the progress of the improvements
which have been made, have long since been destroyed.

Castle-street contained many good shops, and several
dwelling-houses, which were inhabited by some of the higher
classes, but it was confined and ill built; and, though it was
one of the principal streets, it was so narrow in some parts,
that it was with difficulty that two carriages could pass at

---

(1) The Octagon Chapel, in Temple-court, does not form an exception, because it
was built of brick, although it had a stone portico and pediment.

the same time; it was, however, rather wider at the north end.

The Town-hall, then called the Exchange, was a conspicuous object at the north end of Castle-street; but it appeared even more out of the line of perspective at that period, than it has done since the widening of that street, which took place in 1786; and in the open space in front of it, the Corn Market, such as it was, used to be held. Houses and shops, since cleared away, were built close up to it, on its west and north sides; and one or two of them touched it.[1] They were removed many years ago, and on the site of part of them, the additional portion of the Town-hall, on the north side, in which the large ball-room now is, was erected. Behind the Town-hall, at the spot which is now a part of the area of the Exchange-buildings, was a small open space with several houses and shops; some butchers' shambles, of considerable extent, called the Old Shambles, extended to it, from the west side of High-street, which was then a continuation of Oldhall-street, and contained a number of shops. A smaller range of shambles, communicating with the old shambles, and extending very near the west side of the Town-hall, led by a narrow passage into Water-street, the passage being separated from the Town-hall by some of the shops before mentioned. From the west end of the old shambles there was also a short passage, which communicated by an abrupt angle to the right, through Pemberton's-alley into Chapel-street, and to the left, through Clayton's-alley into Water-street. At the spot where the north entrance of the Exchange-buildings now is, and near the third pillar on the right of the centre iron gate, entering from Chapel-street, a portion of the ancient cross,[2] called

---

(1) There was also at the upper end of Water-street, a shop occupied by a hairdresser, named Blackstock, which touched the Town-hall.

(2) Communicated by the late Mr. William Gibson, of St. Anne-street, who

the White Cross, within the memory of persons recently living, stood; and close to it the White Cross market used to be held.

Old Hall-street was ill built, and dangerously narrow, but several families of the higher classes resided there. On the west side, between Union-street and Queen-street, was a long old-fashioned house, which had to the front of Old Hall-street a large and comparatively modern bay window; it was inhabited by Mrs. Stanley, the widow of the Rev. Dr. Stanley, rector of Winwick. This house was called the Old Hall, from which, or rather from an old mansion previously standing on its site, the street derived its name: some remains of the house were to be found as lately as 1847, behind counting-houses erected in front of it.

Tithebarn-street was equally narrow. In an old deed, dated the 4th August, in the twelfth year of the reign of Charles the First, in 1636, which was a conveyance of a portion of a house and land in Tithebarn-street, the street is called "the Moore-street *alias* Tieth barne-street."[1] On the north side of it, and not very far from Highfield-street, an old barn stood, from which the street was supposed to have derived its name.[2] The lower end of Tithebarn-street,

---

remembered it standing there. He once took the trouble of going with the Author, and pointing out the precise spot.

(1) The Author is indebted to the kindness of Mr. Thomas Avison for an inspection of that ancient deed. The name "the Moore-street" is not derived from the ancient family so called, and after whom the old street called Moor-street has for centuries had its name, but is evidently used in the same manner as if "the moss," "the moor," "the waste," &c. &c. were spoken of. The street opening out of Tithebarn-street, still called Moorfields, has evidently had its name from the same source as "the Moore-street." The deed contains general words, which would excite surprise if introduced, in these times, into a deed of conveyance of a house and land in Liverpool, "together with a moiety of all," &c. &c. &c. "rights, members, moores, mosses, mynes, quarries, commons, common of pasture and turbarie," &c. &c.

(2) A barn, which possibly may be the same, is laid down in Yates and Perry's map of the environs of Liverpool, of 1768, and called the "Tythe Barn," as standing

between Hatton-garden and Cheapside, (formerly called Dig-lane,) was then called Patrick's-hill; at the foot of which, and at the end of Pinfold-lane, now Vauxhall-road, stood a portion of St. Patrick's Cross;[1] the Pinfold or Town Pound also stood in that road, on the west side, and near its point of junction with Tithebarn-street. On the south side of Patrick's-hill, and at the spot where Hatton-garden and Great Crosshall-street now meet, was a considerable sheet of water, called the Flashes; and there was a large garden at the corner of Pinfold-lane, at its point of junction with the place now called Marybone, where a country lane commenced, leading by Bevington-hill towards Kirkdale, Walton, and Ormskirk; the way through those three places being then, as now, the great north road out of Liverpool.

Union-street contained some good houses, the residences of respectable persons.

Water-street was considerably narrower than it now is, but it contained some large houses, inhabited by families of respectability.

---

on the north side of the lane leading from Tithebarn-street to Bevington-hill, Its situation seems, however, rather further from the town than that of the old Tithe barn, as it has been described to the Author. Another old barn-like building stood, not many years ago, on the south side of the street, and near the north end of Hackins-hey, which many persons imagined had been the Tithe barn; there seems, however, to be little doubt of that supposition being incorrect.

(1) The remains of it were there three or four years after 1775.—Communicated by Mr. John Wilson, of Orrell, who remembered a portion of it standing.

In former times, besides the White Cross and St. Patrick's Cross, there were two other Crosses in Liverpool; one the High Cross, near where the front of the Town-hall now is, and the other the Town-end Cross, near where St. Stephen's Church, in Byrom-street, now stands. St. Patrick's Cross, and the Pinfold near it, are both laid down in Mr. Perry's Map of Liverpool, of 1769. A large Bowling-green is also laid down in it, on the south side of Patrick's-hill, now part of Tithebarn-street, opposite Milk-street, and close to the spot, now the site of some large warehouses, where the Mersey Iron Foundry, belonging to Mr. John Cragg, formerly stood, but it has not been found practicable to ascertain when the Bowling-green was destroyed.

Brunswick-street did not then exist, and it was not laid out until after the widening of Castle-street.

In Derby-square, and at the south end of Castle-street, were dwelling-houses and shops; and there St. George's Church was a conspicuous object. Derby-square then comprised the open space lying on the northward side of the church, as well as on the eastward of it, as far as the row of houses and shops stood, which were recently pulled down in laying out St. George's-crescent. The most southward houses of that row projected considerably towards St. George's Church, and left a narrow passage between the row and the church, for foot passengers only, called Temple-bar. One or two small houses were standing in what is now an open space, very near the north westward part of the church; and there was, at the westward end of it, near the steeple, a considerable flight of steps, called Kenyon's Steps, which descended towards Preesons-row and James-street. In an open space at the upper end of Pool-lane, (now South Castle-street,) and on the south side of St. George's Church, the pillory, a moveable one, used to be placed, within the memory of numbers yet living, and the public stocks formerly stood there; from that circumstance the spot was formerly called the Stocks Market; and the part of the open space immediately contiguous to Pool-lane, was used for the sale of vegetables, and called the Green Market. A large vaulted cistern of water, collected from the church roof, with a pump attached, was under the obelisk, which stood contiguous to the fish market, then called the fish-stones, in the open space before mentioned, at the upper end of Pool-lane; and the cistern was in existence until the latter end of 1851, when it was destroyed. Fire engines were kept under an arch of the arcade, formed under the raised terrace before noticed, of the church; and the market for butter, bacon, and cheese was principally held under others of the arches.

G. Jarman sc

ST. GEORGE'S CHURCH,

as it appeared in the 18th Century.

James-street was very narrow, with small and inferior dwelling-houses, shops, and public houses in it.

Redcross-street was of its present width, and contained some rather large houses, the residences of respectable families, and also some others of an inferior size.

Moor-street, called after the old family of that name, was, as is still the case, exceedingly narrow, but contained some large ancient-looking houses, as well as others of an inferior description.

Dale-street was very narrow; it was irregularly built, and contained many inferior shops, taverns, and small houses; several of the dwelling-houses were very old and dilapidated, but the most respectable inns were in that street. There were also a few very old houses in other parts of the town, as for example, an old white public-house, at the corner of Chapel-street, fronting the east end of St. Nicholas' Church yard, and some ancient houses in Moor-street and in Tithe-barn-street.

Pool-lane, now South Castle-street, consisted of shops and rather small houses at the upper end, but at the middle and lower end there were several large houses, inhabited by families of respectability.

Castle-ditch, which was destroyed not very long since, to make room for part of the site of St. George's-crescent, was a narrow curved street of shops, then called the Potato Market, and was built, as its name imports, where part of the ditch of the castle had extended.

At that period Lord-street, formerly called Lord Moly-neux-street, was an ill-built and very narrow street, especially on the north side, but contained several good houses, inhabited by respectable families, some tolerably good shops, and several taverns. There was not then any direct road or communication from Lord-street to Dale-street, through John-street, notwithstanding the Post-office was in John-

R

street. The way, which afterwards existed, to the Old Dock
had not then been made through Marshall-street, Love-lane,
and Trafford's-weint; all which were destroyed when South
John-street, which was formed upon their sites, was laid out.
Persons who had occasion to go from Lord-street to transact
business at the Old Dock or the Custom-house, were obliged
to proceed thither by Paradise-street or Pool-lane.

At the Old Dock, on its south side, and very near its
south-east corner, was a remarkable row or block of houses,
similar to those isolated blocks of houses which may yet be
occasionally seen in old cities and towns, entirely detached
from all others, and though much smaller, it resembled
Middle-row, in Holborn. In one of the houses in the row
or block at the Old Dock, Mr. James Aspinall, a plumber
and glazier, resided, and carried on his business, (it was
afterwards conducted under the firm of John and James
Aspinall;) he was the father of Mr. John Bridge Aspinall,
who lived there many years, and afterwards resided in Duke-
street, and was a member of the Council.[1]

Paradise-street, formerly called the Common Shore, contained some large dwelling-houses, which were inhabited by
most respectable families, but there were also some small
houses and shops there.

---

(1) He was elected a member of the Council on the 7th of October, 1801, in the
room of Mr. William Rowe,* and was Mayor of Liverpool, in 1803. During a considerable part of his life he was a merchant, but had retired from business, and resided
in Cheshire, some years before his death. He was much respected, and was a
charitable, kind-hearted and benevolent man. He was a strong Tory, (the word Conservative not being then used in a political sense,) and was a warm supporter of General
Gascoyne, at the Liverpool elections; was accustomed to act as Chairman of the Committees for conducting his elections; and was Chairman of the True-Blue Club, established
in 1818, for electioneering purposes. Many of the readers must recollect Mr. John Bridge
Aspinall presiding at public dinners connected with the elections of General Gascoyne;
and when in the chair, on those occasions, wearing at his button-hole a gold medal of
the Pitt Club, of which he was a member, and though no orator, he generally managed
to get through the duties of chairman to the satisfaction of the company assembled.

* Council Book, vol. 13, page 550.

Whitechapel, formerly called Frog-lane, was not then completely built, and on the eastward side, opposite Spital-fields, it was bounded for some distance by a thorn hedge, which separated it from an adjoining field.[1]   Both White-chapel and Paradise-street were subject to great mischief and inconvenience from floods during heavy rains; the principal drain from the eastward part of the town, and from the fields to the eastward of it, passed through them.   It may be here correct to remind the reader, that those streets extend over a portion of what was the bed or site of the old pool, from which Liverpool derives the termination of its name.

The mud and other vestiges of the bed of the Pool have frequently been exposed to view of late years, in various places, particularly in digging in the old Custom-house yard, to the eastward of the spot where Revenue-buildings now stand, at the east end of King-street, in Coopers-row, at the lowest end of Lord-street, and at the point of junction between that street, Whitechapel, Paradise-street, and Church-street.   When the foundations were excavated a few years ago for the shop at the south side of Church-street, and the corner of that street and Paradise-street, formerly occupied by Mr. Taylor, the bookseller, some squared stones and a number of wooden piles, which had been driven into the mud, were exposed to view, and were calculated to con-vey the impression that a small pier or wharf had, at a remote period back, been formed there.[2]

---

(1) The field formed a portion of a tract of land, usually called Patten's Gardens, within the memory of the Author's father. In the map of Liverpool, published by Mr. R. Williamson, in 1766, the place is called Patten's late Garden; and Whitechapel is, as might be expected, called Frog-lane. In January, 1847, the Author was con-versing with the late Mr. Samuel Staniforth respecting Whitechapel, when he men-tioned that he recollected there being some cabbage gardens between Whitechapel and Williamson-square, before the land was built upon. He died in March, 1851, and the circumstance which he so mentioned existed when he was a little boy.

(2) See *infra*, in this chapter, the communication made to the Author by the late

The Pool, and the stream formerly called the Brook, which flowed into it, formed an important auxiliary to the batteries, mud wall, and fortifications, in the defence of Liverpool, when besieged by Prince Rupert, who took it by storm on the 26th of June, 1644, after a siege of about twenty-four days.[1]

When Edward Moore, of Bank-hall, wrote the Moore Rental, in 1667-8,[2] he little thought, that in a comparatively short time the Pool and Brook would cease to be. It would have been a great affliction to him, if he could have foreseen that the Brook which was so important in his eyes, and from which he foretold such great advantage to his family and to Liverpool, was so soon to be forgotten, that not one person in a hundred, of the present residents in Liverpool, ever heard of it. In mentioning the Brook as flowing from the Mosslake Fields, he proceeds thus :—" and then to supply these dams, so great a fresh from off the Moss Lake, that though my eyes may never see it, yet, I am confident that God Almighty, which makes nothing in vain, hath ordained this to be the greatest good for this town. Therefore, I hope the town will never lose the advantage of the water coming that way ; for if they do, all they are worth cannot procure a stream to cleanse the Pool, as above said."[3]

At the north-west corner of Church-street and south-east corner of Whitechapel, there stood a low-built red brick house of small size, and ancient appearance, with a shop under it, which was afterwards used for many years as a

---

Mr. Samuel Staniforth, as to the discovery, in the last century, of an abutment of a bridge, in excavating the ground at the lowest end of Lord-street, for the foundation of Bates's Hotel.

(1) Most of the garrison, when taken prisoners, were confined in the Church of St. Nicholas, and in the old Tower, in Water-street.

(2) The Moor-Rental, published by the Cheetham Society.

(3) Ibid. page 71 and 72.

toy-shop[1] on the site of which were the shop and museum recently occupied by Mr. Kind. It has been sometimes said to have been a boat-house or ferry-house, where the person lived who had the charge of a ferry-boat, for conveying passengers over the pool, between the lowest end of Lord-street and the end of Church-street,[2] and that at one period the boat was drawn over by means of a rope. Judging, however, from the appearance of the house, it is not probable that it could have been old enough to have been a ferry-house; but it is very likely that it had been erected on the site of an old house connected with a ferry. It is, however, certain that before the end of the 17th century, perhaps much earlier, a stone bridge stood there.[3]

In a part of the excavation made for the foundation of Bates's Hotel, which was erected on the north-east (the lowest) end of Lord-street and south-west corner of White-chapel, on the site of which shops now stand; one of the abutments of the old bridge was discovered.[4]   Besides

---

(1) The Author perfectly recollects its being used as a Toy-shop, at the end of the last or the commencement of the present century, and has been informed by the late Mr. Samuel Staniforth, that it was kept by a Miss Meadows, (he probably meant Miss Matthews, who once kept it,) and that it had previously been a Butcher's shop.

(2) It is stated in Troughton's Liverpool, page 20, that a Ferry-boat was kept there as lately as 1680 ; no authority, however, is quoted in support of the statement, nor does that date seem to carry much probability on the face of it.

(3) There are several instances of repairs recorded as done in the 17th century to a bridge or bridges connected with the Pool : they, however, seem not to be quite con-clusive of the existence of a stone bridge at the spot in question, because there were then not only the bridge at the lowest end of Lord-street, relative to which we are now engaged, but also one at the lowest end of Dale-street, opposite Shaws-brow, (the place was called the Towns-end ;) and also one which could not, from circumstances, have been of any more substantial or durable materials than wood, at the south side of the town, which afforded a communication for foot passengers, from the bottom of the street afterwards called Pool-lane, (now South Castle-street,) over the Pool towards Toxteth-park.

(4) Communicated by the late Mr. Samuel Staniforth. The Hotel must have been erected prior to 1785, because it is laid down in Mr. Charles Eyes' Map of the Town of that date. The corner shop is one of the shops erected on its site.

which, in March, 1851, during the operations of the Gas Company, the workmen made an excavation very near that corner, and exposed to view the arch, or one of the arches of the bridge,[1] (from the width of the Pool, it is probable that there had been more arches than one over it, even if it had been narrowed in some degree by a causeway leading towards the middle of it,) and also a considerable portion of an abutment at the end of the arch nearest to Church-street.

These remains were constructed of rather large squared stones. The crown of the arch was about three feet below the surface. The arch was obtuse, and in pretty good repair, except that the side or parapet walls, which had been above it, were gone. Its span was about 10 feet, and its breadth about 9 feet from side to side. Its westward end was about 10 or 12 feet from the corner of the shop now standing on part of the site of Bates's Hotel, at the point of junction of Lord-street and Whitechapel.[2] It is to be regretted that not any attempt was made by excavations to discover whether there was a corresponding abutment on both sides, or whether there was any other arch.

In Church-street, St. Peter's Church stood conspicuously as at present, on the south side. There was a row of trees in the church yard, on the south, and also on the west side, some of which were recently remaining.

---

(1) The Author examined those remains when they were exposed to view, in March, 1851, with considerable attention, and feels no doubt that they had been connected with the abutment mentioned by Mr. Samuel Staniforth.

(2) Some indications of a breast wall were also discovered extending at right angles with the bridge, on its east side, towards Whitechapel and Paradise-street, but it is very difficult to say whether it was coeval with the bridge or not. It has been suggested from that discovery, that when the Pool was in a great degree filled up, the brook or stream was allowed to remain flowing in an open channel, confined by a wall on each side, as was the case, until within the memory of man, with Fleet-ditch, in London; but there does not appear to be any reason to suppose that any remains of a corresponding breast wall, on the west side, were ever discovered in Whitechapel or Paradise-street; and certainly none such were exposed to view when the recent discovery of the arch of the bridge took place.

The north side of Church-street contained dwelling-houses, several of which were of a large size, and were occupied by families of the higher classes.   In a row of houses on that side of the street, part of which now forms the site of Compton-house, a tea dealer's or grocer's shop was soon afterwards established, which remained the only shop in the row, until after the commencement of the present century.   There was afterwards a confectioner's shop on the opposite side of the street, and at the corner of Church-alley, kept by Miss Furniss, a female of the Quaker persuasion, remarkable for her neatness and skill; this was one of the principal confectioners' shops in Liverpool, during many years both of the last and the commencement of the present centuries.   Close to it, and on the same side of Church-street, and on part of the ground where Mr. Hausburg's bazaar now stands, was a house, afterwards a tavern, the sign of the White Dog; and on another part of the site of the bazaar, and at the corner, where Postoffice-place now is, were some old outbuildings which had apparently belonged to a farm; and further up the street, on the space of ground where the Athæneum and the adjoining house, (now shops) formerly belonging to Mr. George Case, stand, and where the Dispensary stood, was an orchard or garden, which was separated from Church-street by a low wall, and had a large oblong fishpond in it, sometimes used in winter for skaiting. On part of the bed of the pond the Athæneum is erected. The orchard or garden belonged to Mr. Joseph Brooks, the great uncle of the Venerable Archdeacon Brooks, one of the present Rectors of Liverpool.   Mr. Joseph Brooks was one of those praiseworthy characters who delight in doing good, and he used cheerfully to devote a deal of valuable time to the affairs of the parish of Liverpool; and was indefatigable in his exertions and attention to the health and comforts of the parish poor, and to the good order

and regulation of the workhouse. His portrait is still preserved in the board-room of the building.

Hanover-street contained many large and handsome
houses, inhabited by some of the most respectable families,
and on the part opposite the east end of College-lane, stood
the large stone-fronted house of Mr. Seel, a person of
considerable property ; and behind it was his extensive
garden, upon a portion of which Seel-street was afterwards
laid out; the house was recently used as the Branch Bank
of the Bank of England.[1] Four of the houses which are
yet standing on the north-west side of the street, and near
Peter's-lane, were built in a remarkable position, with large
angles projecting towards Hanover-street, in which the
windows were so placed as to face down the street, in
order, as has been said, to obtain a view of the Mersey,
and of Cheshire, before the prospect was obstructed by
the erection of buildings at the south side of the Old
Dock and near the Mersey.

Clayton-square was laid out, but was in an incomplete
state ; a few houses only, at that period, having been
built in it.

Bold-street was not then even laid out; some unbuilt
land[2] and a large oblong field, extending in a south-eastward
direction, formed the site upon which the street was afterwards made ; and at the lowest part of it, on the south side,
close to the corner of Hanover-street, stood a respectable-
looking brick house, which was said to have formerly been
a farm-house. It had a large laburnum tree growing against
the front, and was recessed back with a small court yard
before it, and was the residence of Mr. Joseph Brooks,

---

(1) The establishment of the Branch Bank of England was removed to Castle-
street, on the 6th April, 1849.

(2) The unbuilt land was formerly used as a timber-yard, and extended from and
included the spot where the Lyceum News-room now stands, to Wood-street.

already mentioned.   It had a large garden at the back, or south side, extending to Wood-street, the lowest part of which street had been laid out, and then contained a few dwelling-houses; and in Hanover-street, near the back of the house, there were a watering trough for cattle, and some outbuildings, (which were said to have been in use for farming purposes, at a time when the house was held with a farm;) and a little higher up than the house, on the tract of land which is now part of the site of Bold-street, two limekilns stood.[1]

At the lower end of Ranelagh-street, the then newly-built house of Mr. Thomas Staniforth, the father of the late Mr. Samuel Staniforth, stood; it is now the Waterloo Hotel. Near it, and close to the spot where part of the Lyceum News-room stands, was the small range of Alms-houses before noticed;[2] and on a portion of some land which lay between Renshaw-street and the land and oblong field before mentioned, which were afterwards the site of Bold-street, there were several rope-walks; the principal of which belonged to Mr. Thomas Staniforth.

---

(1) It appears most extraordinary and unaccountable, that the town, with its shops, houses, and buildings, did not extend, and that the tide of population did not set, from Church-street up Ranelagh-street and Brownlow-hill, or Mount-pleasant, instead as was afterwards done, up Bold-street.   The former were wider streets than Bold-street now is, and had been laid out and used as roads, for very many years, before Bold-street was formed or projected: besides which, they led directly to a cultivated country, with a considerable population, and several villages, whilst Bold-street, after having been laid out, merely led from the town through Great George-street to Toxteth-park, (then very sparingly inhabited;) nay, at that time, the most direct way to the Park, from the heart of the town, was up Park-lane, nor was there then any direct way from Toxteth-park to Aigburth or Garston, without going round by and ascending Mosley-hill.   Even after Bold-street was laid out there was not a possibility of going from that part of the town to Allerton or its vicinity, except by a very circuitous route by Brownlow-hill or Mount-pleasant, and through Smeatham or Smithdown-lane, because Crabtree-lane, now called Falkner-street, was not then opened, and fields occupied the site of Upper Parliament-street, until some years after the commencement of the present century.

(2) Chapter I, page 63.

s

Ranelagh-street had some moderately-sized houses erected in it; and, although it may appear extraordinary to those who have not long known the town, it is a fact, that Renshaw-street was formed, and its lowest end was paved and partly built, some time before Bold-street was even laid out. The lower part of Renshaw-street was very narrow, but was some years afterwards widened on its east side. At the upper end there was only one house, which is yet standing, though masked by shops; it is a long low-built brick house, two stories high, and stands on the west side nearly opposite Old-ham-street, which, as many of the readers will recollect, was the residence of Mr. William Goore, a merchant, not very many years ago. At the latter end of the last, and in the early part of the present century, it was inhabited by Mr. John Travis, a person of advanced age, who died in 1811. He resided in Manchester, in 1745, and was one of the very few persons left alive in Lancashire, some years after the commencement of the present century, who had seen Prince Charles Stuart, the Young Pretender, when he occupied Manchester with his forces of Scotch Highlanders, some of whom were quartered in the house where Mr. Travis then resided.[1]

Most of the upper portion of Mount-pleasant (formerly called Martindale-hill) was an unpaved country lane, with fields and hedge rows on each side. In consequence of its elevated and salubrious situation, there were a few large detached houses (which may still be seen there) with extensive gardens on the south side, and about half way up the hill; the largest of the houses was for several years occupied by Mr. James Dawson, and is now occupied by Mr. John

---

(1) The Author had the above account from Mr. Travis, in a conversation which they had together on the subject of the Rebellion; and he is not the only person known to the Author, who had been an eye witness of the march of the Young Pretender and his Highland army, in 1745; for at that date the Author's grandfather was in Staffordshire, and saw them pass through it.

L. Minshull: it was built in 1771, by Mr. Thomas Foxcroft, a merchant, and that date, with his initials, may still be seen on its spouts. In the whole space on the north side of Mount-pleasant, extending from the place where Clarence-street now is, to the point of junction with Brownlow-hill, there was only one house, [1] which was one of the two taverns with bowling-greens belonging to them, which will be afterwards noticed; and the large triangular tract of land between the lowest end of Mount-pleasant and Brownlow-hill, was an open field, called, from its remarkable shape, the Shoulder of Mutton Field. There were also a number of gardens on the south side of Mount-pleasant, many of which had summer houses, of two stories, with fire-places and accommodations for taking tea and refreshments, and one of them still remains, but it is enlarged and used as a small dwelling-house; it stands at the upper end of a timber-yard, of which the entrance is in Renshaw-street, exactly opposite Heathfield-street. From the part of Renshaw-street where Oldham-street now is, to the spot where Mount-pleasant and Renshaw-street meet in a point at Ranelagh-place, the whole side of the hill was covered with gardens of considerable size, except at the lowest end of Renshaw-street, where some small houses had been erected.

Ranelagh Gardens, near the back part of the spot where the Adelphi Hotel, in Ranelagh-place, now stands, have been already mentioned as a place of public amusement, where entertainments of music and fireworks occasionally took place.

There were open fields nearly the whole way on each

---

(1) Not very many years ago there stood opposite the Parish Lunatic Asylum, (recently pulled down) formerly the House of Correction, on Mount-pleasant, a small public house, (the Ship,) and the Author has an impression that he has heard that it stood there in 1775. There were also some small gardens and hovels standing close to, and at the back of it, which have been removed some years ago.

side of Brownlow-hill, or as it was sometimes called, Brownlow-hill-lane.[1]

On the north side of it, at the place which is now the south end of Russell-street, stood an old brick building, which has been before slightly noticed, in the middle of a square space or court, inclosed by a high wall,[2] and with a pair of large gates, opening from Brownlow-hill, opposite the spot which is now the north end of Clarence-street. The building has been pulled down many years ago. It was originally the Liverpool depôt or magazine of gunpowder; the date of its erection is not known, but it was used as a powder magazine at least as early as the year 1737.

A lease of it, dated the 14th January, 1737, was granted by the Corporation of Liverpool to Thomas Pearse, Samuel Underhill and Robert Norman, for three lives and twenty-one years, at a rent of 2s. The following is an extract respecting it from the Register of Leases granted by the Corporation :—[3]

				£ s. d.
1737. Jan. 14	Thomas Pearse, Samuel Underhill and Robert Norman.	A Powder House or building and ground, as sett out in the Close in Lease to Alderman Gildart,[4] on the north side of the way to Brownlow-hill, next to Charles Hilliards on west side, containing in breadth 39 yards ½.	Johnson, James, and Richard, sons of Alderman Gildart.[5]	21 [6]	Highway to Brownlow-hill.	0 2 0

(1) In the Map of Liverpool, by John Eyes, of 1765, it is called the road to Warrington. May not that be a mistake of Mr. Eyes, and be meant for the road to Wavertree, especially as the present London-road is called in that map the road to Prescot ?

(2) It is remarkable that though the building and enclosed space are laid down with care and accuracy by Mr. Charles Eyes, in his Plan of Liverpool, of 1785, he has not given them any name.

(3) Register Book A of Leases of 1737, in the Town-hall.

(4) In Mr. Charles Eyes' Map of 1785, Mr. Gildart's name is inserted as the owner of the land situate both to the eastward and westward of the building and premises; thus appearing to corroborate the above description of them as having been " set out in " (or, in other words, taken from) a close of land in lease to Mr. Gildart.

(5) The three lives named in the lease.

(6) The 21 years after the lives named in the lease.

The same Register also contains an entry of three new leases, dated 5th April, 1744, of one-third of the same " Powder-house and building," to each of the same parties, respectively, but the lives in all the three leases were not quite the same, and more land appears to have been comprised in them, it being described as " containing 56 y^{ds} to ye front of the lane."

It cannot now be ascertained exactly when the building ceased to be used as a powder magazine, or when the Magazines, afterwards established at Liscard, in Cheshire, were first used; but it appears to have occurred before November, 1768, because the first lease which can be found respecting the latter is one from the Corporation of Liverpool to William Penkett, of Bidstone, gentleman, of three compartments of the Liscard Magazines, and is dated the 30th of November, 1768, for three lives and twenty-one years, and the land upon which those magazines were erected, is described as having been " some time since purchased from one Robert Richardson," by the Corporation. The next lease is about ten years later, (1769) of some other compartments, to Richard Taylor.[1]

The land upon which the Magazines at Liscard were erected, was purchased by the Corporation, from Robert Richardson, for £30, and was about an acre in extent, and called the Warringer Close.

The old building on Brownlow-hill was, during the American Revolutionary War, and the war which soon broke out with France, the prison for the confinement of prisoners of war. During the French Revolutionary War, after the Borough Gaol had been built in Great Howard-street, (formerly called Milehouse-lane,) the prisoners of war were confined in that gaol.

---

(1) From the Corporation Muniments, in the Town-hall.

At the commencement of the American Revolutionary War, and before the building on Brownlow-hill was used for the confinement of prisoners, a few American prisoners were confined in a house on the north side of Union-street, at the corner of Lancelots-hey, but it has not been found practicable to ascertain the exact date when the building on Brownlow-hill was first used as a place of confinement, although it is supposed to have been in the year 1776 or 1777.

When the store-place or depôt for gunpowder at Liverpool, was on Brownlow-hill, the trade in that dangerous combustible, and the quantity deposited there, were inconsiderable; but after the removal to the place of deposit at Liscard, the trade in gunpowder increased to a great extent. The quantities which were of late years usually deposited in the powder magazines at Liscard, were so great, and with such trivial and inadequate precautions against explosion, as to excite well-grounded alarm. In a number of insecure buildings, merely covered with slates, in a small yard, under the charge of private individuals, without any military guard, from 700 to 800 tons of this most dangerous combustible were commonly deposited, until within a few months past, in the immediate vicinity of dwelling-houses, and of not a trifling population, close to a part of the Mersey, which is constantly frequented by, and often crowded with, sailing vessels and steamers freighted not merely with merchandise of incalculable value, but with (what is precious beyond all price) human life, and within a little mile of the docks, houses, and buildings of the second port of the British empire. Another generation will scarcely credit the folly and apathy of the local authorities and inhabitants of Liverpool, who, year after year, remained supine and passive, with this terrific nuisance close to them, when at any moment the effects of lightening, the sparks from a neighbouring cottage chimney, the intoxication of a workman, the violation of the rules against smoking tobacco, or a boy's rocket, might cause an explosion terrific and destructive beyond all example, might take away the lives of thousands of human beings, and cause a degree of misery to individuals, and an extent of destruction to property, unparalleled in history. This nuisance was most unjustifiably left as a legacy by the old Corporation of Liverpool, and it might have been expected that the members of the new Corporation, elected under the act for the reform of municipal bodies corporate, would have taken immediate steps to endeavour to remove it; but instead of doing so, the members of the new Corporation, scorning to be wiser than their predecessors, adopted measures to continue it, by renewing the leases of the magazine buildings, to persons who traded in gunpowder, and were accustomed to store it there.

At length some of the people of Liverpool seemed to be roused from their supineness, and in the year 1851, the Corporation showed some signs of being aware of the impending danger. After much discussion and many objections started, an Act of Parliament was passed in the 14th and 15th Victoria, chap. 67, calculated, as was said, in some degree to mitigate the evil.

Instead, however, of removing, as ought to have been done, the nuisance altogether far away from Liverpool, provisions were merely made by that act for changing the place of deposit of the gunpowder, from its dangerous situation at Liscard, to floating magazines on the waters of the Mersey, but still within the port of Liverpool, and very near the town and shipping. Under the provisions of the act, the gunpowder has been removed to the floating magazines. The wisdom, if there be any, of the promoters of such a scheme, seems past finding out. It is true, that the danger to life and property at Liscard, and at the north end of Liverpool, may be decreased, but it must be very much greater elsewhere, and the peril to the shipping, and to the lives of mariners and passengers on the Mersey, will be vastly increased. Under the old system, bad as it was, the gunpowder brought coastwise, was taken to the Liscard magazines, deposited there, and when afterwards shipped for exportation, was removed without passing the town; but now under the new system, a double risk must be incurred, for it must be conveyed up the Mersey, through crowds of ships and sailing craft of all denominations, past the town to the floating magazines; and afterwards, on exportation, it must be taken back, by the same course, past the town and shipping.

The scheme might have been worthy of the wisdom of the sages of Gotham, if that ancient and celebrated place had possessed a body corporate, but something a little more judicious might have been expected from the local authorities of Liverpool.

Higher up Brownlow-hill, on the south side, was the parish Workhouse or Poorhouse, which has been before described.[1] Above it, and near the spot where the Fever Hospital now stands, was a stone quarry, opposite to which, on the north side of the hill, was another quarry near the site of the present Lunatic Asylum.

A foot-path entered a field where Brownlow-street now is, opposite the Workhouse, and ran along the fence of the field, and came out at the bottom of the lane now called Fairclough-lane, leading to Low-hill. Another footpath commenced at a gate in the fields at the upper end of Copperas-hill, which derived its name from some copperas works which belonged to Mr. Hughes, and stood on the north side near the part where Silver-street and White Mill-street now join it; this footpath passed over fields until it joined the path just mentioned, at the bottom of Fairclough-lane.

---

(1) Chapter 1, page 69.

Clarence-street was not then laid out.

A little higher than the point of junction of Pleasant-street and May-street, on the north side of Mount-pleasant, and at the back of the bowling-green, connected with the tavern, which will be shortly noticed, stood an old windmill.

It has been already mentioned that some dwelling-houses were even then built on Mount-pleasant; besides which, at that time, there were two respectable taverns standing there, each of which had a bowling-green attached to it. One was on the north side, a little above the spot where May-street now is, which was for some time kept by Joseph Gleadhill,[1] and which was more recently a lodging-house; the other was much higher up the hill, and on the south side, and at the upper corner of a lane called St. Mary's-lane, now in-closed and built upon.

The latter was an old-fashioned quaint-looking tavern, with a bowling-green attached to it; it was remarkable for an old porch at the front, and was afterwards known by the name of "Richardson's," from a person of that name who kept the tavern, and it had the sign of the grapes. It was the birth-place of an individual of extra-ordinary abilities, self-raised and almost self-educated, who became celebrated as a poet and historian, and though of humble parentage, without fortune, patronage or connections, yet, by his literary attainments, his remarkable talents, and his amiable character, his society was sought after, and his works were admired by the great, the noble, and the learned of the land. The name of that talented individual was WILLIAM ROSCOE. It would be quite foreign to the object of a work of this nature to give even an outline of his life, the particulars of which have been much before the

---

(1) This Tavern was built by Mr. Roscoe's Father, and the Bowling-green attached to it has been occasionally called by the name of Roscoe's Bowling-green.

T

public lately, and even during the time whilst this work has been in the press.[1]

Mr. Roscoe was born on the 8th March, 1753, and died on the 30th of June, 1831, in the 78th year of his age. He was the son of a respectable man, who kept the tavern, and united to the business of a publican that of a market gardener.

Some confusion or doubt as to which was the place of his birth, has arisen from there being two taverns with bowling-greens, in Mount-pleasant, but the one afterwards

---

[1] The 8th of March, 1853, the centenary of the birth of Mr. Roscoe, was celebrated by the inhabitants of Liverpool, in a manner worthy of the memory of so distinguished a literary character, and highly creditable to themselves. A very short notice of its celebration is all that is consistent with the nature and object of this publication; persons desirous of a full account will have to refer to the newspapers of the time. At ten in the morning there was a public breakfast at the Philharmonic-hall, in Hope-street, at which the Earl of Sefton, the Lord-Lieutenant of the county, presided; supported on the right by the Bishop of Chester, and by Mr. Samuel Holme, Mayor of Liverpool, and on the left by Mr. William Caldwell Roscoe, the grandson of the poet and historian, and by Mr. William Rathbone. It is quite impossible to give here even a curtailed account of the speeches delivered on the occasion, but if space will admit of it, that of the Mayor will be found in the Appendix. It was attended by 1500 persons, comprising many literary and scientific characters, and numbers of the ladies and gentlemen inhabitants of Liverpool, as well as not a few visitors from other places.

The next occurrence of interest which took place on that day, was the opening of the Museum of Natural History, at the Union-Rooms, in Duke-street, consisting of a splendid collection of objects, the munificent gift of the Earl of Derby to the town, at which an inaugural address was delivered by the Mayor, and the assemblage was also addressed by several other gentlemen.

At the Royal Institution, in Colquitt-street, a talented and appropriate address was delivered in the Theatre of that Institution, by the President of the Literary and Philosophical Society of Liverpool, (Joseph Brooks Yates, F.S.A.)

In the evening the Mayor gave a splendid entertainment at the Town-hall, to about 820 guests, consisting of the principal inhabitants of Liverpool, and many literary characters from elsewhere. It is not, however, practicable to do more in this place than give a short passing notice of it; an account of it will more correctly come, in the part* where the amusements and entertainments of the inhabitants of Liverpool are mentioned.

* Chapter IV.

called Richardson's, on the south side of it, and at the corner of St. Mary's-lane, was the one in which he was born. The author's father, who was personally acquainted with Mr. Roscoe, recollected him when a young man residing in the lower one (afterwards called Gleadhill's,) with the other members of his family.[1] Mr. Roscoe's father built the latter and removed with his family to it when the future poet and historian, Mr. Roscoe, was quite an infant. Both of the taverns have been for some time demolished.

Mount-pleasant turned off to the north-east at the upper end, as at present, and wound round the back of the land now occupied by the parish Workhouse and Fever Hospital, into the Brownlow-hill road, which was the principal road to Wavertree. In a field on the eastward side of, and immediately behind the old tavern (Richardson's) and bowling-green, and at that part of Mount-pleasant where the corner house stands, in which Dr. Carson, and afterwards Mr. Neill, lived, now the Eye and Ear Infirmary, stood a white windmill, and very near to it, but to the northward of it, was a turnstile by which pedestrians might leave Mount-pleasant and enter a portion of the fields called the Mosslake-fields,[2] and pursuing a footpath leading over them, in the direction where Oxford-street and the north end of Abercromby-square now are,

---

(1) In the life of Mr. Roscoe, by his Son, Mr. Henry Roscoe, the latter states, (page 4,) that "at the period of Mr. Roscoe's birth, his Father kept a public-house, called 'The Bowling-green,' in the neighbourhood of Liverpool," and continued for many years in the same business, to which he united the cultivation of an extensive market garden. Mr. Henry Roscoe also gives a letter from Mr. Roscoe, written shortly before his death, to an old friend, in which he states, (page 6,) that he was "born on the 8th March, 1753, at the old Bowling-green house, on Mount-pleasant," but that in the following year he was removed with the family to the new Bowling-green house, in Mount-pleasant, which his Father was building at the time of Mr. Roscoe's birth.

(2) This tract of land is called "Moss Lake," in the Corporation records of the year 1671.—See the Report of Proceedings, at Liverpool, before the Commissioners of Inquiry into Municipal Corporations, page 287.

and crossing the stream already mentioned in the account of the old Pool, by a wooden bridge or platform which stood near where Grove-street now intersects Oxford-street, might walk to Edge-hill, or to Smeatham-lane. In the Mosslake-fields there was at one period a large turbary or turf ground, from which Liverpool derived a great portion of turf for its fires, and it is rather amusing to observe the import-ance which Edward Moore, of Bank-hall, attached to his portion of it, in the observations which he intended for the guidance of his son, and wrote in 1667-8, thus :— " Remember, that when you get this watercourse opened, it will not only be so advantageous for the town, but will make the turf room so dry, that I dare assure you, you may sell fifty pounds' worth at least of turf to the town in a year ; for, of my knowledge, you have good black turf at least four yards deep ; if so, it may be worth two hundred pounds an acre, and you have ten acres of it ; in a word, you know not what it may be worth, lying so near a great town ; and if you leave half a yard of the bottom ungotten, once in forty years, it swells and grows again.[1]"

There was not a house, in the large tract of ground between the part of Mount-pleasant where Clarence-street now joins it, or where Rodney-street now stands, and the upper part of Duke-street ; but between the place where the St. James' Cemetery chapel and Dr. Formby's house in Sandon-terrace stand, there were a windmill, a small tavern of the sign of the Grapes, and two houses, one fronting the lane now St. James'-road, and the other with an area or small court, in which were two trees ; the latter was a neat

---

(1) The Moore Rental, published by the Cheetham Society, page 72. The Author has seen a person cutting turf there for fuel, rather more than thirty years ago ; and he very recently brought home from thence, by way of experiment, a small quantity which had been dug out of the foundation of a house there, and after drying it, burnt it as turf.

small old-fashioned house, which commanded a view down
Duke-street.   Behind these houses, but nearer the place
where Hope-street now is, was a bowling-green; a sum-
mer-house stood upon part of it, and it now forms a portion
of the site of some of the houses in Sandon-terrace.   A lane
turned off in front of the old-fashioned house just mentioned,
and passed on the east side of a field on a part of which the
south end of Rodney-street was afterwards laid out,[1] and
then made a sharp turn up the hill, forming what is now
part of Mount-street, (then remarkable for a copious spring
of water, which gushed out on the north side of it, and
flowed in a channel across the foot-walk,) and led with a
considerable curvature over the tract of ground which is
now Hope-street, but deviating from it at the north end a
little to the eastward.   The lane then turned in a curved
line past the south side of the bowling-green and tavern
(Richardson's) before mentioned; and it there joined the
upper part of Mount-pleasant.   The place where it made
that curve was afterwards called St. Mary's-lane.

The lane[2] before mentioned, now Hope-street, was the
principal outlet from the south and south-east end of
the town to Edge-hill, and to Wavertree-lane; and was,
in fact, the only direct cart or carriage road to those
places from the neighbourhood of what is now Great
George-street, Duke-street, Park-lane, and St. James'-

---

(1) That part of the lane remained until Pilgrim-street was straightened not many
years ago, when a portion of the site was inclosed, and added to the gardens and yards
of the houses at the south-east end of Rodney-street.

(2) The lane was so crooked or curved in the course of the distance between the
place where it left Duke-street, and where it joined Mount-pleasant, as to have some
slight resemblance to the figure used to signify a note of interrogation.   It has
been suggested, and seemingly with a great degree of probability, that the reason of
this road taking so remarkable a curve to the northward to join the Brownlow-hill-
road to Wavertree and Smithdown-lane, was, to avoid, in former times, the swamp or
marsh of Mosslake-fields.

street. On the east side of the lane before mentioned, now Hope-street, was a small hill, which is now cut away, and upon it, and very near the place where the Unitarian Chapel and the Music-hall stand, between Myrtle-street and Falkner-street, an Observatory stood, to which a short path led from the lane. The Observatory was, however, never used. It was intended to encourage the study of astronomy by means of a convenient place, and a suitable apparatus for astronomical observations. It was built on elevated ground, and in September, 1768, the first stone was laid by the Mayor, who was attended by the Deputy-Recorder, and many other gentlemen. The edifice, though built, never having been used, and the design being neglected, it consequently fell into ruin, and not a vestige of it has been seen for many years. The south end of the lane, now part of Hope-street, terminated at some fields into which a footpath, leading towards Toxteth-park, opened from the lane near the spot where the west end of Canning-street now stands. Crabtree-lane, now Falkner-street, led from the east side of the lane, but it was not then, nor was it for many years afterwards, a thoroughfare for carts, but was merely an occupation road to fields; a footpath, however, led from its eastward end into Smeatham-lane.

St. James' walk, or terrace, originally called Mount Sion, or Sion-hill, and sometimes The Mount, was formed upon elevated ground at one time called the Quarry-hill. There was a coffee-house or tavern upon it, called the St. James' Coffee-house, of considerable repute, kept by Mr. John Bridge, frequented principally by persons of a superior class, and where parties of gentlemen occasionally had dinners and other entertainments; it formed a portion of the present row of houses there, and there was then a garden belonging to the tavern, which now forms part of the Mount-gardens.

Near each end of the terrace stood a windmill, and

behind it was a large stone-quarry, which had been worked during a long period before the time which we are now engaged upon.

The site of the quarry is now St. James' Cemetery; and from the rubbish got out of the quarry, the terrace and small mount, where the present Observatory stands, were formed in 1767, when the poor people, in a season of great scarcity and a severe winter, were employed in making it.   In the quarry was a mineral spring, upon which Dr. Houlston published a pamphlet: it flowed down the rock, about the middle of the east side, and was caught in a little basin cut in the rock, to which a small iron ladle was attached.   It was afterwards lost when part of the rock was cut away ; but it used to flow not far from the present spring in the Cemetery.   There was then a cart-way into the quarry at the south end, and another by a subterranean tunnel commencing at the highest part of Duke-street, near the place where the south end of Rodney-street, and the north end of St. James'-road now meet, and close to the corner house, formerly occupied by the late Mr. Gill, the surgeon.   The tunnel had two eyes to admit light and air, and on each side over the entrance was the figure of a lion carved in stone.

Berry-street did not then exist as a street,[1] but there was a narrow and very indifferent lane at the place where, after being widened, Berry-street was afterwards built, through which carts could proceed from the upper end of Renshaw-street to the upper end of Duke-street.

Duke-street appears to have owed its origin in former times to the necessity of having a road to bring freestone

<hr/>

(1) There was a house on the west side of it, at the corner of Duke-street, where Captain Berry once lived, a relation of the late Rev. Henry Berry, the minister of St. Michael's Church, and from whom it probably took its name.   It should appear from Mr. C. Eyes' Map of Liverpool, of 1785, that before Colquitt-street was built, that name was intended to have been given to the street which is now Berry-street.

from the old quarry, now St. James' Cemetery. Several houses were erected at the upper part of Duke-street, near the corner where it joins Berry-street, and two or three stood on the north end of, and on the east side of, the road leading to Toxteth-park, now Great George-street; but on the west side there were only open fields extending from thence and from the upper part of Duke-street, as far as the continuation of Park-lane, now St. James'-street. The fields remained open until after the commencement of the present century.

Not long before the year 1775, the (south) Ladies'-walk stood on the north side of Duke-street, and extended from below the part opposite York-street, nearly as far as the spot where Colquitt-street now is. It was planted with a row of large trees, the last of which stood in a small garden or yard nearly opposite York-street, and was blown down in January, 1852; and the projecting house in Duke-street, in which, for many years, Mr. Stavert, the surgeon, lived, was built near the lower end of it.

Cleveland-square was built, and at the two ends, it had trees growing at the edge of the foot-walk, one or two of which were standing long after the commencement of the present century. There was an obelisk in the centre where a fountain played, of which the water is said to have been supplied by pipes from some springs near the footpath in the fields, which, until very recently, led from Parliament-street, opposite the end of Catharine-street, towards the tanyard and the lodge in Toxteth-park.

On the land to the eastward of Pitt-street, opposite to and not far from the Methodist Chapel, there was a well, called the Dye-house well, of remarkably pure water, which is still in existence.[1]

---

(1) In the work called the "Stranger in Liverpool," page ii, the well is said yet to exist, under No. 11, in Greetham-street, near Gilbert-street.

The town terminated on the southward side, in Pitt-street and Park-lane, and near the place where Mason-street and Tabley-street now are, and at the north end of Wapping, then called the South Shore; and there were fields and rather extensive gardens to the southward of Tabley-street.

In proceeding to describe the extent and appearance of the town at the eastward and northward sides, the reader must imagine himself to have returned to Mount-pleasant and Ranelagh-place.

Copperas-hill-lane, since called Elliot-street, now Cop-peras-hill, led to some copperas works which stood on the north side of it, near where Silver-street and White Mill-street now are. A little lower down than the copperas-works, on the same side, an ancient windmill stood, which was afterwards blown down in a great storm on the 2nd of February, 1794.

Limekiln-lane (so called from some lime-burners' works, then standing where the London and North-Western Rail-way Station at present is,) now Lime-street, was quite in the country, with fields on the east side.[1] The lime-works were indicted in 1804, by the Corporation, being considered a nuisance and injurious to the patients in the Infirmary, and a verdict was obtained against the owners of them. Between Clayton-square and Limekiln-lane were a number of rope-walks of considerable size. At the upper end of what is now St. John's-lane, and in the open space in front of the London and North-Western Railway Station, but which space was then much smaller than at present, there was an ancient and considerable spring called the Fall-well. It was in a shallow square area, built round with stone; and some years afterwards, when it was disused

---

(1) The Author recollects one of these fields, called Waterworth's, remaining un-built upon as late as 1807.

V

for general purposes, the water from it was conducted by pipes to the garden at the back of the house, where the late Mr. William Rowe then lived, now the Stork Hotel, at the north end of Queen-square, where it rose up in the form of a fountain,[1] and so continued during many years.

The range of alms-houses, before mentioned,[2] stood in the vicinity of the Fall-well, but rather nearer the place where the London and North-Western Railway Station is.

Limekiln-lane passed on the east side of the garden of the Infirmary to the point where Shaws-brow and London-road now meet. On the upper part of the former, and in front of the Infirmary and the Seaman's Hospital, and at the west end of the open space where Islington market was recently held, stood a windmill, called Townsend mill. It was taken down in 1780 or 1781, the mill and adjoining ground having been purchased by the Corporation, in August, 1780, for £600; of which Mr. Peter Rigby was paid £300 for his leasehold interest, and the Earl of Derby £300 for the reversion of the premises.[3]

To the north-eastward of the place where Commutation-row and part of Islington now are, and near the spot where the southward part of Christian-street now stands, there was a tavern with a lofty tower-like building of six or eight stories high, connected with and forming part of it, which commanded a very pleasant and extensive prospect, and was much resorted to by persons intent on recreation. It was called the Folly, and gave that name to the lane, which was for many years called Folly-lane, now Islington and Brunswick-road, leading towards West Derby. The fair has been before mentioned;[4] it was formerly held in the

---

(1) The Author has seen the fountain playing there, about thirty-three years ago.
(2) Chapter I, page 62.
(3) Ledger (No. 3) of 1775 of the Corporation, page 248.
(4) Chapter I, page 113.

neighbourhood of Islington and in London-road, and took its name of Folly Fair from the building called the Folly.

Folly-lane was a rural lane which led towards West Derby, and on the north side of it, near the site of Islington-square, where Carver-street, Shaw-street and Islington now meet, there was a windmill standing close to the lane. The mill, and a formal-looking cottage[1] which stood very near it, are conspicuously laid down, and are near objects on the right side of the view of Liverpool, published in Aikin's Description of the Country from Thirty to Forty Miles round Manchester. The view was taken from the fields then on the north side of the upper part of Folly-lane, now Brunswick-road, and not far from the spot where Brunswick-house now stands.

Shaws-brow was then much more steep than it now is, the hill having been subsequently considerably lowered. On the south side there was a large space of ground formerly waste, and called "The Heath," which had been inclosed and consecrated in 1767, as a Cemetery, now St. John's Church-yard, in which was a small chapel called St. John's Chapel, which was used only for reading the funeral service. It stood near where the lowest gate opens towards the Old Haymarket, now Shaw-place, at the bottom of St. John's-lane. The foundations of St. John's Church were laid in 1775, as will be mentioned elsewhere,[2] but owing to some cause which it is not easy to ascertain, it was not completed and used until several years afterwards. At the bottom of Shaws-brow, on the south side, stood a range of alms-houses, which has been before noticed.[3]

---

(1) The mill was destroyed many years ago, but the cottage remained until within the last thirty years or thereabouts. Many of the readers will recollect its standing near the ends of Carver-street and Haigh-street, and facing towards the eastward.   (2) Chapter V.

(3) Chapter I, page 62.—Behind the houses which stood on the north side of

The south side of Shaws-brow was built as high up the hill as where the old Infirmary stood, and where St. George's-hall now stands, and about the same distance on the north side, but not any part of London-road was then built.

Byrom-street was then little more than a country lane leading towards Walton and the north, and was only partially built; there were one or two tanyards on its western side, supplied with water from the stream which, at that place, was called the Brook, and which has been before mentioned[1] as formerly flowing into the Old Pool. It also supplied the kennel of a pack of hounds, (harriers,) called the Corporation harriers, but they were for a long period at least, a subscription pack; and at one time the Corporation used to subscribe £5 5s a-year towards it.[2] The kennel stood at the foot of Richmond-row, and extended a little up the spot where Downe-street now stands; the brook flowed through the kennel, and before entering it, passed through a kind of valley called the Dingle, on part of which Downe-street now stands.[3]

St. Ann's Church was quite in the country, but there were three or four houses, with gardens in front of them,

---

Shaws-brow, as well as behind those on the westward side of the Old Haymarket, now called Shaw-place, were some earthenware works. There were several others in different parts of the town, one of which was between Duke-street and Wolstenholme-street, now Gradwell-street, from which Pothouse-lane, formerly Pothouse-weint, derives its name.

(1) Introduction, page 17.

(2) Ledger (No. 3) of 1775 of the Corporation, page 103. A receipt has been preserved at the Town-hall, for three years' subscription, signed by Mr. George Case, dated 15th November, 1775, " for three years' subscription to the expense of keeping the hounds of the Liverpool Hunt, due in August last."

(3) The Author has seen an old abstract of a deed of conveyance, dated the 2nd February, 1778, to Richard Gerrard, John Rose, and John Leigh, of a close of land on the eastward side of Byrom-street, containing 1A. 3R. 30P. of the large measure, called " The Dog Kennel Field," or " Field near the Dog Kennel."

built on the elevated part of Richmond-row. From the north end of Byrom-street, part of which is now Scotland-road, a road led past a lane called Sickman's, or Deadman's-lane; where tradition says that a large number of persons were buried who had died in Liverpool of the plague. The place was near where the lowest part of either Sawney Pope-street, or Addison-street now is.[1] The road continued as a country lane, from the lowest end of Rose-place to near the spot where the east end of Burlington-street and the west end of Collingwood-street now stand, not straight, as it at present runs, but it wound round by Bevington-bush and up Bevington-hill, and from thence it led as a rural lane towards Kirkdale and Walton, through which the high way to Ormskirk passed, as at present.

At that time, and for several years after the commence-ment of the present century, the road near Bevington-bush and Bevington-hill, and the first part of the way towards Kirkdale, passed a great number of small gardens, where vegetables, principally cabbages, were grown for the Liver-pool market.

Behind the houses and buildings which stood on the westward side of Byrom-street, and lowest end and middle of Dale-street, on its northward side, there were fields and gardens. Pownall-square, though laid out, was not built. The north ends of Oldhall-street and of Plumbe-street opened to the fields.

Between the north end of Oldhall-street and the North Shore, or North Quay, as it was sometimes called, now Bath-street, was the (North) Ladies'-walk. It was entered

---

(1) In the Annals in Gore's Directory, the circumstance is mentioned, and the date of the event is given as 1651, and "Sickman's-lane, now Addison-street," is mentioned as the place of interment. In Williamson's Liverpool Advertiser, of Friday, the 13th August, 1756, is an advertisement of a "Garden, near Sickman's-lane," to be let, which evidently was the lane above alluded to.

by a gate a little to the northward of Brook-street, then Holding's-weint, at the Oldhall-street or east end, and also by a flight of steps exactly opposite the old Baths, at the west end; and contained two rows of trees and a walk between them, besides a walk on the outside of each row.

There were sea-water Baths for public convenience, on the west side of Bath-street, on the site of the Prince's Dock. They were formerly the property of Mr. Wright, a boat-builder, who erected them about the middle of the last century. The site was held by lease from the Corporation, who purchased the leasehold interest in the property, with the intention of embellishing the baths, and making considerable alterations in the original plan. Great alterations and improvements were accordingly made in them in 1794, as will be mentioned in another chapter.[1]

The open shore extended to the northward from the baths, and was a public road to Bootle and Crosby. A little beyond the baths there were three or four fishermen's cottages, overlooking the shore, which have long since disappeared in the improvements made in that quarter; and still further to the north was a tavern called the Wishing Gate, of some repute, which respectable persons were in the habit of frequenting and of enjoying the marine view from it. There were also the old and the new North-shore Houses, usually called the Half-mile Houses, two taverns standing on the shore, much frequented by bathers.

An account of the outskirts or suburbs of Liverpool, at present so extensive, and containing so numerous a population, may be comprised in a small compass.

In Toxteth-park, now so populous,[2] there was not, in

---

(1) Chapter V.

(2) The census of 1851 showed a population of 61,326 inhabitants, in two of the wards, part only of Toxteth-park, which have been added to the borough of Liverpool, under the Municipal Reform Act, exclusive of the other parts of Toxteth-park, of which the population is considerable.

1775, a village or hamlet, or even a cluster of houses; but the tavern then called the Park Coffee-house, now called the Pine Apple Tavern,[1] on the west side of the High Park-road; and the ancient white and low-built public house, with its old-fashioned porch still remaining, though altered, on the east side of the road, and distinguished by the sign of the Peacock, with two or three small houses near them; and the old chapel used by dissenters, called the Park Chapel, were standing.

At that period, nearly the whole of Toxteth-park belonged to the then Earl of Sefton. It is extra-parochial; but doubts having been suggested, the point was raised in the cause, Bellis against Roberts and another, (a case of prohibition respecting the non-payment of church rates,) tried at the Lent Assizes, at Lancaster, in 1835, and the result was, a verdict establishing that Toxteth-park was extra-parochial, and not subject to the rates of the parish of Walton-on-the-Hill.

In that part of Toxteth-park which was afterwards called Harrington, there was not one house; but a little to the southward of it, and on the South Shore beyond the spot where the south end of Brunswick Dock is now made, and rather to the southward of the end of what is now Park-street, a lofty and unsightly house called the Tall House was erected, about that period,[2] on the open shore. It was built by Mr. Cuthbert Bisbrown, with the sanction of the then Earl of Sefton, and was intended to have been a Ferry-house, corresponding with the opposite ferry (Rock Ferry) in Cheshire, and it was in contemplation to have had ferry boats to ply regularly, between the Tall-house

---

(1) The High-Park Coffee-house was erected at a subsequent period, on the east side of the road.

(2) The exact date of its erection and intended adaptation to the purposes of a Ferry-house have not been ascertained, but it is supposed to have been prior to 1776.

and Toxteth-park, and the Rock Ferry. The scheme was, however, premature, and was soon abandoned; as the population and other matters were not sufficiently ripe for it. The house was afterwards, at one time, used as a ladies' boarding school, and, after being applied to various other purposes, it was pulled down rather more than two years ago.[1]

The small portion of Toxteth-park near the Mersey, and adjoining the south side of Liverpool, called Harrington, was so called in compliment to Isabella, daughter of the Second Earl of Harrington, the wife of Charles William, First Earl of Sefton.

Instead of the large and populous suburb of Edge-hill which now exists, there were only two houses; one was a farm-house belonging to Mr. Fleetwood, and the other stood in a lane which is now Mason-street, but which was then merely an occupation road to some fields. There was one cottage on the north side of Wavertree-lane leading towards Rake-lane, but that was so far down the descent of the hill on the Wavertree side, that it may be doubtful whether it could be considered to be upon the hill; in fact, the district was not then known by the name of Edge-hill.

The only house upon Mount-vernon was Vernon-hall, which is still standing.

At Low-hill there were a tolerably good tavern, (the Low-hill Coffee-house,) two or three respectable-looking houses with gardens,[2] a few small mean-looking cottages, and the old West Derby Workhouse, without any date, but with an inscription on a stone tablet, containing the words,

---

(1) It is laid down in Mr. Jonathan Bennison's Map of the Town and Port of Liverpool and the Environs, of 1835.

(2) One of these houses is still standing, in a garden there, and has the initials M and date A E cut on a stone on its side.
1743.

cut in a style apparently of considerable antiquity, " WEST DARBY WORK HOUSE " on the front. It was pulled down about the end of 1851, and a school-house for boys and girls, called St. Jude's Schools, connected with St. Jude's Church, was erected on its site, and opened on the 13th of July, 1852.

At Everton there were a few large houses, some of which had been erected by merchants of opulence ; besides which, there was the well-known white cottage, on the upper end and south side of Everton-brow, where Prince Rupert is reputed to have established his head quarters, in 1644, during the siege of Liverpool, and which was a few years ago pulled down : there were also three or four respectable-looking houses, and some cottages, on the part now more particularly distinguished by the appellation of Everton-village;[1] these were nearly all that were then standing on Everton-hill. The ancient fire-beacon, however, which had stood for centuries, near where St. George's Church now is, was then a conspicuous object on the hill. It was blown down in the great storm of 1802.

It is said that during the wars between King Charles and the Parliament, marriages were celebrated in the old beacon, by the Episcopal ministers ejected from the church at Liverpool. It is certain that during those troublesome times, marriages were solemnized by justices of the peace;[2] and an Act of Parliament of 12th Charles the Second,

---

(1) On one house, the name and date, " Thos. Heys, 1734," are cut on a stone, and on an adjoining outbuilding, are cut the initials and date, $\frac{T\ H}{1735}$; and on a cottage on the opposite side of the road, there are the following initials and date, $\frac{\text{H}}{\text{I M}}$ 1688. The Cage, or place of temporary confinement for prisoners, was not built; but Everton Cross, now destroyed, was standing on the open space higher up the part of the hill which is often called Everton-brow.

(2) Blackstone's Commentaries, 14th edition, vol. 1, page 440.

W

chap. 33, was passed in 1660, by which such marriages were declared valid without any fresh solemnization. It was a square tower, and at the top it had a large stone receptacle, where faggots and other combustibles were deposited, in order to be lighted in case of invasion or alarm. It was built of dull reddish-brown stone. It was about six yards square, and about twenty-five feet high. There was only one apartment below, which was level with the field, and a flight of stone steps led to the upper part. The roof was a terraced platform, and a stone cistern was at the south-west corner. A gooseberry tree and a thorn bush, at one period, grew in a little soil upon the ledging of the east wall, and flourished there many summers. It communicated with Rivington-pike near Chorley, Billinge-hill near Wigan, and Blackstone-edge, (dividing Lancashire from Yorkshire,) and commanded a view of Snowdon and Penmanmaur mountains westward, with many smaller hills on the north and south. It also commanded a distinct view of Beeston Castle.[1]

Kirkdale certainly then existed, as a small village, but it contained only very few houses; and there were not any houses whatever between the village and the Mersey.

There were Ferries at Seacombe, Woodside, Lower Tranmere, Rock Ferry, New Ferry, and Eastham, but there was scarcely a house near the Mersey at those places, except their respective ferry-houses. The most usual place for the embarkation and landing of passengers to and from Woodside, Tranmere, and the Cheshire ferries higher up the Mersey, was George's pier and slip. Passengers were conveyed across the Mersey between Liverpool and the ferries in small open boats, some with and some without sails, but all of very unsafe construction with reference to the length of the passage, the frequency of strong gales of

---

(1) Underhill's M.S. Account of Liverpool, page 53.

wind, and the strength of the current; and consequently fatal accidents not unfrequently occurred to the passengers.

The ferries of Birkenhead, Monk's Ferry, Egremont, and New Brighton, did not then exist, nor were they established until long after the commencement of the present century, and comparatively only a few years ago.

The extraordinary changes which have taken place since 1775, on the west side of the Mersey, opposite Liverpool, may well excite not surprise merely, but astonishment. Places there, which now possess a redundant population, with handsome churches, streets, squares, docks, and a large market, had at that date, scarcely any houses or cottages to boast of. Within the memories of numbers of persons now living, there was not in the part of the township or chapelry of Birkenhead, where the town of Birkenhead now stands, a house except the old Hall, now destroyed, belonging to the ancient family of Price, the Woodside ferry-house, and two or three small cottages, near the latter, inhabited by boatmen or fishermen.[1]

The ancient chapel, now used as a school, formerly part of the old Abbey of Birkenhead, with the picturesque ivy-clad ruins adjoining, then formed an interesting object when approached from the ferry, at Woodside, or from that at Tranmere. The chapel was used for Divine service, of the Established Church, and marriages were solemnized there, until the opening of the present church close to it, in 1822.

It is unfortunate that no account seems to have been handed down of the number of streets, houses, and families of Liverpool, in 1775; however, an account exists of the number in the year 1773, which, probably, does not differ very much from that of 1775.

---

(1) The Author perfectly recollects Birkenhead being in that state, some time after the commencement of the present century.

In Enfield's Account of Liverpool, published in 1774, it is stated that the number of streets lanes, alleys, &c. in Liverpool, was then about 230; and he gives a list of the former names and of the then names of some few of the streets and lanes, viz :—

THE FORMER NAMES.	THE THEN NAMES.
Castle-hill[1]	Harrington-street
Church-lane	Tower-garden
Dry-bridge	(Part of) Fenwick-street
Glass-house-weint	Hall-street
Great George-street	York-street
Holden's-weint	Brook-street
Lower Stanley-street	Button-street
Old Tower	Castle-ditch
Potato-market[2]	Fazakerley-street
Rosemary-lane	Sea-brow
Sea-bank	Chorley-street
Squire's-garden	Church-alley

And he mentions the following as new streets :—

Bath-street	Henry-street	Millington's-alley
Croston-court	Johnson-street	Orange-street
Dickenson-street	Jordan-street	Sparling-street
Drinkwater-street	Kent-street	Suffolk-street
Flint-street	Kitchen-street	Tabley-street
Hargrave-street	Marsden-street	Tyrer-street

It is evident that in mentioning them as "new streets," Mr. Enfield did not mean that the streets were then built, for that was not the case, but that they were laid out; and he proceeds to state, " a design has been formed and begun

---

(1) Also called Castle-hey.

(2) There seems to be some confusion in Mr. Enfield's Work between Fazakerley-street and the Potato-market. Fazakerley-street may have been called the Potato-market for a short time, but Castle-ditch, (now destroyed,) at the upper end of Lord-street, and where the south part of St. George's-crescent now stands, was called the Potato-market, within the recollection of the Author's Father, several years after 1775 ; it is also so called in Mr. John Eyes' Map of Liverpool, of 1768, and in that of Mr. Perry, of 1769.

to be executed, for erecting several new streets at the south end of the town, under the name of New Leverpool; but how far the scheme will be accomplished is at present uncertain."[1]

It certainly must appear extraordinary to the present generation, to hear that, in the life time of more than one person now living, it was contemplated to call such a district as the streets, lanes and alleys which extend from Park-lane and St. James'-street to the Docks and to the Mersey, by the name of "New Leverpool," yet that is the locality to which Mr. Enfield alluded by that title. Mr. Cuthbert Bisbrown, who has been already mentioned, was the principal projector of most of the new streets subsequently built in that neighbourhood, at the south end of Liverpool.

Although a census was not taken in 1775, it is tolerably certain that the population of Liverpool consisted of rather more than 35,000. It must, of course, have increased in some degree since 1773, in which year it was ascertained by an actual survey, that the number of inhabited houses was 5928, of untenanted houses 412, of families 8002, and of inhabitants 34,407, averaging 5 and 4-5ths to each house.[2] As the increase during the previous twenty years had been about 14,000,[3] and supposing the population to continue to increase in the same ratio, the proportionate increase during the two years which elapsed between 1773 and 1775, would amount to about 1400. On that calculation the population, in 1775 would be about 35,800, which seems to be as close an approximation to perfect accuracy as can reasonably be expected under the circumstances. The increase since that date has been wonderful.

The population of Liverpool, in 1851, was, according to

---

(1) Enfield's Liverpool, page 21 and 22.

(2) Enfield's Liverpool, page 24.   (3) Ibid. page 25.

the census taken on the 31st March, in that year, as follows, viz :—

In the Parish of Liverpool (before the extension of the borough by the Act 5th and 6th William the Fourth, chap. 76, (1835,) usually called the Municipal Reform Act, the borough of Liverpool did not extend beyond the limits of the parish of Liverpool,) Males, 125,960; Females, 129,349: total...255,309

To the above must be added the population of the places now forming part of the borough, but beyond the limits of the parish of Liverpool, viz :—

Everton ....total...25,875		
Kirkdale.................................... „ ... 9,890		
	35,765	
Toxteth-park, two Wards.................. „ ...61,326		
West Derby, one Ward..................... „ ...22,001		
	————...119,092	

Total....................374,401

In addition to the above, it was estimated that the number of persons in the streets, or sleeping on board vessels in the docks, on the night of the 30th March, 1851, (the night previous to the taking of the census,) amounted to about 4000;[1] to which must also be added, the seamen belonging to Liverpool, but then at sea, estimated at 10,000, over and above those who were then in the port.[2]

The Public Walks and Promenades of the town were, George's-parade, St. James'-terrace, occasionally called The Mount, and the Ladies'-walk, which has been mentioned in another place as being at the north end of Liverpool; it remained several years after 1775; but the South Ladies'-walk, in Duke-street, had been destroyed not long previous to that date. The Rope-walks, which were then between Limekiln-lane (now Lime-street) and Clayton-square, and

---

(1) In the 4000, it is fair also to include a considerable number of persons who were in the over-crowded low lodging-houses, who were never included in the returns for the census, the lodging-house keepers being afraid of the numbers being known.

(2) Communicated by Mr. James Eckersley, Superintendent Registrar of Births, Deaths, and Marriages, in Liverpool.

now form part of the site of St. John's-market, were also occasionally used as promenades, especially on the afternoon of Sunday.   Everton-terrace was also a favourite walk; and the upper part of Mount-pleasant, as long as it retained some of the characteristics of the country; the latter had, some time before the close of the last century, the advantage of a white seat and rail for the fatigued, which stood on some vacant ground at the north-east corner of Rodney-street, in Mount-pleasant.

There were then many pleasant rural walks and pathways in the fields, very near the town, amongst which may be particularly named one leading over the fields, where the portion of Toxteth-park called Harrington now stands, on the east bank of the Mersey, past the then copper-works, afterwards the Herculaneum pottery, which stood on the South Shore, and through Knots-hole-dingle to the old chapel, called the Park Chapel.   From the Park Chapel a footpath passed through the fields where Ullet-lane now is, and through an occupation lane in continuation of it, now widened and opened to the public, leading towards Brook-house at the upper end of Smeatham-lane.   An old road, said to be a church road, led also from Walton Church through the fields behind the spot where Walton-priory stands; from thence, below Cabbage-hall and past where Elm-house now is, along Lower Breck-lane and across the fields below where Newsham-house now stands, and from thence, still across fields, to the Prescot-lane, then crossed close to Fairfield-house,[1] and by its stable-yard into Edge-lane, and from thence over the fields into Wavertree-lane, at the spot where the railway now passes, then across the country to the place where the house called the Higher-lodge stands, at the

---

(1) Fairfield-house was built before 1775, having been erected by Mr. Thomas Tarleton, before mentioned, whose daughter, Mr. Edward Falkner, who afterwards resided there, married.

east side of Ullet-lane, and from thence the path diverged in two directions, one leading to the southward, past the row of elms (where Elm-cottage now is) towards Aigburth and Garston, and the other to the westward, by the footpath before mentioned, to the Park chapel and Knots-hole-dingle.

On the shore adjoining Knots-hole-dingle, nets were commonly set by fishermen, who continued the practice until within the recollection of many persons now living.

It may seem scarcely credible to those who have only known Liverpool since it attained its present immense size, to hear of a rural walk commencing in the fields which existed near where the end of the St. James' Cemetery now is, but the fact was actually so. A very pleasant footpath entered the fields at the south end of St. James'-terrace, and of the then stone quarry, now the Cemetery, and following the line where Upper Parliament-street is now built, it passed over the meadows and fields about as far as near the spot where Lodge-lane and Smeatham-lane meet. This walk was remarkable for having on its north side considerable remains of the old Toxteth-park wall. The footpath and some portions of the wall remained after the commencement of the present century; and they were not destroyed until after Parliament-street was laid out. This part of the park wall, as has been already stated, was a boundary of the town on one side, and is so mentioned in the Corporation Records of the year 1671.[1]

The only high roads out of Liverpool, in 1775, on which there were toll-bars, were the present turnpike road through Prescot, and the north road through Ormskirk and Preston; the first Act for repairing and enlarging the former having been passed in 1725, in the 12th George the First, chap.

---

(1) Report of the Proceedings at Liverpool before the Commissioners of Inquiry into Municipal Corporations, page 287.

21, "An Act for repairing and enlarging the road from Liverpool to Prescot, and other roads therein mentioned, in the county palatine of Lancaster;"[1] and the first Act for repairing and widening the latter road having been passed in the year 1771, in the 11th George the Third, chap. 93, "An Act for repairing and widening the road from Patrick's Cross, within the town of Liverpoole, in the county palatine of Lancaster, to the town of Preston, in the same county palatine."[2]

Remains of the more ancient high road from Liverpool to London, through Warrington, might then easily be traced, and there are even yet some small portions of it discernible, turning off to the right, from near the furthest end of Edge-lane-road; and, after crossing Mill-lane, it runs on the right hand of the footpath, which passes across the fields, leading towards Wavertree-nook and the nursery gardens there: it was so narrow that it had evidently been in use when pack-horses were in fashion.

In 1775, the only Inns existing in Liverpool were the Golden Lion, the Angel, the Fleece, the Cross-Keys, and the Bull and Punch Bowl, in Dale-street, and the Talbot, in Water-street,[3] which were all considered as of the first

---

(1) In Troughton's Liverpool, page 107, it is erroneously stated that the first Act for the Liverpool and Prescot road was of the year 1720; no such Act was then passed; he made a mistake of five years in the date. See also the Act 19th George the 2nd, chap. 19, 1746; 26th George the 2nd, chap. 65, 1753; and 11th George the 3rd, chap. 91, 1771.

(2) The Act 11th George the 3rd, chap. 93, 1771, was afterwards repealed. See 26th George the 3rd, chap. 126, 1786, (repealed,) and 50th George the 3rd, chap. 57, 1810.

(3) The Talbot was at the upper end and south side of Water-street, and was, together with the old Exchange-alley, demolished when Castle-street, and a portion of the upper part of Water-street, were widened. Near the site of the old Talbot a new inn or hotel, also called the Talbot, was afterwards erected in Water-street, the entrance to which was on the west, or right hand of Back Castle-street, immediately after passing through the modern archway leading into Back Castle-street, from Water-street: it was destroyed some years ago.

X

class :[1] and at several of the inns post-chaises were kept. Every one of them has since been pulled down.

There were then a number of respectable and much frequented coffee-houses and taverns in the town.

The St. George's Coffee-house stood on the west side of Castle-street; here public dinners, suppers, and other entertainments were occasionally had, and the committee of the Liverpool Library frequently used to hold their meetings : it was pulled down when Castle-street was widened; Pontack's Coffee-house, on the north side of Water-street, and the Merchant's Coffee-house, in St. Nicholas' Church-yard ; all these were highly respectable coffee-houses or taverns, with large news-rooms in them; but they were not generally adapted to the use of travellers. Neptune's Coffee-house was on the southward side of and fronting the shambles before mentioned, near the place where the Sun Fire-office now stands, in what is now Exchange-street West, but the door opened into the passage before mentioned,[2] leading into Water-street, and it had a skittle-ground attached to it ; the Merlin's Cave Coffee-house was to the northward of the old shambles ;[2] but the two latter were merely taverns, and had not any room appropriated to the purpose of reading newspapers. The Buck and Vine Tavern, in Hackins-hey, was much frequented by respectable persons ; at that time the habits of the age, sanctioned persons of respectability, in frequently passing their evenings in coffee-houses and taverns. The St. James' Coffee-house, sometimes called the Mount Coffee-house, has been already mentioned[3] as standing, with a garden attached to it, on St. James'-walk.

---

(1) There had been, a short time previous to that period, a respectable Inn on the east side of Castle-street, called the Millstone, but the Author has been unable to ascertain at what date it was discontinued or destroyed.

(2) Chapter II, page 119.   (3) Chapter II, page 144.

The following is a copy of a bill of Mr. John Bridge, the landlord of the St. James' Coffee-house, for a dinner; from the date of the bill, 15th October, 1775, and from the fact of the Mayor and Corporation being debited with the amount, the entertainment should seem to have been given by the Mayor on some occasion just before he went out of office :—

" *St. James, 15th Octr. 1775.*

" The Worshipfull Mayor &
Corporation of Liverpoole.

	lb.	To John Bridge.		Dr.	
		s.	d.		
1 Tortle	37	.... at 1 6p............	£2	16	6
Wine 7ˢ Butter, Eggs & Seasoning			„	9	6
Gellies, Posets, & Flumery — Sweetmeats.........			„	10	0
Wild fowl of different sorts			„	10	8
A goose, Ham, fowls & Giblet pye			„	14	0
A round of Beef, Fish & Pidgeon pye...			„	12	0
Pudins, Bread & Roots................................			„	7	0
Frutes, grapes comon, & Wall Nutts			„	8	10
Wine			3	0	0
Punch..........................			2	0	0
Beef & Porter..			„	9	0
Servants Punch & Beer			„	12	0

£12 9 6

" At a Committee held the 30th day of Novr. 1775, Allowed to be p^d Jno. Bridge twelve pounds nine shillings & six pence.

Ja⁸ Clemens
Peter Rigby
To Jno. Crosbie, Esqr. Treas^{r.}   Willm. Crosbie, Junr.
John Colquitt
Jno. Hughes.

Rec^{d.} Feby. 24th 1776 from John Crosbie the Contents,
p. John Bridge."[1]

The bill is curious and interesting, as giving some idea of the nature of an entertainment of that description, the viands and dainties introduced on such an occasion, and the cost of them in 1775.

The public Conveyances and means of Travelling, and of conveying goods, may be considered as, in some degree,

---

(1) Copied from the original Bill as it was audited by the Committee and paid, preserved at the Town-hall.

in their infancy. Goods, except those sent by river or canal navigation, were principally conveyed inland, in large and heavy waggons. The conveyance of goods to and from Liverpool, on pack-horses, had ceased before the period now under consideration; but the author's father recollected that strings of them used to come into Cheshire, with Yorkshire goods, when he was a youth.

Considerable quantities of goods were sent from Liverpool by the river Mersey in barges or flats to Runcorn, and from thence to Preston-brook, and inland by the Trent and Mersey or Grand-Trunk Canal, into Staffordshire, or as the case might be, to Manchester, by the Duke of Bridgewater's Canal. The Leeds and Liverpool Canal was then and for several years afterwards, navigable at the Liverpool end, only as far as Wigan, and was principally used to convey coals. The Acts of Parliament for the various navigations and canals then in existence, connected with Liverpool, have been already mentioned.[1]

There was then a considerable coasting trade between Liverpool and other ports of the kingdom, which will be briefly noticed in another chapter,[2] where the trade of the port will be mentioned.

The stage-coaches, carriers, waggons, &c. now claim some attention.

In 1775, there was not any mail-coach running between Liverpool and any other town; and as has been noticed in another chapter,[3] the mail bags of letters were conveyed to and from Liverpool on horseback.

A heavy stage-coach appears to have been then running between Liverpool and London; it certainly ran in the preceding year,[4] and there is not any reason to believe

---

(1) Chapter I, page 103.   (3) Chapter I, page 88.

(2) Chapter IV.   (4) Gore's Liverpool Directory of 1774.

that it had been discontinued. It went, or rather crawled over the road, from Liverpool to London six times only in the week, and in the winter season only four times a week. There was a Liverpool and Manchester coach which ran three days in the week in the summer, and two in the winter season; and there were two coaches to Warrington, each of which ran four days a week.[1]

The particulars of the stage-coaches from Liverpool to other places, about that period, will be gathered from the following advertisement, which appears in the Liverpool Directory of 1774; and when we compare the uncomfortable, dilatory, and ill-arranged public conveyances of the last century, with the railway trains by which the public now travel, the contrast speaks volumes in favour of the advantages of the present system :—[2]

---

(1) Gore's Liverpool Directory of 1774.

(2) As a proof how dilatory and inconvenient even the best public conveyance between Liverpool and London was, until within a comparatively late period, it may be mentioned, that many years after the commencement of the present century, the Royal Mail Coach was the favourite and most rapid conveyance from Liverpool to London ; the mail-coach office at Liverpool was in Water-street, on the east side of the archway near the Talbot Hotel before mentioned.   Certainly as recently as thirty-seven years ago, if not still more recently, the mail-coach used to take its departure from that office at nine o'clock at night ; the passengers breakfasted at Stone, dined at Coventry, supped at some other place, and after being two nights and one day on the road, they were put down at the Swan-with-two-Necks, in Lad-lane, London, about a quarter before six in the morning but one after leaving Liverpool.   It then went round by Congleton, but that circuitous route was abandoned several years before the adoption of railways.   The Author has more than once since he became a man, travelled by the royal mail, when it was so dilatory a conveyance, and went by that circuitous route.   The delays and stoppages on the road were then so great, that on one occasion, during the time allowed, or rather wasted, in changing the horses of the mail, at Lichfield, the Author and another passenger visited and inspected the exterior of the Cathedral.   Travelling by the mail-coach was not even an economical mode, for the Author has paid sometimes as much as five pounds or five guineas for an inside place, after its speed had been accelerated, besides the expense of breakfasting and dining on the road, and some not trifling contributions to guards, coachmen, waiters, porters, &c.

It was considered an admirable improvement when the speed of the royal mail was

"STAGE COACHES."[1]

" The London Stage Coach, on Steel Springs, sets out from the Golden Talbot, in Water-street, Liverpool, every Sunday morning, about nine o'clock, 'and every Monday, Tuesday, Wednesday, Thursday, and Friday, about noon; and from the Swan-with-two-Necks, in Lad-lane, London, on the same evenings, about nine o'clock; lies at Middle-which and Coventry up, and Lichfield down.

" N.B. The same Machine goes four days a week during the Winter Season.

Each inside passenger from Liverpool to Warrington 4s, Litch-field £1 2 0, Coventry £1 9 0, London £2 10 0, Outsides and children on the lap, half-price; one-half to be paid at booking, the other at taking Coach. Each inside to be allowed 20lb. wt. of luggage;

---

afterwards so increased, that it left Liverpool at half-past six in the evening, and being only one night on the road, arrived in London at thirty-four minutes past ten on the following evening.

The celerity of the mail-coach was, however, again increased before the intro-duction of railways, so that it left the post-office, in London, at seven o'clock in the evening, and arrived at Liverpool, at six o'clock on the following evening, and the letters were delivered at a quarter before seven. In April 1836, the Author travelled from London to Liverpool after its speed had been so increased. Its rate of travelling from Liverpool to London was also accelerated in the same degree.

The route of the London royal mail from Liverpool, immediately before the adoption of railways, was through Prescot, Warrington, Knutsford, Newcastle, Stone, Wolsley-Bridge, Lichfield, Coleshill, Coventry, Dunchurch, Daventry, Towcester, Stoney-Stratford, Redburn, St. Albans and Barnet. The distance on the turnpike road, by that route, from Liverpool to London, is 207¾ miles.

On the 15th September, 1830, the Liverpool and Manchester Railway was opened. On the 4th July, 1837, the Grand Junction Railway, between Liverpool and Birming-ham, was also opened; on the 17th of September, 1838, the public had the advantage of the opening of the London and Birmingham Railway; in 1845, the Liverpool and Man-chester Railway was united to the Grand Junction Railway; and, in 1846, the London and Birmingham, the Grand Junction, and the Manchester and Birmingham Railway Companies became amalgamated, and the joint companies assumed their present title of the London and North-Western Railway Company. As a contrast to the old dilatory mode of being conveyed to London by the royal mail, at present passengers travelling from Liverpool to London by that railway, and wishing to breakfast without hurry before the journey, may leave Liverpool at half-past nine in the morning, and arrive at London at half-past four in the afternoon of the same day. The distance by the London and North-Western Railway, through Birmingham, is 210¼ miles, or through the Trent Valley, 201 miles.

(1) Published in Gore's Liverpool Directory of 1774.

outsides, and children on lap, 10lb., all above to pay 3d per pd. to London, and so in proportion. Parcels, &c. to be paid for at booking. A Coach from Kendal meets the above Liverpool Coach at Warrington, every Monday, Wednesday, and Friday afternoon; one goes to Liverpool the same evening, the other returns and lies at Wigan, and goes to Kendal the next day. Fare between Kendal and Warrington £1 1 0. Performed by J. Hanforth and W. Dimock, of London; J. Procter, of Dunstable; W. Webster, of Coleshill; J. Fearn, of Litchfield; J. Morgan, of Stone; Oulton and Cook, of Middlewich; Watson and Baxter, of Warrington. They will not be accountable for cash, plate, jewels, watches, writings, &c. unless entered as such and paid for accordingly; Walter Williams, bookkeeper, No. 26, Cheapside."

" The Manchester Stage Coach[1] comes to the Bull and Punch Bowl, Mr. John Randles's, in Dale-street, every Monday, Wednesday, and Friday, and goes out every Tuesday, Thursday, and Saturday, during the summer Season: Comes in every Monday and Thursday, and goes out every Tuesday and Friday, during the Winter Season, and takes passengers for Warrington, Manchester, &c.

" William Griffith sets out from his own house, in Fenwick-street, with a Coach and four horses every Sunday, Monday, Wednesday, and Friday, at seven o'clock in the morning, for Warrington, and returns the same day.

" John Corner sets out from his own house, in Fenwick-alley, with a Coach and Four horses, every Sunday, Monday, Wednesday, and Friday, at seven o'clock in the morning, for Warrington, and returns the same day."[2]

In 1775, or a little earlier, there was a stage-coach which ran between Liverpool and London,[3] which is believed to have been the same coach which, as before mentioned, was

---

(1) It will be remarked, that it is called *the* Manchester Stage-Coach, from which it is reasonable to infer that, at that date, there was not any other running between Liverpool and Manchester. There was, however, a stage-coach between Liverpool and Manchester, in 1766, which is mentioned in Gore's Liverpool Directory of that year.

(2) Published in Gore's Liverpool Directory of the year 1774.

(3) The Author's Father perfectly recollected this coach running through Cheshire, and has often stated that he did not remember that there was then any other coach which ran between Liverpool and London.

advertised[1] to run from the Golden Talbot, in Water-street; that, however, cannot, after so great a lapse of time, be clearly ascertained. It had a large basket of wicker work behind, for such passengers as were of a humble class, and its route from Liverpool to London was through Middlewich, in which town a person named Oulton[2] kept the White Bear Inn, and was one of the proprietors of the coach.[2] During the Knutsford race week, which was then the last week in July, the coach, instead of proceeding in the direct route from Warrington through Northwich to Middlewich, was sent round by Knutsford, much out of the way, at the close of the races, for the double purpose of accommodating the company attending them, and of conducing to bring customers to the White Bear, at Middlewich. It could scarcely have been much less than three days on the road.

In Gore's General Advertiser of 19th May, 1775, is

---

(1) It ought to be stated, however, that *two* London coaches are mentioned in Gore's Liverpool Directory of 1766, which, at the first view, it seems difficult to reconcile with the above advertisement; but it is possible that two London coaches might run from Liverpool in that year, and being found more than could be supported, one of them might be discontinued. The following is a copy of the paragraph in the Liverpool Directory respecting those coaches, and it also merits notice in consequence of the information which it gives, respecting coaches from Liverpool to Kendal, and to Manchester.

(From Gore's Liverpool Directory of 1766, page 25.)

" STAGE COACHES.

" There are two Stage Coaches which go constantly to London, viz : in three days during the winter season, and in two days during the summer season, one from the Golden Talbot, in Water-street, Thomas Sutton, bookkeeper ; and the other from the Mill Stone, in Castle-street, Samuel Adams, bookkeeper.

" The Kendall Stage Coach comes to the Black Horse and Rainbow, Mr. Cuthbert Cottam's, in High-street, every Saturday, and goes out every Sunday, and takes passenger's for Lancaster, Kendall, &c.

"The Manchester Stage Coach comes to the Golden Lion in Dale-street, every Monday, Wednesday, and Friday; and goes out every Tuesday, Thursday, and Saturday, during the Summer season: comes in every Monday and Thursday, and goes out every Tuesday and Friday, during the Winter season, and takes passengers for Warrington, and Manchester, &c."

(2) Oulton and Cook, of Middlewich, are mentioned in the advertisement respecting the stage-coach which ran from the Golden Talbot, in Water-street, Liverpool, as proprietors of it, from which it may be reasonably inferred that it must have been identical with the coach above mentioned.

1. St. George's Church, Derby Square.

2. The Royal Liverpool Umpire, 1817.

3. View of Everton, 1817.

4. James Street c.1822/23.

5. Old Infirmary and Almshouses.

advertised a public conveyance called the "Flying Machine," to run between London and Kendal, (through Lancaster, Preston, Wigan, &c.); the proprietors of which professed to perform the distance between the two places in three days; the advertisement states, that "Two seats are reserved for passengers from Liverpool who *meets* this Coach at Warrington;" and from the following postcript to the advertisement, it appears that a coach then ran between Liverpool and Preston :—" N.B. A Stage Coach which goes between Liverpool and Preston, by way of Ormskirk, meets the above Machine at Preston, both going up and coming down."

In 1777 there were two stage-coaches which ran between Liverpool and London, one called "The London Stage Coach," and the other "The London Diligence."[1]

Some curious particulars, relative to the public conveyances which then ran between Liverpool and other places are contained in Gore's Liverpool Directory of that date, and are given in the note below.[2]

---

(1) Gore's Liverpool Directory of 1777, page 111.

"STAGE COACHES."

(2) " The London Stage Coach sets out from the Talbot Inn, Water-street, Liverpool, every Sunday morning, at nine o'clock, and every Monday, Tuesday, Wednesday, Thursday, and Friday evenings, at half-past four, and from the Swan-with-two-Necks, Lad-lane, London, every evening, except Saturday, about the same hour.

Each inside, from Liverpool to London........ £1 11 6

Each outside, from Ditto   to   Ditto   1   1 0

Fourteen pounds weight of luggage allowed, all above to pay three pence per pound, small parcels two shillings and six pence each, all above ten pounds at three pence per pound.

Performed by J. Hanforth, London; W. Webster, of Meriden; J. Fern, of Litchfield; J. Morgan, of Stone; M. Oulton, of Middlewich; J. Watson and J. Crossley, of Warrington; J. Baxter, of Preston, and Co.

The Proprietors will not be accountable for Cash, Plate, Jewels, Watches, Writings, &c. nor any parcel above five pounds value, unless entered as such, and paid for accordingly. Full fare to be paid on taking the seats, and if fail going, one half will be returned."

" The London Diligence. Sets out from the Talbot Inn, Water-street, Liverpool, every evening at three o'clock, and from the Swan-with-two-Necks, Lad-lane, London,

Y

A public conveyance, between Liverpool and London, called the "Liverpool Diligence," was advertised in Janu-

at the same time; lies at Stony Stratford up, and Stone down, will have a night's rest of 7 or 8 hours at each place.

Fare from Liverpool to London Two pounds ten shillings, and Three pence per mile any part of the road—allowing 10lb. weight of luggage, all above to pay three-pence per pound.

Full fare to be paid on taking the seats, and if fail going, one half will be returned. Perform'd by John Hanforth, London; J. Crossley, Warrington, and Co."

"The Lancaster Stage. Sets out from the New Inn, in Lancaster, every Monday, Wednesday, and Friday morning, at 6 o'clock, and from the Bull and Punch Bowl, in Dale-street, Liverpool, every Tuesday, Thursday, and Saturday mornings, at 6 o'clock.

		INSIDE.		OUTSIDE.	
	Ormskirk	3s	6d	2s	6d
Fare from Liverpool to	Preston........	8	6	5	6
	Lancaster	13	6	8	6

Fourteen pounds of luggage allow'd, all above to pay one penny per pound. Places taken at the above Inns and regularly entered every evening before the Machine sets out, by nine o'clock, at latest, where due attendance will be given.

Performed by { JOHN WATSON, of Warrington. and JOHN BAXTER, of Preston.

The proprietors will not be accountable for cash, plate, jewels, watches, &c. unless enter'd as such and paid for accordingly."

"Manchester Stage. Sets out for the Summer season every morning at six o'clock, from William Griffith's, the sign of the Cross Keys Inn, in Dale-street, Liverpool, and another coach every morning at 6 o'clock, sets out from Mr. Raffald's the King's Head Inn, Salford, Manchester; the two coaches meet, and passengers breakfast at the George Inn, Warrington, and dine at Liverpool and Manchester, every day.

Each Inside between Manchester and Liverpool	6s	6d
Do. between Manchester and Warrington	3	0
Children on Lap, half-price............................		
Outside between Manchester and Liverpool	4	0

Each inside to be allowed 14lb. of Luggage, outside and children on lap 7lb.; all above one penny a pound, and so in proportion to Warrington. Parcels under 6lb. to pay 6d; all above, one penny a pound, and in proportion to any part of the road.

Perform'd (if God permit) by John Watson and John Crossley, Warrington, and William Griffith, Liverpool.

N.B. They will not be accountable for money, watches, plate, jewels, writings, or any thing above the value of five pounds unless enter'd as such and paid for accordingly.

Places to be taken by nine o'clock every evening, and all parcels are desired to be brought before that time, that they may be regularly entered and taken care of.

Walter Williams, bookkeeper, 26, Cheapside."

"The Warrington Coach sets out from John Corner's, in Fenwick-alley, every

ary, 1776,[1] under the head "Elegant and expeditious
travelling between Liverpool and London," to run from
the Fleece Inn,[2] through the Potteries to London " in

Sunday, Monday, Wednesday, and Friday, at seven o'clock in the morning, and returns
the same day."

" A Diligence likewise sets out from John Corner's every Tuesday and Thursday,
at six o'clock in the morning, for Warrington, and Stockton Quay, and returns the
same day."

" A Warrington Coach, sets out from William Griffith's, the Cross Keys, in Dale-
street, every Sunday, Monday, Wednesday, and Friday, at seven o'clock in the morning,
and returns the same day."

" The Warrington Diligence sets out every morning at eight o'clock, from Mr.
Banner's, the Golden Fleece, in Dale-street, and returns the same day."

"LEEDS AND LIVERPOOL CANAL.

" The Union Packets set off from Liverpool every morning, Sunday excepted,
precisely at seven o'clock, from Lady-Day to Michaelmas, and at eight from Michaelmas to Lady-Day, and carry passengers on the following terms:—

From Liverpool to Gathurst Bridge 32 miles, Front Cabin, 2s 8d, After Cabin,
1s 9d—To Newbrough, 27 miles, Front Cabin, 2s 3d, After Cabin 1s 6d—To Burscough 24 miles, Front Cabin, 2s, After Cabin, 1s 3d.

They are met every day at Burscough by the Union Machine, which conveys
passengers through Preston to Lancaster, the same evening, and returns the morning
following, with passengers to meet the Packet and Diligence at Burscough.   Fare in
the Union Machine :

	INSIDE.		OUTSIDE.	
From Burscough to Preston	4s	6d	2s	6d
From Preston to Lancaster	5	0	3	0 "

The Union Diligence, sets out from the Golden Lion, Liverpool, every morning
at nine o'clock carries passengers at three pence per mile each ; meets the Union
Machine at 12 o'clock, in which they are taken to Preston or Lancaster the same
evening, at the rates above mentioned.

There are likewise four Union Traders employed in carrying Merchandize upon this
Canal ; one of which is constantly at Liverpool, for the reception of goods going to
Preston, Wigan, Chorley, Blackburn, &c. &c.

Expenses of Travelling from Liverpool to Lancaster per Canal, in the Packet to
Burscough, First places, 2s, Second places, 1s 3d ; in the Machine to Preston, inside
4s 6d, outside 2s 6d ; from Preston to Lancaster, inside 5s, outside 3s ; the whole from
Liverpool to Lancaster, insides 11s 6d, outsides 6s 9d.   Expenses per land, in the
Diligence to Burscough, 4s, Machine to Preston, 4s 6d, from Preston to Lancaster,
5s ; the whole, 13s 6d.   THOMAS ATKINSON, Clerk, at the Canal." *

* Gore's Liverpool Directory of 1777, page 111.

(1) Gore's General Advertiser of 5th January, 1776.

(2) The Fleece Inn was in Dale-street, Liverpool.

about 43 hours." It left the Fleece Inn every evening at ten, and the Swan-with-two-Necks Inn, Doctor's Commons,[1] London, at 11 [2] every evening. The proprietors advertised that they discharged the expense of turnpikes, and that the drivers were not suffered " to solicit for any gratuity." From the mode in which this vehicle is mentioned in the advertisement, and from its carrying only three passengers, it may be inferred, that it was not constructed in the form of a stage-coach, but that it rather resembled a post-chaise; the advertisement states that it was attended by a guard, and carried three passengers at threepence a mile each, with 10lbs. luggage allowed; and there is a note added to it, thus, " all parcels sent by this conveyance will be delivered immediately after the arrival of *the Chaise* in London." It would scarcely appear to have been successful, as the advertisement was soon discontinued.

About the period which we are now considering, but the exact date cannot be ascertained, coaches with passengers ran constantly from Liverpool, through Warrington, to the place called London-Bridge,[3] at the Duke of Bridgewater's Canal, a short distance beyond Warrington and on the road to Great Budworth; and the passengers were conveyed by the canal boat from that place to Manchester, and *vice versa* from Manchester, by the canal to London-Bridge, and from thence by coach to Liverpool.

---

(1) This Inn appears not to have had any connection with the well-known Swan-with-two-Necks, in Lad-lane, London.

(2) It is not easy to understand how the journey could have been performed in 43 hours if the vehicle left Liverpool at ten in the evening, and arrived, as is evidently meant to be understood, about eleven on the next evening but one afterwards. There seems to have been some mistake in the advertisement, and perhaps 49 hours were intended.

(3) Although it was usually called London-Bridge, it is believed to have been the same place which is called Stockton Quay in the advertisement in Gore's Directory of 1777, which mentions that a Diligence went from John Corner's, every Tuesday and Thursday, " for Warrington and Stockton Quay."—See supra, page 173, (in notis.)

In 1775 waggons were not merely used for the carriage of goods, but, in consequence of the limited number of stage-coaches, many people, and those not of the humblest rank of society, who did not travel on horseback, and to whom it was not convenient to incur the expense of travelling in post-chaises, travelled in waggons in most parts of England.

It may be interesting to learn what Waggons and Carriers arrived at and departed from the following places in Liverpool about that period, as published in the Liverpool Directory :—[1]

" WAGGONS AND CARRIERS."

" The London Stage Waggons come to, and set out from the Nag's Head, in College-lane, every Tuesday and Friday, with goods and passengers to and from London, or any part of the road: The owners are Joseph Hulse, Thomas Widders, Jonathan Higginson, and W. Widders. T. Sutton, book keeper; who may be spoke with every day upon 'change, at 'change hours."

" William Molding and Thomas Roberts come to the Woolpack, Mr. Edward Woods's, in Dale-street, every Tuesday, Thursday and Saturday, and go out the same days, carry all sorts of goods to and from Warrington, Manchester, Stockport, Macclesfield, Knutsford, and most parts of Derbyshire, Sheffield, and most parts of Yorkshire. Put up at the Three Crowns, in the Corn-market, Warrington, every Monday, Wednesday, and Friday, and at the Woolpack, in Deansgate, Manchester, every Tuesday, Thursday, and Saturday."

" William and Daniel Morris come to the Woolpack, Mr. Edward Woods's, in Dale-street, every Wednesday, and go out every Thursday, with goods for Northwich, Middlewich, Namptwich, Sandbach, Holme's-Chapel, and all parts of Staffordshire; and forward goods to Birmingham, Wolverhampton and Litchfield."

" Henry Farrington comes to the Black Horse and Rainbow, Mr. Henry Forshaw's, in High-street, every Wednesday, and goes out every Thursday, carries goods for Ormskirk, Preston, Garstang, Lancaster, Kendal, York, and all parts of Westmoreland and Cumberland."

---

(1) Gore's Liverpool Directory of 1774, page 71.

"John Hesketh comes to the Old Angel, Mr. John Phithian's, in Dale-street, every Monday, and goes out every Tuesday, carries goods for Ormskirk, Preston, Garstang, Lancaster, Kendal, York, and all parts of Westmoreland and Cumberland."

" Richard Gamon comes to the Ince Boat House, in the Old Church yard, almost every day, and takes goods for Chester, and all the adjacent parts."

"Alice Liptrot comes to the Black Bull, in Lord-street, every Wednesday and Saturday, and goes out the same days, and takes goods for Ormskirk."

"John Nicholson comes to Mr. Richard Clarke's, near the Old Dock Gates, every Tuesday and Friday, and sets out the following days, with goods, for Chester, Whitchurch, Newport, Drayton, Salop, Elsmere, Oswestry, Denbigh, Ruthen, Mold, Wrexham, Holywell, and all other parts of Cheshire and North Wales. He sets out from his own house in Chester, every Tuesday and Friday morning."

" Nicholas Carpenter comes to the Crooked Billet, Mr. Robert Ashcroft's, in Tythebarn-street, once a week, days uncertain, and takes goods for Poulton, Kirkham, and all parts of the Filde."

" John and James Parkinson come to the Millstone and Castle, in Dale-street, once a week, days uncertain, and take goods for Poulton, Kirkham, and all parts of the Filde."

" John Riding comes to the Black Bull, in Lord Street, takes goods for all parts of the Filde."

" N.B.—Every Wednesday and Saturday there are Carts at the Cross Keys, and Millstone and Castle, in Dale Street, which carry goods for Ormskirk."[1]

Post-chaises were kept at the Golden Lion, and at two or three of the other principal Liverpool inns, and were commonly used by persons of a superior class in life, who did not undertake journeys either in their own carriages or on horseback.

It would form an exceedingly interesting contrast with the luxury and expensive habits of the present age, if the exact number of private carriages kept in Liverpool, or its

---

(1) Gore's Liverpool Directory of 1774, page 71.

immediate vicinity, at the commencement of the last quarter of the 18th century, could be ascertained. Some attempts have been made to discover it, but it has been found impracticable to do so with any degree of accuracy. Several of the principal merchants kept private carriages, but the number of them was not considerable. Thomas Knowles, a wholesale and retail brush-maker, whose warehouse and shop were in the Potato-market, afterwards called Castle-ditch, who was living in or about 1782, and who was then an old man, had been a servant in the capacity of coachman to Miss Clayton: he was a person well known, and he informed the author's father, that in his (Knowles's) younger days, he drove her carriage, and that it was the only private one then kept in Liverpool.[1]

It has been stated[2] that in 1750, there was only one private carriage kept in Liverpool, and that hackney-coaches were then unknown there; consequently it will not excite surprise in any one to hear, that for many years, both before and after that date, there was a difficulty in meeting with a carriage of any kind for hire; and that there was for a considerable period only one to be hired there. It was a one-horse chaise with a leathern top; it belonged to one James Dimoke; and a boy, named Watt, was accustomed at one period to drive it, and being a sharp lad, his master placed him at an evening school, to learn reading, writing, and arithmetic. The boy afterwards went to Jamaica, but

---

(1) The circumstance is alluded to in Troughton's Liverpool, page 96, where the date of it is stated as 1750, and the carriage is said to have belonged to *Mrs.* Clayton. It may possibly happen that Mr. Troughton had mistaken Miss for Mrs., or the lady may have then become an elderly maiden lady called by either appellation. It is probable, however, that it was Miss Clayton, because in the letter dated 28th September, 1754, giving an account of the rejoicings on the opening of the New Exchange, it is mentioned that a public breakfast was given on each morning of the festivities, at the expense of Mr. Ellis Cunliffe and Miss Clayton.—Troughton's Liverpool, page 95.

(2) Troughton's Liverpool, page 96.

the date of his going thither cannot be ascertained, and returning about forty years afterwards to Liverpool, he inquired whether any of James Dimoke's family were living, and having ascertained that there were two maiden sisters of Dimoke alive, he, to his immortal honour, settled £100 a year upon each of them. The person who evinced this noble trait and amiable disposition, was Mr. Richard Watt, the eminent Liverpool merchant, who died there, leaving to his nephews above half a million sterling, acquired by his own industry, talents, and integrity. He was buried at Standish, in Lancashire, having been born at Shevington, in that parish.[1]

James Dimoke was succeeded in his business by his relation, Jeffry Whalley, who continued the one-horse chaise, and also kept a post-chaise; besides which, he was a cowkeeper, and kept a farmer's inn, and livery-stables, at the corner of Paradise-street and School-lane, near where the building which was recently the Unitarian chapel was afterwards erected.

---

(1) From a *MS.* note, formerly in the possession of the Author's Father.

CHAPTER III.

SITUATION OF LIVERPOOL, ARMORIAL BEARINGS, SEALS, REGALIA,
BOUNDARIES, CHARTERS, MEMBERS OF THE COMMON COUNCIL,
OFFICERS OF THE CORPORATION, MAGISTRATES, BURGESSES,
LOCAL COURTS, POLICE, ECCLESIASTICAL PATRONAGE, FREE
SCHOOL, LANDED ESTATE AND SOURCES OF REVENUE OF THE
CORPORATION IN 1775.   COMMON HALL, AND CONSEQUENT
LEGAL PROCEEDINGS.

LIVERPOOL is situated in the south-westward part of Lancashire, and on the eastward side of the estuary of the Mersey; in latitude 53° 23' 56" North; the longitude of the Town-hall, West of Greenwich, is 2° 59' 45". The difference of time between Greenwich and the Town-hall is 11' 59". The comparatively small portion of the town which was in existence in 1775, stood upon a stratum of sand and soft sandy rock, except the north end, most of which rested on clay or marl.

Before entering upon the general matters connected with the Corporation of Liverpool, and its municipal affairs, it may be advisable to notice the Armorial Bearings of the Corporation of Liverpool. With the exception of a grant of supporters obtained in 1797, the Armorial Bearings were, in 1775, and probably had been for ages before that date, the same as those which are now used. The following is the heraldic description of them :[1]—" Argent, a Cormorant[2] Sable, beaked and legged Gules, holding in the beak a

---

(1) Edmondson's Heraldry vol. 1, title Liverpool; published in 1780.

(2) The Cormorant, or Liver, as it is often called, when describing the Arms of Liverpool, has been an armorial bearing or device of the town for many centuries; besides appearing on the present seal of the town, the antiquity of which is disputed, it appears on the impression of the seal affixed to an old deed of the 4th and 5th of Philip and Mary, preserved in the Town-hall. The word Liver seems to be either a heraldic or a provincial word for a Cormorant; as "Tod" is for a Fox, "Brock" for a Badger, "Lioncel" for a small Lion, &c. &c.

z

branch of Sea-weed called Laver[1] inverted, vert." Crest, "A Cormorant with wings indorsed, Sable, beaked and legged gules; in his beak a sprig of Laver[1] vert." Motto, "*Deus nobis hæc otia fecit.*"

The following is a copy of an instrument of confirmation of the armorial bearings of the Corporation of Liverpool, issued by the authority of the Earl Marshal of England, and dated the 22nd of March, 37th George the Third, 1797 :—

" To all and singular to whom these presents shall come, Sir Isaac Heard, Knight, Garter Principal King of Arms, and George Harrison, Esquire, Norroy King of Arms, from the river Trent, northwards, send Greeting, WHEREAS, the Mayor, Bailiffs, and Burgesses of the town of Liverpool, in the county palatine of Lancaster, have, in their memorial, signed by Thomas Naylor, Esquire, Mayor, Peter W. Brancker, Esquire, Bailiff, and George Case and Clayton Tarleton, Esquires, Aldermen, represented unto the Most Noble Charles, Duke of Norfolk, Earl Marshal, and hereditary Marshal of England, that the arms assumed and used by the Corporation of the said town are a Cormorant, in the beak a branch of Sea-weed called Laver, and for the Crest, a Cormorant as in the Arms, with wings elevated; but that the same not having been registered in the College of Arms, they requested the favour of his Grace's Warrant for our granting, confirming and exemplifying the said Armorial Ensigns, to be borne and used by the said Corporation of the town of Liverpool, and their successors, on Shields, Banners, Seals, or otherwise, according to the ancient usage and Laws of Arms. AND forasmuch as the said Earl Marshal did by Warrant under his hand and seal, bearing date the twenty-first day of March instant, authorize and direct us to grant, exemplify and confirm the said Armorial Ensigns accordingly: KNOW YE THEREFORE, that we the said Garter and Norroy, in pursuance of His Grace's Warrant, and by virtue of the letters patent of our several offices, to each of us respec-

---

(1) In some places a kind of sea-weed is yet called Laver. " Laver Bread, a sort of food made of a sea-plant, that seems to be oister-green, or *Sea Liver-wort*, used in Wales."—Bailey's Dictionary, 23rd edition, of 1773.

" Laver ;" an aquatic plant.—Crabb's Technological Dictionary of 1823.

" Ulva Lactuca. Green Laver or Oyster-green. Common in the sea, and about the mouths of large rivers, growing under water upon stones and shells."—James Edward Smith's English Botany, vol. 22, page 1551.

tively granted, under the great seal of Great Britain, do, by these presents, grant, confirm, and exemplify unto the Mayor, Bailiffs, and Burgesses of the town of Liverpool, the arms following, That is to say, Argent, a Cormorant, in the Beak a Branch of Sea-weed called Laver, all proper; and for the Crest, on a Wreath of the Colours, a Cormorant, the wings elevated, in the beak a Branch of Laver, proper, as the same are in the margin hereof more plainly depicted; to be borne and used for ever hereafter, by the Mayor, Bailiffs and Burgesses of the said town of Liverpool, and their successors in office, in their corporate capacity, on Shields, Banners, Seals, or otherwise, according to the Laws of Arms, without the let or interruption of any person or persons whatsoever. In Witness whereof, We, the said Garter and Norroy Kings of Arms, have to these presents, subscribed our names, and affixed the seals of our several offices, this twenty-second day of March, in the thirty-seventh year of the reign of our sovereign Lord George the Third, by the Grace of God, King of Great Britain, France and Ireland, Defender of the Faith, &c. and in the Year of our Lord One Thousand Seven Hundred and Ninety-seven.

ISAAC HEARD, Garter [seal] Principal King of Arms.

GEORGE HARRISON, Norroy [seal] King of Arms."[1]

It will be observed, that the instrument of confirmation, of the 22nd of March, 1797, states the arms and crest to be " as the same are in the margin hereof *more plainly depicted*." In the shield of arms blazoned in the margin of the instrument, the cormorant, in accordance with the ancient usage of the town, and with the description given in Edmondson's Heraldry,[2] is correctly depicted, " Sable, beaked and legged gules, holding in the beak a branch of sea-weed called Laver, inverted, vert;" the crest is also correctly depicted in the margin, with "wings indorsed sable, beaked and legged gules, in his beak a sprig of Laver, vert." An

---

(1) Copied from the original, in the Town-hall.

(2) Edmondson's Heraldry, vol. 1, title, " Liverpool." The arms of the Earl of Liverpool contain on a chief the arms of the Corporation of Liverpool, as above described, in Edmondson's Heraldry. The Earldom was created on the 28th May, 1796, being about a year before the dates of the above mentioned instruments.

error seems, however, to have crept into the body of the instrument in describing the cormorant, both in the shield and the crest, as " proper," which it may perhaps be superfluous to remind the reader, signifies in heraldry, of the natural or proper colour. The error seems however, to be of no importance, because the reference to the margin, and the blazonry of the arms, in the margin, where they are correctly depicted, must be considered as qualifying and correcting the error in the body of the instrument; but if that had not been the case, it might some time or other have perplexed the officers of the Herald's College, to decide whether the manner of blazoning the arms according to the usage of centuries, or that set out in the body of the instrument, ought to prevail.[1]

The following is a copy of a grant of Supporters to the Arms of Liverpool, dated the 23rd of March, 37th George the Third, A.D. 1797 :—

" To all and singular to whom these presents shall come, Sir Isaac Heard, Knight, Garter Principal King of Arms, sendeth greeting, WHEREAS, the Mayor, Bailiffs and Burgesses of the town of Liverpool, in the county palatine of Lancaster, have in their memorial, sign'd by Thomas Naylor, Esquire, Mayor, Peter W. Brancker, Esquire, Bailiffe, and George Case and Clayton Tarleton, Esquires, Aldermen, represented unto the Most Noble Charles, Duke of Norfolk, Earl Marshal and Hereditary Marshal of England, That Liverpool is a very ancient Corporation by prescription long before the time of King John,[2] who, in the ninth year of his reign granted to the said town a Charter of Incorporation,[2] and the privileges thereby obtained have been confirmed

---

(1) It is also worthy of remark that in the recital in the instrument, respecting the Arms borne by the Corporation, the word " proper" does not occur. These are points which, in a heraldic point of view, are important, though their importance may not be very apparent to persons unacquainted with heraldry.

(2) The above assertions as to *Prescription* and *Incorporation* have been already shown to be erroneous. See Introduction, and the opinion of Mr. Henry Brown, the legal adviser of the Corporation, referred to in it, page 24 and 25.

by several succeeding monarchs; That, by its extensive and flourishing commerce, Liverpool is become the second port of the kingdom; and as agreeably to ancient usage, the chief cities and some of the principal borough towns of this realm, have borne, and do bear, Supporters to their Arms, they trusted that a place so important to the commerce of Great Britain, as the town of Liverpool, might with propriety receive a similar honourable distinction, and therefore requested the favour of his Grace's Warrant for my granting such Supporters, as might be proper to be borne and used with the Arms of Liverpool, by them and their successors in office, on Shields, Banners, Seals, or otherwise, according to the Laws of Arms: KNOW YE THEREFORE, that I, the said Garter, by virtue of my office, and with the consent of the said Earl Marshal, signified to me by Warrant under his hand and seal, bearing date the Twenty-first day of March instant, have devised, and do by these presents grant and assign unto the Mayor, Bailiffs and Burgesses of the said town of Liverpool, the Supporters following, that is to say, the Dexter, Neptune, with his Sea-Green Mantle flowing, the waist wreath'd with Laver; on his head an Eastern-crown Gold,[1] in the right hand his Trident Sable, the left supporting a Banner of the Arms of Liverpool; on the Sinister, a Triton wreath'd as the Dexter, and blow- ing his Shell; the right hand supporting a Banner, thereon a Ship under sail, in perspective, all proper, the Banner Staves or; as the same are in the margin hereof more plainly depicted, to be borne and used for ever hereafter, by the Mayor, Bailiffs and Burgesses of the said town of Liverpool, and their successors in office, in their corporate capacity, on Shields, Banners, Seals, or otherwise, according to the Laws of Arms, without the let or interruption of any person or persons whatsoever. IN WITNESS whereof, I, the said Garter Principal King of Arms, have to these presents subscribed my name, and affixed the seal of my office, this twenty-third day of March, in the Thirty-seventh year of the reign of our Sovereign Lord George the Third, by the grace of God, King of Great Britain, France, and Ireland, Defender of the Faith, &c. and in the year of our Lord One Thousand Seven Hundred and Ninety-seven.

ISAAC HEARD, Garter [seal] Principal King of Arms"[2]

In the shield of arms and crest blazoned in the margin

---

(1) The error of introducing the English word "gold," instead of the heraldic word "or," exists in the original instrument.

(2) Copied from the original in the Town-hall.

of that instrument, the cormorant is also correctly depicted sable, beaked and legged gules.

An exact copy of the armorial bearings, as they are depicted in the margin of the grant of the 23rd of March, 1797, is given at the foot of this page.

Besides the common seal of the borough, which will be described more fully afterwards, it appeared in the course of the proceedings before the Commissioners of Inquiry into the Municipal Corporations of England, in 1833,[1] that there were then also the seal of the Mayor for powers of attorney and other official documents; that of the Mayor and Bailiffs as judges of the Court of Passage; and that called the Town-clerk's seal, which is mentioned in the charter of the 7th of William the Third.

It is not known at what date Liverpool first had a common seal; and, if the charter of King John be as it is considered, a mere grant of a privilege, and not a charter of

---

(1) See the printed report of their proceedings, at Liverpool, page 21.

incorporation,[1] it would, as has been already mentioned,[2] have been not only useless, but irregular, to have had a common seal, before a complete charter of incorporation had been obtained; a circumstance which seems fatal to the theories of persons, who have imagined that the present common seal is either an original, or a copy of one coeval in point of time with King John's charter.

The common seal of Liverpool is of silver, of an oval form : in the centre appears the cormorant with wings elevated holding in its beak a sprig of sea-weed; beneath its breast is a label or scroll, on which are some letters, which have caused some discussion, and the meaning of which possibly may not yet be satisfactorily ascertained. At the extreme end (the sinister side in heraldry) of an impression of the seal, a crescent and a star appear, and at the opposite end are four pellets. From the form of the letters, and some modern ones being introduced, it appears either to be an incorrect copy of one comparatively ancient, or an old one re-cut.

A paper was written some years ago by Wm. Hamper, F.S.A. which appeared in the Archæologia,[3] in which he showed pretty clearly, that the present seal is not an ancient one, but is merely a blundered copy[3] of some older one, executed by an artist ignorant of the Latin language, and probably worked from an injured impression of the original. Mr. Hamper suggested that the circumscription as it now appears, stands thus, the letters considered erroneous being marked by *italics*.[4] SIC*ILIS* CON*MVN*C *D*ORGESIV*D*LEVE*B*, and, for want of room, *IO*DIS, are added on a subsidiary

---

(1) See the opinion of Mr. Henry Brown, the legal adviser of the Corporation, written in 1789, on that subject, referred to in the Introduction, page 24 and 25.

(2) Introduction, page 23 and 24.   (3) Archæologia, vol. 21, page 543.

(4) On referring to an impression of the seal, affixed to a lease from the Corporation, in the Author's possession, it seems to be a matter of doubt, whether the

scroll. The original circumscription is supposed by Mr. Hamper to have been in contractions, as follows, SIGILLV̄ . COMMVNE . BVRGĒSIVM . LEVERPOLIS: i. e. *Sigillum Commune Burgensium Leverpolis,* or " the Common Seal of the Burgesses of Leverpool." Mr. Hamper's opinion appears to be in some degree borne out by more extended researches. An ancient deed of 7th October, of the 4th and 5th of Philip and Mary, belonging to the Corporation of Liverpool, has been subsequently discovered in the Town-hall,[1] and the impression on its seal contains a circumscription, of which, although two or three of the letters are altogether defaced, yet the remainder of it is quite legible. Even that has not the appearance of great antiquity. Some of the letters appear to be an earlier age, than those of the present seal, and so much of the circumscription as is now legible is as follows: "SIGILL CONMVNE —ORGESI—— LEVERPOL"[2] and in a scroll or label underneath are five additional letters, "IOPIS."

---

artist has intended the third letter in the first word of the circumscription, for c or g. Most of the words of the inscription are so close to each other as to leave scarcely any space between them.

(1) Another, and older deed, (which the Author has not had an opportunity of seeing, but which is said to be of the year 1459, 37th Henry the 6th,) is, or recently was in the possession of Lord Lilford, of which the seal is said to be similar. The Author has a copy of the impression of it which is imperfect, and does not throw any additional light on the subject.

(2) The letter B, with which the third word evidently once commenced, is completely defaced and illegible. At the spot before the word or part of the word " LEVERPOL" the impression is defaced or imperfect, and the Author after more than one examination of the seal appended to the deed, both with the naked eye and with a magnifying glass, ascertained that it was impossible for any person to decide, from an inspection of it, what letters (if any) had been there; but they most probably were the letters v and M, the last letters of the previous word, (intended for *Burgensium,*) and as far as respects that word it seems nearly to tally with Mr. Hamper's solution. The Author again had access to the deed, and carefully examined the impression on its seal, whilst this work was in the press, and, as far as the letters are perfect or can now be read with any degree of certainty, the above copy of the circumscription has been correctly made, and corresponds in all respects with the impression.

It seems, therefore, though it is by no means certain, that the circumscription on the seal used for the deed of 7th October, in the 4th and 5th of Philip and Mary, and from which it is possible that the seal now in use may have been incorrectly copied, was intended (without the contractions) to be read thus, " *Sigillum Commune Burgensium Leverpoliopis,*"[1]—or "the common seal of the Burgesses of Liverpool," a reading perfectly in accordance with the style of many other corporation seals.[2]   This does not differ much from the solution given by Mr. Hamper, which, if not altogether correct, appears to be very nearly so; but as the original seal is not to be found, it appears to be impossible for any person to decide the point.

The present Regalia of the Corporation are modern, but it is evident from the following entry in the Council book, that more ancient regalia were in existence in 1761 :—

"At a Council held the second day of December, 1761,
Ordered, That the Deputy Water-Bailiff do attend and carry the oar on state days, and other proper times.
Ordered, That the Corporation Regalia be new guilt and repaired."[3]

New regalia were ordered in 1763 :—

"At a Special Council held the twenty-second day of December, 1763,
Ordered, That a new Corporation Regalia, viz : a sword, sergeant's mace, and two sub-bailiffs' maces be provided at the expense of this Corporation, and that Mr. Mayor be desired to order the same according to the models thereof sent him from London."[3]

---

(1) It may probably occur to the reader that it is remarkable that, both in the present and the older seal, the word (in contractions) intended for Burgensium, seems to have been spelt Borgensium, contrary to the more usual mode.

(2) The word " Leverpoliopis," if that be the word meant, as there seems reason to believe, is quite as good a genitive case, as many which, in the mediæval times, have been used with respect to cities and towns in England, as for example, the circumscription on the seal of Carlisle, terminates with the words "Civivm Karliolensis," on that of Cambridge, " Villæ Cantabrigiæ," on that of Chichester, " Civitatis Cicestriæ," on that of Rochester, " Civitatis Rofensis," and on that of Pontefract, " Bvrgensivm Pontisfracti," * and various other instances might be adduced.

* Lewis' Topographical Dictionary.

(3) Council Book, vol. 11, page 237 and 288.
A l

In February, 1784, the Exchange was robbed of the regalia, by Charles Coney, who was convicted and executed for the offence at the ensuing March assizes.

The regalia now in use consist of a large mace, of the Sergeant-at-Mace, on which is the inscription :—

> " JOHN GREGSON, Esq$^{re.}$
> Mayor,
> JOSEPH BROOKS, Jun$^{r.}$
> JOHN GREENWOOD,
> Gent$^{n.}$ Bailiffs.
> 1785."

Also two smaller maces of the sub-bailiffs, on each of which are the same inscription and date. Besides which there is the silver oar of the water-bailiff, which has also the same inscription and date, and an additional date on the blade, of 1785. They are all of silver. There is also a handsome sword of state, which was carried before the Mayor, pursuant to the Charter of the 7th of William the Third; a custom which is still kept up. Probably Charles Coney did not consider the sword worth stealing, as it could not be melted down. It is inscribed,

> " 1764,
> GEORGE CAMPBELL,
> Mayor."

Would not some of the readers who take snuff exclaim against the author, if the old snuff-box of the Corporation were to be passed over without notice? May they not say: " True it is, that the snuff-box cannot be strictly considered as forming part of the regalia, but it is, and has been, as long as we can remember it, most deservedly a great favourite. Often when we have dined at the Town-hall, and had inadvertently left our snuff-boxes at home, we have watched the box, after dinner, in its travels round the table, and anxiously waited for its arrival, in order to secure a

pinch of its contents."   Perhaps it would scarcely be right
to omit a brief notice of this old and favourite box.   It is of
silver, of very large size, with a detached lid; and is believed
to have been, in days of yore, the tobacco-box of the Corporation, the members of which, when they became more
refined than to chew tobacco, advanced it to the higher grade
of a snuff-box, and caused it to be introduced at the Town-hall
after the dinners given there.   On its side is the inscription:—

> " The Corporation of Leverpoole's Box—1690."

As connected, to a certain extent, with this subject, the
sword of state, which was carried before Sir William Norris,
of Speke, in his embassy to the Great Mogul, may be here
noticed.   It was presented to the Corporation of Liverpool,
in 1702 in the mayoralty of Mr. John Cockshutt, and is
preserved in the Council-room; and in a frame under it is
the following inscription :—

> " This Sword of State,
> carried before
> His Excellency Sir Wᴹ Norris, of
> Speake, in his Embassy to the Great
> Mogul, was given as a memorial of
> his respect to this Corporation,
> Anno Domini, 1702,
> John Cockshutt, Mayor."

As the Municipal Corporations Reform Act[1] has made
a great change in the ancient boundaries of Liverpool, it
may not be out of place to mention what the extent of the town
formerly was.   The limits of the borough and parish of Liverpool were co-extensive before that act was passed; and when

---

(1) Act 5th and 6th William the 4th, chap. 76:—" An Act to provide for the
Regulation of Municipal Corporations in England and Wales ;" which enacts, by section
7th, that the boundaries of certain boroughs, mentioned in a Schedule to the Act,
including Liverpool, shall be the same as were then settled by the Act of 2nd and 3rd
William the 4th, chap. 64 ; " An Act to settle and describe the divisions of Counties
and the limits of Cities and Boroughs in England and Wales, so far as respects the

the inquiry respecting the Corporation of Liverpool took place before the Commissioners of Inquiry into Municipal Corporations, the following statement respecting the limits, was deposed to before them in November, 1833, by the then Town-clerk, and it will be observed that after allowing for some slight changes made in the boundary at particular points, in order to make the line of demarcation more straight, as will be afterwards noticed, the limits of the borough and parish were very nearly the same in 1775 as in 1833 :—

" SITUATION AND BOUNDARIES OF THE BOROUGH AND PARISH OF LIVERPOOL."

" The borough and parish of Liverpool are co-extensive, and adjoin on the west to the river Mersey, on the south to the township of Toxteth-park, on the east in part to the township of West Derby, and in other part to the township of Everton, and on the north to the township of Kirkdale.

" The Boundaries are as follows :—

" The Western Boundary, commencing at the low-water mark of

Election of Members to serve in Parliament." By Section 35, of the last-mentioned act, and Schedule O annexed to it, Liverpool is now, as to Elections, comprised within the following boundaries, viz :—

"From the western extremity of Dingle-lane, on the south of the town, along Dingle-lane, to the point at which the same meets Ullet-lane ; thence along Ullet-lane to the point at which the same meets Lodge-lane ; thence along Lodge-lane to the point at which the same meets Smithdown-lane ; thence along Smithdown-lane to the point at which the same is met by the boundary of the township of Wavertree ; thence, northward, along the boundary of the township of Wavertree to that point thereof which is nearest to the south-eastern corner of the wall of the new Botanic-gardens ; thence, in a straight line, to the said south-eastern corner ; thence along the eastern wall of the new Botanic-gardens to the point at which such wall reaches Edge-lane ; thence, eastward, along Edge-lane to a point seventy-four yards distant from the point last described ; thence, in a line parallel to the new street called Grove-street, to the point at which such parallel line reaches the London-road ; thence along the London-road to the point at which the same is joined by Deane-street ; thence, in a straight line, to the Boundary Stone in Rake-lane, near the southern extremity of Whitefield-lane ; thence, northward, along the boundary of the township of Everton to the point at which the same joins the boundary of the township of Kirkdale ; thence, northward, along the boundary of the township of Kirkdale to the point at which the same reaches the high-water mark of the river Mersey ; thence, along the high-water mark of the river Mersey, to that point thereof which is nearest to the point first described ; thence, in a straight line, to the point first described."

the river Mersey, where a brook called Beacon's Gutter, enters the river and continuing from thence southward along the low-water mark of the said river to the centre of a certain slip or basin called 'Etna Slip.'

" The Southern Boundary, commencing from the centre of ' Etna Slip,' and running from thence eastwardly across the southernmost end of the Queen's Dock to the western termination of Parliament-street; thence along the south side of the said street and of Upper Parliament-street to the south-eastern termination of Crown-street.

" The Eastern Boundary, commencing at the termination last specified, and running from thence along the east side of a street situate between Upper Parliament-street aforesaid and Pembroke-place, called Crown-street; thence along the line of an ancient ditch or water-course between Pembroke-place and London-road, at the distance of   feet eastwardly from the walls of the yards or inclosures of the houses there; thence along the east side of a street situate between the London-road aforesaid and Upper Islington, called Moss-street, to a boundary-stone at the north-east corner of Carver-street; thence along the north-east side of Carver-street, the east side of certain intended streets to be made through certain land in the several occupations of John Ewart and Henry Williams Ross, and the north side of Mansfield-street as far as Soho-street; thence along the east side and to the north termination of Soho-street; thence across Richmond-row, and along the north side thereof as far as Fox-street, and along the east side of the improved line thereof into Great Homer-street, and along the east side of the same street; thence along the east side of a street of twenty yards wide, continuing from Great Homer-street afore-said to and terminating at the township of Kirkdale.

" The Northern Boundary, commencing at the last-mentioned termination, and running from thence westwardly in a straight line in part along the north side of a certain intended street as far as New Scotland-road; then crossing the said road and running in continuation westwardly along the north side of the same intended street as far as Vauxhall-road; then crossing Vauxhall-road in an oblique direction, and running westwardly (crossing the Leeds and Liverpool Canal) for a space of 460 yards; then turning off at a right angle and running northwardly along the east side of the continuation of such intended street for a space of 248 yards; then turning off at another right angle and running westwardly on the north side of the continuation of such intended street as far as a street intended to form a continuation of Regent-road for a space of 200 yards; then running still further westwardly in a straight line across the shore of the river Mersey along the said brook called Beacon's Gutter to the before-mentioned low-water mark of the said river."[1]

There were some slight changes made in the limits at some particular points, in order to make the line of demarcation more straight, and the boundaries were finally settled and defined by Acts of Parliament, viz: the 1st of George the Fourth, chap. 13, and 11th of George the Fourth, chap. 15; and except those slight changes, and except the alteration in appearance caused by streets, squares, houses and docks having being erected or made, in the places, where formerly there were open fields and unbuilt or waste ground, the boundaries of the borough and parish of Liverpool, remained the same in 1833, when the inquiry took place respecting the Corporation of Liverpool, before the Commissioners of Inquiry, as they had been from 1775 to the close of the 18th century.

In the Corporation records of the year 1671, is a description of the boundaries of Liverpool, as follows:—

" THE BONDARIES OF LIVERPOOLE.

" The Perambulacon is from the Water Street end, to Beeton Guttar on the N——— of Liverpoole, thence to the Grove, and the Meyre Stone in Mr. Moore's mead— thence to Kirkdall Lane, to the Meyre Stone there, overagainst the beakon th—, to a meyre stone in Syres ditch, adioining to the Breck, thence through ——— thence through sev'rall Closses, to a meyr stone up Everton Cawsey, thence through severall Fields to Liverpoole Comon, and soe after the Comon side to the meyr stone at Johnsons field end, on the east side of the Towne, and soe up the Guttar or ——— to the Mosslake, to a place called Hollin hedge, and thence straight to the Park Wall, and all along the Parke Wall, and through two Crofts to Booths Mill, and soe to the sea side, and all along the Sea side over the Poole, and thence along the sea side to Water Street end.

---

(1) Printed Report of the Proceedings before the Commissioners of Inquiry into Municipal Corporations, in November, 1833, page 10.

" Our liberty at Sea to arrest within the flood mark, is on both sides the River of Mersey, as for upward as the same fflowes, with Custome or Toll on either side of the River with other usuall priviledges of the River."[1]

The Charter of King John has been before mentioned as the earliest Liverpool charter of any description. There were also a number of other charters obtained from succeeding sovereigns. The following is a list of the various Charters which have been granted to Liverpool, with their respective dates :—

1st.—9th John, 28th August, 1207.

2nd.—13th Henry the Third, 24th March, 1229, by which Liverpool is declared a free borough for ever, with a guild.

3rd.—6th Edward the Third, 22nd Jan. 1333,} confirming those of King
4th.—5th Richard the Second, 11th June, 1382.} John and King Henry.

5th.—1st Henry the Fourth, 9th May, 1400.   } confirming all the
6th.—2nd and 3rd Philip and Mary, 4th Jan. 1556.} former Charters.

7th.—2nd Charles the First, 4th July, 1626 ; by which an entirely new Charter was granted to the burgesses of Liverpool, by the style and title of " the Mayor, Bailiffs and Burgesses of Liverpool," which was the foundation of the late constitution of the Corporation. A Charter was granted by King Charles the Second, but was afterwards abrogated, and is not in the possession of the Corporation.

8th.—1st James the Second, 1685.   } also abrogated.
9th.—3rd William and Mary, 9th March, 1692.}

10th.—7th William the Third, 26th September, 1695 ; under the great seal, reciting, *totidem verbis*, the Charter of King Charles the First, and it was the governing Charter of the Corporation. Another copy of the same Charter, under the seal of the Duchy, is in the Court of the county palatine of Lancaster.

11th.—25th George the Second, 26th March, 1752. By this Charter the Mayor was empowered to act as a Justice of the Peace for four years next after the expiration of his office, and the four Aldermen next to the senior Alderman were made additional

---

(1) Printed Report of the Proceedings at Liverpool before the Commissioners of Inquiry into Municipal Corporations, in 1833, page 287 and 288.

Justices so long as they might continue members of the Council, and took the same oaths as were prescribed by the Charter of William the Third, for the senior Alderman in the like capacity; power was also given to the Recorder to appoint a deputy in case of absence or sickness.

12th.—48th George the Third, 19th January, 1808; by which all Aldermen, together with the Mayor and Recorder, or his deputy, were made Justices of the Peace; and every person who had served the office of Mayor was made Coroner for the succeeding four years.

13th.—8th George the Fourth, 28th April, 1828, which made the person who had passed the office of Mayor, Coroner for the next year only, and he, with the Bailiffs for the time being, were made Coroners.[1]

These Charters were produced and proved in November, 1833, before the Commissioners of Inquiry into Municipal Corporations; but since the Municipal Corporations Reform Act of the 5th and 6th William the Fourth, chap. 76, (1835,) " An Act to provide for the regulation of Municipal Corporations in England and Wales;" the whole system as respects such Corporations has been changed, and in the main outlines and features of municipal government, nearly all the cities and boroughs in England and Wales have been assimilated.

The Corporation of Liverpool consisted, in 1775, of a Mayor, Bailiffs and Burgesses, who formed the Common Council of the borough, comprising forty-one members, acting under the authority of the governing charter, which has been before mentioned. Of these members, every one who had served the office of Mayor became an Alderman and Magistrate for the borough, whilst he remained a member of the Council.

---

(1) See the printed Report of the Proceedings at Liverpool before the Commissioners of Inquiry into Municipal Corporations in 1833, from which many of the particulars given in this Chapter relative to the Corporation have been extracted.

THE EXCHANGE (NOW THE TOWN HALL)

a.s it was before the Fire in 1795.

G.Jarman. sc.

MEMBERS OF THE COMMON COUNCIL OF LIVERPOOL,
on the 18th of October, 1775.

James Clemens, *Mayor.*
Owen Salisbury Brereton, *Recorder.*

Ralph Peters, *Deputy-Recorder.*
Francis Gildart, *Town-Clerk.*

Thomas Shaw
James Gildart
Charles Goore
Richard Hughes
Sir Robert Cunliffe, Bart.
Lawrence Spencer
John Blackburne, Jun.
John Williamson
William Gregson
John Crosbie
Ralph Earle
John Sparling
Thomas Wilson
Thomas Golightly
John Parr
Peter Rigby

} *Aldermen.*

James Kelsall
William Penkett
Joseph Jackson
John Parr
William Boats
William Crosbie, Sen.
Henry Trafford
William Pickering
   (died in 1775)
John Hughes
William Pole
John Brown
Thomas Birch
Thomas Earle
Richard Statham
Richard Gerard
John Colquit
James Gildart, Jun.
   [*Two Vacancies.*]

William Crosbie, Jun.
George Case
} *Bailiffs.*

The public business of the Corporation used to be transacted in the Exchange, now called the Town-hall. The edifice contained, besides an assembly room[1] and other entertaining rooms, the council room, the magistrates' court room, the offices of the treasurer and the surveyor, the loan office, and other offices[2] connected with the Corporation; and also the hall-keeper's apartments. The Court of Quarter Sessions for the trial of offences, and the Court of Passage for civil causes, were held in the building; and in front of it, towards Castle-street, the hustings on the election of the members of parliament, and of mayors and bailiffs, used to be erected. Public meetings were also held in the edifice, and the mayor's dinners and other entertainments were given in it.

(1) Chapter I, page 73.

(2) At one period, a portion at least of the business connected with the Town-clerk's department, was transacted at an office, on the west side of Fenwick-street.

B 1

By the governing Charter of 7th William the Third,[1]
(26th September, 1695,) the title of the Corporation was
expressed to be, " The Mayor, Bailiffs and Burgesses of
the town of Liverpool, in the county of Lancaster." Pursuant to that charter the Common Council consisted of
forty-one members, including the Mayor, the two Bailiffs,
the Recorder, and a Town-clerk,[2] called in the charter, "the
Common Clerk." The Recorder and Town-clerk were elected
by the Council, and they held their offices " quamdiu se bene
gesserint." Two Sub-bailiffs and a Sword-bearer were also
mentioned in the charter, as to be chosen by the Council;
which completes the list of what may be called chartered
officers.

The Mayor was annually elected from amongst the
members of the Council at a Court of Election, held on the
feast of St. Luke, the 18th of October, without any notice,
for being charter day, it was universally known, and notice
was not necessary. The election took place by the freemen,
or, as they were otherwise called, free burgesses, at hustings,
before the outgoing Mayor and Bailiffs. The new Mayor
might be put in nomination at the hustings by any free
burgess, (the practice being, as was usual in other places,
for one burgess to nominate him, and another to second
the nomination,) and if there were more than one nomination, it was the custom to proceed to a poll, which used to
be taken in tallies of ten at a time, and the member of the
Council so nominated, if returned by the majority of votes,
was sworn in at the same court, or as soon as he attended

---

(1) The Charter is in Latin, but a copy and also a translation have been published
in the printed Report of the Proceedings at Liverpool before the Commissioners of
Inquiry into Municipal Corporations, in 1833.

(2) Prior to the Act for the regulation of Municipal Corporations the person who
held the office of Town-clerk of Liverpool, held also various other beneficial appointments, which will be mentioned afterwards.

afterwards.[1]   The election ought, if possible, to be finished
on the charter day; in a contested election, therefore, the
poll has occasionally been kept open until twelve at night;
on subsequent days there was not the same necessity, and
the usual time of polling was about eight hours a day.   The
contest has been known to last several days; in general,
however, it terminated some time in the course of one day.
It was necessary that the Mayor should be a member of the
Council, but beyond that there was no restriction.   He was
not elected in rotation, and could not serve the office two
years in succession; being returning officer, he could not
elect himself.   The Mayor was elected to hold the office
for one year, and in case of absence or sickness, he had the
power of appointing a deputy to represent him, which was
frequently acted upon.   He was not only a justice of the
peace for the borough, but was, during the mayoralty, also
(after taking the usual oath) one for the county of Lancaster.   He was the chairman at the quarter sessions for the
borough, and also, assisted by the Recorder, at the Mayor's
Court, called the Court of Passage, at which the Mayor presided, for the trial of civil causes, where the cause of action
arose within the borough; he also presided at the meetings
of the Common Council; and was returning officer at the
election of members of parliament for the borough, and at
the election of his successor in office.   He had the privilege
of nominating a burgess after his year of office had expired;
but that appears to have been a matter rather of courtesy
than of right, and it was given by a resolution of the
Council, generally at the first Council after the expiration of
his year of office.

Instances have occurred of serious riots on the occasion

---

(1) The printed Report of the Proceedings at Liverpool, before the Commissioners
of Inquiry into Municipal Corporations, in 1833.

of elections of Mayors of Liverpool. In 1757, at the election of Mr. William Goodwin, a riot took place; the hustings were destroyed, the houses of Mr. Campbell, one of the Aldermen, and of Mr. Carr, were attacked, and the windows of the Exchange were broken. Two remarkable entries appear in the proceedings of the Council relative to it:—

" At a Council, held this sixth day of July, 1768,

Ordered, That Mr. Alderman Campbell be paid the expenses he was at in defending his house and the Exchange from a mob, in the year 1757, who assembled and threatened to pull the said Exchange and buildings down, and in prosecuting the said rioters, being about the sum of forty-two pounds, and that the Treasurer be allowed it in his accounts." [1]

" At a Council, held the 3rd day of August, 1768,

Ordered, That the executors of the late Mr. Laurence Carr, be paid the sum of four pounds for damages done to his house by the mob, in the year 1757, when the 'Change and Mr. Campbell's house were damaged, and that the Treasurer be allowed it in his accounts." [2]

At the close of a contested election for the office of Mayor, it was formerly not unusual to chair, as it was called, the successful candidate from the hustings to his own house. He was carried home in triumph in a chair,[3] borne on men's shoulders, accompanied by a procession of his supporters and friends, with colours, a band of music, &c. The last Liverpool Mayor who underwent that ceremony was Mr. Peter Whitfield Brancker:[3] it took place on Sunday afternoon, the 18th October, 1801; he was carried from the hustings in Castle-street, to his house in Colquitt-street, on the site of which the Apothecaries'-hall now stands; and

---

(1) Council Book of the Corporation, of 1768, vol. 2, page 463.

(2) Council Book, of 1768, vol. 2, page 465.

(3) The Author, when a child, saw Mr. George Dunbar (afterwards Sir George Dunbar, Bart.) chaired, in 1796, and Mr. Peter Whitfield Brancker, in 1801, on their respective elections to the office of Mayor.

the bearers being, as was not unusual on such occasions, drunk, had very nearly overthrown the new Mayor, opposite the Athenæum, whilst the procession was passing through Church-street.

The allowance out of the funds of the town to each Mayor of Liverpool towards the expenses of the entertainments, &c. of his mayoralty, was 300 guineas, prior to the 2nd November, 1774,[1] when the amount was raised to £400, by a resolution of a Council held on that day, viz :—

It is Ordered, That the thanks of this Council be given to the late Mr. Mayor, Alderman John Parr, for his diligent, upright and steady discharge of his said office of Mayor of this Borough and Corporation, during the last year, and that he be paid and allowed the sum of four hundred pounds for and towards defraying the expense thereof, which said allowance shall be continued to all future Mayors during the pleasure of the Council only."[2]

Some years, however, before the close of the 18th century, the allowance to the Mayor was doubled.[3]

In connection with the yearly vote of a sum of money to the outgoing Mayor, there is a circumstance relative to the late Mr. John Shaw, which merits notice here. He was Mayor in 1794, and also in 1800. He was slovenly in his dress, not courteous or polished in his deportment, nor was he always grammatical in his language; but he made an impartial, active and excellent chief magistrate. Many of our readers must recollect the dismal season of scarcity and distress of 1800. Mr. Shaw was then Mayor, and exerted himself, as much as man could do, on behalf of the suffering poor. Once he used a vigour beyond the law : a large quantity of fresh herrings had been imported, and

(1) Council Book, vol. 11, page 634.   (2) Ibid. vol. 11, page 686.   (3) Ibid. vol. 13, page 420.   Ibid. in 1795, page 129 ; in 1796, page 237 ; in 1797, page 289, and in 1798, page 359.

some persons were under an engagement to supply, or, at least intended to supply, some neighbouring place with them ; he however caused the carts when loaded with them to be stopped, and prevented from leaving the town, stating that, as the poor people in Liverpool were in need of them, he would have the town supplied first. He knew that having stopped the carts, the owners of the fish could not wait long to argue the matter, for they must of necessity soon sell them. His motive was a benevolent one, and he was willing to expose himself to all consequences or damages to which he might be liable, at the instance of the persons who had, by his acts, been deprived of profit, upon the sale of the herrings in any other place. He refused to give any entertainments, or, at least, he scarcely gave any, during his mayoralty, and came to the conclusion to devote to the public charities the money which they would have cost: after its termination, the Common Council, impressed with a due sense of the exemplary conduct of Mr. Shaw, during a season of such severe distress and scarcity, passed a resolution,[1]

> " That the thanks of this Council be presented to Mr. Alderman Shaw, the late Mayor, for his very attentive, impartial and disinterested conduct in the duties of his office, and his very particular exertions to keep down the high price of provisions, and render every possible assistance to alleviate the distresses of the honest and labouring poor in a season of most extreme scarcity and difficulty. That the sum of eight hundred pounds, as the usual Mayor's allowance, be paid him by the Treasurer and passed in his accounts, and that he be also allowed the nomination of his Mayor's freeman, according to ancient custom."[1]

Mr. Shaw, in consequence, received the £800, and

---

(1) At a meeting of the Common Council, held on the 6th of January, 1802.—See the Council Book, vol. 13, page 565. After Mr. John Shaw's previous mayoralty, by a vote of the Common Council, of the 4th November, 1794, he had the usual £800 voted to him for the expenses of his mayoralty.—Council Book, vol. 13, page 129.

immediately distributed it amongst the public charities of the town. As he was by no means a general favourite, it is only an act of justice to his memory, to record these good features in his character.

He was for many years a member of the Council, and had a very exalted idea of the importance of the office. It is not necessary to discuss here whether the members of the old Council were, as a body, remarkable for talent or otherwise, but though he did not want abilities, he seemed very averse to men of abilities being admitted into that body. On one occasion, when a person of considerable talents was talked of as a proper man to be proposed for a vacant seat in that body, he was known to say with perfect seriousness, " I don't like clever fellows being admitted into the Council. What is the use of so many clever fellows? There are J——n H——d, G——e D——r, and myself; we are quite a sufficient number for the Council."[1]

The Deputy-Mayor was appointed by an instrument in writing upon a stamp, under the hand and seal of the Mayor, in the nature of a power of attorney, which was destroyed when its temporary object had been effected. The Deputy-Mayor was sworn in, in the same manner as the Mayor; and it is remarkable, that the charter did not expressly direct that the deputy should be a member of the Council; it merely directed that he should be " some one other free burgess of the town."

The Bailiffs were also elected on St. Luke's Day, the 18th October, after being nominated by two burgesses in

---

(1) In 1852 some letters appeared in a Liverpool newspaper, purporting to contain accounts and information respecting Liverpool a few years ago. The Author read some, but not the whole of them, and noticed that the above anecdote respecting the speech of Mr. John Shaw is attributed, in error, to a Liverpool banker, who was too guarded to make any such remark. In fact, it was a matter of notoriety, and caused a good deal of conversation, at the time when Mr. Shaw made the above observation.

the same manner as the Mayor was nominated. They were elected like the Mayor for one year. The instances of a contest and a poll for the Bailiffs were rare, but they have occasionally occurred. They were officers of the court called the Court of Passage, the local court of record for the borough, at which the Mayor presided, for the trial of civil causes; and it was considered that without the presence of one of the Bailiffs, that court could not be legally held.[1]

They had in the borough the functions of Sheriffs, with respect to juries ; one of their duties being to summon grand juries, petty juries, and coroner's juries : the free burgesses only served upon them.

They used also formerly to act as billet-masters, and an allowance was voted to them to cover expenses incurred in executing that office ; and the duty of billeting soldiers in their passage through the town devolved upon them; but many years previous to the Act for the regulation of Municipal Corporations, it was found necessary to appoint a permanent billet-master, after which, the allowance was paid to him, as part of his salary, and was never received by the Bailiffs.

Two Sub-bailiffs were directed by the charter to be chosen by the Council from the burgesses. They were constables of the borough, and their principal duty was to assist the Bailiffs in summoning juries. They were appointed annually by the Council, and were generally re-elected.

The Recorder was appointed by the Council ; he had power to appoint a deputy in case of sickness or absence only. The practice appears always to have been to elect a barrister, but that was not required by the charter, which stated that he should be " one honest and discreet man,

(1) By the modern Charter of 8th George the 4th, (28th April, 1828,) the person who had last passed the office of Mayor, was Coroner for the next year only, and he, with the Bailiffs, for the time being, were made Coroners.

skilful in the laws of England." He was a borough magistrate by virtue of his office. He assisted the magistrates as chairman of the Court of Quarter Sessions, and of the Court of Passage, or Mayor's Court, which were held four times in the year. He also usually assisted the Mayor as Assessor, under a retainer, at elections.

> RECORDERS OF LIVERPOOL IN THE 18TH CENTURY.
> 1709, Bertie Entwistle, *died.*
> 1723, Thos. Henry Ashurst, *resigned 27th Sept.* 1742.
> 1742, Owen Salisbury Brereton.
> 1797, Francis Hargrave.

The Town-clerk, called in the governing charter, the " Common-clerk," was also appointed by the Council ; and that office formerly embraced the several duties of Clerk to the Mayor's Court, or Court of Passage, Clerk of the Peace for the Borough, Clerk to the Coroners, and Clerk to the Magistrates, and he was the legal adviser of the Mayor for the time being. At one period, the Town-clerk was also the Vestry-clerk, for conducting the legal matters of the parish of Liverpool.[1]

Before the passing of the Act 5th and 6th William the Fourth, chap. 76, " An Act to provide for the regulation of Municipal Corporations in England and Wales," the Town-clerk, for the time being, held also various other appointments of a public nature. Pursuant to a resolution of the Council of 1st August, 1832, a report was made by the Select Finance Committee, enumerating the then duties of the Town-clerk as follows :—

" The Town-clerk is the keeper of the Corporation records and

---

(1) Some Advertisements appear in *Williamson's Liverpool Advertiser*, of 1756, signed Francis Gildart, Town-clerk, requiring the immediate delivery at the Workhouse of the Parish, of bills or demands, for provisions, goods, or articles, furnished to it ; and it is tolerably certain that the advertisements would not have been inserted by the Town-clerk, if he had not also been professionally employed by the parish as Vestry-clerk.

C l

title deeds, and has the preparation and registry of the Corporation leases, and purchase deeds.

" He is the Clerk of the Peace at the Licensing and Quarter Sessions.

" He is the officer of the Mayor's, or Civil Court.

" He is the Clerk to the Mayor and Bailiffs as returning officers at elections.

" He may be the Clerk to the Coroners of the Borough, with the approbation of the Coroners for the time being.

" He is the official legal adviser of the Mayor for the time being, in reference to the various duties he is called upon from time to time to discharge, in his municipal character, and is to prepare all documents, and other matters connected with the Mayor's office, (except such as are connected with his magisterial duties in the police office.)

" That as Clerk of the Council he has the custody and arrangement of all minutes and proceedings of that body.

" That he has the conduct and management of all legal and parliamentary business of the Corporation."

It will be observed from the above, that the office of Clerk of the Magistrates had, at the time of that report, been severed from that of Town-clerk, with which it used formerly to be enjoyed.

TOWN-CLERKS OF LIVERPOOL IN THE 18TH CENTURY.

1706, Ralph Peters.
1742, Francis Gildart.
1780, William Gregson, jun.
1781, John Colquitt.

The Sword-Bearer was another officer directed by the governing charter, which empowered the Common Council " to choose and name one honest man within the said town to be Sword-Bearer," and gives power to the Corporation to have a sword, and to cause it to be carried before the Mayor of the town.

The Common Council was composed exclusively of free burgesses or freemen, as they were called. The number was forty-one, including the Mayor, Bailiffs, Town-clerk, and Recorder, according to the governing Charter of 7th William the Third: " Forty and one honest and discreet men of the burgesses of the town aforesaid, who shall be, and be called the Common Council of the said town." In order to constitute a Council it was necessary that twenty-five members must have been present. Instances have occurred of the removal of members of the Council for non-residence or other causes.

The members were self-elected; and it was a remarkable circumstance, that the Charter of the 7th of William the Third, did not expressly define the manner in which the members of the Council were to be elected, but merely stated, that they should be elected in the same manner as was accustomed before the grant of the abrogated Charter of the 29th of Charles the Second; a vague expression, which gave rise to considerable differences and litigation. The Corporation muniments showed that persons were elected by the members of the Council to supply vacancies in it before that charter was granted, and consequently, they continued the usage of self-election after the Charter of William the Third. There have been two decisions in a court of law connected with that subject; namely, the cases of the King against Mr. Richard Walker, and the King against Mr. (afterwards Sir Joseph) Birch, which were tried in 1792 and 1793. The case of the King v. Walker established, that a common councilman, elected (in 1791) at a common-hall or public assembly (called by the Mayor and a Bailiff) of the burgesses, and by their voices, was not elected in the mode accustomed before the granting of the Charter of Charles the Second; and the other, viz: the King against Birch, established, that a common councilman, elected at a court of election, on the Mayor's election day, (not a common-hall as before,) in 1792, by the burgesses, was also not elected in the mode accustomed before the Charter of Charles the Second.[1]

_____

[1] See the printed Report of the Proceedings before the Commissioners of Inquiry

The system of self-election, by which the numbers of the Common Council of Liverpool were kept up, was a very general and great defect in the municipal corporations of that period.   In Liverpool it produced its usual results : family connections, intimacy in private life, or status in society, and not talents, public services, or worth, in nine cases out of ten, were the tests for deciding the admission into Council, or the rejection of any person who might be proposed.   The Council were sadly too exclusive, and, consequently, the affairs of the town got into the hands of a knot of men, many of whom were nearly related to each other by consanguinity or marriage, who, though generally persons of property and respectability, were not superior in those respects to many others who might have been introduced into the Common Council of Liverpool, to the satisfaction of the inhabitants. Mankind are very prone to rush from one extreme to another, and it may be difficult to decide, whether the disadvantage to the town of self-election under the old system, or of too frequent popular elections under the new one, is the greatest. Opinions differ upon that point.

Besides the chartered officers, there were several other officers of the Corporation, some of whose duties were of considerable moment, and all of them were elected by the Common Council.

The principal officer not named in the Charter was the Treasurer, through whose hands the revenue of the Corporation passed.   He was the general Treasurer of all the finances of the Corporation, for keeping the cash and paying all disbursements, and he found sureties for the due performance of his office.

---

into Municipal Corporations, in 1833, pages 51, 52 and 478.   There is some confusion on page 478 in the printed report of those proceedings, as the names of Mr. Walker and Mr. Birch seem, by mistake, to have been transposed.

TREASURERS OF LIVERPOOL IN THE 18TH CENTURY.

31st August, 1716...............Alderman Moorcroft (elected at this
                                        date, but to commence his duties
                                        on the 18th October following.)
13th October, 1720...............Peter Hall.
20th March, 1721...............Henry Trafford.
20th Sept.   1734...............William Pole (in the place of Henry
                                        Trafford who resigned.)
24th Dec.   1759...............Edward Forbes.
21st April   1760...............Matthew Strong.
3rd Nov.   1773...............John Crosbie.
5th August, 1789...............Thomas Golightly.[1]

The Receiver of the Town's Dues was another of such officers, whose duty it was to collect the town's dues for the port of Liverpool, and also the dues arising from the anchorage.

The Surveyor of the Corporation was another officer not named in the charter.

There were besides several other officers, such as the Serjeant-at-Mace, the Water-Bailiff, the Keeper of the Gaol, the Leave-looker of the Markets, the Beadle, and two or three others of minor importance.

The Magistrates of the borough were all members of the Council, and, except the Recorder, who, on being elected to that office, became a borough magistrate, every member of the Council who had passed through the office of Mayor, became an Alderman and a Justice of the Peace for the borough for life, if he continued a member of the Council. The jurisdiction of the borough justices extended throughout the limits of the borough, and also over the waters of the port of Liverpool.[2] Their jurisdiction was not an exclusive one, as county Magistrates might act within the borough. The borough Magistrates had also, at a subsequent period,

---

(1) Extracted from a Book in the Town-hall. On the 5th July, 1820, Mr. John Deane Case was appointed Treasurer, in the place of Mr. Thomas Golightly, resigned.

(2) See the evidence of the then Town-clerk, in the printed Report of the Proceedings before the Commissioners of Inquiry into Municipal Corporations, in 1833.

jurisdiction over a portion of Toxteth-park, by the Act 51st of George the Third, chap. 143. sec. 135, and by the 6th of George the Fourth, chap. 187, sec. 138.

The burgesses or freemen acquired the freedom of the borough in three ways; by birth, by gift of the Common Council, or by servitude under a written instrument for seven years within the borough, to a freeman; the sons of freemen, to become free, must have been born within the borough. The Common Council occasionally presented the freedom to individuals, such as public characters, naval and military officers, or persons who had rendered some kind of service to, or had distinguished themselves in the borough ; to the credit, however, of the members of the Common Council of Liverpool, the fact ought to be here mentioned, that there is not a single instance known, of the Common Council having ever been guilty of the corrupt act of creating freemen for electioneering purposes, as used formerly to be practised at Nottingham and other places, sometimes in a whole batch at a time ; and when honorary freemen of Liverpool have ever been created on any occasion, the practice has been pursued with very great restriction.[1]   It has been before observed, that the freemen were exclusively entitled to vote at elections of members of parliament, and of mayor and bailiffs, and were the only class who served on grand, petty, and coroners' juries.   The greatest privilege, however, of the freemen, was being exempt from payment of the Liverpool town's dues.

The Liverpool freemen were exempt from the dues of Waterford, Wexford, and Bristol ; and freemen of those places respectively, and also the freemen of London, were exempt from the dues at Liverpool.   But in order to obtain

---

(1) Printed Report of the Proceedings before the Commissioners of Inquiry into Municipal Corporations in 1833, page 48 and 49.

exemption from the payment of town's dues at Liverpool, the freemen of the places just before mentioned must be resident freemen, in each place respectively.

At one time a practice prevailed of selling the freedom, but the last time that it was sold was in September, 1792, when the freedom was purchased by a merchant, named Lloyd, a native of Ireland.

The following are the particulars of the sums received from the sales of the freedom of the borough, from 1773 to 1792, which were delivered in November, 1833, on oath, to the Commissioners of Inquiry into Municipal Corporations:—

The Total amount received from that source between 1773 and 1792 was £626 9s 6d, and the prices varied from 12 to 100 guineas.

1773	John Foster ...£12	12s	0d	1780	Wm. Dickson...£21	0s	0d
1775	Cornelius Bourne.52	10	0	„	George Bowden..52	10	0
„	John Bailey......52	10	0	„	Executors of		
„	— Lake............21	0	0		William Greg-		
1776	Thomas Manley..52	10	0		son, late Town-	218 12 10	
„	Chas. Matthews..10	10	0		clerk, on this		
1780	John Beckwith. (admitted 1762)	15 15	0		account.........		
„	John Fazakerley (admitted 1769.)	12 0	0	1792	J. L. Lloyd......105	0	0

Of the item "The Executors of William Gregson, £218 12s 10d," no further account could be given than the conjecture, that it might have been received in payments for the same purpose, and was not handed in until it had amounted to that sum ; or else that it was the amount of the fine of 6s 8d, which was payable upon admission by servitude, and the fine of 3s 4d, which was payable upon admission by birthright.[1]

---

(1) Printed Report of the Proceedings before the Commissioners of Inquiry into Municipal Corporations in 1833, page 53. These sums, however, were nominal, without having ever been demanded or paid ; unless, as seems probable, they might be considered as part of the fee paid on admission, which, in after times was £1, besides £1 for stamp duty. Between 1746 and 1747, the amount of fines paid on the admission of freemen was £322 18s 4d ; twenty-nine persons having received the freedom by purchase, and forty-eight by birthright and servitude. From 1747 to 1758 there

The following is an exact copy of the form of the oath, as it was administered to one of the freemen 110 years ago, during the mayoralty of Mr. Edward Trafford :—

EDWARD TRAFFORD, ESQ. Mayor.

Burgus de Liverpool,
in Com: Pall: Lanc. ss.

YOU shall be a True and Faithful Subject to our Sovereign Lord King George Majesty's his Heirs and Successors, and no Treason do Procure, or Commit, or cause to be Done, Procur'd, or Committed within this Town and Liberties thereof; you shall also from time to time (as Occasion shall require) Aid, Assist, and Obey, as well the Mayor of this Town, as also all other Majesty's officers within the same, under the said Mayor, in the due and Lawful Execution of their several offices, and especially concerning the Preservation of   Majesty's Peace, the observation of good Orders, and the Ancient and Laudable Privileges, Franchises, Liberties, and Customs of the same; which said Liberties and Customs, you shall further and increase to your Knowledge and best Endeavour: You shall likewise by no Covin, Colour, or Deceit, free any Foreigner, or the Goods, Chattels, or Merchandize of any Foreigner or other Person whatsoever, not Free within this Town, in the name of your own proper Goods, Chattels or Merchandize, whereby the Customs of this Town may be impaired, hindred, impeached, delay'd, or imbezled; you shall be liable and contributary at all times necessary and convenient to all reasonable Taxations and Payments, which shall be assest upon you amongst other the Burgesses, Freemen, and Inhabitants of this Town, as well for the Maintenance and Furtherance of the Franchises and Liberties of this Town of Liverpool, and other necessaries thereunto incident and appertaining, as also for the repairation of the

---

appear to have been no fines; and in 1758 only £15 15s was received. It has been suggested that the reason why there was nothing paid on that account, between 1747 and 1758 was, that about the year 1749, a person named Fazakerley being fined for opening a shop without permission, and refusing to pay, a law-suit was commenced against him; and consequently, that persons thinking that the Corporation had no right to sell the freedom, levy town's dues, or exact penalties, on persons opening shops, abstained from buying the freedom for some time. Ibid. page 62.

Parish Church of St. Peter's, and the Parochial Chappel of Our Lady and St. Nicholas within the same.

AND further you shall not Implead or Sue any Freeman of this Town, Inhabiting within the same, for any matter, cause, or thing whatsoever, whereof the said Mayor's Court may hold Plea (out of the Jurisdiction of this Court) unless it be for want of Justice or Right there to be Administered.

AND if you shall know, or hear of any Unlawful Congregations, Conventicles, Riots, Routs, or unlawful Assemblies, or other disorderly Tumults to be had or made, or like to be had, made or procur'd, by Day or by Night, within this Town and Liberties of the same, to the Disturbance of the Peace of our Sovereign King George   Majesty's Heirs and Successors, you shall give Warning and Notice thereof to the Mayor, his Deputy, or Bayliffs with all speed; and all and every other thing or things which shall either touch, or concern the Advancement or Preferment of the Commonwealth and State of this Town, or shall appertain and belong to be done by good and honest Burgesses, Freemen, and Inhabitants of the same: You shall for your part do, accomplish, fulfill, perform and observe, to the best of your Ability, Power, Knowledge and Witt.

So, HELP YOU GOD.

8th June, 1743.

George Parker, Joiner,   Sworn by

FRAN: GILDARDT, Town-clerk.[1]

The Court of Quarter Sessions was the chief criminal court, and was held four times in the year. It discharged the duty of the Court Leet, and Port Moot Court; of the latter there was no trace except the name, and the presentments of the Grand Jury; but by those designations, together with that of the Court of Quarter Sessions, the court continued to be held and called. The borough magistrates presided, two of them, as at other sessions, being sufficient; the Mayor generally as chairman, assisted by the Recorder, who, as before mentioned, was also a magistrate. There is

---

(1) From the original, in the possession of the Rev. John James Moss.

D l

little doubt that many of the corporate officers were formerly elected at these courts.

It was the custom during the last quarter of the 18th century, and even during many years of the present century, for dinners to be provided at the expense of the Corporation, at the Exchange, at the periodical times when the quarter sessions were being held; of which the Mayor, Bailiffs, Recorder, Grand Jury, and others, whose duties required their attendance at the sessions, used, as a matter of course, to partake. The following entry appears in the ledger of the Corporation, for dinners, at the quarter sessions, in 1775 :—

"1775 Sept. 23. | 427 | To cash paid Daniel Dale,[1] for Sessions Dinners £58 15s 10d."[2]

It is remarkable that twenty-five years afterwards, the expenses of the sessions dinners remained much the same as they were in 1775, and there is in the cash book of the Corporation, of 1800, the following entry:—

" 1800 Oct. 18. By Sessions, paid John Bates[3] for Dinners £55 4s."[4]

During the 18th century, as well as in the present century, previously to the Charter of 48th George the Third, (1808) the person who had served the office of Mayor of Liverpool, filled the office of Coroner for the borough during the ensuing year, and the practice was for him to be sworn in accordingly, on St. Luke's day, as Coroner and as a Justice of the Peace for the borough. The Books of Record of the Corporation contain many entries to that effect. The following is a copy of that relative to the Court of Election, on the 18th of October, 1775 :—

---

(1) Mr. Daniel Dale then kept the St. George's Coffee-house, which has been before mentioned, in Castle-street, and afterwards the King's Arms, in Water-street.

(2) Ledger of the Corporation, of 1775, No. 3, (7) page 144.

(3) Mr. John Bates kept the Royal Hotel, at the lowest end and north side of Lord-street.

(4) Cash Book of the Corporation, of 1800, No. 26, page 131.

"At the Court of Election, held on Wednesday, the eighteenth day of October (being Saint Luke's day), in the fifteenth year of the reign of our Sovereign Lord, George the Third, of Great Britain, France, and Ireland, King, Defender of the Faith and so forth and in the year of our Lord One Thousand seven hundred and seventy-five Before the Worshipful Peter Rigby Esq. Mayor, John Colquitt and James Gildart the younger, Gentlemen, Bailiffs of the Borough and Corporation of Liverpool, in the County Palatine of Lancaster, and the Aldermen and Burgesses of the same Borough, assembled in the open Exchange there,

2nd Geo.2nd } Then first read in open court the Act of parliament for the
Cap. 24 } more effectual preventing of Bribery and Corruption in the Election of Members to serve in Parliament

James Clemens, Esquire, is duly elected Mayor of the Borough and Corporation of Liverpool aforesaid, for the year ensuing, and then took the oaths to his Majesty's Person and Government, the oath of the said office of Mayor, and of a Justice of the Peace for the said Borough.

William Crosbie the younger, Merchant, is nominated and Elected Mayor's Bailiff of the said Borough of Liverpool, for the year ensuing, and at the same time took the oaths to his Majesty's Person and Government and the oath of the office of Bailiff of the said Borough.

George Case, merchant, is duly Elected Town's Bailiff of the said Borough, for the year ensuing, and also then took the oaths to his Majesty's Person and Government, and the oath of office of Bailiff of the said Borough.

Peter Rigby Esquire is sworn his Majesty's Coroner within the said Borough, for the year ensuing, and also one of His Majesty's Justices of the peace in and for the said Borough." [1]

The earliest entry in the books which is known, relating to the election of Coroner, is of the date of 18th October, 1694, of which the following is a copy :—

" Jasper Maudit, Esq. Maior.

The Election Court, holden for the Antient Town Corporate and Burrough of Liverpoole, in the county of Lancaster, on Thursday the

_____

(1) Book of Records, vol. 11, 1756 to 1776, page 725.

eighteenth day of October, being the feast of St. Luke the Evangelist, anno domini 1694, Before the said Maj^r., James Townsend and John Gamond, Bailiffs, of the same.

Alexander Norres Gentleman is elected Major, for the year ensuing, who took the oath of allegiance and supremacy, and made subscription as by Law required, and then took the oath of Majoralty.

Jasper Maudit Esq. took the oath of a Justice of the Peace and Coroner, of the said Borough, having first taken the oath of allegiance and supremacy, and made subscription as by Law required."[1]

The jurisdiction of the Coroner's Court extended throughout the borough, and also over the waters of the port of Liverpool. A county Coroner's warrant was of force in the borough, but not any instance was known of inquests respecting deaths, within the borough, being ever held by the county Coroner. The expenses of juries, surgeons, and other requisites, were paid by the Corporation.[2] The Coroner's Jury was exclusively composed of burgesses, who were summoned by the Beadle, and, in cases of importance requiring particular deliberation, the Coroner used to select from the burgesses a jury of merchants, or other persons of equal respectability.

The Court of Passage was, (as it still is,) a civil court of record of the borough of Liverpool. It was always the practice for the Mayor and Bailiffs to preside. The Mayor or his deputy invariably attended, and one Bailiff. The cause of action, in all matters tried in it, must have arisen within the borough.

---

(1) Book of Records, vol. 4, 1671 to 1703, page 678.

(2) It has been already stated* that afterwards, in 1808, the Coroners of the borough were constituted by the Charter of 48th George the 3rd, (19th January, 1808,) which made every person who had served the office of Mayor, a Coroner for the succeeding four years. By the last Charter, 8th George the 4th, (28th April, 1828,) the person who had passed the office of Mayor, was Coroner for the next year only, and he, with the Bailiffs for the time being, were made Coroners. It was not requisite under that Charter that the three should act. The Bailiffs were the officiating Coroners under it, and one of them used to attend; in case of the absence of both, the late Mayor acted.

* Chapter III, page 194.

The power to try actions of ejectment in it, is supposed to have once existed; but if so, it had for a long time fallen into disuse.

The trial of defended causes took place once a quarter, at the same period as the Quarter Sessions. The processes of the Court of Passage were executed throughout all the limits of the borough, and also over the waters of the port of Liverpool.

The Court of Requests was another civil court, which was established under an Act of 25th George the Second, chap. 43, for the recovery of debts under 40s. Commissioners were appointed monthly by the Common Council, consisting of the Recorder, two Aldermen, four Common Councilmen and ten Householders.

There was not any presiding Judge : such an officer was not considered requisite, as the Clerk to the Commissioners had merely to make an entry of the proceedings. Any three of the Commissioners could act. The clerks were appointed by the Council.

The local Police was principally established under the provisions of an Act of the 21st of George the Second, chap. 24, entitled, " An Act for building a Church in the town of Liverpool, in the county palatine of Lancaster, and for enlightening and cleansing the streets of the said town, and for keeping and maintaining a Nightly Watch there :" the powers of the Act were enlarged by the Act of 28th George the Third, chap. 13. The night watch was under the directions of Commissioners of Watch, &c. consisting of all the Aldermen and of eighteen other householders of the borough : none of the Council but Aldermen were Commissioners, as the Act required them to be Justices. Under these Acts the Commissioners appointed watchmen, and directed every thing connected with the nightly police. Besides that description of police, the Corporation paid a few constables and head-constables; but, as has been before mentioned, the police department was in a most inefficient state, and very inadequate to the preservation of the peace of the borough.

The Church Patronage of the Corporation of Liverpool will now be noticed.

The Rectory of Liverpool consisted of two medieties. By the Act of 10th and 11th of William the Third, chap. 36, (1699,) by which Liverpool was made a parish of itself distinct from Walton-on-the-Hill, the Corporation became patrons of the Rectory of Liverpool; and, by virtue of that Act, the Common Council presented to the Rectory on every vacancy. The Rectors were formerly entitled under that Act, as has been before mentioned,[1] to have houses and gardens provided for them by the parish; an advantage which they relinquished in 1786: an increase of their salaries was made by the parish,[2] in consideration of their giving up the small tithes, and other emoluments, belonging to their rectory.

The other ecclesiastical patronage of the Corporation was derived, under specific Acts of Parliament, for the establishment of the different churches which the Corporation either had built or had contributed materially to build, or of which they had given the site. In consideration of those grants and contributions, the Corporation had vested in them, the perpetual advowsons of, and the right of presentation to, the following churches:—

St. George's, built by the Corporation: the perpetual election and choice of a curate or chaplain of which, was vested in them, by an Act of 1st George the First, chap. 21.

---

(1) Chapter I, page 47.

(2) From £200 to £350 from the Parish, which was exclusive of Salaries which they received from the Corporation.

St. Thomas' Church, built by subscription, under an Act of the 21st George the Second, chap. 24, by which, in consideration of the Corporation granting their reversion in the site, and stipulating to support and keep the church in repair, the perpetual advowson was vested in the Corporation, and the right of presenting the ministers given to the Common Council.

St. Paul's Church, for which the Corporation gave the land ; built by the Parish under an Act of the 2nd George the Third, chap. 68, by which the perpetual advowson and right of presentation was vested in the Corporation.

St. John's Church, built by the Parish, on a site given by the Corporation, under the Act of Parliament last mentioned, which vested the right of presentation and nomination of the ministers in the Corporation.

St. Ann's Church, built by three individuals, under an Act of the 12th of George the Third, chap. 36, by which, after three presentations, the patronage of the Church, and the nomination of all future incumbents, was also vested in the Corporation.

There was not any kind of collegiate school, or public school of that nature, in Liverpool. There was, however, a free school ; a grant having been made in the reign of Queen Elizabeth, of a sum of £5 6s 8d,[1] out of the revenues of the Duchy of Lancaster, towards the salary of a schoolmaster, which was received as long as that school existed ; the remainder of the expense of the school was defrayed by the Corporation, and the Common Council had the appointment of the schoolmaster. The last schoolmaster was Mr. John Baines, who died in 1803.[2] His salary, in

---

(1) Stated to have been £5 6s 8d in the printed Report of the Proceedings before the Commissioners of Inquiry into Municipal Corporations in 1833, page 104 ; but some other accounts state it to have been £5 13s 4d.

(2) The date of 1803 is taken from Baines' Lancashire, vol. iv. page 108. In

1775, was £35 per annum.[1] It was in School-lane, on the south side, and next above the Blue-coat Hospital, of which its site now forms part. The school was given up in 1803.

Mrs. Ann Molyneux's Charity has been briefly mentioned before, but is again noticed here in consequence of the Mayor of Liverpool having the distribution of part of its annual proceeds. A sum of money, afterwards invested in land, was originally left, the interest to be distributed in part by the Mayor amongst poor debtors, and in part by the Rectors, amongst poor seamen's widows. The charity is now regulated under an Act passed in 1828, in the 9th of George the Fourth, chap. 39, "An Act for enabling the Trustees of Mrs. Ann Molyneux's Charities, in Liverpool, to grant building and repairing leases, and for better vesting the estates in them; for confirming exchanges, and other purposes, for the benefit of the charities." The land being within the boundaries of the town, the Act authorizes it to be let on building leases: with the increase of the town, the funds will be augmented, and become applicable to charitable purposes, according to the Act of Parliament.[2] Most of the land is already built upon.

The landed estate of the Corporation was, as it now is, extensive and valuable, and comprised a large portion of the land lying within the borough and parish of Liverpool.

It does not clearly appear how the Corporation originally acquired their lands; but the greatest portion has been held

---

1708 the School was used temporarily for the purposes of the Blue-coat School. On the formation of the latter, the first contributors to it met there.

(1) From an original receipt for a quarter's salary, signed by Mr. John Baines; preserved in the Town-hall.

(2) Printed Report of the Proceedings before the Commissioners of Inquiry into Municipal Corporations in 1833, page 99.

by the Corporation for centuries, and a small part has been purchased at different times.

The fines paid, on the renewal of leases of land and buildings, formed a considerable source of the income of the Corporation. In explanation of the system of leasing, it should be mentioned, that the Corporation were accustomed formerly to let out their land on leases, granting it on lease for lives only; and about the beginning of the last century the Corporation books contain the first entries of leases being granted. About 1712, the practice of leasing for lives was deviated from, and an order in Council made, that a term of twenty-one years should be added to the three lives in every lease, on the person taking up the same paying a reasonable fine, and public notice of the regulation was given to all the tenants. The practice of granting leases for lives and years, renewable upon a fine, continued up to 1824, when the Corporation altered their plan, and the present system commenced, of granting leases for a specific term of seventy-five years, which has been the practice ever since. Leases for seventy-five years are now renewable, in almost all cases, (except, for example, when the property is wanted for improvements,) upon fines payable, calculated from a table.

Connected in some degree with this subject, was the income which formerly arose from the sales of the ground rents or small chief rents, which were reserved under the old system of leasing.

Besides that portion of the revenue of the Corporation of Liverpool which arose from their landed estate, there were also various other sources of revenue of which some will be now mentioned.

The Town's Dues were by far the most important. The Town's Dues, and various other rights and beneficial interests in the town, had originally belonged to the Crown, and after

E 1

a lapse of many years they were acquired by the Corporation, by purchase from the ancestors of the Earl of Sefton. In order that this acquisition may be correctly understood, it may be expedient to mention, that the town was originally the property of the Sovereign; afterwards of the Duchy of Lancaster. It then reverted to the Crown. Afterwards, all such rights and beneficial interests as the Crown possessed in it, were sold by Charles the First, in 1628, to the citizens of London, and from them they passed to the ancient family of Molyneux. About the year 1640, it is said that the Corporation became possessed of such rights and interests in it, either under title from the Crown, or from the ancestors of the Earl of Sefton, (the family of Molyneux;) but disputes having arisen between the Corporation and the Molyneux family, as to the ownership, they were terminated by Lord Molyneux (and John Tatlock, his trustee,) granting to the Corporation a lease, dated 27th May, 1672, of all his interest in the town, for 1000 years.[1] From that time may be traced the gradual increase of the town in buildings and prosperity; and a grant of the reversion, dated the 4th of February, 1777, was subsequently obtained by the Corporation from Charles William, Lord Viscount Molyneux, and others.

The Town's-dues were rates paid upon the importation and exportation of goods and merchandise, and collected by the Receiver of the Town's-dues, according to a table of rates. As before mentioned, the Liverpool freemen were exempt from the payment of them, and also from the dues of Waterford, Wexford and Bristol, as the resident freemen

---

(1) Printed Report of the Proceedings at Liverpool, before the Commissioners of Inquiry into Municipal Corporations, in 1833, page 85 ; also, Printed Report of the Proceedings of the Associated Merchants, and of the Bill of Exceptions, in the cause the Corporation of Liverpool against Thomas Bolton and others, page 24 and 25.

of those places respectively, and of London, were exempt from the dues at Liverpool.

The right of the Corporation of Liverpool to those dues was, about twenty years ago, contested ; and, on the 14th February, 1833, the important cause, " The Mayor, Bailiffs and Burgesses of Liverpool against Thomas Bolton and others," involving the right to the Town's-dues, came on for trial, in the Court of King's Bench, in Westminster-hall, before Lord Chief-Justice Denman and a special jury, and occupied two days; when a verdict was obtained by the Corporation. A bill of exceptions was tendered on behalf of the defendant, which terminated in a compromise, on the principle of recognising the right to levy Town's-dues, but on a more satisfactory scale.

The Anchorage-dues, connected in some degree with the Town's-dues, were payable on every vessel, whether British or Foreign, entering at the Liverpool Custom-house. There was no exemption for freemen in regard to Anchorage-dues.

The Corporation claimed the right to Anchorage by purchase, under the same title (derived from the Crown, through the ancestors of the Earl of Sefton) as that before mentioned respecting the Town's-dues. The Corporation received Town's-dues and Anchorage also at Runcorn, in Cheshire, it being a place within the port of Liverpool.

Under the same title as that by which the Corporation are entitled to the Town's-dues, they are also said to claim the right of escheat, or of taking the property of persons dying intestate, and possessed of property within the ancient boundaries[1] of the parish and borough of Liverpool, provided such persons happen to die, without leaving relations legally entitled to it. As it is evident, that instances must occasionally occur of persons dying intestate, in Liverpool, possessed of

---

[1] This does not extend to the modern Municipal boundaries of the town.

property, but without leaving any legitimate heirs or relations, it is extraordinary, if the claim were valid and had
ever been substantiated or enforced, that during the proceedings before the Commissioners of Inquiry into Municipal Corporations, in November, 1833, not any notice was
taken of it, nor does it appear to have even been mentioned
on that occasion. It is said, however, that the claim has
been recently submitted to, without any contest.

Another source of income was from tolls from the
markets, which were altered subsequently by an Act of
59th George the Third, chap. 9. One of the markets, that
of Saturday, was held by prescription, and the other that
of Wednesday, was under a grant by letters patent of
Queen Anne. The inhabitants of Altcar and Prescot were
exempt from the tolls by prescription, and freemen of Liverpool were exempt from one half by custom. The old tolls
which were called ingates and outgates have been abolished,
and others instituted. By the Act just mentioned, double
tolls and stallage are payable during the Liverpool fairs,[1]
on the 25th of July and 11th November, and ten days

---

(1) A Collation was at one time provided by the Corporation at the time of the
occurrence of the Fair, but it is not now known who were the partakers of it. The
following is a copy of a Bill for the expence of the collation in July, 1775 :—

	Corporation of Liverpool	To Thos. Bowman Snack for Fair day	Dr.
1775 26 : July	To Beef	£0 9 4	
	To Ham & Fowles	0 17 0	
	To Tongues	0 3 6	
	To Pigeon Pye	0 8 6	
	Potted and Fresh Shrimps	0 4 0	
	To Apple Pye	0 2 0	
	Cheese, Butter and Bread	0 7 0	
	Sugar, Lemmons and Bread	0 4 6	
	Rum, & Brandy	0 10 0	
	18 Bottles Wine	1 16 0	
		£5 1 10*	

* Copied from the original Bill preserved in the Town-hall.

previously, and ten days subsequently to them, in all the markets except the fish-market.

Graving Docks may also be here mentioned as adding something to the revenue of the Corporation. The Graving Dock No. 1 was constructed in 1756, and those, Nos. 2 and 3, in 1765;[1] all three were subsequently enlarged, and have been some time destroyed in the improvements of the docks.

There were also some weighing-machines for weighing straw, coal, potatoes, &c. by the load, the tolls of which contributed their quota to the Corporation income.

Besides which, there were some other sources of income, but they were trivial, and not sufficiently important to be detailed here.

It has been already mentioned that the members of the Council were self-elected, and, as a natural consequence of that objectionable system, they were in the habit of electing the relations of each other, so as to keep the office as much as possible in three or four favoured families. The Council also had the control over the public purse, and exercised legislative powers in the making of all by-laws, for the regulation and government of the town, without the intervention of the general body of burgesses. In 1735, a Common-hall was held, the burgesses having been called together in the mayoralty of the Earl of Derby, on which occasion various by-laws were declared to be made, but without any effectual result. His Lordship having died in the following year, the intended by-laws were declared by the Council to be nugatory and contrary to the Charter, and two Common Councilmen were expelled from the Council for attending and taking a part at the meeting.

---

(1) Printed Report of the Proceedings before the Commissioners of Inquiry into Municipal Corporations, in 1833, page 94.

In 1791, about 1000 burgesses signed a requisition for calling a Common-hall; a measure which created a great sensation in the town, and eventually gave rise to important legal proceedings. The movement was set on foot by a number of individuals, many of whom were quite as wealthy, talented and respectable, as most of the then members of the Council, and who were desirous to try whether it was by right or by usurpation that the Council exercised the before-mentioned powers. The Mayor, Mr. John Sparling, and the Bailiffs, Mr. Clayton Tarleton and Mr. Robert Moss, accordingly convened the burgesses together, or, as the usual expression is, called a Common-hall. That event, and the proceedings which ensued in consequence, are so closely connected with the Corporation of Liverpool, and with the subjects of the present chapter, that, notwithstanding they occurred long after the year 1775, it is considered to be the most expedient course to give a narrative of them here.

The Common-hall was held, after public notice from the Mayor and Bailiffs, on the 17th of January, 1791, and in consequence of there being some vacant seats in the Council, the burgesses proceeded to elect gentlemen to supply the vacancies,[1] and also declared various by-laws passed at the meeting. Another Common-hall was held on the 16th of June in the same year, when other by-laws were declared to be passed, and amongst others one imposing a penalty of forty shillings on the town's Treasurer, if he should refuse to permit the Mayor and Auditors to inspect the books and papers of the Corporation in his possession. In consequence of those proceedings Mr. Thomas Golightly, the

---

(1) It has been already mentioned, in this Chapter, that the above mode of electing a Common Councilman was contested in the Court of King's Bench, and was held to be at variance with the Charter, and that it could not be legally supported.

Treasurer, was called upon to permit an inspection of the books and papers, which being refused, an action was commenced against him, in the Court of King's Bench, for the recovery of the penalty of forty shillings, and to try the legal right to make by-laws.[1]

It was evident to all, that those proceedings involved points much beyond the mere making of by-laws; points on which the very existence of the Council, as then constituted, depended. The members of the Council were quite alive to the danger with which the exclusive system of electing their own relations and dependants, and the various other powers which they claimed, were threatened, if it should be decided that a Common-hall, so held, was legal, and possessed the powers which its supporters contended for.

It was, therefore, essentially necessary for the Corporation to employ some legal practitioner of superior talents to conduct their case, and to support what they contended to be their rights; but the Common Council of that period had not the good fortune which the present Corporation enjoys, of having a Town-clerk possessing the talents, industry, and information of the gentleman who now fills, and so well fills, that important office,[2] and the Town-clerk of 1791 was not considered quite competent to perform so arduous an undertaking; fortunately for the Corporation, they entrusted it to Mr. Henry Brown,[3] a solicitor of extraordinary learning and talents; and of whom, as has been before stated,[4] the late Lord Chief-Justice Ellenborough, when Mr. Law, K.C. has

---

(1) The Mayor, Bailiffs and Burgesses of Liverpool against Golightly in the King's Bench, 1791. A good account of the trial and of the subsequent arguments are in print, from which the particulars given in this Chapter are principally taken.

(2) Mr. William Shuttleworth, elected Town-clerk in 1844.

(3) Mr. Edward Parr, a solicitor of talent, well known to many of the readers, was employed against him by the supporters of the Common Hall.

(4) Introduction, page 24.

been known to say, that he was the best read Corporation lawyer in existence. This gentleman was the deputy Town-clerk, and solicitor to the Corporation, and both on that and various other occasions[1] conducted most important pro-fessional business for the town with wonderful talents and success.[2]

When this important cause came on for trial at the Lan-caster Assizes, it excited great interest, and gave rise to a splendid exhibition of legal ingenuity and forensic eloquence, on the part of the counsel on both sides, and the points of law which arose were so nice, and so unusual, and the argu-ments so equally poised, that it can scarcely excite surprise that even the judges of the court were rather perplexed.[3]

---

(1) Introduction, page 24.

(2) Mr. Brown was, like many other very learned, deep-read and talented men, eccentric in his manners, slovenly, almost amounting to shabbiness, in his dress, and indifferent to public opinion; but his talents, industry and exertions were on many occasions of great value to the Corporation, and many of his researches at the Tower and elsewhere are said to have been of essential service, in after years, to the Town-clerks of Liverpool, who have had the benefit of them. One instance which has been given of his eccentricity is worth recording. He was many years ago engaged in London on some important business for the Corporation, and with a beard of full growth, dirty, and tired, probably, with researches at the Tower, it has been said, that he entered a barber's shop, in Turnstile, Holborn, and sat down to be shaved, having first put on a dressing-gown belonging to the barber, ornamented with spots like a leopard's skin. The shop commanded a view into Holborn, and after Mr. Brown's face had been well lathered, and one side only of it had been cleaned with the razor, he caught a glimpse of Colonel Gascoyne (afterwards General Gascoyne,) one of the members for Liverpool, passing along the street, and Mr. Brown, after pushing aside the astonished tonsor, rushed out of the shop into Holborn, half shaved, with the morning gown of leopard's spots floating in the air crying out as he ran, " Colonel Gascoyne ! " " Colonel Gascoyne ! " whilst the populace made way for Mr. Brown as if he had been a lunatic.

(3) The points which were urged on behalf of the burgesses, who supported the proceedings of the Common-hall, were, that Liverpool, though a very ancient town, could not be considered a Corporation by prescription, because the first Charter, that of King John, of 1207, was within what is termed the time of legal memory, [the period of the return of Richard the 1st from the Holy Wars, is considered the time of legal memory ;] that neither the Charter of the 2nd year of King Charles the 1st,

The trial took place in 1791, at Lancaster, before Mr. Baron Thompson; and the conflicting parties had the advantage of the distinguished and splendid talents of two of the first advocates in Europe; the leading counsel employed by the plaintiffs, or, to describe the matter more clearly, on behalf of the burgesses who supported the

---

(4th July, 1626,) nor any earlier Charter, ever mentioned a Council as existing or as necessary for the town, and that the Charter of Charles the 1st expressly declared that the power of making By-laws should exist in " the *Mayor, Bailiffs and Burgesses*," for the time being, or the major part of them, of whom the Mayor and one of the Bailiffs should be two, assembled after public notice to be given for that purpose ; that a surreptitious Charter of the 29th of Charles the 2nd, (8th July, 1677,) by which almost all the powers of the burgesses at large were taken from them, and given to the select body, (the Council,) had long been annulled and abrogated by a subsequent Charter, then the governing Charter of Liverpool, of the 7th of William the 3rd, 26th September, 1695, (which recited by inspeximus the Charter of Charles the 1st,) by which Charter King William the 3rd confirmed that of King Charles the 1st, and consequently, that the right of passing By-laws by the Mayor, Bailiffs and Burgesses at large, in the manner mentioned in the Charter of Charles the 1st, was confirmed ; that though it was conceded that a Common Council for Liverpool had existed for ages previously, and had exercised the power of making By-laws, yet that it was a mere usurpation of the rights of the burgesses, not warranted by any Charter ; and that a petition had been sent by the Corporation to King George the 2nd, in 1751, complaining that the Charter of King William, ordaining that there should be a Common Council, omitted to give them " the least power " in express words, and praying for an explanatory Charter.

On the other hand, it was urged on behalf of the Common Council, that Liverpool enjoyed various ancient prescriptive usages and customs, which had existed from time immemorial, amongst which was the existence of a Common Council, which had possessed the right of passing By-laws from the earliest period that could be traced, and that the entries in the Corporation Books, showed that, as early as the reign of Queen Elizabeth, on the 14th January, 1581, in the mayoralty of Edward Halsall, an assembly was held of the Mayor and all his brethren the Aldermen of the town, and a great number of the common burgesses, at which it was declared by the meeting, that, " upon due consideration of the *ancient customs* of this town, it seemed there ought to be, amongst other things, a *Common Council* within the same, of the Mayor, Aldermen and twenty-four others, of the most discreet and substantial free burgesses, inhabitants thereof," for the good government of the town ; and treating some assemblies of the commons or general body of burgesses, as usurpations ; and it was declared by the meeting, " that the said late *usurped assemblies* of the *commons* shall be abolished, and that from henceforth the said *ancient custom* of Common Council shall be restored, and inviolably used and observed." The meeting then proceeded to declare that if any

F l

proceedings of the Common-hall, being Mr. Serjeant Adair; and the leading counsel employed on behalf of the defendant, or virtually, of the Common Council, being Mr. Erskine, (afterwards Lord Erskine). The latter contended, that in consequence of the ambiguities in the Charter (more fully explained in the note at foot) he was entitled by law to

---

vacancy in the Council should happen, the remaining members of the Council should elect another to supply the vacancy, and so as often as any vacancy should occur ; and that the members of the Common Council should take an oath, of which the form was prescribed, and which had continued, for above two centuries before the trial, to be the form of oath used on those occasions ; and the form of oath not only more than once mentions the Common Council, but it distinctly mentions the " Aldermen," who must have had their existence by some ancient usage or forgotten Charter, because they were not mentioned in any known Charter anterior to the date of that meeting ; that the Common Council had always exercised the right of self-election, and of making By-laws by prescriptive usage and ancient custom ; and that the Charter of Charles the 1st, merely used the words " Mayor, Bailiffs and Burgesses " in the same sense as it would be used in a grant of lands, which must necessarily be to them in their corporate name ; that the select body, the Council then existing, were making By-laws and Resolutions under the name of the Mayor, Bailiffs and Burgesses, and by that name were in exercise of the legislative power in the Corporation at the time of the Charter of Charles the 1st, and that it was not then intended to give a power of legislation to the body at large, or to annul the prescriptive usages and customs of the town ; but, on the contrary, that they were expressly recognized by that Charter as subsisting, and that it confirmed all " lawful liberties, *privileges*, franchises, immunities, executions, *customs*," &c. &c. of the town, whether by charter or letters patent, or " *custom, use, or prescription ;*" that that intention of the Charter was corroborated by a passage in it, which stated that the senior Alderman should be one of the two Justices, the Mayor being the other, (" without whose concurrence not a session in the town could be held :")* yet, no Alderman was constituted by the Charter, and consequently, it seemed to recognize the creation of Aldermen by prescriptive usage ; that the Charter of William the 3rd, which was the first Charter which expressly directed the number of the Common Council to be forty-one, (the number having fluctuated previously,) was not intended to revoke or interfere with the prescriptive usages of the town, appeared to be clear from the circumstance that the Charter directed the members of the Council to continue in office, *quamdiu se bene gesserint*, unless any of them should " happen to be *removed* for a reasonable and just cause by the Mayor, Bailiffs and Common Council of the said town, or the major part of them," for the time being ; thereby referring to a power of removing one another, existing by usage in the Council before that time ; that though the Charter

* Per Lord Chief-Justice Kenyon, speaking of the two Justices, on the motion for a third trial of the cause.

give evidence to the jury to show in explanation what were
the immemorial usages of the borough ; Baron Thompson
was of a different opinion, and refused to allow the evidence
of usage, and consequently nothing more could then be
done but for the jury to find a verdict for the plaintiff, with
forty shillings damages ; not that the cause was considered,
even at that time, to be decided by the verdict, for the
Counsel on both sides, as well as the Judge, deemed it
merely a prelude to taking the opinion of the Court of
King's Bench, on argument, at Westminster, and so well
was the Judge assured of that being the case, that before
giving any opinion, he stated to the counsel of the parties:
" I wish to know in what way the opinion I am about to
give, may be put, so as most advantageously to be brought
before the Court." An application was accordingly made
to the Court of King's Bench for a new trial, and it was

---

did not give the Council any express power of making By-laws, (or, in fact, any express
powers whatever, except to appoint a Sword-Bearer and elect Sub-Bailiffs,) yet, it
directed a quorum of twenty-five, of whom the Mayor and one of the Bailiffs were to
be two, " *all* those things to *do, ordain, execute and perform*, in as full a manner and
form as the forty and one Councilmen of the said town, in Common Council present
and assembled, can do, ordain, execute, or perform ;" from which it was contended
that it was not considered necessary, to specify in the Charter the powers of the
Council, and that they were so well defined by usage, that they were notorious, and
needed not any definition ; that the Charter also directed that, if any Mayor, Recorder,
Common Clerk, Bailiff, or *any of the Common Council*, should happen to *die*, or be
removed, or *refuse* to act, that then, in his room and office, from time to time, another
fit person should be *elected* and sworn " by *such persons* in such manner, time and
form, as in that particular was used and *accustomed, before* the abrogated Charter of
18th of July, in the 29th year of Charles the 2nd, thereby referring to the usage and
practice of the election by the members of the Council, as it existed before the Charter
of Charles the 2nd, and that the books of the Corporation showed, that immediately
after the grant of the Charter of Charles the 1st, elections of members of the Council
took place, and also that immediately after the Charter of William the 3rd, vacancies
in the body, caused by refusals to act, were supplied by elections, by the members
of the Council, without any intervention of the burgesses at large ; and that, in like
manner, and without any such intervention, the members of the Council had continued
to elect each other, and to make By-laws up to the time of the trial.

decided unanimously by all the Judges of the Court, (not by Lord Chief-Justice Kenyon, as has been erroneously stated, for no one Judge of the Court of King's Bench could by law grant a new trial,) that the evidence of usage ought to have been received; and the application was accordingly granted, on the 8th of May, 1792; and the cause was sent back to Lancaster for another trial. A second trial took place, at Lancaster, before Mr. Baron Thompson, on the 23rd of August, 1792, when Mr. Serjeant Adair was again the leading counsel for the plaintiffs, and Mr. Law (afterwards Lord Ellenborough) for the defendant. On the second trial evidence was given of an immemorial usage of the making of by-laws by the Council, but a verdict was again found for the plaintiffs, with forty shillings damages. Another application was made to the Court of King's Bench for a third trial; and the matter was argued in April and May, 1793, when the Judges of the Court unanimously granted the application, being of opinion, that the Charter of Charles the First did not abrogate all the old usages, and that the cause ought to be sent to a new trial; the Court being desirous that a special verdict should be found, so that the parties might not be precluded by any opinion which they (the judges) could hold upon the subject, but might go to a higher resort. The cause was, however, never brought again to trial, either in consequence of the funds of the supporters of the Common-hall being exhausted, or of their finding, in the course of the argument, that the opinions of the judges appeared to be unfavourable to the construction put upon the charter by the plaintiff's counsel, and nothing further was done in the matter by the opponents of the Corporation.

CHAPTER IV.

COMMERCE, SHIPPING, TRADES, MANUFACTORIES, DOCK DUTIES, REVENUE OF CUSTOMS, BANKING HOUSES, ISSUE OF NEGOTIABLE NOTES BY THE CORPORATION, PERIODICAL FESTIVALS, OLD CUSTOMS, DRESS, HOURS OF VISITING, PASTIMES, AMUSEMENTS, AND HABITS OF THE INHABITANTS, CROSBY RACES, MUSIC, THE DRAMA, BALL AT THE EXCHANGE, PUBLIC ENTERTAINMENTS, CLUBS AND FIRESIDES, UNANIMOUS CLUB, INEFFICIENCY OF THE POLICE, AND INCREASING POPULATION OF LIVERPOOL, BETWEEN 1775 AND 1800.   LIVERPOOL ELECTIONS.

IT is intended to give in this chapter, some account of the commerce of Liverpool, and of the habits, manners, pursuits, and amusements of its inhabitants, during the period which elapsed from the commencement of the year 1775 to the termination of the year 1799, the last quarter of the 18th century; and in order to prevent any misconception with respect to dates, it may be advisable to observe in the outset, that though in general there is not any great difficulty in ascertaining the time of the erection of any public building, or the establishment of any public work or institution, in Liverpool, yet, with respect to various matters, which will be mentioned in this chapter, it will be obvious, that it must occasionally be impracticable to give dates with exactness; in fact, in some instances, the circumstances detailed may not have been confined to a day, a month, or a year, but may have spread over a considerable period of time.

At the commencement of the concluding quarter of the eighteenth century, the trade of Liverpool was considerable, but it was afterwards far surpassed by the extensive commerce which it enjoyed at the close of it.

A Chamber of Commerce existed in Liverpool, and it was the custom on every Midsummer-day for its members to elect a committee; and as it may be interesting to know who the merchants of Liverpool were, who were elected members of it at that remote period, the following are the names of the committee in the month of June, 1775[1]:—

Nicholas Ashton	Thomas Falkner	A. Nottingham
William Bolden	Arthur Heywood	F. H. Rawlinson
J. Brooks, Jun.	Thomas Hodgson	Gill Slater
Thomas Case	F. Hodgson, Jun.	Thomas Smyth
Edward Chaffers	William James	T. Staniforth
John Chorley	Francis Ingram	T. Tarleton
Edgar Corrie	Richard Kent	G. Venables
John Dobson		

About that period, and for several years afterwards, the merchants of Liverpool usually transacted their own business, and, consequently, the vocation of a broker was but little pursued in Liverpool. For a considerable period the only houses of any note who then called themselves brokers, were Mr. Thomas Ryan, Mr. James Drinkwater, Mr. Woodward, and Mr. George Dunbar, afterwards Sir George Dunbar, Bart.

There were some marine underwriters, and also some insurance brokers, in Liverpool, during the American Revolutionary War. They were not a numerous body, but they were persons of property and respectability.

The principal branches of the trade of Liverpool will be now noticed.

The West India trade, which gave employment to a large number of ships, and in which considerable fortunes were made; it was, however, much connected with, and to a certain extent dependant on the African Slave trade, which will be next mentioned.

---

(1) Gore's General Advertiser of 30th of June, 1775.

The following is a statement of the shipping engaged in the West India trade (in 1787) from and to Great Britain :—

	OUTWARDS.			INWARDS.	
	SHIPS.	TONS.		SHIPS.	TONS.
LONDON	218	61,695	......	252	70,418
LIVERPOOL	87	17,463	......	143	27,578
LANCASTER	37	5,665	......	33	4,943
BRISTOL	73	16,913	......	71	16,209
ALL OTHER PORTS	36	7,216	......	107	1,052
	451	108,952		606	120,200

Statement of Sugar, Coffee, and Rum, the most valuable branches of West India produce, imported into Liverpool, in 1770 :—

1770.	1770.	1770.
SUGAR $\begin{cases} 9998 \text{ hhds.} \\ 2376 \text{ casks, \&c.} \end{cases}$	COFFEE $\begin{cases} 377 \text{ hhds.} \\ 265 \text{ casks} \end{cases}$	RUM $\begin{cases} 2676 \text{ hhds.} \\ 62 \text{ brls.} \end{cases}$[1]

The African Slave trade, an odious and inhuman source of emolument, was a branch of trade in which Liverpool had attained not an enviable degree of notoriety, by the purchase and sale of human beings; however, London, Bristol, and other seaport towns of England were more or less engaged in the traffic, and must share in the odium. One merchant of Liverpool (Mr. James) had, at one time, twenty-nine vessels engaged in the trade, but they were not of large dimensions.

In 1775 the number of vessels cleared out from Liverpool for Africa, employed in that execrable traffic, was 81, burthen 9200 tons.[2] The number and tonnage fluctuated, but in 1799 the number was 134 vessels, burthen 34,966.[3] A striking but lamentable increase. The following table will show the number of vessels engaged in it, which cleared out from Liverpool, not only during the quarter of the century which is now under consideration,

---

(1) Smithers' Liverpool, page 101.

(2) Troughton's Liverpool, page 265.   (3) Ibid. page 265. The above was not the greatest number in any one year about that period, for in 1798 the number was 149.

but including every year, from the earliest records of the numbers, until the abolition of the trade :—

THE NUMBER OF SHIPS WHICH CLEARED OUT FROM THE PORT OF LIVERPOOL TO THE COAST OF AFRICA, TO THE TIME OF THE TRADE BEING ABOLISHED, IN MAY, 1807.[1]

YEAR.	SHIPS.	TONS.	YEAR.	SHIPS.	TONS.	YEAR.	SHIPS.	TONS.
1709	1	30	1767	83	8,345	1788	73	13,394
1730	15	1111	1768	81	8,302	1789	66	11,564
1737	33	2756	1769	90	9,852	1790	91	17,917
1744	34	2698	1770	96	9,818	1791	102	19,610
1751	53	5334	1771	105	10,929	1792	132	22,402
1752	58	5437	1772	100	10,159	1793	52	10,544
1753	72	7547	1773	105	11,056	1794		
1754	71	5463	1774	92	9,859	1795	59	
1755	41	4052	1775	81	9,200	1796	94	
1756	60	5147	1776	57	7,078	1797	90	20,415
1757	47	5050	1777	30	4,060	1798	149	34,937
1758	51	5229	1778	26	3,651	1799	134	34,966
1759	58	5892	1779	11	1,205	1800	120	33,774
1760	74	8178	1780	32	4,275	1801	122	28,429
1761	69	7309	1781	43	5,720	1802	122	30,796
1762	61	6752	1782	47	6,209	1803	83	15,534
1763	65	6650	1783	85	12,294	1804	126	27,322
1764	74	7978	1784	67	9,568	1805	117	26,536
1765	83	9382	1785	79	10,982	1806	111	25,949
1766	65	6650	1786	92	13,971	1807	74	17,806
			1787	81	14,012			

N.B.—From the first day of January, 1806, to the first day of May, 1807, there had sailed from the port of Liverpool 185 African Ships, measuring 43,755 tons, which were allowed to carry 49,213 Slaves.

COMPARATIVE STATEMENT OF SHIPS CLEARED OUT FROM THE PORTS OF LONDON, LIVERPOOL, AND BRISTOL, TO THE COAST OF AFRICA, FOR TEN YEARS, FROM 1795 TO 1804 INCLUSIVE.

YEAR.	LONDON.		BRISTOL.		LIVERPOOL.		TOTAL.		EACH SHIP.
	SHIPS.	SLAVES ALLOWED.	SHIPS.	SLAVES ALLOWED.	SHIPS	SLAVES ALLOWED.	SHIPS.	SLAVES.	MEDIUM SLAVES.
1795	14	5,149	6	2,402	59	17,647	79	25,198	317
1796	8	2,593	1	393	94	29,425	103	32,411	315
1797	12	4,225	2	801	90	29,958	104	34,984	336
1798	8	2,650	3	1,433	149	53,051	160	57,104	356
1799	17	5,582	5	2,529	134	47,517	156	55,628	356
1800	10	2,231	3	717	120	31,844	133	34,722	261
1801	23	6,347	2	586	122	30,913	147	37,846	259
1802	30	9,011	3	704	122	31,371	155	41,086	266
1803	15	3,616	1	355	83	29,954	99	24,925	253
1804	18	5,001	3	798	126	31,090	147	36,899	244
10 yrs.		46,405		10,718		323,770		380,893	

(1) Troughton's Liverpool, page 265.

As few persons, comparatively speaking, in this country ever saw a bill of lading for human beings, shipped on board a British vessel, engaged in this odious traffic, and as an original bill of lading for slaves, shipped for Georgia, is now in the author's possession, a copy of it is here given, as a matter of curiosity:—

"*Shipped, by the grace of God,*[1] in good order and well-condition'd by JAMES[2]   in and upon the good Ship call'd the MARY BOROUGH, whereof is Master, under God, for this present voyage, Captain David Morton, and now riding at Anchor at the Barr of Senegal, and by God's grace bound for Georgey, in South Carolina, to say, twenty-four prime Slaves, six prime women Slaves, being mark'd and

Marked on the Right Buttock
0
0

number'd as in the margin, and are to be deliver'd, in the like good order and well condition'd, at the aforesaid Port of Georgia, South Carolina, (the danger of the Seas and Mortality only excepted) unto Messrs. Broughton and Smith, or to their Assigns; he or they paying Freight for the said Slaves at the rate of Five pounds sterling per head at delivery, with Primage and Avrage accustom'd.—In WITNESS whereof, the Master or Purser of the said Ship hath affirm'd to three Bills of Lading, all of this tenor and date; the one of which three bills being accomplish'd, the other two to stand void; and so God send the good Ship to her desir'd port in safety, Amen.

Dated in Senegal, 1st February, 1766.

DAVID MORTON."

It will be observed from the bill of lading, that those slaves were marked or branded with particular marks. The operation of marking slaves was performed on them by means of a heated iron, with as much indifference as if they had been merely cattle; indeed, when the author was a boy he has seen branding irons, with letters or marks for branding slaves, exhibited for sale in the shops of Liverpool, and no doubt, they were sold in the same manner in other seaport towns of the kingdom.

" HE THAT STEALETH A MAN AND SELLETH HIM, OR IF HE BE FOUND IN HIS HAND, HE SHALL SURELY BE PUT TO DEATH."[3]

It is a remarkable fact, that of the large number of

---

(1) The words, " the grace of God," are supplied here, but have been apparently accidentally torn from the original.

(2) The surname is illegible in the original.

(3) Exodus, chap. 21, verse 16.

G 1

Liverpool persons who made fortunes in the African slave trade, and some of them acquired by that odious traffic considerable wealth, it only remained, in very few instances, in their families, until the third generation, and in many cases it was dispersed or disappeared in the first generation, after the deaths of the persons acquiring it.

Besides the risk of fire and shipwreck which all vessels are more or less liable to at sea, those which were engaged in the African slave trade were exposed to an additional and terrible danger, the mutiny of the slaves. A shocking instance of that nature occurred to the ship Thomas, of Liverpool, belonging to Mr. Thomas Clarke, and commanded by a very brave, respectable, and intelligent man, Captain Peter M'Quie.[1] She had been to the Coast of Africa, and had taken on board, at Loango, 375 picked slaves, was on her voyage to Barbadoes, and, on the morning of 2nd September, 1797, whilst all hands were occupied at breakfast, two or three of the female slaves having discovered that the armourer had incautiously left the arm chest open, got into the after-hatchway, and conveyed all the arms which they could find through the bulkheads to the male slaves, about two hundred of whom immediately ran up the forescuttles, and put to death all of the crew who came in their way. For a little while some of the crew, with their captain at their head, fought desperately with the few arms which were usually kept in the cabin, but were eventually overpowered, and the vessel remained in the hands of the slaves. The captain and many of his brave crew perished in the insurrection, having either fallen in the conflict, or been butchered in the vessel, or been

---

(1) He was a native of Minnigaff, in the county of Galloway, Scotland, but sailed some years out of Liverpool. Some instances of his bravery will be mentioned in Chapter VI. He was the Father of Mr. Peter Robinson M'Quie, merchant, of Liverpool.

driven overboard. Twelve of the crew, however, escaped in the stern-boat, and after enduring the most dreadful hardships, two only survived and landed on the island of Barbadoes; besides those, there were a few who were preserved from death in order that they might steer the vessel to Africa, two of whom afterwards escaped (with two others) in the long-boat, and landed, after having been six days and nights without food or water, in a most wretched state, on Watling's Island, one of the Bahamas; five of the crew still remained on board the Thomas, and were only preserved from death by the negroes not being able to steer the vessel without them; and, after forty-two days of misery and dread, it providentially happened that an American brig, laden with rum, came alongside, of which the insurgent negroes made themselves masters, her crew escaping in their boats. The rum casks were soon broken open, and in the drunkenness and confusion which ensued, several negroes were drowned. The remaining crew of the Thomas immediately took advantage of this occurrence, and retook possession of the rum brig, (the boatswain, with the captain's cutlass, having first killed the ringleader of the negroes,) and set sail for the nearest land, and reached and landed on Long Island, Providence. The Thomas, with the surviving revolted negroes on board, was afterwards re-captured by H.M. frigate the Thames.[1]

The trade from Liverpool to the Mediterranean was considerable during that period, but not any tables are known to exist to show its extent or increase.

The Baltic trade was another important branch of the commerce of the port. Large quantities of salt were exported to the Baltic from Liverpool, and considerable quantities were also sent, during that period, to the Netherlands.

---

(1) Communicated by Mr. Peter Robinson M'Quie, from documents in his possession.

Liverpool also had her fair share of trade to and from other parts of the continent of Europe; though Hull, from its geographical position, perhaps enjoyed a larger portion of the latter, especially of the trade in the importation of timber from the European continent.

The Irish trade was also one of some magnitude and importance to Liverpool, although previous to the Union, the importation of oats and other grain was under various restrictions, and, consequently, was not to be compared in extent to what took place after the Union. Even after that event, the trade with Ireland was for some time regulated much on the same principle as before. The Union did not immediately produce free trade with Ireland; the duties on importation, the drawbacks, as well as the acts of parliament relative to corn, existed long afterwards.

The Greenland Fishery also was then of importance to Liverpool; and one of the principal merchants concerned in it was Mr. Thomas Staniforth, the father of the late Mr. Samuel Staniforth. It fluctuated very much, but at one time there were twenty-three ships from Liverpool[1] employed in it. The seamen engaged in it were, as an encouragement to the Greenland trade, protected by parliamentary enactments, against impressment; and instances were not unfrequent during the war, of a body of seamen engaged in that trade, going to the Liverpool Custom-house armed with harpoons and whaling knives, to defend themselves against the press-gang, until they could reach the Custom-house, where lists of their names being furnished, on oath, by the owners, the seamen gave security to the satisfaction of the Commissioners of Customs, to proceed in the vessels to which they belonged to the Greenland

---

(1) Communicated by the late Mr. Samuel Staniforth to the Author. In Troughton's Liverpool, and in Smithers' Liverpool, the largest number in any one year, is stated to have been twenty-one.

seas, or Davis' Straits, in the whale fishery, in the following season; and they then received a certificate of protection, under the provisions of the Acts of Parliament 13th George the Second, chap. 28, sec. 5; 11th George the Third, chap. 38, sec. 19; 26th George the Third, chap. 41, sec. 17, and 31st George the Third, chap. 43, sec. 5; and they were then privileged from impressment, until after the expiration of the season of the fishery, and until the termination of the voyage.[1]

The first vessel which sailed from Liverpool in that trade was the Golden Lion, in 1750; she had been a prize taken from the French, and was called at the time of capture, "Le Lion d'or."[2]   The following is a copy of proposals, in 1749, for the purchase of the vessel in shares, and for fitting her out for the Greenland trade, with the names or firms of the merchants who subscribed to them, and embarked in the concern, and of the shares which they respectively took :—

"PROPOSALS from GOORE and BULKELEY to all such Persons as shall become Subscribers hereto, for the sale of the Ship GOLDEN LION, now belonging to them, and for fitting her out for the GREENLAND WHALE-FISHING TRADE, for the next Season.

1st.—That they the said Goore and Bulkeley do consent and agree to take the Sum of Two Thousand Pounds Sterling for the Vessel and her Materials, (the Great Guns with their Tackle and Firearms only excepted,) the Persons subscribing hereto do oblige themselves respectively to pay his or their proportion according to the amount of the share subscribed for towards the Payment of the said Sum of two thousand Pounds, in two months from the Date of the Bill of Sale.

2nd.—That the joint Concern in the said Vessel shall be divided into twenty or more equal shares, every Person having the liberty of Subscribing one Share more or less, so that none subscribe for less than half a Share.

3rd.—That twenty shares being subscribed for, the Bargain shall be valid, otherwise void.

---

(1) And every harpooner, line manager, or boat-steerer who had given such security as above mentioned, was allowed to sail in the Colliery or Coasting Trade, without being liable to be impressed during the time of the year that they were not employed in the fishery.

(2) Communicated to the Author by the late Mr. Samuel Staniforth.

4th.—That the Subscription being completed, every Subscriber shall and is obliged to pay his or their Proportion of the Outfit, Disbursements, Wages, or other charges, into the Hands of the Persons appointed Managers, when and as often as by them the said Managers required.

5th.—That the Subscribers or a Majority of them do immediately after the Completion hereof, appoint two or more of the said Subscribers to be Agents for the directing of the whole Proceedings of the Voyage and equipping the Vessel.

Lastly, the said Goore and Bulkeley agree on their Part to hold one whole Share.—In witness whereof, We the Persons willing to be concerned have Subscribed our Names and Shares this eighteenth Day of December, 1749.

SHARES.

Thos. & John Backhouse,—half a Share.
John Nicholson, & Co,—halfe Share.
David Edie.—half a Share.
Joseph Jackson.—half a Share.
Jo: Manesty.—half a Share.
Richd. Nicholas.—half a share.
Jas. Gordon.—half a Share.
Thos. Shaw.—halfe Share.
John Atherton.—half a share.
Heywood Benson & Co.—half a Share.
John Parke.—half a share.
Richd. Golightly,—half a Share.
Owen Prichard.—half a share.
Tho. Mears for self, & John Okill.—half a Share.
Richard Savage.—half a Share.
Charles Goore for William Hurst.—half share.
Charles Goore, for Nathl. Bassnett.—one share.
Thomas Seel.—One Share.
Foster Cunliffe, & Sons.—One Share.
Saml. Ogden.—one Share.
Edwd. Trafford.—One Share.
John Knight.—One Share.
John Brooks.—one Share.
John Hardman.—one Share.
Sam. Shaw,—half a Share.
Jam. Crosbie.—half a Share.
Chas. Lowndes.—half a Share.
Edwd. Cropper.—half a Share.
John Tarleton.—half a Share.
Law^{ce} Spencer.—half a Share.
Edward Lowndes.—half a Share.
Edward Parr.—half a Share.
Edwd. Roughsedge.—half a Share.
Joseph Bird.—half a share.
John Seddon.—half a Share.
James Pardoe.—half a Share.
John Entwisle.—half a Share."[1]

---

[1] From the original in the possession of the late Mr. Samuel Staniforth.

The vessel, after being commanded for a long time by Captain Metcalf was lost, whilst a full ship, as it was termed, in coming out of the ice during one of her voyages. She was accustomed, when in Liverpool, to lie near the south-west corner of the Old Dock; which, from that circumstance, was called the Golden Lion berth. She ought not to be confounded with another well-known but more modern vessel, called after the former, also, the Golden Lion, which was commanded by Captain Thompson; she was employed in the same trade, and belonged to Messrs. T. Staniforth and Sons; she was afterwards withdrawn from that trade and let out to the Government, and employed in the victualling service, and, whilst so employed, in coming home from the Mediterranean, was captured by the French.

The first ship built at Liverpool, and employed in the trade, was launched in the year 1775, from Mr. Sutton's yard.[1]

A building for extracting the oil from the fat or blubber of whales, and provided with boilers for that purpose, was erected by a person named Nathan Kershaw, and was standing for a long time towards the latter part of the last century,[2] at the south end of the Queen's Dock, near the lowest end of Greenland-street; and since the enlargement of the dock, the site of the building now forms a part of it. These works were projected by Mr. Kershaw, who, being of a speculative turn of mind, also endeavoured to establish the manufacture of glue there, from the skin of whales' tails; but the whole of the works were a failure. The odour from them was any thing but agreeable to the neighbourhood.

---

(1) Smithers' Liverpool, page 97.

(2) The exact date when Mr. Nathan Kershaw erected those works cannot be ascertained, but it is certain that they were in existence at least as early as in 1795, because they are laid down in the Map of Liverpool, published in that year, in Aikin's Description of the Country from Thirty to Forty Miles round Manchester.

The Liverpool branch of the Greenland trade gradually declined, until it ceased to exist. One of the last of the vessels remaining in that trade was the Lion, Captain Hawkins, belonging to Mr. Staniforth ; he sold her to Mr. Hurry, and she was afterwards lost in the ice, in 1817, but the crew were saved.

The East India and China trades were not at that time thrown open to Liverpool. The East India Company still enjoyed their charter of exclusive trading ; and a renewed term of twenty years was granted to them from the 1st of March, 1794, when an Act of Parliament was passed in the 33rd year of George the Third, chap. 52, which, amongst other things, continued to that company for the renewed term, the possession of the British territories in India, together with their exclusive trade, under certain limitations. By the Act of 53rd George the Third, chap. 155, passed in 1813, the trade was thrown open to the mercantile public except as to the East India Company's exclusive right to trade to the dominions of the Emperor of China, and to trade in tea with all islands and places between the Cape of Good Hope and the Straits of Magellan, until three years' notice after the 10th of April, 1831.

The exclusive right of trading in tea then enjoyed by the East India Company terminated by law on the 22nd April, 1834; and thereupon the Act of the 3rd and 4th William the Fourth, chap. 101, allowed tea to be imported into any Port of the United Kingdom, (the privilege had previously been confined to London,) provided it was brought from places not nearer than the Cape of Good Hope and Straits of Magellan. And on the 26th June, 1849, by the Act of the 12th and 13th Victoria, chap. 29, (repealing the Navigation Act,) this remaining restriction on tea was abolished, and it now may be imported from any place.

The trade to the British Colonies in North America was

an important one; and even during the American revolutionary war there was an extensive commerce with such parts as were then either occupied by British forces, or as sided with Great Britain in the contest:[1] and, after the termination of the war, the trade with the United States of America soon became very considerable.

Cotton, an article of which the importation is now so immense, was, about that period, imported into Liverpool, in what must be considered as comparatively very insignificant quantities, principally from the British West India Islands, and some from the Mediterranean.

As tending to show at what a recent period the trade in cotton from North America dates its origin, it may be correct to mention here, that, in 1784, eight bags of cotton were imported from the United States of America, in an American vessel into Liverpool, which were seized by an officer of Customs, under the impression, that cotton was not grown in America.[2]   Much more importance, however, seems to have been attached to the occurrence, by different narrators of it, than it merited.   It merely appears to amount to this : that a blundering, and perhaps very young officer, who knew nothing about cotton, had temporarily detained it, (similar mistakes, quite as singular, occasionally occur even now, with respect to other articles ;) but the matter probably was set to rights as soon as the result of his ignorance was known to his superior officers, and there is not any reason

(1) Communicated by the Author's Father.

(2) Recollections of Liverpool; anonymous, but, in fact, published by Mr. Bryan Blundell, on the 25th February, 1824.   Mr. Bryan Blundell was a high authority in the matter, because, he resided in Liverpool at the date of the occurrence, and a public appointment which he afterwards held, would have a tendency to keep it in his recollection.   The authenticity of the anecdote has been confirmed by the Author's Father who also resided in Liverpool, at that date, and who has conversed with the Author on the subject, and expressed himself quite satisfied that the anecdote was substantially correct.

H l

to suppose that any reference on the subject was considered necessary to be made to the Commissioners of Customs. If the eight bags of cotton had not been grown in the United States, it is clear that, according to our navigation laws, they could not legally have been imported in an American vessel into Liverpool.

But another remarkable circumstance connected with those eight bags of cotton remains to be told. It should seem that the importation of the eight bags caused something like a glut in the market, because they lay in the warehouse of Messrs. William Rathbone and Son, who were the consignees of them, for several months, for want of buyers, and were afterwards sold to Messrs. Strutt and Company, of Derby.[1]

For some time after the close of the American revolutionary war, though some little cotton was imported into Liverpool from the United States, it was in very insignificant quantities.[2]

It seems a doubtful point at what date cotton was first grown in, and imported from, the British States of North America; there is, however, some evidence that several years before the American revolutionary war, cotton was an article of importation from the British States in North America, though in very limited quantities, into Liverpool. An account of the imports of merchandise from all places into Liverpool, in 1770, has fortunately been preserved, and amongst other articles the importation of cotton was then as follows:—

From   New York .... 3 bales
  „   Virginia and Maryland .... 4 bags
  „   North Carolina......................... 3 barrels
  „   Georgia .... 3 bags.[3]

---

(1) Communicated by Mr. William Rathbone, whose grandfather and father constituted the above-mentioned firm of Messrs. William Rathbone and Son, the consignees of the cotton.

(2) Communicated by the Author's Father.

(3) Enfield's Liverpool, page 73, 74 and 79.

Whether the cotton had been grown in those States, or had been previously brought there (as is within the scope of possibility) from any of the British West India Islands, cannot now be ascertained.

The total quantity of cotton imported into Liverpool from the British West Indian and North American colonies and Foreign countries, in 1770, was 6037 bags, 3 bales, and 3 barrels.[1] The mode in which some of it was packed may now appear remarkable, as only three bales are mentioned in the list of imports of that year, as coming from the States of North America, and on one occasion some came in barrels.

In 1852 the quantity of cotton imported into Liverpool from all places whatever, was 2,207,016 packages, (such as bales, bags, &c.) of which 1,717,256 came from the United States of America, which presents an astonishing contrast between the importations now, and those of the last century.

The Fishing trade carried on from Liverpool, in 1775, was also of considerable extent. Enfield, in his work on Liverpool, published a short time previous to that year, mentions a list of 44 different species of fish which had been taken in the Mersey, all of which, except five kinds, were eatable. The fisheries gave employment to a number of small Liverpool vessels, and the capture of fish, especially of cod and herrings, was occasionally very great; the latter were caught in large quantities in various places, one of which was near Parkgate, at the mouth of the Dee, from about 1775 to 1780; and a curing-house for them was established at Parkgate. There were also six herring-curing houses in Liverpool about 1775, some of which were on an extensive scale, which were supplied with herrings principally brought from the Isle of Man; but after the com-

(1) Enfield's Liverpool, page 73, 74 and 79.

mencement of the present century, the number of those houses diminished, and of such as remained the business was on a comparatively small scale.

Liverpool had a considerable Coasting trade in 1775. About twelve vessels[1] of good size were employed in the coasting trade, as regular traders, for conveying goods between Liverpool and London ; some also traded between Liverpool and Bristol, Hull, Glasgow, Dumfries, Chester, Preston, Lancaster, Milnthorpe, Ulverstone, Whitehaven, and Carlisle. Such of those vessels as traded between Liverpool and London, were employed to convey, besides other goods, cheese, the produce of the Cheshire dairies, to London, from which circumstance they were often called cheese vessels. One of them, called the *Swan*, was commanded by a person named William Hunter, and on one of his voyages from London to Liverpool, he had occasion to put into Deal, or some other port in that quarter of the coast, and his dog was accidentally left on shore, and found its way to Liverpool, much to the surprise and alarm of the captain's family, who conjectured from the dog's arrival before the vessel, that the latter must have been wrecked, and that the dog had escaped to the shore.

The coasting trade between Liverpool and other parts of the kingdom was considerable during the whole period upon which we are now engaged, and gave employment to a most useful and hardy race of seamen. It is a circumstance to be regretted that authentic tables, or returns, have not been preserved, of the number of vessels or men employed in the coasting or fishing trade, during the period which elapsed between 1775 and 1800.

The articles of export to most of the places with which Liverpool traded, were principally the productions of Man-

---

(1) A list of the vessels is given in Gore's Liverpool Directory of 1774.

chester, Leeds, Sheffield, and Birmingham, with large quantities of earthenware from Staffordshire, and of salt from Cheshire. There is, indeed, no reasonable ground for doubting, that the trade in salt, especially when combined with the facilities afforded to bringing it down by the river Mersey for shipment, laid, in a great measure, the foundation, long ago, of the commercial greatness of Liverpool.

In the Appendix will be found some tables[1] which show the progress and increase of the general trade of the port of Liverpool during a considerable part of the last century.

COALS EXPORTED FROM LIVERPOOL IN 1791.

To Foreign Ports.............................57,000 tons.
Coastways ....40,000 „
                                              _____
                                               97,000 „

Leaving 41,000 tons for Liverpool, exclusive of those brought down the Sankey Canal, and those carted from the various collieries in the neighbourhood.[2]

In 1795, the Commissioners for manning his Majesty's navy completed their quota of men for this port, namely,[3]

Seamen 510
Ordinary Seamen... 365
Land Men 836
                                                          ____
                                                          1711

Inquiries have been made without success by the the Author, in order to have obtained a list of the ships belonging to Liverpool, in 1775; and, from the destruction by fire, in 1814, of the London Custom-house, where the books of Registry of Shipping were deposited, it is believed to be now impracticable to obtain it.

_____

(1) Appendix, No. X. The tables are copied from Troughton's Liverpool, page 259 to 266.

(2) Troughton's Liverpool, page 264.

(3) Ibid. page 195.

It fortunately happens, however, that a printed list is in existence of the vessels belonging to the Port of Liverpool, with the names of their commanders, and most of the trades in which they were respectively employed, in 1752; a copy of it will be found in the Appendix.[1] It appears from it, that there were then 357 vessels of all descriptions belonging to the Port of Liverpool; and upwards of eighty river sloops or vessels engaged principally in the Salt trade between Liverpool and Northwich, of the burthen of from forty to seventy tons each; besides which, there were numbers of vessels which were constantly employed in the Coasting trade to and from the port, which did not belong to it.

It would not come within the object and limits of this publication, nor is it intended, to give a detailed account of all the various trades and manufactures carried on in Liverpool in 1775; it will, therefore, suffice to mention briefly some of the principal of them.

The making of earthenware had been a trade of considerable importance to Liverpool, but before that date most of the potters had removed their establishments into Staffordshire; although some earthenware works for making articles of a common or coarse description, were still carried on in Liverpool, nearly all the Liverpool workers of the finer kinds of earthenware had emigrated into Staffordshire, where a number of them were employed who happened to be freemen, or more correctly called, free burgesses of Liverpool; and it was customary for many years afterwards, and in some cases even up to the passing of the Act[2] for the reform of the

---

(1) Appendix, No. XI. An original printed list is in the possession of Mr. James Boardman, to whom the Author is indebted for access to it, and for permission to copy it.

(2) 2nd William the 4th, chap. 45.

representation, passed in 1832, to send for the survivors to vote on the occasion of contested political elections. The opening of a communication, by canal, with Staffordshire, had given facilities for carrying pipe-clay to that county, which was brought principally from Exeter and Teignmouth to Liverpool, chiefly for the use of the potteries.

Glass-works, sugar-boiling and refining houses, tobacco manufactories, public breweries, copperas works, rope and cable manufactories, ironfoundries, herring curing-houses, and pitch works, as well as a considerable amount of ship-building, and various trades connected with shipping, were carried on at Liverpool.

A cotton-mill was established prior to 1796, in Cheapside, by Mr. Thomas Middleton; and another, a considerable time before the end of the 18th century, in Vauxhall-road, by Messrs. Kirkman and Company, for the spinning of cotton-twist. The former was burnt down, and the latter was kept up for some years, but it did not answer, and was eventually abandoned. The trade of spinning cotton, from some cause or other did not then succeed in Liverpool.

A similar establishment for spinning cotton was also attempted about the close of the last century, in Bolton-street, by Mr. Edward Pemberton, but was also abandoned; and the building was afterwards used as a printing-office, and called the Caxton printing-office, which was burnt down in 1821.

A remarkable fatality seems to have attended the trade of spinning cotton at Liverpool. About 1830 another cotton mill was established on the Canal-bank, in the north part of the town, which was consumed by fire on the 17th of May, 1853.

The progressive increase of the Dock Duties, from the middle to the close of the last century, will be interesting to those who are curious in matters connected with the rise and prosperity of the town.

AMOUNT OF DOCK DUTIES RECEIVED AT THE PORT OF LIVERPOOL, FROM THE
YEAR 1752 TO 1800, ENDING 24TH JUNE IN EACH YEAR.[1]

YEAR.	NO. VESSELS.	£.	s.	d.	YEAR.	NO. VESSELS.	£.	s.	d.
1752	——	1,776	8	2	1777	2361	4,610	4	9
1753	——	2,034	16	2	1778	2292	4,649	7	7
1754	——	2,095	11	0	1779	2374	4,957	17	10
1755	——	2,417	13	11	1780	2261	3,528	7	9
1756	——	2,187	16	9	1781	2512	3,915	4	11
1757	1371	2,336	15	0	1782	2496	4,249	6	3
1758	1453	2,403	6	3	1783	2816	4,840	8	3
1759	1281	2,372	12	2	1784	3098	6,597	11	1
1760	1245	2,330	6	7	1785	3429	8,411	5	3
1761	1319	2,382	0	2	1786	3228	7,508	0	1
1762	1307	2,526	19	6	1787	3567	9,199	18	8
1763	1752	3,141	1	5	1788	3677	9,206	13	10
1764	1625	2,780	3	4	1789	3619	8,901	10	10
1765	1930	3,455	8	4	1790	4223	10,037	6	2½
1766	1908	3,653	19	2	1791	4045	11,645	6	6
1767	1704	3,615	9	2	1792	4483	13,243	17	8¼
1768	1808	3,566	14	9	1793	4129	12,480	5	5
1769	2054	4,004	5	0	1794	4265	10,678	7	0
1770	2073	4,142	17	2	1795	3948	9,368	16	4
1771	2087	4,203	19	10	1796	4738	12.377	7	7
1772	2259	4,552	5	4	1797	4528	13,319	12	8
1773	2214	4,725	1	11	1798	4478	12,057	18	3
1774	2258	4,580	5	5	1799	4518	14,049	15	1
1775	2291	5,384	4	9	1800	4746	23,379	13	6
1776	2216	5,064	10	10					

The Dock Duties of Liverpool, for the year ending
June 24, 1852, amounted to £246,686 5s 8d.[2]

In 1770, Mr. John Colquitt, the then Collector of
Customs for Liverpool, said, "How happy shall I be when
the Customs of Liverpool amount to £100,000 a year." At
that time they were between £80,000 and £90,000 per
annum. For the year ending on the 5th of April, 1850, the
nett remittance from the revenue of customs from the port
of Liverpool alone, was £3,373,890 18s 4d; which was
a larger nett amount than the revenue of customs received
into the Exchequer either from Scotland or from Ireland;
and previously to the duties being taken off cotton, hides,
skins, turpentine, and other articles, by the Act 8th and 9th
Victoria, chap. 12, passed in 1845, (see also the Act 8th

(1) From an account published by the Treasurer of the Dock Trustees, and with
their authority.   (2) Ibid.

and 9th Victoria, chap. 90, passed in the same year,) and the establishment of a custom-house at Manchester, which circumstances naturally reduced the amount of duties collected at Liverpool, the nett revenue of customs remitted into the Exchequer from Liverpool was greater than from all Scotland and Ireland together.

In 1775, the gross receipts from the revenue of customs, at Liverpool, were £274,655 3s 1d; and the nett amount remitted and paid into the Exchequer was £96,159 3s 6d;[1] and in 1800, the gross receipts were £1,058,578 12s 6d, and the nett amount remitted was £734,320 12s 6d,[1] which was a very great increase in twenty-five years.

In 1850 the comparative amount of the revenue of Customs from Liverpool, Scotland, and Ireland, appears in the following account, viz :—

REVENUE OF CUSTOMS.
Account for the Year ending 5th April, 1850.

LIVERPOOL.				SCOTLAND.			
Gross Revenue £3,474,202	3	9		Gross Revenue £1,955,906	15	10	
Deduct 100,311	5	5		Deduct 62,115	0	7	
							1,893,791 15 3
Nett.... £3,373,890	18	4		IRELAND.			
				Gross Revenue £2,180,058	4	6	
				Deduct 57,903	2	6	
							2,122,155 2 0
				Nett........ £4,015,946	17	3	

The nett amount remitted from the Revenue of Customs at Liverpool, for the year ending the 5th of April, 1853, was £3,320,606 5s 3d.

REVENUE OF CUSTOMS
OF LIVERPOOL,
Account for the Year ending 5th April, 1853.

Gross Revenue.......................................£3,451,647 10 0
Deduct the expenses of collection, the drawbacks, and repayments.. 131,041 4 9

Nett........ £3,320,606 5 3

The astonishing progressive increase in the nett revenue of customs, remitted from Liverpool, is shown by the subjoined

---

(1) The nett remittance from the Customs at Liverpool, at that time, was the amount received after deducting the expenses of management and collection, the bounties, and some trifling expenses connected with the Customs.

I l

table, which was proved on behalf of the Corporation of Liverpool, on the trial of the important cause, The Mayor, Bailiffs, and Burgesses of Liverpool against Thomas Bolton and others, in the King's Bench, in February, 1833, which has been before noticed.[1] It will be observed that the subjoined table not only shows the nett sums remitted, but it also contains the gross receipts, which have been furnished to the author from a quarter of full authority in such matters; and that it embraces periods of time considerably before and after the period of which we are treating; but it is considered advisable not to mutilate or curtail so remarkable and curious a document.

LIVERPOOL REVENUE OF CUSTOMS.

YEAR.	GROSS RECEIPTS.			NETT REMITTANCES.		
	£.	s.	d.	£.	s.	d.
1733	92,466	13	4	35,106	14	6
1750	215,961	7	4	58,907	5	3
1755	202,367	9	2	49,661	0	8
1760	248,312	1	9	84,480	8	10
1765	269,435	8	1	70,346	2	11
1770	231,994	12	5	72,987	13	11
1775	274,655	3	1	96,159	3	6
1780	188,830	6	11	108,648	4	2
1785	680,928	19	10	264,771	5	8

1790—Books lost.

YEAR.	GROSS RECEIPTS.			NETT REMITTANCES.		
1795	469,438	18	5	250,462	16	1
1800	1,058,578	12	6	734,320	12	6

Warehousing Act, 1803.

YEAR.	GROSS RECEIPTS.			NETT REMITTANCES.		
1805	1,766,370	5	9	1,468,063	7	7
1810	2,675,766	8	10	2,347,409	10	9
1815	2,360,967	15	11	2,146,448	19	9

{ The Duty on tobacco, coffee, &c. transferred to the Excise in 1819.

YEAR.	GROSS RECEIPTS.			NETT REMITTANCES.		
1820	1,488,072	9	10	1,269,115	1	1
1824	1,984,522	16	0	1,660,971	2	1

{ In 1825, the Excise duties re-transferred.

YEAR.	GROSS RECEIPTS.			NETT REMITTANCES.		
1826	3,087,651	2	7	2,896,535	13	11
1827	3,308,804	4	4	3,113,384	12	3
1828	3,180,503	14	4	2,973,416	19	10
1829	3,315,041	10	3	3,123,758	8	10
1830	3,562,114	14	11	3,333,473	19	6
1831	3,599,206	3	3	3,381,574	19	7
1832	3,925,062	8	2	3,741,382	0	0[2]

(1) Chapter III, page 221.

(2) The nett remittances only were deposed to, on the trial of the before-mentioned cause, the Mayor, Bailiffs and Burgesses of Liverpool, against Thomas Bolton and others, and it was not considered necessary to prove on the trial the gross receipts; however, the particulars of the gross receipts, as above set out, have been subsequently obtained by the Author, from a quarter of full authority on that subject.

Liverpool was, a long time ago, as far as relates merely to the Customs' regulations, under the officers of the Customs of Chester; but the following entry appears on the Liverpool Corporation Records, as early as the 15th January, 1646, from which it should appear that, from that date at least, it was no longer the case :—

"It is desired that, Whereas this port is a free and Independant Port, that all Officers for Customs may be properly belonging to this port; and that the Officers of Chester, may not hereafter usurp anie power, or authoritie, in this port, as from Chester; o^r. Charters and auncient grants and customs are, that we shall enjoy all such liberties and priviledges as anie other port within the King's dominions."[1]

In 1658, is an entry in the Corporation Records referring to a difference which had arisen between the officers of the Customs of Chester and of Liverpool, and stating that—

"The matter having been referred, the 29th October, 1658, to Mr. Samuel Sandford, the Surveyor General for the Customs and Excise, he declared and concluded that the liberties of Liverpool reached to the accustomed place, on the further side of Redstones."[2]

The Banking Houses which existed in Liverpool, in 1775, and for several years afterwards, were that of Messrs. Charles Caldwell and Company (subsequently Messrs. Caldwell, Smythe and Co.) in Paradise-street; that of Messrs. William Clarke and Son, on the east side of Derby-square; and that of Messrs. Arthur Heywood, Son and Co. in Castle-street; the banking hours of the latter were stated in the Directory of 1777, as "hours of attendance from nine to one, and from three to six. No business done on Thursday."[3] Afterwards, Messrs. Thomas, Samuel and Joseph Crane, had at one period a bank in Dale-street, near the Exchange.

(1) Printed Report of the Proceedings at Liverpool before the Commissioners of Inquiry into Municipal Corporations, in 1833, page 284.

(2) Ibid. page 286.

(3) From J. Gore's Liverpool Directory of 1777.

About 1790, the bank of Messrs. William Gregson, Sons and Company, was established, in Paradise-street, near the lower end of College-lane; at the close of 1795, or the commencement of 1796, the firm was changed to that of William Gregson, Sons, Parkes and Clay;[1] in 1805, it was again changed to that of Gregson, Clay and Company; and, in 1807, not being successful, the bank was discontinued. Messrs. Staniforth, Ingram, Bold and Daltera, were also Liverpool bankers in 1793, but did not carry on the business for a long time : their bank was in Pool-lane, now South Castle-street, nearly opposite the end of King-street.

In 1793, in consequence of the prevalence of great commercial distress, both in Liverpool and elsewhere in the kingdom, a plan was taken into consideration, for obtaining a legislative permission for the issue of negotiable notes, by the Corporation of Liverpool, and on that occasion, a statement and explanation were made of the property and income of the Corporation, as being a sufficient security for the payment of the notes, as will be more fully explained in another chapter.[2]

The permanent property of all descriptions, including debts owing to the Corporation, the items of which were exhibited, and after deducting the debt owing by the Corporation, amounted to £821,959 8s, and the gross annual income amounted to £25,000 17s 11d, and an act of parliament was passed May 10, 1793, in the thirty-third year of George the Third, chap. 31, empowering the Corporation to issue negotiable notes, to an extent not exceeding £200,000, for a limited time; which judicious measure had the happy effect of assisting in restoring confidence; not a moiety of that amount was required, and the notes which had been issued were in due time paid off.

---

(1) For a short time about that period, the firm was William Gregson, Sons, Parkes and Morland.   (2) Chapter V.

During the period which elapsed, between 1775 and the close of the 18th century, the periodical observance of old customs, festivals, and holydays, was much more attended to than at present. The recurrence of the time-honoured festival of Christmas, was commemorated in Liverpool, to an extent much beyond what is now the usage, though in a degree inferior to the manner in which it was observed in the age which was gone by.[1] In this town the boar's head, garnished with rosemary, and with a pippin in its mouth, had ceased to be a standard dish at the table, it was not then considered essential for the yule log to blaze on the hearth, and morris-dancers and mummers no longer contributed to the rude mirth of the Christmas guests; but the churches and houses were still profusely decorated with holly, laurel, ivy, and other evergreens, hospitable and convivial meetings, visits of relations and friends, and the Christmas carols, marked the anniversary of the season, which was one of enjoyment, festivity, and

---

(1) The account given in Mr. Washington Irving's Sketch Book, of the manner of celebrating Christmas, in England, is erroneous, and is also objectionable, as having a tendency to mislead persons who may not be conversant with English habits or customs. The Author of this Work had some acquaintance with him and his brother, Mr. Peter Irving, when they resided in Liverpool, in 1817, and is confident that there is not any material difference between the ages of Mr. W. Irving and the Author; and he feels no hesitation in asserting, that the mode of celebrating Christmas, by a combination of so many old ceremonies, observances and pastimes, as are there described, has never existed in England during the life time of either of them. It is true that the Sketch Book is merely a work of imagination and not of history, and that it describes Mr. Bracebridge as an eccentric elderly gentleman, who was fond of keeping up or reviving ancient customs and old pastimes, but it is so expressed that a stranger to English habits, on reading it, can scarcely avoid falling into the error of imagining that such a mode of celebration, was observed at Christmas, in some parts of England, at the time when that book was written, or at least, in very modern times. Even if all the ceremonies, sports and observances which are there described, ever were commonly practised at Christmas, in English families, it was in an age long since past, and there is no reason to believe that the mode of observing or celebrating Christmas, described in the Sketch Book, ever occurred in England, within the last hundred years.

relaxation. The interest excited by the recurrence of this festival did not escape the notice of Shakespeare, who makes a most beautiful, although wild and fanciful, allusion to the night preceding Christmas-day, and who appears desirous to inculcate a degree of religious veneration for the season : in mentioning the disappearance of the ghost of the deceased King, he introduces the following passage :—

> " It faded on the crowing of the cock.
> Some say, that ever 'gainst that season comes,
> Wherein our Saviour's birth is celebrated,
> This bird of dawning, singeth all night long :
> And then they say no spirit dares stir abroad,
> The nights are wholesome, then no planets strike,
> No fairy takes, nor witch hath power to charm ;
> So hallowed and so gracious is the time."[1]

The custom of having supper parties on new year's-eve, to let in, as it was termed, the new year, was then very prevalent ; as the clock struck twelve at midnight, a loyal or appropriate song was commonly sung, and sometimes the ceremony was gone through, of opening the window for a few seconds, to let in the new year. This custom still lingers in some places, though much less observed than formerly. A similar ceremony was not unfrequently observed on Christmas-eve, on letting in Christmas.

The other seasons of enjoyment, Easter and Whitsuntide weeks, were also much more observed in Liverpool, as periods of relaxation and recreation, than they now are.

In Easter week, the fair, called Folly Fair, before noticed,[2] was held in the neighbourhood of London-road and Islington. An idle and blameable practice also existed, on Monday and Tuesday in Easter week, amongst the lower classes, called lifting, which is not yet quite abolished

---

(1) Hamlet, act 1, scene 1. It is remarkable, that in Bell's edition of Shakespeare, a considerable portion of that exquisitely beautiful passage is omitted.

(2) Chapter I, page 113.

in some remote and rude places ; and which consisted in the ceremony of lifting persons into the air, sometimes in a chair, and at other times without one, unless they purchased impunity by a pecuniary gratuity. It is supposed that if there be any meaning at all in so foolish a practice, it is a reprehensible allusion to the resurrection, or the ascension of our Saviour.

The anniversary of the gunpowder plot, the 5th of November, was celebrated by bonfires and fireworks.

That of the restoration of monarchy, the 29th of May, was commemorated by the usual honours of oak leaves; the Liverpool people probably thinking, like many others, that although there was nothing to admire in the conduct or character of a licentious and despotically-inclined monarch like Charles the Second, yet, that the nation in recalling him, and discarding the Puritan Parliament, chose the least of two evils, and not being then sufficiently ripe or experienced to invite over some other prince, as was afterwards done in 1688, who would accept the crown, on the condition of governing on constitutional principles, acted judiciously, in preferring one tyrannical king, rather than remaining under the government of many tyrannical rulers.

During a considerable part of the concluding quarter of the 18th century, the dress of the bankers, merchants, and others, of the upper and middle classes of Liverpool, was very different from anything now seen there. They then commonly wore coats cut much in the form of court dress-coats, often with stand-up collars, and usually with gilt, silvered, twist, or basket buttons; waistcoats of very great length, of the kind called flap waistcoats, the flaps being large, and containing pockets with a small cover or flap over each pocket, and often with ornamented basket buttons ; short breeches, with buckles of gold, silver, or false stones, at the knees, and large buckles of gold or silver, or gilt or plated to resemble those metals, in their shoes. The coat, waistcoat, and breeches were often all of one colour, frequently of a light or snuff colour. Ruffles at the wrists, and white stocks for the throat were almost invariably worn.[1] Cocked hats were commonly used; the kind of cocked hat then in fashion, came to a point or peak in front, and the raised part of the back was higher than the sides, not dissimilar in fashion to the small hat of that description, which is often seen introduced in portraits of King George the Third. The two last residents in Liverpool, who persevered in wearing hats something of that description, appear to have been Mr. Murray, of Duke-street, who was the owner of considerable property near the Old Dock gut, and whom many of the survivors of the congregation of the old chapel in Benns-garden must recollect, as he was regular in his attendance at divine service there, and Mr. Arthur Onslow, the then collector of customs; the latter continued to do so until nearly the period of his death, (which occurred in the year 1807;) and he also wore a tie wig until he died. The young men, and some of the middle-aged men wore their hair dressed with large curls on each side of the face, called cannon curls, and with queues behind, and occasionally thick short queues called clubs. Wigs of various descriptions, such as tie wigs, cauliflower wigs, brown bob wigs,[2] and bush wigs,[3] with hair powder, were also commonly worn by middle aged and elderly persons.

Hair powder was almost always worn by persons in the higher and middle ranks, whether they wore their own hair

---

(1) The Author's Father recollected the dress of the Liverpool merchants being as above described. A portrait of him, in a dress something of that description, taken about 1782, or a short time afterwards, has been preserved.

(2) The pictures and engravings of King George the 3rd, taken when he was advanced in life, usually represent him with a brown bob wig.

(3) The engraved portrait of Dr. Johnson, usually placed at the commencement of his dictionary, is represented with a bush wig; but the bottom or curled part is rather deeper than was worn in Liverpool at the time we are treating of.

or wigs; and the first tax upon hair powder was in 1795, when, by the Act 35th George the Third, chap. 49, a duty was imposed on certificates issued for using hair powder.

The stockings worn by them were generally of silk, sometimes plain, and at other times ribbed or striped, and in the morning occasionally of cotton or of woollen yarn.

Canes and walking-sticks were very generally used, with large heads of gold, and sometimes of silver, amber, or ebony.

Boots were rarely used, except the kind called top-boots, which were commonly worn by equestrians.

In such a costume, merchants, bankers, and persons in a similar station in life constantly went abroad in the morning. It may easily be supposed, what astonishment would be excited on the Liverpool Exchange, if a merchant were now to appear there, attired in the dress which was commonly worn by a Liverpool merchant of those days.

When in full dress for visiting, they usually wore silk, satin, or velvet waistcoats, frequently of a rich colour and pattern, and often much embroidered or worked about the pocket holes and flaps, which were made very long, and silk breeches and stockings, with knee and shoe buckles;[1] in

---

(1) This style of dress was also prevalent in London, and probably in all other parts of the kingdom at that period. In Townsend's Lives of Twelve eminent Judges, vol. 1, page 427, it is stated, on the authority of Dr. Dibden, who narrates the fact from his own observation, that the usual evening dress of the times which he was describing, was as follows:—" Cocked hats and ruffles, with satin small clothes, and silk stockings;" and Mr. (afterwards Lord) Erskine is there stated to have been " attired in the smart dress of the times, a dark green coat, scarlet waistcoat, and silk breeches." This was on the occasion of Dr. Dibdin's calling upon Mr. Erskine, whilst he was at breakfast, to request permission to dedicate a book to him. The precise date is not given, but Mr. Erskine was called to the bar in 1778, and, at the time when that is stated to have been his dress, he is represented as having been on the point of going out of town, to some provincial town, on a special retainer, and as his rise was so rapid, that he had, in the fourth year after being called to the bar, refused to accept junior briefs at Nisi Prius, and had the distinction of a silk gown and a patent of precedency, in 1783, it is fair to infer, that the date cannot have been long after the latter year.

K 1

other respects the dress differed little from the walking or morning costume.

The ladies, when in full dress, wore hair powder, with a cushion upon the crown of the head, over which the hair was turned, and combed smoothly, so as to be raised several inches high.[1] They also wore very high-heeled shoes, the heels being from three to four inches in height. The very large hoops which appear depicted in old pictures and prints[2] were gone out of use, or very nearly so, but they appear to have then been still commonly used on the stage.[2] Small hoops were, however, then constantly worn by ladies when visiting in Liverpool, and they continued to be used for many years after the commencement of the last quarter of that century. Parasols were not then used in Liverpool; indeed, they did not come into general use in England until about 1795; but instead of them, the ladies were in the habit of screening their faces from the sun, by means of immensely large green fans, which they carried with them when walking out; a custom which many ladies continued until about the commencement of the present century.

The customary dinner hour of the merchants and other persons of respectability in Liverpool, during a considerable part of the last quarter of the 18th century, was one o'clock, rarely as late as two, when not engaged with company at home, or not dining from home.

The usual hour of dinner parties was frequently as early as one o'clock, and, as years rolled on, it was commonly at two, or at three o'clock at the latest; and an inconvenient and expensive mode of entertaining resulted from dining so early, the giving both dinner, tea, and

---

(1) In Bell's edition of the British Theatre, published at various periods, between 1776 to 1781 inclusive, many such head-dresses are given, in the engravings of the performers.

(2) Ibid. Where many of the large hoops appear in the engravings.

supper to the visiters. The dinner hour of the Unanimous Club, which was composed of persons of the first families of Liverpool, and which will be mentioned in another place in this chapter, varied from half-past two, in 1775, to three o'clock, in 1777.

The following advertisement shows that, in 1775, it was usual for public dinners of gentlemen to take place, in Liverpool, as early as two o'clock in the afternoon :—

" The Annual Meeting of the Friends of Sir William Meredith and Mr. Pennant, will be held on Friday, the 6th of October, at Mr. Wrigley's, the Golden Lion, in Dale-street.

Mr. Atherton in the chair.

Dinner on table at two o'Clock."[1]

The custom of dining early extended to all classes; even the Mayors of Liverpool were in the habit of inviting guests to dine at the Town-hall, then called the Exchange, at one o'clock. The following is a copy of a card[2] (engraved) of invitation to dinner, issued by the Mayor of Liverpool, in 1776 :—

" Mr. Mayor presents his compliments to Mr. Leece, begs the favor of his company, on Sunday next, to dinner, at one o'Clock, at the Exchange.

An Answer is desired.—12 July, '76."

It cannot be ascertained at this distance of time, how the Mayor entertained his guests on Sunday, at such a dinner as that to which the card refers; but it is fair to surmise, that the attendance of the Mayor and his guests at Divine service in the afternoon was not a very probable event.

It was a common occurrence for the Mayors of Liverpool, after leaving St. George's Church, on Sunday, to have the

(1) Gore's General Advertiser of 22nd and 29th September, 1775.

(2) Copied by the Author from the original card of invitation, in the possession of Mrs. Bourne, the grand-daughter of the gentleman invited.

chaplain and two or three other persons, such as the Bailiffs, Town-clerk, or some personal friends, to dine with them, between the morning and afternoon services; most likely a mere verbal invitation sufficed for those occasions, without the form of a card. Instead of wine, their Sunday beverage, was punch, and censorious persons used to say, (but with what truth it is now impossible to ascertain,) that the person who most excelled in mixing it, was not one of the laymen. It is said that when the time arrived for afternoon service at St. George's Church, the Sword-bearer used to enter the room, and place the wand against the Mayor's chair, or in his hand, as a signal for church going; and if any punch remained, the party returned and finished it after the service.

It, of course, can excite no surprise in any person, to be told, that it was then the custom (a custom which is still kept up,) for the officers bearing the regalia, and for some of the Mayor's male friends to walk and attend divine service with him, at St. George's Church on Sunday; but it is remarkable, that not long before the period we are now engaged upon, the wives of the Mayors also occasionally walked in the procession with their husbands to the church, accompanied by ladies who were their female friends or acquaintances, and who walked with them on those occasions as a mark of respect.

Balls, and parties where dancing was introduced, for young persons, were very common : the dances consisted of country dances and cottillions, and occasionally minuets.

There were public assemblies where both dancing and cards were introduced, which were held in the Exchange, before the fire destroyed its interior; they were afterwards held at one of the inns or hotels.

It may seem extraordinary to persons accustomed to the late hours of the present time, to hear of the company meeting as early as five o'clock, at a card assembly ; but such was the fashion of the age.

THE ARCHERY LODGE
of the Mersey Bowmen.

G. Jarman sc.

The following is a copy of a curious announcement of a card assembly, in 1775 :—

" Liverpool, Sept[r.] 22.

The Card Assembly

will begin on Thursday next, the 28th instant, in the Exchange.

To meet at five o'Clock."[1]

The above particulars are valuable, as giving an insight into the habits of Liverpool people of respectability, in the last century.

The old English and manly practice of Archery was a pastime which was held in estimation, in the last quarter of the 18th century, by the higher classes in Liverpool. An archery ground, with shooting butts, was formed, and respectably supported for some time, before the close of the last century, near the west side of Cazneau-street, which was then quite in the country ; and the members of the society or club which supported it, were called the " Mersey Bowmen." The principal part of the archery ground is built upon, but the lodge belonging to it still exists,[2] and is now altered, and used as a dwelling-house and workshop, occupied by James Macdonald, a cooper, but it is hid from Cazneau-street by other houses; the west part is, however, visible from Grosvenor-street, and is rather conspicuous from having had projecting wings added to it. A view of its east front may be obtained by going up a narrow court of small mean houses, called Cazneau-place, which communicates indirectly with Grosvenor-street, into which the back door of a small yard belonging to the lodge opens. The east front is of brick; and on a stone over a large window, a bow, arrows, and a hunting-horn are appropriately carved ; and on each side of the window is a stone tablet, on which are

---

(1) Gore's General Advertiser of 22nd September, 1775.

(2) The Author has been unable to learn the date of its erection.

carved two arrows crossed, with the initials, in old English letters 𝕸 and 𝕭 for Mersey Bowmen, as in the wood cut at the foot of this page.

In the anonymous work on Liverpool[1] before noticed, published in 1795, its author, in alluding to the club and to the fine manly practice of archery, calls it " the harmless infantine amusement of the bow and arrow," which, he states, was then still pursued " in conformity to fashion," at Liverpool.   There are persons yet living who recollect archery being practised at the archery ground, in 1796 or 1797. The ground, however, had ceased to be so used before April, 1798, and there is reason to believe that the club had then been broken up, because, in one of the title-deeds[2]

---

(1) History of Liverpool, Anon. of 1795 ; printed by J. M'Creery, page 279, the authorship of which has been sometimes attributed to a person named Moss.

(2) The deed is in the possession of Mr. John Bibby ; and from it we learn that in April, 1798, Joshua Rose sold to William Farrall, a parcel of land, " then lately the Shooting Butts," which he had purchased in February of the same year, from Joseph Brooks and Benjamin Bromfield, the property having been exchanged to them in 1797, by the Right Honourable Edward Smith Stanley, Earl of Derby, and the Rev. Geoffrey Hornby, Rector of Winwick.

relating to it, dated in April, in that year, it is described as " lately the Shooting Butts."

Tennis, cricket, skittles, and bowls were favourite games. There was a tennis-court kept up for some years on the east side of Grosvenor-street ; the date of its erection is uncertain, but, eventually falling into disuse, it was purchased and converted into a place of worship, in 1798, by the Rev. Robert Banister, who officiated as the minister there, from that time until near the period of his death, in 1829, as will be afterwards noticed.[1]

Another tennis-court was made at a date subsequent to the making of the former, by Mr. Morgan, a pipe-maker, in Gradwell-street, which was in existence for several years; but has long been disused, and the building has been destroyed or applied to other purposes.

There were bowling-greens and skittle-grounds at various taverns, which were a good deal frequented. One of the latter, Neptune's Coffee-house, has been before mentioned[2] as having a skittle-ground; the locality selected for such a place of amusement seems very remarkable, as it was close to the Exchange, and the door of the Coffee-house opened into a passage leading from the shambles into Water-street.

The use of tobacco and snuff was then very general : both the lower and middle classes, and many in the higher ranks of life, were accustomed to smoke tobacco ; but as cigars were then scarcely known, and certainly were not in use in Liverpool in the early part of the period we are engaged upon, they smoked with long earthen pipes. The first cigars introduced into the town are said to have been brought in some French prizes from the Island of St. Domingo, which were taken in the war in which the

---

(1) Chapter V.   (2) Chapter II, page 164.

United Kingdom was engaged with the States of America and France.

The amusements and habits of the lower classes in Liverpool were then rude and coarse. Drunkenness was a common vice, and was indulged in without concealment. There was not, however, much notorious gambling then practised in Liverpool.

Cock-fighting formed one of the amusements of the Liverpool people; and the then Earl of Derby promoted it to a great extent. There have been, at different periods, several cockpits in the town. A cockpit existed for a short time in Cockspur-street,[1] which was afterwards altered, and was for some years used as a place of worship by a congregation of dissenters, but was subsequently made into shops.

There was another sport, if it can, with propriety, be so termed, of a strange and cruel nature, which may with propriety be mentioned here. In the latter part of the last, and even in the early part of the present century, it was customary in Liverpool, on Shrove Tuesday, to have a cock turned out in Waterworth's Field,[2] before mentioned, in Lime-street, before a number of boys, the arms of each of whom were tied, in order to prevent their seizing the cock with their hands; they pursued it, and endeavoured to catch it, but their arms being tied, their only mode of catching it was to surround it, or run it down, and then throw themselves upon it and try to secure it with their teeth, and whoever succeeded in doing so was the winner of the bird.

Dog-fighting and bull-baiting were frequent in Liver-

---

(1) At one time there was a Cockpit near the Half-mile House, on the North Shore, and there was also one called the New Cockpit near the (then) Infirmary, and there have probably been others, at different periods in the last century, in Liverpool.

(2) Chapter II, page 147, note (1)

pool. The opening of the Queen's Dock was preceded by a bull-bait, which took place in the excavation or bed of the dock. The annual wakes at West Derby village, near Liverpool, exhibited reprehensible scenes of drunkenness and brutality; and amongst other sports there usually was a bull baited there.[1] He was confined by a rope or an iron chain fastened to a strong stake driven into the ground, and in this situation he was assailed by dogs, which were permitted to attack him one by one, that the courage of each might be fully proved. It has occurred, after the bull-bait was over, that the poor animal has been brought to Liverpool in triumph, on the evening of the last day of the wakes, his head being decorated with ribbons of different colours. On one occasion, a party of sailors went to West Derby and brought the bull to Liverpool, and resolved to conclude the frolic by showing him the play, and actually dragged him by means of ropes tied to his horns, into the theatre, and introduced his head into one of the centre boxes; and then, as he had seen (to use their own expression) the play, they led him out.[2] There was no great difficulty in getting him in or out, because the principal entrance door was in the middle of the front of the theatre, with an ascent from Williamson-square, of only two or three steps, and was exactly opposite the centre boxes.

The amusement of horse racing had some votaries in Liverpool, and though it was not very keenly pursued, still some of all classes liked to partake of it. The races were held

---

(1) Bull-baiting continued to be occasionally practised at the West Derby Wakes until not many years ago.

(2) The Author's Father was in the Theatre at the time when this disgraceful and brutal occurrence took place, but he could not recollect the date. In Troughton's Liverpool, page 98, however, the date is given as 1783, which is probably correct.

at Crosby ;[1] they were first established in 1774. A race ball or assembly used to be held during the race week; and the company at the assembly, which was held in the

---

(1) The following is a copy of an advertisement of the Races from Gore's General Advertiser, of July 7th, 1775 :—

" LIVERPOOL RACES, 1775."

"To be run for on Crosby Marsh, near Liverpool, on Monday, the 10th day of July, Fifty pounds in specie by any Five, Six year old, and aged horses, &c. carrying Weight for Age and qualifications, viz: Five years old to carry 8st 7lb. Six years old 9st, and Aged 9st 5lb. a Winner of one fifty pound plate in the present Season, to carry 3lb. extra; and a Winner of two to carry 5lb. On Tuesday, the 11th, will be run for on the same course £50, by any four, five, six years old, and aged horses, &c. that never won the value of £50, (matches and Sweepstakes excepted,) viz. four years old to carry 7st, five years old 8st, six years old 8st 8lb. and aged 9st. The same day will be run for on the same course, a Subscription Purse of Fifty Pounds *only*, by four year old colts, carrying 8st 3lb. and fillies 8st, the best of three two-mile heats; a winner of one fifty in the present year to carry 3lb extra, and a winner of two or more fifties to carry 5lb. extra. On Wednesday, the 12th, £50, give and take, viz: 14 hands aged to carry 8st 7lb, higher or lower weight in proportion, allowing seven pounds for every year under 7. A winner of one £50 plate in the present season, to carry 3lb. extra, and a winner of two to carry 5lb. The Turf upon Crosby Marsh is naturally fine, the Situation exceedingly pleasant, and the Marsh is now very much improved, and the course will be corded all round both inside and out. To run the best of three four mile heats each day, and the second best horse to be entitled to £10. To enter at Nanny Hesketh's, in Great Crosby, on Saturday, the 8th day of July, between the hours of three and seven o'clock in the evening, one guinea only to be paid to the Clerk of the races for weighing, &c.

No entrance at the post without permission of the Stewards, and if any are permitted, to pay four guineas entrance. The Running to be subject to the King's Plate Articles, and the Plates paid without any deduction. Certificates of the Ages to be produced under the hands of the breeders at the time of entrance, otherwise to be deemed aged. To start each day precisely at twelve o'clock. All disputes and differences to be determined by the Stewards, or whom they shall appoint, and their determination to be final. No less than three reputed racers will be admitted to start for any of the above plates, and if only one horse enters to be entitled to £15, if two £10 each. For the greater certainty of distinguishing the horses, &c. and also to prevent disputes arising from not knowing the colours, each rider is desired to declare at the time of entering, the colour he will ride in, that it may be inserted in the list for each day, and it is hoped that the Gentlemen will give directions to their riders, strictly to observe this regulation, and not to mention one colour and afterwards ride in another. No person whatsoever to erect a Booth or Stand, or sell liquor on the course, except such person pay half a Guinea for each Booth, and one Guinea for each Stand.

SIR GEORGE WARREN,   } Stewards.
NICHOLAS ASHTON, ESQUIRE, }

Exchange, in August, 1774, amounted to upwards of 350 persons,[1] which, with reference to the then population of the town and neighbourhood, was a very large number. The races, however, not being warmly supported, lost their attraction, and were finally abandoned in 1786. A dreadful thunder storm which occurred during Crosby races, in 1781, and which marred the amusements of the day, contributed its share to increase the indifference or distaste, which the Liverpool people experienced towards them.

Until the Athenæum News-Room and Library were established, in 1798, there was not, strictly speaking, any public establishment of the nature of a news-room in Liverpool, but during most of the last quarter of the 18th century, there were, as has been before mentioned,[2] several taverns and coffee-houses of respectability, in each of which a room was furnished with newspapers, and called a news-room. Afterwards a large room was used for that purpose in Bates's Hotel, on the north side of Lord-street, and corner of Whitechapel; it is difficult to ascertain exactly when that hotel was opened, or the news-room in it established, but the hotel was certainly erected previous to 1785.[3]

Music was a good deal cultivated in Liverpool, and the opening of the Music-Hall, in Bold-street, will be noticed in another chapter.[4]

There is a large and commodious stand erected upon the Course, and the Theatre Royal will be open every night during the Races, and Assemblies as usual.

There will be an Ordinary at Wrigley's on the Monday; Banner's on Tuesday; and George's Coffee House on Wednesday, and there will be a Public Breakfast at John Bridge's, St. James's Coffee House, on Thursday morning.

The collecting after dinner at the Ordinaries being found very disagreeable to the Company, the Stewards will be obliged to the Gentlemen to send each Race day to the aforesaid places for Admission Tickets."

(1) Troughton's Liverpool, page 153.

(2) Chapter II, page 164.

(3) It is laid down in Mr. Charles Eyes' Map of Liverpool, of 1785.

(4) Chapter V.

A Musical Festival was held in Liverpool, in September, 1784, and the following is a copy of an advertisement[1] announcing it :—

"The Committee for conducting the ensuing FESTIVAL OF MUSIC, wishing to render the Entertainment as easy to Individuals as was consistent with the Design of so benevolent an Institution, trusted that a Subscription of One Guinea would have been sufficient. Finding that Sum however, inadequate, considering *the present state* of the Charities of this Town; they flatter themselves that the generous Public will readily acquiesce in the propriety of altering the Terms of Admission to the following :—

Subscription to the Five Performances,
One Guinea and a half.
Subscribers' Tickets transferable.
A Single Ticket to each Oratorio,
Seven Shillings and Sixpence.
To the Selection of Sacred Music, and each of
The Miscellaneous Concerts,
Ten Shillings and Sixpence.

Liverpool, July 24th, 1784.

For the Benefit of the
PUBLIC CHARITIES OF LIVERPOOL.
On the Mornings of Tuesday, the 14th, Thursday, the 16th, and
Friday, the 17th of September,
Will be performed,
In St. Peter's Church,
Under the Direction of Mr. Isaac,
The Sacred Oratorios
of the
MESSIAH
and
JUDAS MACCHABÆUS,
And the same
SELECTION OF SACRED MUSIC,
From Handel,
Which was performed in Westminster Abby,
On the last day of the Commemoration,
By Command of His Majesty.

---

(1) Gore's General Advertiser of 2nd September, 1784.

And, on the Evenings of Wednesday and Thursday,

Will be performed,

TWO GRAND MISCELLANEOUS CONCERTS,

In the Theatre,

In one of which will be introduced,

ALEXANDER'S FEAST.

Principal Instrumental Performers:

Mr. Cramer,

Mr. Bassett,	Mr. Burchell,	Mr. Ashley, .
Mr. M'Intosh,	Mr. Hackwood,	Mr. L. Crathorn,
Mr. Wainwright,	Mr. Clarke,	Mr. Karst,
Mr. Sergant,	Mr. Fitzgerald	Mr. Ashbridge,

Mr. Parke,   Sig. Gariboldi,

And Mr. Crosdill.

Principal Vocal Performers:

Mr. Harrison,   Mr. Meredith,

Miss Cantelo, Miss Phillips, and Mrs. Kennedy.

The Orchestra will consist of One Hundred and Thirty Performers, and that the Chorusses may be as full as possible, the Trombones, and Double Drum, that were introduced in Westminster Abby, are engaged.

Subscription to the Five Performances One Guinea and a half.

Subscribers' Tickets transferable.

A Single Ticket to each Oratorio, Seven Shillings and Sixpence.

To the Selection of Sacred Music, and each of the Miscellaneous Concerts, Ten Shillings and Sixpence.

Books open for Subscriptions at Mr. Gore's, Mr. Sibbald's, Mr. Crane's, Mr. Hodgson's, and Mrs. Williamson's, Stationers, in Liverpool; Mr. Broster and Mr. Poole, in Chester; Mr. Harrop, in Manchester; Mrs. Bancks, in Warrington; Mr. Binns, in Preston; Mr. Walmsley, in Lancaster; and Mr. Hancock's, Knutsford.

The Subscribers are particularly requested to give in their Names, with the Number of Tickets for which they intend to subscribe, as soon as convenient.

The Tickets will be ready for delivery, and the Subscriptions received the week before the Meeting.

On Tuesday Evening,

Will be an ASSEMBLY,

And on Friday Evening,

A FANCY BALL AND SUPPER,

In the Exchange.

An Ordinary each Day, and Plays at the Theatre-Royal, every Evening in the week, except Wednesday and Thursday.

EARL OF DERBY,
LORD GREY DE WILTON,
SIR W^{M.} STANLEY, BART.
JOHN BLACKBURNE, ESQ.
    Stewards."
(1)

The following is an account of the amusements of the musical festival week, dated 23rd September, 1784;[2] the making arrangements for a race, on one of the days, as part of the amusement, without ensuring the attendance of horses, is curious in its way :—

" LIVERPOOL, SEPTEMBER 23RD, 1784.

" On Saturday last, our festival-week was concluded with a public Breakfast at the Exchange, attended by a numerous company of ladies and gentlemen. Various entertainments were introduced, to render the *fête* as complete, as a Town so far removed from the metropolis can be supposed to admit. On Monday a horse race, but no great diversion; in the evening a play, by a new company in part, his Majesty's servants being called to their respective houses ; the new ones are selected from the Dublin theatre and different quarters. On Tuesday morning was performed the oratorio of the Messiah, and in the evening was a numerous and brilliant assembly. On Wednesday no race, for want of horses ; but the Concert in the evening, in which was introduced Alexander's Feast, amply compensated for the loss of the morning's diversion. On Thursday morning was performed the oratorio of Judas Maccabæus; and the evening of this day concluded with another grand miscellaneous Concert. On Friday morning, the great day of expectation, was performed, the music selected in commemoration of Handel on the 26th of May, in Westminster Abbey ; and the evening of this day concluded with a novelty unknown here before, a Fancy Ball.

" Too much cannot be said in honour of the committee who collected the band, and conducted this various and troublesome business with unremitting ardour, to benefit the charities ; and who strove with every exertion, to maintain peace, regularity, and decorum ; and, at the same time to render proper accommodations to the spectators.[2]

" The principal characters at the fancy ball were, a Sultana, an

---

(1) Gore's General Advertiser of 2nd September, 1784.

(2) Troughton's Liverpool, page 170. A similar account appears also in Gore's General Advertiser of the 23rd September, 1784.

elegant figure; a Turk; an Algerine; America, by a Lady, who displayed the 13 Stripes; 3 Spaniards; a Boatswain, well supported; 2 or 3 Jews, good; 2 Harlequin and Columbine characters; a Market Girl, with flowers; 2 Counsellors; 2 Friars; 2 Mungos; the *Child of Hale*, well attended by an excellent Nurse; a German Merchant; Collegians; a House-maid, with a sweeping brush; a Good Girl, with fowls in a basket; a Country Clergyman; 2 Devils; Eve; a Conjurer; Douglas; Diana; an Ancient Briton; Mother Shipton; a Farmer, well supported; Shepherds; Shepherdesses; Sailors; Dominos of all sorts, &c. &c."[1]

A band of music, of which a person named Langhorne, of Cook-street, was the master, was, either wholly or in part, paid for by the Corporation of Liverpool, and was called " The Waits;" and the performers in it, besides their other performances, occasionally perambulated the town, on Christmas eve, and enlivened it with music; they also were in the habit of going to the houses of the masters of vessels, on the day after that of their arrival in the port, and playing before their doors, by way of welcoming them home.

The following entry of a payment respecting the waits, appears in the ledger of the Corporation, in 1775 :—

" THE WAITS.
1775, March 31. To cash paid them for 1 year's salary...... £24 0s 0d." [2]

The Drama was a favourite source of amusement in Liverpool, and many of the most celebrated London performers trod the boards of the Theatre in Williamson-square,[3] before they had engagements in the metropolis.

---

(1) Gore's General Advertiser of 23rd September, 1784.   It is pretty clear from the characters mentioned, that the entertainment pertook more of the nature of a masquerade than a fancy dress ball.

(2) Ledger of the Corporation, No. 3, [7] page 112.

(3) It has been already mentioned that the Theatre in Williamson-square was opened in 1772, the following theatrical announcements are of the 30th of June, 1775 :—
" Liverpool, June 30.
" The Tragedy of Richard the Third, will be performed this evening, the part of Richard (for that night only) by Mr. Macklin.   Love a la Mode, will be performed after the Opera of the Maid of the Mill, on Monday next.   The Burletta of the

With respect to the London performers, who, from time to time visited Liverpool, it may be here mentioned, that the custom of engaging "the stars" to perform here for a few nights only in the season, was not in general practised about that period ; and it was not uncommon for London performers of celebrity to be engaged here for a considerable part of the summer, and to return to London for the winter season.

Golden Pippin (written by the author of Midas) will be performed on Saturday next, the principal parts by Mr. Mattocks, Mr. Baker, Mr. Wheeler, Miss Brown, Mrs. Taylor, Miss Pearce, and Mrs. Mattocks; an elegant scene representing Juno's Palace, is painted by Mr. Hodgins, for the Burletta.   Mr. Macklin will make his second and last appearance in the character of Shylock, in the Merchant of Venice, on Wednesday night.   The new Comedy of the Rivals is in rehersal, and will be performed as soon as possible : and the Tragedy of Macbeth ; the part of Macbeth by Mr. Macklin."—*Gore's General Advertiser, of 30th June*, 1775.

"By his Majesty's Servants.

Theatre-Royal, Liverpool.

This present *Friday, June* 30, will be presented

A Tragedy called

KING RICHARD THE IIIᵈ.

King Richard, (for that night only,) Mr. Macklin ; K. Henry, Mr. Wroughton ; Richmond, Mr. Clinch ; Buckingham, Mr. Wheeler ; Tressell, Mr. Lewes ; Prince Edward, Master Summers ; Duke of York, Master Jones ; Catesby, Mr. Baker ; Blunt, Mr. Ledger ; Stanley. Mr. Thompson ; Lord Mayor, Mr. Keen ; Lady Ann, Miss Dayes ; Duchess of York, Mrs. Barrington ; Queen Elizabeth, Miss Mansell.

End of the Play, a Comic Dance, called the TAILORS,

By Mr. Dagville, Mr. Blurton, Master Holland, Miss Armstrong, and Mrs. Dagville.

To which will be added a Farce, called,

THE LYING VALET.

Sharp, Mr. Lewes ; Gayless, Mr. Wheeler ; Justice Guttle, Mr. Keen ; Dick, Mr. Baker ; Trippet, Mr. Wewitzer ; Mrs. Gadabout, Mrs. Barrington ; Mrs. Trippet, Mrs. Taylor ; Melissa, Miss Pearce ; Kitty Pry, Mrs. Pitt.

To-morrow,

THE CARELESS HUSBAND,

With (for the first time) a Burletta, called

THE GOLDEN PIPPIN,

(By the Author of Midas.)

Boxes, 3s 6d—Pit, 2s 6d—Gallery, 1s.

Tickets and Places for the Boxes, to be taken at the Stage Door.

No person can be admitted behind the Scenes.

VIVANT REX & REGINA.*

* Gore's General Advertiser of 30th June, 1775.

There was a peculiarity about the gallery, which is worth notice; it was by no means as distant from the stage, or as much elevated from the ground as the present gallery, and was one of the best situations in the house for hearing

---

The following is a copy of the announcement of the performance at the Liverpool Theatre, on the 7th July, 1775 :—

" For the Benefit of Mr. Macklin,
By his Majesty's Servants,
Theatre-Royal, Liverpool,
This present Friday, July 7, will be presented
A Tragedy called
MACBETH.

Macbeth, Mr. Macklin; Macduff, Mr. Clinch; Banquo, Mr. Lewes; Malcolm, Mr. Wheeler; Duncan, Mr. Keen; Lenox, Mr. Thomson; Hecate, Mr. Baker; the Witches, Mr. Shuter, Mrs. Pitt, Mrs. Barrington; Fleance, Master Summers; Seyton, Mr. Wewitzer.—Lady Macbeth, Mrs. Mattocks. With the Original Music, Scenery, and Decorations.

The Vocal Parts by Mr. Mattocks, Mr. Baker, Miss Brown, Miss Dayes, Mrs. Taylor, Miss Summers, &c.

End of the Play, a Pastoral Dance called the Bell and the Lamb, by Mr. Dagville, Mr. Blurton, Mrs. Dagville, Mr. Ratchford, Master Holland and Miss Armstrong, Scholars to Mr. Dagville.

To which will be added (for the third time) a new
Burletta, called
The GOLDEN PIPPIN,
(Written by the Author of Midas.)
The Music compiled from the most eminent Masters.

Paris, Mr. Mattocks; Jupiter, Mr. Baker; Mercury, Mr. Wheeler; Momus, Mr. Hollingsworth;* Venus, Miss Brown; Pallas, Mrs. Taylor; Iris, Miss Pearce; Juno, Mrs. Mattocks.

Tickets to be had of Mr. Macklin, at Mr. Bolton's, Dawson-street; and of Mr. Ledger, at the Theatre, where places for the boxes may be taken.

Boxes 3s 6d—Pit 2s 6d—Gallery 1s.
Tickets and Places for the Boxes to be taken at the stage door.
No person can be admitted behind the Scenes.
VIVANT REX & REGINA." †

† Gore's General Advertiser of 7th July, 1775.

* Mr. Hollingsworth lived so long as to perform on the Liverpool stage when Miss O'Neill performed there about 1815. The Author saw him acting in the same play ("Isabella, or the Fatal Marriage") with her; and he also once, about the same period, saw him perform in the same play ("Lear") with Mr. Kemble. As Mr. Hollingsworth appears, from the above advertisement, to have performed in the character of Momus in the Burletta of the "Golden Pippin," in 1775, he must have been an old man when he performed with Miss O'Neill, and when he left the stage.

M 1

and seeing the performances; the height of the front of the gallery was much the same as that of the present upper boxes; it was frequented by persons of a higher grade in society than such as are now seen in the pit of a Liverpool theatre, and they were accustomed to sit on the left side of the gallery when looking towards the stage, whilst the lower classes, by a kind of tacit arrangement, seldom interfered with them, but took their seats on the right of it, and in the wings, which extended over a part of the upper side boxes.

Amongst the performers of eminence, who, from time to time, appeared on the Liverpool stage during the last quarter of the 18th century, may be enumerated: tragedians, Mr. Macklin, Mr. Henderson, Mr. Kemble, Mr. Cooke, Mr. Wilson, Mrs. Siddons, Mrs. Pitt; comedians, Mr. Quick, Mr. Dodd, Mr. Suett, Mr. Murray, Mr. Munden, Mr. Lewis, (called Gentleman Lewis,) Mr. Lee Lewis, who excelled as harlequin, and in light comedy, in such characters as Marplot, in the Busy Body, &c. &c., Mr. Wilson, who usually personated the characters of old gentlemen, Miss Farren, afterwards Countess of Derby, Mrs. Hopkins, the mother of Mrs. Kemble, Mrs. Mattocks, and Miss Mellon, afterwards the Duchess of St. Albans. The manager of the theatre was Mr. Younger; but afterwards, Messrs. Younger and Mattocks were joint managers.[1]

There was an amphitheatre or circus, as has been before mentioned,[2] in Christian-street, principally for the exhibition of equestrian performances, some years before the close of the last century, but the Author has been unable to discover the precise date when it was first used. It is supposed to have been erected towards the close

---

(1) It has not been ascertained when they became joint managers, but it is certain they were so in 1779.

(2) Chapter I, page 88.

of 1795, because, an advertisement of Mr. Astley, containing a prospectus or proposals[1] for building it by subscription, was published on the 2nd of July in that year, and it announced that he undertook, when the subscription was complete, to have the building ready in four months. The advertisement states that the amphitheatre was intended for "music, dancing, pantomines, equestrian and other exercises, pieces of mechanism, and scenic representations;" for which purpose £5000 would be wanted to complete it, and that it was therefore proposed to build an amphitheatre by subscription by way of tontine. It has been much altered since the period of its erection, and is now the Adelphi Theatre.

On the 26th of March, 1789, on the occasion of the recovery of King George the Third, from a serious and afflicting malady, besides other modes of expressing re-

---

(1) " Proposals for Building

AN AMPHITHEATRE,

In the Town of Liverpool.

Mr. Astley having, for a series of years, rented from Mr. Aickin, the Theatre, and that gentleman having given Mr. Astley a certain form of notice to quit the same, he is under the necessity of immediately building an Amphitheatre, for the following purposes :—*Music, Dancing, Pantomines, Equestrian, and other Exercises, Pieces of Mechanism, and Scenic Representations ;* for which purpose the Sum of Five Thousand Pounds will be wanted to complete the same. It is, therefore, proposed to build an Amphitheatre by subscription, by way of Tontine, viz. one hundred subscribers at fifty pounds each, to have a free admission ticket, on the same plan as the Theatre. The building to be held in trust by six of the subscribers, by way of security. Mr. Astley to keep the same in substantial repair, and pay every incumbrance.

It is intended the Amphitheatre shall be open twice a year, viz. November and and December, also July and August, and to continue three or more days in each week.

Further particulars will be made known on Mr. Astley's arrival in Liverpool. In the meanwhile, such ladies and gentlemen as are inclinable to subscribe, either for themselves or families, are humbly requested to send their address immediately to Mr, Astley, Westminster Bridge, London.

N.B. When the subscription is complete, Mr. Astley will undertake to have the building ready in four months."

Copied from Gore's General Advertiser of 2nd July, 1795,

joicing, there was a general illumination of the town, which commenced at seven o'clock in the evening, on a signal given by the firing of twenty-one pieces of cannon at the Fort, and closed at midnight, on a similar signal, by the discharge of the same number of cannon. The illumination is said to have been very general, and magnificent, particularly at the Exchange, the front of which was adorned with a variety of coloured lamps and transparent paintings. In addition to those public testimonials of loyalty, a ball and supper were given by the Corporation, on the 16th of the following month.

The following account of them, which has been preserved,[1] is given here, as it will inform the curious, how a ball and supper were conducted at the Exchange, [the Townhall,] in Liverpool, in April, 1789 :—

" On this occasion a temporary roof was thrown over the area of the Exchange, and an intermediate floor at the base of the columns on the second story : the upper room formed the grand saloon and promenade communicating with the Town-hall, assembly-room, cardroom, and other apartments. This saloon was brilliantly illuminated by coloured lamps formed into festoons, stars, and other devices ; also by five elegant chandeliers suspended from the ceiling, which were decorated with a multitude of stars, made of polished metal, and so disposed as to produce a luminous appearance. In this room were placed two circular bars, for the purpose of supplying the company with refreshments, and the recesses between the columns were ornamented with glass girandoles. In the central attic window, on one side, was an elegant transparency; and the other attic windows were decorated with devices of the royal cyphers, stars, &c. enriched with lamps.

" The Concert and assembly room were appropriated for dancing, and had a most brilliant and pleasing appearance when viewed from the saloon; the upper room, which occupied the whole ground floor[2] of

---

(1) Troughton's Liverpool, page 177, and Gore's General Advertiser of 23rd April, 1789.

(2) This is supposed to mean that it occupied a space equal in size to the whole ground floor of the interior.

the interior part of the Exchange, including the area, formed the grandest spectacle of the kind, perhaps, ever seen in this country. The Doric order of which this room is composed was correctly preserved, and lighted by a profusion of variegated lamps beautifully arranged; the interior columns being wreathed, and the lines of the pilasters on the side walls and the cornices hung with lamps. In the interior part of the room was a quadrangle of columns, supporting large semicircular arches, brilliantly illuminated. These columns were ornamented with wreaths of artificial flowers, and the ceiling of this interior quadrangle, was elegantly painted in compartments, of laurel and oak devices, from which were suspended five superb glass chandeliers. Over the doors at the entrance, on the east and west sides, were two large regal crowns, in crystal lamps; and in the recesses of the south part of the room, between the pilasters, were introduced nine large emblematic trans-parencies, executed in a masterly style, by artists of the first distinction. The large recess in the centre of the north side of the room was occupied by another emblematic transparency, over which was the royal cypher G. R. in crystal lamps, and from the ceiling were suspended a number of elegant chandeliers with wax lights.

" The tables were arranged in such a manner, that splendid and interesting objects presented themselves, to every part of the company, at the same instant.

" This elegant public entertainment, was under the direction of a committee of the council, who were in the room, at seven o'clock, to receive the company. At nine the country dances began, and the supper was announced at twelve, when eight hundred persons sat down to an elegant repast, in one superb room, illuminated with ten thousand lights. The ladies wore bandeaus, and favours, with devices, and ap-plicable mottos. The gentlemen had crowns, cyphers, and mottos on their breasts, and collars. The toasts given were, the king ; the queen ; the prince of Wales, and the rest of the royal family ; and prosperity to the town and trade of Liverpool. The company, in general, retired at four o'clock, highly gratified with the magnificence of the enter-tainment."

In *Gore's General Advertiser* there is also an account of the ball, from which the following are extracts. It com-mences as follows :—

" In addition to those Public Testimonies of Joy, which have peculiarly distinguished the Town of Liverpool on the happy event of His Majesty's recovery, a Ball and supper was given by the Corporation, on Thursday last, under the direction of a Committee of the Council, consisting of

John Blackburne, Jun. Esq. Mayor.

Mr. John Gregson,	Mr. Staniforth,	Mr. Clayton Tarleton,
Mr. Brooks,	Mr. John Crosbie,	Mr. Steers."
Mr. Statham,	Mr. T. Earle,	

It then proceeds to give an account of the ball, which is substantially the same as that already given, but it contains the following additional particulars:—

"The tables were arranged in such a manner, that splendid and interested[1] objects presented themselves to every part of the Company, (consisting of upwards of Eight hundred) at the same instant; and it is only justice to Messrs. Forshaw,[2] Dale,[3] and Harris and Bates,[4] who supplied the supper, to say, they provided a profusion of every rarity which the season afforded. The confectionery, consisting of near one hundred ornaments, were executed by Mr. Menzies,[5] and, equally arranged on the several Tables; amongst the devices were, Mercury, bringing the joyful information of the King's recovery to Neptune; a transparency of the King's arms; a neat festoon compartment with Mottos; a beautiful transparency, exhibiting an exact representation of the Exchange, illuminated in the same manner as on the night of Public rejoicing, the 26th March; in the interior part of which was seen a transparency of the King, at full length, robed and crowned, and another of Britannia; and on the back part, some lines suited to the occasion. Two transparent urns, with various beautiful devices in ovals; an elegant and beautiful representation of Bidston Light-house and Signals, with applicable mottos to the whole; and a variety of other elegant devices, such as triumphal arches, vases, &c. &c.

---

(1) So printed in the original.

(2) In 1789, Mr. H. Forshaw kept the Hotel, in Lord-street, at the corner of Whitechapel, afterwards kept by Mr. Bates. Mr. Forshaw had previously kept the Golden Lion, in Dale-street, in which he succeeded Mr. James Wrigley.

(3) Mr. D. Dale, then kept the King's Arms Inn, in Water-street; he had previously kept George's Coffee House, in Castle-street.

(4) Messrs. Harris and Bates then kept the Talbot Inn, at the upper end of Water-street.

(5) Mr. J. Menzies was a celebrated confectioner and pastry cook, of the last century; his shop was at the sign of the Pine Apple, on the east side of Castle-street.

" The wines were of a superior quality, and served in great plenty. It is impossible to describe the elegant dresses of the company, which, in novelty and richness, did great credit to their taste. The ladies wore bandeaus and favours, with devices and applicable mottos. The gentlemen had crowns, cyphers, mottos, &c. on their breasts and collars. The toasts given were, The King, The Queen, The Prince of Wales, and the rest of the Royal Family; and prosperity to the Town and Trade of Liverpool.

" The Company in general returned to the Assembly rooms, highly gratified with the entertainment.

" The Committee were in the rooms at seven o'Clock to receive the Company, at nine the Country-dances began, the first of which was led down by Edward Falkner, Esq. High Sheriff for this county, and Lady Henry Murray. The Supper was announced at twelve, and the company in general broke up at four, expressing the highest approbation of the great ingenuity and taste exhibited in the variegated display of the lamps, and other beautiful ornaments."

" Upwards of 10,000 lamps and 1200 wax candles were used on this occasion.

" Yesterday the Supper room within the Exchange, was lighted and opened, by order of the Committee, for public inspection; the prodigious concourse of people which attended on this occasion was astonishing, and they expressed the highest satisfaction.

" We hear that the Committee who conducted the Corporation Ball, on the 16th instant, have it in contemplation not to take down the temporary rooms in the Exchange, but to open them for a ball and promenade on his Majesty's Birth-day, the 4th of June."[1]

A subsequent number (30th April) of the newspaper contains the following additional particulars:—

" Eight hundred well-dressed persons of both sexes, commodiously sat down to an elegant supper, *all* at *one* time, in *one* superb room, splendidly illuminated with ten thousand lights, (as was the case at the late Ball and supper at the Exchange, on the King's Restoration,) was a sight at which even a Cockney would have stared, and his more exalted and refined neighbours of St. James's would have admired, and been surprised at. 'Tis very likely they would have considered themselves under the power of *witchcraft:* indeed how could it be thought

---

(1) Gore's General Advertiser of 23rd April, 1789.

otherwise, under the fascinating influence of five hundred *Lancashire witches !*"[1]

A ball took place according to the before-mentioned intimation, in the Exchange, on the 4th June, to which the company were admitted by tickets, advertised in Gore's newspaper, at 7s each.

" In the Evening was a Ball and Promenade, at the Exchange, in the same grand and splendid style as on the 16th April last, which we formerly described; with this only difference, that instead of a Supper, as before, here was a Concert, in the lower area of the Exchange, which had a fine effect. The Company exceeded 700, who appeared highly gratified with the evening amusement; as the whole was conducted with taste, ease, and regularity. The Band of the 40th Regiment contributed to the entertainment, and the officers seemed emulous to distinguish themselves on the occasion, in honour of their Royal Master."[2]

After reading the account of the ball given by the Corporation on the 16th of April, 1789, how cumbrous, antiquated, and heavy the arrangements appear, when contrasted with the splendour, taste, and elegance displayed at some of the balls and evening entertainments given at the town-hall[3] in comparatively recent times !

---

(1) Gore's General Advertiser of 30th April, 1789.

(2) Ibid. of 11th June, 1789.

(3) There have been three evening entertainments given at the Town-hall, viz. in the respective mayoralties of the late Mr. Thomas Leyland, Mr. John Bramley-Moore, and Mr. Samuel Holme, which, from the admirable manner in which they were conducted, as the Author can testify, are entitled to some notice.

On the 6th of September, 1821, during the third mayoralty of Mr. Thomas Leyland, a ball was given by him at the Town-hall, which, in point of elegance and magnificence, had, perhaps, seldom been equalled out of the metropolis. The cards of invitation had been extensively issued, not only to the higher classes of the inhabitants of Liverpool, but to many of the county gentry of Lancashire and Cheshire, and nearly 1000 persons were present. On ascending the grand staircase, where the fine military band of the 29th regiment was stationed, the guests were received by four gentlemen, to whom that office had been delegated, and by them were conducted to the Mayor and Mrs. Leyland, who stood at the head of the first drawing-

Public Balls of a very different description, also not unfrequently took place in Liverpool in the last, and even for a few years after the commencement of the present century. It was the custom of the dancing masters to have balls at the Theatre-Royal, in Williamson-square, at which the pupils, girls as well as boys, of the first and most respectable families in the town, used to dance in public.   It was an

---

room. Amongst other distinguished individuals present, were the Countess of Derby, Lord Stanley, (afterwards Earl of Derby) Lady Mary Stanley, Captain Phibbs Hornby, and several others of the same family, (the whole of the Knowsley party amounted to fourteen,) Lord and Lady Combermere, E. Bootle Wilbraham, Esq. M.P. (afterwards Lord Skelmersdale) and family, Joseph Birch, Esq. M.P. (afterwards Sir Joseph Birch, Bart.) Lady Henry Murray, General Beckwith, Admiral Murray, Mr., Mrs. and Miss Egerton, of Gresford, Colonel and Mrs. Egerton, of Tarporley, the Rev. Rowland Egerton and his Son, of Arley, Colonel Freeth, and the Staff of the District, Colonel Hodge and most of the Officers of the 29th Regiment, stationed at Liverpool. Many of the ladies were profusely decorated with diamonds, the rooms were brilliantly lighted, and every appendage and decoration appeared to the greatest advantage.   At ten o'clock, the ball was opened by Lord Stanley and Miss Heathcote, niece of Sir Thomas Heathcote, Bart.   When the supper room was thrown open, it presented a *coup d'œil* of splendour and profusion, which even those who were most accustomed to such spectacles, declared was most magnificent and striking.   Dancing was resumed after supper.   The display of beauty, elegance, and fashion, on this occasion, had probably been rarely equalled in the north of England.   Everything that a lavish expenditure, combined with good taste, could do, was freely bestowed upon the entertainment ; but what cannot be done in point of magnificence by a Mayor of Liverpool, who is also a banker and a millionaire, upon such an occasion, in such a suite of rooms ?

On the evening of the 6th of February, 1849, during the mayoralty of Mr. John Bramley-Moore, 1400 guests, consisting of the leading and most respectable inhabitants of Liverpool and its vicinity, were entertained in a magnificent manner by him and Mrs. Bramley-Moore, at a Soirée, in the splendid rooms of the Town-hall.   The rooms exhibited a brilliant scene of magnificence, elegance, and fashion seldom equalled : the refreshments were on a most hospitable scale, and the Mayor, with great good taste, caused some modes of entertaining the guests to be introduced, which were of a very interesting and pleasing nature, as well as being novelties on such an occasion ; for example, there were beautiful dissolving views of Palestine, in the large ball-room, explained by the Rev. H. Higgins ; wires from the Telegraph office were fixed to communicate with the centre drawing-room ; parties were stationed in London, Birmingham, Manchester, and Glasgow, and communications were constantly carried on with all those places.   Speeches were reported to the company every half hour from the House of Commons, and printed and circulated in

N l

interesting and delightful spectacle to see so many young and pleasing children so engaged; and there are many persons yet living in Liverpool who have either witnessed such exhibitions, or have personally taken a part in them at the Theatre. These balls were supposed to be a source of considerable emolument to the dancing masters, because, except paying for the hire of the Theatre, the expenses must

---

the rooms. There were also delightful musical performances, both instrumental and vocal, by professional performers, of which the following is a Programme:—

OVERTURE............... Preciosa.................... Weber.
CHORUS............. " Beauties Praise ".............. Weber.
SONG.............. " As you a nutting go " .... L. Phillips.
TRIO AND CHORUS.... " The Gabre's Glee " .... Bishop.
MELANGE ..from Masnadieri .... Verdi.
AIR................. " In this old Chair ".............. Balfe.
DUET.................. " The Elfin Call " .... Glover.
SOLO AND CHORUS...... " Haste thee, Nymph " .... Handel.
QUARTET.......... " O'er the dark blue waters " .... Weber.
OVERTURE.......... " La Figlia del Reggimento " ...... Donizetti.
CHORUS............. " The Gypsies' Glee " .... Weber.
SONG........... " Away to the Forest Green " .... Linley.
DUET AND CHORUS...... " Country Lasses ".............. Balfe.
POT POURRI.. from La Favorita .. Donizetti—arranged by A. Seume.
ARIA .... " Oh! how shall I triumph ? " ...... Mozart.
SOLO AND CHORUS " Now tramp o'er Moss and Fell " ...... Bishop.
        GOD SAVE THE QUEEN........ arranged by Novello.

On the 8th March, 1853, in the mayoralty of Mr. Samuel Holme, the Centenary of the birth of Mr. Roscoe was celebrated, as has been mentioned in a former Chapter,* by the inhabitants of Liverpool, in a manner at once honourable to his memory and creditable to themselves. The proceedings which took place in the morning and early in the afternoon, have been already described, and it is not necessary to recapitulate them here. A very superb and elegant Evening Entertainment was afterwards given by the Mayor, at the Town-hall; and from the peculiar commemoration connected with which it was given, it excited more than usual interest. The Mayor and Mrs. Holme entertained on that occasion about 820 guests, very much to the gratification of all who were present. The entertainment combined both a Soirée, Concert and Ball, and also the exhibition of various objects highly interesting to the company generally, as well as to the literary and scientific characters who were amongst the visitors, besides the exhibition of some curiosities and novelties which were peculiarly connected with the centenary of Mr. Roscoe. The following is a short extract from the Programme of the evening's entertainment:—

Nine o'clock.
The Reception, Promenade, and Examination of the Specimens of Art and Science,
in the Drawing-rooms and Small Ball-room.
Tea, Coffee, and Ices, in the Centre-room.

* Chapter II, page 140.

have been very trivial. The professors of dancing of celebrity in Liverpool towards the close of the last century, were Mr. Langrish, Mr. Wilson, and Mr. Palmer. From an advertisement, in the year 1796,[1] of a ball of Mr. Langrish, it appears that the ball commenced at half-past three, and that the admittance to the boxes was 3s 6d, and to the gallery 2s.

On the westward side of the ground where Colquitt-street and Back Colquitt-street now stand, an extraordinary exhibition took place in a garden, in the upper part of Fleet-street, on its southward side. The garden was then quite in the country, and Fleet-street though laid out, was not

---

Half-past Nine o'clock.
MUSIC,
By a few Members of the Liverpool Philharmonic Society.
Part I.
MADRIGAL...... " Who shall win my Lady fair ? .... *Purcell.*
SOLO*(Violoncello)*...." Fantasia on National Airs "........ *Lidell.*
FOUR-PART SONG.... " I know a Maiden " .... *Hatton.*
SONG................. " The Skylark " .... *Hatton.*
SOLO *(Piano-forte)* Selection from the " Lieder ohne Worte" *Mendelssohn.*

Ten o'clock.
Promenade and Examination of the Specimen and Microscope Tables.
 Illustrated Books.
 Miscellaneous Zoology and Botany.
 Local Antiquities.
 Rare Manuscripts and Books of Art.
 Architectural and Mechanical Models and Stereoscopes.
 Microscopes.
Half-past Ten o'clock.
MUSIC.—Part II.
MADRIGAL.......... " O'er desert plains " .... *Waebrent.*
SOLO.. *(Violin)*......... " Tremolo " .... *De Beriot.*
FOUR-PART SONG...... "The Nightingale "......... *Mendelssohn.*
SONG........... " Oh listen, dearest Lady " .... *Balfe.*
GLEE........ " The Squirrel ".. (Words by ROSCOE).. *Sir G. Smart.*
 At Eleven o'clock, the Refreshment Room opened.

---

(1) " Theatre-Royal, Liverpool.
Mr. Langrish,
Respectfully informs his friends and the public, his Ball will be To-morrow, (Friday,) the 3rd of June. The doors to open at half-past two, to begin at half-past three o'clock.

No person can be admitted without Tickets, which may be had of Messrs. Gore and Billinge, Mrs. Egerton Smith, Pool-lane, and at the Theatre Tavern.

Box Tickets, 3s, 6d—Gallery Tickets, 2s."

Copied from Gore's General Advertiser of 2nd June, 1796.

a thoroughfare; a person, professing to be a medical practitioner, called Dr. Graham, arrived in Liverpool, and recommended the use of earth baths, as a cure for various complaints.　His plan was to have the patient buried up to the neck in earth, and in order to set the example, he and a female, who was said to be his wife, were buried up to their necks in the garden, with their faces towards each other.　They had their heads dressed with hair powder, as was the fashion at that period, and the public were admitted on payment of a small sum.　There is not any reason, however, to believe that they induced any patient to follow their example.[1]

The Liverpool people did not object to be amused by the sleight-of-hand tricks of the celebrated Breslaw, a native of Berlin.　He was accustomed to show off his amusing feats of legerdemain, in a full-dress court suit, with ruffles and a dress wig.　He exhibited his performances in the Large Room, at the Golden Lion Inn, in Dale-street, on the occasion, at least, of one of his visits to Liverpool.　He died at the Bull and Punch Bowl Inn, in Dale-street, on the 16th April, 1803.

Mr. George Alexander Stevens used to exhibit an entertainment which was very popular and well attended, and was called his "Lecture on Heads," in which he produced busts, representing various characters, in the proper head dress of the personages, on which he used to give an amusing explanatory lecture.　A performer, named Rogers, has been also known to exhibit a similar entertainment, in which he delivered lectures on the same subject, but whether he did so after 1775 has not been ascertained.　A

---

(1) The Author's Father was present at one of these exhibitions, but could not recollect the date, but he thought that the occurrence took place some time between 1780 and 1785.

hand-bill of his performance in 1768, has, however, been preserved, of which the following is a copy:—

" By desire, positively the Last Time of performing.

At the

Buck's Room, the Golden Lyon, in Dale-street, Liverpool,

This present Friday, being the 22nd of January, 1768,

Mr. ROGERS,

(from the Theatre-Royal, in the Haymarket, London,)

Will deliver Mr. Stevens' (so much admired)

LECTURE ON HEADS.

Hard and soft, Thick and paper Sculls, Hoods, Hats, Caps, Brains, &c. &c. &c.

A new comic Satire, in three parts; with several pieces of Mimicry never attempted by any other, in which Mr. Rogers has gained vast applause, in Bath, Bristol, and both the Universities, and most of the principal Towns in the Kingdom.

With a new Occasional Prologue, on the present practice of Inoculation. To censure Folly and expose Vice, does more public service than all the Ministers of State from Adam down to Walpole.

The Characters are,

Part I.

ALEXANDER THE GREAT.

Sachem Swampum Scalpum Tomahawk, or the Head of a Cherokee Chief; a Quack Doctor; the Head of a C * * * * * *; the Head of a Lawyer, with an Oration in Praise of the Law, Daniel against Dishclout, in which Oration Mr. Rogers will mimic several well-known Persons.

A DISSERTATION ON CARD PLAYERS.

Nobody's Head—the Family of Nobody; with a humorous description of two Parish Officers, and an oration lately made in a certain House, on the present scarcity of Corn; in imitation of a Member thereof.

Also, the Heads of HONESTY and FLATTERY.

Part II.

LADIES' HEADS AND HEAD DRESSES.

Riding Hood, Ranelagh Hood, Cannonading Curls, and Billingsgate Hood.

VENUS'S GIRDLE; a Present to the Ladies.

A DISSERTATION ON CURTAIN LECTURES,

The Head of Cleopatra.—French Night-Cap.

FACE-PAINTING.

Young Married Lady,—Old Maid—Old Batchelor.

The Head of a Quaker; with a Quaker's Sermon.

Part III.

Physical Wig—a Dissertation on Sneezing and Snuff-taking;
The Snuff of Self-consequence—and the Snuff of Contempt.
The life of a Blood, and a Woman of the Town.
The Head of an English Captain.
The Head of a Wit, with his Adventures, Death, and Funeral.
The Head of a Methodist, with his Tabernacle Harangue.
To conclude with an Epilogue.

The approbation Mr. Rogers has met with, in the above Performance, induces him to request the Indulgence of the Ladies and Gentlemen of this Town; as they may depend nothing shall be wanting to render the evening's entertainment as agreeable as possible.

Tickets to be had at the Place of Performance, Price one shilling and sixpence.

The Doors to be opened at six o'clock, and begin precisely at seven.

A good fire will be kept in the room."[1]

Another entertainment, something of the same class, but called a "Dissertation on Faces," appears to have occasionally taken place in Liverpool. It was advertised to be exhibited in the large room at Mr. H. Forshaw's, the Golden Lion, in Dale-street, in 1784:—

" For two Evenings in the Oratorio Week.
An entire new Exhibition.
The Lovers of rational and intellectual Entertainment are respectfully informed, that, by desire,
At Mr. Forshaw's Great Room, Dale-Street,
Liverpool,
On Wednesday and Friday Evenings next,
Will be delivered,
The celebrated Serious, Comic, and Satyric

DISSERTATION UPON FACES.

As repeatedly performed at the Theatre-Royal, Chester, Liverpool, Shrewsbury, &c. with universal applause.
Written, and to be delivered, by Mr. Cowdroy.

---

(1) Copied from the original, in the possession of, and kindly lent to the Author by Mr. Thomas Beckett Gibbons.

Part I.

An occasional Exordium.
The Face of an Alderman.
The Face of a Poet.
The Face of a Nabob.
The two Faces of a Lawyer.
The two Faces of his Client, with the striking effects of a Law-suit on his Figure and Countenance.

The two Faces of a Bum-bailiff.
The Face of a Country Parish Clerk.
The Emblematical figure of an Exotic Dancing-master.
The two Faces of a Music-master, and the striking effects of a Discord on his Muscles,

With a whimsical instance of the power of Music over a group of Tailors.

In Part I, An Allegorical Representation of MOUNT PARNASSUS.

End of the first Part, THE CONTRAST; or National Degeneracy, exemplified in the figures of a wounded British Sailor, a Frenchman, and two Beaux; with an allegorical Representation of the Invincibility of GIBRALTER, under the command of the British Salamander and his brave associates.

And a Representation of the ROCK, supported by the Military Atlas, ELIOTT.

Part II.

The Face of Hyder Ally.
The Face of a Highwayman.
The two Faces of a Lottery Office-keeper, (before and after the drawing,) with his Motto.
The Face of a Naturalist.
The Face of an Astronomer.
The two Faces of a modern Politician.
The Face of a learned Pedant, with his speech as President of a Debating Society.
The two Faces of an unlearned Pedant.

The Face of a Man a week before, and three weeks after, Marriage.
The Married Man's Coat of Arms.
The Faces of two Politicians contrasted.
A Dialogue between three English characters, a Debtor, a Porter, and an Old Soldier, on the subject of an Invasion.
The two Faces of a Senator, (in and out of place,) with the powerful influence of a Pension on the Lips.

The Three Faces of a Tabernacle Teacher,—His Street or Public Countenance; his Parlour or Home Countenance; and his Spiritual or Conventicle Countenance:

To conclude with a modern *Tabernacle Harangue.*

** The Faces, Figures, &c. entirely new, and painted by that admired artist, Mr. G. Wilkinson, whose professional abilities are sufficiently evinced in his productions at the Theatre-Royal, Drury-lane, London, and at the Theatre of Sir Watkin Williams Wynne, Bart.

To begin at eight o'Clock.

Admission, Front Seats 2s—Back Seats 1s.

Tickets to be had at Mr. Gore's."[1]

---

(1) Copied from Gore's General Advertiser of 9th September, 1784.

During the concluding quarter of the last century, Clubs, and similar meetings called Firesides, held at taverns and coffee-houses,[1] were numerous in Liverpool : they were not confined to the tradesmen, or to people of an inferior rank in life, but persons of the highest position in society in Liverpool, were accustomed to be members of such convivial associations.

One of the clubs of Liverpool which was in existence in 1775 was called "The Unanimous Society," the members of which used to meet every Saturday evening, from the first Saturday in September, to the last Saturday in April; exclusive of dining together, sometimes in Liverpool, and occasionally in the neighbouring towns of Prescot, Ormskirk and Warrington.

The members were gentlemen of the first families of the town ; many of them were members of the Council, and several afterwards served the offices of mayor and bailiff of Liverpool; they were admitted into the club by ballot only, and by the 6th rule, one adverse vote excluded a candidate.

The club was established in October, 1753, (100 years ago,) and the book of its proceedings and resolutions has been preserved,[2] from which it appears, that the place of the evening meetings of the club was originally the Cross Keys, in Dale-street.

Many of the readers must remember Mr. Thomas Golightly, a gentleman of great age, who had been Mayor, in 1772, and was afterwards Treasurer of the Corporation. He was an original member of the club, and the first who signed the Book of Resolutions, and opposite his signature is the date October 7th, 1753.

---

(1) One of those Clubs was held at the Angel Tavern, at the upper end of Lord-street, near the Potato Market, (afterwards called Castle-ditch,) at which several Performers, such as Mr. Stephen Kemble and Mr. Hollingsworth, occasionally attended, in order to keep up their popularity with the persons frequenting them.

(2) It is in the possession of Mr. John Forshaw, solicitor, who very kindly permitted the Author to have access to it, and take extracts from it.

The rules of the club are valuable, as showing the habits of the higher classes of the inhabitants of Liverpool, not merely in 1775, but one hundred years ago, and giving us an insight into the customs and manners of the age, and a copy will be given in the Appendix.[1]

The members of the club used to meet at seven o'clock in the evening, and if any member did not attend at that hour, he had, by the first rule, to pay a small fine ; if not attending at eight, a larger fine, and if he did not attend at all, unless prevented by sickness or absence from town, a still larger fine.

It is impossible for any person conversant with the literature of one hundred years back, not to gather from the works of various writers that the culpable practice of interlarding conversation with oaths, and the vice of drinking to excess then prevailed to a great extent.   As the founders of the club were persons of the first position in society in Liverpool, they, very properly, framed some of their rules with a view to discountenance those disgraceful practices.

One of the rules imposes a penalty upon any of the members for cursing or swearing, or affronting any other member; and, no doubt, in order to prevent intoxication, a prevalent vice of the age, it also imposes a penalty upon members who should come to the club intoxicated: " disguised in liquor ;" and in order to settle the question, whether a member were intoxicated or not, it declares, that " if any disputes arise about the validity of such disguise, the same to be determined by poll or ballot of the members then present."

Another directs the president to have a supper of bread, cheese, and butter, upon the table, on or before eight o'clock at night, but with a very considerate saving clause in favour of those members who did not like so plain a supper, " and what other supper the members shall think proper to

---

(1) Appendix, No. XII.

appoint, which they are to do on the preceding night;" and, evidently, in order to discourage the culpable practice then prevalent of drinking half-pint bumpers, the fourth rule proceeds to state, " that no one of the said members be compelled to drink any quantity of liquor, but what he shall think proper, (except his own toast,) and that not in a half pint."

The fifth rule directs the president to call for the reckoning at ten o'clock at night, and that each member should pay his " share of the shott, and then leave the society," but it contains a saving clause, which was, of course, very satisfactory to those who wished to remain later, for it adds, " or stay longer if he pleases." It also interdicts immodest songs being sung in the society, but it again contains a very considerate saving clause by the addition of the words, " without the consent of the president;" and it declares, that if any dispute should arise respecting " the time of the night at coming into the society, or at closing of the same, the time of coming in to be determined by the house clock, and the time of closing by the president's watch."

By the ninth rule it is ordered that, if any of the members " do marry, they shall, on the first meeting afterwards, pay unto the president for the time being, the sum of ten shillings and sixpence, which said sum must be paid towards the shott, the first evening upon their appearance after such marriage."

Another rule directs a trifling nominal payment to be made by the members by way of forfeiture, for trivial nonobservances, "instead of drinking a glass of liquor," as was the custom of the age.

By the thirteenth, a fine is imposed upon any member who should talk in an indecent manner, and in case it should be disputed whether any expression used were indecent or not, it directs that "the same shall be determined by a majority of the members present." If any person who may read this rule, should have doubts, whether the style of conversation 100 years ago, was such as to render the rule necessary, it would be advisable for him to refer to the conversations given in some of the novels which were then very much read and admired, such as those of Fielding and Smollet; in which, in very many instances, the language used is exceedingly licentious and incorrect; and, although it is not disputed, that in those of the two writers just mentioned, wit is occasionally to be found, it is too often buried under a heap of filth and indecency, and may truly be considered like a grain of wheat in a bushel of chaff.

On the 18th January, 1766, a change in the place of meeting seems to have been declared; and it was resolved that the meetings of the members should be held on the first Saturday in September, then next, at the house of "Thomas Monkus,[1] in Water-street."

Some of the minutes and proceedings entered in the Club Book are curious. One of the 15th November, 1769, commemorates Mr. Thomas Golightly's liberality in giving an entertainment, probably a dinner, to the club :—

"15th November, 1769.   This day, Mr. Golightly gave the Unanimous Society an elegant entertainment, on Sion Hill, on Accot. of His being chose a Member of the Common Council of Liverpool.

ALEXR. NOTTINGHAM, Prest.
WIL. CROSBIE, Jur. Secrey "

A number of wagers were laid at various periods by the members, and entered in the book, of which the following, amongst many others laid in 1775, are selected :—

"Liverpool, 9th March, 1775.   Received from Mr. William Pole, Ten pounds ten shillings, (for which sum now paid down) I promise to pay to the said William Pole Fifty-two pounds ten shillings on the day of his Marriage.   THOs. TARLETON."

Mr. William Pole, one of the parties to the wager, and

---

(1) Pontack's Coffee-house, in Water-street, was kept by Mr. Thomas Moncas, whose name in the Club Book is erroneously spelt " Monkus."

respecting whose marriage doubts seem to have been entertained by the club, was Mayor of Liverpool in 1778. He appears to have lost the ten guineas, as he died an old bachelor in 1820. In order, as it is presumed, that no dispute should occur as to the wager, the entry was duly authenticated by the signatures of the members of the club who were present, viz :—

" Witness,

Alexr. Nottingham	Geor : Case	George Warren Watts
Tho : Carter	Will : Crosbie, Junr.	H. H. Lake
Charles Pole	Geo : Venables	Hy. Roughsedge
Will : Crosbie	Thos. Hutton Rawlinson	Tho. Golightly
	James Bridge."	

The entries of the following wagers appear to be authenticated by the signatures of the president and the secretary.

" 5th September, 1775, at Mr. Tarleton's.
" Mr. Carter wagers Mr. Chorley six Bottles of Wine that he attends the Club as often as Mr. Chorley.

> GEOR. CASE, Pt.
> Jos : BROOKS, Junr. Secty."

" 23rd September, 1775.
" Mr. Rawlinson wagers Mr. Will. Crosbie, Junr. Six bottles of wine that he attends the Club as often as Mr. W. Crosbie, Junr.

> Jos. BROOKS, Junr. Pt.
> ALEXR. NOTTINGHAM, Secy."

" October 7th, 1775.
" Mr. Brooks wagers Mr. Nottingham a Bottle of Wine that Mr. William Crosbie, Junr. is not made Mayor's Bailiff for the ensuing year.

> Jos : BROOKS, Junr.
> ALEXR. NOTTINGHAM."

Mr. Brooks lost the wager, because Mr. W. Crosbie was elected Mayor's Bailiff on St. Luke's day, in 1775.[1] The entry is struck through with a pen, and a memorandum subjoined to it, stating, that on the 4th November, 1775, Mr. Jos. Brooks, Junr. paid the wager.

It is not requisite to give the dates of the election of the various members of the club, but perhaps it may be allowable to mention the election of three or four, who were

---

(1) See Chapter III, page 213.

well known for many years in Liverpool, and are not yet forgotten. Mr. Thomas Tarleton, an elder brother of General Sir Banastre Tarleton, Baronet, was elected on the 15th October, 1774; Mr. George Case, who was afterwards Mayor, in 1781, was elected a member on the 19th November, 1774; Dr. Brandreth, the father of the present Dr. Brandreth, in September,[1] 1776; Mr. Joseph Brooks, Jun. who was the father of the Venerable Archdeacon Brooks, one of the Rectors of Liverpool, was admitted a member on the 28th of December, 1765; Mr. Mundy Pole, Mr. Charles Pole, and Mr. William Pole, were also members; those three gentlemen were brothers, of an old and very respectable family, and were nephews of Mr. Charles Pole,[2] who was elected one of the members of

---

[1] Dr. Brandreth is recorded as having been proposed as a member on the 7th September, 1776. There is no entry of the actual day of his election, but it is certain that he was a member, because, on the next leaf after that mentioning his nomination, his name is signed with the others who attended a meeting.

[2] The subjoined outline will show the relationship of those gentlemen:—

Samuel Pole, of ═ Ann Mundy.
Radborne Co:
Derby : died
in 1730-1.

other issue. Anne Cunliffe. ═ Charles Pole, Elizabeth Coore. ═ William Pole,
                               of London,   of Liverpool,
                               M. P. for   Stamp Dis-
                               Liverpool :   tributor :
                               died in 1779   died in 1759,
                                                                    aged 60.

other   Mundy Pole,   Ellen Hatton. ═ Charles Pole,   William Pole,   other
issue.   a Major in   Mayor of   of Wavertree,   issue.
            the army :   Liverpool, in   Mayor in 1778;
            died in 1786,   1785 : died   Stamp Distri-
            aged 52.   in 1804, aged   butor for Li-
                                              69.   verpool : died
                                                              in 1820, aged
                                                              83.

            Elizabeth Mary ═ Charles Pole, of
              Pemberton   Abercromby-
                                square, born
                                in 1777 : died
                                in 1832.
                Charles Chandos Pole ═ Anne Constantia Hill.

Parliament for Liverpool on the death of Mr. Salisbury, and afterwards unsuccessfully contested the representation of the borough, at the general election of 1761 ; the first of the three was a member of the Common Council, and was afterwards a Major in the army, he was an uncle of the late Mr. Charles Pole, of Abercromby-square, who was also a member of the Council ; the second of them was Mayor in 1785, and was the father of the last-mentioned Mr. Charles Pole ; and the third was Mayor in 1778, and many of the readers will recollect his afterwards holding the office of stamp distributor for Liverpool.

The club used occasionally to have dinners not only at the coffee-house which has been already more than once mentioned, on Sion-hill, (St. James'-terrace,) kept by Mr. John Bridge ; but also at Mrs. Hooley's, the Legs of Man and Bull Inn, at Prescot ; at Mr. Samuel Hanmers, the Wheat Sheaf Inn, at Ormskirk ; and at Mrs. Dale's, the Red Lion Inn, at Warrington.

The dinner hour of the club varied. It was two o'clock in 1769, half-past two in 1775 ; and the club seems to have become more fashionable in the dinner hour in 1777, for it then got as late as three o'clock.

Not any record of the proceedings appears in the book after the 3rd and 12th September, 1778, when the club assembled at Pontack's Coffee-house, and voted a small sum of money for the relief of a poor family at Wavertree, but there are indications of the leaves containing the subsequent proceedings having been torn out.

With respect to the club dinners, two of the entries are here selected, out of several others, as being worthy of notice :—

" 29th April, 1775.

" Order'd. That the Anniversary be held at John Bridge's, at

Sion-hill, upon Tuesday, the 6th June next, and that Mr. Golightly order dinner for twelve, at 18ᵈ· p. head, at half-past two o'clock, and the Secretary summons the members.

Jos: Brooks, Junʳ· Secʸ·"

Again, at a meeting held at Pontack's Coffee-house, on the 5th April, 1777, the club passed a resolution, from which the following is an extract, for dining together on two successive days:—

" Pontack's, 5th April, 1777.

" Ordered by the Members present, that the Anniversary be held at the Red Lion, in Warrington, upon Tuesday, the 10th June, and that Mr. President order Dinner for Twelve persons, at 2s 6d p. head, at 3 o'Clock : and that dinner be ordered at Mrs. Hooley's, for the same number, on the following day, at 2s 6d p. head, at 3 o'Clock."

The reader will probably exclaim, that the members of the club were not extravagant in ordering dinners at 1s 6d or 2s 6d a head. Gently, good reader, let us not run on quite so fast. Not one word is said in the resolution respecting those sums including the wine, which, like the expense of the carriages to convey the members to Warrington, Prescot, or Ormskirk, certainly must have been paid for in addition. Besides which, those sums were evidently merely paid for a plain dinner, and the members were fond of good cheer, and occasionally seem to have had dainties in addition, as will be discovered on reading a little further in the same resolution, as follows:—

" And if any of the Members have an opportunity of presenting a Turtle, they are desired to send it to Mrs. Hooley's, at Prescott. It is further agreed, that a cask of Limes or a Haunch of Venison will be esteemed an acceptable present."

The mention of the cask of limes seems to show, that they liked to have lime punch with their turtle ; and as some of the members were West India merchants, and, probably, imported their own turtle, it was doubtless expected to be good; or the limes may have been wanted for punch after dinner. The resolution is subscribed by the following members :—

"Will. Crosbie, Junr.   Geo. Venables   John Chorley
Geor. Case   Tho. Hodgson   Wm. Pole
Joseph Brandreth   Jos. Brooks, Junr.   H. H. Lake
T. Carter   Alex^{r.} Nottingham   Charles Pole
Hy. Roughsedge

George Warren Watts, Secretary."

All the members of the club who signed that resolution are now in their graves, but there are several persons yet living who knew nearly all of them.[1]

It is fortunate that the club book, the record of their proceedings, still exists; it is worthy of perusal, because every document and all kinds of information are valuable, which give us an insight, into the habits and manners of an age gone by.

As a proof of the lamentably inefficient state of the police of the town, during the last quarter of the 18th century, if indeed there were then any body of men meriting that appellation, for it consisted only of a few constables and night watchmen, the streets of Liverpool were frequently the scenes of nocturnal brawls, riot, and dissipation : nor were such excesses confined to the lower classes; a number of ill-disposed and hot-headed young men, who were distinguished by the vulgar appellation of bloods,[2] were often engaged in disgraceful affrays ; and inoffensive passengers

   *   *   *   *   *   " loth
" To meet the rudeness and swill'd insolence,
" Of such late wassailers,"[3]

were not unfrequently insulted by them.

On one occasion, some young men of the higher

---

(1) The Author knew five of the members who signed the above resolution.

(2) Troughton's Liverpool, page 152 and 192.

(3) Milton's Comus.

classes, returning from a cotillion ball, engaged in a conflict with the watch, opposite a house of a disreputable kind, in Rainford-gardens ; the result was very shocking ; they killed a watchman ; for which they were indicted, and convicted of manslaughter, at the Lancaster Assizes ; the sentence, however, was lenient, in consequence of the penitence of the parties implicated, and their having liberally provided for the deceased's widow. Mr. Wood, (afterwards Mr. Baron Wood,) one of the first criminal lawyers of the age, was counsel for the prosecution, and drew the indictment, and stated, after reading the depositions, that he saw no reason why the offenders might not be indicted for murder.

Another extraordinary death by violence, under more than usually shocking circumstances, occurred in Liverpool, about the commencement of the last quarter of the 18th century. The body of a gentleman, who was well known,[1] was found near the New Quay,[2] having been deprived of life by a violent blow on the head ; little doubt was entertained of his having been killed whilst engaged in some licentious pursuit in the neighbourhood ; but the person who was suspected to have committed the deed, was, either in consequence of the inefficiency of the police, or the want of evidence, never brought to justice.[3]

The streets of Liverpool frequently exhibited sad scenes of profligacy ; abandoned women paraded them in considerable numbers, indulging in disgusting language, noises, and

---

(1) Mr. Jesse Case.

(2) The body had been thrown down a declivity, and left about high-water mark, and near a glass-house which old persons may recollect standing there.

(3) A female, called Mrs. Lyon, was taken up on suspicion, and she stated, that he used to visit at her house, but that he also used to visit the wife of a flatman or bargeman, in that neighbourhood; and the husband was suspected of having surprised and killed him on the impulse of the moment.

P 1

riotous conduct, without any effectual interference from the police; and one street, Bridge-street, which was not many years since demolished, the site of which is at present part of the open space adjoining the north end of the Salthouse Dock, was almost entirely tenanted by them; and the same remark will apply to many of the houses then on the New Quay. It may, perhaps, be very true, that vice is quite as prevalent now as it was at that period, but certainly it is not so openly displayed or so disgustingly prominent.

Notwithstanding what has been mentioned respecting the excesses and vices of some of the inhabitants, there were many of all ranks who were exemplary in their conduct in the observance of their religious duties, in habits of morality, and the practice of charity. In general, the Sabbath-day, in Liverpool, was a day of cessation from worldly labour, and, it was an uncommon circumstance to meet with the head of a family professing to be respectable, who did not make a point of setting a correct example to his household, by attending to his religious duties, and frequenting, on that day, a place of worship of some Christian denomination, and offering up to the Most High, a tribute of adoration and thanksgiving.

There is a circumstance worth noticing connected with the population of Liverpool, as it was during a considerable part of the period we are engaged upon. It is remarkable when we consider how numerous and respectable the Scotch families engaged in commerce now are, who reside in Liverpool, that there were then scarcely any of them settled there during a considerable part of the last quarter of the 18th century; and that, of course, accounts for the circumstance of the Scotch Presbyterians not having, prior to 1793,[1] any place of worship in Liverpool; and with respect to Irish

---

(1) See Chapter I, page 37, and see also Chapter V.

families, there were comparatively few of any class, either high or low, in Liverpool, until the rebellion of 1798; but afterwards the Union caused a considerable change in that respect. When the facility of coming over from Ireland is taken into account, the previous paucity of the Irish, may well seem extraordinary to those who now witness the vast numbers of Irish, of the lower class, who swarm by thousands in the small courts, alleys, and back streets of some of the districts of Liverpool. A number of Irish, of all classes, came to Liverpool in 1798,[1] who had left Ireland to avoid the miseries of rebellion, and the unhappy state of affairs which then prevailed there. That circumstance would, no doubt, add something to the population of Liverpool; but there were also the widely extending commerce of the port, and many other causes which combined to affect it, so that the increase of the population became very considerable before the close of the 18th century.

The Liverpool Elections now require some notice. Whenever they occurred in Liverpool, before the termination of the 18th century, they were, probably, conducted much as they were in other places, and the reprehensible practice of treating the voters was carried on to a great extent. In contested elections, inns, taverns, and public-houses were open in various parts of the town, such as the Black Horse and Rainbow, in High-street, the Angel, and other houses, in Dale-street, and the Talbot, in Water-street, where the voters were supplied with free drink. Many of the voters, and also numbers of women, remained together at the Black Horse and Rainbow, and other houses in the vicinity of the Exchange, where both the men and women were kept in a disgraceful state of

---

(1) Troughton's Liverpool, page 198.

intoxication for days together, until the men were wanted to go to the hustings. The practice of so keeping the voters together in intoxicated herds, was however not continued after the end of the 18th century; and if treating were practised at elections after the commencement of the present century, it was done in a less indecorous manner.

Besides the scenes just described, there were various public-houses open in other parts of the town, where free drink was supplied to the voters.

At that period the mode of voting was by tallies, and the elections sometimes lasted many days; which plans were well calculated for treating the voters, and for temptations to intoxication and idleness.

Probably Liverpool, in point of electioneering vices of that nature, was then much on a par with most other cities and boroughs of the kingdom.

As it may be interesting to some of the readers to know at what inns or places, in Liverpool, the electioneering matters of rival candidates were principally conducted seventy-three years ago, it may be well to mention here, that at the General Election of 1780, the Angel Inn, in Dale-street, George's Coffee-house, in Castle-street, the Fleece Inn, in Dale-street, and Neptune's Coffee-house, in the Old Shambles, were electioneering houses of the friends of Mr. Bamber Gascoyne, (then called Mr. Bamber Gascoyne, junior); the Talbot, in Water-street, and the White Lion, in Castle-street, the Black Horse and Rainbow, in High-street, and the Peacock, in the Old Shambles, of those of Mr. Henry Rawlinson; and Mr. Forshaw's, the Golden Lion, in Dale-street, was an electioneering house of those of Mr. Richard Pennant.[1]

---

(1) From the Book of Addresses, Pasquinades, &c. of the Liverpool Election of 1780, in the Author's possession.

Mob intimidation appears to have been resorted to, in the last century, as an electioneering auxiliary. The following anecdote is illustrative of the course formerly pursued, in that respect, at a Liverpool election, and is worth notice, although it is rather earlier in point of date than the period we are treating of.

At a general election in 1768, Sir William Meredith and Mr. Richard Pennant were returned to serve as members of parliament for the borough of Liverpool. Prior to this return, a poll was demanded in favour of Mr. John Tarleton, but a great number of blubber-knives (long knives fixed on poles for cutting up whales) appearing held up against him, and he not making his appearance on the hustings, his friends could not get forward to give their suffrages. About two o'clock, the Mayor thought proper to put an end to the business of the day, and the evening concluded with the usual demonstrations of joy.[1]

It was a common practice, after political elections in Liverpool, in the last century, (as it still is in many places,) for public dinners to take place, which were attended by the candidates and their respective friends. After the general election of 1796, the successful candidates, Colonel (afterwards General) Gascoyne and his friends dined together at Bates's Hotel, Lord-street; General Tarleton (afterwards General Sir Banastre Tarleton, Bart.) and his friends, at the Angel Inn, in Dale-street, Mr. Corrie in the chair; and Mr. John Tarleton (the unsuccessful candidate) and his friends, at the King's Arms Inn, in Water-street. As the practice of having dinners on such occasions was very common, it perhaps would not have been considered requisite to mention the dinners which took place

---

(1) Troughton's Liverpool, page 145, quoting as an authority the Liverpool Chronicle, of March 24, 1768.

after the election of 1796, if it had not been for a circumstance which shows the marked difference between the habits and expenses of the last, contrasted with the present century. The tickets of admission to the dinner of General Tarleton and his friends, at one of the principal inns in Liverpool, were only five shillings each.[1]

After the termination of a political election, (and even occasionally after that of Mayor,) it was formerly the custom to chair the successful candidates, and they were carried in procession, with colours, flags, and bands of music, accompanied by their friends and a large crowd, through the principal streets of Liverpool : a custom which was only discontinued a comparatively short time ago.

Although some of the particulars relating to the Liverpool elections which will now be narrated, occurred some years after the termination of the 18th century, yet the subject is so closely connected with the elections of the last century, that it is considered advisable to narrate them here.

As a proof how opinions have changed during the present century, it may be here mentioned, without impropriety, that, in the year 1802, there was a contested election for Liverpool, in which the candidates were General Gascoyne, General Tarleton, Mr. Birch, (afterwards Sir Joseph Birch, Bart. father of Sir Thomas Bernard Birch, Bart. the late member for Liverpool,) and Mr. Francis Chalmer, which terminated in the election of the two former. Mr. Chalmer received no support or encouragement whatever from the higher, and scarcely any from the middle classes, but he addressed himself assiduously to the feelings of the lower

(1) See the advertisement in Gore's General Advertiser of 2nd June, 1796. From what has been already noticed in the present Chapter (page 261), it should appear that at one period the friends of Sir William Meredith and Mr. Pennant, the then members for Liverpool, were in the habit of having an annual dinner.

orders, by dwelling, by way of clap-trap, in his addresses, upon the subject of a large loaf and cheap bread, and having painted on his flags or colours, large loaves of prodigious dimensions. The author perfectly recollects being present when a boy, and hearing Mr. Chalmer speak from a window of the old Bull and Punch Bowl Inn, which was his head quarters, in Dale-street, and in his speech he held forth to the crowd with much emphasis, on the subject of large loaves, independence, and other matters which he thought would have weight with them. It was, however, labour thrown away; the voters of all classes, both high, middle, and low, turned a dull deaf ear to matters which, of late years, have procured such numbers of votes to candidates who resorted to such topics for success. Nay, they were at that time considered actually absurd; and Mr. Chalmer, with all his flags, colours, addresses, and speeches on the topic of cheap bread and large loaves, only obtained the insignificant number of thirty-one votes.[1]

----

(1) Mr. Birch and Mr. Chalmer, upon withdrawing from the contest, issued addresses to the electors, of which the following are copies; and it will be observed that Mr. Birch attributed his want of success to the lateness of the time when he declared himself a candidate; and Mr. Chalmer appeared to consider that his failure was caused by the defection of persons who had promised him their support:—

"To the worthy and independent
Electors of Liverpool.

" Brother Freemen,

" Sensible of the very great value and importance of the interests committed by the Electors of Liverpool to their Representatives in Parliament, and considering it also as the prevailing sentiment of my Fellow Townsmen, that those interests would be best guarded and promoted by Representatives who are Merchants and Residents in it, I obeyed the Summons of many respectable Inhabitants to offer myself to your suffrages as a free and independent man *unconnected with any party*, and desirous only of your welfare and that of the nation. My failure of success is, in the opinion of my friends at least, chiefly to be attributed to the lateness of my appearing as a Candidate. The zeal and support, however, which have been manifested by those friends, during this arduous contest, will impress my mind with sentiments of indelible

At the final close of the poll the numbers were :—

General Gascoyne	 884	Mr. Birch	 477
General Tarleton	 600	Mr. Francis Chalmer	 31

1426 Freemen polled.

The expense of bringing over the out-voters, sometimes from a great distance, was a serious evil, and caused much expense, as their numbers were far from inconsiderable. It has been already mentioned that numbers of the manufacturers of earthenware left Liverpool a consider-

---

gratitude. Having afforded you an opportunity of asserting your just rights, I submit with deference and respect to your decision—for by me the Freedom of Election shall never be violated. To the latest hour of my life, I trust I shall prove faithful to those principles which have, on this occcasion, recommended me to so respectable, disinterested, and distinguished a support.

" Believe me, Brother Freemen,

" With sentiments of the sincerest gratitude and respect,

" Your most obliged and faithful Servant,

" JOSEPH BIRCH.

" Friday, July 9, 1802."

" To the independent Electors of the
Borough of Liverpool.

" Before the late Election, I was solicited by many respectable Inhabitants and Freemen of Liverpool, to present myself as a Candidate, and voluntary offers of support were made to me by many others.—I did present myself—I pledged myself that I would give the truly Independent Electors an opportunity of exercising the Right of Unbiassed Choice, and I was then the only Man who would come forward to give that Pledge.

" The flattering Reception I everywhere met with was a Proof that the Public in general was favourable to my pretensions.

" Notwithstanding the subsequent appearance of another Candidate, I stood true to my Pledge, and until the opening of the Poll I was not informed of any *Defection* of those by whom I had been solicited, and by whom offers of Support had been made.

" The Moment the Poll opened, and not before, it appeared that of those on whom I principally relied for success in my election—some had deserted me—and others done worse.

" When I retired from the hustings, the cause of my Failure was fully disclosed. I found ultimate success impossible ; I therefore abandoned the poll, and I have the satisfaction to know, that the confusion incident to a General Election was not protracted one moment on my account.

" I do not cherish resentment against any man for his conduct on this occasion.

able period before the end of the last century,[1] and went to live in Staffordshire, and that many of them were freemen, who used to be sent for to vote at the Liverpool elections; and it is remarkable that, according to the Poll Book, even as late as the contest for the office of Mayor, between Mr. Thomas Colley Porter and Mr. Nicholas Robinson, in 1827, three or four of them came over from Staffordshire to vote at that election :[1] they must have been very old men.

In the course of the recent investigation before a committee of the House of Commons, on the petition against the return of Mr. Charles Turner and Mr. Forbes Mackenzie, it was stated that some, at least, of the canvassers at their election, were hired to canvass the voters. If that be true, it presents a strange contrast to the spirit and alacrity with which, within the personal knowledge of the author, the young men, of the first families in the town, formerly used to come forward and volunteer their services gratuitously as canvassers at the Liverpool elections. There was another class of persons in Liverpool who used to devote their talents and services gratuitously at elections, viz : the professional gentlemen who were the

---

The suffrages of the majority have been conferred on their former Representatives, and to the decision of that Majority it becomes Me most respectfully to defer.

" Throughout this whole proceeding I have adhered strictly to my original Profession. I have acted with entire Independence ; and, I trust, I shall never forsake those Principles which have induced me so boldly to stand forth, at a time when *no other Man* would appear. Those Principles I have so unequivocally explained, that, I trust, they cannot be mistaken.

" I beg leave most warmly, most cordially and most gratefully, to thank a few, who unexpectedly and disinterestedly came forward at the moment of action, and so far as lay in their power, *performed* what was *promised* by others.

" FRANCIS CHALMER."

(1) The bulk of them must have left Liverpool some time before 1775, consequently, any of them who came over to vote at the election of 1827, must have attained a great age.

Q 1

solicitors and legal advisers of the committees for conducting the elections of the different candidates, (the author
does not offer any opinion or surmise, whether that course
is or is not now pursued at elections, by the present race
of legal practitioners;) but any person who was acquainted
with the late Mr. George Rowe, the solicitor, who acted
professionally for the committee for conducting Mr. Canning's first election; the late Mr. William Stanistreet, the
solicitor, who was employed for that of General Gascoyne;
or the late Mr. Thomas Avison, the solicitor, who acted
for that of Mr. (afterwards Lord) Brougham and Mr.
Creevy, and afterwards for that of the late Earl of Sefton,
must be aware that each of those three gentlemen, (all of
whom were of high respectability, and others might be
named who were equally respectable with them,) would
have felt offended if money had been offered for his professional services.

Such of the readers who remember that they "once
were young," and who, in days of yore, took an active part
in elections, may call to mind what a scene of excitement
a Liverpool contested election formerly was! What rich
humour, and what glorious fun then abounded! The curtailment of the time and the change in the manner of
voting, with the introduction of a different class of electors,
have, doubtless, effected a very great and very desirable
improvement in many respects, and in none more so than
in diminishing the opportunity of treating the voters, and
consequently, the indulgence of the latter in idleness and
dissipation; but although the facilities afforded to those evils
are diminished, the humour, the wit, and the fun of the
Liverpool elections are departed.

That treating and supplying the voters with drink were
formerly openly and reprehensibly resorted to by the influential men of both parties, at the Liverpool elections, both

of Members of Parliament and Mayors, to obtain votes amongst the lower classes of electors, is unhappily too true; but it is not true that either in the latter part of the last, or in the early part of the present century, the freemen of Liverpool (who have often had much more culpability laid to their charge than they merited) were in the habit of receiving money for their votes.[1]   That practice was first introduced in Liverpool amongst the lower classes of voters, to a considerable extent, on the occasion of the municipal election of 1827, when there was the contest for the office of Mayor, between Mr. Thomas Colley Porter and Mr. Nicholas Robinson; and the evil was greatly increased at the political election for the representation of the borough, in 1830, when there was a contest between Mr. William Ewart and Mr. John Evelyn Denison; the former was successful, or to write correctly, he had a majority of votes, but the election was declared null and void on the ground (though it was not brought home to the successful candidate individually,) of gross bribery and corruption on an extensive scale :[2] the cream of the jest is, that both the successful and the unsuccessful candidate, at the

---

(1) If the losing party at the Election of 1812, (when Mr. (now Lord) Brougham and Mr. Creevy were candidates,) or at that of 1818, (when the late Earl of Sefton was a candidate,) found it requisite, when they became distressed for votes, towards the close of those elections, to give any money to voters, in order to fill their broken tallies, it is a matter best known to themselves. The Author knows nothing of their secrets, for, although he took an active part at those elections, it happened to be on the successful side. If such practices, however, were resorted to by the losers, it could only have been on a very limited and trivial scale; they must have formed the exception, not the rule, or the circumstance would soon have got wind and have become a matter of notoriety.

(2) The corruption of those two Elections was notorious, and that of the latter was afterwards proved before a Committee of the House of Commons, otherwise the Author would not have felt himself justified in making such a statement, because he had not any personal knowledge on the subject, as he did not interfere or vote at all in that of 1827, and only gave a quiet vote, without taking any active part, in that of 1830.

latter election, professed the same politics, (whether they now hold the same or different opinions it is not material to consider here,) and were avowed Reformers or Reforming Whigs. Nor is it less droll or remarkable that in the municipal election of 1827, when the system of bribery was also pursued, though on a comparatively small scale, both the successful and the unsuccessful candidate were of the same political principles : both of them were Tories.

It is a considerable number of years since the author took an active part (as he used to do at an earlier time of his life,) at elections in Liverpool, but certainly during the period when he did take an active part in them, one party never was more pure, or less free from the charge of treating the Liverpool electors, than the other. As far as respects treating them goes, all parties, whigs, tories, reformers and conservatives have, formerly, equally set a bad example. The two severest contests which ever took place in Liverpool about that period, within the recollection of the author, were at the election of 1806, when Mr. Roscoe was a candidate on the whig interest, and General Gascoyne and General Tarleton, on the tory interest; and at that of 1812, when Mr. (now Lord) Brougham and Mr. Thomas Creevy were the candidates of the whig party, and Mr. Canning and General Gascoyne of the tory party. Any man of honour and veracity who still survives, and who took an active part for the whig party, in the election of 1806, when the whigs succeeded in getting Mr. Roscoe elected, or in that of 1812, when Mr. (now Lord) Brougham and Mr. Creevy were defeated, must admit that at both of those elections reprehensible means were openly and notoriously resorted to by their whig friends, by opening public-houses and treating and supplying the electors with drink, to endeavour to secure the election of the whig candidates. On the other hand, no honourable man who took an active part at the

former election, on the tory interest, for General Gascoyne
and General Tarleton; or, at the latter election, for Mr.
Canning and General Gascoyne, can deny that precisely
the same reprehensible means were resorted to for the purpose of promoting the success of the tory candidates. In
point of purity, there was not then a pin to choose between
the two parties in Liverpool, nor, probably, in any other
large city or town in this country. Many years have,
however, since elapsed; the corrupt system above mentioned has been discontinued in Liverpool; the curtailment
of the time allowed for voting renders treating, in the
reprehensible manner in which it was formerly practised,
impracticable; and it is now admitted, on all hands, that
Liverpool elections are conducted in a more correct and
commendable manner: and there does not now seem to
be any reason to believe that the elections in other large
cities and towns are generally conducted with more purity,
or in a better manner, than those of Liverpool.

In former days, many of the electioneering pasquinades
and squibs were witty and talented. Not a few of the middle-
aged or elderly readers will recollect some clever songs and
squibs which were published at different elections, some of
which were attributed to two very different but talented men,
both long since dead, one of whom was not a layman. Of
the gentlemen who formerly used to be prominent characters
at different Liverpool elections, as for example, Mr. John
Bolton, who nominated General Tarleton, at the election in
1807, and put Mr. Canning in nomination at several subsequent elections, Mr. Pudsey Dawson, who seconded the
nomination of General Tarleton, in 1807, Mr. William
Harper, a great supporter of the latter; Mr. Thomas Leyland, the banker, who put General Gascoyne in nomination,
in 1807, Mr. John Leigh, Mr. Thomas Parr, and Mr. Joseph
Leigh, who were strong partisans of General Gascoyne;

Mr. Thomas Booth, who was chairman of the committee for conducting Mr. Roscoe's election, in 1806, Mr. Arthur Heywood, the banker, and Mr. Richard Carson, who were active friends of Mr. Roscoe, and between whom he walked in the procession to the hustings; Mr. Nicholas Ashton, who nominated Mr. (now Lord) Brougham, at the election of 1812, and Mr. Charles Lawrence, who was an active supporter of Mr. Brougham and Mr. Creevy, at that election, and was afterwards chairman of the committee for conducting the election of the late Earl of Sefton, in 1818; and a host of other individuals, who were chairmen or committee-men, or took a conspicuous part at elections, and against whom electioneering paper shots were occasionally fired:—where are they now? How very few of them are now alive![1]

There cannot be any doubt that many of the Liverpool squibs, songs, and pasquinades, against individuals, were then coarse and offensive, but on the other hand, there were others which were witty and entertaining; it is even yet well worth the while of those who have preserved them, to take them down from their shelves, and read them once more; much racy humour and wit will be found in them; and even now, after so many years have passed away, the perusal of them, by those who knew the parties, will afford them considerable amusement.

The freemen or free burgesses of Liverpool then possessed the exclusive right of voting for members of parliament and

---

(1) Mr. Thomas Moore, the merchant, and the Author, were above forty-six years ago, active at the Liverpool Election of May, 1807. They accidentally met on the Liverpool hustings at the Election of 7th of July, 1853, but (although some of the canvassers must yet be living) neither of them could recollect that any person was now alive, except themselves, who had taken an active part *on the hustings* at the Election of May, 1807.

mayors,[1] and the mode of voting was by tallies of ten men in each.

The ship-carpenters of Liverpool were a powerful body at political elections, as well as at elections of mayors. Great numbers of them were freemen, consequently, if they would only co-operate, the result of an election was, to a great extent in their own hands. During the latter part of the last century, and for some years after the commencement of the present one, a freeman named George Dykes, who was a ship-carpenter, resided in Liverpool, and though almost devoid of education, he possessed a certain degree of shrewdness and talent, and often uttered very clever and witty remarks. He was a kind of mob-leader, exercised a great degree of sway over his comrades, could do much towards deciding the fate of an election, and was a man of tory principles, the word Conservative, as applied in a political sense, not being then in use. Like many other electioneering characters of his own sphere in life, however, George Dykes, in his old age, became shattered in health, and exhibited strong symptoms of the effects of dissipation and drinking, and was reduced to poverty.

Although the general elections of 1806 and 1807, were subsequent, in point of date, to the period contemplated in this publication; yet, as George Dykes took an active part in them, and as his name was prominently brought before the returning officers at one of them, it may not be altogether out of place to take some notice of those elections and of

---

(1) The exclusive right of voting, formerly possessed by the freemen or free burgesses, and also the system of bringing over the out-voters from a considerable distance, were changed by the Parliamentary Reform Act, 2nd of William the Fourth, chap. 45, "An Act to amend the Representation of the People in England and Wales," which, whilst it extended the elective franchise to other classes of persons, took away the right of voting from such of the freemen or free burgesses of cities and towns, as did not reside within the distance of seven miles.

George Dykes here.   He exerted himself against Mr.
Roscoe.   In the elections of 1806 and 1807, but more particularly in the former year, treating was much practised by
both parties.   In that of 1807, it became a question with both
whigs and tories, whether, if the candidate they respectively
supported were returned, his election might not be vacated.
Mr. Roscoe's friends having already kept the poll open
for more than four days, considered it expedient to put in
nomination a gentleman who was not on the spot, and
against whose voters, few as they might be, no treating
could be proved.   Mr. Richard Downward, a supporter of
the whig party, presented himself on the fifth day, the
12th of May, on the hustings, and proposed Mr. William
Joseph Denison, of London, banker, as a proper person
to represent the borough of Liverpool in Parliament;
this nomination was seconded by Mr. Thomas Leatham,
merchant.   One of the other party, moved by the impulse of
fun, immediately came forward on the hustings, and begged
leave to propose George Dykes, of Liverpool, ship-carpenter,
as a proper person to represent the borough of Liverpool
in parliament.   A brother wag, amidst peals of laughter,
immediately seconded that nomination.   Some person of
the whig party, hoping to put George Dykes *hors de combat*,
then demanded his oath of qualification, which was immediately met by a person from the tory party demanding that
of Mr. Denison.   The former from poverty, and the latter
from absence, were in no condition to comply with any
such demand.   This scene, which occurred in the author's
presence, produced much mirth and great confusion on the
hustings, much to the annoyance of Mr. Richard Statham,
the then Town-clerk, (the father of Mr. William Statham,
the subsequent Town-clerk,) who leaned over to the Mayor,
and, full of consternation at the inconvenience and absurdity
which would ensue from another bar being opened for

George Dykes' voters, whispered to the Mayor, that if the nomination were persevered in, he was bound to open a bar. The consequence was, that after a little coaxing, the nomination of George Dykes was withdrawn; and, on the seventh day, Generals Tarleton and Gascoyne were declared duly elected. Mr. Denison obtained thirty-nine votes.

In the course of that election, the author was present when General Tarleton, in consequence of there happening to be a broken tally at his bar, and of his being a free-man, voted for himself; not a very usual occurrence on the part of a candidate at a political election. Mr. Roscoe's friends immediately put out an electioneering placard or squib, as follows:

> " I have voted for myself.
> BAN. TARLETON."

Mr. Roscoe was not then a freeman, and consequently had not a vote; and it was, therefore, answered by a counter placard from General Tarleton's friends:

> " I wish I could vote for myself.
> WILL. ROSCOE."

The numbers polled at the elections of 1806 and 1807 were as follows:

1806.—Mr. Roscoe 1151
      General Gascoyne 1138
      General Tarleton 986
          2345 Freemen polled.

1807.—General Tarleton 1461
      General Gascoyne 1277
      Mr. Roscoe........................... 379
      Mr. Denison 39
          2014 Freemen polled.

The reason why Mr. Roscoe obtained so few votes in 1807, compared with his numbers at the former election,

R l

was, that prior to the commencement of that of 1807, he had publicly notified that he was not a candidate.

It once occurred that George Dykes had a dispute with the landlord of a tavern or ale-house, called the Globe, which was decided at last before the magistrates, or some other tribunal, in Dykes' favour, and he was much elated at his success.   Afterwards, at one of the elections, he was known to say that Mr. Canning and Lord Nelson were, certainly, great men, and that the Duke of Wellington was also a great man, for he had defeated the French, but that he (George Dykes) was a still greater man, because he had " conquered the Globe."

The last political election at which George Dykes appears to have voted, was in his old age, in the contest of 1812, when, contrary to the principles which he had always formerly professed, he voted for the whig candidates, Mr. (now Lord) Brougham and Mr. Creevy: whether he preferred the liquor and treating of their committee, to those of the committee, of the other candidates, or what was the inducement, was best known to himself; but with a degree of shrewd humour, for which the man was remarkable, he replied, upon being reproached with deserting his political principles, that it was " all right to quarter upon the enemy."

The personation of voters was formerly often practised, by both parties, at the Liverpool elections.

An instance of it occurred at the election of 1812, which is worth recording.   The author was standing with a tally of voters, who were ready to poll at General Gascoyne's bar, and close to him were two gentlemen, now dead, Mr. Roger Leigh and Mr. James Dickson, who used to take an active part at elections, when a man, whom for want of recollecting his real name we may call John Thompson, appeared to vote at Mr. (now Lord) Brougham's bar ; Mr. Roger Leigh or Mr. Dickson immediately called out that the man was an impostor, and that the real John Thompson was at that moment waiting with them, to vote at the other bar; and some person at the hustings stated that the real John Thompson had lost a leg. The man at General Gascoyne's bar immediately presented himself conspicuously, and exhibited a wooden leg. The conscience-stricken impostor instantly made use of his two legs, and fled from Mr. Brougham's bar, and the wooden-legged John Thompson voted in triumph on the other side. The author met Mr. Roger Leigh a short time afterwards, and remarked to him that it was singular that the impostor had been so opportunely detected : " Ah !" said Mr. Roger Leigh, " you are young in electioneering; they were both impostors, but we were fortunate in having got the wooden-legged one."

A very remarkable circumstance and one unprecedented in Liverpool, occurred at the general election of 1818. The candidates were Mr. Canning and General Gascoyne, on the tory, and the late Earl of Sefton, on the whig interest. The mode of voting was by tallies; and it was soon perceived that of the electors on the tory side, the greatest number gave votes to each of the two first, and as the Earl of Sefton's voters merely gave him single votes, or plumpers as they were called, it speedily produced a considerable majority in favour of the two first. In order to counteract, in some degree that disadvantage, Mr. Arthur Heywood, the banker, was also put in nomination by the Earl of Sefton's friends, not with any serious view to Mr. Heywood's election, but in order to obtain an additional bar to vote at. The opposite party then proceeded to nominate another gentleman, Mr. John Bolton. The same proceeding was, on a subsequent day, again and again adopted by the whig party, and again and again by the tory party, until at length, to the astonishment of the voters, there appeared to be in the field, in all, twenty-one candidates,[1] (including the three originally put in nomination,) or to write more correctly, there were twenty-one gentlemen who had been duly nominated and seconded as candidates. A vast deal of amusement, but much confusion in the proceedings, arose in consequence, and it ended at last in a compromise, by all the *nominal* candidates being withdrawn, except Mr. Heywood, at whose bar votes were allowed to be taken, until the Earl of Sefton's friends abandoned the contest, and Mr. Canning and General Gascoyne were declared duly elected.[2]

These extraordinary proceedings had been commenced on a Saturday, but it was on the following Monday that the very great increase in the numbers of the candidates took place, and Mr. Canning, in speaking, as he was accustomed to do, from the balcony of Mr. Bolton's house, in Duke-street, at the close of the fourth day's poll, on the 22nd of June, 1818, alluded to the circumstance in a speech replete with his usual eloquence, wit, and elegance of language, from which the following is an extract :—

" Gentlemen,—If I have been longer than usual this evening in reaching the place from which I am to address you, you are to attribute it to the accident of my being, according to an arrangement agreed to by all the candidates, the last to leave the hustings this day. And, under these circumstances, you will be rather surprised that I am not later still—when I tell you, that the number of candidates for the honour of representing you in Parliament has been, in the course of this day, not less than *twenty-one !—(A loud laugh.)*

" Gentlemen, you have all read, no doubt, the letters of Lord Chesterfield. It is upon the authority of that polite writer, I think, that it has been laid down as a maxim, that, for the perfect enjoyment

---

(1) The Author has a list of their names in his possession.

(2) Mr. Canning was first elected M.P. for Liverpool in 1812, and was afterwards three times re-elected.

of social comfort, a company ought not to be less numerous than the Graces, nor more numerous than the Muses. Gentlemen, your candidates, when we set out, were equal in number to the Graces only; and so long as that analogy was preserved, we went on most courteously together. On Saturday that analogy was abandoned by the addition of two candidates. Disorder immediately ensued; but we had no sooner reached the hustings this morning, than an attempt was made to repair it by raising our number to nine. Bars were actually opened for candidates equal in number to the Muses; but not, that I could see, with any great increase of harmony from that association.—*(Laughter.)*

"Gentlemen, having tried that mystical number for one round, (just time enough to induce Lord Sefton's friends to inscribe "HARMONY AND SEFTON,"[1] on their flag,) it was found that the Muses were anything but a security for harmony. The harmony which followed the adoption of their numbers was, indeed, of that species for which certain concerts, called, I know not how justly, after our neighbours the Dutch, are celebrated, where every man is said to play his own tune upon his own instrument!—*(Much laughter.)*

"Unluckily, the effort to escape from this confusion was not as well considered as it was, no doubt, well intended. By adding to the number nine, nine more, and three more to that, till, by regular progression, we rose to the number that I have stated, twenty-one,—I cannot help thinking, that we rather augmented than diminished the complication of our affairs.—*(Laughter.)*

"The list, however, of twenty-one, which I hold in my hand, but which the excessive state of pressure in which I see you, prevents me from reading to you, contains many names of individuals which you would hear with kindness and respect—*(Cries of 'Read, read.')* But, then, gentlemen, there are others of a different description—*(Cries of 'Read, read.')* No, gentlemen. The concert which I have described is happily terminated; and, as many of the performers were advertised without their own consent, and were never persuaded to take a vocal part in it, I should do unfairly in bringing their names before you for criticism and comparison.—*(A loud laugh.)*" [2]

---

(1) A new flag, with that inscription, was displayed during the day.

(2) Copied from the Liverpool Courier of 24th June, 1818.

Persons whose knowledge of the Right Hon. George Canning's matchless eloquence, arises merely from having heard him deliver his splendid, statesman-like, and classical speeches in the House of Commons, may, possibly, not be aware that he could, when so disposed, excel in playful, witty, and humourous speeches, elsewhere.

Liverpool elections, in those times, used to be conducted with urbanity, politeness, and good feeling; offensive or discourteous remarks never passed the lips of the candidates, and seldom those of the other persons assembled on the hustings, and there was then no occasion for the Mayor, as not unfrequently occurs now, to be obliged to exhort

---

It is well known that Mr. Canning was not an advocate for Parliamentary Reform. Many years ago there was a public dinner given to him at Liverpool, at which Mr. Canning alluded to the question of Reform, in a speech, of which an extract is given below. At that period there was a considerable indifference amongst most classes respecting the question of a reformed Parliament, and the time had not arrived when the nation at large called for it, as was done nine or ten years afterwards, otherwise, Mr. Canning, from his knowledge of the world, and out of deference to public opinion, would have omitted that part of his speech. In order to show with what comic powers, wit, and humour, he could speak upon such a topic, as Mr. Canning has long been in his grave, and any electioneering or political feeling which may once have existed in the minds of his opponents against him, has probably been buried with him, there can be no objection (before quitting the subject of the Liverpool Elections, and of the persons who were the Representatives of Liverpool, in former days) to give an extract from his speech.

The public dinner was given to Mr. Canning, at the Lyceum Room, in Bold-street, Liverpool, on Friday, 30th August, 1822, Mr. Henry Blundell Hollinshead, in the chair.

Mr. Canning, in the course of his speech, adverted to the circumstance that, at a period some years previously, there had been much distress from high prices, and a considerable want of employment amongst the working classes, and that Parliamentary Reform had been urged as a remedy for those evils; but he added, that at the time when he was addressing his auditors, although there was constant and steady employment for the labouring classes of the people, and the poor-rates and crimes were diminishing, yet that what was called Agricultural Distress existed, and the growers of corn were suffering, and that Parliamentary Reform, was recommended as a remedy; and he proceeded thus :—

" So that, in the year 1817, when you suffered under high prices, parliamentary reform was the cure for that calamity; and now, when the landholders are suffering under cheapness, parliamentary reform is necessary the other way. And for what purpose ? To restore, I suppose, the good old times of 1817. Let me not be understood as underrating the pressure of either of these evils; in both states of things there is much to lament, and in that which now exists there is much which I wish I could see the way to cure. But as to parliamentary reform, as the remedy for either— much more as the remedy for both, I will ask any man, whether there is common sense in such a proposition; whether the double clamour for it, be not a presumption rather in favour of the impartiality with which Parliament has acted in both these painful extremes ?

the partizans on both sides to preserve order and good humour, abstain from interruptions, and give a fair hearing to the opposite candidates and speakers.[1]

Besides which, how sadly changed, and what a falling off in point of talent, wit, and eloquence, are the scenes which are now exhibited on the Liverpool hustings, compared with those of from thirty to forty-three years ago!

" But parliamentary reform is the panacea for every evil. I read a few days ago, (I cannot immediately recollect where,) a story of an artist who had attained great eminence in painting, but who had directed his art chiefly to one favourite object. That object happened to be a red lion. His first employment was at a public house, where the landlord allowed him to follow his fancy. Of course the artist recommended a red lion. A gentleman in the neighbourhood having a new dinner-parlour to ornament, applied to the artist for his assistance; and, in order that he might have full scope for his talents, left to him the choice of a subject for the principal compartment of the room. The painter took due time to deliberate; and then, with the utmost gravity and earnestness—' Don't you think,' said he, to his employer, ' that a handsome red lion would have a fine effect in this situation?' The gentleman was not entirely convinced, perhaps; however, he let the painter have his way in this instance; determined, nevertheless, that in his library, to which he next conducted the artist, he would have something of more exquisite device and ornament. He showed him a small panel over his chimney piece. ' Here,' says he, ' I must have something striking. The space, you see, is but small, the workmanship must be proportionably delicate.' ' What think you,' says the painter, after appearing to dive deep into his imagination for the suggestion, 'what think you of a small red lion?'—*(Loud laughter.)* Just so it is with parliamentary reform. Whatever may be the evil, the remedy is a parliamentary reform; and the utmost variety that you can extort from those who call themselves moderate reformers is, that they will be contented with a *small* red lion.— *(Renewed laughter.)*

" Gentlemen, I wish that these theories were only entertaining; but they have mischief in them; and I wish that against them the country should be on its guard. I confess I am against even the smallest of these red lions; I object not to the size, but to the species. I fear the smallest would be but the precursor of the whole menagerie; and that if once propitiated by his smallness, you open the door for his admission, you would find, when you wanted him to turn out again, that he had been pampered to a formidable size in his cage."*

* Copied from the Liverpool Courier of September 4th, 1822.

(1) The Author, when a young man, used to exert himself actively at the Liverpool Elections, and his first appearance and taking an active part upon the hustings was in May, 1807. Of course he has witnessed a great many Elections since that date, and, until very recently, (when there have been some symptoms of a change

Of late years, several persons of only moderate talents, who had never been in parliament, of whose fitness or capacity nothing had previously been known, almost total strangers to the inhabitants of Liverpool, and, perhaps, picked up in some London club-house, have come down and presented themselves as candidates to a constituency who had seldom, or, perhaps, never before heard of them; whilst formerly, public characters of distinguished celebrity and talents, considered it an honour to be invited to become candidates for the representation of Liverpool; and the electors have, in days gone by, listened, upon the hustings, with delight, to the manly, soldier-like, and popular speeches of General Tarleton, whose elegant manners and fascinating conversation caused his society to be courted by princes of the blood royal, and by the great and noble of the land; the persuasive and talented addresses of the scholar and philanthropist Mr. Roscoe; the matchless eloquence, classical taste, and wit, of Mr. Canning;[1] the brilliant and powerful oratory of Mr. Brougham; and the profound and statesman-like speeches of Mr. Huskisson.[2]

---

for the worse,) he has always observed, and, in fact, it is admitted that the Liverpool hustings were remarkable for the courtesy and good humour which prevailed amongst all parties. Another circumstance, which has also been remarked, may be noticed here ; that, although lawyers, and persons who had been lawyers by education, have occasionally been candidates, yet, except in the case of Mr. (now Sir Cresswell) Cresswell, they have, in general, seldom been successful at the Liverpool Elections, and even if occasionally successful, they have rarely been re-elected. The general opinion amongst the mercantile classes, and persons engaged in trade in the town, seems to be, that a lawyer is not exactly the most eligible person to be a representative of such a great mercantile town as Liverpool.

(1) As a proof that the memory of Mr. Canning is still cherished amongst his old supporters in Liverpool, it may be well to mention, that at the General Election for this borough, on the 8th July, 1853, an old Elector tendered his vote for Mr. Canning, (so many years after his death,) and although the inutility of his so voting was mentioned, he recorded his vote for Mr. Canning.

(2) Mr. Huskisson was elected M.P. for Liverpool in 1823, and was afterwards re-elected three times.

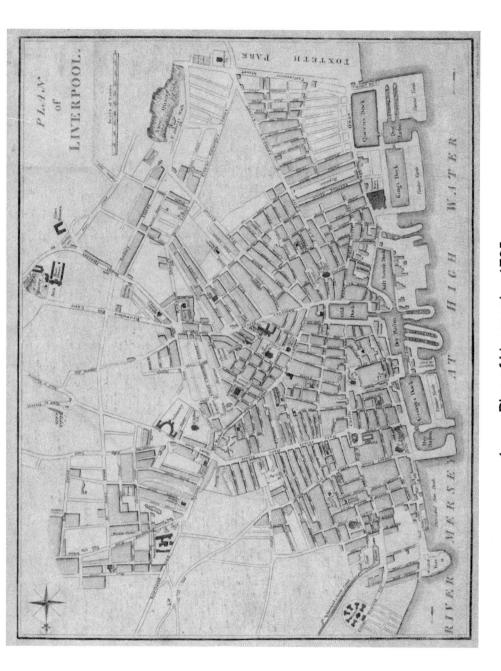

1.   Plan of Liverpool, c.1795.

2.   Chapel Street, 1797.

3. Old Dock and Custom House, 1773.

4. Lord Street, 1798.

5.   Liverpool, 1770.

6.   Sir Banastre Tarleton.

7. High Street, 1797.

8.   Old Fish Market, James Street, 1822.

9.   Blue Coat School and School Lane.

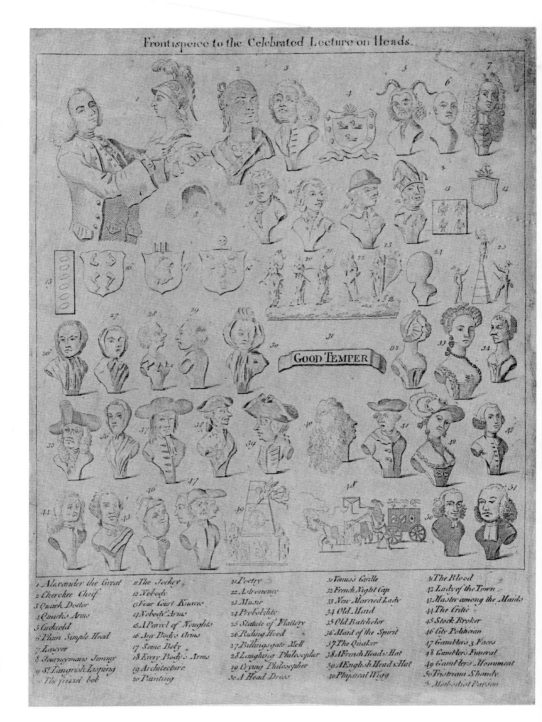

10.   'Lecture on heads', 1766.

11. Custom House (4th) and Old Dock.

12. William Roscoe.

Mr. Palmer Dies at the end of the Third
Act in this Evening in the 4th Act

Positively the LAST TIME of performing the STRANGER this Season.

This present THURSDAY, AUGUST 2d. 1798.

For the Fifth time the new Play of The

STRANGER.

The Stranger,   Mr. PALMER,

The Son
and   } of the Stranger { Master S. WARD,
Daughter,   }   { Miss S. WARD,

Count Wintersen,   Mr.   HAMERTON,
Lord William,   Master HAMERTON,
Baron Steinsort,   Mr   WHITFIELD,
Mr. Solomon, Mr. EMERY,--Peter, Mr. SIMMONS,
Tobias, Mr. ATKINS,--Francis, Mr. CALLAN,
George, Mr. WALKER,--Frederic, Mr. CORFIELD,

Countess Wintersen, Miss GODDARD,
Mrs. Haller, Mrs. WARD,
Charlotte, Mrs. HARVEY,--Teresa, Mrs. FREEMAN,
Annette } With a Duett and Song { Mrs. CHAPMAN,
Maria   }   { Miss WEBB.

The WORDS of the SONG by
R. B. SHERIDAN Esqr.
And the MUSIC by
The Dutchess of Devonshire.

To which will be added a Musical Entertainment called The

DESERTER.

Henry,   Mr. INCLEDON,

Russet, Mr. EMERY,
Simpkin,   Mr.   SIMMONS,
Flint, Mr. MARA--Serjeant, Mr. PATTERSON,
Soldiers, Mr. CALLAN, Mr. LLOYD, Mr. WALKER,
Mr CORFIELD, &c.
And Skirmish, Mr. HOLLINGSWORTH,

Jenny, Mrs. CHAPMAN,
Margaret, Mrs. FREEMAN,

And Louisa,   Miss LEAK.

In the course of the Evening "The Death of Admiral BENBOW,"
By Mr. INCLEDON,
And the new Song "Blue his Little Jacket," by Miss LEAK,

To-morrow, INKLE and YARICO,
With the PADLOCK,
Campley & Leander, Mr. INCLEDON, Wowski & Leonora, Miss LEAK.

13.   Playbill for the Theatre Royal, 2nd August 1798.

14.   Castle Street from the Exchange, 1786.

V. Lunardi Esq. *M.* *Sage G.* *Biggin Esq.*

15.   Balloon ascent, 1785.

CHAPTER V.

PRINCIPAL EVENTS AND OCCURRENCES, PUBLIC BUILDINGS, DOCKS,
CHARITABLE AND OTHER PUBLIC INSTITUTIONS AND UNDER-
TAKINGS IN LIVERPOOL, BETWEEN THE COMMENCEMENT
OF THE YEAR 1775 AND THAT OF 1800.   LOCAL ACTS OF
PARLIAMENT RELATIVE TO LIVERPOOL AND ITS VICINITY.

IT is not pretended to give in this work, a chronological
account of all the events, which occurred in Liverpool,
during the concluding quarter of the 18th century; such
an attempt would be one of great labour, and, after all,
would probably be incomplete : but although it is not considered necessary to detail circumstances which many might
consider as of minor importance,[1] the principal or more
important occurrences, and the establishment, erection, or
opening of public institutions, undertakings, or buildings,
during that period, will be narrated in chronological order,
or as nearly so as can be conveniently done.

In June, 1775, St. James' Church was first opened for 1775.
divine service, which was performed by the Reverend Mr.
Massey.[2]

On the 24th of June, the first stone of St. John's
Church was laid in the cemetery, (on the ground formerly
the heath,) between St. John's-lane and Shaws-brow, and
an account of the ceremony was given in one of the Liverpool newspapers of the time, as follows :—

"Saturday last, the Worshipful the Mayor, with the Aldermen,
Bailiffs, Common Council, &c. went in procession to St. John's Burial

---

(1) Persons who feel much interest in such matters as storms, fires, shipwrecks,
accidents, and occurrences of that nature, at or near Liverpool, in the 18th century,
will find them chronologically recorded in the Annals in the Liverpool Directory: it
does not come within the plan of this work to narrate them.

(2) Gore's General Advertiser of 9th June, 1775.

s 1

1775. Ground, and laid the first stone of the new intended church, on which is the following inscription : ' Hic lapis positus erat septimo die ante Julii Calendas, et anno salutis millesimo septingentesimo septuagesimo quinto, nec non et die festo maxime venerando sanctissimi Johannis Baptistæ, in cujus memoriam, hæ sacræ ædes sunt pietissime dicatæ, et ejusdem nomine reverenter nuncupatæ Petro Rigby, Prætore : Johanne Colquitt, Jacobo Gildart, juniore, Ædilibus : Edvardo Chaffers, Gulielmo Hatton, Custodibus Sacrorum.' "[1]

However, as has been before noticed,[2] a very considerable delay took place before the church was completed, and used for divine service. The cemetery had been consecrated in 1767. A small building where the funeral service used to be read, stood in it, at that time, near the gate opening towards Shaw-place.

St. John's Church is of dark yellow stone and built in a style which is intended for Gothic, but of which it is, in fact, a complete caricature. It is difficult to point out in Liverpool any ecclesiastical edifice of the last century, built in worse taste, or evincing, on the part of the architect,[3] greater ignorance of the principles of the Gothic style, than that church.

In this year, notwithstanding an application to the General Post-office from the inhabitants, only one letter-

---

(1) Gore's General Advertiser, Friday, June 30th, 1775.

(2) Chapter II, page 149.

(3) After looking at the new Palace of Westminster, from the vicinity of Old Palace-yard and Abingdon-street, and viewing its huge entrance tower, (at which the Queen alights on opening and proroguing Parliament,) which resembles a large Gothic warehouse on stilts, elaborately and expensively carved, and seems almost a caricature of the Gothic style, when we compare that unsightly entrance with the simplicity and grandeur of the gateways and entrances of some of the ancient edifices in this country, and reflect upon the enormous sums which it has very recently cost the nation, we may well be pardoned for inferring, that with respect to that style at least, the science of architecture is retrograde, instead of advancing, and we ought to be a little indulgent, with respect to the want of taste or knowledge, evinced in such an edifice as St. John's Church, by an architect of the last century.

carrier was allowed for the delivery of letters in Liverpool ; 1775. and the Post-office authorities gave as a reason for declining to comply with the application for an increased number, that no more than one letter-carrier had then been allowed to any one town in England.[1]

The unhappy disputes depending between Great Britain and her North American Colonies, and the hostilities which commenced between them in 1775,[2] were, as might naturally be expected, attended for a time with considerable injury to the commerce of Liverpool.

On the 11th September, 1775, a Special Council was held in Liverpool, relative to the disputes with the American States, when an Address to the King, was voted from the Corporation, under the common seal of the town, expressive of loyalty and support.[3]

The interruption of the commercial intercourse with the American colonies, the depressed state of the African trade,

---

(1) " We are authorised to acquaint the public, that application has been made at the General Post-office for a remedy to the many and much complained of inconveniences, arising from the dilatory and uncertain delivery of Letters brought by Post to this Town. To this Application the following Answer was immediately returned :—

" ' That no more than one Letter Carrier has as yet been allowed to any one Town in England. That whenever it may be thought necessary to increase the number, there can be no doubt, that the correspondence of a place so considerable as Liverpool will be entitled to every advantage that any Town in the Kingdom can possibly expect. That there are many Applications already of a similar nature, from many of the Great Cities and trading towns in England, which may possibly bring the matter before Parliament this very sessions. Whilst this matter is depending, if the Postmaster-General should not be thought justifiable in the expence of more than one letter carrier in one town, it is recommended to the inhabitants of Liverpool, to pursue whatever may have been their former method till a settlement is made upon some general grounds.' "*

      * Copied from Gore's General Advertiser of 17th February, 1775.

(2) The first blood which was shed in that contest was at Lexington, in April, 1775.

(3) To persons who may feel a desire to know what was said in an Address voted in 1775, from one of the principal mercantile towns of Great Britain, relative to the American States, with which happily, for both countries, so harmonious a feeling now exists, it may be interesting to read a copy of the Address, which

1775. and the return to the port of a number of vessels employed in the Greenland trade, the crews of which were discharged, threw a great number of seamen out of employ, which, combined with other causes, gave rise to very serious disturbances in the town.

In the autumn of 1775, considerable differences existed between the merchants and shipowners of Liverpool engaged in the African slave trade, and the sailors, on the subject of wages; followed by a series of dangerous riots; and

---

is very curious, when contrasted with the friendly relations in which the two countries now stand with respect to each other :—

"At a Special Council, held this Eleventh day of September, 1775,

"*It is Ordered*—That the Address to his Majesty now read be passed, under the Common Seal, and transmitted to the Right Honble. the Earl of Dartmouth, to be presented to his Majesty; and is as follows, viz :

"To the King's Most Excellent Majesty,

"The humble Address of the Mayor, Aldermen, Bailiffs, and Common Council of Liverpool, in the County of Lancaster, in Council assembled :

"Truly sensible of the many blessings we enjoy, in common with the rest of your people, under your Majesty's mild administration and Paternal care, We, your Majesty's Dutiful and Loyal Subjects, beg leave to approach the Throne with all due respect to your Royal Person, the most steady Attachment to the Protestant Succession, and the firmest Zeal for our Glorious Constitution, to Testify our warmest commendations of the Wisdom and Stability of your Majesty's Councils, which have been directed to allay and put an end to the unhappy differences subsisting between Great Britain and her Colonies.

"It is with the greatest concern we reflect that the Measures hitherto pursued to bring our fellow subjects, in America, to a true sense of their Duty and Interest, have not, as yet, had the desired effect, but we ardently hope that they will very soon be sensible of their error, and return to a due acknowledgement of the Power of the British Legislature, that the joys of Peace and tranquility may be restored, and the hearts of all your Majesty's Subjects be re-united in the strictest Bonds of mutual confidence and affection.

"We cannot, however, avoid expressing our abhorrence and Detestation of all Traitorous and Rebellious disturbers of your Majesty's Peace and Government, and assuring your Majesty that we shall ever be ready and willing to exert our utmost endeavours for the discouragement of all such illegal proceedings. And we Pray that your Majesty may long Reign in the Heart and Affections of all your subjects, and that the Crown of these Realms may descend to your latest Posterity."*

* Corporation Book of Records of 1775, vol. 11, page 716-7.

with the exception of the alarming disturbances in the 1775. Metropolis, in 1780, called Lord George Gordon's riots, it seems impossible to mention any popular outbreak in England, which took place during the last century, of so formidable and extraordinary a description, as the riots which occurred in Liverpool.   They were the more dangerous, because the town then had a very inefficient civil force, and there was not a soldier in the place when they broke out; and it is an extraordinary fact, for which no precedent can be found in any other riot in England, that the Liverpool rioters made use of both cannon and other fire-arms, as well as cutlasses and other kinds of weapons, on that occasion.

As the then Mayor and the local authorities were not considered to have displayed either courage or judgment, it is not extraordinary that an account of the riots seems to have been suppressed, as far as practicable, on the spot; but they could not prevent some accounts of them being published in the London and the provincial newspapers, as well as in the magazines of that period.[1]

---

(1) In the following notes will be found, copies of some particulars and accounts of the Riots, which the Author, after several careful searches in the Library of the British Museum, has extracted from some of the London and Provincial Newspapers and Magazines of 1775, preserved there.

FROM THE [London] GAZETTEER AND NEW DAILY ADVERTISER.

" Friday se'enight, some sailors who had been engaged on board a Guineaman, fitting out in one of the Docks at Liverpool, having finished the rigging, demanded their wages at the rate of 30s per month, for which they had engaged; but were given to understand by the owners, that as there were plenty of hands to be had, they would give but 20s, upon which they returned on board the vessel, and in a short time cut and demolished the whole of the rigging, and left it on the deck. A party of constables immediately seized nine of the principals, and brought them before the magistrates, who committed them to prison; upon which a great number of sailors, (supposed to be upwards of 2000,) armed with handspikes, clubs, &c. proceeded to the Gaol, the windows of which they soon destroyed : upon this the Riot Act was read to them, which, having no effect, as they were determined to rescue their companions, or destroy the gaol, eight of them were accordingly dismissed, with whom they marched off in triumph; but on mustering, and finding one had been detained, they instantly

1775. In the latter part of August, serious disputes arose between the Liverpool merchants engaged in the African slave trade, on the Coast of Guinea, and from that circumstance called Guinea or African merchants, and the sailors ; the former, whilst preparing to fit out some vessels at Liverpool for the slave trade, having lowered the sailors' wages from thirty shillings per month, at which the

returned to the prison, and brought him off, together with a woman who had been also committed for aiding and assisting in the riot ; when, after parading and terrifying the inhabitants till near twelve o'clock at night, they dispersed, and on Saturday morning all was quiet.''

" Another letter from Liverpool, dated August 30th, received by Saturday's post, says :—' The whole town is in the greatest confusion. You know there are a great number of Guiney ships that go from this port ; but since the present disturbances in America, as soon as they return they are laid up, there being now no sale for slaves ; this, together with the arrival of several Greenlandmen, have thrown as many as three thousand sailors out of employ in this port. The merchants, on this account, have lowered their wages, which occasioned the sailors to rise in great bodies, and they immediately went to all the ships that were ready to sail, and unrigged them ; this has been practised for four nights successively. Yesterday, they all met in a body, in 'Change time, to offer terms to the merchants ; but on being refused, they threatened to pull down the 'Change that night. The magistrates and merchants planted one hundred and twenty persons armed in the 'Change ; and, at nine o'clock last night, the sailors surrounded it, and were fired on from within. There were two sailors killed, and several wounded. I reckoned, this morning, sixteen holes in one of Miss Williamson's * shutters, and many of the balls were found in the shop ; many other shops round the 'Change shared the same fate. The sailors now grew desperate, on account of some of their party being killed and wounded ; and this morning they have broke open warehouses for powder and musquets. At one o'clock they surrounded the 'Change, all armed, some with musquets and others with cutlasses, together with three cannon ; they then hoisted the bloody flag, and began to fire on the 'Change. How it will end, I cannot tell, but have given you the earliest information ; further particulars you may depend on by Friday's post. Yours, &c.

" P.S. All the houses are shut up.' "

The [London] Gazetteer and New Daily Advertizer of September 4th, 1775.

" An Express arrived yesterday morning at the Admiralty, from Liverpool, for which place some Lieutenants of the Navy set out, on Saturday, to enlist sailors for his Majesty's service.''

" The ' Liverpool Advertiser,' of Friday last, gives only the following short

* Miss [Alice] Williamson, mentioned in the above account, was a bookseller, stationer, and printer. She kept a shop for several years in Castle-street.

sailors contended they had been engaged, to twenty 1775.
shillings per month. The sailors on board a Guineaman,
the Derby, Captain Yates, which was being fitted out for a
voyage to the Coast of Guinea, having finished the rigging,
applied for their wages at the former rate. This was refused
in consequence of there being plenty of seamen in the port,
and in fact, from the then depression of the Guinea trade,

account of the disturbances there, viz: ' For a few days past we have had much disturbance in town, with the sailors, on account of their wages, which is now subsided.' "

" By accounts received from Liverpool on Sunday, we are asured that the sailors
had proceeded in their depredations with great violence ; they, on Thursday, destroyed
the houses of Messrs. James, Yates, Simmons, and Ratcliffe, all Guinea merchants, but
that there was the greatest reason to believe that they would soon be dispersed, as a
party of horse from the adjacent towns, and a large body of foot from Manchester, had
entered the environs of Liverpool."

The [London] Gazetteer and New Daily Advertiser of September 5th, 1775.

" Extract of a Letter from Liverpool, September 1.

" ' My last of the 30th, ended with telling you that the sailors had surrounded the
'Change ; they fired six rounds with musquets, and six cannon, having provided themselves with three pieces more than I mentioned in my letter. One of the cannon was
fixed in Castle-street, between the houses of Mr. Warren and Mr. Cordeux, and being
pretty large, and the street narrow, the houses were so shook by it that there is scarce
a whole pane of glass in the neighbourhood. From the 'Change they went to the
house of a merchant in Whitechapel ; a party forced in, and threw all the furniture
out of the windows, which those in the street broke, and cut to pieces. From thence
they proceeded to another merchant's, hard by, where they repeated the same, and
finding plenty of liquors in the cellar, they drank till they quite disabled themselves,
on which they returned to the Ladies' Walk, their place of rendezvous. Yesterday
afternoon, a party of soldiers arrived here, and, last night and this morning, they have
taken up all they could ; so that there are now between forty and fifty of the sailors in
custody, and the town is somewhat quieter. I shall write again on Monday next.' "—
The [London] Gazetteer and New Daily Advertizer of September 6, 1775.

FROM THE MORNING CHRONICLE AND LONDON ADVERTISER.

" Extract of a Letter from Liverpool, dated August 30, six in the evening.

" ' This place is in a most dreadful situation ; the sailors have quarrelled with the
merchants on account of wages, they wanted to lower. They assembled last night at
the 'Change, (I mean the sailors,) and were somewhat riotous. The merchants had
got a number of people in the 'Change to protect it, and they were so imprudent as to
fire upon the sailors, who were unarmed ; they killed three on the spot, and wounded

1775. in consequence of the loss of the market for slaves in the American States, and of other branches of commerce being also depressed, and also from the circumstance of the crews of the Greenland ships, which had arrived in July and the commencement of August, having, as was the usual practice, been discharged for the season, and from several other causes, the number of seamen out of employ, in the town, was very

---

several; they then dispersed, but assembled again this morning, enraged, and drew up two pieces of cannon, and about one hundred small arms before the 'Change, which they battered as much as they could; they then went to Mr. Ratcliff's, in Frog-lane, and threw all the furniture out of his house, (he is a Guinea merchant); this instant, they have left Mr. James' house, after serving it in the same manner; they have also done a thousand pounds' worth of damage in his house; they are now gone to Mr. Yeates's in New Square, and they mean to go to all the Guinea merchants in town. The magistrates have sent for the military, and everything is in the utmost confusion.' "

" Extract of another Letter from Liverpool, dated Wednesday, six o'clock.

" ' I have scarce time to inform you of the most dreadful thing that ever happened here, last Friday evening. The crew of the Derby, Captain Yates, for Africa, unrigged the vessel, owing to the owners only offering them twenty shillings per month, after they had promised them thirty shillings, a month ago; taking advantage of the great plenty of sailors; however, nine were apprehended, and sent to gaol; the same evening three thousand assembled, broke the gaol open, and took their companions out; they have since paraded the docks, &c. stopping all vessels ready for sailing. On Monday they in a body waited on the magistrates, praying redress and support; they came to no terms, and were to meet next day, which they did, and the merchants agreed to give the wages they demanded: on this they dispersed, and spent the day in the greatest festivity. In the meantime, 300 able bodied men were hired at 10s per day, to apprehend those who had been most forward in the riot. The sailors discovering this, again met at nine o'clock the same evening, unarmed, and went to the 'Change, where some straggler of their party unfortunately broke a pane; on this the new appointed constables fired upon them from the 'Change, (no Riot Act being read,*) and seven were killed, and about forty wounded; † and then a general attack was made with stones, &c. at the windows, when they dispersed: but the cries and groans of the wounded were

---

* The above statement, relative to the Riot Act, evidently appears to be incorrect. The Author has conversed, with persons who were living in Liverpool, at the time of the riots, and never heard any one state that the Proclamation under the Riot Act had not been read; nor is it probable that the Magistrates would have omitted to read it; which is tolerably good negative evidence that it was read. Besides which, in the accounts which will be subsequently copied in these notes, from the "Morning Chronicle and London Advertiser" of the 8th and also that of the 11th of September, the London Chronicle of the 2nd to the 5th, and the 5th to the 7th of September, the Chester Chronicle of 4th of September, and the Annual Register, all of 1775, it is distinctly stated that the Riot Act had been read.

† The number of killed and wounded in the above account seems to be exaggerated.

great, amounting, according to some accounts, to as many as
three thousand.   In consequence of this dispute a violent
commotion was excited, the sailors rose in great bodies, went
to the vessel prepared for sea, and unrigged her, so as to prevent her sailing, by cutting and demolishing her rigging; and
left it on deck ; the same line of conduct was also pursued

---

dismal.   The sailors, this morning, again assembled to upwards of 1000, all with red
ribbons in their hats ; they went to Paris', * the gunsmith, took near 300 musquets,
half of which are burst, also powder, balls, &c. from other places, and about one
o'clock assailed the 'Change with two large cannon, and their small arms.   In this
attack four persons were killed ; they have since entirely destroyed the house, furniture,
&c. of Mr. Ratcliffe, a Guinea merchant, who was active against them, and they are at
this moment battering Mr. James's house, which is fortified.

P.S.   The soldiery who are sent for, are arrived, and are now in engagement with
the rioters.' "—*The Morning Chronicle and London Advertiser, September* 4, 1775.

" The rioting of the sailors at Liverpool, will effectually be put a period to in the
course of this week ; as press warrants, we hear, were issued on Saturday, for securing
all of them, if possible, for his Majesty's service."—*The Morning Chronicle and
London Advertiser of Tuesday, September* 5, 1775.

In that of September 6th, an extract is given from the Liverpool Letter
of 1st September, similar to the one before copied, which appeared
in the " Gazetteer and New Daily Advertiser" of 6th September,
commencing, " My last of the 30th ended with telling you that the
sailors had surrounded the 'Change ;" and with the addition, by way
of postscript, " I shall write again on Monday next."

" Extract of a Letter from Liverpool, Friday, September 1.

" ' This day I have been so frightened as hardly to be able to do anything.   Such
scenes of distress as I have been eye witness to, with the clattering of swords and
cannon, have so terrified me, that I hardly know what I say or do.   To inform you of
the particulars; you must know that in Whitechapel, lived a merchant,† who was said to
be the first that fired upon the sailors ; in consequence thereof, a large number of them
came with a drum, a flag, and armed with guns, blunderbusses, cutlasses, clubs, &c. who
fired on the said merchant's house, which stands in sight of us, where they threw out
the feather-beds, pillows, &c. ripped them open, and scattered the feathers in the air,
broke open the drawers, full of clothes, laces, linen, tore in pieces the house and bed
furniture, together with the stoves, parchments, china, &c. and all that was in the
house.   We were all in a dreadful confusion, but they behaved very well to every one,
excepting those to whom they owed a grudge.   They then marched to a very large

* This appears to be intended for " Parr's, the gunsmith."

† The Merchant above alluded to, as living in Whitechapel, was Mr. Thomas Ratcliffe.

1775. by them, with respect to several vessels which were intended to have gone to sea shortly. The constables secured nine of the offenders, and brought them before the magistrates, who committed them to prison; the old Tower, in Water-street, was at that time the gaol of the town. A large number of sailors, according to one account upwards of 2000, and to another 3000, armed with such weapons as hand-

---

house behind us, belonging to another merchant, whose name is James, and one of the greatest traders here : the family having been apprised of their coming, had left it, and taken some of their most valuable effects with them to a country house they have; but such good furniture they destroyed here, would have grieved any one to see ; they destroyed also the compting-house, with all the papers, goods, &c. The household furniture was very rich, with abundance of china and chintz bed furniture, all of which were torn to shivers, and linen, plate, &c. tumbled into the street, and thrown about in fragments immediately, in the air. During the whole time the cellars were kept quite open, and what liquor they did not drink, they threw away ; our poor Debby would go to see them, and has got her eyelash cut with a candlestick.

" ' It is not possible to form any idea of the distress this place has been in, all this day. The merchants get to the corner of the streets, where, methinks, I yet see them standing, with fear painted in their faces. The 'Change has all its windows broke, and frames forced quite out. They have been firing also at the walls the greatest part of this day, and are now gone to Cleveland-square. I suppose there is not a merchant who has wanted to lower their wages but will be visited by them ; and God knows how long these riots may continue. You will not wonder, after reading this, that I was terrified. I am a coward its true, but I think this would have alarmed any one. They read the Riot Act last night, and then began to fire on them, when they killed three, and wounded fifteen. This has made them so desperate. I could not help thinking we had Boston here, and I fear this is only the beginning of our sorrows.' "

" A Letter from Liverpool, dated the 1st instant, says—

" ' About forty sail of Guinea ships are now laid up, and all that may arrive will be laid up also, for the embargo upon arms prevents any from sailing, even admitting there was encouragement for the sale of negroes in the West Indies, and the payment good.' "—*The Morning Chronicle and London Advertiser, Friday, September* 8, 1775.

" Extract of a Letter from a Gentleman who accompanied the party of Lord Pembroke's Royal Regiment of Horse, that was sent for from Manchester to Liverpool, to quell the disturbances of the sailors, dated September 6 :—

" ' Last Wednesday, at three o'clock in the afternoon, an express was received at Manchester from the Mayor of this place, demanding the assistance of the soldiery, to put a stop to the riotings of the sailors ; and, in the evening, two of the principal gentlemen in the town arrived, praying their immediate march, otherwise, Liverpool would be laid in ashes, and every inhabitant murdered. Upon this, the men were spikes, clubs, &c. went to the gaol in order to rescue their 1775. comrades, and proceeded to break the windows; the riot act was read, but being disregarded, and the rioters being determined to liberate the prisoners or destroy the gaol, its safety was purchased by the liberation of eight of the prisoners, whom the assailants carried off in triumph. On discovering, however, that one of the prisoners was detained, they returned to the gaol and took him out of it, together

---

collected together with all speed, to the number of 100 privates and six officers ; and about three o'clock in the morning, they marched. It rained very hard, and did not cease until they came within six miles of Liverpool, where they were met by the Mayor, who told them the rioters were drawn up in a body to attack them. Before they proceeded any further they examined their arms, which, being very wet, required a short time to put them in order, and when done, they loaded, then marched in six divisions with their horses on each side, to keep the flanks clear, intending to give the sailors the street fairing. They arrived at Liverpool about four o'clock in the afternoon, in good spirits, though somewhat fatigued, amidst the acclamations of the whole town, who now came out of their houses, which they had not done, nor even shewn their faces, for some time before. Immediately upon their appearance, the rioters dispersed, with the utmost confusion, hiding themselves in garrets, cellars, &c. and in short, anywhere they could. The soldiers then surrounded several houses, and in the course of Thursday and Friday, made about sixty prisoners, who were sent to Lancaster jail, and now all remains very quiet.

" ' The cause of the riot was this. The African merchants having lost one or two ships, reduced the men's wages from thirty to twenty-five shillings ; upon this, the sailors applied to the Mayor, but not gaining the redress they wanted, began breaking the windows of the Exchange, and committing many outrages. The Mayor having got a few people together within this building, read the Riot Act, which not being regarded, obliged him to fire from the windows, when two or three of the leaders were killed. This exasperated the others so much, that they fetched pieces of cannon and planted them before the 'Change, and kept a continual fire for two days, which, though somewhat extraordinary, did little other damage than breaking the windows. They then went to the houses of Mr. James and Mr. Ratcliffe, African merchants, and entirely destroyed the furniture, throwing the portable valuables out of the windows, which were carried away by their whores, &c. Mr. James's loss is estimated at upwards of a thousand pounds. Every moment now became more alarming to the inhabitants ; the rioters broke open the gunsmith's shops, and took all the arms they could find, and marched about the streets, presenting pistols at the breast of every person they met, demanding money from them. Their leader they called General Gage, and they held meetings every day.' "—*The Morning Chronicle and London Advertiser, September* 11, 1775.

1775. with a woman who had been also committed for assisting
in the riot, and marched away with them. The rioters
then proceeded to parade about the docks, and continued
doing so until near midnight, terrifying the inhabitants, and
taking measures for stopping such vessels as were prepared
for sailing. One account states, that their violence in
unrigging the ships which were ready to sail, was practised
for four nights successively. Besides other acts of tur-

FROM THE DAILY ADVERTIZER.

The copy of the Letter from Liverpool, dated "August 30," commencing, "The
whole town is in the greatest confusion," and terminating, "all the houses are shut
up;" and the extract from the letter of August 31st, commencing, "Last Friday
evening, some sailors who had been engaged," and terminating, "they dispersed,
and on Saturday morning all was quiet," also appear as given in the [London]
"Gazetteer and New Daily Advertiser" of Monday, September 4th, 1775.

The extract from the Letter from Liverpool, dated Liverpool, Wednesday, 6 o'clock,
(as given in the "Morning Chronicle and London Advertiser" of September 4, 1775,)
appears in the "Daily [London] Advertiser" of September 5, 1775, commencing,
"I have scarce time to tell you of the dreadful affair that happened here last Friday
evening. It was the crew of the Derby, Captain Yates, for Africa, who unrigged the
vessel;" and mentioning the mob having plundered the gunsmith of musquets, and
having assailed the Exchange with two large cannon and their small arms. It, however,
brings down the account somewhat later, with respect to the attack on Mr. James's
house, than the other newspaper, and states:—"This instant they have left Mr.
James's house, after serving it in the same manner; they have done a thousand
pounds worth of damage in his house. They are gone to Mr. Yeates's, in New-square,
and mean to go to all the Guinea Merchants in town. The Magistrates have sent for
the military, and everything is in the utmost confusion."—*The Daily Advertiser,
Tuesday, September* 5, 1775.

Subsequently, on the same page, is the following concise further statement, apparently received from Liverpool:—"Liverpool, Sept. 1. For a few days past we have
had much disturbance in this town, with the sailors, on account of their wages, which
is now subsided."—*The Daily Advertiser, Tuesday, September* 5, 1775.

The "London Chronicle" of Saturday, September 2nd, to Tuesday, September
5th, 1775, and also the "Morning Post and Daily Advertiser" of September 4th,
1775, contain a copy of the Letter from Liverpool, dated 30th August, before copied,
commencing, "The whole town is in the greatest confusion," and terminating, "All
the houses are shut up," as above: besides which, the "London Chronicle" of
Saturday, September 2nd, to Tuesday, September 5th, also contains the following
further particulars :—

bulence and disorder which were committed during several 1775.
days, the rioters went round the town in gangs to the houses
of the merchants, levying contributions of money.   Amongst
many other places which they visited with that object, was
the house of Mr. William Leece, a merchant, in Water-
street: it happened that at that time no person was within
except the female servants, and his daughter, Miss Leece,

FROM THE LONDON CHRONICLE.
" Extract of a Letter from Liverpool, Sept. 1.

" No doubt but you have heard of the dreadful disturbance between the sailors of
this port and the Guinea merchants, relative to their lowering the sailors' wages.   Such
scenes of distress I never before beheld ; the clattering of swords and cannon has so
terrified me that I hardly know what I write.   The first place the sailors proceeded to
was the house of a Guinea merchant in Whitechapel, who, they were informed, was
one of the persons that first fired on them, which house, together with all the furniture,
they entirely destroyed.   They next proceeded to Mr. James's house, the whole of
which, together with great part of his furniture, shared the same fate.   It is impossible
to form an idea of the distress of the inhabitants.   Last night, the Riot Act was read,
which, not having the desired effect, the sailors were fired upon, when three were
killed, and fifteen wounded.   A party of soldiers are arrived, who have secured about
fifty of the ringleaders, and the town is now pretty quiet."—*The London Chronicle,
Saturday, September 2nd, to Tuesday, September 5th*, 1775.

" Extract of a Letter from Liverpool, September 2nd :—

" ' Last night the Riot Act was read, which not having the desired effect, the
sailors were fired upon, when three were killed, and fifteen wounded.   A party of
soldiers are arrived, who have secured about fifty of the ringleaders, and the town is
now pretty quiet.' "—*The London Chronicle, Tuesday, September 5th, to Thursday,
September 7th*, 1775.

" A Letter from Liverpool, dated the first instant, says :—' About forty sail of
Guinea ships are now laid up, and all that may arrive will be laid up also, for the
embargo upon arms prevents any from sailing, even admitting there was encouragement
for the sale of negroes in the West Indies, and the payment good.' "—*The London
Chronicle, Thursday, September 7th, to Saturday, September 9th*, 1775.

" From Liverpool, we hear that the sailors who did the mischief, were not above
sixty, but were attended by a great number of blackguards, who swarm about that seaport ; two of the rioters were killed opposite the 'Change ; a third is since dead."—
The London Chronicle, Thursday, September 7th, to Saturday, September 9th, 1775.

The extract from a Letter from a gentleman who accompanied the party of
Lord Pembroke's Royal Regiment of Horse, that was sent for from Manchester to
Liverpool, to quell the disturbances of the sailors, dated September 6th, commencing,
" Last Wednesday, in the afternoon, an express was received at Manchester, from

1775. and she, with a degree of strength of mind and good sense which characterized her through life, being quite aware that to show symptoms of fear was not the way to deal with a lawless rabble, stepped to the house door, and addressing the mob leader, who was a sailor, she inquired what they wanted.

---

the Mayor of Liverpool," and concluding, " who are sent to Lancaster jail ; and now all remains very quiet," also appears in the " London Chronicle," of Saturday, September 9th, to Tuesday, September 12th, 1775.

Of the six persons whose names are mentioned in the above accounts, extracted from the London Newspapers, Mr. [Thomas] Ratcliffe, resided in Whitechapel, Mr. [William] James, in Rainford-garden, Mr. [Thomas] Yates, in Cleveland-square, and Mr. [John] Simmons, in St. Paul's-square, and were merchants ; Mr. [Samuel] Warren was a goldsmith, and Mr. [Thomas] Cordeux was a hatter and hosier, the shops of the two latter were in Castle-street.

FROM THE CHESTER CHRONICLE.
" Chester, September 4.

" In the beginning of last week, a violent disturbance happened at Liverpool, owing to the imprudence of the merchants attempting to lower the sailors' wages, after they had employed them to fit out some vessels for Africa, and contracted with them at a certain rate per month.   Upon being refused their stipulated agreement, a great mob assembled, and a dangerous riot ensued, which continued several days.   The Riot Act was read, and all other means tried to prevent bloodshed, but in vain.   The military were sent for from Chester and Manchester ; but previous to their arrival the sailors very prudently dispersed, upon having destroyed the windows and furniture of several houses, and committed many other daring outrages."—*The Chester Chronicle, Monday, September 4th,* 1775.

FROM THE SCOT'S MAGAZINE.
" The slave trade having been greatly affected by the order of Council prohibiting the exportation of gunpowder, the sailors of Liverpool, who are unemployed, on that occasion asembled in a body, August 28, and threatened destruction to the whole town.   They had got several pieces of cannon which they fired.   But a party of Light Horse being sent for from Manchester, they were soon dispersed, and about 40 of them lodged in gaol."—*The Scot's Magazine for* 1775, *vol.* 37, *page* 523.

There is an account in the " Gentleman's Magazine " of the month of September, 1775, page 450, which corresponds almost word for word with the last.

Portions of the above accounts, taken from the newspapers, also appear in the " Westminster Magazine " of September, 1775, vol. 3, page 506 ; The " Town and Country Magazine " of September, 1775, vol. 7, page 499 ; The " Universal Magazine " of September, 1775, vol. 57, page 160 ; and The " Gentleman's Magazine " of September, 1775, vol. 45, page 450 ; but as they do not afford any information of

Here a scene ensued highly characteristic of the habits of 1775.
a British seaman. The man, probably, was surprised at and
admired her courage and self-possession, which might have
been then sought for in vain, amongst the local authorities
of Liverpool, and finding himself in the presence of a

moment, beyond the accounts before given, it is not considered necessary to introduce
extracts from those Magazines here. The following account also appears in the
" Annual Register " of 1775 ; it contains little more than the particulars formerly
given in the newspapers, in a more condensed form :—

FROM THE ANNUAL REGISTER.

" Some sailors who had been engaged on board a Guineaman, fitting out in one
of the docks at Liverpool, having finished the rigging, demanded their wages at the
rate of 30s per month, for which they had engaged ; but were given to understand by
the owners, that as there were plenty of hands to be had they would give but 20s,
upon which they returned on board the vessel, and in a short time cut and demolished
the whole of the rigging, and left it on the deck. A party of constables immediately
seized nine of the principals, and brought them before the magistrates, who committed
them to prison ; upon which a great number of sailors, supposed to be upwards of
2000, armed with handspikes, clubs, &c. proceeded to the gaol, the windows of which
they soon destroyed ; upon this the Riot Act was read to them, which having no effect,
as they were determined to rescue their companions, or destroy the gaol, eight of
them were accordingly dismissed, with whom they marched off in triumph ; but upon
mustering, and finding one had been detained, they instantly returned to the prison,
and brought him off, together with a woman, who had been also committed for aiding
and assisting in the riot ; when after parading and terryfying the inhabitants till near
12 o'clock at night, they dispersed ; and next morning all was quiet."

" Some days after, however, there was another rising of the sailors in the same
port, in consequence, some will have it, of the slave trade having been greatly affected
by the late Order of Council, for prohibiting the exportation of gunpowder, &c.; the
sailors out of employment on that account assembled in a body, threatened destruction
to the whole town, and had actually got several pieces of cannon which they fired ; but
a party of light-horse being sent for from Manchester, they were soon dispersed, and
about forty of them lodged in gaol."—*Annual Register*, 1775, *vol.* 18, [*Chronicle*]
pages 146 *and* 147.

" The inability of purchasing and providing for negroes, which the present disputes
had occasioned in our West India Islands, together with the loss of the American
market for slaves, and the impediments caused by the proclamations of Council,
against the exportation of arms and ammunition, had altogether nearly extinguished our
African trade. This loss was more particularly felt in the port of Liverpoole, which
had possessed a much greater part of that commerce than any other in the kingdom.
As the Guinea ships now arrived they were laid up, in an uncertainty of their future

1775. young lady, " Jack " did not forget the proverbial " good manners " of a sailor, but took off his hat, and remained uncovered, whilst, in respectful language, he told his tale and solicited (not demanded) a contribution, and having received it, he thanked her, and retired with the mob from the house, without mischief.[1]

---

disposition, whilst their crews looked in vain for other employment. As other branches of commerce were also slackened in a great degree, and that the crews of the Greenland ships, upon their return in July and the beginning of August, were as usual discharged, the number of seamen out of employ, in that town, became very great, and according to some accounts amounted to about 3000.

" In this situation, the seamen complained that an attempt was made by the merchants, to lower their wages, in consequence of which a violent commotion was excited among them, in which they cut the rigging of some ships to pieces, assaulted some houses, and committed other violences.

" They, however, dispersed again, and all became quiet; but the seizing a number of them and sending them to prison, rekindled the flame with greater violence, so that without any extraordinary bias upon the common course of things in such circumstances, it might well have ended in the destruction of that flourishing town. The sailors immediately assembled, procured not only fire-arms, but cannon, and were proceeding to the destruction of the prison, when its safety was purchased by the enlargement of their companions; but their rage was by this time too high, and they were too much inflamed by liquor, to be appeased by reasonable concessions. They not only proceeded to destroy the houses of obnoxious persons, but they at length marched in a body to demolish the Exchange. This danger was foreseen, or probably announced by themselves, a considerable time before the attempt, so that the Exchange was shut up, barricaded, and well garisoned by the merchants and townsmen. They, however, made several confused attacks, which continued through the course of a night and part of the ensuing morning, during which, through their drunkenness and disorder, they laid themselves so open to the fire of the defenders, (who were themselves safe under cover,) that several of them were killed and wounded. The arrival of a detachment of light-horse, at length put an end to the disorder. It was then apprehended that this would prove only a prelude to other disorders. But the affair was accidental; and sufficient employment for the seamen was soon found in the King's service."— *Annual Register*, 1775, *vol.* 19, [*History*] *page* 44.

(1) Miss Leece was afterwards Mrs. Drinkwater, she having married Mr. James Drinkwater, who was Mayor of Liverpool, in 1810. Her oldest son, Sir George Drinkwater, was Mayor, in 1829; her second son, Mr. William Leece Drinkwater, of the Isle of Man, was a member of the House of Keys and a Magistrate of that Island; her third son, Mr. John Drinkwater, is the father of Deemster Drinkwater, of the Isle of Man; and her daughter (Margaret Drinkwater) married Mr. Peter Bourne, who was Mayor of Liverpool, in 1825. Mrs. Drinkwater was a clever, strong-minded person, an excellent wife and mother, and a valuable friend. The Author feels pleasure in offering this tribute of respect to the memory of a lady, who for many years was his near neighbour, and under whose roof he has passed many happy hours.

In order to put an end to these commotions and dis- 1775. turbances, some negotiations took place with the sailors, but without any satisfactory result; and they went in a body in 'Change time to offer terms to the merchants, and to ask for redress and support; but being either refused, or at least disappointed in their expectations, the sailors threatened to pull down the Exchange (now called the Town-hall) that night. The alarm arising from the threats and violent proceedings of the sailors, naturally caused some of the inhabitants to conceal their most valuable and portable articles, and remove their children to places of greater safety.[1]

So far the outbreak, though violent and lawless, had not been attended with any loss of life; but a very different and shocking scene was shortly after-wards witnessed, and most alarming and dangerous riots ensued. The magistrates being warned of the intended attack on the Exchange, planted a number of persons (according to one account, one hundred and twenty) armed, by way of garrison, in it; and in the evening of the same day, the sailors, joined by the low rabble and dregs of the populace, to whom the hope of plunder was doubtless acceptable, surrounded it in great numbers, assailed it with violence, and broke the windows and window frames with stones, and the proclamation under the riot act having been read without any good effect, they were fired at from within, and two or three of the rioters were killed and several were wounded; and some of the shop windows in Castle-street, exhibited the effects of musket balls, fired from the

---

(1) The Author has been informed by the late Mr. Samuel Staniforth that his father, Mr. Thomas Staniforth, who resided at his house in Ranelagh-street, now the Waterloo Hotel, adopted both of those precautions; in consequence of considering that it was likely that his house would be attacked, his children were sent away, and some articles of silver were carefully hid in his hay-loft.

v 1

1775. Exchange.   The inhabitants of the town had already passed some days of alarm and anxiety, but now, the threats of the rioters were so violent, and their lawless proceedings had attained such a height, that many of the merchants and other inhabitants passed a sleepless and anxious night, looking forward with dread to the morrow.

The next day the houses were shut up, the whole town being in a state of the greatest alarm and confusion, and the rioters, excited almost to desperation in consequence of some of their party having been killed or wounded, mustered again in a violent and tumultuous manner, and proceeded to attack the houses of the merchants and ship-owners who were disliked by them.   In the course of their violence they took several pieces of cannon from one of the ships, broke open gunsmiths' shops, warehouses, and other places, one of which was the place of business of Mr. Parr,[1] a gunsmith, and carried off muskets, ammunition, and balls. About one o'clock they went to the Exchange, all armed, some with muskets, some with cutlasses, and others with what other weapons they could obtain, and brought up the cannon, which are said to have consisted of three pieces, into Castle-street,[2] in front of the Exchange, and made a general attack upon the building with the cannon and small arms. One account states that they had as many as one hundred muskets.   They made several irregular and confused attacks

---

(1) His name is called " Paris" in an account in a newspaper of the time, but it can scarcely admit of a doubt that it was meant for Mr. Parr, who was a well-known gunsmith.

(2) The late Mr. William Stanistreet, father of Mr. John Frederick Stanistreet, solicitor, has informed the Author that he (Mr. William Stanistreet) was in Castle-street when one of the cannon was brought there by the sailors.   The late Mr. Henry Holmes once mentioned to the Author, that the sailors, in order to get one of the cannon to the scene of action, took a horse from the stables of Mr. Blackburne's salt works, at the Salthouse Dock, and that one of them, probably more accustomed to work a gun than to harness a horse to it, happening to have his back to the horse whilst attaching him to the cannon, the animal bit him severely.

on the building, which remained in a state something re- 1775.
sembling that of siege during many hours,[1] in the course of
which the rioters, through their drunkenness and disorder,
laid themselves open to the fire of the defenders from within,
who were safe under cover, and several of the rioters were
killed and some were wounded.

During the continuance of the riots, but whether it was
before or after the attacks on the Exchange cannot now
be clearly ascertained, the rioters also attacked several
dwelling-houses inhabited by merchants. They broke into
the house of Mr. Thomas Ratcliffe, a Guinea merchant,
who lived in Whitechapel, at the south corner of Richmond-street, and was unpopular with them, destroyed the
windows, and threw all the furniture out of them to
others in the street, who broke and cut it to pieces. One
of the inmates of his house, who was escaping towards
the back of the premises, just as the rioters broke in, was
fired at by a sailor armed with a pistol,[2] the ball of which
remained for years, and may probably yet be in the door-
post of one of the front rooms. They also gutted the house
and destroyed the furniture of Mr. William James,[3]
another Guinea merchant, in Rainford-gardens, who was
also unpopular with the sailors; and at the latter place they
got a large quantity of wine or spirits, and in conse-

---

(1) One account says during the night and part of the next morning.

(2) Communicated to the Author by the late Mr. Jonathan Ratcliffe, the son of Mr.
Thomas Ratcliffe, whose house was thus attacked. Many years ago the Author was
informed by a person, that, when he was a very young man, he was one of those who
had taken a part in the attack on Mr. Ratcliffe's house, and that when the rioters
destroyed the bedding there, they found that one (if not more) of the servants'
beds was stuffed with chaff, which the lower classes used as a by-word against
Mr. Ratcliffe for a long period of time afterwards. An account, somewhat similar,
was also communicated to the Author by Mr. Jonathan Ratcliffe.

(3) In destroying Mr. James' furniture, a little negro boy was discovered by the
sailors concealed in the clock case, whither he had fled for safety.

1775. quence, many of them became very drunk; and from thence they proceeded to their place of rendezvous, which was in the North Ladies'-walk. Besides the depredations committed at those houses, the rioters also attacked that of Mr. Thomas Yates, in Cleveland-square, and that of Mr. John Simmons, in St. Paul's-square, Guinea merchants, and committed many other daring outrages, and threatened hostile visits to all the merchants engaged in the Guinea trade.

During the attack upon the Exchange, the concussion of air from the discharges of the cannon broke many of the shop windows in Castle-street. More than one of the marks of the cannon balls fired at the Exchange are even yet visible; one may be seen on the east side of the stone frame (where the stone work has been repaired, and pieced together with cement) of the drawing-room window nearest to Dale-street, and another on the second pilaster from Dale-street, in a line with the same window. The marks of balls were also perceptible, for a long period, on the centre below the pediment of the edifice, before the centre was altered and covered by the present portico; and persons are yet living who remember their being visible on it. There were not any military then stationed in Liverpool. In addition to the civil force, such as it was, the Town-hall was defended by several persons who volunteered for the occasion, some of whom were in a superior rank in life, and others were engaged by the magistrates, and were paid for their exertions. The military were sent for from Manchester, and, as has been said, from Chester also, but only those from the former arrived in time for the suppression of the riot. In the afternoon of the 31st of August, a body of the 1st or Royal Regiment of Dragoons,[1] arrived from Manchester, and

---

(1) Council Book, of 1775, vol. 2, page 717 and 718. In some London newspapers of that period the regiment is called Lord Pemberton's Regiment of Horse. Is that another name for the same regiment?

caused the immediate dispersion of the rioters, (who took 1775.
to flight as soon as they saw the cavalry arrive,) and
from forty to fifty of the rioters were apprehended. It is
said that much more damage would have been done to
the Town-hall by the balls from the cannon, if it had
not been for the circumstance of some one in the crowd,
either from stupidity, or a praise-worthy desire of preventing mischief, calling out to the sailors, when levelling
one of the guns, "Aim at the Goose :" alluding to the
Cormorant (called the Liver,) the armorial device of the
town, which formed one of the figures in the pediment;
and certainly for a bird, it was very large and conspicuous;
the idea was caught at, as enabling them in some sort, to
wreak their resentment, against the local authorities of the
town, by destroying its heraldic ornament, and the cannon
being pointed high, did less mischief than it might otherwise have done.

The number of killed and wounded during the riots
cannot be ascertained, but there certainly were several lives
lost, and a considerable number wounded.

As means appear to have been used to suppress the
account of the riots in the Liverpool papers, it is not remarkable that on referring to one of them,[1] the riots do not
appear to be mentioned until the 5th of April, 1776, when
fourteen sailors, who had been committed to take their trial,
and had been imprisoned during the preceding winter in
Lancaster Castle, were briefly mentioned as having been concerned in the riot in Liverpool, and that they were all
permitted to go on board one of the ships of war.[2]

---

(1) Gore's General Advertiser of 1775 and 1776.

(2) "Thomas Locket, John Hipsley, James Hamilton, George Hill, Thomas
Williams, George Oliver, Joseph Black, Bernard Handwright, Robert Peat, Abraham
Place, John Fisher, James Rosthorn, John Sparks, and Thomas Pearson, for being

1775.   From the following paragraph which appears in one of the Liverpool newspapers, it should appear that a subscription had been set on foot and money had been collected for the sailors whilst lying in gaol :—

' The sailors who have been so long confined in the county gaol, return their most grateful thanks to Alderman Rigby, of this town, and to the ladies and gentlemen of Lancaster, for their charitable contributions, during their distressed situation."[1]

It is supposed that this was the only instance that ever occurred, in England, of a mob using cannon, and also small arms, during a riot.[2]

A resolution, of which the following is a copy, relative to the military who had marched to suppress the riots, appears in the Council Book of the Corporation of 1775 :—

" At a Special Council, held this eleventh day of September, 1775,
[Amongst other Resolutions.]

" It is Ordered, That the expenses incurred on account of sending for the Military to quell the late Riots, in this Town, be defrayed out of the public estate, and that the Freedom of this Town be granted, gratis, to the following Gentlemen :—

Captain Philip Goldsworthy......Sworn 14th Sept. 1775.
Lieuten^{ts:} {Thomas Garth ....Sworn same day.
{William Clive.........
Cornets {David Garrick ....Sworn 14th Sept. 1775.
{S^{r:} John Henry More...Sworn same day.
{William Spencer ......Sworn same day.
John Kinsey, *Quarter Master* ...Sworn 22nd Feb^{y:} 1776.

of the first or Royal Regiment of Dragoons, for their expedi-

---

concerned in the riot at this town, were all permitted to go on board one of his Majesty's ships of war."—*Gore's General Advertiser of 5th April*, 1776.

" Fourteen prisoners, concerned in the riot at Liverpool, were, by the clemency of the Judge and prosecutors, suffered to go on board one of his Majesty's ships of war destined for America."—*Annual Register for* 1776, *vol.* 19, *page* 139.

(1) Gore's General Advertiser of 5th April, 1776.

(2) Of course it is not intended to apply that observation to any outbreak of a more serious nature than a mere riot ; such, for example, as a rebellion : indeed, the Insurgent Adherents to the Pretender in 1715, in defending the neighbouring town of Preston, on the occasion of what was called " Preston Fight," used cannon.

tious March to the relief of this Town, and their great services 1775. in quelling the late Riotous sailors and others, and thereby saving the Town and Shipping from impending destruction, and that Mr. Mayor be desired to entertain them at the expense of the Corporation, in such manner as he shall think proper, till further orders."[1]

The expenses of the officers incurred at the inns, and of the private soldiers at the taverns and public-houses, appear to have been defrayed by the Corporation. The following is a copy of a bill in respect of Cornet Garrick, and his horse, which was sent in by Mr. John Bridge, who kept the St. James' Coffee-house, where the former appears to have stayed whilst the troops were in Liverpool :—

"St. James's Taverne,
4 Sep^{r:} 1775.

" Corporation of Liverpool, ⎱
  David Garrick, Esq.   ⎰

To John Bridge, D^{r.}

	£		
To eating	£1	1	0
Wine & neguse	,,	17	10
Punch, Beer & Porter	,,	7	1
Tea & Coffee	1	12	5
Cyder & Capilaire	,,	9	7
Lodgin 3 weeks & 3 days @ 4s pr	,,	14	0
Horse Corne	1	3	2
Do. Hay	,,	14	0
Paid to the Coachman	,,	3	0
	7	2	1

' At a Committee held the 29th day of Feb^{y,} 1776, allowed to be p^{d.} Jno. Bridge, Seven pounds two Shillings.

To Jno. Crosbie, Esqr.
Treas^{r.}

Richd. Hughes
Thomas Earle
Geor^e Case
Fran^{s.} Gildart
Jno. Hughes'

Rece^{d.} March 6th. 1776, from John Crosbie, the Contents of the above, p. John Bridge."[2]

This bill is curious and interesting, as giving an insight

---

(1) Council Book of the Corporation, of 1775, vol. 2, page 717 and 718.

(2) Copied from the original bill, as it was audited by the committee and paid, preserved at the Town-hall.

1775. into the expenses of an officer of the Royal Dragoons, for above three weeks, at a respectable inn or coffee-house in Liverpool, in 1775. It should, however, seem that the sum of £1 1s, charged for eating, could scarcely include his dinners during the three weeks and three days; if it did, the charge was exceedingly moderate.

The following expenses, ordered to be paid out of the funds of the Corporation, appear to have arisen out of the riots:—

"At a Committee for signing Bills, held 30th. Novr. 1775, *It is Ordered,* that the following Bills be paid by Jno. Crosbie, Esqr. Treasurer, viz:—

"Thomas Swettenham," 7 Bills [amongst others] " Exchange .... £47   0   4"[1]

"At a Committee for signing Bills, held 28th Decr. 1775, *It is Ordered,* that the following Bills be paid by Jno. Crosbie, Esqr. Treasurer, viz:—

Thomas Bowman,[2] For the Soldiers, &c. ....£29   16   10 John Wilson,[3] For the Dragoons 33   5   4"[4]

The Ledger and Cash-book of the Corporation contain many curious entries of payments connected with the riots, as for example :—

	£.	s.	d.
1775 Sepr. 6—To Cash paid for 12 of the Royal Dragoon Soldiers expenses attending prisoners to Lancaster Castle...	9	9	0
„ „ 26—To Cash paid G. Byrom, cartg. Prisoners to Lancaster	5	10	0
„ „ 14—To Cash paid for 2 Expresses to London and 1 to Manchester......	7	5	7[4]

There are also various entries of payments to innkeepers

---

(1) Committee Book, page 207 and 208.

(2) Mr. Thomas Bowman kept the White Lion Inn, in Castle-street.

(3) Mr. John Wilson kept the Angel Inn, sometimes called the Angel and Crown, or New Angel, in Dale-street.

(4) Copied from the Ledger (No. 3) of the Corporation, of 1775, page 114.

and others in the town for the subsistence of the soldiers, 1775.
in September and October, 1775.

The Cash-book contains an entry of 20th September, in
that year, (which is also in a more concise manner posted
into the Ledger,) of " Subscriptions and gratuities paid 114
soldiers of the first Regiment of Royal Dragoons,"[1] opposite
to which is entered the sum of £59 17s.   After the important services rendered by the dragoons, who had so
opportunely come to the rescue, the town, in common gratitude, could not well do less than give them some such substantial proof that their services were gratefully appreciated.

There are also entries in the ledger of payments, about
that period, to a considerable amount, to the glazier and
joiner, employed by the Corporation, which, it is presumed,
were, in part, at least, for repairs at the Town-hall, in consequence of the damages done in the riot.[2]

On the 7th November, in consequence of the hostilities
which had broken out in the States of North America, a

---

(1) Cash-book (No. 23) of the Corporation of 1775, page 72.

(2) Amongst the vouchers preserved in the Town-hall, is a bill from Mr. John
Parr, the gunsmith, for arms and ammunition, most of which seem to have been had
with reference to the Riots, and although the date is 20th November, 1775, it may
relate to arms previously delivered, in consequence of the riots, or possibly, to arms
supplied subsequently to them, in order to be prepared in case of another outbreak.
The brass-hilted hangers, however, evidently were arms for the police, supplied at a
subsequent period, and had no relation to the riots :—

" The Corporation
     of Liverpool.   Bot. of John Parr.

		£.	s.	d.
Novr. 20, 1775.	50 Tower Musqs. with Bayonets, Cartouch Boxes, Belts, froggs formers, &c. —20s pr.	50	0	0
	Discount of, for Present Money 20 pr. Ct. is..........	10	0	0
		£40	0	0
	To Cash paid for 1 Quire & a half Cartridge paper......	,,	1	6
	To Do. for 29 lbs Lead Balls @ 2d. p...............	,,	4	10
	To Do. for 18 lbs Battle Powder @ 1/9 p.............	1	11	6
	To making & filling 450 Catridges, &c..............	,,	7	6
	To 1 Scowring Rod 1/4, 2 Screw drivers 1/4, 200 best flints, 2/6	,,	5	2
	Carried forward....	£12	10	6

W 1

1775. public meeting was called by the Mayor, at which a subscription was resolved upon (which was liberally responded
to by the public) " for such occasional acts of benevolence,
as may be useful to the soldiers who are or may be employed
in his Majesty's service in America, and for affording relief
to the widows and orphans of such brave men as have fallen
or may fall in defending the constitutional government of
this country;" and the following gentlemen were appointed
a committee to receive contributions and carry the object
of the resolution into effect:—

"James Clemens, Mayor, *Chairman and Treasurer.*
William Crosbie, junior,—George Case, *Deputy Chairmen.*

Nicholas Ashton	Rev^d. Mr. Plumbe	Ambrose Lace
James Gildart	Rev^d. Mr Hodson	Henry Blundell
F. Gildart, Town-clerk	Rev^d. Mr. Moore	Charles Pole
Tho. Golightly	Joseph Brooks, jun.	Edward Mason
Robert Richmond	Edgar Corrie	John Myers
Thomas Foxcroft	Richard Heywood	Charles Caldwell
Thomas Earle	Thomas S. Dunn	Hugh H. Leigh
Alex. Nottingham	Thomas Manley	George W. Watts." [1]

In November, 1775, the old Tower in Water-street,
which, in ages long past, had belonged to the Stanley's,
and which has been fully described in a former chapter,[2]

	Brought forward.... £42	10	6	
	To 4 Woodalls & handles 1/2, 2 Quarts of Oyl & Bottles 4/10	,,	6	0
	To 12 yards of wide Bayze to Line Chests & Cover Guns 18^d. p.	,,	18	0
	To 2 dozen of Sand paper 1/- p^r.	,,	2	0
March 10, 1776.	To 32 Neat Brass Hilted Hangars, Money 4/6 p......	7	4	0
		£51	0	6

Mr. Parr agrees to keep all the fire arms, &^c. Belonging to the Corporat^n in
order at 2 g^s. p: annum to be exam^d Quarterly."

" At a Committee held the 28th day of March, 1776, Allowed to be p^d. John Parr,
fifty-one pounds & 6^d.

Jno. Hughes

Ja^s. Clemens
Rich^d. Hughes
Jno. Crosbie
Fras. Gildart.*

To Jno Crosbie, Esqre. Treas^r. "

* Copied from the original Bill, as audited by the Committee, and paid; preserved
in the Town-hall, and charged in the Ledger (No. 3) of 1775.

(1) Gore's General Advertiser of 17th November, 1775.

(2) Chapter I, page 74.

became the property of the Corporation of Liverpool, they 1775.
having purchased it, with the adjoining house, from the then
owners, Sir Richard Clayton and Mr. Clayton, for the sum
of £1535 10s.   It is not known when it was first used as
a gaol, but it certainly was so used some time before the
purchase, and, consequently, it must be presumed, that it
had been previously rented for the purpose.

The following is a copy of the receipt for the purchase-
money, preserved in the Town-hall :—

" Reced. 10th Nov. 1775, from Mr. Ald[r.] Crosbie, fifteen hundred
thirty-five Pounds ten shill[s.] to be paid to S[r.] R[d.] Clayton & his
Brot[r.] for the Purchase of the Gaol, and house adjoining, £1535 10s.

Tho[s.] Hutton."

The following are also entries relative to it in the Cash-
book and Ledger of the Corporation :—

	£.	s.	d.
"1775 Nov. 10 By John Clayton p[d.] him for purchase of Gaol & ho[e.] adjoining...........	1535	10	0"[1]

"1775	£.	s.	d.	1775	£.	s.	d.
Nov. 4 To Cash p[d.] for Purchase of Gaol & ho[e.] adjoining ..	1535	10	0	Nov[r.] 11 By Do. & purchase of the Tower	1560	8	8"[2]
1776 May 25 To Do. for rent in full	24	18	8				

In the same year the Humane Society, for the recovery of
persons apparently drowned, was established, and a house
of reception opened on the north side of the Old Dock, at
the instance of Dr. Houlston ;[3] after some years, however,
the institution was suffered to fall into decay.   A new
society succeeded it in 1823, called the Marine Humane
Society.

(1) Copied from the Cash-book (No. 23) of 1775.

(2) Copied from the Ledger (No. 3) of 1775.

(3) Smithers' Liverpool, page 271.

1775.   In the course of this year a considerable number of privateers were fitted out in the ports of the North American States, engaged in hostilities with this country, which cruized against the British shipping, and caused considerable losses.   Many privateers were also afterwards fitted out, and sailed from Liverpool, to annoy the trade of the enemy, especially after the commencement of the war which soon ensued with France; and several very important and valuable captures were made by the Liverpool privateers, and many remarkable instances of bravery were exhibited by their officers and crews, as will be more conveniently mentioned in another place.[1]

1776.   In the month of March, 1776, the Duke of Bridgewater's Canal, of which the origin and history have been given in a former chapter,[2] was opened for traffic, and has produced most beneficial results to the inland trade of this country as well as to the town of Liverpool.

In this year St. Catherine's Church, formerly the Octagon Chapel, at the lowest end of Temple-court, was purchased by the Reverend William Plumbe, the Rector of Aughton, and licensed by the Bishop of the diocese for divine service, pursuant to the rites and creed of the Church of England.   Some account of it, during the period when it was a place of worship for dissenters, has been given in a former chapter.[3]   A paragraph appeared in a Liverpool newspaper of the 22nd of March, 1776, communicating the intended opening of the church,[4] which took place on the 24th of that month.   An advertisement

---

(1) Chapter VI.   (2) Chapter I, page 109.

(3) Chapter I, page 58.

(4) " We hear that St. Catherine's Chapel will be opened on Sunday morning, by the Reverend Mr. Plumbe ; and that attendance will be given there, for letting the seats, on Monday, Tuesday, and Wednesday mornings following."—Gore's General Advertiser of 22nd March, 1776.

also appeared in the same paper announcing the publica- 1776.
tion of a sermon, preached there on the 25th of February,
1776, preparatory to the dissenting congregation leaving
it, by the Rev. Nicholas Clayton, the minister of the chapel,
from which it should appear that the principal part of its
frequenters then joined the congregation in Benn's-gardens
Chapel.[1]

Mr. Plumbe preached there for many years, and was
very popular as a preacher; and it was remarkable, that
though it was a small edifice, and could not contain a
numerous congregation, there was at one time as large, if
not a larger number of private carriages belonging to the
frequenters of that church than to the congregation of any
other church in Liverpool. The Rev. Mr. Wilmot preached
there for a short time after Mr. Plumbe's death.   The Rev.
Brownlow (afterwards Dr.) Forde then became the incum-
bent. He was a native of Ireland, a man of great talents,
and experienced some remarkable vicissitudes.   In after
life he got the appointment of chaplain or ordinary to the
prison of Newgate, in London, which he held for many
years. After Mr. Plumbe's death, St. Catherine's Church
was sold to the Corporation of Liverpool, in 1786, and
when Mr. Forde left it the Rev. R. K. Milner and the Rev.
Thomas Bold, jointly, became the ministers; and it continued a place of worship of the Church of England until
it was pulled down in 1820, and its site is now occupied by

---

(1) " This day is published, price 6d,
And Sold by John Sibbald,
THE IMPORTANCE OF SINCERITY IN PUBLIC WORSHIP, TO TRUTH,
MORALS, AND CHRISTIANITY,
A SERMON,
Preached the 25th February, 1776,
Before the Society at the Octagon Chapel, Liverpool.
Explaining the Views with which their Liturgy was composed, the Reasons for
laying it aside, and for their union with the Protestant Dissenters at Benn's Gardens."
" BY N. CLAYTON."

1776. part of the lower end of Temple-court, and by the Fire Police Station.

On the 19th of March, in this year, St. Mary's Church, on the south side of Harrington-street, was opened by the Rev. Joseph Bragg, and was licensed as a place of worship of the Church of England. The licence had been obtained for it from the Bishop of Chester about three months prior to the opening of the church, as is shown by the the following paragraph which appeared in a Liverpool paper of 15th December, 1775 :—"The Lord Bishop of Chester has been pleased to license the Rev. Mr. Bragg, minister of St. Mary's Church, in this town.[1]   It was a small brick edifice of unpretending exterior, and was taken down in 1809, and a sugar-house was erected on its site.   The pulpit afterwards used at St. Nicholas' Church, is said to be the same which was formerly in St. Mary's Church.

In this year, the House of Correction on the north-west side of Mount-pleasant, and near the back of the Work-house, was erected, and was used as a place of imprison-ment of disorderly persons, vagrants, &c. until the present Borough Gaol was opened in 1811 ; and the House of Correction then became used as an asylum for pauper lunatics.   It was pulled down in the summer of 1852, in con-sequence of the site being wanted for the alterations and enlargement of the adjoining parish Workhouse.   A person named Widdows was, many years ago, the keeper of this House of Correction.   He was once examined as a witness, at the Lancaster Assizes, in a prosecution arising out of a riot in Liverpool, which occurred at a time when the Mayor of Liverpool was entertaining a dinner party at

---

(1) Gore's General Advertiser of 15th December, 1775.   In that of 20th November, 1778, is an announcement of a Charity Sermon to be preached, on the afternoon of the ensuing Sunday, by the Rev. Mr. Bragg, and a collection to be made for the benefit of the Blue-Coat Hospital.

the Town-hall; and Mr. Scarlett (afterwards Lord Abin- 1776.
ger), the counsel who cross-examined Widdows, having
remarked, that the witness had an absurd habit of almost
always answering in the affirmative to any question put
to him, considered it a good opportunity of deriving
some amusement at the expense of Mr. James Clarke,
the then Deputy-Recorder (afterwards Recorder) of Liverpool, who had been dining at the Town-hall, at the time
when the riot occurred, and who held a brief for the
prosecution; and the following dialogue took place on
the cross-examination of the witness Widdows :—

"*Mr. Scarlett.*—This was a serious riot, I believe?
Witness.—Yes, Sir.
Mr. Scarlett.—Had not the Mayor a dinner party at the Town-hall
on the evening on which it occurred ?
Witness.—Oh yes, Sir! Yes!
Mr. Scarlett.—Mr. Clarke here [*pointing him out in the Court,*]
was of the party, I am told ?
Witness.—Yes, Sir—Yes.
Mr. Scarlett.—He is the Deputy-Recorder of Liverpool, is he not ?
Witness.—Yes, Sir.
Mr. Scarlett.—Did Mr. Clarke go with the Mayor to quell the riot ?
Witness.—Yes, Sir—Yes, Sir.
Mr. Scarlett.—Gown and Wig ?
Witness.—Yes, Sir.
Mr. Scarlett.—In armour ; was he not ?
Witness.—Yes, Sir—Yes, Sir."

Mr. Scarlett having thus succeeded in having it proved
on oath, that the Deputy-Recorder had gone in armour to
quell a riot, brought the matter before the Bar, at the
Grand Court (often called the " Grand Night,") of the
Northern Circuit, much to their amusement; and carried
out the jest by causing Mr. Clarke to be fined or mulcted
by the Bar for going out so unprofessionally accoutered.[1]

Mr. John Howard, the philanthropist, visited this House

---

(1) Communicated to the Author by the late Mr. William Statham, the Town-
clerk.   The penalty inflicted upon Mr. Clarke was, probably, a small quantity
of claret.

1776. of Correction in 1779 and 1782, and has left the following description of it :—

> " This prison was built in 1776. The men and women have separate rooms, courts, &c. The women have six rooms below, and the same number above : the men have four rooms below, and four above. These are twelve feet by ten, and eight feet nine inches high ; are furnished with bedsteads, blankets, and coverlets; but are too close, having no window, only an aperture in the door about nine inches square, and another near the ceiling. They have a work-room, twenty feet by sixteeen feet nine inches."[1]

At the time of Mr. Howard's last visit, the female prisoners were subject to treatment of a very tyrannical and inhuman description, and it may well cause astonishment to find that such disgraceful proceedings were permitted, in any gaol in this country, at that period. Near the work-room in the men's court was a pump, to which the women were tied every week, and received the cruel and unjustifiable discipline of being pumped upon. We have the authority of Mr. James Nield, another philanthropist, that this inhuman treatment of female prisoners was not discontinued even at the commencement of the present century.

Another mode of punishment was practised in this prison, at least as late as the time of Mr. Howard's first visit, in 1779, and which may well excite amazement at the inhumanity of the gaoler who inflicted it, and the callous unfeeling indifference of the magistrates who permitted it : the ducking-stool, a barbarous contrivance derived from a barbarous age, was certainly in use in this prison in 1779, and, perhaps, much later.

It is well known that in former times, the ducking-stool was the punishment in country towns for scolds and brawling women. The ducking-stool used in England consisted of a

---

(1) Howard's Appendix to the State of the Prisons in England and Wales, page 258.

strong upright post or standard, fixed at the entrance of a 1776. pool of water; at the top of this was attached, horizontally, a moveable long pole, at the extremity of which a chair was secured. In this the woman was placed, the extremity of the pole with the chair was suddenly brought down to the water, and the woman underwent a thorough ducking.

In the adjoining county, Cheshire, the ducking-stool was often called the " cucking (supposed to be a corruption of "choaking") stool," or " cuck stool;" and when the author's father was young, there was, in the part of Cheshire where he was at school, in a pond called the " cuck-stool pond," the upright post or standard, which had been part of the apparatus of the ducking-stool. We have also the authority of Mr. James Neild, the philanthropist, that a ducking-stool, within the memory of persons living when he wrote, (in 1803) was in the great reservoir in the Green Park, in London.[1]

There are, perhaps, few persons of intelligence and feeling who can learn without astonishment that this tyrannical, wanton, and inhuman punishment, was still practised in the Liverpool House of Correction during part of the life-time of more than one aged person now (in 1853) living in the town. To make the matter more indecent and revolting, it appears that the men's court, in the House of Correction, was the place where this wicked and unmanly punishment was inflicted on the female prisoners; and we have the authority of Mr. Howard, that it was performed in the following manner, in a tank or bath in that court :—

" At one end of it [the bath] was a standard for a long pole, at the extremity of which was fastened a chair. In this all the *females* (not the *males*) at their entrance, after a few questions, were placed, with a flannel shift on, and underwent a thorough ducking, thrice repeated, an use of a bath which I dare say the legislature never

---

(1) See the copy of a communication from Mr. James Neild, in the " Gentleman's Magazine" of 1803, vol. 73, part 2, page 1104.

x 1

1776. thought of, when in their late Act they ordered baths, with a view to cleanliness and preserving the health of prisoners; not for the exercise of a wanton and dangerous kind of severity. But I was glad to find this use of the bath has been discontinued since my visit in 1779."[1]

It was not possible for the magistrates or the gaoler to justify the practice on the ground of discipline, or attention to cleanliness, otherwise the male prisoners would not have been exempted from it; besides which, some better and more humane plan would have been adopted. It is impossible to view the proceeding in any other light, than as a reprehensible wanton act of buffoonery and cruelty, practised upon the weaker sex, in many cases dangerous to the health and revolting to the feelings of the female prisoners. The severe weekly discipline of the women at the pump in the men's court, was, however, still continued at the time of Mr. Howard's last visit in 1782:[1] and it is certain that though the use of the ducking-stool was abolished, the female prisoners were subject to the discipline of the pump even as lately as 1803.[2] Mr. Howard also informs us that the prison was kept remarkably clean by the matron, and that all the prisoners were employed in picking oakum.

In the remarks upon the gaols of Liverpool, contained in a letter of the 16th of October, 1803, written by Mr. James Neild, the philanthropist,[3] he also alludes to the ducking-stool having been used at the time of his previous visit to Liverpool, and says, " The House of Correction, built in 1776, is much improved since my former visit.[4]   The

---

(1) Howard's Appendix to the State of the Prisons in England and Wales, page 258.

(2) See the copy of Mr. James Neild's communication, published in the " Gentleman's Magazine" for December, 1803, vol. 73, part 2, page 1104.

(3) Published in the " Gentleman's Magazine" for December, 1803, vol. 73, part 2, page 1104.

(4) It is much to be regretted, that the date of the former visit to which he alludes is not given.

wanton severity of the ducking-stool, used upon a woman's 1776. first admission,[1] is now discontinued;" but he informs us that the discipline of the pump in the men's court was (in 1803) still continued, though not inflicted weekly. We are also informed on the same authority, that the prison was " kept very clean by the matron, Jane Widdowes; salary, £63 ;"[2] and that the allowance in that prison was " a two-penny loaf, 2lb. of potatoes, and salt, daily. No chaplain, or any religious attention whatsoever. Prisoners, 75 women, 19 men and boys."[2]

After having been used as an asylum for pauper lunatics for many years, the edifice was entirely taken down in the summer of 1852, in consequence of the alterations and enlargement of the contiguous parish workhouse.

The Duke of Bridgewater's Canal, connecting Liverpool, through Runcorn, with Manchester, having been completed and opened, in March, 1776, as has been already mentioned,[3] the following account then appeared in one of the Liverpool newspapers :—

" We have the pleasure to inform the public that last week, his Grace the Duke of Bridgewater's Canal was completed, and opened through the lands of Sir Richard Brooke, Bart. at Norton, in Cheshire; in consequence of which several barges and other vessels, with numbers of Gentlemen on board, came from Liverpool to Runcorn, passed through the locks there, and navigated completely through the whole course of the Canal to Manchester; the greatest rejoicings were made on this occasion by all ranks of people, and a grand entertainment was given by the Gentlemen and merchants of Manchester."[4]

---

(1) This expression clearly corroborates Mr. Howard's statement, and shows that the ducking-stool had been used to women in this House of Correction.

(2) Published in the "Gentleman's Magazine" for December, 1803, vol. 73, part 2, page 1104.

(3) Chapter I, page 109.

(4) Gore's General Advertiser of 29th March, 1776. The above account was inadvertently omitted on page 350, where it was intended to have appeared.

1776.   At a Common Council held on the 4th December, 1776, it was ordered,—

"That when any future Mayor of this Corporation nominates his Gratis or Mayor's Freemen, every such Mayor shall be confined to nominate a Gentleman or person then not in Trade or likely to be, or follow any Merchandize or Trade in or out of this Town."[1]

1777.   In 1777, the Corporation appear to have taken into consideration the expediency of abandoning the system of selling the freedom of the borough, and at a Common Council, held on the 4th of June, 1777, the following order was passed :—

"Whereas, it has been represented to this Council that the admitting persons to the Freedom of this Borough and Corporation, on purchase for any sum or sums of money, is attended with many great Inconveniences and losses to the publick Estate and Revenue, by greatly lessening the Town Duties and Customs, it is now ordered and agreed, that from henceforth no person or persons shall be admitted a freeman or freemen of this Borough and Corporation, upon purchase for any sum or sums of money, or other valuable consideration for granting such freedom."[2]

It appears difficult to believe that the above order was seriously acted upon for a considerable time after the date of it, because, as has been already mentioned,[3] there were several instances considerably after 1777, of the sale of the freedom of the town to persons who were previously non-freemen, which were deposed to before the Commissioners of Inquiry into Municipal Corporations, in 1833.[4] It is very improbable that those persons could have contracted for the purchase of the freedom of the town prior to 1777, and have neglected to take it up until some time afterwards.

---

(1) Book of Records of the Corporation of 1776, vol. 12, page 42 and 43.

(2) Ibid. of 1777, vol. 12, page 63.

(3) Chapter III, page 209.

(4) See the printed Report of the Proceedings before the Commissioners of Inquiry into Municipal Corporations, in 1833, page 53.

In June, 1777, the Trent and Mersey Canal was com-   1777.
pleted; thus effecting a junction, by inland navigation,
between the German Ocean and the Irish Sea.[1]

In the same year, the reversionary right in the Manor
and Lordship of Liverpool, was purchased by the Corporation from the Earl of Sefton, as has been noticed in a
former chapter[2] when treating of the possessions and
revenue of the Corporation.

In this year, the chapel for Protestant Dissenters, (Independents,) on the west side of Renshaw-street, below Newington, and on the east side of Cropper-street, was built.
The Rev. David Bruce was the first minister there. The
part of Renshaw-street near where it stood was at that time
narrow and imperfectly built, and the principal front of the
chapel was then considered to be in Cropper-street.

In 1778, a regiment of regular soldiers, called the   1778.
Liverpool Blues, 1100 strong, was raised by the Corporation and inhabitants of the town. The Corporation contributed £2000 towards the expenses of raising it.[3] The
Colonel was Lieut.-General Calcroft, and Major Pole was
Lieut.-Colonel. On Monday, the 25th of May, 1778, the
regiment assembled at Bank-hall Marsh, near Liverpool,
when it was presented with its colours, and, on the 17th of
June following, the first division marched out of the town,
and on the 18th and 19th it was followed by the other divisions.[4] It was not the first time that a Liverpool regiment
was so called, for in 1745 a regiment of that name was also
raised there, which was on active service at Carlisle when it
was captured from the insurgent adherents to the Pretender.

---

(1) Gore's General Advertiser of 13th June, 1777.

(2) Chapter III, page 220.

(3) Book of Records of the Corporation of 1777, vol. 12, page 91.

(3) Gore's General Advertiser of 29th of May and 19th June, 1778.

1778.   At a Common Council held on the 4th of November, 1778, an order, with reference to the fort then building, was passed as follows :—

> " On Colonel Gordon's Letter, now read to this Council, of the state of the Fort now building in this town, for the defence and security of the same, the Shipping and trade thereof, and concerning the number of Soldiers or men which will be necessary to ask from Government for the Manning and defence thereof, and other matters relative thereto, that the Mayor and some of the Gentlemen of the Council be desired to wait on Colonel Gordon to consult and advise with him thereon, but not to ask for a less force than four or five hundred men for such purpose."[1]

In 1778, the Liverpool Dispensary was established at No. 25, Princes-street; it had a front on the east side of North John-street, and to the northward of and at the corner of, the opening leading into Princes-street. Its entrance was from the latter street. It was instituted for the purpose of supplying the poor gratuitously with medicines, and medical and surgical advice and assistance. The building remained standing long after the commencement of the present century, and many of the readers will recollect it from its having a plastered white front, which distinguished it from the other houses and buildings near it. Its site is now covered by a warehouse.

The following is a list of the officers of the Dispensary, during the first year of its institution, copied from the original printed report, in the author's possession; and, with the exception of the president, the officers remained the same during the next year :—

" Officers
For the year 1778.
President.
John Blackburne, Junior, Esquire.
Treasurer.
Joseph Brooks, Esquire.

---

(1) Book of Records of the Corporation of 1778, vol. 12, page 122 and 123.

Auditors.
Mr. John Wyke, Mr. William Dickson.
Physicians.
Doctor Joseph Brandreth.
Doctor Jonathan Binns.
Doctor James Worthington.
Surgeons.
Mr. Wright Gleave,
Mr. Edward Alanson,
Mr. James Gerard.
Apothecary and Secretary.
Mr. Thomas Avison.
For the year 1779.
Nicholas Ashton, Esq$^{r.}$ *President.*
The rest of the officers the same as last year."[1]

The statement of the receipts and expenditure, from the time of its being opened on the 31st of August, 1778, to the 25th of March, 1779, published in the first Report of the Charity, and given in the subjoined note, shows a balance of £4 11s 6d against the charity, viz :—

Received from Individual Subscribers	£117	12	0
Received from the Parish of Liverpool	105	0	0
Total....................	222	12	0
Disbursements	227	3	6
Leaving the Dispensary in debt......	£4	11	6

This country being at war, in 1779, not only with the North American States, but with France and Spain, privateering was pursued to a great extent by Liverpool cruisers, and their officers and crews exhibited numerous instances of great bravery, some of which will be more par- 1779.

(1) From the original printed Report of the Dispensary of 1779, in the Author's possession, which appears to be the first which was published relative to that charity. The following is a List of the Subscribers to the Dispensary, in the first year of its establishment: the list is curious and interesting as containing the names of many of the then principal and most respectable merchants and inhabitants of Liverpool; the reader will observe in it several names of individuals, whose descendants follow their example, and are still foremost in works of charity. Subjoined to it is a statement of the diseases, and of the number of patients of the charity during the period between the 31st of August, 1778, when the institution was opened, and the

1779. ticularly mentioned in another place;[1] and it was, in many instances, a lucrative pursuit. Between the end of August, 1778, and that of April, 1779, there sailed from the port of Liverpool 120 privateers, carrying 1986 guns, (from ten to thirty guns each,) mostly six and nine pounders, and 8754 men, and of the burthen of 30,787 tons.[2]

In consequence of the hostilities with France, and the States of North America, and of war also breaking out with Spain, a Special Council was held on the 26th of June, 1779, to take into consideration an address to the King,

25th of March, 1779.   The names of the officers and subscribers, and the other particulars, are taken from the Report :—

"SUBSCRIBERS.

	£.	s.	d.		£.	s.	d.
A				Edgar Corrie, merchant	1	1	0
Nicholas Ashton, Esq.	2	2	0	Rev. Mr. Crigan	1	1	0
S. Aspinwall, attorney	1	1	0	Miss Cropper	1	1	0
James Ansdell, merchant	1	1	0	Wm. Crosbie, Jun. merchant.	1	1	0
Unknown, by E.Alanson,surg.	1	1	0	William Crosdale, ditto .	1	1	0
B				Rev. Mr. Clayton	1	1	0
John Blackburne, Jun. Esq..	4	4	0	Thomas Crosbyn & Co. drug-			
Jonathan Blundell, Esq......	2	2	0	gests, London	1	1	0
Joseph Brooks, Esq........	2	2	0	John Coutts, merchant......	0	10	6
J. and T. Backhouse, merchts.	2	2	0	**D**			
Wm. Barnes, tallow chandler.	1	1	0	Wm. Dickson, merchant	1	1	0
William Bonney, ditto .	1	1	0	Felix Doran, gentleman	1	1	0
James Barrow, merchant	1	1	0	Dr. Matthew Dobson........	1	1	0
John Baines, schoolmaster ..	1	1	0	**E**			
Henry Berry, surveyor	1	1	0	Charles Eyes, surveyor......	1	1	0
Dr. Jonathan Binns	1	1	0	**F**			
Jonathan Blackburne, Esq. ..	1	1	0	Thomas Falkner, Esq..	2	2	0
Thomas Booth, merchant	1	1	0	Rev. Mr. Fishwick..........	1	1	0
George Booth, ditto	1	1	0	David Frearson, ironmonger .	1	1	0
Mrs. Bostock..............	1	1	0	**G**			
Cornelius Bourne, merchant..	1	1	0	Richard Gerard, surgeon....	1	1	0
Dr. Joseph Brandreth	1	1	0	Wright Gleave, surgeon	1	1	0
C. Bromfield, marble cutter..	1	1	0	Guy Green, china painter....	1	1	0
Robert Buddicom, surgeon ..	1	1	0	John Greenwood, merchant..	1	1	0
Rev. Mr. Brereton	1	1	0	**H**			
Dr. W. F. Blencowe........	1	1	0	W. Hutchinson, for two years.	2	2	0
T. B.....................	1	1	0	Arthur Heywood, merchant ..	1	1	0
Donation, unknown, by T. B.	0	10	6	Benjamin A. Heywood, ditto.	1	1	0
C			.	John Houghton, distiller	1	1	0
Thomas Crowder, Esq......	2	2	0	Hillary and Scott, merchants.	1	1	0
Dr. Joseph Camplin........	1	1	0	Capt. Francis Holland	1	1	0
William Calvert, merchant ..	1	1	0				
Scrope Colquit, Esq........	1	1	0				

(1) Chapter VI.

(2) Aiken's Description of the Country from Thirty to Forty Miles round Manchester, page 371.

on the rupture with Spain, and on other special affairs; and 1779.
it was resolved, that an address, under the common seal of
the Corporation, should be presented to the King by Mr.
Bamber Gascoyne, one of the members for Liverpool, and
Mr. Owen Salisbury Brereton, the Recorder, of which the
following is an extract:—

" Permit us, your Majesty's faithful and loyal subjects, the Mayor,
Bailiffs, and Burgesses of your Town of Liverpool, humbly to present to
the Throne a Testimony of our Duty and Affection for your Majesty's
Royal Person, and of our Attachment to the Welfare and prosperity of
your Kingdoms, at the present alarming Juncture; when, from the per-
fidious Alliances of our natural and combined enemies, the House of

	£.	s.	d.		£.	s.	d.
Dr. Thomas Houlston	1	1	0	Wm. Roscoe, attorney	1	1	0
Rev. Mr. Harris	1	1	0	John Renshaw, gentleman ..	1	1	0
R. Hetherington, merchant ..	1	1	0	Edward Rogers, merchant ..	1	1	0
William Hesketh, ditto. ..	0	10	6	Rev. Mr. Roughsedge	1	1	0
J				Unknown, by ditto	0	10	6
T. Jameson, merchant	1	1	0	Mrs. Roughsedge	0	10	6
K				S			
Dr. John Kenion	1	1	0	Samuel Shaw, merchant	1	1	0
John Kennion, merchant	1	1	0	Thomas Staniforth, merchant	1	1	0
L				W			
James Leigh, apothecary	1	1	0	Benedict P. Wagner, merchant	2	2	0
William Lightbody, gentleman	1	1	0	Richard Watt, ditto ..	2	2	0
Mrs. A. Lightbody	1	1	0	Miss Waterworth	1	1	0
Richard Lowndes, gentleman.	1	1	0	Stephen Waterworth, merchant	1	1	0
John Lyon, surgeon	1	1	0	Dr. Wainwright............	1	1	0
Edmund Lyon, merchant....	1	1	0	William Wallace, merchant ..	1	1	0
M				William Whalley, gentleman .	1	1	0
Rev. Mr. Maddock	1	1	0	Thomas Whittaker, merchant	1	1	0
Thomas Manley, merchant ..	1	1	0	John Wilcock, butcher	1	1	0
William M. Mears, ditto	1	1	0	Dr. James Worthington	1	1	0
Rev. Mr. Moore	1	1	0	R. Watson, corn factor......	1	1	0
William Moss, surgeon......	1	1	0	John Wyke	1	1	0
N				Y			
Robert Nicholson, merchant .	0	10	6	Rev. Mr. Yates	1	1	0
P				Z			
Henry Park, surgeon........	1	1	0	Henrick Zinck, merchant....	1	1	0
R.							
Joseph Rathbone, merchant..	2	2	0		£117	12	0
Rev. Mr. Renshaw	1	1	0	Parish of Liverpool ·..	105	0	0
Dr. Henry Richmond	1	1	0				
James Roberts, merchant....	1	1	0	Total......£222	12	0	

EXPENSES.

	£.	s.	d.		£.	s.	d.
Drugs and Fixtures	£113	6	0	Sundry disbursements	£29	6	6
House rent for one half-year..	3	0	0				
Printing and stationery wares.	7	2	0	Total disbursements......	227	3	6
Apothecary's salary	60	0	0	Total subscriptions	222	12	0
Joiner's work..............	4	1	0				
Glass and Spirits	10	8	0	Dispensary in debt £4	11	6	

Y 1

1779.   Bourbon, with your Majesty's revolted Colonies in America, to succour
rebellion against the parent state, this Nation and the most formidable
powers in Europe must be unavoidably involved in all the Calamities
of War."

And the address concludes thus : —

" We shall, on all occasions, with the most determined Resolution,
be ready to stand forth, in the defence of your Majesty and your Kingdoms, against the United efforts of all your enemies, and to aid and
support your Majesty, to the extent of our Ability, to prosecute a War,
on their part so voluntary and unprovoked, until Peace can be restored
with Honour and safety to Great Britain."[1]

At the same Special Council it was also ordered that a
bounty of ten guineas for every able seaman, and five
guineas for every ordinary seaman, should be offered, and
should be paid by the Corporation Treasurer, to every
volunteer who should enter on board any of the King's
ships of war at Liverpool.[2]

In this year considerable alarm was excited in Liverpool

DISEASES.

Fevers	410	Dropsy	20
Ophthalmy	69	Rickets, Scrophula	8
Sore Throats	172	Venereal Complaints	34
Pleurisy	35	Jaundice	10
Consumption	37	Gravel	5
Rheumatism	60	Worms	96
Erysepelas	10	Itch, and other Eruptions	221
Small Pox	59	Burns and Scalds	40
Sore Mouth	13	Tumors, Abscesses, Ulcers	175
Piles	14	Wounds, Bruises, Fractures	87
Hœmorrhage	31	Anomalous	5
Dysentery	5		
Head-ach, Vertigo	40	Patients admitted	2062
Palsy	4		
Stomach Complaints	87	Cured	1439
Epilepsy	2	Relieved	117
Asthma, Coughs	152	Removed to the Infirmary	24
Colick	14	Turned away, being able to pay }	7
Cholera	15	for medicines }	
Diarrhœa	47	Dead	115
Hysteria	19	Remaining on the Books	360
Convulsive Affections	19		
Insanity	3		2062 "
Chronic weakness	44		

(1) Book of Records of the Corporation of 1779, vol. 12, page 148 and 149.

(2) Ibid. page 148 and 150.

by the appearance, in the Irish sea, of some vessels of war 1779.
of the enemy, under the command of the noted and
daring adventurer, Paul Jones, and by his having attacked
Whitehaven, and set fire to the shipping there. A Special
Council of the Corporation was held on the 13th of September, 1779, to take into consideration the most effectual
method of putting the town into a state of defence, and the
following orders were passed; amongst which was one relative
to the removal, upon an emergency, of the buoys upon the
coast, which was an excellent and judicious measure, calculated to expose the enemy to very great danger, in so
intricate and unsafe a navigation as the entrance of the port
of Liverpool is :—

" At a Special Council, held for the Town of Liverpool, this 13th day
of September, 1779, pursuant to Notice, for the particular purpose of
taking into consideration the proper and most effectual means of putting
this Town into a State of Defence at the present alarming Juncture, an
Account having been received by a letter from Administration to the
Mayor, that Paul Jones, with several Ships of Force, and Troops on
board, are now upon the Coast."

"*It is Ordered,* That application be immediately made to the proprietors,
of the best proof gunpowder lodged in the Magazines on the
Cheshire shore, to remove such quantity as can conveniently be lodged in the Magazines at the New Fort and
St. George's Battery, for the use of the Guns upon the
different Forts and Batteries near this Town, for the Defence
of the same, if there shall be occasion ; and that the Officers
of the Magazines be accountable to the Proprietors for the
same, and the Proprietors be at liberty to take it out and
sell it : And that the Treasurers for the Corporation and
the Dock Duties shall respectively pay for such powder
as shall be used at such Forts and Batteries, in the exercise
of the Guns, and for the Defence of this Town and Harbour,
and be allowed the same in their respective Accounts."

" *Ordered,* That the Mayor be, and he is hereby desired and authorised
to apply immediately, in the name of this Council, and
under the Corporate Seal, to the King in Council, as well as

1779.

to the Board of Ordnance, and at the Tower, for a Thousand stands of Arms, for the use of such Gentlemen and private men who may offer themselves, to serve as independent Volunteer Companies, in case of an enemy's landing upon this Coast, which is now much to be feared, from the Account received by the Mayor from Administration."

" And that immediate public Notice be given of this order, and the Gentlemen and other private men willing to serve upon this occasion, be desired to give in their names at the Mayor's office from eleven o'clock till one each day ; and that the Mayor and Bailiffs, with such other Gentlemen of the Council as may choose to attend, be and they are hereby appointed a Committee to receive the same, and that three be sufficient to make a Committee."

" Ordered, That the Mayor do likewise apply to the Secretarys of State for an immediate removal of the French and Spanish Prisoners now confined in the Gaol at Mount Pleasant,[1] to the Castles at Chester, Carlisle, York, and Lancaster, or some other place of safety Inland. And also for the removal of the Prisoners upon Parole at Ormskirk and Wigan, to some more Inland situation ; And that copies of the Letter from Sir George Saville to the Mayor upon this Subject, accompany such application."

" Ordered, That it be recommended to the Pilot Committee to send out a Pilot Boat, with two or three skilful and prudent Pilots on board, to ply as far as the Point of Linas, to give Intelligence, by throwing out signals or otherwise, upon the Appearance of an enemy, and to station Boats at the different Buoys upon this coast, that the same be sunk, in case there should be imminent Danger from the Actual Appearance of an enemy, but that the Pilot Committee be very particular in their directions to the Pilots to be very cautious and circumspect, not to sink them, unless there is the most absolute necessity.

" That Richard Wilding, upon any intelligence of an Enemy, give an alarm at Bidston Lighthouse, and not keep the Lights burning either there or at Hoylake, in such case."

---

(1) The prison above alluded to was on Brownlow-hill, near Mount-pleasant, and has been noticed in Chapter II, page 134 and 135.

"That the Mayor and Bailiffs, with two or three other Gentlemen **1779.** of the Council who may please to attend, be a committee to meet the Pilot Committee, for the better digesting these orders, and carrying the same into execution, and fixing the mode and terms of payment and satisfaction to the Boats and men who may be sent upon this business; the same to be paid by the Treasurer of the Dock Duties."[1]

On the 6th of October, 1779, the Common Council passed an order—

"That the two Rooms in the Exchange, commonly called the Card and the Assembly Room, be furnished at the Expense of this Corporation, and that the Ladies and Gentlemen of the Town have the use thereof for their public nights of assembly."[2]

In this year, a Liverpool Medical Library was instituted by the physicians and surgeons of the Infirmary. In this library is a work of eight volumes, the Reports of the Humane Society of London. In the eighth volume appear manuscript notes in the handwriting of Dr. Houlston, containing statements from 1773 to 1784, of the success attending the plan in Liverpool, kept by Dr. Houlston.[3]

At a Common Council held on the 2nd of February, 1780, **1780.**

"*It is Ordered,* That the old Dock be posted and chained round, at the expense of the Dock Duties, under the Inspection of Mr. William Hutchinson and Mr. Henry Berry, in such manner as they shall think will best prevent many of the like fatal accidents as have happened therein, and as shall be least incommodious to Shipping and business on the Quays."[4]

The expenses of the dinners and suppers, which it was customary at that period to provide, on the occasion of the Court of Quarter Sessions and Court of Passage of the town, were considered sufficiently important to merit the atten-

---

(1) Book of Records of the Corporation of 1779, vol. 12, page 159, 160, and 161.

(2) Ibid. page 162 and 163.

(3) Smithers' Liverpool, page 366.

(4) Book of Records of the Corporation of 1780, vol. 12, page 177 and 178.

1780. tion of the Common Council, and accordingly, at the same Council, (2nd of February, 1780,) the following order was made :—

" That Mr. Mayor and Bailiffs, the Treasurer, Mr. Gregson, Mr. Sparling, Mr. Alderman Hughes, Mr. Williamson, Mr. Brown, and Mr. Peters, or any Gentlemen of the Council who please to attend, be appointed a Committee to inspect and regulate the expence of the Dinners, at the Courts of Quarter Sessions and Passage, and to report to the next Council, at what sum they conceive a dinner for the Court, the two Juries, and the necessary attendants on the Mayor, at those Courts, may reasonably be furnished, one Court with Another; and that the allowance to be fixed by the Council of the four Annual Dinners, after hearing the Committee's report, be deemed (as it is) a part of the expences of supporting the Dignity of Office of the Chief Magistrate, so important to the peace and Good Government of this Town, and be considered in the annual allowance in that behalf, to be made to the Mayors, who are meant to defray the Costs, and to have the sole direction of, and Invitation to such dinners."[1]

At a Common Council, held on the 5th of April, 1780,

" Upon hearing the report now read, of the Committee met the third of April instant, pursuant to the order of last Council, respecting the regulation of Sessions Dinners, this Council do approve thereof, and do order, that the Orders, Regulations, and Articles therein contained, be from henceforth carried into execution, and that the expences of the Sessions Dinners, upon the foot thereof, be experienced for a few Sessions, and afterwards that a standing sum for the expences of such dinners be ascertained upon that foot, to be allowed as part of the Expences of office of the Mayor for the time being ; or that such further Regulations be afterwards made respecting such dinners as in experience shall be found useful."[2]

The following is a copy of the report, which is copied at the end of the proceedings of the same Council :—

" The Report of the Committee touching the Regulation of the Sessions' dinners, referred to in the first order of this day :—

‘ It is the opinion of this Committee that Suppers for the

---

(1) Book of Records of the Corporation of 1780, vol. 12, page 177 and 178.

(2) Ibid. page 184 and 185.

Magistrates, for either Jury, officers, or any other Company, 1780. in the evenings, at Sessions times, are inconvenient, retard the attending at Court next morning, are rather a restraint upon the Mayor and Bailiffs, and that it would be of utility to abolish them.

> *Resolved.*—That Mr. Rothwell, the Treasurer's clerk, assisted by the Sword Bearer, do attend at the Inn, at every sessions, and take in and deliver out all Wines and Rum for Punch, and keep an account of all Liquors taken in and delivered out, and in what respective Rooms the same shall be used, and keep also an account of all persons who shall dine at the several tables each day.

It is understood that the Innkeeper takes back all Wines and Rum, the corks whereof are not drawn.

The Committee approves of the establish'd Method of allowing the officers five shillings a Head, per sessions, in Lieu of Meat, drink, and entertainment.' "[1]

In 1780, on the occasion of a general election, a contest for the representation of Liverpool in parliament took place; the candidates were Mr. Bamber Gascoyne, at that time usually called Mr. Bamber Gascoyne, junior, in consequence of his father Mr. Bamber Gascoyne, of Childwall-hall, being then living, Mr. Henry Rawlinson, a Liverpool merchant, much respected, and Mr. Richard Pennant, afterwards Lord Penrhyn. On Saturday, the 16th of September, the two former were elected after a poll of five days, the votes being :—

Mr. Bamber Gascoyne, junior	608
Mr. Henry Rawlinson...........................	572
Mr. Richard Pennant...........................	462

1173 Freemen polled.

After the proclamation for closing the poll, Mr. Bamber Gascoyne, junior, and Mr. Henry Rawlinson, were chaired, as was then customary, from the Exchange to some other places,

---

(1) Book of Records of the Corporation of 1780, vol. 12, page 190.

1780. in the town, amidst the acclamations of several thousand people, with music playing and colours and flags flying. On the Monday following, in consequence of Mr. Bamber Gascoyne, senior, having intimated that it would give him pleasure, to see the freemen who had voted for his son, at Childwall-hall, Mr. Bamber Gascoyne, junior, was again chaired, from the house of Mr. Baker, in School-lane, accompanied with music, and nearly thirty colours, elegantly painted with different arms and inscriptions, and attended by some thousands of persons, to Childwall, about four miles distant, where they expected to have been abundantly supplied with provisions and liquor. Great confusion however arose, from their immense numbers; and a multitude of people, who had nothing whatever to do with the election, but who hoped to have their share of the treat, flocked in from the neighbouring country, so that it was impossible to maintain complete order; besides which, Mr. Gascoyne gave offence by having a number of men armed with poles, whose office it was to prevent the visiters from walking upon some parts of the lawns, or going into some of the plantations. He also offended them from the circumstance of having promised, that an ox should be roasted whole, and the meat distributed; but an idea went forth, (whether true or not cannot now be ascertained,) that it was only a tough old bull which he caused to be killed, roasted, and served up for the occasion; there was also something wrong about the vegetables;[1] and the upshot was, that the intended treat was a complete failure, and the bulk of those who had gone out in

---

(1) The lower classes long entertained feelings of displeasure and disappointment respecting the entertainment at Childwall, and some of the Electioneerers are yet alive who used to take a part for General Gascoyne, at Elections, who must recollect during what a long time afterwards the lower classes have been known to hoot and try to affront them, by calling out to them to remember the " Bull Beef and Cabbage Stalks " of Childwall.

procession, returned heartily disappointed. Mr. Bamber 1780.
Gascoyne, after the death of Mr. Bamber Gascoyne, senior,
was for many years the owner of the estate at Childwall,
and resided there. His daughter Frances Mary was married
in 1821 to the Marquis of Salisbury, who, by Royal permission, assumed the surname of Gascoyne before that of
Cecil, and through that lady he became the possessor of the
Childwall estate. His brother, Colonel, afterwards General
Gascoyne, at a subsequent period (1796) became one of
the representatives of Liverpool in Parliament, and continued
to represent it, as will be mentioned afterwards, in successive parliaments for many years.

In 1781, a Fort, Barracks, and Store-houses were 1781.
erected on the west side of the road on the North Shore,
(on part of which Bath-street now stands,) opposite the end
of Denison-street. The fort presented a circular front
towards the river, mounted with guns, viz. eighteen and
thirty-two pounders. The entrance was on the side towards
Bath-street, by a gateway, over which, on one side, was the
figure of a lion, and on the other the heraldic device of
the town, the Liver (Cormorant.) The whole of the fort
and buildings were destroyed in 1820 in making the
Prince's Dock, (which was opened on the 19th of July,
1821,) and the site forms part of that dock. A new fort
was afterwards built on the shore, more to the northward,
which in its turn, in consequence of the increase of the town
and the extension of the docks, has also been demolished.

In the month of May, in this year, an important case
came before the Court of King's Bench for argument, in
which the Revd: Claudius Crigan was plaintiff, and the
Revd: Robert Brereton and Thomas Maddock, co-rectors of
Liverpool, were defendants, which arose in consequence of
the loose manner in which the Act of Parliament for building
St. Ann's Church, noticed the solemnization of marriages

z 1

1781. there; and the question for decision was, whether Mr. Crigan had or had not a right to solemnize marriages in that church. The court were unanimously of opinion that all marriages previously solemnized, or afterwards to be solemnized there, were good and valid.[1] Thus effectually setting to rest doubts, which had been suggested, in consequence of the ambiguous or loose manner in which the act had been worded, and removing all feeling of uneasiness, from the minds of those persons, who had been or might afterwards be married there.

1782.   In the year 1782, a new Dispensary having been built on the south side of Church-street;[2] it superseded the old building in John-street and Princes-street, which ceased to be used; and that building was converted to other purposes, and was afterwards pulled down; and a warehouse now stands on its site. In 1829, the Dispensary in Church-street was sold, and the establishment was afterwards removed to the new dispensary in Vauxhall-road, called the North Dispensary.

In 1782, a communication by canal was opened between Liverpool and the river Ribble, and goods were regularly forwarded between Liverpool and Preston.

In the autumn of this year, a volunteer corps, or armed association, was raised in the town. Mr. Gill Slater was appointed captain, and Mr. Joseph Brooks, jun. lieutenant of it; and in the month of September, they received their commissions;[3] and on the 20th of February, 1783, a pair of colours, one of which was the gift of the King,

---

(1) Gore's General Advertiser of 31st May, 1781.

(2) It had a court in front, inclosed with iron rails, extending from the corner of Post-office Place, in the direction towards the spot where the Athenæum now stands, but not quite so far.

(3) Gore's General Advertiser of 26th September, 1782.

and the other of Mrs. Rawlinson, were presented to the 1782.
corps.[1]

In 1783, an Act of Parliament, rather material with 1783.
reference to the trade of Liverpool, was passed, empowering the proprietors of the Leeds and Liverpool Canal to
purchase the Douglas Navigation from the Ribble to Wigan.
The Act is of the 23rd of George the 3rd, chap. 47.

In consequence of Mr. John Brown, who had been
elected Mayor of Liverpool, having declined to serve the
office, a notice was issued by the Bailiffs, appointing the
7th of April, 1783, at the Exchange, for the burgesses
to proceed to the election of a Mayor, in his room.[2]   The
circumstance of any person who had been elected Mayor
declining to act, is, in itself, a very unusual one in Liverpool; but it is rendered still more remarkable, by the fact,
that, on the day so appointed for the election, Mr. Brown
was again elected, but he would not take the oaths or serve
the office, until the 12th of September following.

The following entry appears in the Records of the Corporation relative to the proceedings at the Court of Election,
held on the of 18th October, 1782, at which Mr. Brown was
first elected to the office of Mayor :—

"John Brown, Esq. is duly elected Mayor of the Borough and
Corporation of Liverpool for the year ensuing, but being required to
take the oath of his said office, did refuse to do so, and did refuse to
stand."[3]

The Records of the Corporation, of the 26th of March,
1783, contain entries, setting out a copy of one of the notices

---

(1) Gore's General Advertiser of 27th February, 1783.   Mrs. Rawlinson, mentioned in the above account, is believed to have been the wife of Mr. Henry Rawlinson,
one of the then members for Liverpool.

(2) Gore's General Advertiser of 27th March, 1783.

(3) Book of Records of the Corporation of 1782, vol. 12, page 317.

1783. of the intended election, as published by the bailiffs, and stating that the notices had been read and proclaimed in all the churches and chapels of Liverpool, and publicly proclaimed throughout the town " by the Common Cryer or Bellman of the said town," and affixed on conspicuous parts of all the churches and chapels, on the Market-house, and on the new market, and in the inside and on the outside of the Custom-house, and in the inside and on the outside of the Exchange ; and also contain entries of the proceedings of the 7th of April, 1783, of which the following are extracts,[1] viz :—

" Memorandum, that on the said seventh day of April, 1783, the aforesaid John Brown, Esquire, was at a Meeting or Assembly of many of the Burgesses of the said Town, held in pursuance of the aforesaid notice, at and in the said Exchange, re-elected Mayor of the same town, until next St. Luke's Day."[2]

" Memorandum, that on the twelfth day of September, 1783, after solemn Proclamation made for silence, the said John Brown, Esq. did on the Publick Hustings of the Exchange, of the said Town, before George Case, Esq. the last Mayor," and before the then Bailiffs, and many Burgesses assembled there, " take the oath of his said office of Mayor, (unto which office he was elected on the 18th day of October last,) and did also then and there take the oath of a Justice of the Peace of the same Borough, and the oaths to his Majesty's person and Government."[2]

It therefore appears that during the long interval which elapsed between the 18th of October, 1782, and the 12th of September, 1783, Mr. Brown refused to serve the office, and the town was without a Mayor.

At a meeting of the Common Council held on the 3rd of December, 1783:—

" Mr. Brown having made an apology in Council for the trouble and

---

(1) Book of Records of the Corporation of 1783, vol. 12, page 320.

(2) Ibid. of 1783, vol. 12, page 321.

expence to which this Corporation was put, on account of his refusing 1783.
to take upon himself the office of Mayor;—ordered, that such his
apology be accepted of."[1]

At the same meeting of the Common Council, in consequence of the representation of the engineer of the new Fort,
that the barracks were then completed for the reception of
100 men, it was ordered that an application should be made
to the Secretary of War to furnish them with that number :—

" And that the present Batteries, called the George's Battery and
Queen's Battery, be taken down, and the timber sold, and the money
arising therefrom be appropriated for the use of the Docks."[2]

On the 5th of June, in this year, a prospectus or outline
of a scheme was published, " For the establishment of a
Coffee-room, Hotel and Tavern, at Liverpool, upon a Tontine Scheme, with benefit of Survivorship."[3]   It resulted
in the erection of the hotel at the lowest end and north
side of Lord-street, and corner of Whitechapel, which was
at one time called the " New Hotel," and afterwards the
" Royal Hotel " or " Bates' Hotel."   It is difficult to ascertain the exact date when it was opened, but it was erected
in 1784.   A large room in it, called the Coffee-room, was
furnished with newspapers, and used as a news-room,[4]
which was frequented by subscribers, until it was superseded
by the Athenæum News-room and Library.

In 1784, on the occurrence of another general election, 1784.
a new candidate appeared on the stage.   Colonel Tarleton,
(afterwards General Sir Banastre Tarleton, Bart.) declared
himself a candidate.   He was the son of Mr. John Tarleton,
of Water-street, in Liverpool, who resided at a large

---

(1) Book of Records of the Corporation of 1783, vol. 12, page 344 and 348.

(2) Ibid. of 1783, vol. 12, page 344 and 347.

(3) Gore's General Advertiser of 5th of June, 1783.

(4) Chapter IV, page 269.

1784. house which was afterwards the King's Arms Hotel, on
the south side of the street, and corner of Fenwick-
street, which is now pulled down and counting-houses are
erected on its site. Colonel Tarleton was born in that
house. His father, Mr. John Tarleton, was a merchant
of eminence and consideration in the town, and was
Mayor in 1764: he was often called (especially in
electioneering pasquinades) by the *sobriquet* of "Great
T." He married Jane, eldest daughter of Mr. Banastre
Parker, and died in 1773, and his wife died in 1797.
They were buried on the westward side of St. Nicholas'
Church-yard, in a portion which is on a lower level than
the older part of it. The place of interment of the
Tarletons is on the eastward side of the portion alluded to,
close to the more elevated and older part of the church-
yard, and is easily distinguishable, by two gravestones lying
contiguous to each other, containing memorials of the
deceased members; and the armorial bearings of the family
are carved upon one of them. The issue of the marriage
of Mr. John Tarleton and of his wife were as follows :—

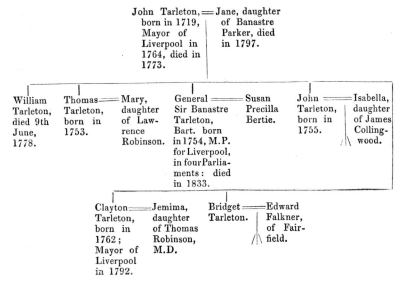

Colonel Tarleton had served and distinguished himself 1784. in America, and had been a clever, active and enterprising cavalry officer in the campaigns of the American revolutionary war. A strong proof of his great popularity in Liverpool and its vicinity, on his arrival from America, in 1782, will be found in the following paragraphs, which appeared in a Liverpool newspaper announcing his arrival:

> " Late on Saturday evening last, a messenger came to town with an account of the arrival of Colonel Tarleton, at Fairfield, near this place, on which occasion the bells rung all night and the next day. At one o'clock, Sunday, the Colonel arrived here on horseback : he was met on the road by a great number of persons, who accompanied him to the Exchange, where he was received by a large concourse of gentlemen and tradesmen, whose repeated acclamations and congratulations testified their joy and satisfaction.   The Colonel's politeness and affability, gains him the esteem of all ranks; but the short time he stays in town makes it impossible for every one who is desirous to show him distinguishing marks of their approbation, as he intends to leave Liverpool on Sunday evening."

> " Extract of a letter from Warrington, February 17.

> "Last night, between seven and eight o'clock, Col. Tarleton, (in his way to Liverpool,) stop'd at the Red Lion Inn, to exchange horses, it was soon made publick by the ringing of bells, the house illuminated, and a number of gentlemen assembled, who took the horses from the carriage, drawed him through the streets, amongst crowded numbers, who echoed, " *Long live brave Tarleton.*" He was very polite; said, don't be afraid of taking hold of my hand, tho' I have lost two fingers, I can use my pen, and will draw my sword when I can do my country service, and when I appear next in the field, my utmost endeavours shall not be wanting to be more successful."[1]

After his return from America to Liverpool, his military services and his being a native of the town, coupled with his prepossessing manners, fine soldier-like appearance, and good address, made him very popular ; and he was induced to declare himself a candidate for the representation of

---

(1) Gore's Liverpool Advertiser of 21st February, 1782.

1784. Liverpool at the general election of April, 1784. At that time, however, he failed in attaining his object, the final state of the poll showing the numbers thus:—

Mr. Bamber Gascoyne, junior 960
Lord Penrhyn 869
Colonel Tarleton 856
1950 Freemen polled.[2]

On that occasion, therefore, Colonel Tarleton was defeated, but a very different result was destined ere long to await his canvassing and exertions. He was elected one of the members for Liverpool in 1790, 1796, and 1802; was a candidate in 1806, was then defeated, and was again elected in 1807, but was once more unsuccessful in 1812. He was exceedingly popular in Liverpool for many years, was a very expert electioneerer, and could accommodate himself to all classes. He had been wounded in the hand when serving abroad, had lost two fingers in the service, and was in the habit of holding up his maimed hand on the hustings, so as to let it be visible to such of his opponent's voters as he thought the exhibition of it might have weight with, and it sometimes procured him votes from the opposite bar. Amongst other classes with whom he was a great favourite were *les Dames de la Halle*, the fish women, and market women; and when he arrived in Liverpool, preparatory to an election, he used immediately to drive in his gig to the fish-market, and kiss the fish girls. It was astonishing how popular he was with them: during the elections when he was a candidate, numbers of them (as many of the readers must recollect) used to go in procession, with not a little noise, to the hustings, carrying green boughs and shrubs, and

---

(2) Sir William Meredith is stated, in the modern Poll Books, to have had 36 votes, but that is not mentioned in Gore's General Advertiser of the time, (15th April, 1784,) from which the above numbers are taken.

wearing green ribbons, as a mark of regard and attachment 1784.
to him; green being the colour of his uniform, and that
which was adopted by his supporters at the elections.

Little can be said in his favour as a member for Liverpool; he was unacquainted with mercantile matters, in-
attentive, fond of pleasure, and mixed a great deal with
the gay world, and was not at all suited to the representation of a large and important commercial town ; it is only
strange that he was allowed to represent it so long.   Before
dismissing the subject of Colonel (afterwards General) Tarleton, it may be well to mention that, at one period, he was
very intimate with the Prince of Wales, afterwards King
George the Fourth; and it is remarkable that two gentlemen,
both closely connected with Lancashire, General Tarleton,
and Colonel Cawthorne, of Wyersdale, in that county, (who
was several times elected member for Lancaster,) were
the last, or very nearly the last survivors of all the intimate
acquaintances of the Prince, in his early life.

In 1784, St. John's Church, on the north-east side of St.
John's-lane, was completed.   The foundation had been laid
long before, but a delay, as has been already mentioned, from
some cause or other occurred, before the church was finished.

In September, in this year, a Grand Musical Festival
took place in St. Peter's Church, of which the receipts were
£2000.   It has been already fully noticed in another chapter,
where the musical and other tastes, and pursuits of the
inhabitants of Liverpool, at that period, were described.[1]

A subscription list was opened in 1784, for contributions
for the laudable purpose of establishing Sunday Schools
in Liverpool for the children of the poor.   The following
paragraphs on the subject appear in a Liverpool newspaper
of November and December, in that year :—

---

[1] Chapter IV, page 270.

1784.

"LIVERPOOL, November 25.

"The Clergy, Gentlemen, Merchants, and others, who are desirous to contribute to the institution and support of SUNDAY SCHOOLS, are requested to meet the MAYOR, in the Council-chamber, on Monday next, at eleven o'clock, to consider on the means of extending an undertaking of such public utility.

Heads of the Plan for SUNDAY SCHOOLS.

It is proposed to have 30;[1] one or more Masters or Mistresses to each school, as the number of scholars may require.

The Children to go to school at one o'clock, and to be kept till the evening comes on, according to the Season of the year. When they have learned to read, and are brought into order and decorum, to be conducted by their respective Masters and Mistresses to church.

The Clergy, and all other persons who wish well to this laudable scheme, to visit the schools at their pleasure and give advice and encouragement.

Proper objects, are all, whose parents are not able to pay for instruction; and particularly those poor children who are employed in rope-walks, tobacco-warehouses, &c.

SUBSCRIPTIONS.

	£	s.		£	s.
Corporation, per ann....	21	0	Mr. Cazneau	1	1
John Gregson, Esq. Mayor	1	1	Mr. Thos. Crook............	1	1
Geo. Case, Esq.	1	1	Mr. Geo. Crooke...........	1	1
W. Crosbie, Jun. Esq......	1	1	Mrs. Dawson	1	1
Wm. Hesketh, Esq.........	1	1	Mr. Daulby, Jun............	1	1
Rev. Mr. Dannett	1	1	Mr. Fuhrer	1	1
Rev. Mr. Hodson	1	1	Mrs. L. Gildart	1	1
Rev. Mr. Moore	1	1	Mr. Wm. Heys	1	1
Rev. Mr. Roughsedge......	1	1	Mr. B. A. Heywood	1	1
Rev. Mr. Formby	1	1	Mr. Houghton..............	1	1
Mr. Brooks	1	1	Mr. Jackson..................	1	1
Mr. Jos. Brooks, Jun.......	1	1	Mr. Kent	1	1
Mr. Thos. Booth............	1	1	Dr. Lyon	1	1
Mr. Bevan	1	1	Mr. Staniforth..............	1	1
Mr. Lace	1	1	Mr. Twemlow	1	1
Mr. Thos. Moore............	1	1	Mr. Wilding.................	1	1
Mr. Nelson	1	1	Mr. Rich. Woods............	1	1
Mr. Rogers	1	1	Mr. Wallace..................	1	1
Mr. Rawson..................	1	1	Mr. Watt, Jun..............	1	1
Mr. Slater	1	1	Mr. G. W. Watts............	1	1
Mr. Chaffers	1	1			

---

(1) It is printed "30" in the newspaper, but there seems to be some mistake of the press there, for that appears to be an unreasonable number of Schools with reference to the then population of the town.

Subscriptions are received by the Rev. Mr. DANNETT, Treasurer, 1784. or JOHN GORE.

N. B. Bibles, Testaments, and Common Prayer Books, will be useful presents.

The Community will certainly be benefited in proportion as this undertaking is prosecuted; and though all may not be effected as could be wished for, yet the generous and liberal mind will have the satisfaction of concurring in an attempt which has in prospect much good, and may possibly be crowned with that success which few persons have any conceptions of, from its present infant state."[1]

The following additional subscriptions were afterwards announced :—

"Subscriptions to SUNDAY SCHOOLS, Continued.

Anonymous	£1 1		Mr. W. C. Lake	£1 1
Mr. Jona. Brooks	1 1		Mr. Meyers	1 1
Mr. J. Blundell	1 1		Mr. North	1 1
Mr. H. Berry	1 1		Mr. Pole	1 1
Mr. Clowes	1 1		Mr. J. Percival	1 1
Edw. Falkner, Esq	1 1		Rev. Mr. Renshaw	1 1
Mr. R. Fisher	1 1		Mr. Ruete	1 1
Mr. France	1 1		Robert Scott, Esq.	1 1
Mr. John Gildart	1 1		Mr. Waterworth	1 1"[2]
Mr. R. Lightbody	1 1			

In one of the Liverpool newspapers of the 8th of June, 1786, the following paragraph appears :—

" The collection for Sunday Schools is now upwards of £500."[3]

It appears from the following advertisement of the 22nd of June, 1786, that eleven Sunday Schools were accordingly opened in different places in Liverpool, under the management of a committee, of which the Revd. Brownlow (afterwards Dr.) Forde, the minister of St. Catherine's Church, was the Secretary :—

" SUNDAY SCHOOLS.

" Notice is hereby given, that Schools will be opened at the following places on Sunday next, at eight o'clock in the morning, and continued

---

(1) Gore's General Advertiser of 9th of December, 1784.

(2) Ibid. of 23rd of December, 1784.

(3) Ibid. of 8th of June, 1786.

1784. every Sunday throughout the year, for the reception of the Children (male and female) of such persons as cannot afford to pay for their education, viz :—

> Mr. Winstanley, at the Free School
> Mr. Gelder, at Mr. Johnson's School room, Peter's Lane
> Mr. and Mrs. Peacock, Union Street
> Mr. and Mrs. Eyre, No. 49, Shaw's Brow
> Mr. Burland, No. 38, Mersey Street
> Mr. Dickens, No. 11, Plumbe Street
> Mr. Hodgson, Clayton's-alley
> Mr. Blake, No. 64, Plumbe Street
> Mr. and Mrs. Hodgson, Stanley Street
> Mr. and Mrs. Jeakins, Thomas's Street
> Mr. Dickinson, Trueman Street

The Committee will meet at the Exchange every Wednesday till further notice.

June 22ᵈ· 1786.   B. FORDE, Sec." [1]

And in an advertisement in a subsequent newspaper, in August, 1786, it is stated that the schools at the above-mentioned places had been opened, and that they would be continued : [2] and at a meeting of the Committee held on the 1st of November, 1786, a resolution was passed calculated to obtain the assistance of the laity, as well as of the clergy, in visiting them. [3]

1785.   A Mail-coach for the conveyance of the bags of letters and of passengers to London, was first established on the 25th of July, 1785 : it has been already mentioned in a former chapter, that the mail bags used previously to be conveyed to and from the town on horseback; and the following announcement of the establishment of the mail-coach appeared in a Liverpool newspaper of that date :—

> " Golden Lion, Dale-street,
> The Original Mail Coach,
> With a Guard all the way,

will set off on Monday next, the 25th instant, at Four o'clock in the Morning, and so continue every day.—To go in 30 hours.— Fare, £3 13s 6d.

---

(1) Gore's General Advertiser of 22nd of June, 1786.

(2) Ibid. of 3rd of August, 1786.   (3) Ibid. of 14th of December, 1786.

Notice is hereby given,

That all Carters, Chaise Boys, &c. betwixt Liverpool and London, are to observe, that, when they hear the Horn of the Guard to the Mail-coach, they are immediately to turn out of the Road, and make way for the same.—If this caution is not strictly attended to, by the parties above-mentioned, they will assuredly be prosecuted as the law in that case directs."[1]

On the 20th of July in this year, Lunardi, the æronaut, ascended in a balloon, from the Fort, and descended at Simmonswood, in Lancashire; and again ascended from the Fort, on the 9th of August following, and descended near Tarporley, in Cheshire. The dates are noticed here, in consequence of those being the first ascents in any balloon which had ever taken place at Liverpool. The following is a copy of Lunardi's announcement of his intended ascent :—

" Mr. Lunardi

" Respectfully informs the ladies and gentlemen of Liverpool, that he arrived on Tuesday evening, and, in the course of yesterday, happily succeeded in procuring all the necessary materials and apparatus to fill his Balloon, and in obtaining permission to *launch* it from the Fort, where the company will be accommodated at *Five Shillings* the first and *Half-a-Crown* the second places, to see the process of filling his Balloon, and his ascension into the atmosphere on Wednesday next, between *Twelve and One o'clock,* if the Wind and Weather permit.

The Balloon, with its appendages, continues to be exhibited at the temporary Pantheon, in Lydia Ann-street, where, To-morrow and

---

(1) Gore's General Advertiser of 21st July, 1785.—Although the establishment of a Mail-coach was a great advantage, and tended to a more certain and regular communication between Liverpool and London, yet that never could be effected by the Royal Mail so as to receive a reply to a letter through the Post-office under four days, until about twenty-four years after the commencement of the present century ; and the communication was liable to be interrupted by various accidents. Early in the year 1814, the winter being one of unusual severity, the snow drifted to so great an extent at Chalk-hill, near Dunstable, as to stop the Mail-coaches, and nearly four days elapsed without letters or tidings being received in Liverpool from London, and, strange to say, the first intelligence from London afterwards, came round by the Bristol mail through Bristol. It would have excited astonishment and incredulity in those days, if the wonderful celerity of communication by the Electric Telegraph had been prognosticated.

1785. Saturday, Mr. Lunardi *will attend,* to gratify the curiosity of those ladies and gentlemen who may favour him with their company, by explaining the principles of ærostation, and the construction of his balloon.—Admittance to the Pantheon, One Shilling.

Subscriptions are opened at Mr. Gore's, stationer; Mr. Egerton Smith's, Pool-lane; the New Hotel,[1] Mr. Forshaw's; and at Messrs. Walley and Jones', near the Exchange; at which places tickets for the Fort will be delivered at 5s. each."[2]

In the same year,[3] an Act of Parliament of the 25th of George the Third, chap. 15, was passed to enlarge the powers of several acts relating to the harbour of Liverpool, and for making two additional docks and piers. This is the Act under which the King's and Queen's Docks were made. The former was opened on the 3rd of October, 1788. The old Tobacco warehouse was not long afterwards erected on the east side of the King's Dock, and extended to the west side of Wapping; it was a long low brick building, erected by the Corporation, and let by them to the Government, at a rent of £500 per annum. For a building of that description it was rather handsome, having rustic gateways ornamented with stone, and surmounted by a neat cornice. The west or dock front had the King's Arms carved in stone, in the pediment, over the central or principal gate, and the front to Wapping had also a uniform pediment with a figure in stone of the Liver.

The dimensions of the building were 210 feet by 180; and it was calculated to contain 7000 hogsheads of tobacco, but it was found too small. Most of it was taken down after the erection of the present one on the west side of the

---

(1) This Hotel was then kept by Mr. Henry Forshaw, and was at the bottom of Lord-street, and corner of Whitechapel, and was afterwards called the Royal Hotel, or Bates' Hotel.

(2) Gore's General Advertiser of July 14th, 1785.

(3) The date, 1785, is in the Statute Book, but it appears probable that the Royal assent was given to it early in the Session in 1784.

Queen's Dock, in 1824; a part of it was, however, after- 1785.
wards used as sheds for goods, and particularly for saltpetre,
but it has been recently pulled down.

In June, 1786, the Music-hall, on the south side of Bold- 1786.
street and corner of Concert-street, was opened,[1] with the
oratorio of the "Messiah." It was calculated to accommodate 1300 persons.[2] It was a plain brick building, and had,
in the centre of it, a small portico of stone, which extended
over the foot-walk in Bold-street; it was for many years
used for concerts, vocal and instrumental. The ground floor
of the building was afterwards altered and made into shops,
with a large room over them used for public meetings, and
occasionally as a dissenting place of worship. It has been
recently pulled down, and a new building and shops have
been erected on its site.

In 1786, the Corporation very laudably came to the
conclusion to adopt measures for widening some of the
streets near the Exchange, and for the improvement of
the town, in various other respects, on a large scale, and
for that purpose determined upon applying to Parliament
for an Improvement Act. At a Special Council, held
in the Mayoralty of Mr. Charles Pole, on Tuesday, the
10th of January, 1786, it was resolved,—

" That it is the unanimous opinion of this Council that a bill be
drawn and brought into Parliament for the purpose of improving and
widening the streets."[3]

And at a Common Council held on the 1st of February,
in the same year, Mr. Richard Statham, Mr. John Gregson,
and Mr. Joseph Brooks, jun. were deputed by the Council to
proceed to London, to solicit the intended bill for improving

---

(1) Gore's General Advertiser of June 8th, 1786.

(2) Troughton's Liverpool, page 326.

(3) Book of Records of the Corporation for 1786, vol. 12, page 460.

1786. the streets.[1]   In consequence of which, the Improvement Act of the 26th of George the Third, chap. 12, was passed.

Under that Act, Castle-street and parts of Water-street, Dale-street, Fenwick-street, Derby-square, and Preeson's-row were widened and improved.   Temple-bar was removed, so as to make the houses and buildings lineable from Derby-square to the end of Cable-street.   Kenyon's steps, and the buildings which stood close to St. George's Church, were removed.   An area of considerable width was made round the Exchange, so as completely to isolate it from other buildings.   A number of small old streets, courts, alleys, and passages, such as the Old Shambles, Johnson's-alley, Pemberton's-alley, Clayton's-alley, Ogden's-court, Smock-alley, Leadenhall-market, Fenwick-alley, Falcon-alley, [old] Exchange-alley, and several others, in the vicinity of the Exchange,[2] were either wholly or partially pulled down, stopped or inclosed; and, eventually, Brunswick-street was made down to the Goree.

No time appears to have been lost in commencing the improvements after the act was passed, for the books of the Corporation contain a resolution of the Select Committee of the Council of the 13th of April, 1786, " that all the houses and buildings on the west side of Castle-street be taken down as they become vacant."[3]

It has been already mentioned[4] that Castle-street had previously been so narrow in some parts, that two carriages

---

(1) Book of Records of the Corporation of 1786, vol. 12, page 462 and 463.

(2) Special Council Book of the Corporation for 1786, vol. 1, page 12 to 55 aud 61.

(3) Ibid. page 62.   The same resolution also directs, " that Mr. Blackstock's house adjoining the Exchange, and the house next to it, belonging to the Corporation, late in the possession of —— Hodgson, printer, with the back buildings to the same, and also the butcher's stalls and shops as far to the northward as the north range of the Exchange, be immediately pulled down and laid open for further improvement."

(4) Chapter II, page 118.

could with difficulty pass.   After being widened, it assumed, 1786.
with the exception of some very recent alterations, its
present appearance.   It was originally intended that the
east side should have been brought forward, and that the
same extent of the front of the Town-hall should be
covered by the new buildings in Castle-street on that
side as on the west; but that plan was abandoned in
consequence of the expense, and the loss of so much space
in the street, and consequently the front of the Town-
hall, viewed from the street, is not quite in the centre.   A
portion of the right wing is veiled by the houses on the
west side of the street; whilst on the east an opening
presents itself, through which, a view is now obtained of
High-street, on the east side of the Town-hall, and of part
of the Exchange-buildings.

In noticing the Improvement Act of 1786, (26th of
George the Third, chap. 12,) it is proper to mention that this
is the act[1] under which the water-works, called the Liverpool Corporation Water-works, (afterwards the Liverpool and
Harrington Water-works,) were subsequently established.

Although the Act of 1786 empowered the Council of
the borough to construct water-works, dig for springs, &c.
scarcely any steps were taken by the Corporation to carry
out the powers of the act until 1799, when the formation
of the Bootle Water-works Company acted as a stimulus to
the Corporation of Liverpool, and the latter accordingly
issued proposals for a scheme for supplying the town with
water, to be taken up in shares of £200 each, by subscribers.
It was eagerly responded to by the public, the shares were
taken within a few hours after the scheme was promulgated;
and, by a deed of 15th January, 1800, the Corporation
transferred to the subscribers all their rights and privileges

---

(1) Sections 26 to 30.

1786. under the Act of 1786, retaining, however, a per-centage share of the profits, (which never accrued,) and a share in the management of the concern.

Under the powers of the act, pipes for the conveyance of water were laid in 1800; they were originally of wood, and many years afterwards cast-iron pipes were substituted for those of wood. The offices for transacting the business, the well, and the steam-engine for pumping and propelling the water, were on the east side of Berry-street, almost opposite to the end of Seel-street. They have long since been destroyed.

The Corporation Water-works were carried on under the deed until 1823; doubts were, however, entertained whether the Corporation had the power to make the transfer professed to be done by that deed; but, be that as it may, the proprietors of the shares were incorporated by an Act of Parliament, in 1822, the 3rd George the Fourth, chap. 77, under the name of "The Company of Proprietors of the Liverpool Corporation Water-works;" and, in 1827, the incorporated company obtained a second Act, the 7th and 8th George the Fourth, chap. 36, extending their powers to Toxteth-park, and changing the name of the company to that of "The Company of Proprietors of the Liverpool and Harrington Water-works." Those Acts were amended in 1846, by an Act of 9th and 10th Victoria, chap. 35.

At length, in 1847, an Act was passed of the 10th and 11th Victoria, chap. 261, "An Act for better supplying with Water the borough of Liverpool, and the neighbour-hood thereof, and for authorising the Mayor, Aldermen, and Burgesses of the said borough, to purchase the Liverpool and Harrington Water-works and Liverpool Water-works," [the Bootle,] by which both the Liverpool and Harrington Water-works, and the Bootle [called Liverpool] Water-works, were transferred to the Corporation of Liverpool; and the companies previously established for 1786. carrying them on ceased to exist.

In the same year, 1786, the Corporation of Liverpool purchased, as has been before mentioned, St. Catherine's Church.

In July, 1786, an association (in which Mr. Roscoe took an active part) for the promotion of the arts, and the encouragement of the works of living artists, was formed in Liverpool, and an exhibition of works of art was the result. An anniversary dinner took place on the 4th of November, 1786, and a second exhibition took place, but the institution soon afterwards was abandoned.[1]

In 1787, the Alms-houses in St. Mary's-lane, Hope- 1787. street, were built, for old and indigent persons, and the edifices which had been erected for similar purposes, and which existed in other parts of the town, were pulled down. The inscription upon the new alms-houses is a curious specimen of the literary attainments, either of some committee, or of some of the officials of the Corporation of Liverpool, in 1787; and what makes it more remarkable, the inscription still appears on each of the wings of the building. It is too singular to be abridged, and therefore is here given entire :—

" These Alms Houses were built by the Corporation of Liverpool, in the year 1787, in lieu of others formerly erected, for certain charitable purposes, more particularly explained by other inscriptions. The former houses were in confined places, but removed altogether to this healthy situation, for the benefit of the inhabitants, and the accommodation of the Public : the patronage being secured to the original Trustees, agreeable to the intentions of the first Benefactors."

As if to make the wings, containing such an ill-judged

---

(1) Smither's Liverpool, page 337.

1787. and absurd inscription, the more conspicuous and objectionable to the eye, about the end of 1847, or the commencement of 1848, the western wing was altered and considerably enlarged, so as to be out of all proportion when compared to the other.

In 1787, the Welsh Methodist Chapel, in Pall-mall, was opened. It has been re-built and altered in 1816; and is now entered from Prussia-street.

A Woollen-hall or mart, sometimes called the Richmond Fair, was erected for the sale of woollen goods, near Richmond-row, sometime in 1787; the exact date has not been ascertained, but in a deed of conveyance, dated 21st July, 1788,[1] it was called "The New Woollen-hall," and consequently it must have been built prior to that date. It was erected in the Richmond-row district, between the town and Everton.

The edifice has a communication both with Richmond-row and Fox-street, but is not visible from either, it being

---

(1) The Author is indebted to the kindness of Mr. Henry Braun, the owner of part of the property, for access to the deed of conveyance :—

1788, 21 July.—Indenture of Appointment made between Joshua Rose of the first part, Robert Lowthian of the second part, and John Brown of the third part: Reciting a Deed of Conveyance by Lease and Release of the 1st and 2nd February, 1786, from Thomas Plumbe to the said Joshua Rose, (amongst other property,) of a Field used as a Garden, lying on the north side of the Public Road or Highway leading from Liverpool to Everton, opposite to the Field near the Loggerheads—And also reciting that Robert Lowthian was under contract with the said Joshua Rose for the purchase of a piece of Ground at Richmond, being part of the Land conveyed to the said Joshua Rose by the said Deed, on which the said Robert Lowthian had erected and built several small shops, and that the said Joshua Rose had consented, at the request of Robert Lowthian, to convey unto the said John Brown, the two shops and premises thereinafter particularly mentioned, the said Joshua Rose accordingly conveyed unto the said John Brown, his heirs and assigns, "All those two shops, the one on the ground floor, and the other over the same, both mentioned, marked and distinguished by the figure 25, situate and being on the north side of *the new Woollen Hall* bounded on the west by the common Warehouse there, and on the east by No. 26," &c. &c.

separated from them by houses under which access is 1787.
obtained to it by passages, which are built over, leading
from the streets. The interior has not been much altered,
and still gives a good idea of what the building originally
was. The area within was a spacious irregular quadrangle
of about 1200 square yards, or, including the ground built
upon, about 2800 square yards, with an upper and lower
range of shops. A gallery, most of which still remains,
supported on pillars, from which the upper range of shops
was entered, extended all round the interior of the building,
forming a colonade, under which was the lower range of
shops. The gallery had a small canopy as a protection
from the weather.[1]   The building was opened for the
sale of woollen cloth, Manchester and Birmingham goods,
on the 10th November, 1787;[2] and it was constantly used
during many years as a cloth-hall, and a fair was also
held there four times in the year for the sale of woollens,
linens, and muslins; but from some cause, probably the
distance from the central and business parts of the town,
those markets, although at one time much frequented,
did not ultimately succeed, and the shops are now converted into dwellings for the lower classes.

Whether the Common Council considered that the pro- 1788.
moters of the undertaking intended to use the edifice for
the purposes of a general market, or that they had no right
to have even a cloth hall, or cloth market, so near the town,
the following order entered in the Council book, shows that,
in 1788, the Common Council contemplated adopting
measures to endeavour to suppress the undertaking; but as
no legal proceedings seem to have been resorted to, the
attempt to suppress it appears to have been abandoned.

---

(1) M.S. Account of Liverpool, by J. Underhill. The building was erected by
Mr. Dobb and others.

(2) Gore's General Advertiser of 25th of October and 15th of November, 1787.

1788.   At a Common Council held the 2nd of April, 1788, it was ordered, " That the records be searched, and a case be stated for the opinion of counsel, respecting the proper mode to be pursued in order to suppress the attempt now making to hold a market or fair, for the purpose of vending different manufactures, at a place erected by Messrs. Dobb and others, near Saint Anne's Church, called the Woollen Hall."[1]

On the 7th of September, 1788, the Roman Catholic Chapel, on the south side of Seel-street, a plain brick edifice, without exterior ornament, was opened. It is dedicated to St. Peter. The first priest was the Rev. Archibald M'Donald, whom many of the readers must recollect; he was a native of Scotland, and was a kind-hearted and much-respected man, and officiated many years at the chapel. About five years after it had been opened, he was joined by the Rev. W. Digby, and was succeeded by the Rev. William Tarleton. The chapel was considerably enlarged in 1818.

The Council book of the Corporation of 1789 contains the following order relative to it :—At a Common Council held on the 1st of April, 1789, it was ordered, " that a new Lease be granted to the Rev. Archibald M'Donald, of the Roman Catholic Chapel, lately erected by him, and situate in Seel-street, for three lives of his own nomination, and for 21 years afterwards ;" under the reserved yearly ground rent of twelvepence per yard for the front; and that for the above purpose only, a perpetual lease should be granted of the Chapel, on the death of any life, on the persons entitled, applying for the renewal of each lease, within six calendar months after each such death : " But it is further ordered, that whenever the said Chapel shall cease to be used as a chapel for Roman Catholics, that thenceforth, the said right of perpetual renewal, shall cease, and the lessees shall only be entitled to the said premises for the then

---

(1) Book of Records of the Corporation of 1788, vol. 12, page 545 and 546.

existing term therein, subject to the said yearly reserved 1788.
rent."[1]

"Also ordered, that the said Archibald M'Donald have a
Lease for three Lives, of his own naming, and twenty-one
years, of his house and school, in Seel-street aforesaid, on
paying a fine of Three pounds three shillings ; and twelve
pence per yard, yearly, ground rent, for the front."[2]

In 1788, several new streets were laid out, particularly
on the north-east side of the town, and so great was the
influx of strangers, that the new houses became occupied as
soon as they were habitable.[3]

In this year the King's Dock was opened, on the 3rd
of October, for the reception of vessels.   The Port-a-Ferry
frigate, which was one of the three vessels that carried
troops from this port to raise the siege of Londonderry in
1688, entered this dock on the first day of its being opened
in 1788, after a lapse of 100 years: she was still in
existence in 1810, and was then a trader between Liverpool and Ireland.[4]

In 1789, the Liverpool Marine Society, for the benefit 1789.
of masters of vessels, their widows and children, was
established, of which the first president was Mr. Thomas
Staniforth.[5] Mr. William Hutchinson, the dock-master,
who has been mentioned in a former chapter, was a liberal
contributor to it, he having subscribed one hundred guineas.

In the same year the Lunatic Asylum was opened; it
joined the rear of the old Infirmary on Shaws-brow ; was
erected on part of its garden, and was entered from St.

---

(1) Book of Records of the Corporation of 1789, vol. 12, page 594 and 601.

(2) Ibid. page 594 and 601.

(3) Troughton's Liverpool, page 176.

(4) Ibid. page 276.

(5) Gore's General Advertiser of 5th of March, 1789.

1789. John's-lane. It was disused when the present Lunatic
Asylum on Brownlow-hill was established many years
subsequently; was for a short time used as barracks, and
soon afterwards was pulled down, and on its site part of
St. George's-hall now stands.

In March of this year, the inhabitants of the town
commemorated the King's recovery from a lamentable state
of mental affliction, by a general illumination and other
modes of rejoicing. On the 16th of the following month
a ball and supper were given by the Corporation, as has
already been more particularly mentioned in another place.[1]

At a Special Council, held on the 14th of March, 1789,
it was unanimously resolved, that an Address (the form of
which was then agreed upon) to the King from the Corporation, under the common seal of the town, congratulating him
upon his recovery from his late severe indisposition, should
be presented to the King, by the Members for the Borough
and the Recorder.[2]

In this year the Baptist Chapel on the east side of
Byrom-street, and corner of Gerard-street, was erected,[3]
and the congregation removed thither from their former
chapel, now St. Stephen's Church, in Byrom-street. The
Rev. Samuel Medley was the minister for several years.
In 1849 the congregation quitted the chapel for one in
another part of the town. The chapel is again occupied
by a small congregation of Baptists.

1790.   The establishment of Sunday Schools in this town
occurred, as has been already mentioned, in 1786; but there
are good grounds for believing that the first establishment
of any Sunday and Daily School, peculiarly intended for the

---

(1) Chapter IV, page 278 to 282.

(2) Book of Records of the Corporation of 1789, vol. 12, page 592 and 593.

(3) Memoirs of the Rev. Samuel Medley, written by his Son, page 91.

children of the poor, who frequented any particular place of 1790.
worship in Liverpool, was carried into effect by the congregation of protestant dissenters of the Benn's-garden Chapel.
A printed prospectus relating to it, issued by that congregation, is in existence, but it is to be regretted that it does
not give the date when it was published : it has, however,
been ascertained that a Sunday and Daily school connected
with that chapel was established in October, 1790.[1]   A
Sunday and Daily school was accordingly instituted on the
plan as stated in the prospectus :—" That tho' the Benefits
of this Charity be designed more directly and immediately
for the Children of the Poor of Benn's Garden Chapel, yet
that this be not meant to exclude the Children of other
Societies, provided that its Funds be sufficiently extensive."[2]

In 1790, the opening by Brunswick-street from Castle-
street to George's Dock was completed. This event was
almost a natural consequence of the improvement in its
neighbourhood, by the widening of Castle-street. Previously
to the opening of Brunswick-street, there was not any street
between Water-street and Moor-street, through which access
could be had, from Castle-street to George's Dock.

In this year, the Methodist Chapel, on the north side of
Mount-pleasant, was built. It was opened on the 7th of
November, on which occasion a sermon was preached by the
Rev. William Miles.[3]   It is a plain brick edifice, and has
remained without any alteration in its exterior, ever since its
erection.   Not long afterwards, the Methodist Sunday and
Daily Schools were established.   They have since branched

---

(1) Communicated by Thomas Thornely, Esq. M.P.   The date of the commencement of the School, 10th of October, 1790, is given in the first printed report of the
receipts and payments of the school, lent to the Author by Mr. James Thornely, Solicitor.

(2) The Prospectus was lent to the Author by Thomas Thornely, Esq. M.P.

(3) See Gore's General Advertiser of the 4th of November, 1790, announcing the
intended opening of the Chapel.
    c 2

1790. off into three different establishments, viz : the Brunswick schools, the Leeds-street schools, and the Jordan-street schools.

There was also, before the close of the 18th century, a chapel in Edmund-street, belonging to the Methodists, but the author has been unable to learn when it was opened, or during what period it was frequented. It must, however, have been opened prior to the 8th of February, 1798, because collections were announced in a newspaper of that date as having been made for the benefit of the Infirmary, at the Methodist Chapels in Pitt-street, Mount-pleasant, and Edmund-street.[1]

A general election took place in June, 1790, when, in consequence of a coalition having been previously arranged between the friends of Lord Penrhyn[2] and Mr. Bamber Gascoyne,[3] and the taps having been stopped rather precipitately, the electors took the alarm, and concluded that it was intended to deprive them of the free drink and indulgences usual on such occasions, at that period : Mr. George Crump,[4] a solicitor of eminence, availing himself of the excitement occasioned by it, called together a number of the electors at the upper end of Water-street, and caused a cask of ale or porter to be rolled into the street, the head to be knocked out, and the contents to be distributed, and harangued the electors upon the injustice of the coalition, and the expediency of supporting Colonel Tarleton, (afterwards General Sir Banastre Tarleton, Bart.)   Colonel Tarleton had previously declared himself

---

(1) Gore's General Advertiser of the 8th of February, 1798.

(2) Formerly member for Liverpool, as Mr. Richard Pennant, afterwards created a Peer of Ireland, on the 10th September, 1783, by the title of Lord Penrhyn.

(3) He had been twice elected on former occasions, when he was called Mr. Bamber Gascoyne, jun. in consequence of his father, Mr. Bamber Gascoyne, of Childwall, being still living.

(4) He was the brother of the late Mr. John Gregory Crump, solicitor.

a candidate, but, on hearing of the coalition, he had despaired 1790. of success, and had left the town.

Whether the liquor or the speech was the most powerful, may admit of some doubt, but certain it is that the freemen there assembled, determined to support Colonel Tarleton, and resist the coalition; and the result was, that Colonel Tarleton was sent for, came back amidst the acclamations of the populace, and was elected by a large majority; the numbers at the close of the poll being as follows :—

Colonel Tarleton	1269
Mr. Bamber Gascoyne	888
Lord Penrhyn	716
Mr. Thomas Townley Parker	4

1967 Freemen polled.

The great bulk of Colonel Tarleton's numbers of 1269 consisted of single votes, or plumpers as they were called. He was chaired, according to the usual custom, through the town ; but, as far as respects Mr. Gascoyne, in consequence of his being unwell, that ceremony was done by proxy.

In September, 1790, a Musical Festival was held in Liverpool, and the following is a copy of the advertisement announcing it, and detailing the nature of the performances :

"FESTIVAL OF MUSIC,
at Liverpool, 1790.

Stewards.
Lord Grey de Wilton.
Hon. Thomas Fitzmaurice.
Sir Richard Brooke, Bart.
Sir George Warren, K.B.
Colonel Tarleton.
John Blackburne, Esq.
Bamber Gascoyne, jun. Esq.

On the Morning of Tuesday, the 14th September, and of the three succeeding Days, will be performed,
In St. Peter's Church,
The following celebrated Compositions of Handel, viz.
On Tuesday Morning,
The Sacred Oratorio of the MESSIAH.
On Wednesday Morning,
A Selection of SACRED MUSIC.

1790.

On Thursday Morning,
The Sacred Oratorio of REDEMPTION.
Compiled by Dr. Arnold, from those great and favorite
Works of Handel, that were performed at his Commemoration
in Westminster Abbey, and in the Pantheon.
And, on Friday Morning,
A Second Selection of SACRED MUSIC.
Also, on the Evenings of *Wednesday and Friday,* will be performed,
In the Music Hall,
TWO GRAND MISCELLANEOUS CONCERTS;
in the first of which will be introduced, a Part of
ALEXANDER'S FEAST,
and the PASSIONS, from Solomon.

The Band will be more numerous than on any former occasion.
PRINCIPAL VOCAL PERFORMERS:
Mr. Harrison, Mr. Meredith,
Miss Cantelo, Mrs. Shepley,
and Mrs. Billington.
PRINCIPAL INSTRUMENTAL PERFORMERS.
Messrs. Cramer, Cervetto, Parke,
Wilton, Billington, Ashley, Mountain, Haigh,
Cramer, jun. Clarke, Sarjeant, Cantelo, &c. &c. &c.
The Organ by Mr. Wainwright,
And the Double Drums by Mr. J. Ashley.

Subscription to the Six Performances, £1 11s 6d. (Tickets transferable.)
Single Tickets to the Oratorios and Selections of Sacred Music, 7s. To the
Miscellaneous Concerts, 10s 6d.
Assemblies at the Exchange on Tuesday and Thursday Evenings;
And an Ordinary at the Hotel every Day.
Books will be open to receive subscriptions at the usual Places.
₊ The Committee request that such as wish to be accommodated with
Lodgings will apply to Mr. John Gore, Stationer, who will recommend good
Lodgings, on terms approved of by the Committee.
The Committee for conducting the ensuing Festival of Music, have the
pleasure of informing the Public, that they have engaged Mrs. Billington as
first Singer. Signora Storace being prevented, by a prior engagement at
Drury-lane, from attending this meeting, the Committee again applied to Mrs.
Billington, who has politely consented to give her assistance on the occasion."[1]

The musical festival took place accordingly; the oratorio
and sacred music were performed at St. Peter's Church, and
the concerts at the Music-hall, and the whole were well
attended, and gave great satisfaction to the company.[1]

Early in 1791, or thereabouts, for the exact time has
not been ascertained, the old Church Sunday and Daily
Charity Schools were established, in Leather-lane. The

---

(1) Gore's General Advertiser of the 26th of August and of 23rd of September, 1790.

institution has since been removed to Moorfields, where the 1790
schools are still carried on. They do not differ much from
other Sunday and daily schools, and are for the instruction
of boys and girls in a humble rank of life.

On the 17th of January, 1791, in pursuance of a requi- 1791.
sition subscribed by 1028 persons, who were free burgesses,
or represented to be free burgesses of Liverpool, a Common
Hall was held, the result of which was, that the trials at
Lancaster, and the other legal proceedings took place, which
have been fully mentioned in a former chapter.[1]

In this year, the Unitarian Chapel, on the eastward side
of Paradise-street and corner of School-lane, was opened
for public worship. The congregation came from the chapel
in Key-street, which was afterwards licensed as a place of
worship of the Church of England, and called St. Matthew's
Church, and which has been lately pulled down to make
room for the station of the Lancashire and Yorkshire and
East Lancashire Railways.   The first minister of the
Paradise-street Chapel was the Rev. John Yates: he
had previously officiated in Key-street, and he continued
to officiate at the Paradise-street Chapel until 1825, when
he retired, and was succeeded by the Rev. John Grundy.
It was disused in 1849, the congregation having erected
the new handsome stone edifice of the Gothic style, on
the east side of Hope-street, to which they then removed.
The Paradise-street Chapel was a handsome building of
brick, with stone ornaments: its form was octangular, with
a projecting front ornamented with stone semi-detached
columns of the Corinthian order, and it was separated from
Paradise-street by an open space with iron rails and
gates, and it had a light and elegant, but small cupola.
The building still remains, but is now called the Royal

---

(1) Chapter III, page 225 to 230.

1791. Colosseum, and is used for concerts, spectacles, and other public entertainments.

It should appear from the date of the following order of the Common Council, for a new lease of the ground on which the chapel was afterwards erected, that the ground must have been purchased by the congregation in 1788. At a Common Council held on the 3rd of December, 1788, it was ordered:—

" That the Society of the Protestant Dissenters, in Key-street, in this town, have a lease for three lives of their own naming, and twenty-one years, granted to them, of the piece of land, with the dwelling-houses, stables, and other buildings erected thereon, situate on the east side of Paradise-street, and running from thence, backwards, along School-lane, up to Manesty's-lane ; "

with a covenant on the part of the Corporation, for the perpetual renewal of the lease within six months after the death of each life :

" but that, in each of such leases, it shall be expressly inserted, that the same is granted for the purpose of a Protestant Dissenting Meeting-house, and that whenever the building to be erected on the aforesaid ground shall cease to be applied to that use, the lease of the said premises shall wholly determine and be void." [1]

In 1791, the School for the Blind was first established, on the east side of Commutation-row,[2] where two contiguous houses were rented for the purpose. The object of it was to instruct the indigent blind in various trades ; and to enable the scholars to learn some occupation or business, in order to maintain themselves ; such of them as

---

(1) Book of Records of the Corporation of 1788, vol. 12, page 571 and 575.

(2) The Row was then remarkable for each of the houses in it, having one large window on the ground floor, built of a particular uniform size, the object being to avoid the tax on two windows ; and having been built prior to 1785, the act imposing a tax upon large windows, did not then make them liable to the additional duty, payable on windows of that description. They are all or nearly all now altered, and made into shop-windows.

have a taste for it are instructed in music and singing, 1791. or prepared for the situation of organists. The establishment was removed to London-road, in 1800, and again to Hardman-street, in 1851. Four persons have been respectively named[1] as having been the first to suggest this institution. The Rev. Henry Dennett was said to have been one of them, and he certainly was an early and active promoter of it. It is said that the first idea of it was suggested to him by Henry Arnold, of Ormskirk, a blind lad, who was afterwards admitted into the school. Another person, who has been so named, was Mr. John Christie, who lost his sight at nineteen years of age. It is also stated by the Rev. Dr. Shepherd, in his account of the life and poetical works of Mr. Edward Rushton, (the father of Mr. Edward Rushton, the late worthy and talented Stipendiary Magistrate of Liverpool,) who laboured under all but a deprivation of sight, that Mr. Edward Rushton was the person to whom the merit of the original suggestion is due. Mr. Pudsey Dawson also devoted much time and gave his active services on its formation.

The old Meeting-house, in Hackins-hey, of the Society of Friends, not being sufficiently large for their increased numbers, and the cemetery attached to it having become nearly filled, it became necessary to provide more extensive and commodious accommodations; and accordingly the society purchased a piece of land in Hunter-street, in 1788, and ever since that period, all or nearly all of the Liverpool interments of the Quakers have been in the cemetery formed upon that piece of land. Their present Meeting-house, in Hunter-street, was also erected upon it, and was opened on the 2nd of October, 1791.[2] It has

---

(1) Smithers' Liverpool, page 240.

(2) The first conveyance of the old Meeting-house, in Hackins-hey, belonging to

1791. been the only place of worship in Liverpool used by the Quakers ever since that date.

1792.   In the year 1792, the growing wealth and prosperity of Liverpool, caused its merchants to consider that they were possessed of sufficient capital, and were in other respects competent to carry on a trade to the East Indies, with advantage. A public meeting of the merchants and inhabitants was accordingly held[1] in the Exchange, at which Mr. Clayton Tarleton was the chairman, and resolutions in furtherance of their objects and wishes were passed. A committee was also appointed consisting of—

The Mayor of Liverpool.

Nicholas Ashton	Thomas Earle	William Rathbone
John Dawson	Willis Earle	Francis Trench
William Smythe	William Earle	Thomas Hodgson
Jonas Bold	Edward Rogers	Thomas Hodgson, jun.

A subscription for defraying the expenses was resolved to be opened, and Messrs. Charles Caldwell and Co. bankers, were appointed treasurers.[1]

A correspondence was entered into by the committee with other committees or firms, in various trading towns, to which it was thought that the monopoly of the East India Company, by charter, was injurious; but in a short time afterwards, in consequence of an uncommon degree of agitation prevailing at home, the prospect of an immediate war with France, the general distress of the com-

---

the Society of Friends, was in the year 1711, and in the deed of conveyance, the edifice is called "The Meeting-house." The Cemetery, adjoining to it, was added in 1752, and, in the deed relating to it, it is declared to be "for a burial Ground for the people called Quakers, belonging to Liverpool Meeting." From the wording of the former deed it seems clear that the Meeting-house had been erected and used prior to 1711, (indeed it is said that it was first used in 1709,) but it has not been found practicable to learn on what terms the Society of Friends occupied the building as a place of worship prior to 1711. The above information has been kindly communicated by Mr. Isaac Hadwen and Mr. Joseph Malcomson.

(1) Aikin's Description of the Country from Thirty to Forty Miles round Manchester, page 608.

mercial world, and the numerous bankruptcies which 1792. took place, of which Liverpool had its share, the minds of men became occupied with other matters, the subject was allowed to drop, and was not again seriously entered upon until many years afterwards.

In this year, the Hunter-street Free Schools (Sunday and Daily Schools), connected with the Established Church, were built by Mr. Stephen Waterworth, sugar refiner, and supported by voluntary subscription until 1803, when his sister, Frances Waterworth, died and endowed them with the sum of £4000, to educate 160 boys in reading, writing, and accounts, and 120 girls, in reading, writing, knitting, and sewing; making a total of 280 boys and girls in humble life.

In the same year, St. Stephen's Church, in Byrom-street, formerly, as already mentioned,[1] a chapel for a congregation of Baptists, was first licensed for divine service as a place of worship for the members of the Church of England.

In this year, the covered Fish-market, a building at the upper end of James-street, and on the north side of it, was erected, and was used for about thirty years. After the removal of the general market from Derby-square to St. John's-market, in 1822, this building ceased to be occupied as a fish market, but was for a short time used as a general market, and called St. George's market. The building, although but little notice has been taken of it, was a neat and handsome structure. Its dimensions were 90 feet by 50 at the west, and 45 feet at the east end, or front. The roof was supported by twenty-four Doric columns, resting upon a basis of rough stone work. The spaces between the columns were railed, and were in part closed with wooden shingles, and windows

---

(2) Chapter I, page 57.

D 2

1792. were afterwards placed in them to give light to the interior; but the principal light was derived from the roof, the middle compartment of which was elevated so as to admit of two ranges of windows. The cornice was surmounted by a balustrade; and over the entrance was a small but handsome dome, supporting a neat cupola, in which the fire alarm-bell was at one time placed. There were five entrances to this market, the principal at the east end, and by two archways, the angles of this end being squared off, and the front supported on five arches, the others in Moor-street.[1]

In the same year, Trinity Church on the east side of St. Anne-street, was consecrated, having been built by three private individuals, Mr. Isaac Hodgson, Mr. John Brown, and Mr. Henry Holt, under an Act of Parliament of the 32nd George the Third, chap. 76, "An Act for building a new Church or Chapel within the town and parish of Liverpool, in the county palatine of Lancaster." The act declares that the new church shall be a perpetual cure and benefice, and shall be called by the name of "the Church or Chapel of the Holy Trinity in Liverpool." The Rev. R. Formby was the first minister of it.

The Manesty-lane Charity Schools (Sunday and Daily Schools) for boys and girls were established in 1792, in a building behind and adjoining the Unitarian Chapel in Paradise-street, and supported by the members of its congregation. On the chapel being disused, in consequence of the erection of the present new edifice in Hope-street, on the 18th of October, 1849, the school-rooms in Manesty-lane were abandoned, and, in lieu of them, the present school-rooms, attached to the Hope-street Chapel, were first used in November, 1851.[2]

---

(1) Underhill's M.S. Account of Liverpool, page 110.

(2) In the interim between closing the Schools in Manesty-lane, and using those

In 1793, the Scotch Kirk, on the south side of Oldham- 1793.
street, the first place of worship in Liverpool for the Scotch
Presbyterians, was opened for public worship.   It is a plain
brick building, without the slightest pretension to beauty
or architectural merit.   Prior to its erection, the Scotch
Presbyterians, for want of a place of worship for persons of
their creed in Liverpool, were in the habit of attending the
Presbyterian or Unitarian Chapels, such as those in Key-
street, Benn's-gardens, Paradise-street, or Toxteth-park, and
some frequented the chapel of Independents in Renshaw-
street.   Several natives of Scotland formed themselves into
a society to raise the necessary funds for erecting a Scotch
Kirk, in Oldham-street, by means of shares, amongst whom
Mr. Gladstone, (afterwards Sir John Gladstone, Bart.) who
was at that time a merchant residing in Liverpool, took an
active part.   The Rev. William (afterwards Dr.) Kirkpatrick
was the first minister; he resided for many years at a small
house, which is now a shop, in Renshaw-street, the next
above the corner of Upper Newington.   He resigned his
charge, on account of a paralytic attack, in 1815.

The year 1793 was a season of great general commercial distress.   Vast numbers of mercantile houses, and many
provincial banks, in England, suspended payment, and
amongst others, the Liverpool Bank of Messrs. Charles
Caldwell and Co.   Every exertion was given by the Corporation and the merchants of the town to remove the alarm
which prevailed, and restore confidence; and a public meeting was held to take into consideration the steps which should
be adopted for that purpose, at which some valuable and
judicious resolutions were passed, with the object of restor-

---

attached to the present Chapel in Hope-street, temporary School-rooms were provided
in the counting-house formerly used by Messrs. Charles Tayleur, Sons and Company,
in Seel-street.

1793. ing public confidence.   The Corporation also applied to the Legislature and obtained an Act of Parliament of the 33rd George the Third, chap. 31, "An Act to enable the Common Council of the town of Liverpool, in the county of Lancaster, on behalf of the Corporation of the said town, to issue negotiable notes, for a limited time, and to a limited amount," which empowered them to issue local promissory notes (a Municipal Corporation, cannot legally do so, without the sanction of an act of parliament,) for the respective sums, of £50 and £100, with interest, and for the respective sums of £5 and £10, without interest; but not to exceed, in the whole, at any one time, the sum of £300,000, for the payment of which the Corporation property became pledged.

The following is a copy of a notice issued by the direction of the Common Council to the merchants and inhabitants of Liverpool, prior to issuing any of the promissory notes :—

" CORPORATION LOAN OFFICE.
" To the Merchants and Inhabitants of Liverpool.

GENTLEMEN,

The Committee for carrying into effect the Act lately passed for issuing Negotiable Notes by the Corporation, on laying before you the Rules and Regulations by which the Plan will be conducted, and the Terms on which Loans will be granted by the Common Council, beg leave to observe, that they have framed both, with a View to give every Accommodation to the Public, consistent with due Safety to the Corporation Estate.   This was indispensibly their Duty, and they flatter themselves their Endeavours to unite those Objects will be found effectual, and be viewed and received with Candour.

The Business of a Loan Office, on the Principles intended by the Act, is without a Parallel; and there being no Institution from which the Committee could derive Information to Aid their Deliberations, they do not suppose that the Rules and Regulations now laid before you, are the best possible; a little experience may point out their Defects, and those Defects will be remedied and removed as they are discovered.   The mode of attaining a Loan will be found unembarrassed, easy, and expeditious; the Terms are as moderate as the expences

which will unavoidably attend the Institution would permit, and fixed on **1793.**
that sure Basis which will protect the Corporation Estate from Injury.

It now rests with you to second the Endeavours of the Corporation.
The Inconveniences resulting from a Convulsion before unknown in the
Commercial History of this Country, all have been exposed to, all have,
in a greater or less Degree, experienced; the Remedy, in a considerable
Degree, is now within your power, and that is, by receiving the Notes
to be issued, in Discharge of all your simple contract Debts.

That you may inspire each other with Confidence in this respect,
it is recommended that you signify your Assent to do so, Publicly and
without Reserve: It has been suggested that this Intention will be
most easily collected by signing your Acquiescence at Mr. Gore's Shop,
near the Exchange.

The Notes will be ready to be issued in a few days, and Notice
will be given of the Day on which the Public Office will be opened in
the Exchange.

The Committee, and all persons employed under them, will be
bound to observe an inviolable Secrecy on all Applications to the Office
for Loans, or in any other respect.

By Order of the Committee,

Corporation Loan Office, }   JOHN COLQUITT, Secretary.[1]
Liverpool, 28th May, 1793."

The engraved form of one of the promissory notes,
which is preserved in the library of the Athenæum, at
Liverpool, is as follows :—

" No.   Liverpool,   179
Twelve months after date I promise to pay to   or
bearer One hundred pounds, with interest for the same after the rate
of   p Cent by the year.
For the Corporation of Liverpool

£ One Hundred
Ent^d."

The plan had the desired effect of restoring confidence;
it was not found requisite to issue more than a portion of the
notes authorized by the Act, and they were all eventually
paid by the Corporation.

---

(1) Copied from the original printed notice preserved in the Library of the
Athenæum, Liverpool. The Rules and Regulations to be observed in carrying into
effect the Act of Parliament are printed and subjoined to the above in the original.

1793.   Prior to obtaining the Act of Parliament the Corporation were obliged to exhibit a statement of their affairs to parliament, which was to the following tenor :—

"GENERAL ACCOUNT AND VALUATION OF THE ESTATE AND REVENUE BELONGING TO THE CORPORATION OF LIVERPOOL, TAKEN THE 21ST OF MARCH, 1793.(1)

INCOME FOR 1792.

	£.	s.	d.
Fines received for renewal of Leases	2,270	14	4
Ground rents received for 1792	1,027	1	10
Rents for buildings in possession, let to tenants at will	5,166	17	6
Rents for land in possession, let to ditto	1,349	1	0
Amount of town's duties	12,180	7	0
Graving docks	1,701	16	5
Anchorage	211	15	3
Small tolls called ingates and outgates	321	9	7
Weighing machine	143	4	0
Rents of seats in St. George's Church	268	11	0
Arrears of interest from the Parish of Liverpool	360	0	0
	£25,000	17	11

INTEREST AND ANNUITIES PAID IN 1792.

	£.	s.	d.
Annual interest upon the bond debts, principally at 4½ per cent. per annum	15,835	14	3
Annuities upon bond	2,109	12	10
	£17,945	7	1
Balance in favour of the Corporation	£9055	10	10
Valuation of the above articles, adding that of land not built on, and the strand of the River	1,044,776	0	0
Valuation of the debt	367,816	12	0
Balance in favour of the Corporation	676,959	8	0
Exclusive of a balance due from the Trustees of the Docks and of the Reversionary interest of certain lots of ground laid out for building, both together estimated at	60,000	0	0
Exclusive also of Public Buildings and ground appropriated to public purposes, valued at	85,000	0	0"
The last three sums show a nett amount of property of the Corporation at that period of	....£821,959	8	0

(1) Aiken's Description of the Country from Thirty to Forty Miles round Manchester, page 378.

In the spring of 1794, the Corporation completed some very considerable alterations and improvements in the public sea-water baths, on the west side of Bath-street, before mentioned.

The entrance was by a neat facade or screen, exhibiting rusticated doors, of which one on the northward led to the gentlemen's bath, and one on the southward to that of the ladies.

On entering the gentlemen's bath there was a passage which, by a private door, led to the open river, in which such as were inclined might conveniently bathe, there being a good flight of steps leading to the water; by these means a person might bathe at such height of the tide as he pleased. The private baths, to which access was obtained by descending a few stone steps, were rendered not only secure, but also private and eligible, to such as were disposed to bathe unseen; for which purpose there were six partitioned baths or closets, with doors, which might be fastened on the inside, by which a person might be concealed from any of the company in the public bath, with which it was connected by means of an aperture, through which bathers passed to the public bath, if so inclined; or, if disposed to be private, they might be perfectly so, by means of a screen, so contrived as to exclude all communication with the rest of the bathers. Those who were disposed for the public bath would find a large square resorvoir of water (33 feet by 30 feet) enclosed by high walls, which rendered it at once private and secure; these walls, imitating stone, gave a cool, neat appearance to the whole; the entrance to this large bath was by stone steps, which went to the bottom, and by which bathers might descend to what depth of water they pleased, which was marked for six, but was seldom raised above five feet. Under a sort of covered way or piazza were rooms, with

1794. fire-places, well matted, and furnished with chairs, tables, &c. which were dressing-rooms, and were very conveniently situated for that purpose. The ladies' bath being an exact counterpart of what has been already described, needs no explanation.[1]

In the same building the bather could also be accommodated with warm salt-water baths.

The building and baths were all destroyed about 1817, in making the excavation for the Prince's Dock.[2]

Besides the public baths, there were before the close of the last century, (and also during many years of the present century,) bathing machines in use on the North Shore, at a short distance from the town;[3] and it appears from a paragraph in one of the Liverpool newspapers of 1794,[3] that the bathing, and the attractions of the theatre, music meetings, and other amusements, were then expected to bring a great resort of company to the town, during the summer.

The following statement, which has been preserved, relative to the Parish Workhouse, in 1794, is interesting and curious :—

"STATE AND EMPLOYMENT OF PEOPLE IN THE WORKHOUSE, 25TH MARCH, 1794.

Governor	1	
Matron and Chamberlain ...	2	
House Servants	3	
Hall and Stair Cleaners	5	
Keeper of Lock and Servants	4	
Two Cooks and six Servants	8	
Two Salters and ten Washerwomen	12	
Milk Mistress and Porter ...	2	
Mistress and Kneaders of Bread		11
Nurses and Servants for Infants		6
Nurses for Lying-in Women, for Sick, Infirm, Venereal, Fever, and Lunatic Wards		14
Bread Cutter and Doctor's Assistant		2

(1) Underhill's M.S. Account of Liverpool, page 180.

(2) Some time before the close of the last century there was a Bath on the Shore of the Mersey at the lowest end of Parliament-street; but it consisted merely of a large vat, in a covered shed; and the water was pumped up into it at high water. It was called Dwerryhouse's Bath, after the proprietor of that name.

(3) Gore's General Advertiser, 29th May, 1794.

Brewer, Warehouseman, and Assistant	4	Yeomen of the Smithies......	2
Two Carters, two Swineherds	4	Spinners of Wool, Thread and Linen	59
One Coalman, ten Labourers	11	Knitters and Seamstresses ...	51
Bell-ringer, Clerk, and Messengers........................	5	Four Sawyers, seven Taylors	11
Gardener and Assistant, ten Pumpers	12	Cotton Pickers...................	266
Keeper of Lock's Family......	6	Ditto Spinners, &c.	42
Schoolmasters and Mistresses	4	Tambour Workers	45
Book-keepers	2		
Barber and Painter	2	Matron's Family	4
Bricklayers, Plasterers, and Blockmaker...................	5	Turnkey	1
Flax-dresser, Leather-cutter, and Glazier...................	3	Working People	663
Shoemakers	9	Lunatics, Idiots, Sick, Lame, Infirm, very old, very young	524
Boys—ditto	9		
Weavers...........................	3	In the House............1197	
Boys—Weavers	4		
Ropers and Knotters.........	9	Average number from 31st March, 1793 to 21st March, 1794............................1032	
Coffin-makers, Joiners, and Boys...........................	6	Ditto, 29th March, 1792 to March, 1793 826	
Boatbuilders	4		
Two Smiths, and Eighteen Boys, making Nails, *for Sale*, and own use.........	20	Average increase......206"[1]	

1794.

1795.

On Sunday, the 18th of January, 1795, about half-past four o'clock in the morning, a fire broke out in the Exchange, on the west side. It commenced in the floor adjoining the fire-place in the Council-room, and in the ceiling of the Loan-office underneath, which in a short time destroyed the whole of the roof, dome, furniture, and the interior of the edifice, except the rooms on the basement story, and the new building on the north side, which escaped. The exterior walls of the Exchange did not sustain any material damage. The fire spread with great rapidity, which was in part accounted for from the timbers in the dome and roof having been coated with rosin or turpentine, which was intended by the architect to preserve them from decay, but which contributed to the rapid spreading of the flames.

---

(1) Aikin's Description of the Country from Thirty to Forty Miles round Manchester, page 352.

E 2

1795.   From a report of Mr. Henry Brown, the Deputy Town-clerk, dated the 2nd of February, 1795, it however appeared that all the charters, council books, and the most important and principal portion of the title-deeds belonging to the Corporation, had, fortunately, been preserved from the fire. The Corporation Seal, and the books and papers belonging to the Treasurer's office, and to the Corporation Loan-office, also escaped destruction.

When the alarm of fire was given, Mr. Henry Brown was early at the scene of devastation, and was active in saving some valuable books and papers. Much praise was also due to Mr. James Holme, the father of the present Mayor, Mr. Samuel Holme, who forced his way, at great personal risk, through a window into the building, and, assisted by other persons, contrived to open some of the cases in the repository of the Corporation muniments, and notwithstanding the smoke and heat, saved many books and documents of importance.

The most remarkable thing connected with the fire is, that it might have been prevented by common precaution ; a warning, nearly two days before, having been given by an unusual smell and smoke issuing from between the grate and the fire-place in the Council-room; apparently indicating that some beam or woodwork had been improperly placed too near the fire-place, and that fire was smouldering there: this occurred during the time when there was a meeting of the Revenue Committee in the Council-room, on the afternoon of Friday, the 16th of January, and the smoke and smell became so great and offensive, as to oblige the members of the committee to quit the room, and retire to and transact their business in the Treasurer's office.[1] Although the members of the committee and also the

---

[1] Book of Records of the Corporation of 1795, vol. 13, page 87 to 95.

Exchange keeper were aware of the circumstance,[1] it seems **1795.** never to have occurred to any one, that it was expedient to have the grate taken down, and the suspicious appearances investigated. The edifice was soon restored, and its re-opening will be noticed afterwards.

In June, in this year, on the opening of the Ellesmere and Chester Canal, the first boat with passengers proceeded through it to Chester.

In April, 1795 the Queen's Dock was opened for the reception of vessels; and though the fact may not be to the credit of the magistrates or police, or to the orderly habits of the inhabitants of that period, a bull was baited[2] before the opening of the dock, in the excavation which formed its bed. This occurred immediately before the admission of the water into it; the circumstance has been before alluded to when treating of the sports and amusements of the inhabitants of Liverpool.[3] The Queen's Dock was constructed under the same powers with the King's Dock, and was completed at an expense of £35,000. It has since been considerably enlarged to the southward.

It was, and still is, a principal depôt for timber vessels, and for those from the Continent, viz : Prussian, Dutch, Swedish, and French.

The first vessel which entered it, was the American brig Baltimore, Captain Johnson, on the 17th of April. On the 6th of April, 1796, Mr. Thomas Naylor, the Mayor, and Mr. Arthur Onslow, the Collector of the Customs of Liverpool,

---

(1) Book of Records of the Corporation of 1795, vol. 13, page 87 to 95.

(2) The poor animal was kept in a stable (now altered and used for other purposes) then belonging to the coffee-house or tavern, at the lowest end of Parliament-street, and corner of Sefton-street, formerly called the South Shore Coffee-house, and now the Transatlantic Hotel, until the preparations for the barbarous amusement were completed.

(3) Chapter IV, page 267.

1795. attended by other principal officers of the Corporation and Customs, who were appointed by a commission for the purpose from the Court of Exchequer, met at the Queen's Dock, and measured and set out the quays of that dock as legal quays, for loading, unloading, examining, and despatching all kinds of goods.

In consequence of an attack made upon the King, by the rabble, and various missiles having been thrown at him, and a shot from an air-gun having broken the window of the state coach, on the 29th of October, 1795, whilst he was proceeding to the House of Lords to open Parliament, a loyal address from the Corporation of Liverpool, and also one from the inhabitants of the town, were presented on the 11th of November to the King, by Mr. Peter Baker, the Mayor, and Mr. Owen Salisbury Brereton, the Recorder.[1]

1796. At the commencement of 1796 the Ladies' Charity was instituted; two meetings having been previously held of its promoters, on the 18th and 24th of December, 1795, for the purpose of establishing it, at which Mr. Thomas Staniforth took the chair.[2] It is an admirable charitable institution for the relief of poor married women in childbed, at their own homes.

The general election of 1796 was remarkable in Liverpool from the uncommon circumstance of two brothers opposing each other. The candidates were Colonel Isaac Gascoyne, the brother of the late member Mr. Bamber Gascoyne, who, from some feelings of disgust, declined to become again a candidate; General (formerly Colonel) Tarleton; and Mr. John Tarleton, a Liverpool merchant,

---

(1) Gore's General Advertiser of 5th and 19th November, 1795.

(2) Gore's General Advertiser of 31st December, 1795.

the brother of General Tarleton. At the final close of 1796. the poll the numbers were :—

Colonel Gascoyne	672
General Tarleton......................	506
Mr. John Tarleton....................	317
Total Freemen polled...1195.	

Colonel (afterwards General) Gascoyne was, from a variety of circumstances, for a long series of years, remarkably fortunate as a candidate at the Liverpool elections; he having been returned a member in nine successive parliaments. Besides being returned to parliament for Liverpool, in 1796, he was also successful at the general elections of 1802, 1806, 1807, 1812, 1818, 1820, 1826, and 1830, but was defeated in 1831. It would be incorrect to pass over a person who was so long and so closely connected with the town, and who had been elected and sat for it in nine parliaments, without a little more notice. He entered the army early in life, but never saw very much military service ; however, he served in the campaign in Holland of 1799, and was there wounded in the heel, which, in after years, furnished a good subject for the squibs and songs of electioneering poets, and not a little merriment used to arise from their dwelling upon the circumstance of a British officer of rank being wounded in that part, which, as his opponents affected to think, seemed at all events as if he had not been facing the enemy. He was not a man of considerable talents, and was only a common-place orator, but he was generally allowed to be a zealous and active member, serviceable on parliamentary committees, and useful as a representative of the town. He certainly was not generally considered to be a man of good judgment, or knowledge of the world; and a remarkable instance of his want of those requisites once came to light, in the author's presence. The author, when young, was a supporter of

1796. General Gascoyne, and, on the occurrence of one of the elections, accompanied him and the late Mr. John Leigh,[1] in canvassing in a remote part of the town: and in the course of their canvass it became requisite to drive to a tavern where there were some voters, and on their entering it, one of the men assembled there, very coolly took a letter from his pocket, unfolded it, showed it to General Gascoyne, and then quietly replaced it in his pocket. It was evident that something had disconcerted the General; and afterwards, when the canvassing party had left the house, he told Mr. Leigh, that, in order to save himself trouble in answering applications from his constituents, respecting such matters as he could not comply with, he had got some letters printed, in which he stated that he regretted, that it was not in his power to effect what the applicant had requested, but that he hoped on some future occasion to be more fortunate. The General added, that " finding it gave offence," (and well it might,) he had discontinued the practice of using them; but that the man whom he had just encountered, made a point of producing to him at elections one of the offensive printed letters. Mr. Leigh was one of the most valuable, and influential supporters, perhaps without any exception the most valuable, and influential supporter whom General Gascoyne had, and, without whose aid, he could not have been re-elected so often. Mr. Leigh was a cool-headed, clever man, who was accustomed to let other people put themselves prominently forward, in such capacities as chairmen, deputy-chairmen, committee-men, &c. &c. at elections, whilst he quietly remained behind the scenes and pulled the wires which regulated their motions. He was also a gentleman of first-rate talents and information, and it may easily be

---

(1) The Father of Mr. John Shaw Leigh.

imagined that he was not quite pleased by the discovery, 1796. that a candidate whom he was supporting, had displayed to his constituents, so little judgment or knowledge of mankind.   It must, however, be evident, that General Gascoyne could not have been elected so many times, if he had not possessed a considerable degree of popularity in the town. His strength at the Liverpool elections arose from his being popular amongst many of the freemen, and having the support of the Corporation, as well as that of a considerable number of men of property, of professional men, and of many individuals of the leading old Liverpool families, besides a great number of the master tradesmen who had no inconsiderable proportion of the freemen in their employ.

On the 10th of December, 1796, the new and extensive Pottery (formerly the copper-works), which was afterwards called the Herculaneum Pottery, situated on the South Shore, near the town, was opened, and an entertainment given on the occasion to upwards of 60 persons employed in the manufactory.[1]   Most of its site is now occupied by a dock.

An express was received at Liverpool on the evening of 1797. Saturday, the 25th of February, 1797, with the intelligence that some French vessels of war had landed a large body of troops near Fishguard, in Wales, and had put to sea again, and that an attack might be expected to be immediately made by the enemy upon Liverpool. This was no idle rumour, because two frigates of 44 guns each, a corvette, and a lugger, had actually landed troops, of which the number could not then be ascertained, and the vessels having again put to sea, their destination was not known. The next morning (Sunday, the 26th) a meeting of the inhabitants was called by the Mayor, and active exertions were made

---

(1) Gore's General Advertiser of 15th of December, 1796.

1797. to repulse the enemy, in case of an attempt on the town or port. The Mayor was requested to apply to government for a reinforcement of troops, and for two ships of war of considerable force to be stationed in the Mersey. Volunteers were invited to come forward, and pilot-boats were ordered out to the westward, for the purpose of descrying the enemy, if any should appear on the coast. The Liverpool Yeomanry (light horse) placed themselves on active duty; a large number of men took up arms as a corps of Volunteer Infantry, offered their services and mustered on the same day under arms, at the fort, (and in the course of four days upwards of 1000 names were enrolled); to the credit of Mr. Nicholson, the eminent flute player, who resided in Liverpool, (the father of the late Mr. Nicholson, also highly celebrated for his admirable performance on the flute,) it should be recorded, that a difficulty being experienced in finding, on the spur of the moment, a man competent to play the fife, Mr. Nicholson kindly offered his services, and acted as fifer to the volunteers, on the first day: a suitable man, accustomed to play that instrument, was afterwards engaged, and relieved Mr. Nicholson from an office, which, at a period of emergency, he had not thought it derogatory to undertake.[1]

The officers of the navy and army having command here, as well as those who happened to be in town not upon any particular duty, very cheerfully and spiritedly offered their services. Several of the merchants, who had war-like

---

(1) In the course of the Spring the Volunteers of Liverpool consisted of one troop of Cavalry, commanded by Mr. Edward Falkner, besides Infantry, which at first, consisted of eight independent companies, commanded respectively by Mr. George Case, Mr. Jonas Bold, Mr. George Dunbar, Mr. Henry Blundell, Mr. Joseph Birch, Mr. Thomas Earle, Mr. Felix Doran, and Mr. George Goring. All of the men found their own arms, clothing, and accoutrements, and the cavalry found their own horses.— Gore's General Advertiser of the 23rd and 30th of March, 1797.

vessels, nearly equipped for sea, offered them as floating 1797.
batteries, to be placed at the entrance of the river, and
temporary batteries, of five and seven guns each, were
erected at commanding points on the river Mersey, with a
furnace to each, for the purpose of heating shot.[1]

The town and port were, in the course of one week,
put into a complete state of defence, for, in addition to
twenty guns, (32 and 18-pounders,) mounted on their
carriages in one day at the fort, there were, in the
course of the week, ten more 18-pounders mounted there,
and twenty-six of the same weight of metal placed on temporary batteries of wood, &c. erected upon the occasion, at
the commanding and projecting points of the river and dock
piers, making in the whole a strong line of fortification of
56 heavy guns, with 570 men, being well appointed and
manned, with ten and twelve men to a gun ; masters, mates,
and seamen, all volunteers.[2]

As it must be obvious to most men, that the near neighbourhood of an extensive depôt of gunpowder, exposed life
and property, the shipping, and the defenders of the town to
awful dangers, in case of a hostile attack, measures were
immediately adopted to remove the gunpowder from the
Magazines, in Cheshire, in small vessels, higher up the
river, so as to be beyond the chance of doing much injury.

---

(1) Gore's General Advertiser of 2nd of March, 1797.

(2) Ibid. of 9th of March, 1797. Besides other points where batteries were constructed, to act against the enemy's vessels if they should approach the town, a battery
was formed on the North Shore, on part of a field at a place called Hogo Nook, near
the Half-mile House. Although not expressly mentioned in the Records of the Corporation, we may fairly presume that orders were issued on that occasion (as occurred
in 1779,* when a visit from the enemy under the command of Paul Jones was expected)
for sinking the buoys on the coast, and extinguishing the light at the Light-house,
upon the appearance of the enemy, because those judicious and requisite measures
were too important to be overlooked : which seems corroborated by the following passage,
which appears in a Liverpool newspaper of the time : "The Committee have paid particular attention to the important circumstances of the Buoys, the Pilots, and the signals
upon the Light Houses."—Gore's General Advertiser of the 9th of March, 1797.

* Chapter V, page 366.

F 2

1797.   The meeting also unanimously elected a committee to conduct the arrangements for the defence of the town, consisting of

George Dunbar, *Mayor.*

Thomas Golightly	Thomas Staniforth	William Earle
John Sparling	Moses Benson	Nicholas Ashton
Henry Blundell	William Dickson	Edmund Rigby
Clayton Tarleton	George Case	Richard Walker
John Shaw	John Gregson	Edward Chaffers
Thomas Naylor	Admiral Smith	John Brown
Jonas Bold ⎱ *Bailiffs*	Captain Child	William Harper
Thos. Leyland ⎰	Captain Whyte	Daniel Backhouse
Joseph Birch	Major M'Bean	Major Sawbridge
Thomas Earle	Major Crowder	James Gregson
Pudsey Dawson	Joseph Brooks	Arthur Heywood
Edward Falkner	William Neilson	Thomas John Parke
Thomas Hinde, jun.	John Bolton	William Peatt Litt.
	Richard Statham	

The utmost unanimity and spirit prevailed amongst all ranks and descriptions of people ; each vying with the other to stand forward in the general cause ; and, when the volunteers, who had mustered in the fort, marched out of it under arms, on Sunday afternoon, the 26th, they were received by the populace with loud cheers ;[1] and there were indications amongst the journeymen ship-carpenters of Liverpool, the most muscular and powerful race of men in the world, that they were ready, if it had been deemed requisite to call upon them, to arm themselves with their own rude weapons, the axes and adzes used in ship-building. They voluntarily came forward and made an offer of their services and assistance against the enemy.[2]

Lieutenant John Cheyné, of the Royal Navy, in a spirited manner, offered himself as a volunteer to take the charge of a pilot-boat, to go out and watch the motions of the enemy, in case of his appearance near the port, and to arrange the signals. Lieutenant Cheyné unfortunately

---

(1) Communicated by one of the Volunteers who was under arms on that occasion.

(2) Gore's General Advertiser of 2nd of March, 1797.

died a few months afterwards; but in consequence of his 1797. meritorious services on this occasion, the Council ordered[1] a complimentary donation of fifty guineas to be paid to his widow, Mrs. Ann Cheyné, as a mark of respect to his memory. And it was also ordered, that his son, John Cheyné, who was born in Liverpool on the 8th of August, 1797, should be complimented with the freedom of the borough, when he should attain the age of twenty-one years.[2]

---

(1) At a Meeting of the 1st November, 1797. Book of Records of the Corporation for 1797, vol. 13, page 289.

(2) The following Statement of some of the proceedings on the occasion of the above-mentioned hostile descent and alarm are extracted from the Books of Record of the Corporation :—

"At a Common Council, held in the Council-room, in Brunswick-street, on
Wednesday, the first day of March, One thousand seven hundred and ninty-
seven, being the first Wednesday in the month, pursuant to ancient custom,
[Amongst other matters,]

"Upon the Mayor's Statement of his having received a letter on Saturday last, from Lieutenant-General Whyte, with an Account of a French Force, consisting of two forty-four Gun Frigates, a Corvette, and a Lugger, having appeared in Cardigan Bay, and landed about twelve hundred Troops, and the probability of their proceeding to this Port, and that he had used every exertion in his power, with the advice and assistance of the Navy and Army officers in Town, and the magistrates and merchants, immediately upon the spur of the occasion, to adopt such measures as were thought most advisable for putting the Town into the best possible state of Defence, and had called a general Meeting of the Inhabitants, upon Sunday, the twenty-sixth instant, which meeting had appointed the following Merchants and other Gentlemen a committee for that purpose, viz : "

[Here follows a list of the names which have been already given on page 420.]

"which Committee had proceeded (with the particular countenance of the Mayor, and as the proper ostensible person) to give and sign the orders for carrying their Resolutions into effect, to direct Pilot Boats to go out to the Westward for the purpose of descrying the enemy, if any should appear upon the coast, and making signals accordingly. And had also proceeded to give Directions for taking Possession of the Cannon and Ammunition at the Fort (two distinct Applications having been made by the Mayor so long ago as the fourteenth of January, and fourteenth of February last, to the Board of Ordnance, for its orders respecting the same, without any reply or Notice taken thereof,) and for the Removal of the Powder, from the Magazines in Cheshire, into Flats, to proceed with the same up the River above the Town. And also

1797.   The history of the landing of the French troops in Wales, is soon told.   In February, 1797, a corps of about 1400 men[1] was embarked by the government of the French Republic, at Brest, in two frigates, a corvette, and a lugger, which stood round the coast of England, and entering the Bristol channel about the 20th of February, anchored in the harbour of Ilfracombe, on the north of Devonshire, where

for the erecting and forming Batteries with the Guns belonging to the Corporation, at different Places upon the Dock Piers, and proper commanding Points of the River, and particularly in a Field or close of Land at Hogs Hey Nook, belonging to Thomas Plumbe, Esquire; and, in every other Particular, use all possible exertion which the time and circumstances would admit, for the safety and defence of the Town, its Docks, and Shipping.

" *Resolved and Ordered*,—That it is the unanimous Opinion of this Council that the Mayor shall, and he is hereby indemnified, and to be indemnified and kept harmless by and out of the Corporation Funds and Estate, from and Against all Losses, Costs, Charges, Damages, and Expenses, occasioned, or to be occasioned for or by reason of any of the steps and measures hereinbefore mentioned, and alluded to, which have been, or shall be adopted by the said Mayor, or by his order during the present alarming Crisis, for the safety and defence of the Town, its Docks, and Shipping."

[After some resolutions and orders relative to the Carriages for the Guns being put in order, and relative to obtaining the acquiescence of Mr. Plumbe, the owner, and Mr. Edward Lyon, the lessee of the field, on the North Shore, on part of which a Battery was to be constructed, and of the sub-tenant, which it is not considered necessary to copy here, the Resolutions proceeded as follows :—]

"*Also Resolved and Ordered*,—That the Mayor be desired to write to the first Lord of the Admiralty requesting that two Ships of War, of not less Force than forty-four Guns each, with proper Mooring chains to secure them from the Rapidity of the Tide in the River Mersey (but not to be considered as receiving ships) be immediately ordered to Liverpool for the safety and defence of the Town, its Docks, and Shipping.

"*Also Resolved and Ordered*,—That the Mayor be desired to continue and repeat, if he shall see necessary, in the name of the Council, the Application already made by him to his Grace the Duke of Portland, his Majesty's Principal Secretary of State for the Home department, for a further Reinforcement of Troops for the Defence of the Town, and the safe custody of the French Prisoners now confined in the new Gaol in

---

(1) Annual Register of 1797, vol. 39, page 88. Their numbers have been variously stated, but the despatch from Lord Milford, Lord Lieutenant of Pembrokeshire, in announcing their surrender, states their number to be 1400.—See Gentleman's Magazine of 1797, vol. 67, part 1, page 243. Lord Cawdor, in his despatch, says, that he had positive intelligence that they disembarked 1200 men.—Ibid.

they scuttled several merchantmen, and would, probably, 1797. have destroyed all the merchant vessels there, if they had not learnt that a body of troops was marching against them. This was the North Devon Regiment of Volunteers, commanded by Colonel Orchard.   The enemy then leaving Ilfracombe, stood over to the headland off St. David's, and came to an anchor in Fishguard bay, on the coast of Pembrokeshire.   Here the troops were disembarked, at

---

this Town : And for the removal of such Prisoners or some part of them from the said Gaol to one or more Places of safety in the interior part of the Country.

"*Also Resolved and Ordered,*—That the said Committee hereinbefore particularly mentioned, (appointed on Sunday, the twenty-sixth of February last, as the General Committee for the safety and defence of the Town, its Docks, and Shipping) be considered, and is hereby allowed and confirmed, as the Committee for that purpose, with full power for such committee, or any seven of them, (George Dunbar, Esquire, the present Mayor, being the Chairman, and any other Gentleman the Committee shall think proper to appoint as Deputy-Chairman, being always one,) to consider and adopt such measures as shall be thought most advisable for the purposes aforesaid, and particularly for raising the Money which hath been, or shall be incurred upon the present occasion : And also, the Propriety of applying to Parliament for an Indemnity from Government against such expenses."*

* Extracted from the Book of Records of the Corporation of 1797, vol. 13, page 246.

At a Meeting of the Common Council, on the 3rd of May, 1797, the Freedom of the Borough was voted to General Whyte, by the following resolution :—

"At a Common Council, held in the Council Chamber, in Brunswick-street, on Wednesday, the third day of May, One Thousand seven hundred and ninety-seven, being the first Wednesday in the Month, pursuant to Ancient Custom,
[Amongst other matters,]

"*Ordered,*—That the Freedom of this Borough be presented to Lieutenant-General Richard Whyte, late Commander of the North West District, resident at Chester, for his watchfulness and attention to the Welfare of the Town of Liverpool, at the time of the late alarm upon the Landing of the French Force, in Cardigan Bay, by sending the most early intelligence of that event to the Mayor, and, afterwards, coming over to Liverpool himself, to examine into the state and situation of the Fort and Batteries, and giving the necessary directions for putting the Town into the best possible State of defence ; and that the Mayor be desired to transmit Lieutenant-General Whyte a copy of this order."*

* Extracted from the Book of Records of the Corporation of 1797, vol. 13, page 252.

1797. Abevelen, in the parish of Llanwnda, about three miles west of the small town of Fishguard, but being totally unacquainted with the locality, their landing was attended with great difficulty, and they came on shore at a place full of rocks. The landing of the enemy is often stated to have been in Cardigan bay, from the contiguity of Fishguard to that bay. They did not land any field pieces, but brought a large quantity of gunpowder and ball, sufficient to load many (one account states seventy) carts; and on the 23rd, the vessels which had brought the troops got under weigh and left the coast.

The enemy's troops advanced a very short distance from the place where they had disembarked, but their landing, gave the Welshmen, a hardy race, proverbial for their loyalty, an opportunity of showing the spirit, courage, and patriotism of the gentlemen and peasantry of the principality. Great numbers of the latter assembled, armed with scythes and other rustic weapons, and some of them with musquets and fowling-pieces, and evinced their readiness to attack the enemy, even before the arrival of the British troops. In the course of the day, three thousand men were collected, of whom seven hundred were well-trained Cardigan Militia, with Lord Cawdor at their head. An ingenious device was adopted to induce the enemy to suppose that the British troops were more numerous than they really were : in several parts of Wales, the farmers' wives were accustomed to wear red cloaks, and it has been said that many of the women so clad, were posted on the hills at a distance, to induce the enemy to mistake them for military ; but a more probable version of the tale may be, that numbers of the red cloaks were purposely thrown over the clothes of the countrymen, and miners, who had joined Lord Cawdor, and when they were posted in the passes in the hills, it would give them, as seen in the distance, very much the appearance of a body 1797, of military.

It was said at the time, that the French expected to have been joined by many of the inhabitants,[1] which may account for the large quantity of ammunition brought on shore; but if so, they were wofully disappointed, as well they might. The French troops, being deserted by the vessels, their retreat by sea cut off, and in the presence of a force numerically superior, found no alternative but to surrender. Upon the night setting in, on the 23rd, a French officer came to Lord Cawdor with a letter from Tate, the French commander: a copy of which, and of Lord Cawdor's reply, have been preserved, as follows, viz:—

" Cardigan Bay, 5th of Ventose, 5th year of the Republic.

" Sir,—The circumstances under which the body of the French troops under my command were landed at this place, render it unnecessary to attempt any military operations, as they would tend only to bloodshed and pillage. The officers of the whole corps, have therefore,

---

(1) In the Gentleman's Magazine of February, 1798, vol. 68, page 163, is published, what purports to be an extract, from the official orders of General Hoche to Tate, the Commander of the French forces, previously to their landing in Wales. If it be genuine, it proves, because it distinctly states, that raising an insurrection in this country was contemplated by the enemy, and that may easily account for the landing of so large a quantity of ammunition. Besides which, the intended surprise and destruction by fire, of Bristol, are also directed in the orders, from which we may understand the reason why the enemy's vessels first appeared in the Bristol Channel. Even Chester and Liverpool, hazardous as the approaches to those ports may be to an enemy, were not passed over in the orders without notice. One of the objects of the expedition is stated in the orders to be, besides attempting to raise an insurrection in this country, to prepare and facilitate the way for a descent by distracting the attention of the English government. If the extract from the official orders be genuine, they reflect the greatest disgrace upon the memory of Hoche. The pillage, destruction of property, murders, and cruelties which appear to have been encouraged in those official orders, are so unsoldier like, that instead of being such as might be expected to be issued, by a general officer to a body of European soldiers, they rather resemble orders given by some barbarous Asiatic chieftain, to a horde of savages and robbers. They are, however, well worth reading, as giving information in what an inhuman and atrocious manner the enemy would then, if it had been practicable, have carried on war in this country.

1797. intimated their desire of entering into a negociation, upon principles of humanity, for a surrender. If you are influenced by similar considerations, you may signify the same by the bearer; and in the mean time hostilities shall cease.

Salute and respect,

To the Officer Commanding his
   Britannic Majesty's Troops."

TATE, Chief of Brigade.

" Fishguard, Feb. 23.

" Sir,—The superiority of the force under my command, which is hourly increasing, must prevent me treating upon any terms short of your surrendering your whole force prisoners of war. I enter fully into your wish of preventing an effusion of blood, which your speedy surrender can alone prevent; and which will entitle you to that consideration, it is ever the wish of British troops to shew an enemy, whose numbers are inferior.

My Major will deliver you this letter; and I shall expect your determination by 10 o'clock, by your officer, whom I have furnished with an escort that will conduct him to me without molestation.

CAWDOR.

To the Officer Commanding the
   French Troops."[1]

The French forces accordingly surrendered unconditionally, at two o'clock, on the 24th, about two days after their landing, and laid down their arms on Goodwick Sands, about a mile to the north-west of Fishguard. One half of them were picked veterans, but the other half were said to be galley slaves, and men taken out of prison, on condition of their engaging in this attempt;[2] and it was supposed that the French government was glad to get rid of them on those terms.

It is said that one life only was lost on this occasion. Some of the invaders soon commenced plundering the

---

(1) Gentleman's Magazine, 1797, vol. 67, part 1, page 243 and 244.

(2) Annual Register of 1797, vol. 39, page 89. In Gore's General Advertiser of the 9th of March, 1797, it is stated that "they had two Grenadier Companies; the men that composed them were remarkably stout, and the whole, in general, able men."

inhabitants; and one of the French ventured on a maraud- 1797. ing expedition into the farm-yard of a small farmer, and the honest Welshman, in a violent passion at the enemy's confused ideas on the subject of the law of property, struck him dead with a spade or hoe.[1]

Various motives, on the part of the French government, have been conjectured for the expedition. The most probable seems to be what was supposed, at the time, that the motive of that government was to ascertain the practicability of effecting a landing of troops in this country, notwithstanding the naval force which guarded its coasts, and whether an insurrection could be effected amongst the lower classes. In a trial of that importance, they might be willing to risk the small number of men that were sent to make it; besides which, as the French had designs against Ireland at that time, it may also have been intended as a feint to distract attention, and draw the British troops to a spot distant from the place of the intended operations. They might not, however, imagine that their forces would surrender immediately, and possibly hoped that they would occasion much mischief and con-fusion, and perplex the British government before they were subdued.

This remarkable event in our annals gives rise to another observation. It not unfrequently happens, that persons argue that it is impossible for a hostile army to invade this country. It is not necessary here to discuss the misery, alarm, injury to private credit and to public confidence, which even a partial or temporary occupation of a small spot upon the coast would inevitably produce; but it

---

(1) One account, however, states that there had been two Welshmen killed, and also, that several of the French had been destroyed in the act of plundering.— Gore's General Advertiser of the 9th of March, 1797.

1797. would be well for those persons to reflect upon the fact, that, in the author's life time, and before the use of steamships, the descent in February, 1797, by the enemy, upon the coast of Wales was safely accomplished, and that a body of French troops, under General Humbert, landed in safety at Killala Bay, in Ireland, on the 22nd of August, 1798, and, although not numerous, they succeeded in keeping the British troops at bay for a considerable time. It was only by the providential occurrence of a storm, which injured and dispersed the enemy's fleet under Admiral Bonvet, in 1796, that General Hoche, with 25,000 men, was prevented from effecting an invasion of Ireland. Nor were the voyages in those instances very short or easy, yet no vessels of war intercepted the enemy in either case, nor was any thing conclusive known of the movements of the latter until the respective landings had been effected. Those facts should convince the British nation and government that over-confidence amounts to folly, and that the surest way to prevent any hostile descent in this country, is to be always on the guard.

In this year, the Exchange (Town-hall), having had its interior re-built, and having been renovated after the fire of 1795, was re-opened on the 4th of June.

On the 18th of October, 1797, a severe contest occurred on the election of the Mayor for the ensuing year. Mr. Thomas Staniforth and Mr. Joseph Brooks were the candidates, and although keeping the poll open at such elections more than one day, has not frequently occurred at Liverpool, the poll was kept open on that occasion three days. The voting was as follows :—

	Mr. Staniforth.	Mr. Brooks.
First day	328	294
Second day	579	355
Third day	597	357

Majority in favour of Mr. Staniforth, 240.

In the same year, Christ Church, on the south side of 1797.
Hunter-street, was built by Mr. Houghton, and cost £22,000.
It is a brick edifice, and contains what is not common, both
a lower and upper gallery.

So many inconveniences were experienced by the subscribers to the News-room already mentioned, which was
then at the hotel (Bates') at the lowest end of Lord-street,
that it was considered advisable to endeavour to establish a
News-room elsewhere, combining also the advantage of a
Library. Dr. Rutter, Mr. Edward Rogers, and Mr. Thomas
Taylor, were the first to take steps towards establishing such
an institution; and they considering a piece of vacant ground
in Church-street an eligible site, and having obtained a plan
and elevation of the contemplated building, invited four
other gentlemen, viz:—Mr. Roscoe, Mr. Joshua Lace,
solicitor, Dr. Currie, and Mr. William Clarke, banker, to
meet them, at the Theatre Tavern, in Williamson-square,
on the 22nd of November, 1797, in order to take the
subject into consideration. All those gentlemen met there
accordingly, except Dr. Currie, who was prevented from
attending by professional engagements. The scheme was
approved of by the meeting, a prospectus was printed and
distributed, and, on the 27th of November, a public meeting
of the supporters of the measure was held, at which Dr.
Currie presided, and a committee was appointed to carry
the scheme into effect. Books were opened to receive the
names of subscribers, and in a very short time the number
proposed, 350, was filled up, which was, subsequently,
increased to 500, the present number.[1]

The result was, that, in 1798, the Athenæum, an edifice 1798.
with a front of stone, but without either portico, pillars, or

---

[1] From a communication by Dr. Rutter, given in the Appendix to Currie's
Life of Dr. Currie, page 485.

1798. pilasters, to relieve its sameness, was erected on the southward side of Church-street.   This was the first public News-room, distinct from a room in a hotel or tavern in Liverpool.   The Athenæum contains both a news-room and a library.   This institution has, ever since its formation, been a favourite resort for persons of the higher ranks of life, and is supplied with newspapers, reviews, magazines, pamphlets, and other periodical works.   The books in the library, which is over the news-room, do not circulate.   It contains a large and valuable collection of books, in the learned, foreign, and English languages, and now consists of about 21,500 volumes.   The rules for the government of the institution were arranged and drawn up by a committee, on the 2nd of November, 1798.

In August, 1798, Mr. John Palmer, a performer of considerable merit, was taken suddenly ill in the Liverpool Theatre, whilst acting in Kotzebue's play of "The Stranger," and died shortly afterwards.   This gave rise to a statement which has appeared in print in "Troughton's Liverpool," and in the Annals in "Gore's Directory," and was at one time generally believed, that he dropped down dead, immediately after uttering the words, "Yet there is another and a better world."[1]   Narrating the catastrophe, as if it had occurred in that manner, certainly made an interesting tale, (if it had been true,) but it has been publicly contradicted. In the notices to correspondents, in August and September, 1838, in the *Liverpool Mercury,* edited by the late Mr. Egerton Smith, it is distinctly mentioned that Mr. Palmer was not taken ill until one of the scenes succeeding that in which the sentence in question occurs.   It is also an important point that it is stated in the *Mercury* that the

---

(1) "The Stranger," Act I, scene 1st.   See Troughton's Liverpool, page 199 and 323.   The words are erroneously quoted in that work.

G.Jarman.

THE OLD THEATRE IN WILLIAMSON – SQUARE,

as it appeared when it was first opened.

writer of the paragraph contradicting the statement, was 1798. in the theatre at the time when Mr. Palmer was attacked by the illness of which he died.[1]

It is worthy of observation, that if Mr. John Palmer uttered those words at all in the play, he could not have been performing the character of " The Stranger " (Wald-bourg,) but must have been performing that of Tobias, who utters the words, " Yet there is another and a better world,"

---

(1) The following paragraphs, contradicting the above-mentioned account relative to the death of Mr. John Palmer, appeared in the *Liverpool Mercury* of the 31st of August and 21st September, 1838, and appear to be conclusive on the point; for every one who knew the strict veracity of the late Mr. Egerton Smith, the then editor, must be aware that he never would have inserted or sanctioned the insertion of those paragraphs in his newspaper, if they had not been perfectly correct :—

" ' There is another and a better world.'—A correspondent, who signs ' Dramaticus,' and who witnessed Mr. Vandenhoff's masterly personification of the Stranger, last week, enquires if it be true, as he has repeatedly heard asserted, that the celebrated John Palmer expired on the Liverpool stage, immediately after repeating the line, ' There is another and a better world.' We know that such is a pretty general impression, and Mr. Roscoe's pathetic verses on the subject of Palmer's death, may have tended to confirm the mistake. The writer of this paragraph was present at our Theatre, when the appalling catastrophe occurred, and he can assure ' Dramaticus,' that the fancied coincidence did not take place. Mr. Palmer died in one of the scenes succeeding that in which the sentence in question occurs."—*The Liverpool Mercury of 31st of August*, 1838.

" John Palmer's death.—In a recent number of the *Mercury*, in reply to the query of a correspondent, we corrected a mistake or misrepresentation respecting the death of Mr. John Palmer, on the Liverpool stage, whilst he was performing the character of the Stranger, in Kotzebue's play of that title, in the year 1798. The current story is, that he expired immediately after exclaiming, in the words of the author, ' There is another and a better world.' The entry in the Annals appended to Gore's Directory, appears to countenance this rumoured coincidence, It is as follows :—' 1798. Mr. John Palmer died on the stage after having given utterance to Kotzebue's memorable words, in the Stranger, ' There is another and a better world.' The alleged coincidence has been, perhaps, strengthened, by a passage in Mr. Roscoe's Monody on the deceased. With respect to the precise circumstances attending the death of Mr. Palmer, we have nothing to add to what we stated in our former note. Our correspondent wishes to know at what particular part of the performance Mr. Palmer died ? We cannot, at this distant period, recollect all the facts; but we repeat with perfect confidence, that the catastrophe did not happen in that scene where the expression which has been considered so singular a coincidence occurs."—*The Liverpool Mercury of 21st September*, 1838.

1798. very early after the commencement of the play, in the 1st scene of the 1st act.

He was interred in Walton Church-yard. A performance at the Liverpool Theatre, for the benefit of his family, took place on the 18th of August, 1798; the receipts of which, after defraying the funeral expenses, were £412; and an appropriate and pathetic address was spoken by Mr. Holman on the occasion.[1] The address was written by Mr. Roscoe.

On the 7th of November, 1798, an address of congratulation was ordered by the Common Council to be presented to the King, by the Recorder and Members for the borough, on the glorious victory obtained by Admiral Lord Nelson, over the French fleet at the mouth of the Nile; and it was accordingly presented on the 14th.

In 1798, the building in Grosvenor-street, formerly the Tennis Court, before mentioned, was converted into a place of worship, called All Saints' Church, by the Rev. Robert Banister, a clergyman of the Church of England, who officiated as the minister there from 1798 until a short time before his death in 1829. He was educated at Cambridge, and was afterwards Curate of Upholland Church, near Wigan; he then came to Liverpool, and was Curate at St. John's, St. Paul's, and St. Peter's Churches, successively. When Christ Church was built by Mr. Houghton, he intended Mr. Banister to officiate there; a difference, however, occurred between him, the then Bishop of Chester, and Mr. Houghton, which induced Mr. Banister to purchase the Tennis-court, and he opened it for Divine worship, as All Saints' Church; but in consequence of the difference with the Bishop it was not consecrated or licensed, whilst Mr. Banister officiated there, although he used the whole

---

(1) Troughton's Liverpool, page 199, (where the address is given,) and page 324.

of the Church of England service, including that of 1798,
baptism and of funerals. In 1832 it was licensed by
the Bishop of Chester, and the Rev. John Lyons officiated
at it for some years.[1] When Mr. Banister opened it, it
would hold 2600 persons.[2] In 1845 the building was sold
to the Roman Catholics, and is now used by them as one
of their places of worship, and dedicated to St. Joseph.

In this year a subscription list was opened in various
cities and towns for voluntary contributions for the defence
of the country, and for the raising of further supplies for the
government. At that period this country was engaged in a
war, of which, from the aggressive designs and implacable
feelings of the enemy, there seemed to be little chance of
a termination; a dangerous mutiny had recently existed in
the fleet; a rebellion had broken out in Ireland, and a hostile
invasion on a large scale was contemplated, and eventually, in part, attempted by the enemy in that country; the
national distress and public anxiety were very great; and
the £3 per Cent. Consols, the depression of which is a sure
index to the feelings of uneasiness in the public mind,
fell down to £48. Liverpool very liberally responded to
the scheme of a voluntary contribution or self-taxation, and
in a remarkably short time, upwards of £17,000 was subscribed and remitted; the contributions of persons of all
parties, opinions, and modes of thinking, who harmoni-
ously united in the time of danger.[3]

---

(1) Communicated by Mr. W. C. Fairclough, a gentleman who married the
daughter of the Rev. R. Banister.

(2) Troughton's Liverpool, page 384.

(3) The unanimous and harmonious feeling which prevailed in Liverpool on the
above subject, amongst contributors of all parties, will be apparent on a reference
to the Liverpool newspapers of the time, in which a list of their names has been
preserved. Amongst the contributors in the city of London, the house of Boyd,
Benfield and Company, merits notice; they subscribed the munificent sum of £3000,
with the promise of an annual contribution during the continuance of the war.—
Gentleman's Magazine for February, 1798, vol. 68, page 165.

1798.   A regiment of volunteers was raised in this year, in Liverpool; and on the 13th of May, the newly-enrolled regiment, upwards of 800 strong, mustered for examination and approval in Mosslake Fields.[1]

1799.   In 1799, (13th of June,) the Royal assent was given to the Bootle Water-works Act, of the 39th of George the Third, chap. 36, entitled, "An Act for better supplying the Town and Port of Liverpool with Water, from certain springs in the Township of Bootle, in the county Palatine of Lancaster." The act incorporated the company by the name and style of the "Company of Proprietors of the Liverpool Water-works."

This was only the revival of a very old scheme for that purpose; for as long ago as in 1709, an Act of the 8th of Queen Anne, chap. 25, was passed on the application of Sir Cleave More, or Moore, Bart. of the old family of More of Bank-hall, entitled, "An Act to enable the Corporation of Leverpoole to make a Grant to Sir Cleave Moore, Baronet, for liberty to bring fresh water into the said Town of Leverpoole."[2]

---

(1) Gore's General Advertiser of the 17th of May, 1798. The Author has been unable to discover whether the Regiment was distinct from the independent companies of Volunteers before mentioned,(*) which were raised in the Spring of 1797, or whether any of those companies combined to form the Regiment, or a portion of it. In Gore's General Advertiser of the 17th of May, 1798, Mr. George Case is mentioned as the Lieutenant-Colonel Commandant of the first battalion of Liverpool Independent Volunteers.   (*) Chapter V, page 480, (note 1.)

(2) The following is a copy of a grant or certificate, of an allotment of a two-thousandth share in the contemplated undertaking, by Sir Cleave More, or Moore, to Mr. Samuel Whitfild, of London, gentleman. The original is in the possession of Mr. Thomas Moore, of the family of Sir Cleave Moore, Baronet. It is printed, except as to names, &c. and is on parchment:—

"No. 179.   Lib: C: Fol: 90.

| [*Impressed with a Stamp duty of*] VI PENCE VI PENCE VI PENCE | Pursuant to an Act of Parliament in Octavo Annæ Reginæ for enabling Sir Cleave More, Bart: to furnish the Town of Liverpool with fresh water, from Springs within his Mannor of Bootle; and pursuant to a Settlement for that purpose made by him of |

In 1799, pipes for supplying the town with water were 1799.
laid down by the Bootle Water-works Company. The
pipes at first used by the company were of wood; iron
pipes not being then in common use for those purposes.

The powers of the Bootle Water-works Company were
enlarged in 1810 by an Act of the 50th of George the
Third, chap. 165, "An Act to alter, amend and enlarge the
powers of the Act of the 39th George the Third, chap. 36";
and again, in 1813, by an Act of the 53rd of George the
Third, chap. 122, "An Act for enlarging the powers of the
before-mentioned two Acts."

The districts supplied with water under these acts comprised Bootle, Kirkdale, Everton, West Derby, Walton-on-
the-Hill, and Liverpool. In 1847, both the Bootle Water-
works and the Liverpool and Harrington Water-works
ceased to be carried on by their respective companies, and
were transferred to the Corporation of Liverpool, under the
powers of an Act passed in the 10th and 11th of Victoria,
chap. 261.

---

his interest in the said Water-works, dated the 20th Day of August, Anno: Dom:
1720, enroll'd in the High Court of Chancery in Great Britain; and in consideration of Ten Pounds lawful money of Great Britain, paid by Samuel Whitfild, of London, Gentl[n] as the first of the five Payments of Ten Pounds each, in
the said Settlement mention'd; the said Sir Cleave More doth hereby (pursuant to the
same settlement) grant, bargain, and sell unto the said Samuel Whitfild, his Heirs
and assigns, (being owners or Possessors of these presents for the time being,) for ever,
One equal Two Thousandth Part (the whole in Two Thousand Equal Parts being
divided) of and in the interest in the said Water-works, and the Rents, Dividends,
and Profits thereof for ever, together with the additional Fund to be purchased with
the * Surplus Moneys, and annexed to the said Water-works as in | * This surplus
the same settlement is mention'd; Subject to the four subsequent | will be 6000 l.
Payments following, viz: Ten Pounds more on or before Lady-Day, 1721, Ten
Pounds more on or before Michaelmas-Day, 1721, Ten Pounds more on or before
Lady-Day, 1722, and Ten Pounds residue on or before Michaelmas-Day, 1722.

CLEAVE MORE.

Receiv'd the Ten Pounds } Sign'd by Sir Cleave in Presence of
first payment above-
mention'd.   E. POTT.
    H 2

1799.   In 1799, an Act of Parliament of the 39th of George the Third, chap. 59, was passed, for altering the powers of the Acts relating to the harbour of Liverpool, and for making two additional docks and piers, to the northward of George's Dock basin. In this act, the site of the intended docks is described as extending " from north to south, (videlicit) from the north side of George's Dock basin, northwardly, to the north boundary of the township of Liverpool." After a delay of many years, the Prince's Dock was the first dock which was constructed under the powers given by that act. The first stone was laid on the 17th of May, 1816, and the dock was opened on the 19th of July, 1821.

On the 4th of June, 1799, the colours were presented to the Royal Liverpool Regiment of Volunteers, commanded by Mr. Pudsey Dawson. It had been intended that the ceremony of presenting the colours should have taken place in the Mosslake Fields, and a stage had been erected, and accommodations provided there for that purpose, but the heavy rain, and the boisterous state of the weather during the day, caused an alteration in the arrangements, and the colours were presented at Mr. Dawson's house, in Rodney-street, by Mrs. Dawson, supported by the Mayor and General Nicolls, the general of the district. In the previous month of April the regiment (which had been raised some time previously) mustered upwards of 1000 strong, and received two brass field-pieces, which were ordered by the last annual vestry meeting of the parish, to be presented to the regiment.[1]

In September, in this year, a Musical Festival was held in Liverpool; the names of the stewards, and the nature of

---

(1) Gore's General Advertiser of the 2nd of May, and the 6th of June, 1799.

the performances, are given in the advertisement announcing 1799. it, from which the following is an extract :—

"FESTIVAL OF MUSIC AT LIVERPOOL.

Stewards.

The Right Hon. the Earl of Uxbridge.
The Right Hon. Lord Stanley.
The Right Hon. Lord Viscount Milsintoun.
Sir John Fleming Leicester, Bart.
Sir George Armitage, Bart.
Sir Edward Price Lloyd, Bart.
Colonel Gascoyne, M.P.
Colonel Patten, M.P.
John Blackburne, Esq. M.P.
Edward Wilbraham Bootle, Esq. M.P.
John Dent, Esq. M.P.
Henry Blundell, Esq. of Ince.

On the morning of Tuesday next, the 10th, Wednesday the 11th, and
Friday, the 13th of September, 1799,
Will be performed,
In St. Peter's Church,
The following celebrated Compositions of Sacred Music.

On Tuesday Morning,
The sacred Oratorio of REDEMPTION,
Compiled by Dr. Arnold, from those great and favorite works of Handel,
that were performed at his Commemoration,
in Westminster Abbey, and at the Pantheon.

On Wednesday Morning,
A Selection of SACRED MUSIC,
From Handel, Purcell, Boyce, Pergolisi, Leo, Graun, &c.

And on Friday Morning, the 13th,
The first and the third Acts of the
Sacred Oratorio of the MESSIAH,
With a Miscellaneous Act.

Also, in the Evenings of Tuesday and Friday,
Will be performed,
In the Music Hall,
Two Grand Miscellaneous CONCERTS,
Consisting of Overtures, Solo Concertos, and Songs,
By the Principal Performers,
With the addition of the most popular Glees, and other Compositions,
which have been introduced at Messrs. Harrison and Knyvet's Vocal
Concerts.

Principal Vocal Performers.
Madame Mara,
Miss Leake,   and   Miss Poole,
Mr. Harrison.   Mr. W. Knyvett,
Mr. Meredith,   Mr. Bartleman, &c.

Among the principal Instrumental Performers are Messrs. Yaniewicz,
Lindley, Dragonetti, Holmes, Nicholson, Harvey, Ware, Clarke, Watts,
Lindley, jun. Hime; Messrs. Athertons, Crathorne, Entwistle, Sudlow,

1799. Evans, Langhorne; Messrs. Humphreys, Erskine, Hughes, Surr, Beale, Tomlins, &c. The Organ by Mr. Wainwright. The Piano-Forte by Mr. Webbe; the Harp by Mr. Meyer, jun. and the Double Drums by Mr. J. Ashley.

Subscription, to the five performances, £2 2s, (Tickets transferable.) Single tickets, to any of the performances, 10s 6d."[1]

This Musical Festival was very well attended, and besides the vocal and instrumental performances, there was a public ball at the Athenæum, on the evening of Thursday, the 12th of September.[2]

In the same year, in consequence of the great prevalence of commercial distress, in Liverpool, an Act Parliament of the 39th and 40th of George the Third, chap. 5, was passed, enabling the government to issue Exchequer Bills, upon receiving security, for the relief of the merchants of Liverpool; a measure which was of great benefit to the town.

On the 20th of April, in this year, an important cause was decided, by the Court of Exchequer, relative to that portion of the revenue of the Corporation of Liverpool which arose from the Town's-dues. In consequence of a Charter of Henry the First, exempting the goods of the citizens of London from payment of tolls, dues, passage, &c. throughout all England, and parts of the sea, several Liverpool merchants became freemen of some of the London companies, in the expectation that as such, they would be exempt from the Liverpool Town's-dues, and this important point at last came before a legal tribunal for adjudication. On the 10th of April, 1799, a Trial at Bar took place before the Barons of the Court of Exchequer, in a cause between the Lord Mayor, Aldermen, and Commonalty of London, and the Mayor, Bailiffs, and Burgesses of Liverpool, respecting the

---

(1) Gore's General Advertiser of the 5th of September, 1799.

(2) Ibid. of the 12th and 19th of September, 1799.

exemptions claimed by the non-resident freemen of London. The leading counsel for the Corporation of London was Mr. Le Blanc (afterwards Mr. Justice Le Blanc), and the one for the Corporation of Liverpool was Mr. Serjeant Shepherd. The jury found by their verdict that the exemption of the citizens, by charters and customs, was good and valid, but that " it belongs exclusively to such as are resident freemen within the liberties, paying scot and bearing lot." Thus deciding that a merchant residing in Liverpool, though a freeman of London, is not exempt from payment of the Liverpool Town's-dues. The decision was said to have involved a question at that time of not less than £20,000 annually. For this important result the Corporation were greatly indebted to the talents, learning, and attention of Mr. Henry Brown, the Deputy Town-clerk, who has been more than once mentioned in the earlier part of this work.[1]

The following is a copy of a resolution of the Council on the result of the trial. At a Common Council, held on the 2nd of October, 1799 :—

" The Council, now Taking into Consideration the late favourable Issue in His Majesty's Court of Exchequer, of the very important Cause relating to the Town Duties belonging to this Corporation, and well knowing how much the success of that cause was promoted by the professional knowledge, laborious researches, and continued attentions of Mr. Henry Brown, a Member of this Council : And being also well aware of the great advantages derived from Mr. Brown's zeal and exertions upon several important former occasions, in defence of the Rights and Privileges of this Corporation,

Unanimously Resolved, —That the Thanks of this Council be given to Mr. Brown for such his services, and that he be presented with a Gold Snuff Box, having an appropriate Inscription, as a further mark of Approbation of his conduct, the same to be ordered and executed

---

[1] Introduction, page 24—Chapter III, page 225.

1799. under the directions of the select Finance Committee, paid for by the Treasurer, and allowed in his Accounts."[1]

Mr. Henry Brown's great talents, learning, and exertions were very valuable to the Corporation on various other occasions during many years.   At length an important office, that of Town-clerk of Liverpool, which was in the gift of the Corporation, became vacant; he was a candidate, and the Corporation rewarded him for his important services—by passing him over, and electing another person who possessed greater interest, but inferior attainments.[2]

---

(1) Book of Records of the Corporation of 1799, vol. 13, page 410.

(2) Mr. Brown was, as might naturally be expected, most indignant at the want of gratitude with which he had been treated by the Corporation.   Even after he had become an old man, he had an acute recollection of it; and on one occasion, the Author heard him say to the effect, that his services had been rewarded by "the gift of a Snuff Box, which was, *vox et nihil præterea.*"   A person who was present, and was fond of a joke, suggested an alteration in the expression, and that Mr. Brown had better have said, "*box et nihil præterea.*"

THE BOROUGH GAOL.

The following particulars relative to the Borough Gaol, in Great Howard-street, were not obtained, until after the principal portion of this Chapter had been printed.   They ought properly to have been introduced on page 379.

1784. The old Tower, in Water-street, having been found ill adapted to the purpose of a prison, and unfit for such an increasing Town as Liverpool, the Corporation came to the conclusion, to erect a new Gaol, in a different and more healthy and open situation, and Great Howard-street being then quite in the country, and without any intervening buildings between it and the estuary of the

Mersey, was fixed upon for the site of the new Gaol. The ground, or at least **1784.** a large part of the ground on which it stands, was purchased for the purpose in 1784, and the following entries are in the ledger of the Corporation for that year : —

" Dr.   New Gaol.

1784.

July 28, To Cash paid Joseph Jackson, purchase of land £735   0   0

Oct. 18, To   ditto,   Stephen Waterworth................   492   5   0

                                              _____

                                              £1227   5   0"(*)
                                              ==============

The erection of the Gaol appears to have been commenced in the Spring of 1785, and the first item in the ledger relative to the construction of it, is of the date of the 31st of May in that year.(†)

The Balance Ledger (which contains entries of payments made by the Corporation, in a great variety of accounts, and comprises a long period of years) has, under the head " Borough Gaol," an account of the various payments relative to it; the first of which is the before-mentioned item of £1227 5s, entered under the date of the 18th of October, 1784. But besides many large payments made for erecting the Gaol, the account evidently includes very considerable payments for subsequent alterations and improvements in it, and the dates extend far into the present century, and entries respecting it appear in various years from the 18th of October, 1784, to and including the 18th of October, 1812, amounting altogether down to that date, to the sum of £53,955 12s 5d.(‡)

There is reason to believe that several years elapsed after the purchase of the land, before the Goal was completed.(§)

_____

(*) Ledger 7 (No. 3) of the Corporation of 1784, page 308.

(†) Ledger 8 (No. 4) of the Corporation of 1785, page 160.

(‡) Balance Ledger of the Corporation, page 48.

(§) The Corporation did not appoint a Gaoler until many years after the erection of the Gaol. Possibly that may be accounted for, from the circumstance of its being at first used, for a considerable time, as a place of confinement for prisoners of war, and at that period it may have been altogether in the hands and under the control of the Government.

LIST OF

THE PRINCIPAL ACTS OF PARLIAMENT

RELATING TO LIVERPOOL AND ITS VICINITY,

FROM 1699 TO THE CLOSE OF THE PARLIAMENTARY SESSION OF 1853.

10 & 11 Wm. 3rd, c. 36...For building St. Peter's Church, and separating Liverpool from the Parish of Walton-on-the-Hill.

8 Anne, c. 12...The Old Dock, (1st Act.)

" ... c. 25...The Bootle Water Act, (1st.)

1 Geo. 1st, c. 21...St. George's Church.

3 ... c. 1...The Old Dock, (2nd Act.)

6 ... c. 28...The Douglas Navigation.

7 ... c. 10...The Weaver Navigation.

" ... c. 15...The Mersey and Irwell Navigation.

12 ... c. 21...The Road from Liverpool to Prescot.

7 Geo. 2nd, c. 28...The Weaver Navigation,—Extension to Nantwich.

10 ... c. 9...The Worsley-Brook Extension to Nantwich.

11 ... c. 32...For enlarging the time granted for making a Dock, (now the Canning Dock,) and building a Pier at Liverpool.

19 ... c. 19...The Road from Liverpool to Prescot and St. Helens.

21 ... c. 24...St. Thomas' Church, and Lighting, Watching, &c.

25 ... c. 43...The Court of Requests.

26 ... c. 65...The Road from Liverpool to Prescot and Warrington.

28 ... c. 8...The Sankey-Brook Navigation.

32 ... c. 2...The Duke of Bridgewater's Canal Act,—Salford to Worsley.

33 ... c. 2...The Duke of Bridgewater's Canal Act,—Worsley Mill to Manchester.

" ... c. 49...The Weaver Navigation Improvement.

2 Geo. 3rd, c. 11...The Duke of Bridgewater's Canal Act,—Longford Bridge to Halton.

" ... c. 56...The Sankey-Brook Navigation Improvement.

" ... c. 68...St. Paul's and St. John's Churches, &c. (1st Act.)

" ... c. 86...George's Dock.

6	Geo. 3rd,	c. 17...The Duke of Bridgewater's Canal Act,— Salemoor to Stockport.
"	...	c. 61...The Pilots' Regulation, (1st Act.)
"	...	c. 96...The Duke of Bridgewater's Canal Act,— Trent and Mersey.
"	...	c. 97...The Severn, Trent, and Mersey Communication.
7	...	c. 80...St. Paul's and St. John's Churches, (2nd Act.)
8	...	c. 51...The Wavertree Inclosure.
10	...	c. 102...The Trent and Mersey Navigation Amendment Act.
"	...	c. 114...The Leeds and Liverpool Canal.
11	...	c. 16...The Liverpool Theatre.
"	...	c. 91...The Road from Liverpool to Prescot.
"	...	c. 93...The Road from Liverpool to Preston.
12	...	c. 36...St. Ann's Church.
14	...	c. 94...St. James' Church.
15	...	c. 20...The Trent and Mersey Navigation Amendment Act.
16	...	c. 32...The Trent and Mersey Navigation Amendment Act.
19	...	c. 33...The Altcar, Sefton, &c. Drainage.
23	...	c. 33...The Trent and Mersey Navigation Amendment Act.
"	...	c. 47...The Leeds and Liverpool Canal,—Purchase of the Douglas Navigation.
25	...	c. 15...The King's and Queen's Docks.
26	...	c. 12...The Liverpool Improvement Act.
"	...	c. 15...The Rectors' Incomes.
"	...	c. 126...The Road from Liverpool to Preston.
27	...	c. 93...The Road from Woodside to Chester.
28	...	c. 13...Watching, Lighting, and Cleansing the Streets.
30	...	c. 65...The Leeds and Liverpool Canal,—varying the line.
32	...	c. 76...Trinity Church.
33	...	c. 31...To enable the Corporation to issue Negotiable Notes.
"	...	c. 91...For making a Canal from the river Severn, at Shrewsbury, to the Mersey,—the Ellesmere Canal.
34	...	c. 37...The Mersey and Irwell Navigation Incorporation Acts.
"	...	c. 94...The Leeds and Liverpool Canal,—varying the line, &c.
35	...	c. 44...The Duke of Bridgewater's Canal Act,—cut from the Worsley Canal to Pennington, near Leigh.
36	...	c. 71...Shrewsbury to the Mersey,—The Ellesmere Canal,—altering and varying the Act.
37	...	c. 36...Trent and Mersey Navigation,—additional powers.
"	...	c. 78...The Liverpool Pilots' Regulation, (2nd Act.)

I 2

37	Geo. 3rd,	c. 81...	The Trent and Mersey Navigation,—to extend several branches.
"	...	c. 94...	The Ditton Inclosure.
"	...	c. 158...	The Road from Liverpool to Prescot, Ashton, and Warrington,—enlarging the powers of the former Act.
38	...	c. 58...	Quarter Sessions for the county of Lancaster.
"	...	c. 72...	Defence of the Town of Liverpool.
39	...	c. 36...	The Bootle Water-works, (2nd Act.)
"	...	c. 59...	For making two additional Wet Docks, to the Northward of George's Dock Basin.
39 & 40	...	c. 5...	For the issue of Exchequer Bills, for the relief of the Merchants of Liverpool and Lancaster.
"	...	c. 33...	The Croston, Mawdsley, Rufford, Tarleton, &c. Drainage.
"	...	c. 53...	The Hale and Halewood Inclosure.
"	...	c. 106...	Christ Church.
41	...	c. 70..	Shrewsbury to the Mersey,—The Ellesmere Canal Extension Act.
42	...	c. 20...	Shrewsbury to the Mersey,—The Ellesmere Canal Amendment Act.
"	...	c. 25...	The Trent and Mersey Navigation, Amendment Act.
"	...	c. 71...	The Liverpool Exchange.
"	...	c. 82...	The Road from Liverpool to Prescot, Ashton, and Warrington Amendment Act.
43	...	c. 93...	The Road from Woodside to Chester,—altering the powers of the Act.
45	...	c. 60...	The Childwall and Woolton Inclosure.
"	...	c. 62...	Improving the passage between Liverpool and the Rock Ferry.
47	...	c. 82...	The Weaver Navigation.
49	...	c. 73...	The Trent and Mersey Navigation.
"	...	c. 103...	The Liscard Inclosure.
50	...	c. 57...	The Turnpike Road from Liverpool to Preston.
"	...	c. 165...	The Bootle Water-works, (3rd Act.)
51	...	c. 143...	Improvement of the Port and Town,—the Brunswick Dock,—filling-up the Old Dock.
52	...	c. 6...	The Crosby Marsh Inclosure.
53	...	c. 114...	St. George's Church, Everton.
"	...	c. 122...	Bootle Water-works, (4th Act.)
"	...	c. 151...	The Aughton Inclosure.
"	...	c. 156...	To authorise the Advance of Money for carrying into effect the Acts for the Improvement of the Port and Town of Liverpool, and to amend the Acts.
54	...	c. 87...	The Wallasey and West Kirby Enclosure.
"	...	c. 111...	St. Michael's Church, Pitt-street.
"	...	c. 192...	As to appointing a Curate to St. Mary's Church, Edge-hill.
55	...	c. 70...	St. Michael's Church, Toxteth-park.
56	...	c. 65...	St. Mark's Church.
58	...	c. 66...	The Coal Gas Company.

59	Geo. 3rd,	c.	9...Regulating the Markets of Liverpool.—Tolls called Ingates and Outgates.
"	...	c.	30...Amendment of the Dock Acts,—Extension of the powers.—Anglesea Light.
"	...	c.	105...The Leeds and Liverpool Canal.
1	Geo. 4th,	c.	2...St. Philip's Church.
"	...	c.	13...For the further Improvement of the Town.
"	...	c.	15...The Road from Chester to Woodside.
1 & 2	...	c.	15...The Road from Liverpool to Prescot, Warrington, &c.
3	...	c.	19...St. Luke's Church, and St. Thomas' Church.
"	...	c.	77...Corporation Water-works Act, alteration of.
4	...	c.	39...Oil Gas Company.
"	...	c.	89...St. Michael's Church.—Also, as to the Interments in the Public Cemeteries.
5	...	c.	73...The Liverpool Pilots' Regulation, (3rd Act.)
6	...	c.	29...The Weaver Navigation.
"	...	c.	75...The Buildings Regulation Act.
"	...	c.	187...Further Improvement of the Port, Harbour, and Town.—Extension of the powers of the Dock Acts.
7	...	c.	49...The Liverpool and Manchester Railway.
"	...	c.	51...St. David's Church.
"	...	c.	52...St. James' Cemetery.
"	...	c.	57...Improvement Act.—Weighing Machines.—Fire Police.
7 & 8	...	c.	21...The Liverpool and Manchester Railway,—Enlarging powers.
"	...	c.	35...The Road from London to Holyhead, and London to Liverpool.
"	...	c.	36...The Liverpool and Harrington Water-works.
9	...	c.	7...The Liverpool and Manchester Railway,—to alter the line and enlarge the powers.
"	...	c.	39...Trustees of Mrs. Molyneux's Charities.
"	...	c.	55...To enable the Dock Trustees to raise money.
"	...	c.	75...The Road from London to Holyhead, and London to Liverpool.
"	...	c.	114...The Dock Acts,—Extending the powers.
10	...	c.	11...St. Martin's Church.
"	...	c.	15...The School for the Blind, Incorporation Act.
"	...	c.	16...Wallasey, &c.—Embankment.
"	...	c.	35...The Liverpool and Manchester Railway,—To alter the line and enlarge the powers.
"	...	c.	51...St. Catharine's Church, in Abercromby-square.
"	...	c.	70...The Weaver Navigation, Amendment.
11	...	c.	14...The Dock Acts,—Extension and Amendment Act.
"	...	c.	15...Paving and Sewerage—Boundaries.
"	...	c.	40...St. Augustine's Church.
"	...	c.	50...The Sankey-brook Navigation, Amendment Act.
"	...	c.	51...The Ellesmere and Chester Canal, Amendment Act.

1	Wm. 4th,	c.	21...Small Tenements Assessment.
"	...	c.	34...The Road from Liverpool to Preston.
"	...	c.	51...The Liverpool and Manchester Railway, Amendment Act.
"	...	c.	54...The Birmingham and Liverpool Junction Canal, Amendment Act.
"	...	c.	55...The Trent and Mersey Canal, Amendment Act.
1 & 2	...	c.	29...The Road from Liverpool to Prescot, Warrington, &c.
"	...	c.	49...St. Bridgett's Church.
2 & 3	...	c.	1...The Liverpool Marine Assurance Company.
"	...	c.	8...The New Cattle Market, at the Old Swan Village.
"	...	c.	14...The Custom-house and Revenue-buildings.
"	...	c.	46...The Liverpool and Manchester Railway, Amendment Act.
3 & 4	...	c.	34...The Grand Junction Railway.
"	...	c.	36...The London and Birmingham Railway.
"	...	c.	40...The Road — Chester, Neston, and Woodside Ferry.
"	...	c.	68...The Birkenhead Improvement Act.
4 & 5	...	c.	1...To empower the Oil Gas Company to produce Gas from Coal, &c.
"	...	c.	3...The St. Helens and Runcorn Gap Railway.
"	...	c.	6...To Repeal the Act of 1st Wm. IV, c. 21— Small Tenements Assessment Act.
"	...	c.	21...Enabling the Birmingham and Liverpool Junction Canal Company to raise further money.
"	...	c.	55...Enabling the Grand Junction Railway Company to extend their Line, &c.
"	...	c.	92...The Liverpool Court of Passage.
5 & 6	...	c.	8...Incorporating the Warrington and Newton Railway with the Grand Junction Railway.
"	...	c.	9...To enable the Grand Junction Railway to alter the Line.
"	...	c.	54...The Buildings Regulation Act.
"	...	c.	56...To enable the London and Birmingham Railway Company to extend and alter the Line.
6 & 7	...	c.	93...The Fire Police.
"	...	c.	119...The Liverpool Fire and Life Insurance Company.
"	...	c.	135...The Court of Passage, Amendment Act.
7	...	c.	27...The Liverpool and Manchester Railway Company,—Enlarging powers, and enabling the Company to raise more money.
7th Wm.& 1st Vict.		c.	107...The Chester and Birkenhead Railway.
"	...	c.	115...The Liverpool Improvement, Opening and widening Streets.
1	Vict.	c.	98...The Liverpool Improvement, Amendment Act.
1 & 2	...	c.	33...The Birkenhead Improvement, Amendment Act.
"	...	c.	98...For uniting the Medieties of the Rectory, &c.

1 & 2	Vict.	c.	99...The Court of Passage.
2 & 3	...	c.	33...St. Mark's, St. Luke's, and St. Michael's Churches.
"	...	c.	41...The Liverpool and Manchester Railway, Extension of the Line, &c.
"	...	c.	92...The Buildings Regulation Act.
3 & 4	...	c.	2...The Chester and Birkenhead Railway, Amendment Act.
"	...	c.	6...The Liverpool East India Warehouse Company.
"	...	c.	89...To enable the Common Council to raise money upon Bonds.
"	...	c.	120...The Herculaneum Docks at Liverpool.
"	...	c.	121...The Harrington Dock Company.
4 & 5	...	c.	9...The Winwick Rectory Division.
"	...	c.	28...The Coal Gas Company, Amendment Act.
"	...	c.	30...For enlarging the powers of the Dock Acts,—Transit Sheds, Warehouses, &c.
"	...	c.	37...As to completing a new Church at Birkenhead.
5 & 6	...	c.	5...The Birkenhead Commissioners,—Woodside Ferry.
"	...	c.	26...The Liverpool Paving and Sewerage, Amendment Act.
"	...	c.	30...For re-building Bridgewater House, and improving the Bridgewater Canal Act.
"	...	c.	33...The Ellesmere and Chester Canal, Amendment Act.
"	...	c.	44...The Health of the Inhabitants of Liverpool and Regulation of Buildings.
"	...	c.	52...To restrict the removal of certain Actions from the Borough Court.
"	...	c.	88...For the Administration of the Laws relating to the Poor of the Parish of Liverpool.
"	...	c.	105...The Toxteth-park Paving, Sewerage, &c. Act.
"	...	c.	106...For the Regulation of the Police of Liverpool.
"	...	c.	108...The Liverpool and Manchester Railway, Extension and Amendment Act.
"	...	c.	110...Preserving the Navigation of the Mersey.
6 & 7	...	c.	13...The Birkenhead Commissioners,—Extending the powers.
"	...	c.	24...Birkenhead Cemetery.
"	...	c.	75...Paving, Sewerage, and Watering of the Streets of Liverpool, and Extinguishing Fires.
"	...	c.	98...The Dock Acts, Amendment.
"	...	c.	109...The better protection of Property in Liverpool from Fire.
7 & 8	...	c.	13...The Gas and Coke Company (New).
"	...	c.	17...For enabling the Manchester and Birmingham Railway Company to vary the line to Macclesfield.
"	...	c.	32...The purchase of Monks' Ferry by the Birkenhead Commissioners.

7 & 8	Vict.	c. 51...	To alter and amend the Act of 6 & 7 Vict. chap. 109, Fire Protection.
"	...	c. 79...	The Birkenhead Dock Act.
"	...	c. 80...	For amending and extending the Liverpool Dock Acts.
8 & 9	...	c. 4...	The Birkenhead Dock Act.
"	...	c. 4...	Partition of William Molyneux's Estate, Amending the Act of 4 & 5 Wm. IV, c. 19.
"	...	c. 6...	The Wallasey Paving, Lighting, Watching, &c.
"	...	c. 9...	For the division of the Rectory of Winwick, to amend the Act of 4 Victoria.
"	...	c. 11...	The Liverpool Dock Acts, Amendment.
"	...	c. 26...	Church Act (Claughton), William Jackson's.
"	...	c. 27...	Ditto (ditto), William Potter's.
"	...	c. 29...	To enable the carrying into execution of an Agreement between the Duke of Bridgewater's Trustees and Lord Francis Egerton.
"	...	c. 60...	For constructing Docks, Walls, Warehouses, &c. in Birkenhead.
"	...	c. 99...	The Chester and Birkenhead Railway Company, Extension Act.
"	...	c. 117...	For uniting the Sankey Brook Navigation with the St. Helens and Runcorn Gap Railway.
"	...	c. 123...	The Liverpool and Manchester Railway, Extension Act.
"	...	c. 166...	The Liverpool, Wigan, Bolton and Bury Railway Act.
"	...	c. 198...	For consolidating the Bolton and Leigh, the Kenyon and Leigh Junction, and the Liverpool and Manchester and Grand Junction Railway Companies.
9 & 10	...	c. 5...	To enable the Proprietors of the Ellesmere and Chester Canal to raise further money.
"	...	c. 28...	For altering the Birkenhead, Claughton, &c. Improvement Act.
"	...	c. 35...	To amend the Acts for the Supply of Water to Liverpool, Harrington, and Toxteth-park, of 3 Geo. IV, c. 77, and 7 & 8 Geo. IV, c. 36.
"	...	c. 109...	For amending the Liverpool Dock Acts, and raising a further sum of money.
"	...	c. 120...	To amend the Liverpool Improvement Act of 1 Vict. c. 115.
"	...	c. 127...	For the improvement of the Sewerage and Drainage, and for the Sanatory regulation of Liverpool.
"	...	c. 146...	For constructing Docks, Walls, Warehouses, &c.—the Herculaneum Docks.
"	...	c. 183...	To enable the St. Helens Canal and Railway Company to make a Railway to Garston, with Branches and Docks at Garston.
"	...	c. 193...	To enable the Grand Junction Railway to make a Branch from Huyton to Warrington.

9 & 10 Vict. c. 204...To consolidate the London and Birmingham, Grand Junction, and Manchester and Birmingham Railway Companies.

" ... c. 261...The Grand Junction Railway,—Huyton, &c. Branches.

" ... c. 282...Liverpool and Bury and Manchester and Leeds Railway Incorporation.

" ... c. 312...The Liverpool and Bury Railway, Amendment Act.

10 & 11 ... c. 105...The Liverpool, Crosby and Southport Railway

" ... c. 187...For making a Railway from Parkgate to join the Chester and Birkenhead Railway at Bebbington.

" ... c. 228...Enlargement of the Stations at Liverpool and Crewe of the London and North-western Railway.

" ... c. 261...Authorizing the Corporation of Liverpool to purchase the Water Works.

" ... c. 264...For constructing an additional Dock at Birkenhead.

" ... c. 265...The Birkenhead Docks Act, Amendment.

" ... c. 268...To change the Name of the Liverpool Fire and Life Insurance Company.

" ... c. 294...To empower the London and North-western Railway to make Branches in Lancashire.

11 & 12 ... c. 9...The Birkenhead Dock Company, sale or lease of Land by.

" ... c. 10...The Liverpool Docks,—to build Warehouses, construct Wet Docks, &c.

" ... c. 12...To alter and amend the Duke of Bridgewater's Canal Act of the 8 & 9 Vict. c. 29.

" ... c. 38...The Gas Companies, Amalgamation.

" ... c. 42...To enable the Herculaneum Dock Company to sell or lease Lands.

" ... c. 144...To amend the Acts relating to the Birkenhead Commissioners' Docks—and transfer powers to Trustees.

12 & 13 ... c. 71...To amend the Act relating to the East Lancashire Railway.

13 & 14 ... c. 3...Giving further powers to the Birkenhead Improvement Commissioners for purchasing the Woodside Ferry, &c.

" ... c. 28...For supplying Childwall, &c. with Water.

" ... c. 80...The Liverpool Corporation Water-works—extension of time for the purchase of Land, &c.

" ... c. 95...Authorizing Alterations in the Line of the Liverpool, Crosby, &c. Railway.

" ... c. 99...To enable the Liverpool, Crosby, &c. Railway Company to sell or lease their Railway to the Lancashire and Yorkshire Railway Company.

13 & 13 Vict.	c. 100...To carry into effect arrangements made between the Commissioners of the Woods and Forests and the Trustees of the Birkenhead Docks, and for other purposes.
14 & 15 ...	c. 64...Altering the constitution of the Committee for the affairs of the Liverpool Dock Estate, authorizing the establishment of an Emigrants' Home, and amending the Dock Acts.
" ...	c. 67...Relative to the Gunpowder Magazines near Liverpool.
15 & 16 ...	c. 3..For establishing a Public Library, Museum, and Gallery of Arts at Liverpool, and making provision as to Specimens of Natural History, presented by the Earl of Derby.
" ...	c. 47...Amending the Acts of 9 & 10 Vict. c. 127, and 10 & 11 Vict. c. 261, relating to the Liverpool Corporation Water-works, authorizing Deviations, and the construction of Reservoirs.
" ...	c. 167...To consolidate and amend the Acts relating to the Birkenhead, Lancashire, and Cheshire Junction Railway.
16 & 17 ...	c. —...The Liverpool Court of Passage Procedure Act.
" ...	c. 107...The Customs Consolidation Act; [in which Liverpool is named as to the entry of goods on importation, in section 60; and as to the entry and clearance of goods for exportation, in section 125.]
" ...	c. ...The Birkenhead Dock Company,—to enable the Company to make a Railway for their Works, and for other purposes.—"The Birkenhead Dock Company's Act, 1853."
" ...	c. ...Authorising arrangements for the Completion of the Birkenhead Docks.
" ...	c. ...To enable the Warrington and Altrincham Junction Railway Company to make Deviations and Branches at Warrington, and to use certain Railways.
" ...	c. ...For enabling the London and North-western Railway Company to construct a Railway from Crewe to Shrewsbury, and for other purposes.
" ...	c. ...The Liverpool, Crosby and Southport Railway, Amendment Act, 1853.

CHAPTER VI.

LIGHTING, PAVING, SEWERAGE, WATCHING, SUPPLY OF WATER, HACKNEY COACHES, SEDAN CHAIRS, MODES OF TRAVELLING, SHIP-BUILDING, PRIVATEERING, BRAVERY OF THE SAILORS, AND PLACES OF RESIDENCE OF SOME OF THE INHABITANTS OF LIVERPOOL, BETWEEN THE COMMENCEMENT OF THE YEAR 1775 AND THAT OF 1800.   INCREASE OF THE REVENUE OF THE CORPORATION, EXTENT AND LIBERTIES OF THE TOWN, AT THE CLOSE OF THE EIGHTEENTH CENTURY.

IN 1775, the application of gas to the lighting of streets being unknown, the town was lighted with oil lamps, and those far asunder; a very inefficient and gloomy method of lighting it, but it was the best which was then known.   Many of the houses inhabited by persons of a superior grade in society had private lamps over or adjoining their doors; and flambeaux-extinguishers, of iron of a large size, for the extinguishing of torches and flambeaux, were generally appendages to private lamps, and were affixed to the lamp irons or to the wall near the door-posts: the Liverpool lamp-lighters extinguished their torches by means of them.   Within a very few years past there were a number of extinguishers of that description in Duke-street; now not one is left; but there is a pair of them affixed to some iron-work in front of a modern house on the east side of Chatham-street, and there is also a pair of them at the Welsh Baptist Chapel on the north side of Stanhope-street, both of which have evidently been brought from some older buildings.

During the last quarter of the eighteenth century, the paving of the town was in a very objectionable state. The pavement of the foot-walks consisted of pebble stones set on end; a method, perhaps, approved of by the brethren of St. Crispin, and by chiropodists, but by no means agree-

K 2

able to pedestrians; and there was not, until nearly the close of the 18th century, a street or a square, or even a continuous row of houses, in the town, which had a foot-walk entirely flagged, except Clayton-square and the lower end of Islington on the north side, called, *par excellence*, from that circumstance, "Islington Flags." In 1799, the owners or occupiers of houses and shops in Lord-street commenced flagging the foot-walks opposite them.[1] As it was not the custom to have streets macadamized, the middle of every street in Liverpool was paved in a rough and slovenly manner with large paving-stones.

The sewerage of the town was in a most deplorable state. Great numbers of the principal streets had not any sewers; and such as existed were very small and ill-constructed. In consequence of the lowness of the ground, and of the defective construction of the sewers in White-chapel and Paradise-street, those streets, as well as the lower ends of most of the streets which communicated with them, were very frequently inundated after thunder-storms and heavy rains, especially if they occurred during the time of high water, much to the injury of property, and causing great distress amongst the persons who resided there; and on one occasion, in 1789, the poor people of Whitechapel were so distressed by a flood of water, that the vacant wards of the Infirmary were fitted up as temporary residences for them.

The watching of the town was entrusted to a few watch-men, generally ignorant and inefficient,—frequently men who were advanced in life, and inactive. They used, whilst

---

(1) Gore's General Advertiser of the 11th of July, 1799. During several years prior to the close of the last, as well as after the commencement of the present century, the footwalks of Castle-street were paved either with white bricks of a large size, or white stone cut in a long square form, (the Author cannot recollect which of those materials were used) and those footwalks were first flagged about 1821.

walking their rounds, to proclaim, or "cry," as it was termed, the hour and weather, from time to time, during the night; a custom which was advantageous to house-breakers and thieves, because the voice of the watchman gave them notice to suspend their operations, and retire until his departure afforded them an opportunity of resuming them; and it had also the effect of rousing quiet people who were in bed, and disposed to sleep. When not employed in going their rounds, the watchmen used to remain in little unsightly watch-boxes, very like military sentry-boxes, where they often indulged in a quiet nap; and it has not unfrequently occurred, that riotously-disposed or half-intoxicated young men, returning from their nocturnal revels, have discovered watchmen in that state, and upset the watch-boxes, in such a manner as to cause it to fall with the door or entrance upon the ground, and so effectually to imprison them for a time, in the watch-boxes.

The supply of water was very defective in the last century; pipes were not laid by any water company until, as already mentioned, about the close of the century, when the Bootle Water Company and Corporation Water-works were established. The supply of water from Bootle, near Liverpool, had many years before been projected, and an Act of Parliament, of the 8th of Queen Anne, chap. 25, had been passed, to enable Sir Cleave More to supply Liverpool with water; but that undertaking had been allowed to remain dormant until about the close of the last century. The various Acts of Parliament which relate to the supply of water by the water companies, and the purchase of the powers and exclusive rights of those companies by the Corporation of Liverpool, have been noticed in a former chapter.[1]   As there were not any pipes laid to

---

[1] Chapter V, page 387, 388, 389, 434 and 435.

the houses and buildings, the water was carried in water-carts, each formed of a large cask placed on wheels, with the axle-tree, bottom frame, and shafts of a common cart, and drawn by one horse. With this contrivance, the house-keepers were daily supplied with water, procured from a spring on the south side of Copperas-hill, and from another, at a rather later date, on the east side of Berry-street, near Roscoe-lane. The water-carts were driven from house to house, and the water was supplied from the carts by women; and, defective as such an arrangement may now seem, it is considered to have been more efficacious in extinguishing fires before the flames had obtained the mastery, than the system which was afterwards pursued of relying upon a supply of water from pipes or mains; because the water-carts were left filled at night ready for use, and, (instead of the firemen being dependent upon the mains or pipes, and frequently having to wait for a supply of water from them,) as soon as an alarm of fire was given, numbers of water-carts, filled with water, were to be seen on the scene of danger almost as promptly as the fire-engines; additional rewards being paid for the arrival of the earliest water-carts. It is undeniable that it is a point of first-rate importance on such occasions, to have an adequate supply of water before the fire has got to a head; a few gallons on the outset being more useful than cisterns full afterwards.

In 1775, (as well as during all the concluding quarter of the 18th century,) hackney coaches were in use in Liverpool, although at the former date they were not numerous. Some were kept by Mrs. Lewis, in Frog-lane (now Whitechapel); William Griffith, in Fenwick-street; John Corner, in Fenwick-alley; John Evans, in Fenwick-street; and John Brown, in Church-street.[1] Soon after the widening

(1) Gore's Liverpool Directory of 1774.

of Castle-street, a stand for them was established in that street, near the Town-hall.

Sedan chairs were also very commonly used in Liverpool, and there was a regular stand of them at the south-east corner of the Town-hall in 1775, and for many years afterwards; but, eventually, they were in a great measure superseded by the more general use of hackney coaches, which in their turn now seem likely to be set aside in favour of cabs.

It has been already mentioned that in 1775 there was not any mail coach which ran in or out of Liverpool. There were then some stage coaches, in which persons travelled between different towns; but those conveyances were very limited in number, and about that period there were only one or two running out of Liverpool.[1] From there being so few public conveyances, persons of the higher and middle classes who did not keep carriages, usually travelled, at that date and for many years afterwards, on horseback or in post-chaises; and as has been already mentioned, some persons, and those not in the humblest rank of society travelled in waggons.[2] When travelling on horseback, they frequently carried their clothes and linen in saddle bags, and generally wore top boots. It was not unusual, however, for persons considerably above the common classes, to wear, when riding, what were called boot stockings, which were strong worsted hose, strapped under the feet, and reaching over the breeches and common stockings, half-way up the thighs: they may yet occasionally be seen worn by farmers travelling on horseback. As a proof that people in a respectable sphere of life adopted such a fashion about that period, the author has been informed by a

---

(1) Chapter II, page 166 to 175.

(2) Chapter II, page 166 to 175. See also the advertisement in Chapter II, page 175, respecting a waggon to and from the Nag's Head in College-lane, Liverpool, "with goods *and passengers* to and from London, or any part of the road."

person who had ridden so equipped from Liverpool to Lancaster, in August, 1778, that on arriving at the Royal Oak Inn at Garstang, where he was to sleep, he passed the evening in the public room with several persons of respectability, amongst whom was Thomas Stanley, Esq. M.P. who was one of the representatives for Lancashire in several parliaments, and was a cousin of the then Earl of Derby. Mr. Stanley was also going to Lancaster, and so different were the habits of that age from the present, that, as he had arranged to sleep at the inn, he considered it not any disparagement to himself, although one of the members for the county, to join the company in the public-room in the evening, instead of having a private sitting-room, and whilst there, to contribute his share of conversation and amusement, to while away time.

Gigs were then scarcely known in Liverpool; but a large, heavy vehicle of that nature, called a whiskey, was not unfrequently used in travelling; it was a singular looking carriage, upon two wheels, with shafts, and drawn by one horse; it would hold three moderately sized persons, and had a hood and leathern apron to protect them from the weather.

Curricles and phaetons do not appear to have been used in Liverpool much before the close of the last century, if so early.

A large trade in shipbuilding, of vessels of every description, was carried on at Liverpool during the American revolutionary and French war; and besides merchant ships, there were a considerable number of frigates and other vessels of war built for the government, by shipwrights at Liverpool.[1]　Several of the king's ships, built there, were of considerable size.

---

(1) The following list of vessels of war, built there between 1778 and 1785, is given in Smithers' Liverpool, page 190 :—

During the early part of the American revolutionary war,[1] it is believed that some, but not many privateers were fitted out at Liverpool. On the breaking out, however, of the war with France, in 1778, so energetic were the exertions of individuals in the equipment of private ships of war, that, as already noticed, between the end of August in that year, and of April in 1779, no less than 120 privateers sailed out of the port of Liverpool.[2] The largest of these vessels was a frigate, carrying thirty-nine pounders, that of the heaviest metal; one of sixteen eighteen-pounders;[3] the guns carried by the other vessels being principally six-pounders and nine-pounders.[3] This formidable armament proved a considerable annoyance to the hostile powers, and captured several French ships, from the East and West Indies, of great value. It is said that one of them, called the *Active*, Captain Powell, in one cruize, captured fourteen prizes.

The riotous behaviour of the crews of different privateers on coming into port was, in several instances, so serious as to demand the interference of the magistracy; insomuch that, towards the close of the year 1778, during the mayoralty

1778	The Hyæna ...... guns	24	1781	The Racehorse .... guns	16
1779	The Ulysses	44	——	The Success	32
1780	The Adamant	50	1782	The Grampus..........	58
——	The Dædalus..........	32	——	The Trusty............	50
——	The Nemeses..........	32	——	The Seraph	44
——	The Alligator..........	16	——	The Echo	16
1781	The Assistance	50	——	The Phaeton	38
——	The Arethusa	38	1783	The Charon	44
——	The Ceres	32	1784	The Andromeda........	32
——	The Ariel	16	1785	The Squirrel	24

(1) Thirteen of the Colonies of North America declared themselves independent of Great Britain, on the 4th of July, 1776; but hostilities had commenced in April, 1775, above a year before. This event was followed by the war with France, which commenced on the 6th of February, 1778; with Spain, on the 17th of April, 1780; and with Holland, on the 21st of December, 1780.

(2) Aikin's description of the Country from 30 to 40 miles round Manchester, page 371. See also supra, Chapter V, page 362.

(3) Troughton's Liverpool, page 161.

of Mr. William Pole, the following notice was published under his authority :—

" Great complaints having been made to me, as your chief magistrate, that of late, numbers of seamen and others, engaged and entered on board the several privateers, and letters of marque vessels, equipping at this port, to cruize against his Majesty's enemies, do frequently assemble themselves, and go armed, in a riotous and unlawful manner, through the town, and its environs, as well in the day as in the night time, without any commission or other officer being in company, or to command them, to the great annoyance of the inhabitants and others, and who have committed several outrages thereby against his Majesty's peace, and the laws of our country in particular, in forcibly breaking open, and rescuing several impressed seamen, out of the houses for the reception of them.   These are, therefore, in his Majesty's name, for the future to caution all such persons, assembling themselves, in such an unlawful manner and mode, and from committing such unlawful breaches of the peace, and violations of the laws, otherwise I shall be under the most disagreeable necessity of calling unto my assistance, for the preservation of the lives and property of his Majesty's peaceable subjects in this town, the military stationed here, of which I hereby require all such persons to take notice, at their peril."

This remonstrance had its proper effect in deterring the offenders from the continuation of their outrages.[1]

The undaunted courage and gallantry of the crews of both the privateers and armed merchant vessels of Liverpool, command our applause, and, on numerous occasions, excited the admiration of the enemy.

After the commencement of the war with France, in 1778, which was almost a natural consequence of the hostilities existing between this country and the States of North America, the seamen of Liverpool, both in privateers and merchantmen, nobly supported their national character for courage.   The year 1779 was memorable for the numerous instances of intrepidity which they displayed; and the following may well be selected from amongst many.   In the beginning of that year,

(1) Troughton's Liverpool, page 162 and 163.

Le Modeste, a French letter of marque, was taken by the *Dragon*, privateer, of Liverpool.   When *Le Modeste* struck, the sea ran so high that it was impracticable to board her, upon which she was ordered to steer towards Ireland, and carry a light, the *Dragon* keeping close on her quarter. When the weather became more moderate, an attempt was made to man the prize, in which all the boats belonging to each ship were stove.   The impatience of the *Dragon's* crew was now raised to the utmost pitch, and, regardless of all danger, five seamen stripped themselves, leaped into the sea, swam to the prize, and took possession.   This unparalleled instance of British courage so astonished the French, that they declared none but Englishmen would have thought of such an expedient, much less have carried it into effect.[1]

The particulars of an engagement between the armed ship *Nanny*, of Liverpool, and an American privateer, of superior force, are given in the following letter, from Captain Beynon, to his owners, dated Cadiz, June 2nd, 1779:—" On the 20th of May, off Cape Finisterre, saw a ship in chase of us.   Being resolved to know the weight of his metal, before I gave up your property, I prepared to make the best defence I could.   Between eight and nine o'clock he came alongside, with American colours, hailed, and told me to haul my colours down; I desired him to begin and blaze away, for I was determined to know his force before I gave up to him.   The engagement began, and lasted about two hours, our ships being close together, having only room to keep clear of each other; our guns told well on both sides; we were soon left destitute of rigging and sails; as I engaged him under my topsails and jib, we were sadly shattered below and aloft.   I got the *Nanny* before the wind, and fought an hour that way,—one pump

---

(1) Troughton's Liverpool, page 165 and 166.

going,—till we had upwards of seven feet water in the hold : I thought it then almost time to give up the battle, as our ship began to be water-logged. We were so close that I told him I had struck, and hauled my colours down. The privateer was in a sad shattered condition. By the time we were all overboard the *Nanny*, the water was up to the lower deck. When Captain Brown heard the number of men I had, he asked me what I meant by engaging him so long ; I told him as I was then his prisoner, I hoped he would not call me to any account for what I had done before the colours were hauled down. He said he approved of all I had done, and treated my officers and myself like gentlemen."[1]

Captain Seddon, of the *Molly*, of Liverpool, who was killed in an engagement, in September, 1779, with an American frigate, of superior force, also displayed the most undaunted courage :[2] the frigate carried twenty-two guns on deck, besides quarter-deck and forecastle guns :[3] she was eventually beaten off by the *Molly*.

In the French revolutionary war, which broke out in 1793, privateering was not carried on to so great an extent, comparatively, from Liverpool, as during the American revolutionary war. Many acts of bravery were, however, performed by the officers and crews of the merchants' ships which sailed out of Liverpool during the French revolutionary war, some instances of which will now be given.

In January, 1795, a French privateer, of six guns and seventy men, attempted to board the *Mary Ann*, Captain Bushell, from Jamaica, and ran on board her starboard quarter, where the former lay thirty minutes, but was

---

(1) Troughton's Liverpool, page 165 and 166.

(2) Ibid. page 166.

(3) Gore's General Advertiser of 24th September, 1779.

repulsed after a severe conflict. The slaughter on board the privateer was very great.

In November, 1795, the *Wilding*, Captain Pemberton, engaged a French privateer, of 18 guns, and full of men, for two hours, when the privateer blew up, and all on board perished. Captain Pemberton died of his wounds received in the action.

As a just tribute paid to his memory, a tablet was erected by Mr. Moses Benson, in St. James' Church: it bears the following inscription :—

> " To the Memory of
> Captain George Pemberton, Commander
> of the Ship *Wilding*, of Liverpool,
> who died on the 20th day of November, 1795, of the wounds
> He received in a most Gallant Action with a French Privateer,
> of superior Force, when bound on a Voyage to Jamaica,
> In which Captain Pemberton did Honor to the Character
> of a British Sailor.

> This Monument is erected by the order of Moses Benson,
> In testimony of the High respect he entertained
> for Captain Pemberton,
> During many years faithful services."

In November, 1796, the ship *Tarleton*, Captain Ratcliff Shimins, succeeded in beating off a French privateer, of 28 guns, (20 guns nine-pounders on her main-deck, and 8 guns on her quarter-deck,) after an action of three hours.

In March, 1797, the *Barton*, Captain Richard Hall, was attacked by a heavy Spanish privateer, of 16 guns (nine-pounders), and 120 men, which was repulsed after an action of twenty minutes; and the next morning, the ship *Agreeable* coming up, the privateer engaged both ships for an hour and forty minutes, and then sheered off, much shattered in her sails and rigging.

In June, 1797, the *Signora del Carma*, a Spanish privateer, of nine guns (nine-pounders), and a number of brass swivels, and 70 men, was brought in a prize, to the *Harlequin*, Captain Topping, which he had captured off Cape Finisterre, after a running fight of an hour and-a-half.

In July, 1797, the *Backhouse*, Captain Flanagan, beat off a French privateer, of 16 guns (six-pounders), and full of men, after an action of two hours and-a-half. Captain Flanagan had only 15 men on board, including officers, and when the action terminated, he had expended nearly all his ammunition.

In October, 1797, the *Backhouse*, Captain James Hunter, repulsed a French privateer, of 16 guns (twelve-pounders), after an engagement of three hours.

In November, 1797, a French privateer, of 16 heavy guns, was beaten off by the *Nereus*, Captain Williams, after an action of two hours.

Captain Peter M'Quie, who commanded the ship *Thomas*, of Liverpool, and whose melancholy fate has been noticed in a former chapter,[1] was as brave and respectable a man as ever commanded a vessel sailing out of Liverpool ; and he several times signalized himself in engagements with vessels of the enemy, of superior force : the *Thomas* carried sixteen guns, of heavy calibre, and sailed from Liverpool, under his command, with a crew of 78 men, and, besides being adapted for the regular trade in which she was employed, she was completely equipped as a privateer. On the 2nd of January, 1797, she encountered a French national corvette, mounting eighteen guns, 12-pounders, and four carronades, of very heavy metal, and between 200 and 300 men, and a severe engagement took place, the vessels being so close together that the enemy's bowsprit was entangled in the fore-shrouds of the *Thomas*,

---

(1) Chapter IV, page 236.

and so remained 47 minutes, whilst the enemy threw on board her, hand granades, stink pots, and other missiles, besides keeping up an incessant fire from the tops upon her deck.   After making some attempts to board, and after sustaining considerable injury, and much loss of life amongst her crew, the French vessel was beaten off.

This well-fought action was soon followed by another, which occurred off Monte Video, in April, in the same year, when the *Thomas* fought a Spanish vessel of war, full of troops, and mounting between thirty and forty guns.   The action commenced at eight in the morning, and lasted until half-past twelve, with scarcely any intermission, at no greater distance than musket or pistol shot.   The *Thomas* suffered considerably in her hull and rigging, and in the loss of several of her brave crew; and her quarter-deck at one time took fire, in consequence of an explosion of gunpowder; yet Captain M'Quie succeeded in preserving his vessel, and beating off the enemy's ship.[1]

In March, 1798, a large French schooner, of fourteen guns and 180 men, was beaten off by the *Abigail*, Captain Williams, after an action of seven hours.

Early in the same year, a French privateer brig, which mounted sixteen 9 and 6-pounders, full of men, (supposed not less than 100,) ran alongside the brig *Betsey and Susan*, Captain J. H. Morgan, and engaged her in close action within pistol shot, above two hours, when the privateer sheered off.

In 1700, the ship *Polly*, Captain John Ainsworth, fell in with a large Spanish brig, and captured her after a running engagement of four hours and-a-half, during which the *Polly* expended 160 cannon cartridges, and upwards of 400 musquet and musquetoon cartridges; and on the 16th of

---

(1) From papers in the possession of Mr. Peter Robinson M'Quie.

March, in the same year, the *Polly* was attacked and attempted to be boarded by a French schooner privateer, which was repulsed with considerable loss, it being supposed that the privateer had twenty men or upwards killed and wounded.

The places of residence of several of the Liverpool families will now be noticed; and the great changes which have taken place in the town, will appear very striking when the reader adverts to the situations in which some of the principal families resided, during some parts of the period between the commencement of the year 1775 and the termination of 1799; and it will be the most convenient course to mention the names of a few of the streets, squares, and places at present almost entirely occupied by shops, warehouses, manufactories, counting-houses, or taverns, in the heart of the town, and, in some instances, in what would now be considered most disagreeable situations for residences, where, however strange it may appear to the present generation, many persons of the first consideration and respectability,[1] some of whom were of considerable opulence, and of the old families of Liverpool, then resided.

The following is a list of some of the streets and squares, with the names of several of the principal inhabitants who resided in them:—

CASTLE-STREET.

Mr. James Gildart, (one of the family of the town-clerk of that name,) a Virginia merchant, mayor in 1750; he inhabited the large house on the east side, which was afterwards the shop of Messrs. Parker and Swann, subsequently made into two shops, one of which Mr. Lathbury, the chemist and

---

(1) Of course it is not pretended to give the exact year of the residence of each person, which would be impossible; but to state the fact, that at some time or other between the commencement of 1775 and the termination of 1799, each of the persons mentioned, resided in the street, square, or place indicated.

druggist, occupied not many years ago; they are now pulled down, and the site is part of the Commercial Bank; Mr. Gill Slater, a merchant; and Mr. Clarke, the father of Mr. James Clarke, formerly the recorder of Liverpool. Messrs. Heywood, Sons and Company, bankers,[1] had their bank there.

THE OLD CHURCH-YARD.

Mr. William Pole, mayor in 1778; he was, within the recollection of numbers who are now living, agent for several years to the commissioners of stamps; and Mr. Charles Goore, mayor, in 1754.

DRURY-LANE.

Mr. William Boats, one of the principal merchants of the town.

WATER-STREET.

Mr. John Parr, who had been mayor of Liverpool in 1773, and resided in Water-street when he served that office; Mr. Henry Blundell (afterwards Mr. Henry Blundell Hollinshead); he subsequently lived at the Canal basin; he was Mayor in 1791, 1793, and 1807; Mr. Jonathan Blundell; Mr. Hugh Hindley Leigh; Mr. Case, who succeeded the latter in the house which he had occupied; Mr. Jonathan Blackburne; Dr. Kennion; Mr. Thomas Tarleton, who has been mentioned in a former chapter,[2] (the brother of General Sir Banastre Tarleton, Baronet,) lived in the house (afterwards the King's Arms Inn, kept by Mr. Daniel Dale;[3] the site is now occupied by counting-houses), on the south side of the street, and at the north-east corner of Fenwick-

---

(1) At that time the street had not been widened; and foot-passengers had often, from its extreme narrowness in some places, to get upon the steps, in order to allow carriages to pass without risk to themselves.

(2) Chapter V, page 376. The street was comparatively very narrow when Mr. Thomas Tarleton lived in it, but it has been subsequently considerably widened.

(3) Mr. Thomas Tarleton must have left the house, and it must have been kept

street; Mr. Thomas Parke, a merchant, afterwards a banker, father of Mr. Baron Parke; and Mr. William Leece, a merchant; he resided at a house, now pulled down, on the north side of the street, and at the east side of Tower-garden, and the next above the old Tower. Many of the readers must recollect his house, which was remarkable from the circumstance of the large Gothic arch before noticed,[1] extending from it across Tower-garden to the east side of the Tower. The ancient Tower, which occupied the site between Tower-garden and Stringer's-alley (now called Prison-weint), was purchased by the Corporation, as has been before mentioned,[2] in 1775.

OLDHALL-STREET.

Mr. Edward Falkner, afterwards of Fairfield; he was high-sheriff of Lancashire, in 1788, and was related, by marriage, to General Sir Banastre Tarleton, Bart. by having married the General's sister, Miss Bridget Tarleton; Mr. Thomas Falkner; Mrs. Stanley, noticed before; Mr. Jonathan Brooks, the grandfather of the venerable Archdeacon Brooks; the Rev. Thomas Maddock, one of the rectors of Liverpool; and Mr. Edward Nicols, a merchant; he succeeded to the estate of the ancient family of Trafford, of Swithamley, in Staffordshire (mentioned in a subsequent part of this chapter), under the will of one of that family, to whom, by the female side, he was nearly related.[3]

---

by Mr. Daniel Dale as an inn and tavern prior to August, 1786, because an advertisement appears in a Liverpool newspaper of the 3rd of August, in that year, announcing that Mr. Dale had removed from George's Coffee-house "to that spacious mansion, lately occupied by Thomas Tarleton, Esq. in Water-street, now the King's Arms Inn and Tavern," and soliciting a continuance of the favours of the public.—*Gore's General Advertiser of 3rd August*, 1786.

(1) Chapter I, page 75.   (2) Chapter V, page 349.

(3) Some of his descendants in Staffordshire many years afterwards took the name of Trafford. He was also related, by marriage, to the family of Leigh, afterwards Trafford, of Oughtrington, in Cheshire.

THE OLD TOWER AND WATER STREET

as they appeared in the 18th Century.

G. Jarman sc.

LANCELOTS-HEY.

Mr. John Williamson, mayor in 1761; one of his daughters married General Gascoyne, who was for many years one of the representatives in parliament for Liverpool; and another married John Dent, Esq. who was, during several parliaments, member for Lancaster: both of the ladies were celebrated for their beauty. His house was standing not many years ago; it was a very handsome large brick mansion, and stood on the west side. Mr. Williamson afterwards built Roby-hall, and resided there; and the house in Lancelots-hey was then occupied by other persons in succession, one of whom was the late Rector Roughsedge. It is now pulled down, and warehouses are erected on its site.

SAINT PAUL'S-SQUARE.

Mr. Edward Chaffers, a merchant; and Mr. Ambrose Lace, a merchant, the father of the late Mr. Joshua Lace.

CHAPEL-STREET.

Mr. William Hesketh, a merchant; he was mayor of Liverpool in 1783; Mr. Laurence Spencer, formerly a merchant, afterwards deputy-customer of Liverpool, mayor in 1759; and Dr. Thomas Houlston, a physician of talents and considerable extent of practice; he was the author of several clever medical works, and was one of the founders of the Humane Society already mentioned, in the success of which he took a warm interest.

RIGBY-STREET.

The Rev. Robert Brereton, one of the rectors of Liverpool.

UNION-STREET.

Mr. Edmund Lyon, a merchant, the grandfather of the late Mr. Lyon, of Neston; Mr. Samuel Riley, a West India merchant; Mr. Edward Brock, a retired merchant; Mr. Thomas Booth, a merchant; Mr. Henry Newsham; and Mr. Atkinson.

CUMBERLAND-STREET.

Mr. Francis Gildart, town-clerk.

M 2

DALE-STREET.

Mr. John Leigh, afterwards of Sandhills.

PREESON'S-ROW.

Mr. Bryan Blundell, brother of Mr. Jonathan Blundell, before mentioned.

REDCROSS-STREET.

Mr. Jonas Bold, in a large house now pulled down, which recently stood at the lower end of the south side, communicating also with Strand-street, and which had a large court in front of it; he was mayor of Liverpool in 1802; Mr. Richard Downward; Messrs. John and Thomas Hodgson, merchants; Mr. Joseph Broster; and Mr. William Hamilton.

HARRINGTON-STREET.

Dr. Matthew Dobson, a physician of celebrity and extensive practice; he retired from Liverpool to Bath, where he resided at the time of his death, which occurred on the 25th of July, 1784; he was a fellow of the Royal Society; and several of the volumes of the transactions of that eminent Society contain some ingenious papers, written by him; he was also a member of the Philosophical Society at Bath, and was an occasional contributor to their transactions.

POOL-LANE, (now SOUTH CASTLE-STREET.)

Mr. William Crosbie, senior, mayor in 1776; Mr. William Crosbie, junior, mayor in 1779; Mr. Peter Rigby, mayor in 1774; and Mr. Francis Ingram, a merchant, who inhabited a large house, on the west side, at the corner of Litherland-alley, now converted into shops and counting-houses.

JOHN-STREET.

Mr. Richard Hughes, who was mayor of Liverpool in 1756; he was a proprietor of the copperas works, on Copperas-hill, from which it derived its name. Mr. Thomas Statham, the post-master, afterwards of Lord-street; and his brother, Mr. William Statham (father of Mr. Richard Statham, the town-clerk, and grandfather of Mr. William

Statham, afterwards also the town-clerk); the latter resided on the east side of the street, at the north corner of Mathew-street.

TEMPLE-COURT.

Mr. Joseph Fowden, a merchant of large extent of business, of the firm of Messrs. Fowden, Ker and Berry; he resided at the large house, now made into offices, at the corner of Temple-street, near the Fire Police Station, of which the doors and windows were intended to have some humble resemblance to the Gothic style. He retired from business to Cheadle, in Cheshire, and was buried at the Parish Church there. His former partner, Mr. Thomas Berry, afterwards lived in the same house in Temple-court.

RAINFORD-GARDENS.

Mr. William James, a merchant, (the grandfather of Mr. James, of Barrock-lodge); he afterwards removed to Clayton-square. His house in Rainford-gardens was subsequently occupied by Messrs. Aspinwall, Roscoe and Lace, solicitors; Mr. Roscoe,[1] one of the firm, was afterwards the well-known poet and historian of that name; and was once (in 1806) returned to parliament as one of the members for Liverpool : another of the firm was the late highly-respected and talented Mr. Joshua Lace, the senior of the legal profession in Liverpool. The house, which was a large and conspicuous brick one, stood exactly opposite to and looked down Button-street; after being occupied for various purposes, some of which were of a very disreputable nature, it was at last made into a warehouse, and still remains so.

LORD-STREET.

Mr. Thomas Golightly, who was mayor in 1772; Mr.

---

(1) It is remarkable that in Mr. William Bailey's Liverpool Directory of 1787, (which was kindly lent to the Author by Miss Leatham, of Liverpool,) although Mr. Roscoe's firm of Aspinwall, Roscoe and Lace is mentioned, yet his name and residence are not given; from which it may be inferred, that at that date he could not have been a housekeeper, or if so, that he resided beyond the limits of the town.

Thomas Statham, the post-master, previously of John-street; Mr. Edmund Rigby, the comptroller of customs; Mr. William Willock, a merchant; Mr. John Thompson, a merchant; and Mr. Roscoe; he resided in Lord-street during part of the time whilst he practised as a solicitor, and afterwards, as already mentioned, in Rainford-gardens.

MATHEW-STREET.

The Rev. Thomas Fishwick, chaplain of St. George's Church.

WHITECHAPEL.

Mr. Thomas Ratcliffe, a merchant, mentioned in a former chapter,[1] in the account of the riots of 1775.

LEIGH-STREET.

Mr. Charles Pole, a merchant, mayor in 1785.[2] He was the father of the late Mr. Charles Pole, of Abercromby-square.

TARLETON-STREET.

Mr. George Dunbar, afterwards Sir George Dunbar, Bart.; he subsequently lived in Dale-street, near the Exchange, and afterwards in Mount-pleasant, where he resided when he was mayor, in 1796.

CHURCH-STREET.

Mr. Henry Midgley, a merchant; Mr. Henry Clay, a merchant, father of the late Mr. Henry Clay, the banker; Mr. Richard Gerard, mayor in 1780; he was a surgeon, and the father of the late Dr. Gerard; Mr. Thomas Holding; Mr. Edward Forbes; Mr. John Backhouse; and Mr. Thomas Backhouse, merchants; Mr. George Rowden; and, at a more recent date, Mr. William Rutson, father of Mr. Rutson of the firm of Messrs. Ewart, Rutson and Company; Mr. George

---

(1) Chapter V, page 341.

(2) This gentleman appears to have resided, in 1787, in Hunter-street, " Charles Pole," a merchant, being mentioned as residing there, in Mr. William Bailey's Liverpool Directory of 1787.

Case, a merchant, who was mayor in 1781, and Dr. James Currie, the eminent and well-known physician.

WILLIAMSON-STREET.

Mr. Thomas Shaw, mayor in 1747.

WILLIAMSON-SQUARE.

The Rev. Thomas Dannett, one of the rectors of Liverpool; Mr. Moss, father of the late vicar of Walton, of that name; Mr. Victor Busigny, a merchant, who built the large house on the south side, afterwards occupied by Mr. Terry; and Mr. James Bridge, a merchant (of the firm of Messrs. Gregson, Bridge and Company); he built the house at the south corner of Upper Dawson-street.

BASNETT-STREET.

Mr. Henry Park, a surgeon of great talents and extensive practice; he went to reside there in 1776, and Basnett-street was then considered so much in the outskirts of the town, that his friends thought him indiscreet in establishing himself in a situation where his patients would have to follow him to so great a distance.

PARKER-STREET.

Mr. George Venables, a merchant.

CLAYTON-SQUARE.

Mr. Nicholas Ashton (formerly of Hanover-street, and afterwards of Woolton); he was high-sheriff for the county of Lancaster in 1770. Mr. William James (after leaving Rainford-gardens); Miss Clayton; Mr. John Wright, a merchant; Mr. Arthur Onslow, collector of the customs; Mr. Richard Statham, solicitor; Mr. Henry Parry, a merchant, of the firm of Messrs. Clay, Hoding and Parry; Mr. John Dobson; and Mr. Thomas Seaman, both merchants.

CASE-STREET.

Mr. Richard Walker, an eminent merchant, afterwards of Duke-street.

RANELAGH-STREET.

Mr. Thomas Staniforth, a merchant, mayor in 1797; his

house is now the Waterloo Hotel; he was the father of the late Mr. Samuel Staniforth.

HEATHFIELD-STREET.

Mr. John Crosbie, who was mayor in 1765; he was afterwards treasurer to the Corporation.[1]

FLEET-STREET.

Mr. Ralph Peters, who was at one time deputy recorder of Liverpool; and Mr. Henry Hardwar, collector of the customs.

SCHOOL-LANE.

Mr. Peter Baker, at the large recessed house at the corner of Manesty-lane, he was mayor in 1795; Mr. Ralph Earle, mayor in 1769; and Dr. Brandreth, the father of the present Dr. Brandreth.

HANOVER-STREET.

Mr. Nicholas Ashton, mentioned before; Mr. Henry Rawlinson, previously of York-street, a merchant, who was once member for Liverpool; Mr. Thomas Seel, a gentleman of large property, to whom the present Mr. Molyneux Seel is related; Mr. John Blackburne, senior; he was of the family of the Blackburnes of Hale, and was mayor of Liverpool in 1760; Mr. John Blackburne, junior,[2] son of the former, he was mayor in 1788; Mr. Robinson; Mr. Benjamin Heywood; Mr. Arthur Heywood; one of whom was the father,

---

(1) Mr. Crosbie, the treasurer, is mentioned in Mr. William Bailey's Liverpool Directory of 1787, as residing in Newington-row, but, in fact, his house was opposite to Newington-row, and at the spot where Heathfield-street now is. St. Andrew's Church stands on the site of the garden belonging to his house. There was a square paddock in front, inclosed with white rails, which extended along Renshaw-street as far as Newington. The house is the one in which Mr. Henry Matthews once lived, and which was afterwards the Female School of Industry; it is now made into shops.

(2) He lived with his father Mr. John Blackburne, senior, in the house of the latter, in Hanover-street, near where the lower end of Seel-street now is, until the latter died; but before his death he had built and nearly completed the large house, now the Girls' School of the Mechanics' Institution, in Hope-street, at the corner of Blackburne-place; and, after his father's death, Mr. John Blackburne, junior, completed and went to live at that house. He afterwards went to reside at Wavertree-hall, and ultimately went to live at Hawford Hall, in Worcestershire.

and the other the uncle of the late Mr. Arthur Heywood, the banker; their houses were contiguous, and were afterwards made into the Excise Office, which was used until that establishment was removed to its present situation in the new Revenue-buildings, the houses are still standing; Mr. John Brown, afterwards of Everton, a merchant, who was mayor in 1782; Mr. Samuel Lenox; Mr. Thomas Barton, both merchants; Mr. Clegg, a solicitor, of extensive practice; Mr. John Colquitt, who was the town-clerk before Mr. Richard Statham held that office; Mr. John Chorley, and Mr. John Copeland, both merchants; Mr. Joseph Daltera, a merchant, Mr. Nowland Holland, a merchant; Mr. John Tarleton, a merchant, afterwards of Duke-street, brother of General Sir Banastre Tarleton, Bart; Mr. Thomas Rumbold, a merchant; his house was the large one recessed back at the west corner of Peter-lane, in which Mr. Banning, the post-master, afterwards resided, early in the present century; Mr. Joseph Brooks, (the great uncle of the venerable Arch-deacon Brooks,) his house has been already noticed;[1] it stood at the extreme north-east end of the street, and at the spot which is now the corner of Bold-street.[2]

WOLSTENHOLME-SQUARE.

Mr. Kendall (whose daughter Mr. Moses Benson afterwards married,) lived at the large brick house on the north-east side; and Mr. John Parr, a merchant.

PARADISE-STREET.

Mr. Charles Caldwell, and Mr. Thomas Smythe, bankers;

---

(1) Chapter II, page 130.

(2) The following account of the death of Mr. Joseph Brooks, appears in one of the Liverpool newspapers of 1788 :—" On Tuesday last died, aged 82, Joseph Brooks, Esq. a gentleman of great uprightness and integrity. Many years since he retired from business, with an affluent fortune; but his inclination to usefulness and an active life led him to accept the care and management of the Poor of this Parish, who reside in the general Workhouse, which his liberal proposals induced the public to erect, and his

their bank was also in that street; Mr. Smythe was mayor
in 1789; Mr. Thomas Moss, the father of Mr. Moss, of
Otterspool; Mr. Daniel Backhouse; Mr. Myers; Mr. Peter
Kenyon, merchants; Mr. Henry Brown, the deputy town-
clerk, whose legal learning and talents have been already
more than once mentioned; Mrs. Bostock; and, more
recently, Mr. James France, a merchant, lived in the house
which she had occupied.

CORN-HILL.

Mr. William Rathbone, a merchant, the grandfather of
Mr. William Rathbone, of Greenbank; his house in Corn-hill
has not long since been destroyed, and its site forms a portion
of the south-western part of the Albert Dock.

LIVER-STREET.

Mr. William Rathbone, a merchant, afterwards of Corn-
hill, the father of Mr. William Rathbone, of Greenbank.
The former died on the 11th of February, 1809, but he
still lives in the recollection of many Liverpool persons;

---

attention and economy in the discharge of this arduous office will ever be remembered
with gratitude."——*Gore's General Advertiser of the 14th of February*, 1788.

The families of Brooks, Ashton, and Yates, were nearly related, and the relationship will be seen by a reference to the subjoined outline of the pedigree :—

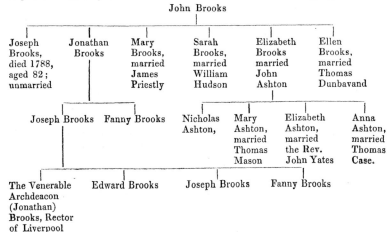

John Brooks

| Joseph Brooks, died 1788, aged 82; unmarried | Jonathan Brooks | Mary Brooks, married James Priestly | Sarah Brooks, married William Hudson | Elizabeth Brooks married John Ashton | Ellen Brooks, married Thomas Dunbavand |

Joseph Brooks   Fanny Brooks   Nicholas Ashton,   Mary Ashton, married Thomas Mason   Elizabeth Ashton, married the Rev. John Yates   Anna Ashton, married Thomas Case.

The Venerable Archdeacon (Jonathan) Brooks, Rector of Liverpool   Edward Brooks   Joseph Brooks   Fanny Brooks

he was a fine venerable-looking man, with dark eyebrows and flowing silvery hair. He was very highly respected; and it is believed that he was not surpassed by any contemporary individual in Liverpool in acts of benevolence and charity.[1]

PITT-STREET.

Mr. Thomas Birch, a Virginia merchant; he was mayor of Liverpool in 1777; was the father of Sir Joseph Birch, Bart. and grandfather of Sir Thomas Bernard Birch, Bart. lately M.P. for Liverpool.

BRIDGEWATER-STREET.

Mr. Henry Trafford, a merchant, a member of the Council; he served the office of bailiff in 1766. Several members of his family served the offices of mayor and bailiff of Liverpool in the course of the 18th century.[2] He was

---

(1) It is a remarkable fact, that in his family there have been seven William Rathbones, in successive generations; and that the Author's father, in the course of his long life, knew five of them, viz: a great great grandfather, a great grandfather, grandfather, father, and son.

(2) His uncle, of the same name, (Henry Trafford,) mayor of Liverpool in 1740, died during his mayoralty. Only one or two houses had been built in Bridgewater-street when Mr. Henry Trafford resided there; it was laid out merely as far as Simpson-street, a field intervening between the latter street and the shore of the Mersey. Mr. Trafford's house is still standing; it is a remarkable-looking house, four stories high, built, as is still perceptible, at two different times. It was afterwards altered into two dwelling-houses; and the present tall door-cases, adjoining each other, were made on that occasion. After it had been divided into two dwelling-houses, one was occupied by Mr. Bramwell, and the other by Mr. Breeze, both merchants: the houses stand on the south side of the street, near the corner of Simpson-street. The house, when entire, had a considerable garden at the back, a portion of which is now built upon. Several of the family of Trafford were Liverpool merchants, trading to North America, and apparently ship-owners also, as there are some advertisements in *Williamson's Liverpool Advertiser* of 1756 and 1757, announcing the intended sailing of the ship *Trafford*, " Captain Joseph Clarke, for Philadelphia," and containing a reference " to Messrs. Traffords, merchants." She is mentioned in the list of Liverpool vessels, in 1752, given in the Appendix,* as then commanded by Captain Thomas Goodaker.

* Appendix, No. XI.

nearly related to the ancient family of Trafford, of Swith-amley, in Staffordshire; and the Liverpool branch of the family also became connected with that of Leigh, of Ough-trington, John Leigh, Esq. of Oughtrington, having married, in 1762, Mr. Henry Trafford's sister, Susannah Trafford, the daughter of Mr. Edward Trafford, of Liverpool; and their son of that marriage, Trafford Leigh, Esq. of Oughtrington, now Trafford Trafford, Esq. in pursuance of the will of his maternal uncle, (Richard Trafford,) assumed, in 1791, the name and arms of Trafford.

PARK-LANE.

Mr. Johnson Gildart, a merchant.

KING-STREET.

Mr. John Zuill, a merchant, afterwards of Tabley-street; he occupied a large house on the south side of King-street, and at the corner of Trafford's-weint,[1] afterwards called Trafford's-lane, now part of South John-street; it was nearly opposite to the spot where Messrs. Leyland and Bullins' bank now stands; and in that house some of the members of the family of Mr. Henry Trafford, before men-tioned, had recently resided, viz : Mr. Edward Trafford, who had been mayor of Liverpool in 1742, and his sons, Mr. Richard Trafford, a merchant, and a member of the Council, who served the office of bailiff in 1755, and Mr. William Trafford, a merchant.[2]   It was subsequently tenanted for many years as a counting-house by Messrs.

---

(1) Trafford's-weint, afterwards called Trafford's-lane, was a narrow street called after old family of Trafford, and was a continuation of Love-lane, and extended from Atherton-street, past King-street to the Old Dock; and its site now forms part of South John-street, where it joins Canning-place.   Trafford's-lane was destroyed when South John-street was made.   A small opening or alley near its site on the west side of South John-street is now occasionally called Trafford's weint.

(2) All the three above-named gentlemen are mentioned in the Poll Book of the general Election of 1761, as having voted at that election, and as then residing in King-street.   The Author is indebted to the kindness of Mrs. Pole for the loan of that

Webster and Forshaw, brassfounders. Mr. Samuel Board-man, agent to Messrs. Wedgewood and Company, also resided in King-street.

TRAFFORD'S-WEINT, (AFTERWARDS TRAFFORD'S-LANE.)

Mr. Thomas Wilson, mayor in 1771.

DUKE-STREET.

At the lowest end of the street, Mr. Richard Walker, (previously of Case-street,) a merchant, and the nephew of Mr. Richard Watt,[1] who was a merchant of great eminence. Mr. Walker's house was the large one recessed back on the north side; it was afterwards used as the show rooms of the

---

Poll Book, now a very scarce work.   Mr. Richard Trafford is also mentioned in the printed List of Subscribers to the Liverpool Library, published in 1760.

The following particulars from the pedigree of the family of Trafford, of Swithamley, will show the relationship of the above-mentioned Liverpool gentlemen of that name, to that family :—

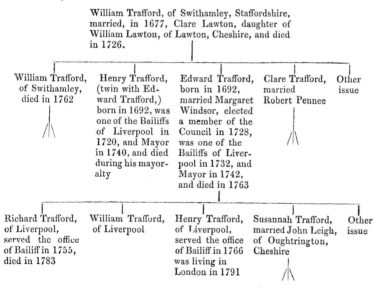

William Trafford, of Swithamley, Staffordshire, married, in 1677, Clare Lawton, daughter of William Lawton, of Lawton, Cheshire, and died in 1726.

William Trafford, of Swithamley, died in 1762

Henry Trafford, (twin with Edward Trafford,) born in 1692, was one of the Bailiffs of Liverpool in 1720, and Mayor in 1740, and died during his mayoralty

Edward Trafford, born in 1692, married Margaret Windsor, elected a member of the Council in 1728, was one of the Bailiffs of Liverpool in 1732, and Mayor in 1742, and died in 1763

Clare Trafford, married Robert Pennee

Other issue

Richard Trafford, of Liverpool, served the office of Bailiff in 1755, died in 1783

William Trafford, of Liverpool

Henry Trafford, of Liverpool, served the office of Bailiff in 1766 was living in London in 1791

Susannah Trafford, married John Leigh, of Oughtrington, Cheshire

Other issue

The Author is indebted to the politeness of Mr. William Brocklehurst, the present owner of the Swithamley Estate, for a copy of the pedigree of the family of Trafford of Swithamley.

(1) Mr. Watt built the mansion called " Oak-hill," near the Old Swan village.

Herculaneum Pottery Company, and subsequently as a barrack for soldiers; rather higher up the street, on the opposite side, Mr. Richard Watt, another nephew of the merchant of that name resided; Mr. John Sparling, a merchant, who was high sheriff of Lancashire in 1785, and mayor of Liverpool in 1790; he lived in a large house, the second below York-street, on the south side; he built the mansion at Everton, called "St. Domingo," where he resided at the time of his death;[1] Mr. Richard Kent, a merchant, who lived in the large house, not many years since pulled down, on the south side of Duke-street, and at the east corner of Kent-street, which was afterwards occupied for some years by Mr. Moses Benson, and still later, by Mr. Ralph Benson; Mr. James Gildart, sen. who was mayor of Liverpool in 1750; Mr. James Gildart, jun. who was mayor in 1786, he resided during his mayoralty in the next house above the one standing at the corner of Pothouse-lane; Rev. George Hodson, one of the rectors; Mr. William Lake, a merchant; Mr. William Bolden, a merchant; Mr. Thomas Naylor, a merchant, who succeeded to the mayoralty on Mr. Peter Baker's death, in 1796; Mr. Joseph Birch, afterwards Sir Joseph Birch, Bart.; Mr. Thomas Leyland, a banker, afterwards of Walton-hall, he was mayor in 1798, 1814, and 1820; Mr. William Wallace, grandfather of the late Mr. William Wallace Currie; Mr. John Bridge Aspinall, mentioned before; Mr. Stephen Hayes, a merchant; Mr. Thomas Manley, a merchant; Mr. Patrick Black, a merchant; the latter died at a very advanced age, and was one of the last, if not the last person of that period in Liverpool, who persevered in wearing a large blue cloth cloak, nearly the

---

(1) There had been another house, called " St. Domingo," previously standing on or near its site.

counterpart of which was re-introduced by the military during the Peninsular war; Mr. Edward Hinde; and Mr. Richard Carson, both merchants; Mr. Clayton Tarleton, a merchant, who was mayor in 1792, a younger brother of General Sir Banastre Tarleton, Bart.; Mr. John Tarleton, a merchant, also a younger brother of the General, both of whom have been mentioned in a former chapter;[1] Mr. John Gregson, a banker, afterwards of Everton, who was mayor of Liverpool in 1784; he resided at the large house at the south-east corner of Slater-street, and north side of Duke-street, now used as a glass warehouse.

Although the individual who will now be mentioned was not a native of Liverpool, nor was he a person of any consideration or prominent position in society, or even much known in the town, yet, as he resided for a short time in Duke-street, and acquired an unenviable degree of criminal notoriety, it is considered advisable to mention here, that on the north-eastward side of Duke-street, and in the eighth or ninth house above Slater-street, resided at one period, (1812,) John Bellingham, who was executed on the 18th of May, 1812, for the murder of Spencer Perceval, Esq. M.P.; and the following particulars, respecting the former, may perhaps be worthy of notice.

John Bellingham was a native of St. Neot's, in Huntingdonshire, and was born about 1771. His father was a land-surveyor and miniature painter; his mother was Elizabeth Scarbrow, the daughter of a respectable country-gentleman of St. Neot's, in comfortable circumstances. They were married in 1768 or 1769, in London, and had two children; their eldest, Mary, a dressmaker, and a well-disposed young woman, died unmarried. John was their second child. The father purchased a house at St. Neot's, and resided in it until

---

[1] Chapter V, page 376.

about 1775, when he returned to London, and lived in Titchfield-street, Oxford-street. In 1779, he discovered marks of mental derangement, and was placed in St. Luke's Hospital; at the end of a twelvemonth he returned home as incurable, and died soon afterwards. At the age of fourteen, John Bellingham was placed as an apprentice with Mr. Love, a jeweller, a man of excellent character, in Whitechapel. Here he was first very perverse and troublesome; and at last ran away from his master. His mother's sister, Mary, had married Mr. William Daw, many years clerk of the King's silver, in the Court of Common Pleas. His mother's property did not produce £56 annually; and, having two children to bring up, she could do but little for them: but Mr. Daw possessing a very good independent income, was continually pestered by the mother to do something for him. At length, in 1786, Mr. Daw expended money in fitting him out for the East Indies; and, in the spring of 1787, he sailed as a subaltern, in the service of the Company, on board their ship, the *Hartwell*, which, on her outward passage, was wrecked in the month of May off Bona Vista, one of the Cape Verde Islands. Being thus prevented from pursuing his voyage, he was one of those who got back to England. Mr. Daw, by that misfortune, not only lost all he had expended on his account, but felt himself again burthened with him; and, after much entreaty, he was induced to advance a pretty large sum, which enabled him to take the shop of a tin-plate worker in Oxford-street. During his residence there, his house got on fire, not without suspicion falling on Bellingham himself. The damage done was not great; but he took occasion to report that he had lost a great many bank-notes: this did not obtain any credit with Mr. Daw. In March, 1794, he became bankrupt, and was gazetted of Oxford-street, tin-plate worker. His creditors were not sufficiently satisfied with either his report of the fire, or his conduct, to grant him a certificate; nor did he ever obtain one under this commission.   It was after this period, and not until after, that he was received into a merchant's counting-house, where he formed connexions; and his employers were induced to commission him beyond seas. Archangel was his first and chief place of business, where he continued three years.   Having formed a connexion with Dorbeker and Co. of Archangel, in the timber line, he returned to England; and entered into a contract with the merchants of Hull for a supply of timber, to the amount of £12,000, for which bills were accordingly accepted and paid, but produce to the value of £4000 only was obtained. In the meanwhile his partner became bankrupt, the vessels returned in ballast, and Bellingham, who remained in Hull, was arrested and thrown into prison.   On the recovery of his liberty he returned to Archangel, and, as appears by his memorial, was arrested for debt by one Solomon Van Briemen, and thrown into prison, where he remained many months. He accused the Russian judges of corruption, and claimed the protection of Sir S. Sharpe, consul, and Lord L. Gower, ambassador, as a British subject; but they, finding that his arrest was legal, declined interfering. He afterwards repaired to England full of complaints against the Russian government. It was in Ireland where he married Miss Mary Anne Neville, daughter of Mr. John Neville, merchant and ship-broker, formerly of Newry, but afterwards of Dublin. His mother died at Liverpool in 1803. His aunt, Mrs. Daw, who lived in Brompton-row, and died in December, 1804, left, by will, £400 to him. He took up his abode at Liverpool, where he commenced business as an insurance broker; whilst his wife pursued that of a milliner. He continued at intervals to present memorials to the British government requiring to be indemnified for his losses, on the ground of his being a British subject, and that he had suffered by the injustice of Russian individuals; but was told that they could not interfere; General Gascoyne returned a similar answer to an application of this kind. It is said that he would have shot Mr. Ryder, or Lord Leveson Gower, had either of them presented themselves before him. To Sir W. Curtis he answered, " I have been fourteen days in making up my mind to the deed; but never could accomplish it until this moment." On the morning of the assassination he went with a lady to the European Museum; he parted with her between four and five, and went down immediately to the House of Commons, without having dined, and with his pistols loaded. It is said that he was so anxious not to be disappointed by the failure of the weapons, that after he had bought his pistols, for which he gave four guineas, he went to Primrose-hill to try how they would go off.[1] Whether that be correct or not, it was certainly proved on the trial, in order to show the malice prepense, that he had employed J. Taylor, of North-place, Grays Inn-lane, a tailor, to make a side pocket for him in his coat, within the breast on the left side, so that he could conveniently get at it with his right hand; the pocket was directed to be of a very particular depth. This coat he had on when he committed the murder, and he was seen previously to the crime, by the witnesses, with his hand in the side-pocket, waiting with evident anxiety near the outer lobby door, for the arrival of some person. He was then within arms length of all who entered.

On the afternoon of Monday, the 11th of May, 1812, he posted himself near the door of the lobby of the House of Commons, through which any person would naturally pass on his way to the body of the house; and a little after five

---

(1) Gentleman's Magazine of 1812, vol. 82, page 664 and 665.

o'clock, on Mr. Perceval entering the lobby, Bellingham shot him with a pistol, and he fell and died almost immediately. The assassin did not attempt to escape or deny the offence, and was immediately secured by General Gascoyne, one of the members for Liverpool, who took the pistol from him.

His trial for the offence took place at the Old Bailey, on the 15th of May, 1812, when he was convicted, and on the 18th of the same month he was executed.

The Rev. Dr. Forde, the ordinary of Newgate,[1] made several visits to Bellingham, on Saturday, the 16th, and Sunday, the 17th. He persisted in defending his crime; and, on one occasion remarked, that "life had been a weary pilgrimage to him; the bliss fleeting and illusory, the misery permanent and real: in laying it down, he had no vain regrets to make." About 11 on Sunday night, Mr. Butterworth, bookseller, of Fleet-street, obtained access to him, accompanied by Mr. Newman: his object appears to have been to interrogate him as an acquaintance, and to pray with

---

(1) It has been mentioned in a former Chapter * that the Rev. Dr. Forde had been the minister of St. Catherine's Church in Liverpool, and that he was a gentleman of great talents. He appears to have left St. Catherine's Church in 1798. On the 24th of April, in that year, he was first appointed by the sheriffs of London to discharge the duties of ordinary of Newgate, in London, during the indisposition of the Rev. Mr. Villette, which appointment was subsequently approved of by the Court of Aldermen. He held for many years the appointment of ordinary; and attended the executions of Colonel Despard, John Bellingham, and other noted offenders. He resigned the office on the 5th of July, 1814, and on the 29th of July the Rev. Horace Salisbury Cotton was elected in his stead. † Dr. Forde died on the 23rd of February, 1824. His death is noticed in the Gentleman's Magazine of 1824, vol. 94, part 1, page 644, as follows :—

"Feby. 23, Aged 80, the Rev. Dr. Ford, formerly Ordinary of Newgate. He was a very worthy man, and was much and deservedly esteemed by the City Magistrates, who, on his retirement from office, settled on him an annuity which provided for the comforts of his latter days."

The Author's father was intimately acquainted with him, and was a member of the congregation of St. Catherine's Church whilst he was the minister of it; in the course of that period the Author was baptized by Dr. Forde, and from those circumstances has felt a considerable degree of interest in the events of his life. In the Gentleman's Magazine his name is erroneously spelt "Ford." The correct manner of spelling it is "Forde": the Author has in his possession a letter, and also a short printed paper, sent to his father by Dr. Forde, in which his name is so spelt.

* Chapter V, page 351.
† Communicated by Mr. Serjeant Merewether, town-clerk of London.

him. He asked him if any person was concerned with him in the murder, to which he answered, "I do most solemnly declare there is not." The pistols he acknowledged he bought at Mr. Beckwith's, in Fleet-street.

At six o'clock on Monday morning, the 18th, Bellingham dressed himself with great composure, and read for half-an-hour in the Prayer Book. Dr. Forde being announced, he shook him by the hand, and left his cell for the room allotted for the condemned criminals. After a few minutes spent in prayer, the sacrament was administered to him. After this was ended, and both he and Dr. Forde had prayed fervently, the prisoner was informed that the sheriffs were ready. He answered in a firm tone, "I am perfectly ready also." The sheriffs and under-sheriffs, and their friends, then proceeded to the press-yard, and the prisoner was brought out.

The executioners bound his hands, during which he said to one of them, "Do everything properly, that I may not suffer more than is necessary:" to another, "Draw the cord tighter; I wish not to have the power of offering resistance." He ascended the scaffold with a confident, calm air. Some of the mob huzzaed him, but it escaped his notice. On the cap being put over his face, which he at first objected to, but afterwards acquiesced in, he prayed fervently with Dr. Forde, adding, in reply to an interrogatory, that "he thanked God for having enabled him to meet his fate with so much fortitude and resignation." The executioner then retired; a perfect silence ensued; the clock struck eight; and whilst it was striking the seventh time, the clergyman and Bellingham fervently praying, the supporters of the internal square of the scaffold were struck away, and Bellingham dropped! The body hung until 9 o'clock, when it was conveyed to St. Bartholomew's Hospital.[1]

---

(1) Gentleman's Magazine of 1812, vol. 82, page 662 to 664.

His wife carried on the business of a milliner at Liverpool, and was respected; and the public appeared to feel great sympathy for her; so much so, that after his death a subscription for the benefit of herself and her children was opened, and the amount was presented to her.

KENT-STREET.

Mr. Cornelius Bourne, a merchant, more recently of Duke-street; he had four sons, all of whom were afterwards on the commission of the peace, at the same time, and qualified as magistrates for the county of Lancaster; a circumstance which is, perhaps, unprecedented in the family of any other Liverpool merchant.

YORK-STREET.

Mr. Henry Rawlinson, afterwards of Hanover-street, a merchant, mentioned in a former chapter[1] as having been at one time one of the members of parliament for Liverpool; and Mr. Peter Ellames, a solicitor of eminence.

A surprising increase occurred in the Revenue of the Corporation of Liverpool during the concluding quarter of the 18th century. The increase will be better understood by a comparison of the amount of the income of the Corporation in 1775, with that in 1800, viz :—

"Gross Income of the Corporation for the year ending on the 18th of October, 1775[2]	£12,417	8	11½
Outgoings[1]	10,745	9	8½
Surplus	£1,672	19	3
Gross Income of the Corporation for the year ending on the 18th of October, 1800[2]	82,393	17	9½
Outgoings[1]	64,383	10	2
Surplus	£18,010	7	7½
Increase in the net Income of the Corporation at the end of the 25 years	16,337	8	4½

(1) Chapter V, page 369.

(2) Communicated from the Treasurer's Office, Town-hall.

Net amount received for Town's Dues (included in the £12,417 8s 11½d) for the year ending on the 18th of October, 1775[1]...............	£4,192	7	1
Net amount received for Town's Dues (included in the £82,393 17s 9½d) for the year ending on the 18th of October, 1800[1]...............	19,668	7	2½
Difference between the net amount of the Town's Dues received for the year ending on the 18th of October, 1775, and the net amount received for the year ending on the 18th of October, 1800	15,476	0	1½"

At the end of the year 1799, some streets had been laid out on the southward side of the town, to the east-ward of the Queen's Dock, which was then much smaller than at present, but there was a considerable extent of vacant land adjoining the quay on the east side, and not a single warehouse or counting-house had then been erected there. The west side of St. James-street was built, but only two or three buildings existed on the east side of that street. Greenland-street, Stanhope-street, and the lower end of Parliament-street were laid out, but contained only a few scattered houses. Blair-street, the north-side of Nile-street, and the east side of Great George-street were partly built. The west side of Great George-street was open to the fields, and completely unbuilt; and on the celebration of victories and other occasions of rejoicing, the troops were not unfrequently drawn up and fired, in Great George-street, and the artillery were placed in the fields, which extended from the west side to St. James-street, for the purpose of firing into the open space, where the discharges could not do harm.[2] On the occasion of the battle of the Nile,

---

(1) Communicated from the Treasurer's Office, Town-hall.

(2) The North Shore, a little beyond the Old Fort was another place for similar military displays on rejoicing days. The troops which met there about the close of the last and the commencement of the present century used to wear hair powder and pomatum, or some substitutes for them; and some regiments of cavalry wore the immense three-cornered cocked hats which are seen in old prints.

the military assembled there late in the afternoon, and the firing being after dark, the effect was very fine. The last, or nearly the last time that the troops met there and fired on such an occasion, was in consequence of Lord Nelson's victory at Copenhagen, in 1801 ;[1] after which the erection of houses, on the west side, prevented such military displays; and then they generally selected the open ground which is now Crown-street and its adjoining streets, below Edge-hill, for such purposes.

On the eastward, the town extended to Rodney-street, which was imperfectly built on each side, and to Hope-street, which, however, had then very few houses, but the north end contained some dwelling-houses in gardens; and there were two of large size on its east side, at the west end of Falkner-street, then Crabtree-lane, in one of which Mr. John Blackburne, before mentioned, lived after leaving Hanover-street, and before going to live at Wavertree-hall, and which is now the school for girls of the Mechanics' Institution, and Mr. John Thomas afterwards lived many years in the other, which is now occupied by Mrs. Pemberton and Mrs. Pole. Mount-pleasant was only partially built. Clarence-street and the south side of the lower end of Brownlow-hill were in an incomplete state; and there was not a house, or any thing besides open fields, between the north end of Clarence-street and the south end of St. Anne-street. Copperas-hill, which was for a short time about that period called Elliot-hill, was partly built. Lime-street was in an unfinished state, but the south end was completed; and at the north end there were one or two houses,—the Old Infirmary gardens, the east side of the Seamen's Hospital, and an old public-house opposite. There was an open field called Waterworth's field,

---

[1] The Author was present, in Great George-street, on that occasion.

mentioned in a former chapter,[1] on the east side of the street where the present London and North-western Railway Station, and the lower part of Gloucester-street now are. A few houses stood at the west or lowest end of London-road. Commutation-row, a portion of Camden-street, and nearly all of the west end of Islington, between Shaws-brow and St. Anne-street, were built. There were a few houses and gardens on the north side of Islington, between St. Anne-street and Soho-street and Birchfield. Part of Soho-street and most of Richmond-row were completed; in the latter, several of the houses had gardens which formed a considerable portion of the frontage to the street; and at the back of the north side, and at the upper end of it, stood the woollen-hall, or market, for the sale of woollen cloth, linens, &c. called the Richmond-hall, before mentioned. Fox-street was laid out and partially built. Some parts of Beau-street, Cazneau-street, Rose-place, Grosvenor-street, and Chaucer-street were built; all those streets were in an incomplete state, although they contained some inhabited houses and other buildings.

On the northward side, the town extended to the spot where the south end of Scotland-road now is, which was partly built; but it was not then opened in a line through the gardens mentioned in a former chapter[2] to Mile-end, Great Nelson-street, and Burlington-street, as at present; the new and straight line was, however, then projected and marked out. Bevington-bush, Freemasons-row, and Banastre-street were partially built; the south end of Vauxhall-road contained some houses and buildings, but it was in an unfinished and incomplete state. Some houses

---

(1) The lime-works mentioned in Chapter II, page 147, formerly adjoined this field on its north side.

(2) Chapter II, page 151.

stood at the north end of Westmoreland-street; and the west side of Smithfield-street was erected. Highfield-street and Plumbe-street were built, and Leeds-street nearly completed; the north side of Denison-street was built; the south end of Great Howard-street was laid out, and contained a few buildings, of which the only prominent or important one was the Gaol, now called the Borough Gaol. There the northern limits of the town, so far as the streets and buildings extended, terminated. Two or three intended streets, however, had been marked out beyond them; and here and there a few straggling houses had been recently erected.

During the French revolutionary war, in the last and at the commencement of the present century, a considerable number of prisoners of war were confined in the Borough Gaol. A most ill-judged place of confinement, when its contiguity to the coast and to the shipping, and the facilities afforded to the escape of the prisoners, in case of the appearance of an enemy off the coast, are considered. In general the prisoners were ill-clad, and appeared dispirited and miserable; and the mortality amongst them was very considerable : the hearse was constantly in requisition to convey from the gaol the corpse of some poor Frenchman to the public cemetery at St. John's Church.[1] Soon after the peace of Amiens, in 1802, the prisoners of war, in number about 1100, some of whom had been confined in the Borough Gaol for several years, were liberated, and sailed from Liverpool for France. Amongst other amusements, some of the French prisoners, during their confinement there, performed plays in a small theatre constructed for that purpose within the walls, and, in some instances they raised in a single night £50 for admission money.[2] Many of the readers

---

(1) A part of St. John's Church-yard was then used as a place of interment for the corpses of parish paupers, of unknown drowned persons, and of prisoners of war.

(2) Troughton's Liverpool, page 226.

will recollect that, with the usual ingenuity of the French, they manufactured a variety of snuff-boxes, rings, trinkets, crucifixes, slippers, little carved boxes, and toys of various kinds, which were exhibited on a stand in the entrance of the gaol, and sold for their benefit.

The Municipal boundaries, usually called the Liberties of the Borough, were marked out in the last century by boundary stones, placed at irregular intervals, and extended into the open fields a great distance beyond the then streets and buildings; and were co-extensive with the limits of the parish of Liverpool. It was the custom for the Mayor, attended by the Bailiffs, and occasionally by one or two other officers of the Corporation, and generally by some of his personal friends, (all on horseback,) with the regalia and a band of music, to ride round the limits of the town, a few days (usually on Monday) before St. Luke's day (the 18th of October); the ceremony was called, "riding the liberties;" and it was continued until the Municipal Corporations Reform Act of the 5th and 6th of William the Fourth, chap. 76, (1835), rendered it superfluous. That ceremony was of use, as the annual visit to the line of demarcation between the borough and the adjoining townships, and to the boundary stones, kept in public remembrance all the exact boundaries, and prevented their becoming matters of dispute. The boundary stones generally had the initials of the Mayor, in whose mayoralty they were placed there, with the year in which he served the office, cut upon them, and one or two of them yet remain.[1]

It was customary to have a tent pitched at Low-hill, near the Coffee-house, where a cold collation was set out, of which

(1) The stones have been in more modern times generally superseded by iron.

the Mayor, the Bailiffs, and some of the persons who accompanied them, partook, before the cavalcade dispersed.

The following entries in the ledger of the Corporation will give some idea of the expense of the ceremony in 1775 : it is believed that the sums charged included the payments for the band of music, the hire of horses, the tent, the collation, and some trivial expenses :—

		£	s.	d.
" 1775. Oct. 18.	To Cash paid expenses at Low Hill on Liberty day	2	13	8
1775. Oct. 18.	To do H Forshaw, expenses on Liberty day	3	10	0
„ „	To do Thos. Moncas, Ditto on Do.	7	9	10 "[1]

The following are entries of the expenses of the ceremony in 1800 :—

	£	s.	d.
" 1800. Oct. 18, pd. Jas. Creary, expenses Liberty day	£5	0	0
1800. Oct. 18, pd J. Barrow, Expenses Liberty day	£16	9	6 "[2]

The following is a copy of the bill of Mrs. Jane Barrow who kept the Lowhill Coffee-house, which gives the items, amounting to the £16 9s 6d, and which is curious and also of some value, as giving an insight into the habits and expenses of the times :—

" Low Hill, 18 Octr. 1800.

Corporation of Lpool.

To Jane Barrow, Dr.

	£	s.	d.
To roast & boiled beef......................	£1	13	6
Hams fowls & tongues	2	15	0
Veal pies	0	8	0
Pidgeon do.	0	15	6
Potted & fresh Shrimps..................	0	11	0
Milk Punch..............................	2	18	6

---

(1) Ledger of the Corporation, No. 3, (7) page 144. In 1775, Mr. Henry Forshaw kept the Black Horse and Rainbow Inn and Tavern, in High-street, and Mr. Thomas Moncas kept Pontack's Coffee-house, in Water-street.

(2) Cash Book of the Corporation for 1800, (26) page 131. The Coffee-house is still standing, and for many years has been called, from its sign, " the Coach and Horses Tavern." Mr. James Creary, mentioned above, kept a tavern in High-street, near the Exchange, in 1800.

Rum & Brandy punch	£1	15	0
Wine...	0	17	6
Brandy......................................	0	16	6
Rum..	0	19	0
Ale, Porter, &c.	1	8	0
Labourers' Wages, Canvas, Cartage, &c.	1	12	0
	£16	9	6"[1]

Copy of the receipt for the amount of the bill :—

" Rec[d.] Dec[r.] 1800, from Tho. Golightly, sixteen pounds nine shillings & six pence, for expenses attending riding the libertys, as p Bill annexed.

Rec[d.] the above by me Jane Barrow,

£16 : 9 : 6   for Mother."[1]

Having now described the appearance, changes, and increase of Liverpool during the last and most eventful quarter of the 18th century, a remarkable circumstance presents itself to notice, calculated to excite surprize, which is, that notwithstanding two expensive and sanguinary wars[2] which occurred during that period, and were attended, as wars almost always are, with much individual distress, and commercial injury, still Liverpool, though it occasionally experienced fits of depression, and stagnation of trade, increased rapidly in size, population, and shipping.

" There where your argosies with portly sail,
    Like signiors and rich burghers on the flood,
    Or as it were the pageants of the sea,
    Do over-peer the petty traffickers,
    That curtsy to them, do them reverence,
    As they fly by them with their woven wings."[3]

Commerce has usually made grateful returns to every

---

(1) From the original bill and receipt preserved in the Town-hall.

(2) The war with the British North American Colonies, afterwards the United States of America, is usually considered as having broken out in 1775, as hostilities had then commenced, but the Declaration of Independence only took place on the 4th of July, 1776 ; it was followed by a war with France in 1778, with Spain in 1780, and with Holland in the same year. The French revolutionary war broke out in 1793.

(3) Shakespeare's Merchant of Venice, Act 1, Scene 1.

nation which has devoted its energies to it.   In the middle ages, it was neglected or despised: the English, blind to the advantages of their situation, and ignorant of the source from which opulence was destined to flow into their country, were so little attentive to their commercial interests, as hardly to attempt those manufactures, the materials of which they furnished to foreigners;[1] and the feudal system rendered the great nobles almost independent of the sovereign and of the laws, kept the common people in a state of vassalage, and was naturally attended by oppression, misery, and disorders; but, as has been justly observed by a talented writer, Commerce and Manufactures gradually introduced order and good government, and with them, the liberty and security of individuals.[2]   Besides having been a principal cause of the emancipation of Western Europe from the darkness and barbarism of the middle ages, the certain effect of commerce in modern times has been to promote civilization; to unite nations together; to produce a species of intimacy between the natives of distant climes; to supply their mutual wants by the interchange of the superfluous articles of one country for the productions of another; and to give industrious employment, and the means of living, to millions of human beings; and, in whatever state, or nation, commerce has flourished, besides being a source of opulence, increased knowledge, useful arts, and intellectual pursuits, have almost constantly attended its progress.

Within the memory of man, Liverpool was a seaport town comparatively unimportant.   The industry, skill, and enterprize of the merchants and other inhabitants of Liverpool, aided, it may be admitted, by the favourable locality of the port, have, however, received their well-earned reward.

---

(1) Robertson's Charles V. vol. 1, page 69.

(2) Smith's Wealth of Nations, vol. 2, page 119.

At the date (1775) at which the author has commenced this account, the town was very limited in point of trade, population, and size : under the blessing of Providence, however, the talent, enterprise, and industry of the mercantile and trading classes of Liverpool have been, as they merited, well rewarded ; and, at the close of the 18th century, the town had become a "Mart of Nations," a "Merchant City," eminent for its extent, prosperity, and commerce.

" This quondam village, which is now fit to be a proud capital for any Empire in the world, has started up like an enchanted palace, even in the memory of living men."[1]

---

(1) From Mr. (afterwards Lord) Erskine's Speech, on the Trial of the cause, The Mayor, Bailiffs, and Burgesses of Liverpool against Golightly, at Lancaster, in 1791, before Mr. Baron Thompson. The cause is mentioned in Chapter III, page 227 and 228.

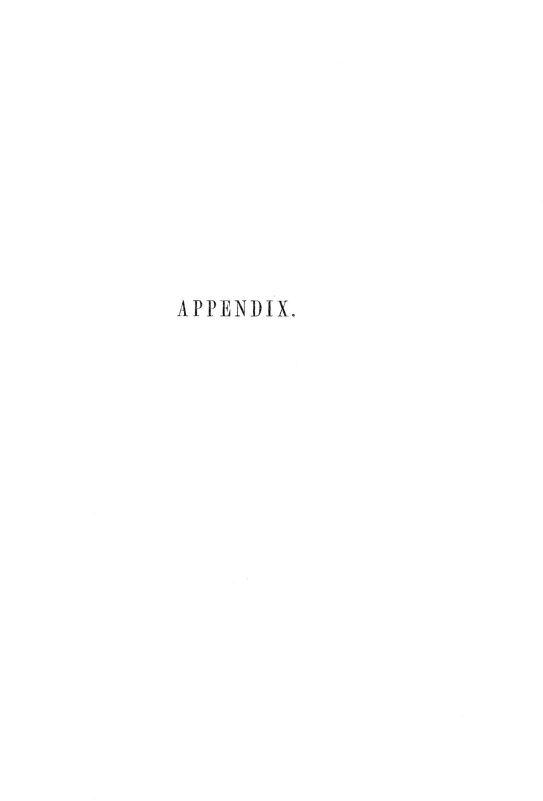

APPENDIX.

APPENDIX.

No. I.

LANCASTER.

Sheriff's Account, 13 John, 1212. Gilbert Fitz Reinfred, Adam Fitz Roger, as custos for him, renders account for him for two hundred pounds for the Farm of Lancaster. In the Treasury.

And in lands given to William Fitz Walkelin, 9 pounds, in Stavenby; and to Nigel de Gresley, 4 pounds and sixteen shillings, in Drakelawe; and to Victor de Wallingour, 58 shillings; and to William Marescall, 32 pounds, in Kartmel; and to Yervert de Hilton, 24 shillings, in land of Penelton; and to William de Huntingefeld, 15 pounds, in Mendham; and to Robert Ruff, six pounds and ten shillings, in Navembi; and to the Earl of Derbi, 10 pounds; and to Geffry Lutrel, 13 pounds, in Croxton, in land which was of Hugh the Porter; and to the same, ten marks, in the same land, which was of Hugh de St. Albin; and, in default of the Issues of the Forest of Lancaster, ten pounds; and in the Town of Lancaster 20 marks, for which the men of Lancaster are respited within; and in acquittance of the land of R., Constable of Chester, 70 pounds; and to the Heirs of William de Valeines, 10 pounds in Corfho; and Hugh de Morton 28 shillings in Fornebi.

And for 400 Hogs bought and sent to the army in Wales 40 pounds, by the King's Writ; and for 100 cows bought and sent there 22 pounds and 10 shillings, by the same Writ; and for 200 spades, 26 shillings, by the same Writ; and for 200 axes, two marks and a half, by the same Writ; and for two thousand hand nets 27 shillings and 9 pence; and in payment of 15 Knights and 60 servants on horseback, and four hundred and sixty six footmen and four score and 16 carpenters in the army of Wales 106 pounds 9 shillings by the same Writ; and in the Work of the Castle of Lancaster, one hundred and four score pounds and 18 shillings by the same Writ; and in payment of four master Huntsmen, with their forty-nine men with 10 horses, and 249 Hares, and with two packs of Dogs, and fifty-two spaniels £16 : 9 : 10½. by the same Writ; and in payment of five prisoners of Ireland for one year and a half and seven weeks, ten marks, by the same Writ; and in the carriage of all the aforesaid from Lancaster unto Liverpool and so to Chester, 9 pounds and 5 shillings, by the same Writ; and for three weighings of cheese by the same Writ, 20 shillings; and his surplusage for the year last past, 41 pounds 12 shillings and eleven-pence.

Of which one hundred four score and two pounds eight shillings and two-pence are allowed to him in various debts, and there remain to be placed to him one hundred and four score pounds thirteen shillings and a half-penny.[1]

---

[1] From a copy in English in the Town-hall.

No. II.

25th March,
13 Henry III.
1229.

Amongst the Records in the Court of Chancery, preserved in the Tower of London, to wit, on the Patent Roll of the 13th year of the Reign of King Henry the Third, membrane 9, is thus contained :—

Henry, by the Grace of God, King of England, &c. To the Sheriff and all his Bailiffs of the County of Lancaster, Greeting: Know Ye, That we have granted to our honest men of Liverpul Our Town of Liverpul, to be held at Farm from the Feast of Saint Michael, in the thirteenth year of our Reign unto the end of four complete years, rendering therefore unto us in each of the aforesaid years at our Exchequer by the Hands of the Sheriff of Lancaster at two terms, Ten Pounds ; to wit, at Easter in the thirteenth year of our Reign, Five Pounds, and at the Feast of Saint Michael in the same year Five Pounds, and so from year to year at the same terms Ten Pounds as is aforesaid.—In Witness whereof, We have caused these our Letters thereof to them to be made Patent.—Witness ourself at Malborough, the 25th day of March in the same year of our Reign.[1]

No. III.

A. D. 1323.
An. 17 Edw. II.
_____
Pat. 17 Edw. II.
p. 1. m. 15. d.
in Turr. Lond.

Contra fingentes miracula fieri apud Bristoll ' ad loca ubi corpora rebellium adhuc suspensa remanent, per inimicos Regis.

Rex, dilectis & fidelibus suis, Johanni de Stonore, & Johanni de Bousser, salutem.

Sciatis quod, cum nuper Henricus de Monte Forti & Henricus de Wylyngton, nuper inimici & rebelles nostri, eâ occasione, per considerationem curiæ nostræ, per equos tracti, & apud Bristoll ' suspensi fuisssent ; & virtute considerationis prædictæ, in furcis pendentes, remansuri quamdiu corpora eorum subsisterent ; ut alii vitarent mala et facinora talia contra nos perpetrare ; Reginaldus de Monteforti, Willielmus de Clyf, Willielmus Curteys, & Johannes frater ejus, unà cum quibusdam aliis malefactoribus, & pacis nostræ perturbatoribus, causas fraudulosas, per quas affectionem populi a nobis elongare, & populum eundem contra nos movere possent, malitiosè fabricantes, apud Bristoll', ad loca, ubi corpora dictorum inimicorum & rebellium nostrorum adhuc suspensa remanent, pluries accesserunt, & miracula ibidem fieri falsò fingentes, idolatriæ figmenta ibidem fecerunt & publicârunt, & per alios fieri & publicari procurârunt :

Et illos qui ad locum prædictum, pro hujusmodi figmentis idolatriæ faciendis, accesserunt, contra alios, qui sic accedentes pro nostro & regiæ dignitatis nostræ honore repellere nitebantur, vi & armis manutenuerunt et defenderunt :

Et alia enormia ibidem fecerunt, in nostri, & regiæ dignitatis nostræ, & considerationis prædictæ opprobium & scandalum manifestum, & contra pacem nostram ;

---

(1) From a copy in English in the Town-hall.

Nos, nolentes contemptus & transgressiones prædictos, si taliter perpetratæ fuerint, transire impunitos, assignavimus vos Justiciarios nostros ad inquirendum, per sacramentum proborum & legalium hominum de comitatu Glouc', per quos, &c. de nominibus malefactorum prædictorum, qui, unà cum præfatis Reginaldo, Willielmo, Willielmo, & Johanne, contemptus & transgressiones prædictos perpetrârunt; & de contemptibus & transgressionibus illis pleniùs veritatem, & ad eosdem contemptus & transgressiones audiend' & terminand' secundum legem, &c.

Et ideò vobis mandamus, quod, ad certos dies & loca, quos ad hoc provideritis, inquisitionem illam facietis, & contemptus & transgressiones prædictos audiatis & terminetis in formâ prædictâ, facturi, &c. salvis, &c.

Mandavimus enim vicecomiti nostro comitatûs prædicti, quod, ad certos dies & loca quos ei sciri faciatis, venire faciat coram vobis tot, &c. per quos, &c.

In cujus, &c.

Teste Rege, apud Skypton' in Craven', secundo die Octobris.

Per ipsum Regem.[1]

<table>
<tr><td>

A. D. 1323.
An. 17 Edw. II.
Pat. 17 Edw. II.
p. 1. m. 23.
in Turr. Lond.

</td><td>

De fingentibus miraculis prosequendis.

Rex, dilectis & fidelibus suis, Johanni de Bousser, Radulpho de Bereford, & Johanni le Botiller de Lamiltyt, salutem.

</td></tr>
</table>

Sciatis quod, cum nuper Henricus de Monteforti & Henricus de Wylyngton, nuper inimici & rebelles nostri, eâ occasione per considerationem curiæ nostræ, per equos tracti, & apud Bristoll' suspensi fuissent. &c. *prout supra, de secundo die Octobris, usque hæc verba, viz :—*

Mandavimus enim vicecomiti nostro comitatûs prædicti, quod, ad certos dies & loca quos vos, vel duo vestrûm ei scire faciatis, venire faciat coram vobis, vel duobus vestrûm tot, &c. per quos, &c.

In cujus, &c.

Teste Rege, apud Liverpol xxiiii die Octobris.[1]

No. IV.

<table>
<tr><td>

19 Edw. II.
1325.
(In the Fœdera,
modern edition,
Vol. 2, part 1,
page 642, it is
stated, as of the
20 Edward II,
1326.)

</td><td>

The King to his dear and faithful Robert de Kendale, Constable of the Castle of Dovor and keeper of the Cinque Ports, Greeting: Whereas, often before these times we have commanded you as well by Writs under the Great Seal as by Letters under our Privy Seal, that you should make diligent search in the Ports aforesaid over all Letters brought from Foreign Parts into our Realm, and to be carried from the same Realm to out-

</td></tr>
</table>

ward Ports, and that all and singular Letters prejudicial to us or to the right of our Crown, or suspected thereof, should be sent to us

---

(1) Fœdera, (17 Edward the 2nd,) modern edition, Vol. 2, part 1, page 536 and 537.

Q 2

before execution of the same should be done; We, on account of some rumours which have newly come to our ears, willing that the premises should be strictly observed, command you under our heavy forfeiture, firmly enjoining that the search aforesaid you shall make in the ports aforesaid, with all the diligence you can, according to the form of our Mandates aforesaid to you many times thereupon directed. Also all and singular persons to us or to our Kingdom worthily suspected, if any you shall find in the Ports aforesaid, you shall without delay cause to be arrested, and in our prison to be safely kept until otherwise you shall thereupon have in command from us; and of the names of them whom you shall have so arrested, and from what cause they shall have so been arrested, you shall from time to time distinctly and openly certify us; holding yourself so in this behalf that through your negligence or default in this behalf, no perils shall arise by the premises through which we ought heavily to lay to you.

Witness the King at Maresfield, the 24th day of September.[1]

In the same manner it is written to the underwritten, that is to say:
To the Barons, Bailiffs, and Commonalty of the Town of Romney.
To the Mayor, Bailiffs, and Commonalty of the Town of Portsmouth.
To the Bailiffs and Commonalty of the Town of Lyverpol. &c. &c.[1]

No. V.

Extracted from the Scotch Roll preserved amongst the Records of the Court of Chancery, in the Tower of London, of the 7th year of King Edward the Third.

1333.
7 Edwd. III.

The King to his beloved and faithful William de Clynton, constable of his Castle of Dover and warden of his cinque ports, or his deputy, greeting: whereas we are given to understand that the Scots, our enemies and rebels have made and cease not daily to enter into confederacies and alliances with men of foreign lands, in order to make war upon us and our people, as well by sea as by land, we being desirous to obviate their malice and to provide for the safety and defence of our kingdom and lands, do command you that all ships carrying the burthen of fifty tons of wine and upwards, in the ports and places within your bailiwick, now being in those ports and places, you do cause to be detained, and all and singular the owners of Ships of the like burthen, of the said ports and places which now are without those ports and places, you cause to be warned that they cause the same ships to be brought back to those ports and places with all the dispatch possible, and that they cause all the said ships to be made ready without delay and to be furnished with double equipment and other things and necessaries for war, so that they be ready and prepared to depart in our service for the defence of us and our kingdom, in manner as by us and our council shall be ordained, when we shall cause you or the owners or masters of the said Ships to be thereupon warned, and of

------

(1) From a copy in English in the Town-hall.

the number of such ships now being in the ports and places aforesaid, and of others now absent, you do certify, distinctly and openly by your letters, with all the dispatch in your power. And this as you value us and our honour and the salvation of our said kingdom, you in no wise omit.

Witness the king, at Twedemouth, the 26th day of June.

By the king himself and the council.[1]

A like writ is directed to Gilbert de Wygeton, constable of the king's castle at Karesbroke, in the Isle of Wight, for providing ships in the ports within the island aforesaid; "Witness," as above :—

The king to his beloved the mayor, barons, and bailiffs of the port of Sandwich, greeting: whereas, we are given to understand, &c. as above, unto "there carrying," and then thus, "in the same port now being in that port you cause to be detained, and all and singular the owners of ships of the like weight of the same port which now are without the said port, you cause to be warned that those ships to the said port with all the dispatch possible," &c. as above, unto, "there we shall cause you to be warned"; and then thus, "and of the number of such ships now being in the port aforesaid," &c. as above, "Witness," as above.

By the king himself and the council.

The like writs are directed, amongst others,

To the Bailiffs of the Town of Liverpool.[1]

No. VI.

Pat. 29 Edw. III   The King to all to whom &c Greeting : Know ye, That
1356.   of Our special grace We have granted and given License
                for Us and Our heirs, as much as in Us is, to Our beloved
the Mayor and Commonalty of the Town of Liverpul in the Duchy of Lancaster, that they, the Ten pounds of lands tenements and rents, with the appurtenances, by the year, according to the true value of the same in the Duchy aforesaid, which they are bound to Our beloved and faithful Henry Duke of Lancaster as it is said to acquire, and the same lands, tenements, and rents, with the appurtenances may give and assign to certain Chaplains, to celebrate Divine service every day, for the Souls of all the faithful deceased, in the Chapel of the Blessed Mary and Saint Nicholas, of Liverpull, according to the order of the Mayor and Commonalty aforesaid. To have and to hold to the same Chaplains, and their successors chaplains, to celebrate Divine Service in the Chapel aforesaid in form aforesaid for ever, and to the same Chaplains, that they the lands tenements and rents aforesaid, with the appurtenances, from the before-named Mayor and Commonalty may receive and hold to them, and their successors Chaplains, to celebrate Divine Service in the Chapel aforesaid for ever, the Statute concerning lands and tenements not to be put to Mortmain edited notwithstanding.

---

(1) From a copy in English in the Town-hall.

By the Inquisitions thereon in due form to be taken, and to be rightly returned into the Chancery of Us or our heirs it is found that the same may be done without the Hurt or prejudice of Us or of our heirs, or of others whomsoever. In testimony whereof &ᶜ. Witness, the King at Westminster, the nineteenth day of May

By Writ of Privy Seal [1]

No. VII.

Amongst the Records of the Court of Chancery, preserved in the Tower of London, that is to say, the Patent Roll of the 35th year of the Reign of King Edward the Third, part 2, membrane 24, is thus contained :—

Concerning the coming of the Earl of Ulster to Ireland.　　The King to the Justice, Chancellor, Treasurer, and others of our Council in the land of Ireland, Greeting : Recalling to memory how our Irish Enemies and Rebels, and others, have in great number destroyed our faithful subjects of the land aforesaid, and have wasted their lands and places and cease not daily to commit such evil and wicked acts, and in process of time much greater are dreaded to be done, unless their wickedness be sooner restrained. We, for the cause aforesaid have determined to send our most dear Son Lionel, Earl of Ulster, with a competent armed force to the land aforesaid, and for the comfort and solace of our adherents and faithful supporters in the said Land, we have resolved to send beforehand our beloved Clerk, Thomas de Baddeby, on whose faithfulness and circumspection we can depend, to announce to you and them the news of the Coming of our said son ; and to excite, and on our behalf to lay the charge on you, that the whole Navy of the Land aforesaid, competently armed, shall be sent with all speed to the Ports of Litherpoole and Chester, and other ports lying between (them), for the Passage of our said Son to those parts, so that it be there seven days before the Feast of St. Peter *ad vincula*, next coming at the latest, and to ascertain from you, and to provide those things which for such his coming you shall judge useful and necessary, and with all the dispatch in your power to report to us, or to cause to be reported by some other, your advice concerning all the premises. And therefore we command you that to the same Thomas, in the doing and executing the premises, you be attending, advising and assisting, and communicating to him your advice upon the said affairs, so that being thereof well-advised, he may be able to return to us in England to relate what things you shall decree to be so done, and that the same our son (the Lord willing) may be able more happily and more advisedly to depart to the Land aforesaid. In testimony whereof, &c. Witness the King at Westminster, the tenth day of May.

By the King himself and the Council.[1]

---

(1) From a copy in English in the Town-hall.

No. VIII.

Amongst the Records of the Court of Chancery, preserved in the Tower of London, that is to say, the Close Roll of the 42nd year of the Reign of King Edward the Third, membrane 4, is thus contained :—

The King, to his Justice Chancellor and Treasurer of Ireland, Greeting: We command you firmly enjoining that all ships of the Burthen of Twenty tons and beyond unto two hundred tons, which in the Ports of Dublin, Drogheda, and Waterford you can find, you shall immediately and without delay cause to be arrested and sent to the Port of Liverpool, in the County of Lancaster, in England, so that they may be there in the Feast of St. Hilary next coming at latest ready and prepared for the passage of our dear and faithful William de Wyndesore, and of the men at arms, archers and others, whom to the parts of Ireland for the salvation of the same, we are about to send to the same parts in our obedience, at our charges about to depart. And this as we and our honour and the salvation of the said land of Ireland you desire, you will in no wise omit. Witness the King at Westminster the first day of November.

By the King himself and the Council.(1)

The King, to his dear and faithful the Mayor and Bailiffs of his City of Dublin, Greeting : We command you firmly enjoining that all the Ships of the Burthen of twenty tons and beyond unto two hundred tons, which in the Port of the City aforesaid you can find, &c. as above.

Witness as above.

Like Writs are directed to the under-written, namely,
To the Mayor and Bailiffs of the City of Drogheda.
To the Mayor and Bailiffs of the City of Waterford.(1)

No. IX.

Amongst the Records of the Court of Chancery, preserved in the Tower of London, to wit, on the Patent Roll of the 47th year of the King Edward III, p. 2, m. 4, is thus contained :—

Concerning the pressing of Ships (Wyndesore) The King to all and singular Admirals, Sheriffs, Mayors, Bailiffs, Ministers, Owners, Masters and Mariners of Ships and other his faithful Subjects to whom &c Greeting : Know Ye that We have assigned Our beloved Simon Charwellen Clerk and Walter de Eure jointly and severally to press without delay all ships of the Burthen of Twenty Tons and upwards to 200 Tons, in the Port of Bristol, and in all ports and places from thence to the Port of the Town of Liverpool and to cause [*the same*] to be brought to the said Port of Liverpool, so that they be there with all the dispatch possible, ready and equipped for the passage of our beloved and

---

(1) From a copy in English in the Town-hall.

faithful William de Wyndesore Governor and Guardian of our Realm of Ireland, and of the Men-at-Arms and others about to depart in our service, in the retinue of the said William, at his wages and expenses, and there to remain for the preservation and defence of our aforesaid Realm according to the order of the said William; and also to take and arrest all those, whom they shall find opposers or Rebels to the said Simon and Walter, or to either of them, in the execution of the premises, and to commit them to our Prison there to remain until We shall cause to be otherwise demanded of them. And therefore we command you that to the said Simon and Walter and to each of them, in the doing and executing the Premises, you be intendant counselling and aiding as often as they or either of them shall make known to you, or either of you, on our behalf. In Witness &c. Witness the King at Westminster the 8th day of October.

By the King himself.[1]

No. X.

A Comparative Statement of the NUMBER OF SHIPS that have arrived at, or sailed from the port of Liverpool for Six Years, preceding the year 1751.[2]

| The Number of Ships that have arrived at or sailed from the port of Liverpool for Six Years. | | | | | Ships belonging to the Port for the same time. | | |
| INWARDS. | | | OUTWARDS. | | | | |
YEARS.	SHIPS.	TONS.	SHIPS.	TONS.	SHIPS.	TONS.	MEN.
1709	374	14,574	334	12,636	84	5,789	936
1716	370	17,870	409	18,872	113	8,386	1376
1723	433	18,840	396	18,373	131	8,070	1114
1730	412	18,070	440	19,058	166	9,766	1710
1737	402	17,493	435	22,350	171	12,016	1981
1744	403	22,072	425	20,937	188	13,772	2621

(1) From a copy in English in the Town-hall.

(2) From Troughton's Liverpool, page 259.

No. X.

A Comparative Statement of the NUMBER OF SHIPS, to and from the ports of Liverpool and Bristol, for the year 1764.[1]

LIVERPOOL.			BRISTOL.		
	INWARDS.	OUT-WARDS.		INWARDS.	OUT-WARDS.
Africa, directly ...	7	... 74	Africa	0	... 32
America	188	... 141	America	137	... 105
Denmark	0	... 19	Canaries	3	... 3
Flanders	4	... 7	France..............	1	... 5
France..............	2	... 5	Germany...........	3	... 1
Germany...........	7	... 14	Guernsey & Jersey	6	... 7
Greenland	3	... 3	Holland	7	... 5
Holland	4	... 14	Ireland	79	... 107
Ireland	418	... 455	Italy	5	... 0
Isle of Man	46	... 56	Levant..............	1	... 0
Italy	4	... 5	Newfoundland ...	6	... 14
North Fishery ...	1	... 1	Norway	13	... 14
Norway	19	... 7	Poland	3	... 4
Portugal...	11	... 3	Portugal	15	... 8
Prussia	18	... 12	Russia..............	5	... 2
Russia..............	21	... 2	Saxony	5	... 8
Spain	5	... 3	Spain	30	... 28
Sweden	8	... 2	Sweden	9	... 0
			Tuscany	3	... 1
	766	823		332	343

(1) From Troughton's Liverpool, page 266.

No. X.

The NUMBER OF SHIPS, and their TONNAGE, that have cleared Outwards, and entered Inwards at the Port of Liverpool, from the year 1751 to 1793, and for 1801.[1]

	INWARDS.				OWTWARDS.			
	BRITISH.		FOREIGN.		BRITISH.		FOREIGN.	
YEAR.	SHIPS.	TONS.	SHIPS.	TONS.	SHIPS.	TONS.	SHIPS.	TONS.
1751	523	29,178	20	2,535	588	31,185	20	2,508
1752	529	29,137	46	5,430	561	31,777	48	5,884
1753	584	34,221	28	3,515	601	34,689	22	3,085
1754	577	32,255	44	5,710	588	33,435	42	5,843
1755	507	33,159	29	3,425	519	30,660	27	3,315
1756	522	29,793	48	5,195	607	35,426	42	4,542
1757	554	32,386	68	7,300	609	37,881	57	7,268
1758	602	36,263	63	7,296	641	38,502	56	6,277
1759	519	33,006	112	17,789	551	35,079	117	14,498
1760	556	36,884	76	10,535	592	37,157	81	11,663
1761	529	32,899	80	11,043	654	40,268	60	8,223
1762	623	45,540	94	12,344	614	39,304	102	13,844
1763	574	39,714	78	11,584	700	44,863	92	13,596
1764	695	46,387	71	10,112	772	50,709	58	8,132
1765	738	53,030	65	8,134	795	53,807	70	9,811
1766	646	51,623	54	7,825	708	51,012	69	9,370
1767	663	51,690	70	8,011	784	57,376	66	9,482
1768	727	54,949	57	7,225	826	60,379	59	7,950
1769	759	58,348	77	10,784	907	62,499	78	11,329
1770	743	46,062	63	7,965	942	66,516	79	10,381
1771	764	59,734	55	6,924	959	73,432	65	10,366
1772	857	68,812	68	8,401	1022	81,689	73	11,284
1773	970	70,392	57	7,111	1022	76,588	64	9,366
1774	989	79,315	61	8,032	973	76,892	64	8,744
1775	1016	86,382	56	7,294	983	76,686	57	7,494
1776	901	74,140	81	12,991	937	68,488	75	11,616
1777	893	70,792	101	11,627	979	71,295	96	11,852
1778	838	76,277	100	13,342	857	63,420	95	11,782
1779	742	57,103	136	17,623	908	64,836	149	19,379
1780	739	58,769	133	17,087	880	61,573	151	19,202
1781	801	58,914	169	22,569	1021	65,477	182	25,899
1782	847	66,290	169	23,107	968	64,481	213	30,295
1783	1165	96,089	206	28,376	1355	105,074	222	32,294
1784	1217	122,263	162	26,091	1333	113,481	160	26,958
1785	1427	127,388	129	21,576	1446	122,195	129	21,990
1786	1381	140,224	150	27,611	1337	128,766	140	28,194
1787	1348	153,625	161	26,903	1474	159,834	180	31,715
1788	1570	140,812	152	25,600	1673	186,355	156	26,973
1789	1603	171,672	89	15,202	1486	170,369	87	14,456
1790	1864	205,440	200	35,677	1779	201,641	196	36,143
1791	1814	220,318	254	46,878	1904	225,641	263	46,839
1792	1832	225,242	215	41,166	1926	231,277	212	41,213
1793	1704	188,286	215	41,177	1739	169,770	240	47,719
1801	1331		641		1694		705	

(1) From Troughton's Liverpool, page 260.

No. X.

An Account of the NUMBER OF VESSELS, with the Amount of their Tonnage, that have entered Inwards and cleared Outwards, in the Port of Liverpool, in the following years, distinguished according to the places whence and to which they made their voyages (N.B. Coasters excluded).(1)

	1788								1789							
	INWARDS				OUTWARDS				INWARDS				OUTWARDS			
	BRITISH		FOREIGN		BRITISH		FOREIGN		BRITISH		FOREIGN		BRITISH		FOREIGN	
Place	SHIPS	TONS	SHIPS	TONS	SHIPS	TONS	SHIPS	TONS	SHIPS	TONS	SHIPS	TONS	SHIPS	TONS	SHIPS	TONS
AFRICA	18	3,310	..	..	73	13,394	..	..	12	1,432	..	..	66	11,564	..	..
AMERICA, viz: BRITISH COLONIES	4	1,016	..	..	14	2,745	..	..	3	220	..	..	8	1,807	..	..
UNITED STATES	58	11,644	49	7,170	66	14,243	51	7,245	62	12,083	37	5,206	110	20,471	39	5,689
WEST INDIES	168	34,988	..	..	112	23,442	..	..	156	33,492	..	..	76	16,195	..	..
BRITISH FISHERY	19	722	..	..	..	..	..	..	41	1,318	..	..	..	..	..	..
SOUTH FISHERY	..	..	..	..	1	320	..	..	1	320	..	..	..	..	..	..
GREENLAND FISHERY	22	6,774	..	..	22	6,774	..	..	13	3,915	..	..	18	5,605	..	..
HONDURAS BAY	4	575	..	..	..	..	..	..	2	434	..	..	1	77	..	..
IRELAND	970	64,131	18	1,684	999	63,764	..	..	968	67,784	13	1,662	890	57,114	..	..
ISLE OF MAN	99	3,686	1	80	112	4,522	..	..	105	4,383	..	..	111	4,240	1	82
GUERNSEY	1	93	..	..	3	196	..	..	1	72	..	..	5	430	..	..
JERSEY	..	..	..	..	..	..	..	..	2	166	..	..	6	324	..	..
DENMARK AND NORWAY	5	963	15	2,563	15	5,293	21	3,553	1	91	5	740	23	6,989	19	3,067
RUSSIA	68	21,346	1	120	22	8,608	1	112	47	14,771	..	..	18	6,417	..	..
SWEDEN	5	593	3	382	1	113	2	240	12	1,105	..	..	1	100	..	..
GERMANY	10	1,447	9	1,086	25	5,037	18	2,258	10	1,508	5	616	23	4,482	5	679
HOLLAND	19	1,818	1	120	7	847	47	11,375	6	696	..	..	11	980	..	..
POLAND AND PRUSSIA	26	8,590	46	11,208	17	6,917	7	1,336	37	12,407	21	6,010	20	7,487	16	4,239
FLANDERS	3	491	1	200	57	9,978	8	1,278	5	539	1	156	70	12,604	1	156
FRANCE	29	2,958	5	520	78	8,278	8	947	82	8,394	4	517	69	6,756	1	159
PORTUGAL	29	2,871	4	367	22	2,470	3	198	51	5,160	3	295	24	2,797	5	385
SPAIN	18	2,026	2	100	15	1,713	..	..	19	2,109	..	..	19	1,915	..	..
ITALY	14	1,492	..	..	12	1,563	..	..	10	1,026	..	..	18	2,092	..	..
TURKEY	..	..	..	..	..	..	..	..	..	..	..	..	..	..	..	..
TOTAL	1589	171,534	155	25,600	1673	180,217	166	28,542	1646	173,425	89	15,202	1587	170,446	87	14,456

(1) From Troughton's Liverpool, page 261.

No. X.

An Account of the Number of Vessels—*continued.*(1)

	1790 INWARDS BRITISH Ships	Tons	1790 INWARDS FOREIGN Ships	Tons	1790 OUTWARDS BRITISH Ships	Tons	1790 OUTWARDS FOREIGN Ships	Tons	1791 INWARDS BRITISH Ships	Tons	1791 INWARDS FOREIGN Ships	Tons	1791 OUTWARDS BRITISH Ships	Tons	1791 OUTWARDS FOREIGN Ships	Tons
AFRICA	11	1,833	..	..	91	17,917	..	..	10	1,622	..	..	102	19,610	..	..
AMERICA, viz: BRITISH COLONIES	1	52	..	..	20	3,731	..	..	8	1,550	..	..	22	4,650	..	..
UNITED STATES	78	14,675	60	9,679	77	16,151	67	10,276	62	14,587	103	18,491	97	21,844	105	17,945
WEST INDIES	155	32,158	1	150	91	19,622	..	..	185	38,196	..	..	98	19,945	..	..
BRITISH FISHERY	31	930	..	..	..	..	..	..	31	932	..	..	..	..	..	..
SOUTH FISHERY	..	..	..	..	1	320	..	..	1	320	..	..	1	459	..	..
GREENLAND FISHERY	14	4,053	..	..	13	4,401	..	..	15	4,373	..	..	15	4,373	..	..
HONDURAS BAY	3	564	..	..	..	..	..	..	2	255	..	..	4	731	..	..
IRELAND	1112	78,491	15	1,991	1037	69,351	..	..	998	74,551	18	2,149	1064	76,353	..	..
ISLE OF MAN	87	3,810	..	..	95	4,270	..	..	103	4,522	..	..	101	4,258	..	..
GUERNSEY	1	218	..	..	8	992	..	..	1	70	2	330	4	471	..	..
JERSEY	1	25	..	..	1	25	39	7,500	3	437	..	..	..	..	46	8,281
DENMARK AND NORWAY	9	1,586	20	3744	31	5,852	2	463	122	33,129	18	3,075	35	8,302	1	199
RUSSIA	81	22,328	1	110	55	18,390	1	150	8	1,035	6	738	62	18,365	6	726
SWEDEN	7	604	14	1,529	5	515	23	2,883	12	2,525	20	2601	3	547	25	3,791
GERMANY	9	980	7	707	24	3,788	3	215	23	2,409	10	784	30	5,669	1	47
HOLLAND	25	2,647	65	15,742	9	1,158	38	10,741	84	20,409	72	18,083	7	839	57	14,868
POLAND AND PRUSSIA	83	23,174	3	435	30	10,450	10	2,300	1	113	..	..	32	9,926	12	2,670
FLANDERS	2	91	7	920	68	11,270	1	172	41	4,273	2	307	67	10,165	3	362
FRANCE	47	5,371	4	394	50	5,515	5	514	84	9,923	3	313	50	5,533	4	486
PORTUGAL	64	6,914	2	201	39	4,367	2	246	27	3,110	..	..	46	5,682	3	464
SPAIN	19	2,014	1	75	17	1,788	5	683	15	1,882	..	..	33	3,940	..	..
ITALY	21	2,619	..	..	15	1,859	..	..	9	1,027	..	..	30	3,656	..	..
TURKEY	3	303	..	..	..	..	..	..	..	..	..	..	1	323	..	..
TOTAL	1863	205,440	200	35,677	1779	201,741	196	36,143	1845	221,250	254	46,878	1904	225,641	263	49,839

(1) From Troughton's Liverpool, page 261 and 262.

No. X.

Account of the Number of Vessels—*continued.*(1)

	1792								1793							
	INWARDS				OUTWARDS				INWARDS				OUTWARDS			
	BRITISH		FOREIGN		BRITISH		FOREIGN		BRITISH		FOREIGN		BRITISH		FOREIGN	
	SHIPS	TONS	SHIPS	TONS	SHIPS	TONS	SHIPS	TONS	SHIPS	TONS	SHIPS	TONS	SHIPS	TONS	SHIPS	TONS
AFRICA	11	1,643	..	..	132	22,402	..	..	14	2,260	..	..	52	10,544	..	..
AMERICA, viz: BRITISH COLONIES	13	3,290	..	..	26	6,318	..	..	6	1,411	..	..	22	4,337	..	..
UNITED STATES	52	11,834	102	18,964	71	15,844	103	18,796	37	9,115	117	21,061	17	4,807	117	21,429
WEST INDIES	195	38,902	..	..	115	24,317	..	..	127	38,911	..	..	108	22,996	..	..
BRITISH FISHERY	26	776	..	..	..	..	..	..	22	670	..	..	..	..	..	..
SOUTH FISHERY	1	459	..	..	..	..	..	..	2	419	..	..	3	710	..	..
GREENLAND FISHERY	14	3,971	..	..	14	5,971	..	..	11	2,978	..	..	11	2,978	..	..
HONDURAS BAY	4	823	15	2,026	3	591	..	..	7	1,463	32	5,347	1	253	..	..
IRELAND	1039	79,965	..	..	1055	76,191	..	..	1073	82,718	..	..	1289	95,250	..	..
ISLE OF MAN	100	4,159	..	..	118	4,826	..	..	136	5,734	3	365	151	6,860	..	..
GUERNSEY	..	..	..	..	1	59	..	..	..	..	..	..	..	..	..	..
JERSEY	1	102	12	1,884	1	40	..	..	..	..	..	..	..	..	..	..
DENMARK AND NORWAY	142	41,535	4	440	25	6,068	31	5,376	4	429	9	1,343	28	7,964	15	2,772
RUSSIA	11	1,365	..	..	83	27,011	1	380	52	16,168	..	..	28	9,811	1	230
SWEDEN	16	2,267	15	2,413	2	522	4	494	3	235	5	611	..	..	5	419
GERMANY	18	2,282	11	1,083	31	5,648	13	1,917	6	941	3	608	22	4,194	16	2,570
HOLLAND	46	12,964	29	13,628	16	2,026	5	242	12	1,273	2	270	10	1,416	6	928
POLAND AND PRUSSIA	..	..	..	..	15	5,517	34	10,571	71	15,740	34	10,456	30	8,531	30	10,127
FLANDERS	27	2,391	1	96	71	13,096	11	1,788	..	..	..	..	25	5,715	32	6,519
FRANCE	84	10,164	4	304	32	3,078	3	724	4	467	3	340	..	..	11	1,068
PORTUGAL	29	3,108	2	328	55	6,921	7	594	33	3,830	5	494	17	2,250	3	194
SPAIN	29	4,018	..	..	26	2,920	1	331	21	2,166	2	282	7	650	1	194
ITALY	..	..	..	..	34	3,911	..	..	15	2,029	..	..	15	1,895	3	469
TURKEY	..	..	..	..	..	..	..	..	..	..	..	..	..	..	..	..
TOTAL	1858	226,018	215	41,166	1926	231,277	212	41,213	1726	188,957	215	41,177	1836	191,191	240	47,719

(1) From Troughton's Liverpool, page 262.

No. XI.

"October 30, 1752.

A List of all the Ships belonging to Liverpool, with their Names, their present Commanders' Names, and in what Trade employ'd.

Vessels from * to * inclusive, are employ'd in the Guiney Trade.

    † to †   do.   in the West India, American, and Foreign Trade.

    ‡ to ‡   do.   commonly take Freight for different Parts of Europe.

    ‖ to ‖   do.   Coasters, and in the Irish Trade, [frequently take Freight for different Parts.]

    § to §   do.   in the London and Cheese Trade.

‡† The Clayton was taken by the Three Sisters, Capt. Jenkin's Long-Boat; whose Crew turn'd Pirates, and carried her to Pernambuco, where a Portuguese Man of War retook her, and has brought her to Lisbon. Capt. Jenkins was shipwreck'd on the Coast of Wexford, October   and he with most of the Crew perished.

  *‖ Sailed from Jamaica twelve months ago for Liverpool, but not since heard of.

  ‖‡ There has been no Account of her these twelve months.

---

* Africa, — Harrison
African, John Newton
Annabella, Wm. Harrison
Antigua Merchant, Rob. Thomas
Anglesey, James Caruthers
Alice Galley, Rich. Jackson
Ann Galley, Nehemiah Holland
Adlington, Tho. Perkin
Allen, James Strangeways
* Achilles, Thomas Patrick
† Alice and Betty, Rich. Hutchinson
Aaron, Samuel Woodward
Anson, Wm. Pemberton
Austin, Matthew Holme
Allen, David Clatworthy
Allerton, James Wallace
Achilles, John Bissbrown
America, George Nicholson
† Ann & Margaret, Law. Mac Leane
‡ Ann, Patrick Strong
Annandale, William Johnston
‡ Adventure, Stephen Reed
‖ Abigail, James Mac Loughlane
Annabella, Alexander Drumgold
‖ Argyle, James Mac Targot
§ Alexander, Edward Howard
* Betty, Samuel Sacheverelle
Blake, Alexander Torbet
Barbadoes Merchant, John Wilson
Boyne, William Wilkinson
Beverley, William Lowe
Brooke, Thomas Kewley

Barclay, John Gadson
Bulkeley, Christopher Baitson
Britannia, James Pemberton
* Bridget, Anthony Grayson
† Britannia, William Day
Brownbill, James Neale
Betty and Peggy, Philip Nagle
Betty, George Drinkwater
† Baldwin, George Mathews
‡ Ball, David Guthrie
‖ Bidston, Christopher Hindley
Betty, Thomas Ward
Betty and Peggy, William More
Betty, Robert Wallace
Betty and Peggy, Joseph Martin
Boyne, James Lampart
Betty and Peggy, Ambrose Sharp
Bank-Key, John Abram
‖ Betty, Thomas Ward
* Cumberland, John Griffin
Chesterfield, Patrick Black
‡† Clayton, —— ——
Charming Nancy, Tho. Roberts
* Cavendish, Robert Jennings
† Cunliffe, John Cleater
Charming Peggy, —— ——
Carter, Samuel Lea
Cæsar, Joseph Wayles
Cato, Charles Slater
Charles, Thomas Nunns
Choptank, Edward Barnes
† Catherine, John Matthews

‡ Clare, David Welch
‡ Concord, John Barrow
|| Charming Molly, Nich. Shimin
Charming Jenny, George Geddes
|| Catherine, John Hamilton
* Duke of Cumberland, John Crosbie
* Dolphin, Joseph Pedrick
† Deane, Christopher Bretargh
Darby and Joan, David Scott
† Draper, Thomas Benn
‡ Duke of Cumberland, Jn. Houston
Diana, James Hurst
‡ Diana, Wilfred Inman
|| Dublin Trader, George Hartwell
Dean Swift, John Murdoch
Dorcas, Galan Hamilton
Draper, Robert Moore
Drogheda Merchant, John Hayes
Duke, Thomas Deaz
Dreadnought, —— Barnes
|| Devonshire, John Janny
§ Diligence, Rowland Hunter
§ Deacon, William Taylor
* Elizabeth, William Heys
Elijah, —— ——
*|| Enterprise, Sam. Greenhow
* Ellis and Robert, Rich. Jackson
‡ Expedition, John Gaff
Elizabeth, Nathaniel Sayers
Eagle, William Copell
Eaton, —— —— —
Everton, Thomas Kelly
Elizabeth, Jonathan Howard
Entwisle, John Smith
Earl of Holderness, Wm. Simpson
Elizabeth, Giles Heysham
Esther, Gilbert Rigby
† Edward, John Murdock
‡ Endeavour, William Cooke
‡ Elizabeth, Alexander Jolly
|| Ellen, Daniel Graham
Endeavour, Richard Barry
Elizabeth and Ann, W. Midgley
Experiment, Walter Young
|| Ellenor, Richard Parker
§ Elizabeth, Charles Howard
Elizabeth and Rebecca, Jos: Deane
§ Edward and Mary, John Littler
* Fanny, William Jenkinson
Florimel, Samuel Linaker
Frodsham, James Powell
Fortune, Hugh Williams
* Foster, Edward Cropper
† Fanny, James Brown

|| Friendship, Alexander Robb
|| Fairplay, Charles Griffin
§ Friendship, Samuel Hunter
* George, Charles Cooke
Grace, —— ——
* Greyhound, Maurice Roach
† Good Intent, Richard Rimmer
Granville, James Lesley,
Greyhound, Isaac Wakely
Golden Lyon, John Metcalf
Gildart, Geo: Sweeting
George, John Gass
Goodman, James Hagarty
† Grampus, Job Lewis
|| Gwydier, Christopher Roshall
Game Cock, James Neale
|| George and William, J. Crocket
* Hesketh, James Thompson
Hector, Brook Kelsall
* Hardman, Joseph Yoward
† Hillary, Timothy Wheelwright
Hopewell, Francis Bare
Happy Return, James Waugh
Henry, William Ross
Hothersall, Thomas Bruce
Happy, James Barrow
† Hopewell, Alexander Caterwood
‡ Happy Chance, John Boggs
‡ Hope, Benjamin Kirby
|| Hibernia, Andrew Moreton
Hawke, Hugh Cunning
Hopewell, James Shutter
|| Henry, Francis Ellis
§ Halsey, Thomas Harrison
* Jenny, Thomas Darbyshire
Judith, Nicholas Southworth
* James, John Sacheverelle
† Jenny, John Quay
John and Hannah, John Triplet
Isaac, John Mac Neale
Jonathan, James Nottingham
James Galley, James Walling
Jenny, John Scorfield
† Joseph and Jane, Wm. Worsdale
‡ John and Thomas, Thomas
Rymer
Isaac and Barbara, Anth. Piper
Isabella, Henry Hinde
Jennet, John Gardner
‡ Jane, Anthony Cocks
|| John, William Weston
Industry, Richard Kenyon
John and Alice, William Jackson

John, Matthew Johnson
John and Robert, James Semple
John and Thomas, Tho. Johnston
Industry, John Moore
Judith, William Semple
Jolly Cooper, James Robinson
|| Jane, James Heslep
§ John and Mary, William Barrow
* Knight, Wm. Boats
† Kingston, John Jump
‡ Kirkham, James Shaw
* Lintott, Ralph Lowe
Lord Strange, Edward Smith
Lovely Betty, George Jackson
* Little Billy, Thomas Dickenson
† Lamb, ⸺ ⸺
Lamb, James Kennedy
Lucy, Nicholas Bolton
Liverpool, Thomas Stamper
Loyd, Samuel Venables
† Liverpool Merchant, S. Matthews
|| Lamb, William Carlisle
Liverpool, Samuel Rimmer
|| Lamb, Peter Wright
§ Lyon, Edmund Lyon
* Mersey, John Gee
Middleham, John Welch
Methwen, John Coppell
Minerva, Thomas Jordan
Mercury, John Walker
* Molly, Richard Rigby
† Monmouth, Henry Twentyman
Melling, John Mathews
Mercury, ⸺ Hutton
Mary Ann, John Quay
† Molly, John Stanton
‡ Marq: of Rockingham, W. Briggs
|| Molly, John Moore
Mary Anne, Joseph Furlong
Morning Star, Solomon Hog
Mary Jane, James Costollo
Martha and Mary, Tho. Howell
Manchester, Ranald Mac'Donald
Martin, Tho. Priest
Martha, Thomas Mac'Kewn
Margaret, Samuel Dawson
Medlicot, Michael Chevers
Martin, Joseph Maynard
Mawbray, Andrew Miller
Mary, Bartholomew Murray
|| Margaret, John Atkinson
§ Manchester, Francis Cooke
* Neptune, Tho. Thompson
Nelly, Joseph Drape

Nancy, John Honeyford
* Nancy, Robert Hewin
† Nancy, Elliot Cooke
Nancy, Thomas Midgeley
Nassau, John Gawith
Nancy, John Foster
† Neptune, Geo. Johnston
|| Newton, John Cartwright
Nancy, Christopher Baker
Newry Trader, Arch. Mac'Donald
Nathaniel, Patrick Withers
New Draper, Edward Semple
|| Nancy, Robert Stevenson
§ Nathaniel, Samuel Hunter
* Orrel, James Griffin
* Ormond Success, ⸺
|| Owners Endeavour, Ja. Stevenson
* Pardoe, ⸺ ⸺
Priscilla, William Parkinson
Phœbe, William Lawson
* Prince William, John Valentine
† Polly, James Clements
Parkside, James Foley
Preston, James Simpson
Pemberton, ⸺ ⸺
Prince of Wales, Robert Gordon
Prospect, Richard Hutchinson
Providence, Rich. Micklethwaite
Providence, Joseph Taylor
Panther, Leonard Benson
Prescot, Bryan Smith
Peggy and Molly, James Oates
Phœnix, Samuel Kelly
Prince, Richard Overton
Pri. of Orange, Constantine
  Hodson
Prince Edward, ⸺ ⸺
† Penelope, John Chubbard
‡ Princess of Wales, Justin Kingston
‡ Parker, John Harrison
|| Prince William, John Chisolm
Ponsonby, Robert Linekar
Phœnix, Robert Johnson
Prosperity, James Doyle
Prince William, James Clinden
Prince of Orange, Ar. Mac'Combe
Prince Edward, ⸺ ⸺
Prosperity, John Wilson
Prince William, Rob. Mac'Makin
Peggy, William Jackson
|| Peter, Peter Swainson
§ Prince Henry, Edward Daniel
* Rider, Michael Rush
* Ranger, James Sanders

† Recovery, Jonathan Slade
Recovery, John Robinson
Robert, Peter Kennedy,
Recovery, William Robinson
Ross, William Potter
Richard, John Platt
† Radbourne, Thomas Ward
‡ Rawleigh, John Grove
‖ Royal Oak, John Thompson
Robert & David, Hugh M‘Nab
Ross, George Duncan
Resolution, John Warburton
‖ Recovery, William Jackson
§ Richmond, William Taylor
§ Robert, John Salisbury
* Sarah, Alexander Lawson
'Salisbury, Thomas Marsden
Sterling Castle, Charles Gardner
Samuel and Nancy, James Lowe
Swan, Peter Leay
* Sammy and Biddy, Rob. Grayson
† Spencer, Rob. Whitlow
Shaw, James Bennet
Stronge, Thomas Cubbin
Susannah, Edward Pryer
† Speedwell, John Thornton
‡ Stadtholder, John Johnson
Sarah and Martha, Rob. Atkinson
‡ Susannah, Robert Durham
‖ Stanhope, Murdock Mac'Ever
Success, Charles Lace
Sugar-house, Richard Hughes
Salford, John Andrews
Speedwell, Nathaniel Allen
Seaflower, Joseph Pugmore
Sankey, —— ——
‖ Sally and Betty, Rich. Hutchinson
§ Smith, Samuel Salisbury
Sally and Betty, Stephen Serjeant
§ Salmon, Henry Ashton
* Tarleton, Jn. Thompson
Triton, Charles Jenkinson
Thomas, James Hutchinson
True Blue, Benjamin Wade
* Thomas and Martha, Jn. Gillman
† Tayloe, John Gaitskill

Tryton, Robert Boyd
Tyger, Gawan Burrows
Telemachus, Robert Feartlough
Trafford, Thomas Goodaker
Tryal, Peter Johnson
† Tryal, Patrick Harrold
‡ Tryal, Richard Newton
‡ Two Brothers, John Clements
‖ True Love, Robert Miller
‖ Thomas and Nancy, John Brooks
§ Trout, John Urmson
* Vigilant, Wm. Freeman ‖ ‡
* Union, Tim. Anyon
† Vine, Robert Makin
Volunteer, Tho. Naylor
† Upton, John Gardiner
‡ Unity, Abraham Williams
‖ Vernon, John Barrowdale
* William and Betty, Th. Barclay
† William, William Nobler
Windsor, —— ——
Wheel of Fortune, Tho. Middleton
William and Robert, J. Chambers
William and Nancy, Wm. Settle
Warren, Robert Loxam
William, Alexander Cutter
† Willoughby, Richard Parker
‖ William, James Ward
William and Nancy, Wm. Settle
William and Betty, Wm. Quirk
Worthington, Samuel Lang
William and Sarah, Adam Weet
‖ Warrington, John Sherwin
§ William, William Vinor

Total, 357 Ships."

"N.B. There are upwards of eighty River Sloops employ'd in the Salt Trade, &c. Burthen from 40 to 70 Tons each, and Numbers of Vessels which use the Coasting Trade constantly that don't belong to the Port."

Liverpool: Printed and sold by E. Owen, in Moore-street."(1)

---

(1) From an original printed list in the possession of Mr. James Boardman.

No. XII.

RULES OF THE UNANIMOUS SOCIETY.

At a Meeting at Liverpool, this twenty-sixth day of October, in the year of our Lord One thousand seven hundred and fifty-four, it is agreed by us, whose names are hereunto subscrib'd, being a special and select Company nominated amongst ourselves THE UNANIMOUS SOCIETY, that we meet every Saturday evening, at the sign of the Cross Keys, in Dale-street, or at any other House, appointed by a Majority of Members present, from the first Saturday in September, to the last Saturday in April inclusive, every year successively.

And in order that no disputes may arise in the regulation of the same, it is agreed that the following Articles be observed, thorough the course and Term of the said Meetings.

In Ratification of which, we have hereunto Subscribed our Names, the Day and Year aforesaid.

First.—We agree if any one, or more, of the said Members, whose names are hereunto affixed, do not come, at the time and place afore-mentioned, on or before seven o'clock, on each evening whereon the said Society is intended to meet as afs^d, that he, or they, shall forfeit & pay into the hands of the President, for the time being, the sum of one penny, and if not 'till eight o'clock or after, the sum of two-pence, and if not on any time of the said night, the sum of three-pence except prevented by Sickness or Absence from Town.

Second.—That if any of the Members, Curse or Swear by or upon anything Solemn, or give any affronts to any of the said Members, that he or they shall forfeit and pay to the said President, for each default, the sum of one penny. That if any of the Members shall, at any time come into the said Society disguis'd in Liquor, he, or they shall pay into the hands of the President then being, the sum of Sixpence, if any dis-putes arise about the validity of such disguise, the same to be determined by Poll or Ballott of the Members then present, and in case of refusal of paying such fine, he or they to be disfranchised out of the said Society.

Third.—That no person resident in Town shall, on any account be admitted into the said Society without being a Member thereof, But any Member of the said Society shall have liberty to bring with him into the same, a Stranger, or one not resident in Town.

Fourth.—That the President shall order and have Bread, Cheese and Butter, and what other Supper the Members shall think proper to appoint (which they are to do the preceding night) upon the Table, on or before Eight o'clock on each night of the said Meeting. That each Member shall have free Liberty to call for what Liquor he chooses, and that the reckoning shall be equally collected from every Member then present. And that no one of the said Members be compelled to drink any quantity of Liquor, but what he shall think proper (except his own Toast), and that not in a half pint.

Fifth.—That the said President call for the reckoning at ten o'clock, on each night of their said Meeting, under forfeiture of one penny. Each Member is to pay his equivolent share of the Shott, and then leave the Society, or stay longer if he pleases. And that no Lewd Songs be introduced into the said Society without the consent of President, under forfeiture of Sixpence; and if any dispute shou'd arise about the time of the Night at comeing into the Society, or at closeing of the same, the time of comeing in to be determined by the House Clock, and the time of closeing, by the President's Watch.

Sixth.—That no person be admitted a Member of this Society without the Unanimous consent of all the Members present. And that the admission of every new Member be determined by Poll or Balott of the Members then present, and if one of such Members shall be against his admission, then the person so proposed shall not be admitted on any account whatsoever. But if the person so proposed be admitted a Member, he shall take such Oaths as are affixed, and in case of refusal, the said person not to be admitted. And in order for the better regulation of the said Society, one of the said Members shall be chose, by a Majority, to be President thereof, which Member so chose shall continue in office for the space of four nights, and at the conclusion of the fourth night, he shall nominate two Candidates, one of which shall be chose by Poll to succeed him, and so continually. The Member so acting as President shall be call'd and distinguish'd by all the Society by the name and title of Mr. President and no other. And the said President may be at liberty to nominate a Deputy, who is to be distinguish'd by the title of Secretary, and he in the absence of the President shall act as such, and have the like power as the President. And in default of the observance of any of the aforesaid Articles, the person so offending shall forfeit and pay to the said President for each default, the sum of one half penny. And it is further agreed that the President shall always be distinguished by wearing his Hatt during his attendance on the said Society. And that the said President attends the last night of his office under the forfeiture of Sixpence extraordinary, unless prevented by Sickness, or absence from Town.

Seventh.—That no Member or Members of the said Society, shall disclose any Secrets of the same, (except to a Brother Member) on any account whatsoever, and upon information and full conviction of such disclosure, the person so offending to pay two shillings.

Eighth.—That the said President shall keep a Book in a regular manner, and enter all fines and forfeitures receiv'd by him, which shall be at the inspection of any of the Members at pleasure; and that the said fines and forfeitures shall be to such use and uses, as a Majority of the said Members present shall direct—and in case of any of the said Members refuseing the payment of any of the said fines, and demand made thereof, by the President, or his deputy, or shall refuse to comply with and be subservient to all the Rules hereinbefore or after written, that the Member or Members so offending shall be disfranchis'd from the said Society, and be for ever afterwards excluded from being a Member of the same untill he has fully comply'd with the same, and paid such fine as a Majority of the Members shall think proper to inflict upon him.

Ninth.—It is Order'd by the Members of this Society, that when any of them do marry, they shall, on the first Meeting afterwards, pay unto the President for the time being the sum of ten shillings and sixpence, which said sum must be paid towards the Shott the first Evening upon their appearance after such Marriage.

Tenth.—It is Order'd by the Members of this Society, that all the Rules and Orders relateing to and observ'd by this Society, shall be read over by the Secretary, on the first Saturday in September, the first Saturday in December, and the first Saturday in March, immediately after Supper.

Eleventh.—It is order'd by the Members of this Society, that all for-

s 2

feitures shall be paid with one half-penny, instead of drinking a Glass of Liquor; and 'tis agreed that all Wagers laid in this Society shall go towards the Shott upon the first Meeting after the said Wager is determined.

Twelfth.—It is Ordered by the Members of this Society, that in case any person be proposed as a Member of this Society, the said person shall not be voted for untill the following Meeting; and that each absent Member shall be inform'd by the Secretary, in writeing, (the Monday after the said person is propos'd) of his name, who is desirous of being admitted, and in case of their non-attendance that evening, they shall have liberty of sending their Votes by a Brother Member; And if said person be chosen a Member, he shall, before his admission, pay Ten shillings and six-pence, otherwise not be admitted: and that such new Member shall be excused from paying any part of the Reckoning the first night of his attendance, when the half Guinea shall go towards the Shott or Reckoning, and be in lieu of paying any proportion of Fines.

Thirteenth.—It is order'd by the Members of this Society, that one penny shall be paid by every person that shall talk * * * * *, and if it shall be disputed what is * * * * *, the same shall be determined by a Majority of the Members present.

Fourteenth.—In case any disputes or arguments arise in this Society, not herein provided for or against, the same shall be left to the decision and determination of a Majority of Members present, and be fully observ'd under the penalty aforesaid: that all disputes which are to be determined by Poll, the President be allow'd a casting Vote, when the Poll is equal. And that there be no challenging of Toasts in this Society upon any account. And if the President, Secretary, and a Majority of the said Members, shall at any time during the continuation of this Society, think proper to alter or make any other new Laws, Articles or Rules, that shall be thought conducive to the regulation of this Society, and the same be enter'd in the Book or Books kept by the President, and sign'd by him and the Secretary for the time being, the same shall be observ'd, and kept to all intents and purposes by all the said Members, as if the same had been herein before inserted, and in case of any alterations in the aforesaid Rules or any new Rules made, the same not to be made till nine by the House Clock.

Witness our approbation & unanimous consent to the afore-written Rules, by signing our names hereto, in presence of each other the day and year before mentioned.

October	7, 1753	Tho. Golightly Joseph Jackson Will. Crosbie John Fairfax Tho. Holden
November	8, 1754	John Giball
September	4, 1756	Thos. Greenup
April	7, 1759	H. Lake
September	22, 1759	Geor: Warren Watts
September	21, 1760	Wm. Pole
November	20, 1761	Alexander Nottingham
September	18, 1762	Thomas Carter
October	—, 1763	Hornby Roughsedge
———	———	Wm. Ker
———	1763	James Bridge

November —,	1763	Robt Bromley
December 22,	1764	Will: Crosbie Junr
January 4,	1766	Jos.^h Brooks Junr
October 25,	1766	John Lyon
November 1,	1766	John Chorley
November 8,	1754	Mundy Pole
November 10,	1770	Geo: Venables
November 10,	1770	Clayton Case[1]

No. XIII.

SPEECH of Mr. SAMUEL HOLME, Mayor of Liverpool, at the Public Breakfast which took place at the Philharmonic-hall, in Hope-street, on the 8th of March, 1853, to commemorate the CENTENARY of the BIRTH of Mr. ROSCOE.[2]

My lords, ladies, and gentlemen, it is a gratification to me, in my official capacity, to be present here this day, to commemorate a name which is imperishably associated with my native town; and it is also a gratification, in these days of excitement, that there are bright and neutral spots where men of all parties may meet in friendship and in amity, without the sacrifice of a single principle, but for the purpose of doing honour to those who have been celebrated and illustrious. Such an occasion is that which has assembled together this magnificent meeting to-day, and as such I have availed myself of my privilege of being present. Distinguished men and remarkable objects are the milestones of time, which sweeps along in its resistless course and carries away the monarch and the subject, the learned and the ignorant. Our memories revert not so much, in taking a glance at the passing events of time, to particular years, as to particular epochs. The ages of Sesostris, of Leonidas, of Tarquin, of Scipio, of Cæsar, of Adrian, and in later periods, the age of the Medici, illustrated as their history was by our illustrious townsman; and, again, in later times, the period when the great German Reformer sounded the trumpet of intellectual and religious freedom; the period of the Revolution, when a new dynasty was called to the throne of England; the revolution of a neighbouring country, when fields were deluged with blood, and when Europe obtained peace for thirty years on the field of Waterloo,—those are all prominent epochs in time, and all deserve to be remembered. I would ask if any man could find himself in the region where the battle of Lepanto was fought without his mind dwelling upon the mighty achievements of that glorious

---

(1) From the original club-book, in the possession of Mr. John Forshaw. After 1770, it does not seem to have been the practice of the Club, for the Members who joined it to sign the club book, and consequently the signatures of the subsequent members do not appear after that date.

(2) See Chapter II, page 140, note (1).

conflict? I would also ask, if any man could view the plains of Marathon, or the pass of Thermopylæ; could see the bridge of Lodi, or the fields of Austerlitz and Marengo, without having extraordinary feelings excited within him, or without feeling that he was treading upon no common ground? And I think that no one could visit Stratford-upon-Avon, and see the birth-place of our great English poet, no one could tread in solitude the park of Abbotsford, or the field where Burns, at Mossgiel, turned up the daisy or disturbed the mouse, without feeling that such places were consecrated by genius, and have become localities that are celebrated to the whole world. Such men, by the lustre of their genius, throw a halo over the localities where they were born, and it is with such associations and such kindred feelings that we revert to a name and a reputation which are so connected with our town. Whether we agreed in the political or the religious opinions of our illustrious townsman or not, all of us can join in a tribute of admiration of the benevolence of his character,—the singular elegance and cultivation of his mind; and I see—and I see it with pleasure—that there is an attachment to the limited monarchical institutions of our country apparent throughout all the writings of our illustrious townsman; and as he never obtruded his religious opinions upon others, that theme is too sacred to be touched upon while he is mouldering in the grave. But his career was most remarkable. Although born of respectable parents, yet he was a poor boy. He was born within a few yards of the place where we are at present assembled; and as we read in his life—and it was a subject of no shame to him afterwards—he probably derived his first botanical lessons from cultivating the potatoes in his father's garden, which his son and biographer, with admirable courage and fidelity, tells us his father carried upon his head to sell in the public market. Then we trace him as a boy in a bookseller's shop. From that he was removed to the office of an attorney; and thus he gathered information in every position. He conquered the dead languages; he made himself master of many living tongues; and then, emerging as a poet and a historian of the first class, displayed an erudition which left behind many of the achievements of those who had enjoyed a university education. He exhibited a stamp of originality and an elegance which is seldom seen, and, as his grandson has said, he was sought out by the illustrious and the learned of every land, and he achieved a world-wide reputation, leaving behind him a name seldom surpassed. All these wonderful attainments deserve notice from those who can call him their townsman. But what do they show? They show that intellect cannot be chained, that perseverance can overcome all difficulties, and that quiet determination will accomplish its objects, step by step, whenever it may be exercised. To Roscoe we are indebted for our Botanic Garden; to Roscoe we are indebted in a great measure for our Athenæum, and certainly to him for its splendid library; to him we are indebted for our Royal Institution; and to him, too, in a great measure, are we indebted for a better taste in architecture, and for the introduction of the beautiful Grecian Doric into the town. Roscoe taught us that elegance is not incompatible with commerce, that the Athenæum was an adjunct to the Exchange, and that our Botanic Garden and our Royal Institution were perfectly consistent with our commercial transactions, docks, warehouses, and counting-houses. His writings display the greatest benevolence of character; and even when dilating upon a subject which has warmed and roused the ire of poets and of statesmen—I mean the wrongs of Africa, which have been already alluded to—we find that Roscoe, though indignant, was benevolent, and that his indignation was rather directed against the offence than personally against the offenders. Roscoe was not like the volcano, streaming forth lava to devastate and destroy; he was rather like the gentle and cultivated hill, which receives the fructifying showers of heaven upon its head, and distributes them into a thousand rills, for the purpose of delighting, invigorating, and improving mankind. And many years ago I found in Italy that the name of Roscoe was a password in all cultivated society. Washington Irving has stated that when he was at Stratford-upon-Avon he inquired of the sexton if he had ever seen opened the tomb of Shakspeare, when the sexton said he had once opened it and saw nothing but dust. Washington Irving's commentary was that he thought it *something* to have seen the dust of Shakspeare; and I in like manner felt, when I had the pleasure of a sojourn in Italy, amid the scenes which he had so admirably depicted, that it was something to be a townsman of Roscoe. Differing, then, as we may do on points of importance, we dwell not on such topics, they are buried with him in the tomb; but admiration of the grasp of intellect of our townsman—considering his name imperishably connected with Liverpool—looking upon him as a philanthropist, a man of genius, a poet, an essayist, and a historian, we embrace the period of his centenary as a reunion for those who knew him and admired him while living,—for the purpose, too, of meeting those now commencing the struggles of life, and to whom he offers a bright example, which I trust the young men who hear me this morning will follow, that they, too, may be of service in their generation. My lord, it was never my gratification, so far as I can remember, to see Roscoe. It is always a misfortune when we do not preserve the likeness of those we love. When they are removed from us, their outward lineaments may be forgotten; but the lineaments of the mind of the great men of the earth can never be forgotten, for their works stamp them on the minds of their fellow-countrymen when they attain, like Roscoe, a world-wide reputation. And now, when we have to lament that " the silver cord is loosed, and the golden bowl broken," and that Roscoe has been carried to the grave, yet still the memory of this great man, I trust, will remain and be useful for years to come, in the town where he was born and where he lived; and although the vase may be broken, that there will be fragrance preserved amongst the fragments which will delight millions for generations yet to come. It is with these sentiments that I have availed myself of the invitation the committee have given to attend in my public capacity, as the noble chairman has in his private capacity, to do honour to the memory of a man whose name is so imperishably connected with the town of Liverpool.[1]

---

(1) From the Liverpool Mercury of 11th March, 1853.

No. XIV.

On the DEATH of MR. BROOKE,[*] the Father of the Author, *(From the Liverpool Courier of the 16th of June, 1852.)*

It is our painful duty to have to record the death of Richard Brooke, Esq. one of the oldest inhabitants of Liverpool, an event which occurred on the 15th instant. There are some circumstances respecting this gentleman, and the vast and extraordinary changes which he witnessed in Liverpool, of so remarkable a nature as to be well worthy of notice. He was born on the 14th of June, 1761, and at the time of his death he had just entered his 92d year. He is believed to have been the oldest landowner in Cheshire, having been for nearly 78 years the owner of an estate (which has for a very long period belonged to his family) at Handford, in that county; and he had been married during a period of more than 60 years. He was a native of Cheshire, (his family was for many years located at Buglawton and Smallwood, in the parish of Astbury;) but he came to reside in Liverpool on the 13th of January, 1776, which was not very long after the commencement of hostilities in the American revolutionary war; and he was the last surviving person, or at least one of the last, who had resided in this town, some time before the declaration of independence of the American States, of the 4th of July, 1776.

During that eventful contest, he was a contemporary with, and knew Mr. Roscoe; Mr. William Rathbone, grandfather of the present Mr. Rathbone; Mr. Thomas Tarleton, elder brother of Colonel Tarleton, afterwards member for Liverpool, and well known at a still later period as General Sir Banastre Tarleton, Bart.; Mr. Rawlinson, at one time member for Liverpool: Mr. Thomas Staniforth, father of the late Mr. Staniforth; Mr. Birch, grandfather of Sir Thomas B. Birch, Bart. member for Liverpool; Mr. Blackburne; Mr. Sparling; Mr. Boats; Mr. Watt; Mr. Walker; Mr. Seel; Mr. Kent; Mr. Bolden; Mr. Gildart; Mr. Joseph Brooks, great uncle of the Venerable Archdeacon Brooks; besides many other individuals of the old Liverpool families, who have long been in their graves.

The information which Mr. Brooke possessed respecting the former state, and the subsequent changes and increase of Liverpool, was exceedingly extensive and valuable. He was gifted with a clear and retentive

---

[*] It has been mentioned in the Preface, that the Author obtained a considerable degree of the information contained in this Work from his Father, who, during his long life, had opportunities of acquiring a vast deal of curious and valuable information relative to Liverpool. By far the largest portion of the manuscript of this Work was written before his death, and was submitted (although, of course, in an incomplete state) to him, and corrected in some respects, by him.

memory, and, unlike most other aged persons, he could remember circumstances both of a remote and recent date; and when he was examined some years ago as a witness on the important and well-known trial before Lord Chief Justice Denman, relative to the right of the Corporation of Liverpool to their large revenue from the town dues, it was the opinion of many persons competent to form a correct judgment, amongst whom we believe that we are justified in including one of the eminent counsel employed on behalf of the Corporation, who is now one of the judges of the Court of Common Pleas, that the result of that trial was in no small degree to be attributed to the accurate knowledge which Mr. Brooke possessed relative to Liverpool.

He witnessed wonderful and astonishing changes in the town and port. He knew Liverpool at a period when it possessed only three floating docks; Castle-street was so narrow, that it was with difficulty that two carriages could pass; Clayton-square, though laid out, had only a few houses erected in it; the town could merely support two weekly newspapers; there was only one chapel (Pitt-street) belonging to the Methodists; one very small meeting-house of the Society of Friends, in Hackins-hey; one Roman Catholic chapel, which was of exceedingly limited size, in Lumber-street; and not one place of worship of the Scotch Presbyterians; there was one theatre, but neither amphitheatre, circus, or music-hall; the population of the town and parish was little more than 35,000, the result of the last census gave 255,309, and including the portions of the out-townships added to Liverpool by the parliamentary reform act, and the seamen, it is believed now to exceed 400,000; between the house called the Three Sixes, in Toxteth-park, and the village of Garston, a large district now covered with splendid mansions and beautiful villas, there were only three dwelling-houses; of the public buildings used for secular purposes there were only two built of stone, the present Town-hall, and the Old Tower, in Water-street, all the others in the town being built of dingy brick; and there were only seven places of worship of the Church of England in Liverpool, or within three miles of the Exchange on the Lancashire side; there are now forty-seven.

The changes in all those respects, which occurred in the lifetime of one individual, have been astonishing.

It has been frequently remarked, with regret, that on the deaths of several Liverpool persons, who might easily be named as having possessed talents and information, all the valuable knowledge which they had acquired, relative to the town perished with them. That inconvenience, however, is not likely to occur, with respect to the extensive information, possessed by the gentleman whose death we are recording, because it was stated without any reserve, several years ago, in an address delivered by a member of his family, at a general meeting of one of the literary societies, at which the then mayor, T. B. Horsfall, Esq. presided, that measures had been adopted, to prevent the information which this venerable patriarch had acquired, from being lost.

By the death of this gentleman, it may be truly said, that Liverpool has lost the last individual of the " old school." Blessed by Providence with good health, and with length of years, far beyond the usual lot of mortals, Mr. Brooke had also the rare happiness, of retaining his memory and knowledge of persons and events, until the period of his death. He possessed a vast amount of interesting information, relative to the former inhabitants of Liverpool; and it has happened in more instances than one, during his long life, that he has known five successive generations in a

Liverpool family. It is always a solemn, and not unfrequently an affecting event, when the grave closes upon an aged man; and in concluding this brief account of this venerable individual, we may be permitted to observe, that in one respect the void created by his death, can never be supplied, because we have now lost the last person who knew "old Liverpool," and possessed from his own observation, at so remote a period back, an extensive and valuable fund of information respecting it; and he may, without impropriety, be said to have been a link connecting the past with the present race of men, and to have stood between the dead and the living.

ADDITIONS AND CORRECTIONS.

Page.

19 In Note (1), for "mislead," read, "misled."

29 After the seventh line introduce, " There are also amongst the muniments preserved in the Tower of London some other proofs of the visit of Edward the 2nd to Liverpool, and also of his having remained at least three days there. Letters patent were issued by him, containing a grant to the Priory of Cartmel, concluding, ' Teste Rege apud Liverpool 26º die Octobris ;'[1] and amongst the writs of Privy Seal is one addressed to the Chancellor, relative to the lands of John de Patesmere, and Ralph de Bukton, concluding thus, ' don' souz nostre prive seal a Liverpol' le xxvi jour d' Octobre, l'an de nostre regne xviime"[2]

38 For " lower end," read, " lower ends."

49 For " 1721," read " 1725," and add,

The following are copies of entries in one of the Books of Records of the Corporation, of the 7th and 15th of April, 1725, from which it is evident that at that date, some, at least, of the walls and buildings of the old Castle had not been removed, when the Council concluded to erect St. George's Church on its site :—

1725, } " Present in Council, &c."
April 7. } " Ordered, That such part of the Buildings and Ground of the late Castle as the Council shall think fitt to let out, shall be putt into small lotts, of six yards in a lott, and publick notice to be given, that the same are to be

---

(1) Pat. part 1, 17 Edward 2nd, membrane 11.

(2) Writs of Privy Seal of Edward 2nd, No. 8. The Author inspected the originals of the two last-mentioned instruments, in the Tower of London, on the 28th of May, 1853 : and has much pleasure in expressing his thanks to Mr. Hardy, the talented and learned assistant-keeper of the Records there, for the assistance which the Author, whilst pursuing his researches in the Tower, received from that gentleman : it is only an act of justice to bear testimony to the talent, attention, and courtesy with which the duties of a public department, and one which is very important in a national point of view, are conducted by him. After Edward the 2nd left Skipton, the letters patent in the Tower show that he visited several places before his arrival at Liverpool, amongst which may be named Blackburne, in Lancashire, and also a place called Holland (the latter within about a day before his arrival at Liverpool). Quære, was not that Up Holland, near Wigan ; and if so, where could the King have been entertained ? Was it at the Abbey of the Black Friars there ? Or, as a castle of the Hollands is said to have once existed there ; was that the place where he stayed ? His visit to Lancashire most probably had reference to the possessions of the late Earl of Lancaster, situated in that county, and recently forfeited by his attainder. From the same authority we learn that very shortly after the time when Edward the 2nd was at Liverpool, and apparently on his way southward, he was at Nottingham, and remained there for at least a fortnight in the next month (November). With respect to the document of 24th of October, in the 17th of Edward the 2nd, Mr. Hardy stated to the Author that there was an error in the reference in the printed copy in the Fœdera ; but that in other respects reliance might be confidently placed in the accuracy of it, as it is given in Fœdera. vol. 2, part 1, page 537.

T 2

Page.

49   sold to the highest bidder, for three lives and twenty one years, paying 12d.
pr. yard, rent to the front."[1]

In the margin is a memorandum, "The Comittee to ascertain the lotts."[1]

1725,   ⎫ "At a Special Council, &c."
April 15. ⎭ " An Estimate, and Sectional plans of a new Church, to be erected in
the late Castle, upon the Ground where the old large square stone tower, and
the stone buildings adjoining to the same northward, now stand, being now
laid before this Council, by Mr. Thomas Steers and Mr. James Shaw, and
this Council having taken the same into consideration, and being very desirous
to promote so pious a work, which is now much wanted, and with all possible
speed to erect a convenient Church with a proper spire steeple doe agree that
a new Church be there built and a spire steeple at the West side or end, and
an Alcove for a Chancel on the East side or end ; and in order to perfect the
same it is now ordered that a Comittee be appointed, to agree with Workmen,
and contract for building the same, and a Comittee is now appointed, viz.
Mr. Mayor and Bailiffs, and all the Aldermen, Mr. Thos. Steers and Mr. Jas.
Shaw, or any five of them, who are to meet every Monday and Thursday at
four o'clock in the afternoon, in the Exchange, and public notice be given
thereof."[2]

In the margin are two memoranda, viz: "The estimate amounts to
£1488 : 3 : 2," and, " Mr. Shaw to make a Modell in Wood."[2]

54   (Note 1.) On the 9th of July, 1783, the spire of St. Thomas' Church
was struck by lightning.[3]

60   After the words, " faces Edmund-street," add, " At one period, but
probably only for a short time, a Roman Catholic Chapel existed
in Chorley-street, as we find in Gore's Liverpool Directories, of 1777
and of 1781, under the head ' Roman Catholic Chapels,' that (after
mentioning the one in Lumber-street) it contains the following
passage, ' Chorley-street, Rev. John Price.' "

The following paragraph also appears in a Liverpool newspaper, of 1780 :

" A few days since was paid into the hands of Mr. William Hesketh,
one of the Deputy Treasurers of the Infirmary, the sum of £10 14s 3d,
being a collection from the Roman Catholic Chapel, in Edmund-street ; and
the further sum of £8 19s 10d was collected at the Roman Catholic Chapel,
in Chorley-street, for the said charity.[4]

60   (Note 2.) For several years before the close of the last century, and after
the commencement of the present one, the Roman Catholics used
the chapel on the south side of Sir Thomas'-buildings. In Gore's
Directory of 1790, under the head " Roman Catholic Chapels," the
following passage occurs :—

" Sir Thomas's-buildings.
Rev. John Price, Sir Thomas's-buildings."

From which we may reasonably infer that the chapel in Chorley-
street had ceased to be used, and the Rev. John Price had left it, and
then officiated at the one in Sir Thomas'-buildings ; and some other
instances are mentioned in the newspapers of the latter part of the last
century, of charity sermons being preached at the latter by the Rev.
John Price, and collections made for the benefit of the Infirmary.

---

(1) Book of Records, containing the Resolutions and Proceedings of the Council
of 1725, vol 9, page 89.

(2) Ibid. page 91.

(3) Gore's General Advertiser of 10th July, 1783.

(4) Ibid. of 14th April, 1780.

Page.

60 After the words, " Cumberland-street, on the south side," add, "imme-diately below the spot where the street widens."

61 After the words, " but by lapse of time," add, " There was originally a passage which formed a communication between Stanley-street near the spot where the Baptist Chapel stood, and Cumberland-street."

61 (Note 2.) In the Rev. Dr. Thom's work on the Churches and Chapels of Liverpool, he has adverted to the circumstance that it had been said, that the Jews had originally a Synagogue in Mathew-street; and he accounts for its being mentioned as if it had been situated in that street, and reconciles the two statements thus :—

> "Mathew-street, in 1765, and even now, assuming Derby-place to be a part of it, reaches from North John-street to Derby-street, called, in 1765, Lower Stanley-street. This last-named street leads into Whitechapel. Almost close to that part of Derby-street, (in its entire length a very short thoroughfare, by the way,) which is at the northern end of what was once Mr. Johnson's Chapel, and runs into Brokers-alley, stood the first Jewish Synagogue. Without being chargeable with any great inaccuracy, a person who had occasion to speak of this building seventy or eighty years ago, when there were scarcely any houses between it and Mathew-street, and when, nearly as soon as the Baptist Meeting House was passed, which was in Mathew-street, one found oneself at the edifice in question, might, correctly enough for ordinary purposes, describe it as in that street, or, at any rate, at the end of it. Besides, to mark still further a sort of loose or general propriety in speaking of the synagogue, as having been in Mathew-street, it may be added, that in 1765, there was no street or lane leading from it to the north, east, or west, it having stood close to the fields intervening between it and Sir Thomas'-buildings : Cumberland-street, on the west, having reached no farther than Poplar Weint, now Poplar-lane, and on the east only about four or five houses from Whitechapel; and, therefore, ingress to it, and egress from it, having been obtained, if not exclusively, at all events principally, from Mathew-street. It was situated towards the eastern extremity of Mathew-street; its position resembled what the French call a *cul de sac*, and as having been in some respects a continuation of the street just named, it might fitly enough be regarded as in it."—*The Rev. Dr. Thom's Work on Liverpool Churches and Chapels, page* 105.

65 Mr. Bryan Blundell had the merit of being one of the earliest promoters of the Blue Coat Hospital; he was a liberal contributor to the erection of the building, and an active supporter of, and Treasurer and Trustee of the Charity.

68 For " they extended," read, " the trenches extended."

73 The present north front, which contains the large ball-room, and forms the south side of the square of the Exchange-buildings, seems to have been added to the Exchange in 1788, as several items appear relative to it in the ledger of the Corporation, the first of which is of the 19th of July, 1788, viz :—

> " 1788, Dr. The north front of Exchange enlarged.
> July 19. To cash paid John Woods .... £15 15s 0d."[1]

73 A balustrade of stone was added in 1804 to the front of the Town-hall, over the blocking stone at the top.

76 In Note (2) add, " In Gore's General Advertiser of 15th of December, 1775, one Elizabeth Ferguson is mentioned as living in a house "near the Gallows Mill," and add also,

---

(1) Ledger 8, No. 4, of the Corporation of 1788, page 246. Mr. Woods, men-tioned above, is believed to have been the architect.

Page.

"In an order of the Common Council of the 2nd June, 1779, for reducing the fine for adding a life in two fields belonging to Mr. William Calvert, they are described as " near the Gallows Mill."[1]

76 (Note 2.) The Gallows Mill, on the north side of the Prescot-lane, now London-road, was purchased by the Corporation in 1788, in order to remove it, as is shown by the following entry in the Corporation Ledger of that year :—

"1788.   Dr.   Gallow Mill, N. side Prescot-lane.
Sept. 10.   To Cash paid purchase thereof ....£700   0   0"[2]

On the opposite or credit side of the account are items as follows :—

"1789, Feb. 24. By Cash received on account of old materials, £20   0   0
       July   9. By Do.   Do.   Do.   ..   51   0   0

                                  £71   0   0"[2]

76 (Note 2.) The Gallows Mill appears to have been destroyed early in 1789, as the materials were advertised to be sold by auction, at the house of Mrs. Murphy, in Whitechapel, on Monday, the 23rd of February, in that year. "The materials of the mill, known by the name of the Gallows Mill, situate on the Prescot-road, near Liverpool."[3] The advertisement contains a reference for further particulars to the Treasurer's-office, in the Exchange, from which it appears clear, that it was pulled down by order of the Corporation.

79 For " Although neither of the prisons which will now be mentioned was used as such," read, " Although it is certain that one at least of the prisons which will now be mentioned was not used as such ;" and after the words, "the old Bridewell of Liverpool," omit the words, "which was not built in 1775; and," and also omit the words, " during a considerable period," and substitute the words, " during many years ;" and after the words, " which formerly stood near it," at the foot of page 79, add as a note, [4] as follows, " [4] In the Ledger of 1775,[4] of the Corporation of Liverpool, there are several entries of payments to watchmen on duty at a prison on the North Shore. As the old Bridewell was built on the north side of the basin of George's Dock, which was at the northern extremity of the docks in 1775, and in fact there was not any dock or pier on the shore beyond it, it appears to have been correct to describe it at that period as situated on the North Shore. There are three entries in the Ledger on that subject, of the respective dates of the 6th, 13th, and 20th of May, 1775, as follows, viz :—

"To Cash paid Watchmen attending North Shore Gaol..£2 : 12 : 6."[4]

It therefore seems reasonable to conclude that the old Bridewell, on the north side of George's Basin, was the Gaol meant in those entries, and that it had been erected and was in use at least as early as 1775.

91 (Note 1.) For "St. George's Coffee-house," read, "George's Coffee-house."
98 For " wheys," read, " ways."
100 For "slip near this place," read, "slip at the north end of George's-parade."

---

(1) Book of Records of the Corporation 1779, vol. 12, page 142 and 147.
(2) Ledger 8 (No. 4) of the Corporation of 1789, page 164.
(3) Gore's General Advertiser of 12th February, 1789.
(4) Ledger 7 (No. 3) of the Corporation of 1775, page 116 and 144.

Page.

100 (Note 2.) At a Common Council held on the 2nd of June, 1779, it was ordered,

> "That a Pier Head be run out on the South side of the entrance of the North [George's] Dock to extend westwards about seventy yards under the direction of a Committee of the Mayor and Bailiffs and such Gentlemen of the Council as choose to attend for that purpose on notice to be given by the Mayor in that behalf."[1]

110 To Note (3) add, "Although the Ellesmere Canal was not projected until long after 1775, it is considered advisable to mention it with the other canals, as that course brings at once under notice, all the principal canals of the 19th century, with which Liverpool had an immediate or considerable connexion.

113 After the words, "ground on which the fair was held," add, "On the fair days in July and November, it was customary formerly, but not within the recollection of any one now living, for the Mayor and Bailiffs, in their gowns, attended by other persons, to go in procession, with a band of music, from the Exchange to Dale-street, where they passed round a large stone, whitewashed for the occasion, and thence proceeded to the other large stone before mentioned in Castle-street, and back to the Exchange.[2]

114 (Note 1.) After the words, "near St. George's Church," add, "There are entries in the books of the Corporation of 1723, describing it as the "New Market, in Derby-square." In the Book of Records of the Corporation an order of the 6th of November, 1723, is entered for regulating the market in Derby-square, in which it is called the "New-Market in Derby-square," and the order directs, "that no goods whatever be retailed in Derby-square, but butter, cheese, potatoes, fowles, eggs, bacon, and all sorts of victualls, (except butcher's meat,) and that Mr. Mayor be requested to grant his warrant to the Bayl[s] for that purpose.[3]

115 For "supp[l]. mate .. £3," read, "supp[l]. mate   ,,   .. £3."

116 (Note 1.) By a resolution of the Common Council of 4th September, 1776, it was "ordered that the Mayor be authorized to get the fishstones and market altered and removed according to the plan now produced, to make it more roomy and convenient."[4]

117 At the commencement of Note (2) insert as follows:—The subjoined para-

---

(1) Book of Records of the Corporation of 1779, vol. 12, page 142 and 143.

(2) Troughton's Liverpool, page 94. It is there stated, that on the return of the Mayor, Bailiffs, and others in procession, to the Exchange, they dined there. Instead of a dinner, it probably was merely a collation of which they partook at the Exchange; and certainly the bill, dated the 26th of July, 1775, sent in by Mr. Thomas Bowman, who then kept the White Lion Inn, Castle-street, which was paid by the Corporation, and which is copied in Chapter III, page 222, (Note 1) was for a collation merely, and not for a dinner; nor has the Author, in the course of his investigations of the books and documents at the Town-hall, ever met with anything to support that statement; for which, by the way, not any authority is given in Troughton's Work.

(3) Book of Records of the Corporation, (No. 9) of 1723, page 49; and Book of Records, (No. 6) of 1723, page 497, where the order is also set out, though somewhat differently worded, and the market is called the "New Market in Derby-square."

(4) Book of Records of the Corporation of 1779, vol. 12, page 23.

Page.
117 graph respecting the cattle market, near St. James' Church, appears in a Liverpool newspaper of 1780:—

"It is with pleasure we can inform our friends and the public, that on Wednesday last, at the fair in Harrington, adjoining the south boundaries of this town, there was a most pleasing and numerous show of fat oxen and other cattle, together with an incredible number of sheep and lambs. The whole of the reputable butchers attended the fair, and expressed their highest approbation of its establishment, and particularly of the accommodations both for the gentlemen dealers, their customers, and their goods. The quantity of land in a good ring fence, well watered, and necessary building for the reception of cattle, added to the vicinity of the flourishing town of Liverpool, we should not wonder if it became in a short time the first fair in England of its kind."[1]

And add immediately afterwards:—" A cattle market, on a very small scale, used to be held, early in the present century, once a-week, in Church-lane."

120 In Note (2), for " possibly may be," read, " possibly may have been."

121 For " stood in that road," read, " stood in that lane."

121 (Note 2.) The Pinfold, near Patrick's-hill, must have been existing at least as late as 1784, because, in the Ledger of the Corporation of that year, there is an entry of a payment to Richard Marsh, the keeper of it, " being a year's allowance," of £2 10s 0d.[2]

122 (Note 1.) The Author has on one or two occasions, many years ago, seen an offender suffering in the Pillory, near St. George's Church.

123 (Note 1.) In 1786, whilst the improvements and alterations were in progress, pursuant to the Act of Parliament for improving the town, a paragraph, of which the following is a copy, appeared in one of the Liverpool newspapers:—

"Who, in viewing the plan of its present state, will then hardly believe that in the year 1786, near the middle and to the front of Dale-street, then stood a little mansion, whose elevation from the ground was scarcely six feet, and whose roof was covered with straw?"[3]

123 After the words, " narrow curved street," add, " principally."

123 Instead of " an ill-built and very narrow street," read, " a very narrow and ill-built street."

126 (Note 2.) For " Moor rental," read, " Moore rental."

129 For " tea-dealer's or grocer's shop," read, " tea-dealer's and grocer's shop, kept by a person named William Brocklebank;" and for " Miss Furniss," read, " Mrs. Furness."

135 For " the next lease is about ten years later," read, " the next lease is about a year later."

139 (Note 2.) The tavern, afterwards called Richardson's, appears, from the following order of the Common Council, to have been called Martindale's Tavern in 1779:—

"At a Common Council held this sixth day of January, in the year of our Lord, 1779,
"Ordered,—That Mr. Joseph Brooks have leave to add one life to two lives in being, in his two Closes of Land, adjoining to Martindale's Bowling

---

(1) Gore's General Advertiser of 4th August, 1780.

(2) Ledger 7 (No. 3) of the Corporation of 1784, page 160.

(3) Gore's General Advertiser of 23rd February, 1786.

Page.

139   Green, containing three acres and a quarter, held by Lease in his own name, paying a fine of Fifty pounds, and the present Ground rent."[1]

It is evident that it was the one on the south side and upper end of Mount-pleasant; because, in Mr. Charles Eyes' Map of Liverpool of 1785, the two adjoining closes of land are laid down as belonging to Mr. Brooks.

144   (Note 1.) The Mount, or St. James'-walk, was at one period called Quarry-hill. An order of the Common Council of the 6th of October, 1779, directs that Richard Trafford, Esq. should have leave to add a life in a close of land near Quarry-hill, held by lease to Richard Gildart, Esq. deceased, containing four acres and a quarter; and another order directs, that he should have leave to add two lives in two closes of land to the eastward of Quarry-hill, called the Further Slate Pitt Fields, containing four acres and a quarter.[2]

147   For "some copperas works," read, "the copperas works before mentioned."

151   For "through which the highway to Ormskirk passed, as at present," substitute, "and was, as it still is, the highroad to Ormskirk."

154   After the words, "of Edge-hill," add, "in West Derby."

159   After the words, "south end of Liverpool," add, "He was a surveyor, and was unfortunate in his undertakings. On the 2nd of February, 1776, an advertisement was published[3] calling upon the creditors of "Cuthbert Bisbrown, of Liverpool, surveyor," to send in accounts of their demands to Mr. Peter Rigby, or Mr. Samuel Livesley, the trustees of his estate; and on the 6th of September, 1776, another advertisement appeared, announcing the sale of a considerable quantity of land, near the shore of the river, and elsewhere, in Toxteth-park, with a reference to the "assignees of the estate of Cuthbert Bisbrown, late of Liverpool, aforesaid, a bankrupt."[4]

160   Before the words "Reform Act," add, "Corporations."

160   (Note 1.) In 1801, the total number of the population of Liverpool, exclusive of Kirkdale, Everton, Low-hill, Edge-hill, and Toxteth-park, but including seamen, was only 83,708.

163 Instead of the passage commencing, "In 1775 the only Inns existing in
&   Liverpool," and terminating with the passage, "every one of them has
164   since been pulled down," substitute as follows: "In 1775 the principal Inns in Liverpool were the Golden Lion,[A] kept by Mr. James Wrigley; the Fleece,[B] often called the Golden Fleece, by Mr. Thomas Banner; the Cross Keys,[B] by Mr. John King; the Angel,[A] (not unfrequently called the Angel and Crown, and also the new Angel;) kept by Mr. John Wilson; another Inn, also called the Angel, kept by Mr. John Phithian; and the Bull and Punch Bowl,[B] by Mr. John Randles, all in Dale-street; the Talbot, or Golden Talbot, by Mr. William Pryer or Prier, on the south side of and upper end of

---

(1) Book of Records of the Corporation of 1779, vol. 12, page 135 and 136.

(2) Ibid. page 162 and 164.

(3) Gore's General Advertiser of 2nd February, 1776.

(4) Ibid. of 6th September, 1776.

(A) The Golden Lion and the Angel Inns were on the south side of Dale-street.

(B) The Fleece, the Cross Keys, and the Bull and Punch Bowl, were on the north side of Dale-street.

163   Water-street; and the Mill Stone, by Mr. William Cockshutt, on the
&   east side of Castle-street;[c] most of them were considered as of the first
164   class, and at several of them post chaises were kept. Every one of them
     has since been pulled down. There were also the Woolpack, kept
     by Mrs. Woods, and the Red Lion, by Mr. Ralph Hoult, both in
     Dale-street; the Black Horse and Rainbow, by Mr. Henry Forshaw,
     in High-street;[D] the White Lion, by Mr. Thomas Bowman, in
     Castle-street; and the Castle, in Lord-street."

164 Omit note (1).

164 Instead of "the St. George's Coffee-house," insert, "George's Coffee-
     house, kept by Mr. Daniel Dale."

164 After "Pontack's Coffee-house," add, "kept by Mr. Thomas Moncas."

164 After the words, "on the north side of Water-street," insert, "the Exchange
     Coffee-house, in Water-street."

164 After the words, "St. Nicholas' Church-yard," add, "the sales by auction,
     and meetings of various kinds, used to take place at most of those
     houses;"

164 After the words, "Neptune's Coffee-house," add, "kept by Mrs. Howell,
     in the Old Shambles;"

164 After the words, "a skittle ground attached to it;" add, "and the Peacock,
     kept by Mrs. Ann Howel, in the Old Shambles;"

165 For "beef and porter," read, "beer and porter."

167 (Note 2.) Instead of "at nine o'clock," read, "at half-past nine o'clock."

177 (Note 1.) Mr. Thomas Knowles, the brushmaker, seems to have died on
     the 15th of March, 1787, according to the following paragraph which
     appeared in one of the Liverpool newspapers :—"Thursday last,
     died Mr. T. Knowles, brushmaker.[1]

180 (Note 1.) "On the coasts of this county [Pembrokeshire], as well as on those
     of Glamorganshire and the Severn Sea, is found a kind of alga or laver,
     which is gathered in spring, and of which the inhabitants make a sort
     of food."—*Encyclopædia Britannica, title,* "*Pembrokeshire.*"

180 (Note 1.) "Laver or sea liverwort is found growing on the rocks and
     stones, in creeks overflowed by the tide, and is frequently gathered,
     well boiled, and put into jars with a little salt, in which state it is
     occasionally exported."—*Lewis' Topographical Dictionary of Wales,
     title,* "*Pembrokeshire.*"

187 Instead of "the style of many," read, "the style of those on many."

188 (Note 1.) "On Monday, March 28th, came on at Lancaster, the trial of Charles
     John Coney, for robbing the Exchange of this place, and stealing there-
     out the silver cup, parts, &c. of the regalia. Moses Solomon deposed that
     he had been acquainted with Coney about two years, during which

---

(c) The Mill Stone Inn was discontinued or destroyed soon afterwards : advertisements of a sale of property, intended to take place at that Inn, appeared in Gore's
General Advertiser of the 3rd and 10th of February, 1775; and on the 6th of September,
1776, it contains an advertisement of a sale of the furniture of Cockshutt, the landlord,
at "the Mill Stone," which it may be fairly presumed is near the date of its being discontinued. From an advertisement in that newspaper, of the 20th of November, 1778,
calling upon his creditors to send in their accounts, and to execute a trust deed, he
appears to have been unfortunate in business.

(D) Unless there were more persons than one, of the name of "Henry Forshaw,"
who kept Inns or Taverns in Liverpool, in the last century, Mr. Henry Forshaw kept
successively the Black Horse and Rainbow, in High-street, the Golden Lion, in Dale-
street, the Hotel in Lord-street, and the Globe Tavern, in John-street.

(1) Gore's General Advertiser of 22nd March, 1787.

Page.

188　　time he had bought several articles which he (Coney) had stolen. That on Saturday, the 30th of October last, three days after the robbery was committed, Coney came to his house in London; but it being the Jews' Sabbath, an appointment was made to meet after sun-set at a tavern. Solomon met Coney at the appointed time, and found him alone, with a small hair trunk lying by him, containing four small parcels, which Coney said was the regalia of Liverpool Exchange, he had stolen; and which robbery he had committed by secreting himself in a room while some workmen employed in making alterations in the Exchange were at dinner; that he sawed them in pieces, put them in his pocket, and in the middle of the night descended by means of a rope fastened to the staircase, through a window into the street; that the plate was melted down at Solomon's house, during which process Coney kept guard at the inside, and Solomon's brother at the outside of the door; that the silver, before it was melted, weighed 25 lbs. and after 17 lbs. and a-half; that he then gave Coney £5 in part, and the following day he paid him £15, and two bills of £10 each, which he had received from the refiner, to whom he had sold the silver for £55. Solomon likewise swore to one square piece of plate, having on one side a crown, and on the other a bird. Coney pleaded in his defence, that he bought the plate at Holyhead; and after a trial of five hours and a-half, he was brought in guilty. He has since received sentence of death, and is to be executed on Saturday, the 23rd instant."[1]

　　" Last Saturday, Charles Coney, for robbing the Exchange in this town, was executed at Lancaster. He made no confession; but in many instances discovered an obstinacy of temper, and at some times principles of resentment."[2]

201　After the words, " Charities of the town," add, " viz :—

"To the Infirmary £300	To the School for the Blind. £50
„　Blue Coat Hospital. 200	„　Marine Society 30
„　Dispensary........ 200	„　Ladies' Charity 20

£800 "

218　Mr. Baines' salary continued to be £35 per annum until 1786, when it was raised.[3]　Besides Mr. Baines, there was an usher, Mr. W. Winstanley, and a writing-master, Mr. William Whiteside, belonging to the School in 1785, paid by the Corporation : the former had a salary of £30 per annum, and the latter £25 per annum. The following items are from the ledger of the Corporation of 1785 :—

" 1785.{Feb⁹ 3.} To Cash paid W. Winstanley a quarter's Salary .. £7　10　0 "[4]

" 1785.{Jan⁹ 6.} To Cash paid Wᵐ Whiteside a qʳˢ Salary ...... £6　5　0 "[5]

225　(Note 1.) For " are in print, from which," read, " is in print, from which."

---

(1) Gore's General Advertiser of 7th April, 1785.

(2) Ibid. of 28th April, 1785.

(3) Ledger 8 (No. 4) of the Corporation of 1786, page 100.

(4) Ibid. of 1785, page 101.

(5) Ibid. of 1785, page 102.

Page.

226 Instead of "that he was the best read Corporation lawyer," read, "that there was not a better Corporation lawyer."

245 (Note 2.) The art of fishing by the Liverpool fishermen was much improved at a late period of the 18th century, by fishermen from Torbay, who were accustomed to fish in much deeper water than the former, and were sent for in order to instruct them. It is conjectured that the Corporation caused the Torbay fishermen to be sent for in 1785, and that a bounty or premium was paid on the occasion out of the Corporate funds (but during what period of time, or for what particular services, is not known); and the following entry appears in the ledger of the Corporation of 1785 :—

"1785.
May 24.} Cash paid towards supplying the Town with Fish. . £200   0   0"[1]

249 (Note 1.) "On Friday night last, a little before twelve o'clock, a most alarming and dreadful fire broke out in a warehouse to and adjoining the brewery of Messrs. Harvey and Fairclough, in Cheapside. The fire began in the top room, occupied by Mr. Middleton, as a cotton spinning factory, nor could it be got under until the whole of the building, with its valuable contents, viz. Mr. Middleton's stock of cotton, machinery, &c., 12,000 bushels of wheat, 6000 ditto barley and oats, with a stock of hops, malt, &c., belonging to the brewery concern, and amounting in the whole to the value of £15,000 were entirely destroyed."[2]   A lamentable accident also occurred on the occasion, by the fall of a wall, by which several lives were lost.

249 (Note 2.) The cotton mill of Messrs. Kirkman and Co. was called the Union Cotton Mill, and must have been established prior to 1795, because the Mayor, on behalf of the Corporation, publicly expressed their "thanks to Mr. Kirkman," one of the proprietors of the Union Cotton Mill," for the assistance rendered by means of his engines and men when the lamentable fire took place at the Exchange.[3]   The building occupied by Messrs. Kirkman and Company yet exists as an ironfoundry.

249 (Note 3.) Besides the cotton mill mentioned above, there was also, about the close of the last century, a cotton mill in the street called Summerseat, which runs from Limekiln-lane, Bevington-hill, to Arley-street; it was not a large building, and the establishment was abandoned from its not being remunerative.[4]

254 For " £200,000," read " £300,000."

264 " On Thursday, the 2nd instant, the Mersey Bowmen held their annual meeting, when the silver medal was shot for, at one hundred yards, and won by William Nicholson, Esq. of Braze-nose College, Oxford."[5]

264 " On Thursday last, the Mersey Bowmen held their autumn meeting, when an elegant bugle horn, presented to that society, by Captain Pickering, of the Royal Lancashire Fencibles, was shot for, at targets,

---

(1) Ledger 8 (No. 4) of the Corporation of 1785, page 159.

(2) Gore's General Advertiser of 22nd September, 1796.

(3) Ibid. of 22nd January, 1795.

(4) Communicated by Mr. James Boardman.

(5) Gore's General Advertiser of 16th July, 1795.

Page.

one hundred yards distance, and won by Mr. Horsman, he having the most central shot in the gold."[1]

265 Add after the words, "lately the Shooting Butts," An Archery Society, or Club, seems to have been in existence in 1781, as an advertisement appears in a Liverpool newspaper of the 22nd of March, in that year, offering a reward for the discovery of the offenders who had destroyed "a quantity of young Trees and Fence, inclosing a plot of ground in the Park, belonging to the Archers' Society."[2]

266 (Note 1.) "A main of cocks was advertised to be fought in the North Shore Cock-pit, on the 12th of May, 1789, for 20 guineas a battle, and £200 the main or odd battle. To show 50 cocks each."[3]

It seems probable that the Cock-pit in Cockspur-street was erected in 1789, because it is called the *new* Cock-pit in an advertisement which appears in one of the Liverpool newspapers in that year, announcing,

"A Main of Cocks to be fought at the new Cock Pit, in Cockspur-street, on the 23rd of June, for thirty pounds a battle, and Three hundred pounds the main or odd battle. To shew 41 Cocks."[4]

266 (Note 3.) The custom of throwing at cocks on Shrove Tuesday existed to some extent, at least, in 1787, as it is mentioned in one of the Liverpool newspapers of that year as decreased, but not as entirely laid aside.[5]

269 Instead of "the hotel was certainly erected previous to 1785," read, "the hotel was erected in 1784."

276 (Note 1.) A paragraph relative to the Theatre, appears to the following effect, in one of the newspapers of 1779 :—

"On Wednesday, Mr. Dunning moved the Court of King's Bench, on the part of Messrs. Younger and Mattocks, the patentees of the Liverpool Theatre, to discontinue an action, on payment of costs, which they had commenced against several of the most eminent merchants in that town, for a supposed riot and disturbance in the play-house. The rule was accordingly granted, when the Court was informed, 'That the defendants wished to meet the plaintiffs in issue, in order to evince the propriety of their conduct, and to maintain the exercise of their judgment, to approve or disapprove individually, during the representation of theatrical performances ; but as they are not influenced by personal or by hostile motives towards Mr. Younger, they had directed their solicitor to return Messrs. Younger and Mattocks their costs, after the discontinuance of the action.' "[6]

277 A paragraph in one of the Liverpool newspapers, in March, 1796, mentions the preparations making at the Circus, by Mr. Astley, for the opening of it; and an advertisement appears in another of them, in the same month, announcing that equestrian performances, feats of strength, pantomimical representations, pony races, &c. at the Circus, Liverpool, would take place on the 1st and 2nd of April, 1796.[7]

286 Instead of " one of his visits," insert, " one or two of his visits."

---

(1) Gore's General Advertiser of 1st October, 1795.

(2) Ibid. of 22nd March, 1781.

(3) Ibid. of 9th April, 1789.

(4) Ibid. of 18th June, 1789.

(5) Ibid. of 15th February, 1787.

(6) Ibid. of 2nd June, 1779.

(7) Ibid. of 24th and 31st March, 1796.

Page.

288 (Note 1.) For "in the possession of and kindly lent to the author by Mr. Thomas Beckett Gibbons," read, "in the possession of and kindly lent by Mr. Thomas Beckett Gibbons to the author."

290 (Note 1.) "We hear that the anniversary of the Free and Easy Potatoe Market Society, will be held at the usual place, this evening, the 22nd instant."[1]

351 For "the Rev. Mr. Willmot," read, "the Rev. Robert Wilmot."

351 (Note 2.) Mr. Plumbe died at Fareham, in Hampshire, in November, 1785, where he was buried.

369 A good judgment may be formed of the uninteresting and unsightly appearance of Liverpool, in 1780, from the following account, left by an unprejudiced stranger, who visited it on the 12th of June in that year :—

"Entered the city of Liverpool, so celebrated for its commercial character; houses by a great majority, in middling and lower style, few rising above that mark; streets long, narrow, crooked, and dirty in an eminent degree. During our short abode here, we scarcely saw a well-dressed person, nor half-a-dozen gentlemen's carriages; few of the shops appear so well as in other great towns; dress and looks more like the inhabitants of Wapping, Shadwell, and Rotherhithe, than in the neighbourhood of the Exchange, or any part of London above the Tower. The whole complexion nautical, and so infinitely below all our expectations, that naught but the thoughts of the few hours we had to pass here rendered it tolerable. The docks, however, are stupendously grand, the inner one, called Town Dock,* lying in the centre of it, and filled with vessels exhibiting a forest of masts; besides this are three very large ones † lying in front of the city, communicating with each other by flood gates, intermixed with dry ones, for repairing;** the lower or new one ‖ has a fine wide quay on its outer side; an agreeable walk, being lined with trees on either hand; †† below this, on the river, is now building, nearly finished, a circular battery,††† with embrasures for thirty cannon. Parade and barracks are in hand, and when completed, will afford a charming walk and prospect, if allowed to the inhabitants."—*Extracted from the interesting Journal and Letters of the late Samuel Curwen, Judge of Admiralty, &c. an American Refugee in England, page 246 and 247.*

The above account of his visit to Liverpool, in 1780, corroborates the observation made at the commencement of Chapter II, page 118, of the unsightly, narrow, and mean appearance of the streets and alleys of Liverpool, early in the concluding quarter of the 18th century.

371 After the words "fort, barracks, and store-houses were erected," read, "were completed."

376 For "the place of interment," read, "one of the places of interment."

390 For "the exact date has not," read, "the exact date of its erection has not."

390 In 1787 a Society existed for the promoting of Painting, &c. of which Mr. Nicholas Ashton was the president; the meetings of which used to be held in the new room at the Liverpool Library, in Lord-street. The first meeting appears to have been held on Thursday, the 28th of January, in that year.[2]

390 There were two societies of the nature of Debating Societies in Liverpool, in 1787; one called the Free Conversation Society, met at Mr. Ban-

---

(1) Gore's General Advertiser of 22nd June, 1786.

(*) The Old Dock. (†) George's Dock, the Dry Dock, (now part of the Canning Dock,) and the Salthouse Dock. (**) The Graving Docks. (‖) George's Dock. (††) The North Ladies' Walk. (†††) The Old Fort.

(2) Gore's General Advertiser of 18th January, 1787.

Page.

390   ner's large room, at the Fleece Inn; and the other called the Free Debating Society, used to meet at Mr. Forshaw's large room, at the Hotel, in Lord-street.[1]

414   A commission appears to have been received several years previously, for setting out quays at Liverpool; because in one of the Liverpool newspapers of Thursday, the 10th of June, 1790, there is an announcement that his Majesty's Commission had been received on the preceding Saturday, for setting out further quays for the landing and shipping of merchandize.[2]

414   In 1795, the Strangers' Friend or Benevolent Society was established, for the relief of strangers and distressed families.

426   (Note 3.) Since the particulars of the hostile descent of the French in 1797, near Fishguard, were printed, in Chapter V, the author has had access to an account of that event which has appeared in print, and gives considerable additional information, to the following effect :—

The enemy's vessels of war were observed on Wednesday, the 22nd of February, 1797, at ten o'clock a m. by Mr. Thomas Williams, of Trelethin, near St. David's Head, a magistrate of the county of Pembroke, who had been a sailor in his youth, and who recognised the vessels, although sailing under British colours, to be enemies' vessels. He had the merit of being the first to send messengers to the town of St. David's and elsewhere to give the alarm. At two P.M. the enemy came to anchor in Fishguard Bay, on the coast of Pembrokeshire, and soon afterwards the British colours were struck and those of France hoisted. By this time a general alarm prevailed, and expresses were despatched in all directions, and vehicles of every description were employed in transporting articles of value into the interior. The inhabitants of St. David's stripped off the lead from buildings, cast it into bullets, and all the gunpowder that could be obtained from the various shops was divided amongst those who bore fire-arms ; and thus prepared, they proceeded *en masse*, clergy and laity, to meet the enemy ; their number being augmented by hundreds of country people, who joined them on their march, in fact by every one, old and young, capable of bearing arms.

The enemy accomplished their landing at Fishguard Bay in sixteen boats; their numbers were 1400 men and two women, with large quantities of ammunition in casks, ball cartridges, and spare arms, besides one long-boat overladen, with ammunition, which upset, and the whole of that was lost. Small parties of the enemy immediately proceeded on marauding expeditions, about four miles along the coast and nearly the same distance inland, and commenced pillaging; much intoxication and disorder in consequence prevailed amongst them, and many of them were speedily taken prisoners, drunk. In the mean time thousands of Welshmen assembled, armed with guns, swords, pistols, some with scythes fixed on long poles, and almost every description of offensive weapons were brought into use on this memorable occasion.

After Chapter V. of this work was printed, it was ascertained that the account on page 426 of that chapter, as to there having been only one life lost on this occasion, is erroneous. On Thursday, the 23rd, at six o'clock in the morning, Mr. Whitesides, a Liverpool gentleman, who

---

(1) Gore's General Advertiser of 18th January, 1787.

(2) Ibid. of 10th June, 1790.

Page.
422

erected the Smalls Lighthouse, mustered the inhabitants of Solva, a little seaport on the Pembrokeshire coast, in the parish of Whitchurch, and the masters and seamen of the vessels there, with their guns and ammunition; they were joined by one or two Welshmen, armed with scythes fixed on poles; and with Mr. Whitesides, on horseback, at their head, they commenced their march towards the enemy, and were joined on the march by several hundreds of the Welsh, and advanced within half a mile of the enemy's advanced post. A little detachment of these brave men had the honour of soon smelling powder, and of drawing the first blood. Five Welsh seamen of Mr. Whiteside's little corps, encountered five French soldiers; the sailors advanced boldly, the Frenchmen fired, and the seamen returned the fire with good effect. One Frenchman was killed, two badly wounded, and the other two fled; the seamen remained masters of the field and buried their dead enemy. One of the seamen, Captain Thomas Beynon, was wounded in the foot, for which he received a pension during his life.

This skirmish took place within the sight of General Tate, who commanded the enemy, and who is represented as having expressed his surprise at finding raw undisciplined men showing so bold and steady a front, and fighting so well. The field where this occurred is now called the French Park.

The British troops, under Lord Cawdor, were now rapidly assembling, and at length consisted of

The Cardiganshire Militia;

The Castlemartin troop of Yeomanry Cavalry;

Lieut.-Colonel Knox's Fencible Infantry;

Captain Ackland's Fencible Infantry;

Lieuts. Mears and Perkins, with their companies of seamen and artillery;

Besides the country gentlemen, and the vast numbers of brave men who, as already mentioned, came forward as volunteers, and took up arms in defence of their country.

On Thursday, the 23rd, at twelve o'clock at noon, the French vessels sailed unexpectedly, to the great surprise of the forces who had landed.

The enemy's advanced post was at Garn-Unda, a rock, which stands upon a streak of rocky land half way between the French camp and Fishguard. It has upon it a hollow flat wide space, which could contain six or seven hundred men; being well protected by a circle of solid rock, and accessible only on one side. From the top the enemy had a full view of Fishguard and the camp, with the two turnpike roads leading from Haverfordwest and Cardigan to Fishguard. Near this place two Welshmen attacked several of the enemy, but were both slain; not, however, without having killed one of the Frenchmen.

The part of the country which was occupied and plundered by the French, is called Pencaer, in the parish of Llanwnda, and the French head-quarters were there, at a house called Trehowel, the residence of Mr. Mortimer. That part is divided in the middle by a streak of high rocky mountain running from east to west three miles in length. Every house, twenty-two in number, on the exterior side of this streak, and also Llanwnda Church, besides a great number of cottages, were plundered by the French. On the interior of the streak, there were nineteen farms, all of which were also pillaged by them, besides many small houses. So closely did the French search and pillage, that at Mr.

Mortimer's house (Trehowel), they took away every moveable article which they could make any use of, and even emptied the feather beds of the feathers, and carried off the ticking for trousers.*

The French found themselves doomed to severe disappointments. They had been told when they embarked, that the people in this country were very disaffected; and that if a landing could be effected, the whole country would join them, and that they could march to London with wooden swords. But, instead of being received as friends with open arms, they found nothing but brave and determined opposition. They were landed and deserted to their fate, without any means of retreat; they found no conveyance for their ammunition and baggage, no provisions, and all the live stock in the neighbourhood were driven into the interior. There appeared, therefore, to be no other alternative than to capitulate. At ten o'clock on the 23rd, two officers, one of whom was the aide-de-camp (Leonard), with a flag of truce, arrived at Fishguard, and inquired for Colonel Knox.

Lord Milford, Lord-lieutenant of the county, Lord Cawdor, Colonel Knox, Colonel Colby, Colonel Ackland, Colonel Dan Vaughan, Colonel James, Colonel George Vaughan, Governor of Fishguard Fort, and other officers, held their preliminary meeting at the Royal Oak Inn, the house of Mr. Hugh Meyler, in Fishguard.

The French officers made an offer of the surrender of the French army, prisoners of war, on condition that they should be sent back to Brest, at the expense of the British government. This being rejected, at length an unconditional and immediate surrender of the French forces was agreed upon, and the French officers, blindfolded with large shawls, were safely guided from Fishguard.

On Friday, the 24th of February, at noon, the British troops were drawn up in line on Windyhill Farm. The time being nearly expired, Lord Cawdor despatched his aid-de-camp, the Honourable Captain Edwardes, with a flag of truce, borne by Mr. Millingchamp, one of the Yeomanry Cavalry, to the French, with a message that "his troops were ready, and unless they surrendered immediately he would attack them at every point." When they arrived at Trehowel, the enemy's head-quarters, 600 of the enemy were drawn up in line, and ordered to "open pans and shed priming," and to march peaceably. The remaining part of the army marched up to the head-quarters to join their comrades, leaving the whole of the ammunition and spare arms in the camp. At two o'clock in the afternoon, the enemy appearing without their colours, the Cardiganshire Militia and the Fishguard Fencibles, were ordered to receive them. When the French reached the top of Goodwick Hill they played their music and proceeded down to the sands, their brass drums echoing through the hills. They were marched up in front of the English in columns, where they laid down their arms very peaceably, and were marched off.

The dispersed plunderers finding that all was over, returned in the evening or the next morning, and were secured; and the prisoners were sent to different prisons, where the sick and hurt immediately received

---

* Mr. Mortimer escaped with his money and some valuable papers; and Ann George, his servant, secured his silver spoons in her pocket, being all that was saved from the house. Ann George remained near the house until the Frenchmen entered the premises; they smashed the parlour windows with the butt ends of their musquets, and shivered the front door to pieces: she then thought it high time to leave.

medical assistance, but several of them died. One Frenchman fell over a precipice and was killed. Several of them appear to have been much injured by the Welsh, in the attempts of the latter to make them prisoners ; and on one occasion, two of the Welsh peasants observed that two of the marauders were enjoying themselves by the side of a hedge, sprang upon them, and one of the Frenchmen seized his musket, but before he could bring it to his shoulder, one of the Welshmen struck him to the earth with a bludgeon, and killed him by piercing him with his own bayonet through the body in several places, the other Frenchman fell on his knees, and his life was spared. On another occasion, two Welshmen observing a musket outside a cottage door, took possession of it, a Frenchman rushed out to recover his musket, a desperate struggle ensued, and the Frenchman was dreadfully beaten and his head nearly scalped, before he yielded, and was secured.[1] It is, however, only reasonable to believe that others of the French forces either lost their lives or were seriously injured when marauding, of whom no account has been preserved: because exasperated Welsh farmers, labourers, and miners could not be expected to submit, without some retaliation, to the robberies, violences, and outrages of a licentious foreign soldiery.

This ill-fated expedition demonstrated the folly of the French government, in expecting that the people of this country would rise in insurrection, or make common cause with men who, at that time, were their bitterest foes; it showed that the same courage and spirit which had animated the brave David Gam and his followers from Wales, at the battle of Agincourt, nearly 382 years before, still existed amongst the Welsh, when called upon to fight their enemies; and the result was the loss to France of the services of a considerable body of soldiers, who surrendered as prisoners of war, after committing a series of robberies and outrages against a number of industrious farmers and poor cottagers.

The following paragraph connected with the subject of the outrages of the French forces on that occasion, appeared in a London newspaper of the 24th of September, 1853 [2]:—

"Died, at Fishguard, on the 12th instant, aged 88 years, Mary Williams, better known as Matty Carham. On the French landing near this place, in Feb. 1797, she was maltreated by one of the soldiers, being then far advanced in pregnancy. Her case was represented by the late Lord Cawdor, (to whom the French troops surrendered, amounting to about 1400 men,) to his Majesty George 3rd, who granted her a pension, by sign manual, of £40 per annum, which she has received for 56 years."[2]

428 After the words "movements of the latter," add, "in February, 1797, and August, 1798."

434 For "page 480, (*) read, "page 418, (Note 1.)"

441 For "in a great variety of accounts," read, "on a great variety of accounts."

475 (Note 1.) For "knew five of them," read, "recollected five of them."

498 For "Malborough," read, "Marlborough."

---

(1) From an account of "The Invasion by the French Troops, under the command of General Tate, on Carrig Gwasted Point, near Fishguard, on Wednesday, the 22nd day of February, 1797, and their Surrender," printed at Haverford West, by Joseph Potter, printer, High-street.

(2) Bell's Weekly Messenger, of 24th September, 1853.

INDEX.

w 2

PAGE.

F.

I.

J.

x 2

X. Y. Z.

ILLUSTRATIONS.

ENGRAVINGS.

WOOD-CUTS.

THE END.

PRINTED BY J. MAWDSLEY AND SON, CASTLE-STREET, LIVERPOOL.

List of Subscribers to the 2003 Edition

Abbott, Edna
Abernethy, Ian
Ablewhite, Miss R
Adams, Geoffrey
Adamson, Mrs Lyn
Afford, Jack
Alcock, John
Alecock, Cynthia & Ethel
Ammundsen, P A
Ancient Chapel of Toxteth
Andrews, Morton
Andrews, Rena
Ardrey Family
Armitage, Ian
Atherton, Mike & Sue
Atherton, Roger
Atkinson, C M
Aubrey, Matthew
Ayre, Joan
Bailey, Mrs F G
Bailey, Trevor
Baker, Mrs Anne
Balshaw, Lisa, Mark & Zoë
Bancroft, George
Barklem, George
Barry, Michael
Barry, Doreen
Basnett, S E
Bayley, Dr T J
Bebington Family History Group
Belchem, Prof John
Benham, Mrs Margaret
Bennett, Wendy & Ian
Bernard, Stephen F
Bernhardt, C H
Berry, George
Bertelson, Bertel
Bird, D
Blackwell, Ruth
Blanchard, Edward
Blease, A & J

Blennarhassett, Paul & Jill
Boardman, Dr Frank
Boardman, Joyce & Mark
Boardman, Terry & Margaret
Bolger, Mr & Mrs P
Bonney, Mr James
Bowen, M
Bowyer, Susan
Boxer, Graham
Bradshaw, Eric
Brazendale, David & Hilary
Brellisford, G G
Brennen, M M
Brett, Margaret & Bernard
Brian, Michael E
Brinkman, M
Briody, Terence
Briody, Margaret & Thomas
Broad, Callum & Maddy
Broadfoot, Barbara
Brocken, Christine A
Brogden, Anne
Brooks, Walter
Browning, Barbara M
Brundrit, Christine
Bryson, Colonel Graeme
Bryson, Mr Gerald Joseph
Burden, Mrs Z B
Burgess, Anna
Burgess, Norman
Burman, Lionel
Burquest, A F
Burton, Kenneth V
Butler, Gordon J
Butler, Paul E
Butler, Peter A
Butterworth, Michael
Button, N
Buxton, Alfie
Byrne, Joseph
Byrne, Mr Denis V

Cadman, Carol & Eddie
Cahill, Peter
Callaghan, Edie
Callan, Paul (in Loving Memory of)
Callender, Mr B R
Campbell, I J F
Canty, Tom
Carr, Mavis & George
Carrick, Mrs S
Carter, Edward John
Carter, T G
Cartin, Peter
Casey, Alan
Cato, Joyce
Cave, W A
Cawley, John C
Chaffers, Ada & George
Chaffin, Eileen
Chapman, Alan
Chapman, I M
Cherry, Joe
Chown, Iris Crosbie
Christall, Norah
Christie, Stuart
Clark, Elaine
Clark, Margaret
Claydon, Tim
Clein, Councillor Jan
Cliffe, Patrick & Alison
Cliffe, Tek Lee & Richard
Clough, Dr C H, (Liverpool)
Clubmoor Youth Centre
Coghlan, Brian
Cohen, Mrs Rhona
Colley, M
Collier, Charles
Conlan, Joseph
Cook, K Clifford, OBE, FCA
Cooke, Anne
Cooper, Alan T P
Copeman, Mark
Corbett, Peter
Corkish, John A
Cosser, Michael

Couche, Mary
Coulshed, Olive
Cowman, A
Cox, Alastair & Linda
Cox, Antony
Cox, Dianne & Les
Cox, Reg & Ina
Cragg, Margaret J
Crawford, Ray & Marie
Creech, David & Vanessa
Cregeen, Mr W A
Crimes, Ralph
Crist, Joan M
Crompton, Arthur Gordon Ellis
Cropper, Michelle E
Crosby, T J
Cross, Lady
Cross, Dave
Crossey, Paul
Cull, Alfred
Culling, Harold
Cunningham, Roger & Doreen
Dale, John & Anne
Dalziel, Ann
Davidson, A S
Davis, John B
Dawe, Noreen
Dawes, George F
Day, A F
Dennis, Mrs Freda
Devitt, Stephen
Dewhurst, Barbara
Dewhurst, Ronnie C
Dickins, Alan, Chairman,
        Liverpool Central R A F A
Dolman, Francis & Margaret,
        Fairfield
Donaldson, Daniel Vincent
Douglas, Corinna & Ray Balmer
Downham, Dr P A
Driessen, Frank
Dring, Mark
Duggan, Mona
Durkin, Len
Earnshaw, Rosemary

Edwards, John
Edwards, Paul
Edwards, Stephen
Ellwood, John
Emery, Rosalind
Emery, W A (Bill)
England, G
Evans, Miss Christine
Evans, T P A
Everett, Mrs Cherie E, MBE
Evetts, Naomi
Fairbrother, Victor E
Fairfax, Margaret
Fairhurst, John
Fairhurst, Mrs E
Fane, John
Farthing, Mrs D & Mr G
Fawcett-Smith, Maralyn
Fazakerley, M Eleanor
Fellows, Sheila
Fenerty, Moira
Fennah, R Mark
Ferns, Arthur Dominic
Fletcher, Duncan
Flood, Dennis
Floyd, Maisie
Ford, Graham
Forrest, F T
Forshaw, Roy
Forster-Dean, Peter
Foster, J
Foster, Mrs J
Fowler, Myra & Ray, Skelmersdale
Fox, Laura
Fraser, Marjorie
Freckleton, Thomas
Fredson, Joan
Gabriel, L W
Gallimore, Peter & Ann
Gambles, David
Gane, Ken
Garrity, Kathleen & Michael
Gee, David
George, William & Susan
Gersten, Florence E

Gilbertson, Dr A A F
Gill, J
Gilmore, A F
Gilmore, John
Gleave, Kenneth
Goodall, Mrs P
Goodier, Diana
Goodman, Dr Mervyn
Goodwin, Peter
Gooseman, Marj & Bill
Gorman, David Jack
Gowans, Barbara
Gray, S A
Greenland, Alfred
Greenwood, E F
Greenwood, Mrs Veronica & Ben
Griffiths, Joe
Grundy, Mrs Patricia
Gustafson, Helen L
Guy, Stephen
Hanrahan, M A
Hardcastle, E
Harper, Jean
Harrison, G J C
Hart, Michael
Haskell, David T
Heath, Margaret & Graham
Heath, Barry Clarke
Heaton, James Mulgrave
Heaton, Ron
Hedley, Doreen & Bill
Henley-Smith, Pam
Hennessy, Gillian
Heyes, B M
Hibbert, J & E
Higgins, J P
Hill, Jean
Hind, Veronica
Hiscox, Rosemary L
Hobbins, Ruth
Hobson, John "West Derby"
Hodges, Frank & Dorothy
Hodgetts, Lilian
Hollinshead, J C
Holmes, Mary Ann

Holmes, Teresa
Holt, Jennifer S
Hopner, S A, R P
Horn, Aelred
Hosker, Donald
Housbey, Valerie
Howard, Michael & Tommy
Hudd, Mr G
Hughes, Emrys & Jane
Hughes, Glynne
Hughes, John
Hughes, Ken
Hughes, Linda
Hughes, Mary Kathleen
Hughes, Mr Jeffrey Vernon
Hull, Roger C
Hulse, Enid
Hunt, Mrs Margaret
Hunt, Robert
Hunton, Maureen
Hunwick, Christopher L &
      Geraldine C White
Hunwick, Mrs Joan E
Hurst, David
Hurst, Mrs Pauline
Hussey, Anthony
Hussey, John
Hyland, Peter
Ingram, G
Ireland, Raymond,
      Margaret & Janet
Irving, Cllr Dave
Irwin, Margaret & Eric
Isherwood, K H C
Jackson, Bernard
Jackson, Mrs V
James, Lynden
James, Edward & Sylvia
James, Pauline
Jenkins, Barbara
Jennings, John & Annette
Jennion, Arthur
Jerabek, Fred
Johnston-Breen, Jackie
Jones, Geoff

Jones, June
Jones, Marjorie
Jones, Mary & Peter
Jones, Peter Gerald
Jones, Trevor
Kay, Margaret
Kelly, Ivy
Kelly, Tom
Kennedy, Ron
Kidd, Ian G
Kidd, Professor Bill
Kincart, Peter
King, Andrew William
King, Neville
King, Sara Elizabeth
Kirwan, Mrs Elaine
Knowles, Miss J I
Knowsley Historical Society
Lamb, Charles J
Lamden, Mr R J
Lancaster, Mr R P
Lancaster-Smith, nee
      Collins, Marjorie
Lancelyn Green, June & Richard
Lane, Diana M
Latham, Trevor
Lawson, Nora
Lea, Norman William
Leach, Dave
Lee, William
Leech, Harry
Lennon, Michael
Lever, Alan
Levin, Ann & David
Levitt Family
Lewis, Arnold S
Lewtas, Marcus & Muriel
Lindsay, Betty & Sid
Lister, William
Liston, Andrew John
Little Family
Littlewood, Kevin
Liverpool World Heritage Bid
Livingston, Ray
Lloyd, Heather M

London, Diana & Jack
Longworth, Frank
Loughran, Sue & Brendan
Lowe, John
Lucy, E G
Lunt, Peter John
Lyons, Mrs Anne
Macardle, Robert
Mace, Councillor Barbara
Maddocks, Katy
Maginn, Lisa
Mahoney, Mrs Ethel
Mallon, Matthew
Manion, Ellie & Sophie
Manning, J A
Maritime Archives & Library,
Merseyside Maritime Museum
Martin, Douglas & Ailna
Martin, R
Matthews, Alan S
Matthews, Barbara
McArdle, Edward Terence
McCann, Jo
McCarthy, Jean
McCarthy, Professor K
McConville, Simon James
McCormack, Breffni
McDonald, Diane
McDonald, Philip
McDonough, Brian
McFarlane/Hesketh, Margaret
McGhee, Ronald
McGovern, Peter John
McKenzie, Mrs I S
McLoughlin, Joseph
McNally, M
McNicol, Alisdair
McParlin, Patricia
McShane, Mrs Pat
McTigue, Vincent
Meeson, Mrs Jean
Meldrum, R
Mercer, Bessie
Moffat, Dave
Molyneux, Henry

Molyneux-Berry, D B
Molyneux-Johnson, Russell
Moore, Ann & James & family
Morgan, Mrs Joan Elizabeth
Mothershaw, Diana
Muraski, Patricia
Murphy, J H
Murphy, John
Navickas, K
Naylor, Doreen
Neillie, Sandra
Netherway, Robert
New, N H
Norris, Heather
Northway School, Wavertree
Nugent, William Thomas
O'Brien, Melanie
O'Brien, Peter A
O'Brien, Peter N
O'Connor, Freddy
O'Reilly, Frank
Organ, E E
Orrom, Martin
Osgood, Paul William
Owen, Teresa
Owen, J D
Owens, G R
Park, George P
Park, James
Park, Robert
Parkes, Mrs S E
Parkins, Gillian
Parrott, Kay & Tim
Parsons, Philip J
Paterson, Bill
Patterson, Stuart W & Norma
Pearce, Andrew
Peers, Barbara
Peers, Leonard
Peers, Lewis
Perry, Kate
Perry, Mr S
Peters, Joseph
Petris, Evaris
Phillips, Andrew James

Phillips, Harold
Pierpoint, Brian
Pitt, Bill
Platt, Peter
Plumbley, Mr   A
Poole, Norman
Pooley, Robert J
Powell , T G & P
Power, Henry
Power, Tony
Price, Dr Geoffrey L
Pritchard, Ian
Pritchard, Steve
Pritchard, Walter
Procter, Margaret
Purcell, Margeret
Quade, Anne
Quinn, Michael
Radley, Gordon
Rawes, Jean
Redman, Don
Rees, Elisabeth
Reeves, Jim
Regan, Mr Vincent
Renshaw, Sue
Richards, Fiona
Riley, Martin Robson
Rimmer, G M
Roberts, Alan, Julie, Kenny
Roberts, Edward W
Roberts, Margaret
Roberts, Margaret
Roberts, Paul
Robertson, Mr Alec
Robinson, Diane
Robinson, Eileen
Robinson, Robert
Roche, Joseph A
Rockliff, Richard Austin
Rose, Samuel
Rothwell, Kirsty
Ruüd, Rose
Ryder-Jones, Angela & Peter
Sanders, Edward
Sarsfield, Ian M

Sarsfield, Rod C
Sayonas, Master Gary &
        Miss Hannah
Scott, Kenneth Michael
Seabrooke, Herbert
Seddon, Tracey
Shirley & Jimmy
Shuttleworth, Thos H
Sinclair, Roy
Sixsmith, Ian
Smethurst, John B, M A
Smith, Maralyn
Smith, Charles H
Smith, Pamela F
Smith, Miss C V
Smith, Alexander
Smith, Joan Geddes
Southern, K
Spenceley, Rita
Spencer, Stephen Joseph
St Finbar's Catholic Primary School
St Francis Xavier's College
Stannard, Madeline
Steel, G Anne
Stock, William
Stoker, Patricia & Terry
Stoker Family
Storrie, Robert
Strauss, Mr & Mrs J M
Street, David
Stubbs, John & Pat
Sunners, D C
Sunners, Sheila
Sweet, Nanora
Taylor, John
Taylor, Lyn-Marie
Taylor, Ms M Iris
Taylor, Paula
Taylor, Thomas S
Teasdale, Anthony
Thomas, Irene
Thomas, Maureen
Thomas, Michael
Thompson, Madeline
Thompson, S N

Threlfall, Alan
Thwaite, Roy
Tiernan, Andy
Tiernan, John & Diane
Tinkler, Ken
Tufnell, Gordon F
Turner, A
Turner, Ethel & Family
Turner, Peter & family
Tweedie, Philip
Upton, Gilbert
Urquhart, Peter
Vaughan, J E
Ventin, Rev Andrew
Vera B
Walker, Michael
Walsh, M A
Walsh, Margaret
Walsh, Philip
Walsh, Roger
Walsh, Ross
Walton, Anne F
Watson, Mrs Ivy
Weatherley, Mr Craig D
Webb, Neville & Eileen
Webster & Shearson Families
Westgaph, Laurence
Wharton, Bernard
Whelehan, Andrew James
White, Mr Alan E
White, Mrs June
Whitfield, "Grandad Matt"
Whitlow, Mr C R (Senior)
Whittaker, Frank & Helen
Wilcott, Thomas
Wilkinson, Dave
Willan, W Ken
Williams, A
Williams, Beryl
Williams, Jacqueline Barton
Williams, Michael
Williams, Pam & Bob
Williams, Shelagh
Wilson, Mr & Mrs A D
Wilson, Paul

Winder, Bob
Winstanley, Frederick
Wolfenden, John L
Woodbridge, Brian
Woodcock, Nora
Woodworth, P L
Woosey, Elizabeth
Workman, Joanne Elisabeth
    & Judith Victoria
Worthington, Bill
Younis, Eileen